Wolfgang Hafner • Heinz Zimmermann (Eds.)

Vinzenz Bronzin's Option Pricing Models

Wolfgang Hafner • Heinz Zimmermann (Eds.)

Vinzenz Bronzin's Option Pricing Models

Exposition and Appraisal

Springer

Wolfgang Hafner
Gartensteig 5
5210 Windisch
Switzerland
whafner@wolfgang-hafner.ch

Heinz Zimmermann
WWZ Abteilung Finanzmarkttheorie
Peter Merian-Weg 6
4002 Basel
Switzerland
heinz.zimmermann@unibas.ch

ISBN: 978-3-540-85710-5 e-ISBN: 978-3-540-85711-2

Library of Congress Control Number: 2008934324

Cover design: WMX Design GmbH, Heidelberg
Cover photo: "Trieste Canal Grande 1898" by courtesy of Libreria Italo Svevo di Franco Zorzon, Trieste

Printed on acid-free paper

9 8 7 6 5 4 3 2 1

springer.com

Contents

Preface

The doctoral dissertation of the French mathematician Louis Bachelier, accepted by the *École Normale Supérieure* and published in 1900, is widely regarded as the seminal, rigorous work in option pricing theory[1]. However, the work remained undiscovered for more than half a century, until Paul A. Samuelson, based on an inquiry by Leonard J. Savage, discovered the piece, and an English translation of the entire thesis was published in the book of Cootner (1964).[2] Clearly, the merits of Bachelier's work are beyond option pricing; he can be credited for having developed the first mathematical theory of continuous time stochastic processes (the Brownian motion), a few years before Albert Einstein's (1905) well-known contribution.

Each scientific discipline needs – and creates – its Patron Saint. In the fields of financial economics and financial mathematics, Bachelier takes this incontrovertible position. This book does not intend to dethrone Bachelier and his seminal achievement, but aims at directing the attention to a different theoretical foundation of option pricing, undertaken by an essentially unknown author, Vinzenz[3] Bronzin, only a few years after Bachelier's work was published (1908).

This tiny booklet is entitled *Theorie der Prämiengeschäfte* (Theory of Premium Contracts), is written in German and some 80 pages long. While it received some attention in the academic literature in the time when it was published, it seems to have been forgotten later. For example it was mentioned in a standard banking textbook from Friedrich Leitner (1920), who was a professor at the *Handels-Hochschule* of Berlin. Moreover, the book got a short review in the famous *Monatshefte für Mathematik und Physik* in 1910 (Volume 21). But more recent academic mentions are

[1] There are numerous references honouring Bachelier's work, e.g. Samuelson (1973), Bernstein (1992), Taqqu (2001), Bouleau (2004), Davis and Etheridge (2006) and others.

[2] A second, more recent translation has now been published by Davis and Etheridge (2006).

[3] Bronzin was originally born with the Italian name "Vincenzo" but is known as a mathematician with the German version of his name Vinzenz. We therefore refer in this book to the German version.

virtually inexistent[4]. Also, only a few biographical details about Bronzin are known to us: he was a professor and later, in the 1920s, the Director of the *Accademia di Commercio e Nautica* in Trieste. As a director of this academy he got also a mention in the famous *Jahrbuch der gelehrten Welt* (Yearbook of the Scientific World).

Bronzin's methodological setup is completely different from Bachelier's, at least in terms of the underlying stochastic framework where he takes a much more pragmatic approach. He develops no stochastic process for the underlying asset price and uses no stochastic calculus, but directly makes different assumptions on the share price distribution at maturity and derives a rich set of closed form solutions for the value of options. This simplified procedure is justified insofar as his work is entirely focused on European style contracts (not to be exercised before maturity), so intertemporal issues (e.g. optimal early exercise) are not of premier importance. From a probabilistic standpoint, the work is no match for Bachelier's stochastic foundations, but from a practical and applied perspective, it is full of important insights, results, and applications.

It would be interesting to know the professional or academic setting which motivated Bronzin to develop his option pricing theory. Unfortunately, not much is known about this. There is no foreword to the book, no introduction, no information about the author except a short mention as "Professor". But from a book published two years earlier (Bronzin 1906) we know that he was a professor for actuarial theory at the *K. K. Handels- und Nautische Akademie* (which after the First World War took the aforementioned Italian naming and was later divided in two separate schools, one specializing on commerce: the *Istituto Tecnico Commerciale "Gian Rinaldo Carli"*, and the other focusing on nautical studies: the *Istituto Tecnico Nautico "Tomaso di Savoia Duca di Genova"*). Trieste was at this time a true melting-pot of people from different nations – James Joyce lived in Trieste from 1905 until the beginning of the First World War – and the window of the *Donaumonarchie* to the Mediterranean Sea. As a center for oversea trading Trieste became an European center for insurance. The headquarter of *Generali* is still located in Trieste. There are not any references at the end of the book. While the publisher (*Franz Deuticke*, Vienna) is still in business, the company was not able to provide any information, and even the worldwide web does not provide any meaningful information on Bronzin either[5].

[4] Except a recent reference from our colleague Yvan Lengwiler (2004), we are aware of only one modern reference on Bronzin's book in a German textbook on option pricing (see Welcker et al. 1988). The authors do not comment on the significance of Bronzin's contribution in the light of modern option pricing theory. A short appreciation of Bronzin's book is also contained in a recent monograph of one of the authors of this volume, Hafner (2002).

[5] By the time when we started our research (in 2004), a worldwide Google search request on "Vinzenz Bronzin" gives 5 entries: one refers to a website of the authors of Welcker et al.

A general difficulty in the attempt to write about Bronzin's book is that the text is written in German, and many of his finance related expressions (which may or may not reflect the commonly used terms at the time being) cannot be translated easily. We therefore have to find English terms as adequate as possible, and add the original German wording in parentheses where it seems to be useful[6]. Moreover we have adapted Bronzin's mathematical notation with only minor changes. In discussing, or extending certain results (particularly in Section 5, Subsection 5.6), we have tried to make a clear distinction between the results of Bronzin and our own.

Both works, Bachelier and Bronzin, shared the fate of being largely (although not completely) unrecognized during the time of publication. In view of the dramatic relevance of option pricing theory as a driver of financial and analytical innovation after 1973, the publication year of the Black-Scholes-Merton models and the launch of the first exchange traded standardized financial options (at the Chicago Board Options Exchange, CBOE), this is an incomprehensible observation indeed. However, this is not an isolated instance in the history of science. There were always ignored, overlooked, undervalued, or simply forgotten scientific works – which should become fundamental from a later perspective. This is the natural consequence of the evolutionary nature of the scientific process. Even the field of finance offers, apart from the case of option pricing, several examples: The mean-variance approach of portfolio theory was developed by Bruno de Finetti in the 30s (see de Finetti 1940), more than a decade before the seminal contribution by Harry Markowitz, before getting adequately recognized[7]; furthermore, an alternative and very accessible approach to portfolio selection was published by Andrew Roy in the same year as Markowitz's work without getting any academic credit until the 90s[8]. The random walk model and major insight about efficient markets (without naming it so) were advanced by the French Jules Regnault in the 60s of the 19th century (see Regnault 1863), without being noticed by Bachelier, Samuelson, Fama and other advocates of the market efficient literature altogether[9]. A final example is the development of expected utility theory where the earliest – and according to Y. Lengwiler (see Chapter 20 in this volume) most powerful – statements date back to Gabriel Cramer and Daniel Bernoulli in the 18th century.

(1988), where the book is quoted in the footnotes, the other four are related to documents released in our own academic environment. Also, searches in electronic archives such as JSTOR did not provide results.

[6] Occasionally, interested readers find important sentences in the full original German wording in footnotes.

[7] See Chapter 19 by F. Pressacco in this volume.

[8] See Roy (1992) for his own contribution after 40 years after his original publication.

[9] See Jovanovic (2006) for an appreciation.

About this Book

This volume includes a facsimile reproduction of Bronzin's original treatise as well an English translation of it. We are grateful to the publisher Franz Deuticke, Vienna, and the still living heirs of Bronzin, Giorgio Raldi and Gherardo Bronzin, for the permission to reproduce the work. Ralf Lemster Financial Translations in Frankfurt on the Main, in particular Igor Uszczapowski, provided an excellent translation of the book; in particular, they succeeded in adapting the old-fashioned German wording to a contemporary writing style and yet conserving the character of the original text.

In addition, the volume offers contributions to the scientific, historical and socio-economic background of Bronzin's work, as well as papers covering the history of derivative markets and option pricing. All these chapters represent original contributions, and we are extremely grateful to the authors for their effort to discuss and redraft their text over several stages.

This work would not have been possible with the support of many people and institutions. First and foremost, we are grateful to the Bronzin families in Trieste, who helped and supported us in our research in any respect, and made us available private documents. We are particularly grateful to Stellia and Giorgio Raldi, to Vinzenz Bronzin's son Andrea Bronzin (who passed away in 2006) and Gherardo Bronzin. The first contact to the Bronzin family was kindly established by Anne Perisic.

In Trieste, the following persons were extremely helpful with respect to contacts, information, and suggestions: Anna Millo, Anna Maria Vinci, Ermanno Pitacco, Arcadio Ogrin, Patrik Karlsen; Sergio Cergol and Clara Gasparini from *RAS*, and from *Generali*: Barbara Visintin, Alfred Leu, Alfeo Zanette, Marco Sarta, Ornella Bonetta (*Biblioteca*). The staff of the *Archivio di Stato di Trieste*, of the *Biblioteca Civica di Trieste*, and the *Biblioteca dell'Assicurazioni Generali*, Trieste, was extremely helpful and supporting. In addition we are grateful to Marina Cattaruzza for helpful advice.

Partial financial funding by the *WWZ-Förderverein* at the *University of Basel* is gratefully acknowledged under the projects No. B-086 and B-107. Without this seed money, the project could not have been started. The *Eurex*, represented by Andreas Preuss, provided the essential funding of the second stage of the project, in particular the translation of Bronzin's treatise.

We are extremely grateful to the *Springer Verlag* for its interest and support for including this book into its publishing program. Special thanks go to Dr. Birgit Leick, the responsible editor, who supported this venture with continuous encouragement, suggestions and helpful comments which significantly improved the final product. Tatjana Strasser and Kurt Mattes did a highly professional job in the production of the final manuscript. Hermione Miller-Moser, Roberta Verona and her staff from *Key Congressi* in Trieste, and again Igor Uszczapowski provided linguistic advice and excellent translations of individual chapters. The assistance of Yves Straub was extremely helpful along the entire editorial process, from the earliest versions until the proofreading of the individual chapters.

Prior to this publication, we had the opportunity to make our research accessible to an international audience by a chapter contributed to Geoffrey Poitras book about *Financial Pioneers* (2006), and a paper in the *Journal of Banking and Finance* (2007).[10] We are grateful to its editor, Giorgio Szegö, for his support and interest. Part of the material included in our Chapters 5, 6, 7 and 9 in this volume is based on these publications.

In 2007, the *Comitato in Onore del Prof. Bronzin* was founded in Trieste under the auspices of Prof. avv. Vittorio Cogno with the secretary Stellia Raldi and the scientific adviser Ermanno Pitacco, representatives of the Bronzin family, of the *Istituto Tecnico Nautico "Tomaso di Savoia Duca di Genova" and of the Istituto Tecnico Commerciale "Gian Rinaldo Carli"* in Trieste. This work of the committee accelerated the public perception of Bronzin's work, and a *Giornata di Studi* was organized on December 13, 2008, in Trieste with the moderation of Lorella Francarli. We are grateful to the organizers and sponsors of this conference for their effort and support. Barbara Visintin provided excellent translations of the non-Italian talks.

We conclude this foreword by quoting Espen Haug from Chapter 17:

> "The history of option pricing and hedging is far too complex and profound to be fully described within a few pages or even a book or two, but, hopefully, this contribution will encourage readers to search out more old books and papers and question the premisses of modern text books that are often not revised with regard to the history option pricing".

We hope that our readers share this insight, and that this book contributes another piece to a fascinating puzzle.

Windisch and Basel, Switzerland, January 2009

Wolfgang Hafner
Heinz Zimmermann

[10] The respective references are Zimmermann and Hafner (2006, 2007).

References

Bachelier L (1900) Théorie de la spéculation. Annales Scientifiques de l' Ecole Normale Supérieure, Ser. 3, 17, Paris, pp. 21–88. English translation in: Cootner P (ed) (1964) The random character of stock market prices. MIT Press, Cambridge (Massachusetts), pp. 17–79

Bernstein P (1992) Capital ideas. The Free Press, New York

Bouleau N (2004) Financial markets and martingales. Observations on science and speculation. Springer, Berlin, (Translated from French original edition, Odile Jacob Edition 1998)

Bronzin V (1906) Lehrbuch der politischen Arithmetik. Franz Deuticke, Leipzig/ Vienna

Bronzin V (1908) Theorie der Prämiengeschäfte. Franz Deuticke, Leipzig/ Vienna

Cootner P (ed) (1964) The random character of stock market prices. MIT Press, Cambridge (Massachusetts)

Davis M, Etheridge A (2006) Louis Bachelier's theory of speculation. Princeton University Press, Princeton

de Finetti B (1940) Il problema dei pieni. Giornale Istituto Italiano Attuari 11, pp. 1–88 (English translation: Barone L (2006) The problem of full risk insurances, Ch. 1: 'The problem in a single accounting period'. Journal of Investment Management 4, pp. 19–43)

Einstein A (1905) Über die von der molekular-kinetischen Theorie der Wärme geforderte Bewegung von in ruhenden Flüssigkeiten suspendierten Teilchen. Annalen der Physik 17, pp. 549–560

Hafner W (2002) Im Schatten der Derivate. Eichborn, Frankfurt on the Main

Jovanovic F (2006) A 19th century random walk: Jules Regnault and the origins of scientific financial economics. In: Poitras G (ed) (2006) Pioneers of financial economics: contributions prior to Irving Fisher, Vol. 1. Edward Elgar Publishing, Cheltenham (UK), pp. 191–222

Leitner F (1920) Das Bankgeschäft und seine Technik, 4th edn. Sauerländer

Lengwiler Y (2004) Microfoundations of financial economics. Princeton University Press, Princeton

Poitras G (ed) (2006) Pioneers of financial economics: contributions prior to Irving Fischer. Edward Elgar Publishing, Cheltenham (UK)

Reganult J (1863) Calcul des chances et philosophie de la bourse. Mallet-Bachelier, Paris

Roy A (1992) A man and his property. Journal of Portfolio Management 18, pp. 93–102

Samuelson P A (1973) Mathematics of speculative price. SIAM Review (Society of Industrial and Applied Mathematics) 15, pp. 1–42

Taqqu M (2001) Bachelier and his times: a conversation with Bernard Bru. Finance and Stochastics 5, pp. 3–32

Welcker J, Kloy J, Schindler K (1988) Professionelles Optionsgeschäft. Verlag Moderne Industrie, Landsberg

Zimmermann H, Hafner W (2006) Vincenz Bronzin's option pricing theory: contents, contribution, and background. In: Poitras G (ed) (2006) Pioneers of financial economics: contributions prior to Irving Fisher, Vol. 1. Edward Elgar, Cheltenham (UK), pp. 238–264

Zimmermann H, Hafner W (2007) Amazing discovery: Vincenz Bronzin's option pricing models. Journal of Banking and Finance 31, pp. 531–546

1 Vinzenz Bronzin – Personal Life and Work

Wolfgang Hafner and Heinz Zimmermann

Vinzenz (later: Vincenzo) Bronzin was born in Rovigno (today: Rovinj), a small town on the peninsula of Istria (Croatia), on 4th May 1872, and died in Trieste on the 20th December 1970 at age 98. He was the son of a commandant of a sailing-ship. After completing the gymnasium (high school) in Capodistria, a town on Istria, he became a student in engineering at the University of Polytechnics in Vienna, where he made his exams after an enrolment of two years. He then studied mathematics and paedagogics at the University of Vienna, and at the same time, he took courses for military officers in Graz.

In his obituary, his nephew Angelo Bronzin reports that he was a well known gambler and a champion in fencing during his time in Vienna. In 1897 he became a teacher in mathematics at the Upper High School of Trieste (*Civica Scuola Reale*

Vinzenz Bronzin at the gymnasium in Capodistria in 1891. Bronzin is the first in the upper row from left

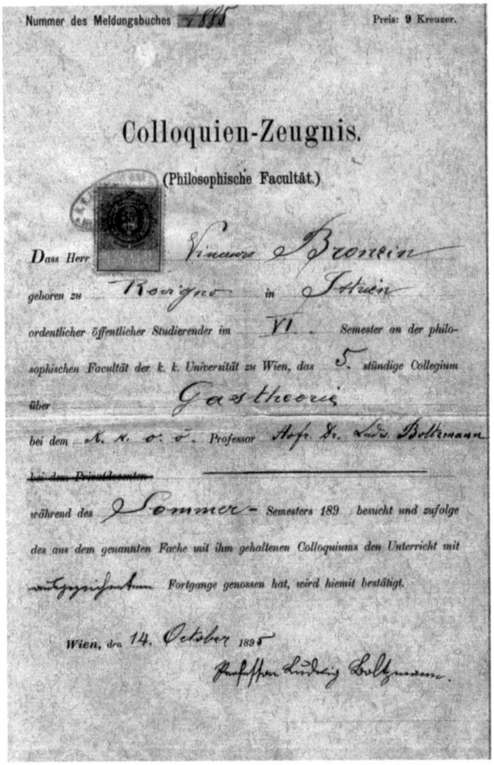
Nummer des Meldungsbuches [illegible] Preis: 9 Kreuzer.

Colloquien-Zeugnis.

(Philosophische Facultät.)

Dass Herr Vincenzo Bronzin

geboren zu Rovigno in Istrien

ordentlicher öffentlicher Studierender im VI. Semester an der philosophischen Facultät der k. k. Universität zu Wien, das 5. stündige Collegium

über Gastheorie

bei dem k. k. o. ö. Professor Hofr. Dr. Ludw. Boltzmann

~~bei dem Privatdocenten~~

während des Sommer- Semesters 189 besucht und zufolge des aus dem genannten Fache mit ihm gehaltenen Colloquiums den Unterricht mit ausgezeichnetem Fortgange genossen hat, wird hiemit bestätigt.

Wien, den 14. October 1895

Professor Ludwig Boltzmann.

In 1895 Bronzin attended lectures on the *Gastheorie* by the famous physicist Ludwig Boltzmann at the University of Vienna

Superiore di Trieste). In 1900 he was nominated professor for commercial and political arithmetic at the *I.R. Accademia di Commercio e Nautica*. He was the director of this institution from 1910 to 1937. Apparently, his reputation was overwhelming. In a book published in 1925, he was euphorically called "a jewel of humanity" (*eine Zierde der Menschheit*) and "heroic scientist".[11]

Why was V. Bronzin interested in probability theory? Why was he interested in derivative (option) contracts? We have only partial answers to these questions, sometimes only hypotheses, even though we had the opportunity to talk with his son in March 2005, Andrea Bronzin (1912–2006).

Many questions remain open because Andrea was born after the time period most relevant for our research (1900–1910), and because, apparently, finance and speculation was no topic his father used to talk about or deal with in later years. In accordance with his son Andrea Bronzin we suggest that Vinzenz Bronzin wrote his (1908) book for educational purposes.[12] This seems to be true for all his earlier

[11] De Tuoni (1925).

[12] From a letter dated 17/01/2005: "*Mio padre ha scritto la teoria delle operazioni a premio perché attinenti al suo insegnamento presso l'Accademia di Commercio di Trieste ed alter Accademie di Commercio austriache.*"

Bronzin and his son Andrea in 1916

publications (e.g. 1904, 1906, 1908), which grew out of subjects of his lectures at the *Accademia di Commercio e Nautico* in Trieste, where he was a professor for "Political and Commercial Arithmetic". Both fields were part of the mathematical curriculum and also included actuarial science and probability theory – however, on a rather applied level. The term "Political Arithmetic" was used to characterize the application of basic mathematics and statistics to a wide range of problems arising in areas such as civil government, political economy, commerce, social science, finance, and insurance. In particular, the field included topics like compounding, annuities, population statistics, life expectancy analysis et al., which had certainly a focus on the needs of the insurance companies[13]. "Commercial Arithmetic" was more accomplished to the needs of the banking industry and international orien-

[13] The program at the Accademia included: "*Elementi di calcolo di probabilità (probabilità assoluta, relativa, composta. Probabilità rispetto alla vita dell'uomo. Durata probabile della vita. Aspettativa matematica e posta e posta legittima nei giuochi di sorte).*" Source: (1917), pp. 163–164.

The building of the *I.R. Accademia di Commercio e Nautica* of Trieste at the beginning of the 20th century

tated trading companies.[14] At this time, it was a well established tradition among professors to publish books about the topics they covered in their lectures[15].

The first publication of Bronzin which is documented in his own curriculum is a short article entitled "*Arbitrage*" in a German journal for commercial education (Bronzin 1904)[16]. The paper is about characterizing relative price ratios of goods across different currencies and associated trading (arbitrage) strategies. While interesting per se, it is unfortunately not directly related to the "arbitrage valuation principle" of derivatives valuation – which Bronzin, ironically, uses as a key valua-

[14] For example: "*Arbitraggio di divise, effetti, valuti e di riporto. Borse. Affari commerciali secondo le norme di Borsa in merci ed effetti. Arrangement ... Spiegazione delle quotazioni di divisen e valute sulle piazze commerciali d'oltremare più importanti per l'importazione ed esportazione europea.*" Source: Subak (1917), p. 164.

[15] See Subak (1917), pp. 257ff, and Piccoli (1882).

[16] We found only one reference to this paper, in Subak (1917), p. 274. The aim of the journal was to publish critical and original surveys on subjects relevant for educational purposes, contributed by the leading scholars in the field ("*Die 'Monatsschrift für Handels- und Sozialwissenschaft' berichtet über alle das Gebiet ... (des) Unterrichtswesen betreffenden Fragen in kritisch zusammengefassten Originalartikeln von ersten Fachleuten*"); Source: *Monatsschrift für Handels- und Sozialwissenschaft 12* (15 December 1904), pp. 356–360.

tion principle (based on his "principle of equivalance") in his option pricing book, however whithout using this term[17].

Bronzins second publication (Bronzin 1906) is a monograph on Political Arithmetic (*Lehrbuch der politischen Arithmetik*); it was approved by the ministry of education as an official textbook to be used at the commercial schools and academies in the Empire[18]. Bronzin had not – in contrast to many of his colleagues at the Accademia – published extensively. It is therefore more than surprising, if not strange, that he did not quote his (1908) option pricing piece in a publication (a festschrift) released for the centenary of the school[19]. Had it become such a "queer" subject in the meantime? As shown in Chapter II.3, it was indeed unusual to apply probability theory to speculation and financial securities pricing in these times, but why should he suppress his major scientific contribution he had produced so far? Was the subject too complicated for the target audience, or did he get frustrating responses?

It is true that gambling, speculation, or trading with derivatives did not enjoy a major popularity around this time[20]. In the last decade of the 19th century, derivatives were more and more blamed to cause exuberant market movements and to be socially harmful. Furthermore, in 1901, a court of justice accepted the "gambling" argument (*Spiel und Wette*) in a legal case in Vienna. Thereafter, forward trading declined and got more and more unimportant.[21] At the rather small stock-exchange of Trieste, premium contracts have not been traded at all during these years.[22] But was this practical limitation a sufficient reason for Bronzin to suppress this publication? Was his interest in derivatives (and finance in general) so much determined by practical matters[23], or was it more on the theoretical side? Unfortunately, we do not have definitive answers.

Writing books must have been hard work for Bronzin anyway. Beside his academic position, Bronzin was nominated director of the *Accademia* in 1909, but he

[17] The closest statement to what we now call "aribtrage strategy" (providing a riskless profit without positive net investment) can be found in his *Theorie der Prämiengeschäfte*, in the last sentence on p. 38.

[18] This is reflected in the subtitle of the book: "... *zum Gebrauche an Höheren Handelsschulen (Handelsakademien) sowie zum Selbstunterricht*".

[19] See Subak (1917)

[20] See Stillich (1909), pp. 1–18, pp. 181–227, for a representative discussion of these issues at that time.

[21] Schmitt (2003), p. 145.

[22] Archivio dello stato di Trieste, atto "*Listino Ufficiale della Borsa di Trieste*" from 1900 to 1910.

[23] At least, all but one of his option valuation models just require pencil and paper to compute option prices; only one model requires a probability distribution table (the law of error, i.e. the Normal distribution) which the author reproduces in the Appendix of his book.

Bronzin at the celebration of his retirement as president, circumvented by alumnies of the commercial school *I.T.C. "Gian Rinaldo Carli"*. The alumnies gifted him a sailing-boat at this occasion

was not yet able to accept the nomination, because he was suffering from a strong nervousness, apparently caused by his efforts of writing the two books ("*in forte nervosità*" because of "*compilazione e publicazione di libri matematici*").[24] One year later he was offered the same position again, and he then accepted. Shortly afterwards, there were plans to launch a Commercial College (*Handelshochschule*) in Vienna, and Bronzin had good chances getting an appointment as a professor[25]; however, with the outbreak of the First World War, the project had to be abandoned. Bronzin resigned from his positions at the *Accademia* in 1937, at the age of 65.

[24] Archivio dello stato di Trieste, atto *Accademia di Commercio e Nautica in Trieste*, b 101 e regg 273, 1909, AA 345/09, from the 31.07.1909. In August 1909, also one of his beloved daughters died.

[25] Based on private communication with Andrea Bronzin.

Piazza della Borsa di Trieste (Square of the Stock Exchange) in the fourth quarter of the 19th century

His major achievement as a director of the *Accademia* was seen in his ability to guide the school through a time of big political turbulences before, during and after the first world war. He still preserved a great reputation as mathematician. As we mentioned above, at least during his study years in Vienna, he had the reputation of being a successful gambler.[26] Combining mathematics with gambling seem to have been a perfect fit to write his option pricing theory. Interestingly, no consulting activities are known or documented. He was several times asked to join insurance companies but preferred to stay in academia.[27]

References

Bronzin, Vinzenz (1904), Arbitrage, *Monatsschrift für Handels- und Sozialwissenschaft* **12**, pp. 356–360

Bronzin, Vinzenz (1906), *Lehrbuch der politischen Arithmetik*, Franz Deuticke

Bronzin, Vinzenz (1908), *Theorie der Prämiengeschäfte*, Franz Deuticke

De Tuoni, Dario (1925), *Il Regio Istituto Commerciale di Trieste*, Saggio Storico, Trieste

[26] Obituary of his nephew, Angelo Bronzin.

[27] Letter as of December 30, 2004, from Arcadio Ogrin, summarizing a conversation with Andrea Bronzin.

Piccoli, Giorgio (1882), *Elementi di Diritto sulle Borse e sulle operazioni di Borsa secondo la Legge Austriaca e le norme della Borsa Triestina, Lezione*, Editrice la Gazetta dei Tribunali in Trieste

Schmitt, Johann (2003), *Die Geschichte der Wiener Börse – Ein Vierteljahrtausend Wertpapierhandel*, Wien Bibliophile Edition

Stillich, Oskar (1909), *Die Börse und ihre Geschäfte*, Karl Curtius

Subak, Giulio (1917), *Cent'Anni d'Insegnamento Commerciale – La Sezione Commerciale della I.R. Accademia di Commercio e Nautica di Trieste*, Presso la Sezione Commerciale dell' I.R. Accademia di Commercio e Nautica, Trieste

Index of pictures

pages 7, 8, 9, 12: Courtesy of Raldi family, Trieste
page 10: Courtesy of Arcadio Ogrin, from the collection of the Istituto Nautico, Trieste
page 13: Courtesy of Libreria Italo Svevo di Franco Zorzon, Trieste

Stefan Zweig: A Representative Voice of the Time

When I attempt to find a simple formula for the period in which I grew up, prior to the First Word War, I hope that I convey its fullness by calling it the Golden Age of Security. Everything in our almost thousand-year-old Austrian monarchy seemed based on permanency, and the State itself was the chief guarantor of this stability. The rights which is granted to its citizens were duly confirmed by parliament, the freely elected representative of the people, and every duty was exactly prescribed. Our currency, the Austrian crown, circulated in bright gold pieces, an assurance of its immutability. Everyone knew how much he possessed or what he was entitled to do, what was permitted and what forbidden. Everything had its norm, its definite measure and weight. He who had a fortune could accurately compute his annual interest. An official or an officer, for example, could confidently look up in the calendar the year when he would be advanced in grade, or when he would be pensioned. Each family had its fixed budget, and know how much could be spent for the rent and food, for vacations and entertainment; and what is more, invariably a small sum was carefully laid aside for sickness and doctor's bills, for the unexpected. Whoever owned a house looked upon it as a secure domicile for his children and grandchildren; estates and businesses were handed down from generation to generation. When the babe was still in its cradle, its first mite was put in its little bank, or deposited in the savings bank, as a "reserve" for the future. In this vast empire everything stood firmly and immovably in its appointed place, and at its head was the aged emperor; and were he to die, one knew (or believed) another would come to take his place, and nothing would change in the well-regulated order. No one thought of wars, of revolutions, or revolts. All that was radical, all violence, seemed impossible in an age of reason.

This feeling of security was the most eagerly sought-after possession of millions, the common ideal of life. Only the possession of this security made life seem worth while, and constantly widening circles desired their share of this costly treasure. At first it was only the prosperous who enjoyed this advantage, but gradually the great masses forced their way toward it. The century of security became the golden age of insurance. One's house was insured against fire and theft, one's field against hail and storm, one's person against accident and sickness. Annuities were purchased for one's old age, and a policy was laid in a girl's cradle for her future dowry. Finally even the workers organized, and won standard wages and workmen's compensation. Servants saved up for old-age insurance and paid in advance into a burial fund for their own interment. Only the man who could look into the future without worry could thoroughly enjoy the present.

from: *The World of Yesterday*, Viking Press, 1943
Chapter 1: The World of Security
Translated edition, The University of Nebraska Press, 1964

2 How I Discovered Bronzin's Book

Wolfgang Hafner*

It was in the 1990's when my joint project with Gian Trepp on "Money Laundering through Derivatives", which had been financed by the Swiss National Science Foundation, was under way. The research for this project was eye-opening. It helped me to understand how derivative instruments work and how they were steadily gaining more importance. I then met people in charge of dealing with these instruments, however working more on the scarcely lit side of this maverick world of modern finance. Among them there were some interesting people from the World Bank and from the International Monetary Fund. I also got the chance of talking to the Senior Advisor to the Under Secretary Enforcement of the US-Treasury, Michael D. Langan with his staff in summer 1998.

The meeting with the US-treasury people was revealing. It gave rise to my impression that the administration was a little bit helpless when confronted with the possibilities for using derivatives for money-laundering. I outlined the system to them, giving them examples. A terrorist organization, or an individual criminal may own two accounts and use them to simultaneously buy and sell financial derivatives. On the first account, which contains the dirty money, a forward transaction may be initiated which would be in complete opposition to market expectations and to all odds. The second account would serve as the counterpart for the deal. Upon exercise, the first account would lose while the second one would in turn make money. Thus, as a result the losses in the dirty money account will have been transformed into legitimate profits in the clean money account. Through this process the dirty money could be laundered. Meanwhile, the inevitable transaction costs, chalked up as business expenses, keep the banks and brokers happy.

In London I also met the responsible compliance manager at Credit Suisse Financial Products (CSFP), Tony Blunden, who at that time confirms their full control of the issue. Some months later he was kicked out of his job as a scapegoat. CSFP has been fined by the Japanese Banking Authorities (FSA) for their maverick instruments they had sold to Japanese companies. These derivative contracts helped "to fly away" financial losses either to special purpose entities located offshore or, otherwise, by making use of a type of contracts that were based on the

* This chapter partly relies on a blueprint of a forthcoming book by George Szpiro, which is gratefully acknowledged.

ancient Japanese accounting system for companies. Each company had its own key date for reporting, and with fraudulent contracts based on derivatives it was possible to repeatedly roll over the loss from the balance sheet of one company to another. A perfect hideaway for the loss.

In this process I gained a more critical approach towards these instruments. Yet on the other hand I was also amazed and surprised by the possibilities that were offered to the financial community through derivative constructions. This made me curious to learn more about these double-edged instruments. As an economic historian I started to dig into the past. I read Edward J. Swan's book "Building the Global Market" (Kluwer 2000), and then Peter Bernstein's bestseller "Against the Gods" (Wiley 1998) about the history of risk-management. I was astonished about the great importance that Bernstein attributed to the contribution of the – namely – American mathematicians to the development of models for the calculation of option-prices and to portfolio-theory. As a historian I was also familiar with the strong trading of derivatives in Europe at the end of the 19th and the start of the 20th century. I was skeptical to believe that it should have been only Louis Bachelier to have successfully worked on a model for computing option prices.

In the meantime I was convinced that it would prove worthwhile to publish a popular version of my research about money-laundering through derivatives along with its glimpse on the history of derivatives. The German publisher Eichborn was interested in this venture, and the book *Im Schatten der Derivate* ("In the Shadows of Derivatives") appeared in 2002.

I continued my historical research and became aware of the great importance of derivative contracts in Europe at the end of the 19th century. In an article published by R. Gömmel on *Entstehung und Entwicklung der Effektenbörsen im 19. Jahrhundert bis 1914* ("Emergence and development of security exchanges in the 19th century until 1914")[28] we read that 60 percent of the trading activity at the German stock-exchanges were transactions for future delivery (forward contracts mostly). I intensified my research focusing on this issue and also asked my antiquarian bookseller to search for the major historical books about banking and speculation published in these days. I hoped through his help to find some contemporary textbooks for students in finance that would specifically follow a practical approach. I was also amazed about the huge production of books about derivatives (*Termingeschäfte*) that have been published at this time.

One of the books I found was written by Friedrich Leitner, a professor at the Handels-Hochschule Berlin, entitled *Das Bankgeschäft und seine Technik*, 4th edition, published in 1920. On some 60 pages, Leitner wrote about the different types of derivative contracts as *Prämiengeschäfte*, *Stellage*, *Nochgeschäfte* and so on. He also used different diagrams, for example, to illustrate put-options

[28] published in: Deutsche Börsengeschichte, edited by Hans Pohl, Fritz Knapp Verlag, 1992, pp. 133–207.

and other trading-tactics. In a footnote he mentioned Bronzins book, *Theorie der Prämiengeschäfte*, and noted that it "deals with the subject from a mathematical point of view".

I got hold of Bronzin's book through my library and was truly amazed. Bronzin showed formulas that were apparently similar to the famous formula of Black-Scholes with which I was then already familiar. I needed to be both certain and scientifically backed in case the issue would turn out to be a rediscovery of an up to then forgotten book. This made me write an email to Professor Heinz Zimmermann from the Department of Finance at University of Basle who I knew from a panel discussion and estimated as an outspoken academic, asking him whether he had ever heard of this obscure professor. Zimmermann had not and was at first extremely doubtful. He knew, of course, Bachelier's early contribution to the theory of finance which had been laying dormant for so long. Now, all of a sudden another forgotten pioneer should appear out of nowhere? The question came: How often can the wheel be *pre*-invented? Zimmermann was close to dismiss the information I had sent him. Yet the more he read, the more surprised he became. Soon his initial skepticism gave way to keen interest and fascination. In fact, after the re-discovery of Regnault, Lefèvre and Bachelier, no less than a new pioneer was on stage.

Part A

Theorie der Prämiengeschäfte

Vinzenz Bronzin

THEORIE

DER

PRÄMIENGESCHÄFTE.

VON

VINZENZ BRONZIN,
PROFESSOR.

LEIPZIG UND WIEN
FRANZ DEUTICKE
1908.

Verlags-Nr. 1394.

K. u. K. Hofbuchdruckerei Karl Prochaska in Teschen.

Inhaltsverzeichnis.

Erster Teil.

Die verschiedenen Formen und die gegenseitigen Beziehungen der Zeitgeschäfte.

I. Kapitel.

II. Kapitel.

III. Kapitel.

Zweiter Teil.

Untersuchungen höherer Ordnung.

I. Kapitel.

II. Kapitel.

Tafel I.

I. Teil.

Die verschiedenen Formen und die gegenseitigen Beziehungen der Zeitgeschäfte.

I. Kapitel.

Normale Prämiengeschäfte.

1. Einleitung. Die Börsengeschäfte teilen wir in Kassa- und in Zeitgeschäfte ein, je nachdem bei denselben die Lieferung der gehandelten Objekte sofort nach Abschluß des Kontrakts oder erst an einem späteren bestimmten Termin zu erfolgen hat. Die Zeitgeschäfte sind ihrerseits entweder feste oder, wie man zu sagen pflegt, Prämiengeschäfte: Bei ersteren müssen die gehandelten Stücke am Lieferungstermin unbedingt abgenommen resp. geliefert werden, bei letzteren hingegen erlangt einer der Kontrahenten, durch eine beim Abschlusse des Geschäftes geleistete Zahlung, das Recht am Lieferungstermin entweder auf Erfüllung des Kontrakts zu bestehen oder von demselben gänzlich resp. teilweise zurückzutreten.

2. Feste Geschäfte. Haben wir einen festen Kauf resp. einen festen Verkauf zum Kurse B, welcher natürlicherweise mit dem Tageskurse nahe oder vollkommen übereinstimmen wird, abgeschlossen, so haben wir bei einem Kurse $B + \varepsilon$ am Lieferungstermin offenbar einen Gewinn resp. einen Verlust von der Größe ε, während bei einem Kurse $B - \eta$ ein Verlust resp. ein Gewinn von der Größe η entstehen wird. In graphischer Darstellung erhalten wir folgende unmittelbar verständliche Gewinn- und Verlustdiagramme, wobei die Figur 1 dem festen Kaufe, die Figur 2 hingegen dem festen Verkaufe entspricht.

Es braucht kaum der Erwähnung, daß die dreieckigen Diagrammteile rechts und links von B als äquivalent anzunehmen sind, da sonst entweder der Kauf oder der Verkauf von Haus aus vorteilhafter sein sollte.

Bei n gleichen Käufen hätten wir bei den betrachteten Marktlagen am Lieferungstermin offenbar die Gewinne

$$n\varepsilon \text{ resp. } -n\eta,$$

wobei wir nämlich den Verlust als einen negativen Gewinn eingeführt haben; ebenso wären die Gewinne bei n gleich großen Verkäufen durch

$$-n\varepsilon \text{ resp. } n\eta$$

dargestellt. Wir ersehen hieraus, wie der Effekt von n Verkäufen dem Effekte von $-n$ Käufen vollkommen äquivalent ist, so daß bei

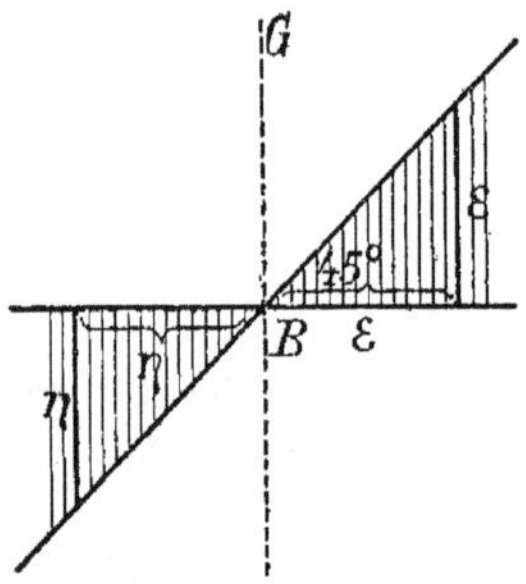

Fig. 1.

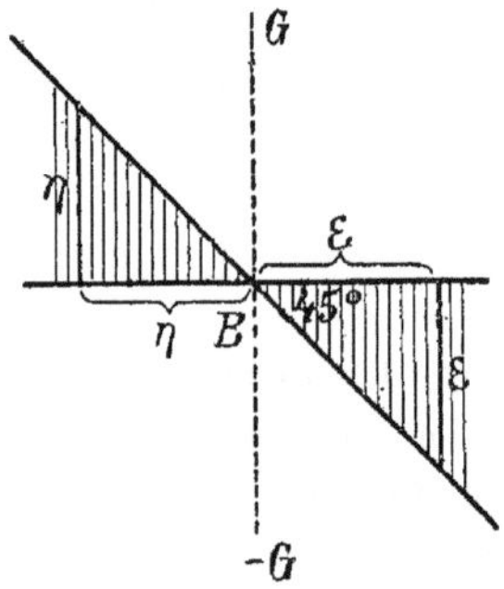

Fig. 2.

analytischen Betrachtungen der einzige Begriff des Kaufes resp. des Verkaufes eingeführt zu werden braucht: in der Folge werden wir durchgängig den positiven Wert für den Kauf reservieren. So wird z. B. der Buchstabe z eine gewisse Anzahl Käufe, $-z$ hingegen ebensoviel Verkäufe bedeuten; ein Resultat $z = 5$ wird z. B. als 5 Käufe, hingegen ein solches $z = -7$ als 7 Verkäufe zu interpretieren sein.

3. Einfache Prämiengeschäfte (Dontgeschäfte). Schließen wir einen Kauf zum Kurse B_1 ab und zahlen eine bestimmte Prämie (Reugeld) P_1, um die Wahl zu erlangen, am Lieferungstermin das gehandelte Objekt wirklich abzunehmen oder nicht, so werden wir von einem Wahlkaufe sprechen; für den anderen Kontrahenten, welcher nach unserer Wahl liefern muß oder nicht, liegt ein Zwangsverkauf vor. Hätten wir einen Verkauf à B_1 abgeschlossen, durch Zahlung aber einer gewissen Prämie P_2 uns das Recht reserviert, am Lieferungstermin nach unserem Belieben wirklich zu liefern oder nicht, so wäre von einem Wahlverkaufe die Rede: der andere Kontrahent, welcher das gehandelte Stück, je nachdem es uns beliebt, abnehmen wird oder nicht, schließt einen Zwangskauf ab. Die hier geschilderten Geschäfte nennen wir nun einfache Prämiengeschäfte; sie stellen gleichsam die Bausteine, aus denen sich alle anderen Prämiengeschäfte zusammensetzen, dar.*)

Der Wahlkauf sowie auch der Zwangsverkauf, falls sie wirklich zu stande kommen, erscheinen offenbar à $B_1 + P_1$ abgeschlossen, wovon (dont) P_1 als Prämie hinzugefügt wurde; ebenso kommen der Wahlverkauf und der Zwangskauf à $B_1 - P_2$ abgeschlossen vor, wovon (dont) P_2 als Prämie nachgelassen wurde.

Um die Gewinnverhältnisse bei den verschiedenen denkbaren Marktlagen am Lieferungstermine darzustellen, verfahren wir auf folgende Weise:

Bei einem Wahlkaufe zahlen wir die Prämie P_1, welcher Betrag offenbar als Verlust bei jeder möglichen Marktlage auftritt; infolge aber des erworbenen Rechtes wirklich zu kaufen oder nicht, werden wir jede Marktschwankung über B_1 zu unserem Vorteile ausnützen können und bei Marktschwankungen unter B_1 vor weiterem Verluste geschützt sein; bei den Marktlagen $B_1 + \varepsilon$ resp. $B_1 - \eta$ werden somit unsere Gewinne

$$\varepsilon - P_1 \text{ resp. } - P_1$$

sein. Bei einem Wahlverkaufe würde P_2 bei jeder Marktlage als Verlust auftreten; hingegen würde jedes Fallen des Kurses unter B_1 einen korrespondierenden Gewinn, jedes Steigen aber desselben über B_1 keinen weiteren Verlust hervorbringen können; wir hätten sonach bei den Marktpreisen $B_1 + \varepsilon$ resp. $B_1 - \eta$ die Gewinne

$$- P_2 \text{ resp. } \eta - P_2.$$

So hätten wir bei n Wahlkäufen derselben Quantität die Gewinne

$$n(\varepsilon - P_1) \text{ resp. } - n P_1,$$

bei n Wahlverkäufen hingegen die Gewinne

$$- n P_2 \text{ resp. } n(\eta - P_2).$$

*) In der Praxis findet man für die geschilderten einfachen Prämiengeschäfte folgende Bezeichnungen: Kauf mit Vorprämie für unseren Wahlkauf, Verkauf mit Vorprämie für den Zwangsverkauf; Verkauf mit Rückprämie für den Wahlverkauf und Kauf mit Rückprämie für den Zwangskauf; wir haben uns zur Einführung unserer Ausdrücke deswegen entschlossen, weil sie kürzer sind nnd jedenfalls die Natur des entsprechenden Geschäftes besser charakterisieren.

Da nun für die anderen Kontrahenten unsere Gewinne ebenso große Verluste und umgekehrt bedeuten, so ergeben sich bei n Zwangsverkäufen die Gewinne

$$-n(\varepsilon - P_1) \text{ resp. } n P_1,$$

bei n Zwangskäufen aber

$$n P_2 \text{ resp. } -n(\eta - P_2).$$

Auch hier ersehen wir, daß die Effekte von n Zwangsverkäufen resp. Zwangskäufen jenen von $-n$ Wahlkäufen resp. Wahlverkäufen vollkommen äquivalent sind; bei algebraischen Untersuchungen werden wir daher auch hier mit den einzigen Begriffen des Wahlkaufes und des Wahlverkaufes auskommen, sobald nur etwa negativ ausfallende Werte als Zwangsverkäufe resp. als Zwangskäufe aufzufassen sein werden.

Bedeuten also x resp. y eine gewisse Anzahl Wahlkäufe resp. Wahlverkäufe, so werden $-x$ resp. $-y$ ebensoviel Zwangsverkäufe resp. Zwangskäufe repräsentieren; so wird z. B. ein Resultat $x = 4$ als 4 Wahlkäufe, ein solches $y = -6$ hingegen als 6 Zwangskäufe zu betrachten sein.

Wollen wir die ermittelten Gewinnverhältnisse graphisch darstellen, so erhalten wir folgende Diagramme:

α) Für den Wahlkauf:

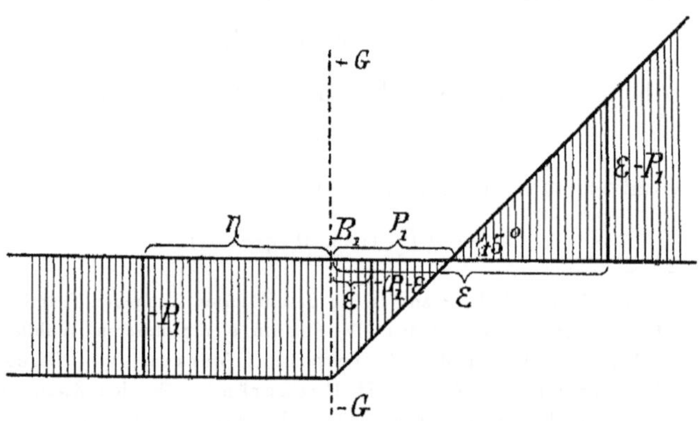

Fig. 3.

— 5 —

β) Für den Zwangsverkauf:

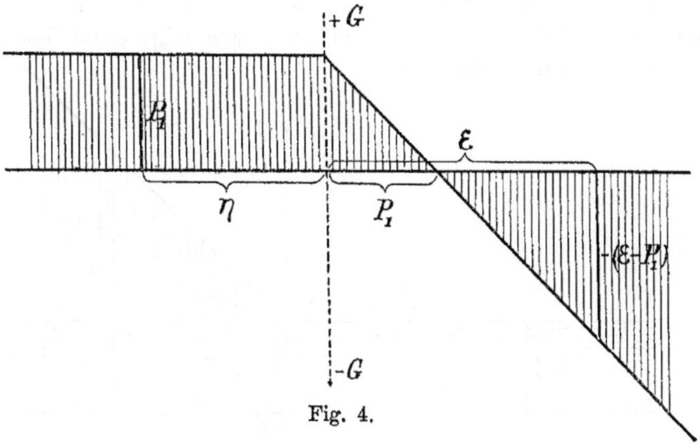

Fig. 4.

γ) Für den Wahlverkauf:

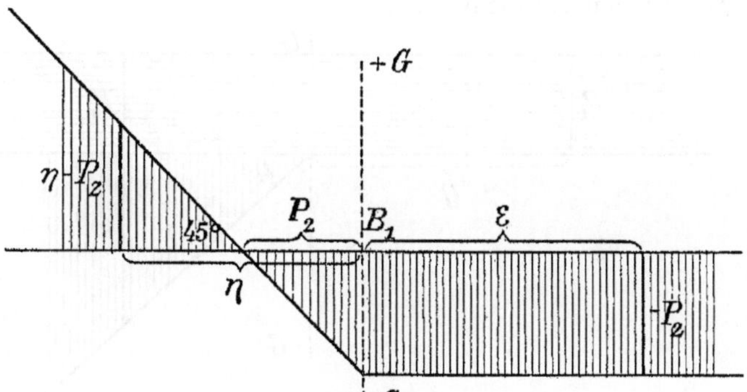

Fig. 5.

δ) Für den Zwangskauf:

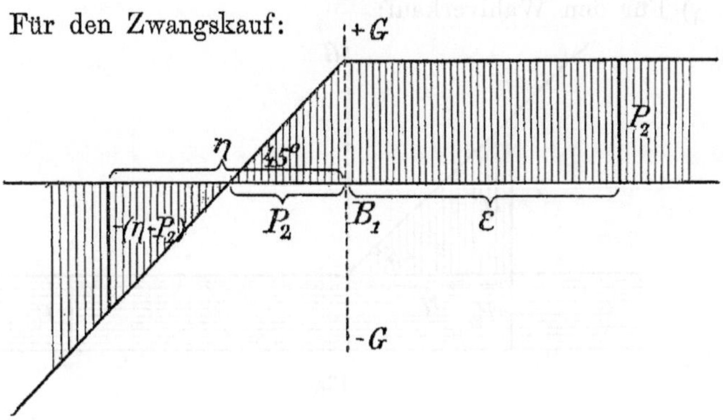

Fig. 6.

In viel bequemerer und übersichtlicher Weise lassen sich aber die vorstehenden Diagramme offenbar auch wie folgt darstellen:

α) Für den Wahlkauf:

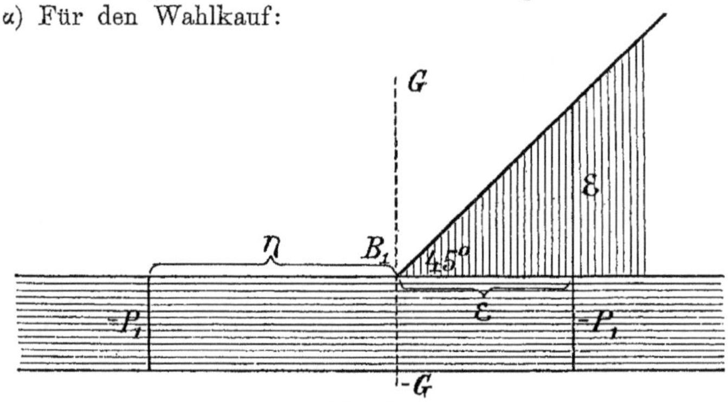

Fig. 7.

β) Für den Zwangsverkauf:

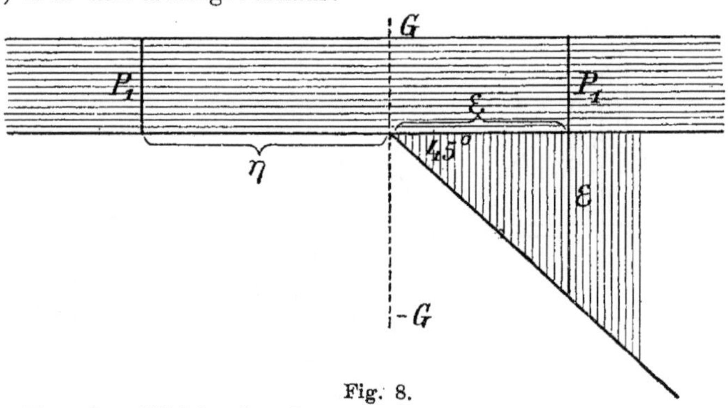

Fig. 8.

γ) Für den Wahlverkauf:

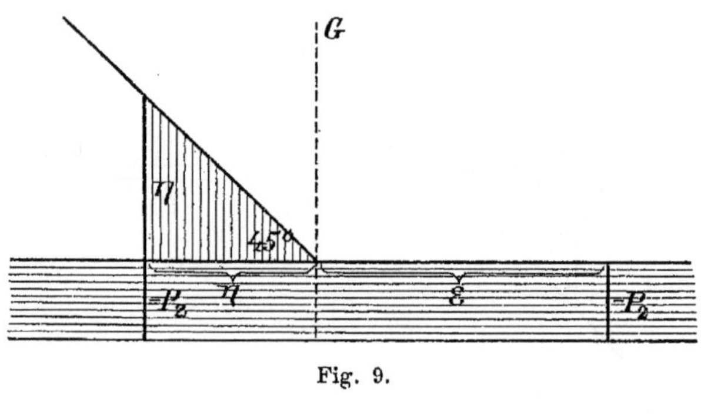

Fig. 9.

— 7 —

δ) Für den Zwangskauf:

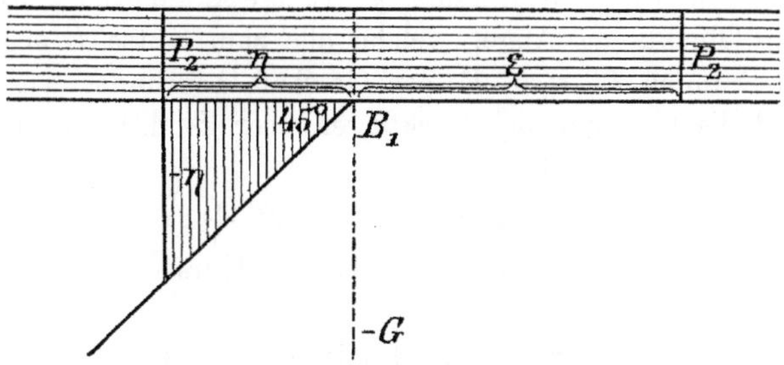

Fig. 10.

Bei den vorhergehenden Betrachtungen haben wir die Geschäfte à B_1 abgeschlossen angenommen, ohne über diesen Wert irgend welche Voraussetzung zu machen; es ist nun von der größten Bedeutung, ob der Kurs, zu welchem das Prämiengeschäft abgeschlossen wird, mit dem Kurse B der festen Geschäfte (dem Tageskurse) zusammenfällt oder nicht. Von diesem Gesichtspunkte aus teilen wir die einfachen Prämiengeschäfte in normale und schiefe Geschäfte ein, je nachdem dieselben zum Kurse B der festen Geschäfte, oder zu einem hievon verschiedenen Kurse, etwa $B + M$, abgeschlossen werden. Die Größe M nennen wir die Schiefe des Geschäftes.

4. Die Deckung bei normalen Geschäften. Sowohl aus den mathematischen Ausdrücken als auch aus den dargestellten Gewinndiagrammen sehen wir unmittelbar ein, daß bei den Wahlgeschäften der Gewinn, bei Zwangsgeschäften hingegen der Verlust unbegrenzt wachsen kann, während bei ersteren der Verlust, bei letzteren hingegen der Gewinn eine bestimmte Grenze, d. h. die Größe der gezahlten Prämie, nicht übersteigen kann. Es ist nun klar, daß der Abschluß von lauter Zwangsgeschäften unter diesen Verhältnissen sehr gefährlich werden und geradezu einen finanziellen Ruin herbeiführen könnte: Ein kluger Spekulant wird somit seine Prämiengeschäfte so zu kombinieren trachten, daß ihm bei keiner der möglichen Lagen des Marktes ein allzu großer Verlust drohe; er wird in anderen Worten suchen, sich auf irgend welche Weise zu decken. Wir werden einen Komplex von Geschäften dann als gedeckt betrachten, wenn bei jeder nur denkbaren Marktlage weder Gewinn zu erwarten noch Verlust zu befürchten ist.

Um die allgemeinen Deckungsgesetze bei normalen Prämiengeschäften mit eventueller Heranziehung von festen Geschäften zu ermitteln, fassen wir x Wahlkäufe, y Wahlverkäufe und z feste Käufe desselben Objekts ins Auge, welche alle zum Kurse B abgeschlossen und mit Prämien P_1 resp. P_2 per Geschäft begründet wurden. Alsdann sind die Gewinne bei Marktlagen über B, d. h. bei einem Kurse $B + \varepsilon$, durch die Gleichung

$$G_1 = x(\varepsilon - P_1) - y P_2 + z \varepsilon,$$

hingegen bei Marktlagen unter B, also bei Kursen $B - \eta$, durch die Gleichung

$$G_2 = - x P_1 + y(\eta - P_2) - z \eta$$

dargestellt; beide Ansätze bringen wir beziehungsweise in die Form

$$\left.\begin{aligned} G_1 &= (x + z)\varepsilon - x P_1 - y P_2 \\ G_2 &= (y - z)\eta - x P_1 - y P_2 \end{aligned}\right\}, \qquad (1)$$

in welcher sie zu weiteren Betrachtungen zu benützen sind.

Die vollständige Deckung im früher definierten Sinne wird offenbar dann erreicht sein, wenn für jeden beliebigen Wert von ε resp. von η die Ausdrücke für G_1 resp. für G_2 identisch verschwinden, also wenn die Gleichungen

$$\left.\begin{aligned} (x + z)\varepsilon - x P_1 - y P_2 &= 0 \\ (y - z)\eta - x P_1 - y P_2 &= 0 \end{aligned}\right\} \qquad (2)$$

beständig erfüllt sein werden; bei der Willkürlichkeit von ε und von η ist dies aber nur dann möglich, wenn ihre Koeffizienten identisch null sind, so daß wir als unerläßliche Bedingungen zunächst die Gleichungen

$$\left.\begin{aligned} x + z &= 0 \\ y - z &= 0 \\ x + y &= 0 \end{aligned}\right\} \qquad (3)$$

gewinnen, wobei die letzte als eine unmittelbare Folge der zwei anderen hinzugefügt wurde. Was nun von den Gleichungen (2) noch übrig bleibt, d. h.

$$x P_1 + y P_2 = 0,$$

nimmt infolge der Bedingungen (3) offenbar die Form

$$x(P_1 - P_2) = 0$$

an, woraus, da im allgemeinen x von Null verschieden ist, die weitere Relation

$$P_1 = P_2 = P \qquad (4)$$

resultiert. Es hat sich somit bei dem Deckungsproblem normaler Geschäfte folgendes Prinzip herausgestellt: Die Summe der Wahlgeschäfte muß, wegen $x + y = 0$, identisch verschwinden, wie es auch, wegen $x + z = 0$ oder $y + (-z) = 0$, mit der Summe aller Käufe oder aller Verkäufe überhaupt der Fall sein muß. Es müssen in anderen Worten Wahlgeschäfte in gleicher Anzahl als Zwangsgeschäfte vorkommen; zu gleicher Zeit müssen aber, wegen $z = -x$, ebenso viele feste Verkäufe desselben Objekts vorgenommen werden, als Wahlkäufe vorhanden sind, oder, was auf dasselbe hinauslaufen muß, wegen $z = y$, ebensoviel feste Käufe abgeschlossen werden, als Wahlverkäufe vorhanden sind. Ferner müssen die Prämien des Wahlkaufes, „die sogenannten Vorprämien", jenen des Wahlverkaufes, „den sogenannten Rückprämien", nach Gleichung (4) gleichgehalten werden.

Auf graphischem Wege lassen sich diese Resultate auf sehr einfache Weise bestätigen und überblicken. Es entspricht nämlich unserem x, je nachdem es positiv oder negativ ausfällt, eine gewisse Anzahl von Diagrammen der Figur 7 resp. der Figur 8; freilich wird x im allgemeinen als eine Differenz von Wahlkäufen und ihren entgegengesetzten Geschäften, d. h. Zwangsverkäufen, die sich in gleicher Anzahl vollständig aufheben, aufzufassen sein; fürs Endresultat ist offenbar diese Differenz einzig und allein in Rechnung zu ziehen. Ebenso liefert y eine gewisse Anzahl von Diagrammen der Figur 9 resp. der Figur 10, je nachdem es positiv oder negativ sein wird, d. h. je nachdem die Wahlverkäufe die Zwangskäufe überwiegen werden oder nicht. Sollen sich nun diese x- und y-Diagramme mit eventueller Heranziehung von festen Geschäften vollständig aufheben, so ist dies nur dann möglich, wenn sich die rechteckigen Diagrammteile für sich und desgleichen die dreieckigen Diagrammteile für sich annullieren; schon die Eliminierung der rechteckigen Teile erfordert eine gleiche Anzahl von Diagrammen der Figuren 7 und 10 resp. der Figuren 8 und 9, in denen überdies die Höhen P_1 und P_2 einander gleich sein müssen; in diesen Erfordernissen sind offenbar die Bedingungen der gleichen Anzahl von Wahl- und von Zwangsgeschäften und der gleichen Höhe der Vor- und der Rückprämien zu erkennen. Nach Aufhebung der Rechtecke bleiben aber noch 2 x oder, was dasselbe ist, 2 y dreieckige Diagrammteile übrig, welche, zu zwei verbunden, x- oder y-Diagramme von der Form der Figur 11,

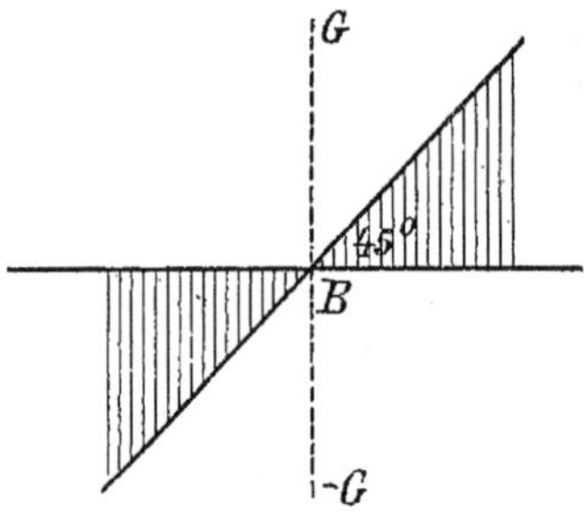

Fig. 11.

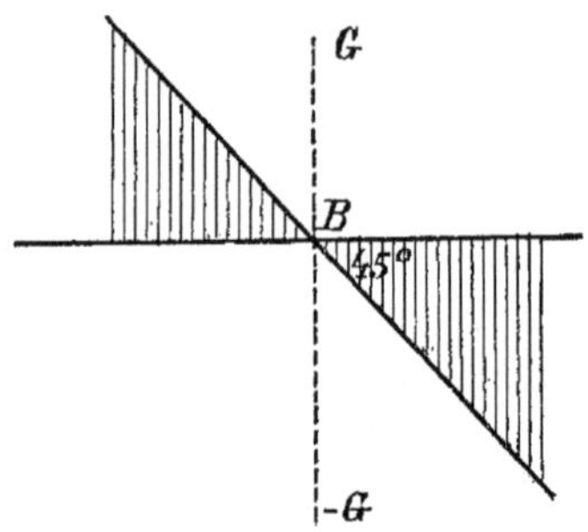

Fig. 12.

wenn x positiv, von der Form der Figur 12 hingegen, wenn x negativ ist, liefern werden. Zur Deckung dieser übrig gebliebenen Diagramme sind nun offenbar entweder ebensoviel feste Verkäufe oder ebensoviel feste Käufe erforderlich, denen eben genau entgegengesetzte Diagramme entsprechen; hierin ist aber der Inhalt der Gleichungen $z = -x$ resp. $z = y$ zu erblicken.

5. Äquivalenz von normalen Geschäften. Mit dem Problem der Deckung ist auch jenes der Äquivalenz gelöst. Zwei Systeme von Geschäften nennen wir nämlich dann einander äquivalent, wenn sich das eine aus dem anderen ableiten läßt, in anderen Worten, wenn dieselben bei jeder nur denkbaren Lage des Marktes einen ganz gleichen Gewinn resp. Verlust ergeben. Nach dieser Definition erfahren wir unmittelbar, daß wir sofort zwei Systeme äquivalenter Geschäfte erhalten, wenn wir nur in einem Komplexe gedeckter Geschäfte einige derselben mit entgegengesetzten Vorzeichen betrachten; das so gewonnene System ist sodann dem System der übrigen Geschäfte vollkommen äquivalent, und zwar aus folgendem Grunde: Es decken sich z. B. die Geschäfte x, y, z, u etc; wir betrachten etwa $-x$ und $-z$ Geschäfte, welche offenbar mit x und z einen in sich gedeckten Komplex bilden; es bringen somit $-x$ und $-z$ denselben Effekt hervor wie die übrig gebliebenen Geschäfte y, u etc.; das System $-x$ und $-y$ muß folglich dem System y, u . . . äquivalent sein. Es ergibt sich hieraus eine einfache Methode, um zu einem gegebenen Geschäftssystem das äquivalente System resp. die äquivalenten Systeme zu ermitteln; man braucht nur nämlich in den Deckungsgleichungen die Geschäfte des gegebenen Systems mit entgegengesetzten Zeichen zu substituieren und erstere nach den übrig gebliebenen Größen aufzulösen, um die äquivalenten Systeme unmittelbar zu erhalten. Bleiben ebensoviel Größen übrig, als Bedingungsgleichungen vorhanden sind, so wird sich ein einziges dem gegebenen äquivalentes System ergeben, da unsere Gleichungen ersten Grades sind; sind aber mehr Unbekannte als Gleichungen vorhanden, so werden im allgemeinen unendlich viele Systeme möglich sein, welche dem ins Auge gefaßten System äquivalent sein werden. Wären endlich mehr Gleichungen als unbekannte Größen vorhanden, so würde sich im allgemeinen das gegebene System aus den übrig bleibenden Geschäften nicht ableiten lassen.

Diese allgemeinen Betrachtungen wollen wir auf die bisher betrachteten normalen einfachen Geschäfte, welche durch die Deckungsgleichungen

$$x + y = 0$$
$$x + z = 0$$

geregelt sind, anwenden. Auf Grund dieser Bedingungen sind offenbar unendlich viele gedeckte, somit auch unendlich viele äquivalente Systeme möglich, welche derart zu bestimmen sind, daß man eine Art von Geschäften wählt und die zwei anderen Arten durch Auflösung der zwei Bedingungsgleichungen ermittelt.

Es handle sich z. B. um die Deckung von 200 Wahlverkäufen. Wir setzen $y = 200$ ein und lösen die Gleichungen

$$x + 200 = 0$$
$$x + z = 0$$

auf; es folgt $x = -200$ und $z = 200$, d. h. 200 Zwangsverkäufe und 200 feste Käufe, so daß 200 Wahlverkäufe, 200 Zwangsverkäufe und 200 feste Käufe ein gedecktes System bilden müssen, sobald nur die Prämien der Wahl- und der Zwangsgeschäfte einander gleich gehalten werden. Das wollen wir an einem numerischen Beispiel erproben. Die gehandelten Stücke seien Aktien mit Kurs 425 K und etwa 6 K Prämie pro Stück. Steigt nun am Liquidationstermin der Kurs z. B. auf 458 K, so erfahren wir bei den 200 Wahlverkäufen, da wir offenbar nicht verkaufen und die eingezahlten Prämien verlieren werden, einen Verlust von 1200 K; ebenso verlieren wir bei den 200 Zwangsverkäufen, da ja unsere Kontrahenten wohl kaufen werden, 27 K pro Stück (nämlich 33 K Kurserhöhung weniger 6 K Prämie), mithin 5400 K; unser ganzer Verlust ist also 6600 K, welcher durch die 200 festen Käufe (33×200 K Gewinn) genau aufgewogen wird.

Kommt es auf die Ableitung eines Geschäftes aus den zwei anderen an, so werden wir in den Gleichungen, je nach der Natur des abzuleitenden Geschäftes, für eine der Größen x, y oder z die positive oder die negative Einheit substituieren und durch nachherige Auflösung die Geschäfte, aus denen das betrachtete sich ableiten läßt, ermitteln.

Wir wollen z. B. finden, wie sich ein fester Kauf durch einfache normale Prämiengeschäfte ableiten läßt. Wir substituieren an Stelle des z den Wert -1, worauf die Gleichungen

$$x + y = 0 \text{ und } x - 1 = 0$$

die Werte $x = 1$ und $y = -1$, das heißt einen Wahlkauf und einen Zwangskauf als jenes Geschäftssystem ergeben, welches dem einen festen Kaufe äquivalent ist. Zur Ableitung eines Wahlverkaufes hätten wir statt y den Wert -1 einzusetzen; wir erhielten dann $x = 1$ und $z = -1$, d. h. einen Wahlkauf und einen festen Verkauf. So müssen wir zur Bestimmung des Systems, welches einem Zwangsverkaufe entspricht, in unseren Gleichungen für x den Wert $+1$ substituieren; alsdann ergibt sich $y = -1$ und $z = -1$, d. h. ein Zwangskauf und ein fester Verkauf u. s. w.

6. Stellgeschäfte oder Stellagen. Beim Stellgeschäfte hat der sog. Käufer der Stellage durch eine beim Abschluß des Kontrakts geleistete Zahlung das Recht erworben, am Lieferungstermin das gehandelte Objekt nach seiner Wahl zum festgesetzten Kurse B entweder zu kaufen oder zu verkaufen; kaufen wird er offenbar, wenn der Kurs über B gestiegen, verkaufen aber, wenn derselbe unter B gefallen sein wird; der andere Kontrahent, welcher das Objekt entweder liefern oder abnehmen muß, tritt als Verkäufer der Stellage auf. Die Gewinnverhältnisse des Verkäufers sind offenbar denjenigen des Käufers vollkommen entgegengesetzt; bezeichnen wir daher mit σ eine bestimmte Anzahl von Stellagenkäufen eines und desselben Objekts, so wird $-\sigma$ eine ebenso große Anzahl von Stellagenverkäufen bedeuten; ein Resultat $\sigma = 3$ wird z. B. einen dreifachen Stellagenkauf, ein solches $\sigma = -5$ hingegen einen fünffachen Stellagenverkauf darstellen.

Aus der Definition der Stellage geht nun unmittelbar hervor, daß sich diese neue Geschäftsform aus zwei einfachen Prämiengeschäften zusammensetzt, und zwar der Stellagenkauf aus einem Wahlkaufe und aus einem Wahlverkaufe, der Stellagenverkauf dagegen aus einem Zwangsverkaufe und aus einem Zwangskaufe desselben Objekts; folglich wird auch die Prämie einer normalen Stellage der doppelten Prämie des einfachen normalen Geschäftes gleichkommen müssen. Es ist weiter klar, daß bei der normalen Stellage der Kauf des Objekts à $B+2P$ zu stehen kommt, während der Verkauf à $B-2P$ geschieht. Die Differenz dieser Preise nennt man die Tension der Stellage und beträgt also, wenn letztere normal ist, $4P$; das arithmetische Mittel derselben, welches bei normaler Stellage mit dem Kurse B der festen Geschäfte zusammenfällt, heißt die Mitte der Stellage. Es sei endlich bemerkt, daß bei diesem Geschäfte der Gewinn des Käufers erst bei Marktschwankungen über oder unter B, die größer als $2P$ sind, beginnt und von da ab unbegrenzt wachsen kann; bei Marktschwankungen, die kleiner als $2P$ sind, hat der Käufer immer Verlust; letzterer nimmt mit der Abnahme der Schwankungen zu und erreicht bei der Schwankung Null, d. h. wenn der Kurs am Lieferungstermin gleich dem festgesetzten Kurse B ist, seinen maximalen Wert $2P$.

Wir können nun sehr leicht, ohne irgend welche direkten Betrachtungen anzustellen, unsere Deckungsgleichungen (3) dahin verallgemeinern, daß sie auch die Stellagengeschäfte explizite enthalten. Treten nämlich zu x Wahlkäufen, zu y Wahlverkäufen und zu z festen Käufen noch σ Stellagenkäufe desselben Objekts hinzu, so liegen im ganzen offenbar $x+\sigma$ Wahlkäufe, $y+\sigma$ Wahlverkäufe und z feste Käufe vor, die sich unter allen Umständen decken müssen; die direkte Anwendung der Bedingungen (3) liefert somit unmittelbar das Gleichungssystem

$$\left.\begin{aligned} x+y+2\sigma&=0\\ x+z+\sigma&=0\\ y-z+\sigma&=0 \end{aligned}\right\}, \qquad (5)$$

durch welches zunächst die Lösung der Deckungsprobleme gegeben und weiter, nach den in Nummer 5 enthaltenen Erörterungen, die Bildung beliebiger äquivalenter Geschäftssysteme ermöglicht ist.

In den Gleichungen (5), von denen eine die unmittelbare Folge der zwei anderen ist, kommen vier unbekannte Größen vor, so daß immer zwei von ihnen beliebig gewählt werden können; es lassen sich somit aus den betrachteten Geschäften zweifach unendlich viele Kombinationen, welche vollständig gedeckt sind, konstruieren. Auch das Problem der äquivalenten Systeme hat hier eine große Erweiterung erfahren. Wollten wir nämlich eine Geschäftsart aus den übrigen drei anderen ableiten, so würde dies darauf zurückkommen, daß wir eine der in den Gleichungen (5) vorkommenden Größen durch eine bestimmte gegebene Zahl zu ersetzen und hierauf zur Ermittlung der ihr äquivalenten Geschäftssysteme zwei Gleichungen mit drei Unbekannten aufzulösen hätten; wir erhielten unendlich viele Systeme, welche der ins Auge gefaßten Geschäftsart äquivalent wären, so daß sich also eine Geschäftsart durchaus nicht auf bestimmte Weise aus den drei anderen ableiten läßt. Nur ein beliebiges System von zwei Geschäftsarten läßt sich aus den zwei anderen auf eindeutige Weise ableiten; haben wir nämlich das abzuleitende System von zwei Geschäften gewählt, so ist hiedurch eine Substitution von zwei der in den Gleichungen (5) enthaltenen vier Größen vorgeschrieben, so daß die zwei übrig gebliebenen aus den Gleichungen vollkommen bestimmt resultieren werden.

Wollen wir z. B. das beliebige System „1 Stellagenverkauf und 3 Wahlverkäufe" aus den zwei übrigen Geschäften ableiten, so haben wir in (5) für σ und y beziehungsweise die entgegengesetzten Werte $+1$ und -3 zu substituieren und hierauf die Gleichungen

$$x-3+2=0$$
$$x+z+1=0$$

aufzulösen. Wir erhalten

$$x=1 \text{ und } z=-2,$$

d. h. einen Wahlkauf und zwei feste Verkäufe als jenes System, welches dem betrachteten vollständig äquivalent ist.

Handelte es sich aber darum, z. B. einen Stellagenkauf aus den drei übrigen Geschäftsformen abzuleiten, so müßte man in (5) für σ den entgegengesetzten Wert -1 substituieren und zur Ermittlung der äquivalenten Systeme die Gleichungen

$$x+y-2=0$$
$$x+z-1=0$$

auflösen; es leuchtet aber ein, daß dies auf unendlich viele Weisen geschehen kann, so daß sich für den betrachteten Stellagenkauf unendlich viele äquivalente Geschäftskombinationen ergeben; eine von diesen wäre z. B. $x=3$, $y=-1$ und $z=-2$, d. h. drei Wahlkäufe, ein Zwangskauf und zwei feste Verkäufe u. s. w.

Wird aber das Problem mit der Einschränkung gestellt, ein Geschäft aus zwei anderen abzuleiten, so tritt hiemit eine Bestimmtheit ein, da ja durch diese Einschränkung das eben ausgedrückt ist, daß eine von den drei Größen, die nach der Substitution des abzuleitenden Geschäftes übrig bleiben, der Null gleich zu setzen ist, wodurch offenbar zur weiteren Behandlung zwei Unbekannte zwischen zwei Gleichungen zur Verfügung stehen.

So können wir z. B. einen Stellagenkauf entweder α) aus Wahlkäufen und Wahlverkäufen oder β) aus Wahlkäufen und festen Käufen oder endlich γ) aus Wahlverkäufen und festen Käufen auf eindeutig bestimmte Weise ableiten. In allen diesen drei Fällen ist in (5) für σ der Wert -1 zu setzen und überdies bei α) $z=0$, bei β) $y=0$ und bei γ) $x=0$ anzunehmen. Alsdann erhalten wir ad α)

$$\begin{aligned} x+y-2&=0 \\ x-1&=0, \end{aligned}$$

somit $x=1$ und $y=1$, d. h. einen Wahlkauf und einen Wahlverkauf, welches Resultat laut Definition a priori klar ist. Ad β) ergibt sich

$$\begin{aligned} x-2&=0 \\ x+z-1&=0, \end{aligned}$$

nämlich $x=2$ und $z=-1$, d. h. zwei Wahlkäufe und ein fester Verkauf. Ad γ) findet sich endlich

$$\begin{aligned} y-2&=0 \\ z-1&=0, \end{aligned}$$

mithin $y=2$ und $z=1$, d. h. zwei Wahlverkäufe und ein fester Kauf. Offenbar würden einem Stellagenverkaufe genau dieselben, nur entgegengesetzt genommenen Systeme entsprechen.

Wollten wir noch einen Zwangskauf aus Stellagen und festen Geschäften ableiten, so müßten wir in (5) für y den Wert $+1$ und überdies, da ja Wahlkäufe ausgeschlossen sind, für x den Wert Null einsetzen; es ergäbe sich

$$\begin{aligned} 1+2\sigma&=0 \\ z+\ \sigma&=0, \end{aligned}$$

mithin $\sigma=-\frac{1}{2}$ und $z=\frac{1}{2}$, d. h. ein Stellagenverkauf und ein fester Kauf je der Hälfte der in Rede stehenden Quantität.

Dieses Resultat wollen wir an der Hand eines numerischen Beispiels bestätigen. Statt eines einzigen nehmen wir 100 Zwangskäufe an, denen also 50 Stellagenverkäufe und 50 feste Käufe äquivalent sein müssen: es handle sich um eine Aktie, deren Kurs 682 betrage; die Prämie der einfachen Geschäfte sei 14 K, mithin jene der Stellage 28 K. Ist der Kurs am Liquidationstermin 645 K, so bringen die 100 Zwangskäufe, da ja die anderen Kontrahenten verkaufen werden, offenbar den Verlust

$$(37-14).100=2300 \text{ K}$$

hervor. Übrigens entsteht bei 50 Stellagenverkäufen ein Verlust von

$$(37 - 28) . 50 = 450 \text{ K},$$

weiter bei 50 festen Käufen ein solcher von

$$37 \times 50 = 1850 \text{ K},$$

so daß wirklich eine vollkommene Äquivalenz resultiert.

Bei einer Kurserhöhung sagen wir von 68 K lieferten die 100 Zwangskäufe offenbar

$$14 \times 100 = 1400 \text{ K Gewinn};$$

die anderen Geschäfte würden ihrerseits ergeben:

50 Stellagenverkäufe . . . . . . $(68 - 28) \times 50 = 2000$ K Verlust
50 feste Käufe . . . . $68 \times 50 = 3400$ K Gewinn

im ganzen also dasselbe Resultat.

Es leuchtet unmittelbar ein, daß es Ableitungen von einem Geschäfte aus zwei anderen der bis jetzt betrachteten Geschäfte, wenn man von den entgegengesetzten absieht, genau 12 an der Zahl gibt.

II. Kapitel.

Schiefe Prämiengeschäfte.

1. Deckung und Äquivalenz bei einfachen schiefen Prämiengeschäften. Wir betrachten h Wahlkäufe, k Wahlverkäufe, welche sämtlich zum Kurse $B + M$ auf Grund der Prämien P_1 resp. P_2 abgeschlossen sind, und überdies l feste, zum Tageskurse B abgeschlossene Käufe. Untersuchen wir die Gewinnverhältnisse bei den beliebigen Marktlagen $B + M + \varepsilon$ resp. $B + M - \eta$, so erhalten wir, wenn wir die in Nummer 3 des vorigen Kapitels vorausgeschickten Erörterungen in die Erinnerung zurückrufen, beziehungsweise die Gleichungen

$$\left.\begin{aligned} G_1 &= h(\varepsilon - P_1) - k P_2 + l(M + \varepsilon) \\ G_2 &= - h P_1 + k(\eta - P_2) + l(M - \eta) \end{aligned}\right\} . \qquad (1)$$

Zur vollständigen Deckung ist es nun notwendig und hinreichend, daß bei jeder nur denkbaren Lage des Marktes weder Gewinn noch Verlust vorhanden sei, in anderen Worten, daß die Gleichungen

$$h(\varepsilon - P_1) - k P_2 + l(M + \varepsilon) = 0$$
$$- h P_1 + k(\eta - P_2) + l(M - \eta) = 0$$

beständig erfüllt seien. Bringen wir dieselben auf die Form

$$\left.\begin{aligned} \varepsilon(h+l) - h P_1 - k P_2 + l M &= 0 \\ \eta(k-l) - h P_1 - k P_2 + l M &= 0 \end{aligned}\right\}, \qquad (2)$$

so erfahren wir unmittelbar, daß bei der Willkürlichkeit von ε und η als erste unerläßliche Bedingung der beständigen Erfüllung der Gleichungen (2) das Verschwinden der Koeffizienten

$$h + l \text{ und } k - l$$

ist. Wir gewinnen somit, ganz analog wie bei normalen Geschäften, das Gleichungsystem

$$\left.\begin{aligned} h + l &= 0 \\ k - l &= 0 \\ h + k &= 0 \end{aligned}\right\}, \qquad (3)$$

wobei aber nur zwei Gleichungen von einander unabhängig sind; es kann also immer eine der hierin vorkommenden drei Größen beliebig gewählt werden, so daß sich aus diesen einfachen Geschäften unendlich viele gedeckte Systeme aufstellen lassen. Infolge der Bedingungen (3) schrumpfen nun die Gleichungen (2) in die einzige Relation

$$-h P_1 - k P_2 + l M = 0$$

zusammen, die sich wegen (3) etwa auf die Form

$$k(P_1 - P_2 + M) = 0$$

bringen läßt. Da nun, wie früher erwähnt, eine der Größen in (3) beliebig gewählt werden kann, so ist k als von Null verschieden anzunehmen, so daß aus letzterer Gleichung die weitere bemerkenswerte Bedingung

$$P_2 = P_1 + M \qquad (4)$$

resultiert. Die Prämie des Wahlverkaufes ergibt sich nämlich um die Schiefe des Geschäftes größer als die des Wahlkaufes. Bei zum Kurse $B - M$ abgeschlossenen Prämiengeschäften hätte man, wenn wieder mit P_1 die Prämie für den Wahlkauf bezeichnet wird, offenbar die Relation

$$P_2 = P_1 - M \qquad (4_a)$$

erhalten.

Es haben sich also bei schiefen Geschäften ganz analoge Deckungsgleichungen ergeben wie bei normalen Geschäften; es müssen auch hier Wahlgeschäfte in gleicher Anzahl als Zwangsgeschäfte vorkommen, denen noch ebenso viele feste Verkäufe als Wahlkäufe, oder was auf dasselbe hinauslaufen muß, ebenso viele feste Käufe als Wahlverkäufe vorhanden sind, hinzugefügt werden müssen. Es müssen überdies zwischen den Prämien der Wahlkäufe und der Wahlverkäufe, damit überhaupt eine Deckung möglich ist, die aufgestellten Bedingungen (4) resp. (4_a) eingehalten werden, welche wenigstens in qualitativer Beziehung unmittelbar verständlich sind.

Auf graphischem Wege können die erhaltenen Gesetze etwa auf folgende Weise gezeigt werden: Es sei h, welches als Differenz der Wahlkäufe und der ihnen entgegengesetzten Zwangsverkäufe aufzufassen ist, sagen wir positiv, es stelle also eine gewisse Anzahl wirklicher Wahlkäufe dar, denen bekanntlich eine gleiche Anzahl Gewinndiagramme folgender Form

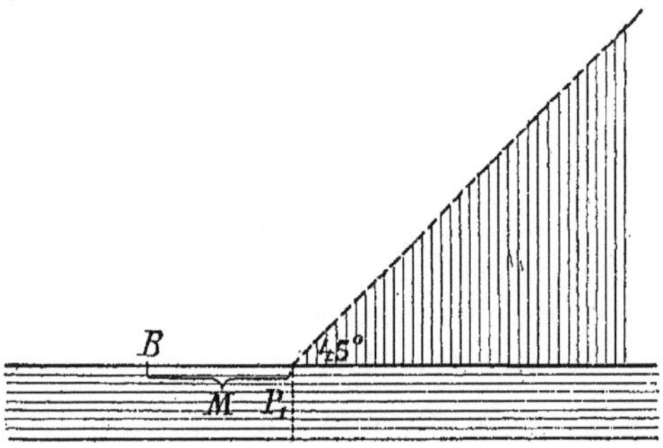

Fig. 13.

entsprechen wird. Die Eliminierung dieser Diagramme erfordert offenbar das Vorhandensein von solchen, deren rechteckige Teile als Gewinn auftreten. Diagramme dieser Art können uns aber, infolge der Bedeutung von h, nur durch Zwangskäufe, d. h. durch ein negatives k, zur Verfügung stehen; ihre Form wird somit die folgende

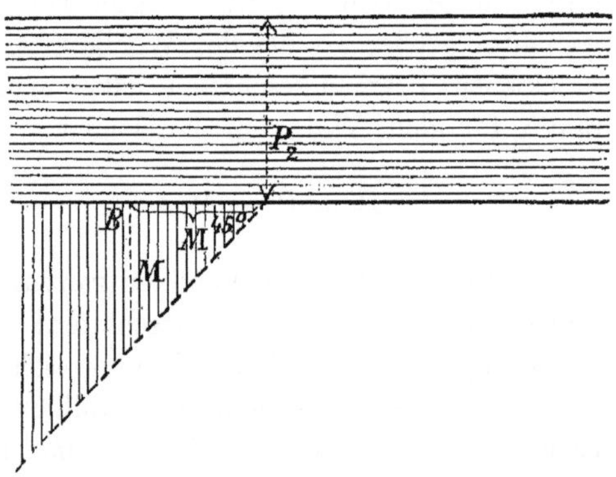

Fig. 14.

sein. Um jetzt die auf analytische Weise gefundenen Gesetze zu bestätigen, nehmen wir an den vorstehenden Diagrammen passende Transformationen vor. Das Diagramm in Fig. 13 ersetzen wir durch das folgende,

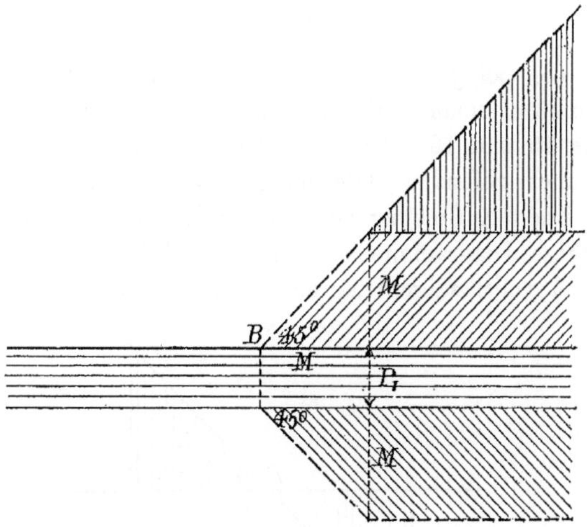

Fig. 15.

das sich aus ersterem durch Hinzufügung der entgegengesetzt gleichen trapezförmigen schraffierten Teile ableiten läßt. Ebenso geht aus einem Diagramm der Figur 14 ein solches von der Form 16

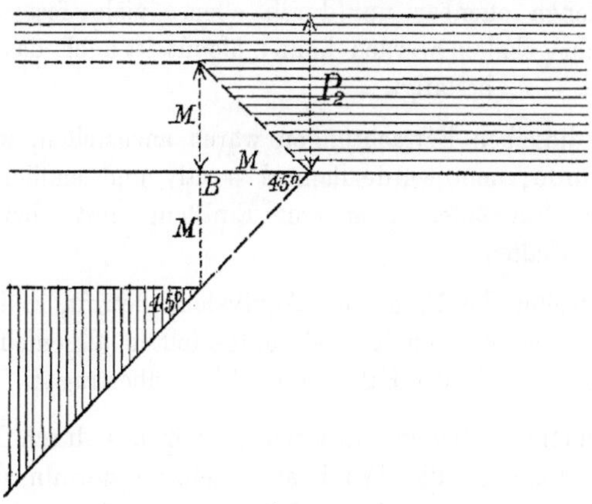

Fig. 16.

hervor, und zwar durch Wegnahme der ganz gleichen trapezförmigen unschraffierten Stücke sowohl aus dem Gebiete des Gewinnes als auch aus jenem des Verlustes. Aus den so transformierten Diagrammen ersehen wir nun unmittelbar, daß sich, wenn nur die Bedingung

$$P_2 = P_1 + M$$

erfüllt ist, die polygonalen Teile in je zwei Diagrammen aufheben werden; zu ihrer totalen Eliminierung ist somit notwendig, daß die Diagramme 15 und 16 in gleicher Anzahl vorhanden seien, was eben auf die früher gefundene Gleichung $h = -k$, d. h. $h + k = 0$ zurückführt. Nach Aufhebung der polygonalen Teile bleiben nun noch 2 h dreieckige Diagrammteile im ganzen übrig, welche, zu je zwei verbunden, h vollständige Diagramme von der Form 17)

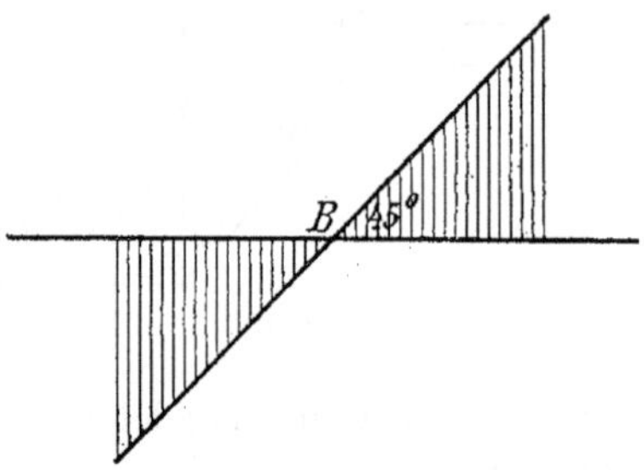

Fig. 17.

erzeugen, denen offenbar nur durch ebenso viele feste Verkäufe das Gleichgewicht gehalten werden kann; hiemit ist auch das letzte Gesetz, nämlich $l = -h$, bestätigt.

Ganz dieselben Betrachtungen wären anzustellen, wenn h negativ ausfallen würde; man würde dann k positiv und endlich feste Käufe statt fester Verkäufe, in stetem Einklang mit den analytischen Resultaten, erhalten.

Was weiter die Frage der Äquivalenz betrifft, so lassen sich die in Nummer 5 des vorigen Kapitels aufgestellten allgemeinen Prinzipien offenbar auch auf diesen Fall vollinhaltlich übertragen.

2. Schiefe Stellagen. Reservieren wir uns durch Zahlung einer gewissen Prämie S_1 die Wahl, am Lieferungstermin das gehandelte Objekt entweder kaufen oder verkaufen zu dürfen, und geschieht dies auf Grund des Kurses $B+M$, so sagen wir, daß wir den Kauf einer schiefen Stellage abgeschlossen haben; den Ekart M vom Kurse B der festen Geschäfte, der offenbar positiv oder negativ ausfallen kann, nennen wir die Schiefe der Stellage. Für den anderen Kontrahenten, welcher sich durch Bezug der Prämie zum vereinbarten Preise das Objekt zu liefern resp. abzunehmen verpflichtet, liegt ein Stellagenverkauf vor. Da die Gewinnverhältnisse des Stellagenkaufes jenen des Verkaufes völlig entgegengesetzt sind, so brauchen wir auch hier einzig und allein vom Begriffe, sagen wir, des Kaufes auszugehen, um durch negativ ausfallende Werte auch den Begriff des Verkaufes repräsentiert zu haben. Wir werden somit in der Folge stets mit s eine gewisse Anzahl von Käufen schiefer à $B+M$ abgeschlossener Stellagen bezeichnen, so daß $-s$ ebenso viele unter denselben Modalitäten abgeschlossene Stellagenverkäufe bedeuten wird.

Bei näherer Betrachtung dieser Geschäfte ersehen wir sofort, daß sich dieselben auch hier aus zwei einfachen schiefen Prämiengeschäften zusammensetzen, und zwar der Stellagenkauf aus einem Wahlkaufe und aus einem Wahlverkaufe, der Stellagenverkauf hingegen aus einem Zwangsverkaufe und aus einem Zwangskaufe, welche Geschäfte alle zum selben Kurse $B+M$ abgeschlossen sind. Drum wird auch die Prämie S_1 für den Erwerb einer Stellage der Summe der Prämien für den Wahlkauf und für den Wahlverkauf gleichzuhalten sein, so daß der eventuelle Kauf des Objekts zum Kurse $B+M+P_1+P_2$, während der eventuelle Verkauf eigentlich zum Kurse $B+M-P_1-P_2$ geschehen wird. Die Differenz zwischen den eigentlichen Kaufs- und Verkaufspreisen, nämlich

$$2\,S_1 \text{ oder } 2\,(P_1+P_2),$$

nennt man die Tension T_1 der schiefen Stellage, während das arithmetische Mittel derselben, welches offenbar mit dem zu Grunde liegenden Kurse $B+M$ koinzidiert, die Mitte der Stellage heißt.

Es gelingt nun, auf graphischem Wege sehr leicht zu zeigen, daß die Gewinnverhältnisse bei einer schiefen Stellage größer als jene bei einer normalen Stellage derselben Größe sind, so daß auch die Prämie für die erstere größer als jene für letztere anzunehmen ist.

Das Gewinndiagramm der normalen Stellage ist offenbar aus nachstehender Figur

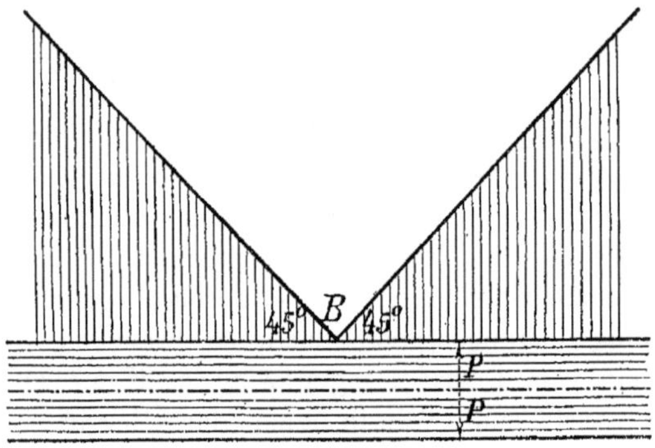

Fig. 18.

zu entnehmen, während jenes bei schiefer Stellage durch das folgende

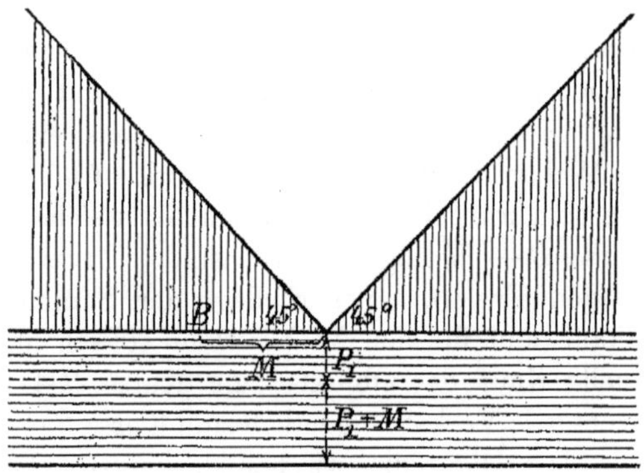

Fig. 19.

dargestellt ist. Wollten wir nun am letzteren Diagramm seinen rechts liegenden dreieckigen Teil nach B verschieben, so hätten wir, wie es aus nachstehendem Schema

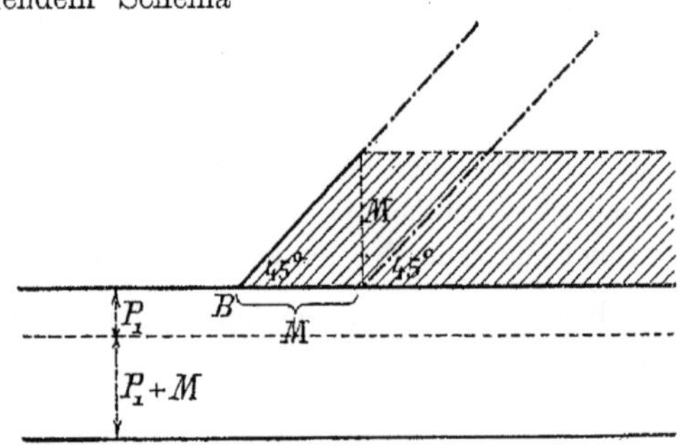

Fig. 20.

unmittelbar hervorgeht, den schraffierten Teil hinzuzufügen, während zur Verschiebung des linksstehenden dreieckigen Diagrammteiles, wie aus folgender Figur

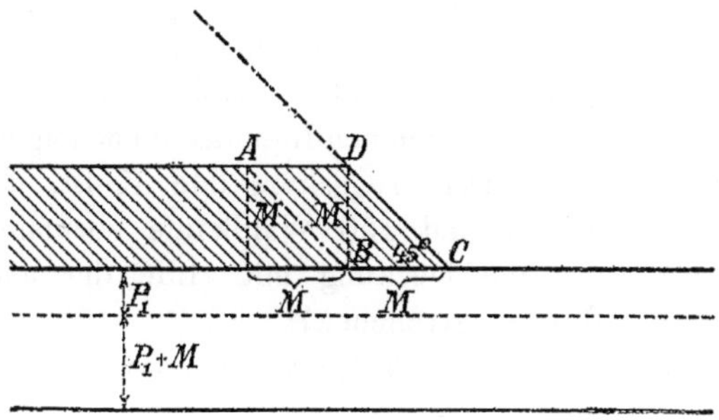

Fig. 21.

zu ersehen ist, die Wegnahme des schraffierten Stückes notwendig wäre. Da nun, wie es der Vergleich der schraffierten Stücke zeigt, das wegzunehmende Stück um den Teil $ABCD$ größer als das hinzuzufügende ist, so ergibt sich unmittelbar, daß die dreieckigen Diagrammteile der Figur 19 zusammen bedeutender sind als die Summe der dreieckigen Teile in dem Schema 18, so daß also in der Tat die schiefe Stellage dem Gewinne größeren Raum gibt, daher auch dieselbe teurer zu bezahlen sein wird. Leider unterliegt die Beantwortung der Frage, welche Beziehung zwischen den naturgemäßen Prämien der normalen und der schiefen Stellage stattfinden muß, unüberwindlichen Schwierigkeiten, die in dem Mangel eines mathematischen Gesetzes, nach welchem die Marktschwankungen erfolgen sollten, ihren Grund haben; die nähere Betrachtung dieser und anderer hieher gehöriger äußerst wichtiger Fragen soll hier nicht weiter verfolgt werden, sondern dem zweiten Teile der vorliegenden Arbeit vorbehalten bleiben.

Wollen wir nun das Bedingungssystem (3) dahin verallgemeinern, daß es auch s Stellagengeschäfte berücksichtigt, so haben wir aus früher dargelegten Gründen zu bedenken, daß durch s Stellagen ebenso viele Wahlkäufe und ebenso viele Wahlverkäufe weiter eingeführt werden (es braucht kaum der Erwähnung, daß alle diese Prämiengeschäfte à $B + M$ abgeschlossen angenommen sind), so daß die bloße Substitution von $h + s$ und $k + s$ statt h und k das verallgemeinerte System

$$\left.\begin{aligned} h+k+2s&=0\\ h+l+s&=0\\ k-l+s&=0 \end{aligned}\right\} \quad (5)$$

liefern wird, welches dem System (5) im vorigen Kapitel vollkommen analog ist und somit alle dort angeknüpften Betrachtungen in bezug auf gedeckte und äquivalente Geschäftskombinationen zuläßt.

Zur Erläuterung der allgemeinen Resultate diene folgendes Beispiel

Von einer Aktie, deren Tageskurs 548 K ist, hat einer 200 Stellagen à 654 verkauft und 150 Wahlkäufe ebenfalls à 654 abgeschlossen; wie kann die Deckung mit Hilfe der anderen bisher betrachteten Geschäftsarten geschehen?

Setzen wir im obigen Gleichungssystem $s = -200$ und $h = 150$ ein, so finden wir

$$\begin{aligned} 150+k-400&=0\\ 150+l-200&=0, \end{aligned}$$

d. h. $k = 250$ und $l = 50$. Die Deckung geschieht also durch 200 Wahlverkäufe, welche ebenfalls zum Kurse 654 abzuschließen sind, und durch 50 feste Käufe zum Tageskurse; die Höhe der Prämien muß selbstverständlich der Relation (4) genügen.

Zur numerischen Bestätigung nehmen wir als Prämie des Wahlkaufes 7 K und am Lieferungstermin z. B. den Kurs 680 an. Da in diesem Falle die Prämie der Wahlverkäufe $7+6=13$ K, jene der Stellagen hingegen $13+7=20$ K betragen muß, so ergibt sich folgendes:

α)	Bei 200 Stellagenverkäufen:	$200\,(26-20) = 1200$	K	Verlust
β)	„ 150 Wahlkäufen:	$150\,(26-7) = 2850$	„	Gewinn
γ)	„ 250 Wahlverkäufen:	$250 \times 13 = 3250$	„	Verlust
δ)	„ 50 festen Käufen:	$50 \times 32 = 1600$	„	Gewinn.

Das Gesamtergebnis dieser Operation ist in der Tat weder Gewinn noch Verlust, wie man es eben wollte.

3. Kombination einfacher auf Grund verschiedener Kurse abgeschlossener Geschäfte. Wir wenden uns nun zur Lösung der wichtigen Frage, ob und wie Geschäfte, welche nicht auf denselben Grundlagen abgeschlossen sind, sich decken können. Zu diesem Behufe nehmen wir an, es seien zu den Kursen $B_1, B_2, \ldots B_r, B_{r+1} = B, B_{r+2}, \ldots$ und B_{n+1} beziehungsweise die einfachen Prämiengeschäfte h_1 und k_1, h_2 und $k_2, \ldots$ h_r und k_r, $h_{r+1} = x$ und $k_{r+1} = y$, h_{r+2} und k_{r+2}, $\ldots$ h^{n+1} und k_{n+1} abgeschlossen, wobei, wie es immer bisher geschehen ist, die verschiedenen h sich auf Wahlkäufe, die verschiedenen k hingegen auf Wahlverkäufe beziehen; für erstere seien respektive die Prämien $p_1, p_2, \ldots p_r, p_{r+1} = p, p_{r+2}, \ldots p_{n+1}$, für letztere hingegen die Prämien $P_1, P_2, \ldots P_r, P_{r+1} = P, P_{r+2}, \ldots P_{n+1}$, bedungen worden. Den so charakterisierten Prämiengeschäften seien respektive die festen Geschäfte $l_1, l_2, \ldots l_r, l_{r+1} = z, l_{r+2}, \ldots l_{n+1}$ hinzugefügt, welche alle zum Tageskurse $B_{r+1} = B$ abgeschlossen anzunehmen sind. Nachstehendes Schema diene die angenommene Situation zu veranschaulichen:

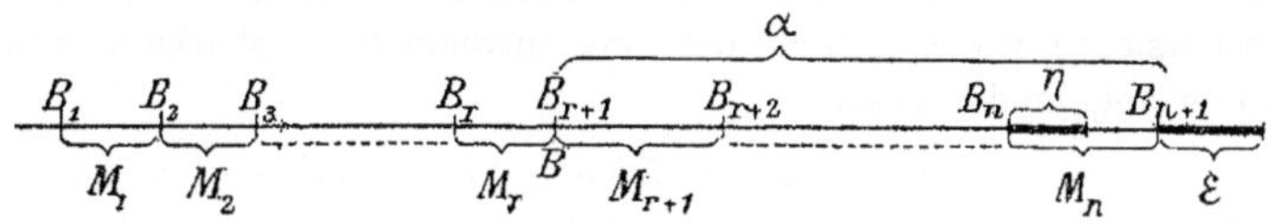

Fig. 22.

Untersuchen wir nun die sich bei den verschiedenen möglichen Marktlagen ergebenden Gewinnverhältnisse. Beim Markte $B_{n+1} + \varepsilon$ wäre der Gesamtgewinn offenbar gleich der Summe folgender Teilgewinne

$$G_{n+1} = h_{n+1}(\varepsilon - p_{n+1}) - k_{n+1} P_{n+1} + l_{n+1}(\overbrace{M_{r+1} + M_{r+2} + \cdots + M_n}^{\alpha} + \varepsilon)$$
$$G_n = h_n(\varepsilon + M_n - p_n) - k_n P_n + l_n(\alpha + \varepsilon)$$
$$G_{n-1} = h_{n-1}(\varepsilon + M_n + M_{n-1} - p_{n-1}) - k_{n-1} P_{n+1} + l_{n-1}(\alpha + \varepsilon)$$
$$\cdots\cdots\cdots$$
$$G_{r+2} = h_{r+2}(\varepsilon + M_n + \cdots + M_{r+2} - p_{r+2}) - k_{r+2} P_{r+2} + l_{r+2}(\alpha + \varepsilon)$$
$$G_{r+1} = G = h_{r+1}(\varepsilon + M_n + \cdots + M_{r+1} - p_{r+1}) - k_{r+1} P_{r+1} + l_{r+1}(\alpha + \varepsilon)$$
$$G_r = h_r(\varepsilon + M_n + \cdots\cdots + M_r - p_r) - k_r P_r + l_r(\alpha + \varepsilon)$$
$$\cdots\cdots\cdots$$
$$G_2 = h_2(\varepsilon + M_n + \cdots\cdots + M_2 - p_2) - k_2 P_2 + l_2(\alpha + \varepsilon)$$
$$G_1 = h_1(\varepsilon + M_n + \cdots\cdots + M_1 - p_1) - k_1 P_1 + l_1(\alpha + \varepsilon).$$

Ebenso wäre der Gesamtgewinn bei der Marktlage $B_n + \eta$ durch die Summe folgender Teilgewinne dargestellt

$$g_{n+1} = -h_{n+1} p_{n+1} + k_{n+1}(M_n - \eta - P_{n+1}) + l_{n+1}(\alpha - M_n + \eta)$$
$$g_n = h_n(\eta - p_n) - k_n P_n + l_n(\alpha - M_n + \eta)$$
$$g_{n-1} = h_{n-1}(\eta + M_{n-1} - p_{n-1}) - k_{n-1} P_{n-1} + l_{n-1}(\alpha - M_n + \eta)$$
$$\cdots\cdots\cdots$$
$$g_{r+1} = g = h_{r+1}(\eta + M_{n-1} + \cdots + M_{r+1} - p_{r+1}) - k_{r+1} P_{r+1} + l_{r+1}(\alpha - M_n + \eta)$$
$$\cdots\cdots\cdots$$
$$g_1 = h_1(\eta + M_{n-1} + M_{n-2} + \cdots + M_1 - p_1) - k_1 P_1 + l_1(\alpha - M_n + \eta).$$

Auf diese Weise fortfahrend, erhielten wir für jede beliebige Marktlage zwischen den verschiedenen B_λ und unter B_1 ein ähnliches System partieller Gewinne, deren Summe den Gesamtgewinn bei den angenommenen Marktlagen liefern würde; es ließen sich offenbar $n+2$ solche Systeme aufstellen.

Sollen nun die betrachteten Geschäfte eine vollständig gedeckte Kombination ergeben, so ist die unerläßliche Bedingung hiefür, daß die Gesamtgewinne bei jeder beliebigen Marktlage der Null gleich seien, wodurch $n+2$ Gleichungen zu stande kommen, von denen die zwei ersteren, wie es sich aus den zwei entwickelten Systemen unmittelbar ergibt, in die Form

$$\left.\begin{aligned} \varepsilon(\Sigma h + \Sigma l) - \Sigma h p - \Sigma k P + \alpha \Sigma l + Q = 0 \\ \eta(\Sigma h - h_{n+1} - k_{n+1} + \Sigma l) - \Sigma h p - \Sigma k P + (\alpha - M_n)\Sigma l + Q_1 = 0 \end{aligned}\right\} \quad (6)$$

gebracht werden können; hiebei sind für Q und Q_1 beziehungsweise die Ausdrücke

$$Q = h_n M_n + h_{n-1}(M_n + M_{n-1}) + \cdots + h_1(M_n + M_{n-1} + \cdots + M_1)$$
$$Q_1 = k_{n+1} M_n + h_{n-1} M_{n-1} + h_{n-2}(M_{n-1} + M_{n-2}) + \cdots + h_1(M_{n-1} + \cdots + M_1)$$

zu verstehen. Ganz analog erhielte man

$$\left.\begin{aligned} \xi(\Sigma h - h_{n+1} - h_n - k_{n+1} - k_n + \Sigma l) - \Sigma h p - \Sigma k P + \\ + (\alpha - M_n - M_{n-1})\Sigma l + Q_2 = 0, \end{aligned}\right\} \quad (7)$$

wobei

$$Q_2 = k_{n+1}(M_n + M_{n-1}) + k_n M_{n-1} + h_{n-2} M_{n-2} + h_{n-3}(M_{n-2} + M_{n-3}) + \cdots + h_1(M_{n-2} + \cdots + M_1)$$

gesetzt wurde u. s. w.

Bei der Willkürlichkeit der Größen ε, η, ξ etc. müssen nun, wenn die Gleichungen (6) und (7) beständig erfüllt sein sollen, ihre Koeffizienten identisch verschwinden; wir erhalten zunächst

$$\Sigma h + \Sigma l = 0,$$

somit auch beim Verschwinden des Koeffizienten des η

$$h_{n+1} + k_{n+1} = 0,$$

und weiter beim Verschwinden des Koeffizienten des ξ

$$h_n + k_n = 0$$

und so weiter fort, so daß wir sukzessive das bemerkenswerte System von Bedingungsgleichungen

$$\left.\begin{array}{l} h_{n+1}+k_{n+1}=0 \\ h_n \quad +k_n \quad =0 \\ h_{n-1}+k_{n-1}=0 \\ \quad\quad / \\ \quad\quad / \\ h_2 \quad +k_2 \quad =0 \\ h_1 \quad +k_1 \quad =0 \\ \Sigma h \quad +\Sigma l \quad =0 \end{array}\right\} \quad (8)$$

gewinnen, an welche als unmittelbare Folge noch die Gleichung

$$\Sigma k - \Sigma l = 0$$

anzuschließen ist.

Aus diesem Gleichungssystem läßt sich nun die merkwürdige Tatsache entnehmen, daß die zu verschiedenen Kursen abgeschlossenen Prämiengeschäfte für sich selbst gedeckte Systeme bilden müssen, so daß bei einer Kombinierung von solchen schiefen Geschäften eine bloße Supraposition von an und für sich gedeckten Komplexen stattfinden kann, wodurch die Unmöglichkeit nachgewiesen wird, Prämiengeschäfte einer einzelnen Gattung durch andere auf Grund verschiedener Kurse abgeschlossene Geschäfte zu decken resp. abzuleiten. Bei der erwähnten Kombinierung solcher an und für sich nach bekannten Regeln gedeckter Geschäftskomplexe geht freilich eine Reduktion der festen Geschäfte vor sich, die unter gegebenen Umständen sich sogar vollständig aufheben können. Die festen Geschäfte sind also die mächtigen Vermittler, durch welche auf verschiedener Basis abgeschlossene Prämiengeschäfte in Berührung gebracht werden können, letztere jedoch immer derart gruppiert, daß für je eine Basis eine gleiche Anzahl von Wahl- und von Zwangsgeschäften vorhanden sein muß.

Die weitere Verfolgung der Gleichungen (6) und (7) ergibt nach dem Verschwinden der mit den willkürlichen Größen ε, η, ξ ... behafteten Glieder eine Reihe von Gleichungen nachstehender Form:

$$\left.\begin{array}{r} -\Sigma hp - \Sigma kP + \alpha \Sigma l + Q = 0 \\ -\Sigma hp - \Sigma kP + (\alpha - M_n)\Sigma l + Q_1 = 0 \\ -\Sigma hp - \Sigma kP + (\alpha - M_n - M_{n-1})\Sigma l + Q_2 = 0 \\ \cdots\cdots\cdots\cdots \\ -\Sigma hp - \Sigma kP + (\alpha - M_n - M_{n-1} - \cdots - M_1)\Sigma l + Q_n = 0, \end{array}\right\} \quad (9)$$

deren Erfüllung das Stattfinden der Relationen

$$\left.\begin{aligned} Q &= Q_1 - M_n \quad \Sigma l \\ Q_1 &= Q_2 - M_{n-1} \Sigma l \\ Q_2 &= Q_3 - M_{n-2} \Sigma l \text{ etc.} \end{aligned}\right\}$$

erfordert. Ein Blick auf die Ausdrücke für die verschiedenen Q zeigt, daß letztere Relationen identisch erfüllt sind, in anderen Worten, daß die Gleichungen des Systems (9) alle äquivalent sind. Zur Herleitung weiterer Schlüsse ist alsdann vollkommen gleichgültig, welche auch von diesen Gleichungen verwendet werden mag. Gehen wir von der ersten derselben aus und bedenken wir, daß für das Endresultat die Verteilung der festen Geschäfte vollkommen gleichgültig ist, sobald nur deren Summe gleich $-\Sigma h$ resp. Σk ist, so nehmen wir die Verteilung

$$\begin{aligned} l_{n+1} &= -h_{n+1} = k_{n+1} \\ l_n &= -h_n = k_n \\ &\;\;\vdots \\ l_1 &= -h_1 \quad = k_1 \end{aligned}$$

an, wodurch die genannte erste Gleichung des Systems (9) in die Form

$$\begin{aligned} &-h_{n+1} p_{n+1} - h_n p_n - \cdots - h_1 p_1 + h_{n+1} P_{n+1} + h_n P_n + \cdots h_1 P_1 - \\ &- \alpha h_{n+1} - \alpha h_n - \cdots \alpha h_1 + h_n M_n + h_{n-1}(M_n + M_{n-1}) + \cdots + \\ &+ h_1 (M_n + M_{n-1} + \cdots + M_1) = 0 \end{aligned}$$

gebracht werden kann; das liefert weiter

$$\begin{aligned} &h_{n+1}(-p_{n+1} + P_{n+1} - \alpha) + h_n(-p_n + P_n - \alpha + M_n) + h_{n+1}(-p_{n-1} + \\ &+ P_{n-1} - \alpha + M_n + M_{n-1}) + h_1(-p_1 + P_1 - \alpha + M_n + M_{n-1} + \\ &\cdots + M_1) = 0. \end{aligned}$$

Da nun die verschiedenen h, indem man in jedem der an und für sich gedeckten Systeme eine Größe willkürlich wählen kann, alle als willkürliche Größen aufzufassen sind und daher ihre Koeffizienten verschwinden müssen, so zerfällt letztere Gleichung in das System

$$\left.\begin{aligned} P_{n+1} &= p_{n+1} + \alpha \\ P_n &= p_n \quad + \alpha - M_n \\ P_{n-1} &= p_{n-1} + \alpha - M_n - M_{n-1} \\ &\;\;\vdots \\ P_1 &= p_1 \quad + \alpha - M_n - M_{n-1} - \cdots - M_1 \end{aligned}\right\} \qquad (10)$$

welches die in einem speziellen Falle abgeleitete Relation (4) in aller Allgemeinheit wiedergibt.

Wollten wir in dem Gleichungssystem (8) auch die Stellagengeschäfte explizite darstellen, so erhielten wir offenbar

$$\left.\begin{array}{llll} h_{n+1} & + k_{n+1} & + 2\, s_{n+1} & = 0 \\ h_n & + k_n & + 2\, s_n & = 0 \\ & \cdots & & \\ h_1 & + k_1 & + 2\, s_1 & = 0 \\ \Sigma h_1 & + \Sigma l & + \Sigma s & = 0 \\ \Sigma k & - \Sigma l & + \Sigma s & = 0 \end{array}\right\}. \qquad (11)$$

Die hier abgeleiteten Prinzipien werden sich von der höchsten Wichtigkeit bei den im nächsten Kapitel zu behandelnden Geschäftsformen erweisen.

Wollten wir z. B. zwei Wahlkäufe à B_1 und drei Zwangskäufe à B_2 durch eventuelle Heranziehung fester und einfacher Prämiengeschäfte auf kürzeste Weise decken, so hätten wir in dem System

$$\left.\begin{array}{r} h_1 + k_1 = 0 \\ h_2 + k_2 = 0 \\ \Sigma l + h_1 + h_2 = 0 \end{array}\right\}, \qquad (12)$$

für h_1 den Wert 2, für k_2 den Wert — 3 zu substituieren und nach den Größen h_1, k_1 und Σl aufzulösen; die Lösung ist diesmal eindeutig und liefert

$$h_2 = 3,\; k_1 = -2,\; \Sigma l = -5,$$

d. h. 3 Wahlkäufe à B_2, 2 Zwangskäufe à B_1 und 5 feste Verkäufe zum Tageskurse; überdies ist stillschweigend anzunehmen, daß die festgesetzten Prämien den Bedingungen (10) Genüge leisten.

In dem früher durchgeführten Beispiel hätten wir außer den angenommenen gewählten Geschäften noch einige feste Geschäfte, z. B. vier feste Käufe, willkürlich wählen können. Das System (12) hätten wir alsdann in der Form

$$\begin{array}{r} 2 + k_1 = 0 \\ h_2 - 3 = 0 \\ 4 + l + 2 + h_2 = 0 \end{array}$$

gebraucht; es hätte sich

$$h_2 = 3,\; k_1 = -2,\; l = -9$$

ergeben, d. h. dieselbe Gesamtkombination wie oben.

Auf ähnliche Weise würde man mit dem ergänzten System (11) verfahren, wenn man auch mit Stellagen operieren wollte.

III. Kapitel.

Nochgeschäfte.

1. Wesen der Nochgeschäfte. Es liegt ein Wahlkauf von einem bestimmten Objekt mit m-mal Noch dann vor, wenn das Objekt zum Tageskurse B fest, und zwar ein einziges Mal gekauft wird und sich überdies der Käufer durch Entrichtung einer gewissen Prämie N das Recht reserviert, am Liquidationstermin dasselbe Objekt noch m-mal, und zwar zum Kurse $B+N$, verlangen zu dürfen; ebenso spricht man von einem Wahlverkaufe eines m-mal Nochs, wenn die in Rede stehende Quantität ein einziges Mal zum Tageskurse B fest verkauft werden muß, vom Verkäufer aber durch Zahlung einer bestimmten Prämie N überdies das Recht erworben wird, dieselbe Quantität noch m-mal, und zwar zum Kurse $B-N$, liefern zu können oder nicht; es ist klar, daß diese Kontrahenten von ihrem erworbenen Rechte dann Gebrauch machen werden, wenn im ersteren Falle der Kurs am Liquidationstermin über $B+N$ gestiegen, im anderen Falle aber, wenn derselbe unter $B-N$ gefallen sein wird.

Es ist weiter klar, daß die anderen Kontrahenten mit genau entgegengesetzt gleichen Gewinn- und Verlustverhältnissen auftreten, so daß die Zwangsnochgeschäfte als negative Wahlnochgeschäfte aufgefaßt werden können; bedeuten u resp. v bestimmte Anzahlen von m-mal Noch-Wahlkäufen resp. Wahlverkäufen, so werden unter $-u$ resp. $-v$ ebenso viele Noch-Zwangsverkäufe resp. Zwangskäufe derselben Ordnung zu verstehen sein.

Betrachten wir nun die geschilderten Geschäftsformen etwas näher, so erfahren wir sofort, daß sich die m-mal Nochkäufe aus einem festen Kaufe zum Tageskurse B und überdies aus m schiefen Wahlkäufen à $B+N$, und ebenso, daß sich die m-mal Nochverkäufe aus einem festen Verkaufe à B und überdies aus m schiefen Wahlverkäufen zum Kurse $B-N$ zusammensetzen. Aus diesem Grunde werden daher die zu leistenden Prämien N offenbar aus der Relation

$$N = m P_1 \tag{1}$$

hervorgehen, wenn P_1 die für den einfachen schiefen Wahlkauf à $B+N$, resp. für den einfachen schiefen Wahlverkauf à $B-N$ festgesetzte Prämie repräsentiert. Erinnern wir uns noch an die Relation

$$P_2 = P_1 + N,$$

welche in diesem Falle in bezug auf die für den Wahlverkauf à $B+N$

resp. für den Wahlkauf à $B-N$ zu zahlende Prämie bestehen muß, so erhalten wir auch

$$N=\frac{m}{m+1}P_2. \tag{2}$$

Die Einführung der Stellagenprämie

$$S_1=P_1+P_2,$$

ergibt mit Hilfe von (1) und (2)

$$N=\frac{m}{m+2}S_1 \tag{3}$$

oder, durch die Tension T_1 derselben ausgedrückt,

$$N=\frac{m}{2m+4}T_1. \tag{4}$$

Nach Entwicklung dieser wichtigen Relationen, die zwischen den bei Nochgeschäften und bei schiefen Prämiengeschäften zu verlangenden Prämien bestehen müssen, wollen wir einige Betrachtungen ganz allgemeiner Natur über die Umwandlungen und Kombinationen vorausschicken, welche zwischen Nochgeschäften und den in früheren Kapiteln besprochenen Geschäften zu erwarten sind.

Die Anwendung der im vorigen Kapitel entwickelten Prinzipien läßt unmittelbar erkennen, daß an eine eigentliche Deckung resp. Äquivalenz der Nochgeschäfte, die ja nichts anders als einfache schiefe Prämiengeschäfte sind, nur durch schiefe, und zwar auf derselben Basis abgeschlossene Geschäfte zu denken ist; so wird die Deckung resp. die Ableitung von Noch-Wahlkäufen nur auf Grund von Prämiengeschäften à $B+N$, von Noch-Wahlverkäufen hingegen nur auf Grund von Prämiengeschäften à $B-N$ geschehen können. So erkennen wir als ein Ding der Unmöglichkeit, speziell Noch-Wahlkäufe aus zwei Geschäftsarten abzuleiten, von denen z. B. eine aus Noch-Wahlverkäufen (sog. Geschäften mit Ankündigung), die andere hingegen aus beliebigen Geschäften besteht, obwohl in Lehrbüchern, auf welche noch heutzutage verwiesen wird, genau das Gegenteil gelehrt und durch horrend verballhornte Formeln dargestellt zu finden ist.

Dies vorausgeschickt, wollen wir die Gleichungen aufzustellen trachten, welche zur Bildung gedeckter, resp. äquivalenter Systeme zwischen allen bisher eingeführten Geschäften notwendig und hinreichend sind. Es liegt nun unmittelbar nahe, wie das Gleichungssystem (5) im vorigen Kapitel dahin verallgemeinert werden kann, daß es auch die

Nochgeschäfte einbezieht und somit das gestellte Problem in seiner ganzen Allgemeinheit löst.

Es seien zunächst Noch-Wahlkäufe, und zwar u an der Zahl, in Betracht zu ziehen. Mit u Noch-Wahlkäufen treten offenbar u feste Käufe zum Kurse B und $m\,u$ zum Kurse $B+N$ abgeschlossene einfache Wahlkäufe hinzu; damit also das erwähnte Gleichungssystem (5) auch diese u Geschäfte explizite darstelle, haben wir bloß hierin statt h den Wert $h+mu$ und statt l den Wert $l+u$ einzusetzen; k bleibt dabei unverändert. Alsdann erhalten wir

$$\left.\begin{aligned} h+k+2s+mu&=0 \\ k+s-l-u&=0 \end{aligned}\right\}. \qquad (5)$$

Sind aber v Noch-Wahlverkäufe zu berücksichtigen, so verfahren wir folgendermaßen: Da durch v Noch-Wahlverkäufe offenbar v feste Verkäufe à B und mv à $B-N$ gehandelte einfache Wahlverkäufe hinzukommen, so substituieren wir in das System (5) des vorigen Kapitels statt k den Wert $k+mv$ und statt l den Wert $l-v$; dabei bleibt h unverändert; es ergibt sich

$$\left.\begin{aligned} h+k+2s+mv&=0 \\ h+s+l-v&=0 \end{aligned}\right\}. \qquad (5_a)$$

Zur Ableitung der Systeme (5) und (5_a) haben wir bloß zwei Gleichungen, und zwar jene, die sich durch ihre Einfachkeit auszeichnen, beibehalten. Das System (5) gilt also jenen Kombinationen, bei denen Noch-Wahlkäufe im Spiele sind, und enthält Prämiengeschäfte, die alle à $B+N$ abgeschlossen sind; das System (5_a) gilt hingegen den Kombinationen mit Noch-Wahlverkäufen und setzt sich aus lauter à $B-N$ gehandelten Prämiengeschäften zusammen. Der Bau dieser getrennten Systeme ist übrigens sehr leicht zu erkennen und zu merken. Es wiederholt sich ja in ihnen das einzige, durch die ganze Theorie sich hindurchziehende Gesetz, es müsse die Summe der Wahlgeschäfte der Nulle gleich sein, wie es auch mit der Summe von Wahlkäufen und festen Käufen oder mit der Summe von Wahlverkäufen und festen Verkäufen der Fall sein muß.

In diesen Gleichungssystemen, welche aus je zwei Gleichungen zwischen fünf Unbekannten bestehen, sind die unendlich vielen Kombinationen und Umwandlungen enthalten, die durch die bisher an der Börse eingeführten Prämiengeschäfte möglich sind; es können immer drei Geschäftsarten beliebig gewählt und hierauf durch eine höchst einfache Rechnung die weiteren zwei Geschäftsarten bestimmt werden, die mit den beliebig gewählten ein vollkommen gedecktes Geschäftssystem ergeben. Auf ganz gleiche Weise kann auch die Bildung äquivalenter Systeme ins Unendliche fortgesetzt werden. So kann eine bestimmte Geschäftsart auf unendlich viele Arten aus den vier übrigen oder aus drei der vier übrigen abgeleitet werden; ein Komplex von zwei bestimmten Geschäftsarten läßt sich auch auf unzählig viele Weisen aus den drei übrigen Geschäften ableiten. Nur das Problem, einen Geschäftskomplex aus zwei anderen Geschäften abzuleiten, wird zu einem eindeutigen Problem; es handelt sich ja in einem solchen Falle offenbar um die Bestimmung von zwei Größen allein, die offenbar auf eindeutige Weise aus den zwei Gleichungen der in Anwendung kommenden Systeme (5) oder (5_a) hervorgehen werden; die drei übrig bleibenden Größen können entweder alle gegeben oder einige von ihnen der Nulle gleichgesetzt sein.

Wir wollen hier die Ableitung eines Geschäftes aus zwei anderen weiter verfolgen. Jedes der Systeme (5) und (5_a) liefert je 30 Ableitungen, da ja jede der fünf Geschäftsarten

$$h,\ k,\ s,\ l,\ u \text{ resp. } h,\ k,\ s,\ l,\ v$$

auf sechsfache Weise durch zwei der vier übrig gebliebenen Größen sich herleiten läßt. Bedenken wir nun, daß die Ableitungen, bei denen Nochgeschäfte nicht vorkommen, als vollständig gleichartig anzusehen sind, gleichviel ob sie aus dem einen oder aus dem anderen der Systeme (5) und (5_a) resultieren, so erhalten wir im ganzen nicht etwa 60 von einander verschiedene Ableitungen, sondern bloß 48, da sich ja die erwähnten Kombinationen ohne Nochgeschäfte auf zwölffache Weise aufstellen lassen.

2. Direkte Ableitung der in voriger Nummer erhaltenen Resultate. Es dürfte nicht als unzweckmäßig erscheinen, wenn wir die Gleichungssysteme (5) und (5_a) so wie auch die aufgestellten Beziehungen zwischen den Prämien bei Nochgeschäften und bei schiefen Prämiengeschäften noch einmal, und zwar durch Anwendung der Methode der willkürlichen Koeffizienten, ableiten wollen. Liegt ein Wahlkauf von einem m-mal Noch mit Prämie N vor, so ist der Gewinn bei diesem Geschäfte, wenn der Kurs am Liquidationstermin auf $B + N + \varepsilon$ gestiegen ist, offenbar

$$N + \varepsilon + m\varepsilon - N, \text{ d. h. } \varepsilon + m\varepsilon,$$

da ja in diesem Falle von dem Rechte, m-mal das gehandelte Objekt à $B + N$ nachfordern zu dürfen, Gebrauch gemacht werden wird.

Würde aber der Kurs bis $B+N-\eta$ fallen, so wäre der Gewinn

$$N-\eta-N, \text{ d. h. } -\eta,$$

da ja hier nur der Gewinn des festen Kaufes und der Verlust der eingezahlten Prämie N in Betracht zu ziehen sind. Bei u solchen Geschäften würden sich für die betrachteten Marktlagen offenbar die Gewinne

$$u\,(\varepsilon+m\,\varepsilon), \text{ resp. } -u\,\eta$$

ergeben. Auf gleiche Weise verfahrend, würden wir bei v Noch-Wahlverkäufen für die Marktlagen $B-N+\varepsilon$, resp. $B-N-\eta$ am Liquidationstermin die Erfolge

$$-v\,\varepsilon, \text{ resp. } v\,(\eta+m\,\eta)$$

erhalten. Für die anderen Kontrahenten wären offenbar die Gewinne genau die entgegengesetzten.

Fassen wir nun u Wahlkäufe von m-mal Noch, l feste Käufe *à* B, h Wahlkäufe und k Wahlverkäufe *à* $B+N$ ins Auge, so ergibt sich beim Markte $B+N+\varepsilon$ ein Gesamtgewinn

$$G_1=h\,(\varepsilon-P_1)-k\,P_2+l\,(N+\varepsilon)+u\,(\varepsilon+m\,\varepsilon),$$

während derselbe bei einer Marktlage $B+N-\eta$ den Betrag

$$G_2=-h\,P_1+k\,(\eta-P_2)+l\,(N-\eta)-u\,\eta$$

erreichen wird. Eine einfache Reduktion liefert

$$G_1=\varepsilon\,(h+l+u+m\,u)-h\,P_1-k\,P_2+l\,N$$
$$G_2=\eta\,(k-l-u)-h\,P_1-k\,P_2+l\,N.$$

Sollen sich nun die betrachteten Geschäfte vollkommen decken, so müssen erstens einmal die Koeffizienten von ε und η identisch verschwinden, d. h. die Gleichungen

$$\left.\begin{aligned} h+l+u+m\,u&=0\\ h-l-u&=0\\ h+k+m\,u&=0 \end{aligned}\right\} \tag{6}$$

erfüllt sein, wobei die dritte aus der Summe der zwei ersteren resultiert. In diesen Gleichungen finden wir das System (5) wieder, wenn wir nur dasselbe mit Einführung von Stellagen ergänzen und bloß die zwei letzten Gleichungen beibehalten.

Zweitens muß offenbar auch die Relation

$$-h\,P_1-h\,P_2+l\,N=0$$

beständig erfüllt sein; werden nun hierin für h und l die aus (6) resultierenden Werte substituiert, so findet sich zunächst

$$(k + m\,u)\,P_1 - k\,P_2 + N(k - u) = 0$$

oder reduziert,

$$k(P_1 - P_2 + N) + u\,(m\,P_1 - N) = 0.$$

Da aber zwischen den Größen h, l, k und u bloß zwei von einander unabhängige Gleichungen bestehen, so sind jedenfalls zwei der erwähnten veränderlichen Größen willkürlich; nehmen wir als solche k und u an, so müssen in der letzten Gleichung die Koeffizienten derselben identisch verschwinden, wodurch die Relationen

$$N = m\,P_1 \text{ resp. } P_2 = P_1 + N,$$

die wir an anderer Stelle a priori hinschreiben konnten, wiederzufinden sind.

Auf ganz ähnliche Weise würde man zum System ($5_{,,}$) gelangen, wenn man von v Noch-Wahlverkäufen den Ausgang nehmen würde.

3. **Beispiele.** Es handle sich um die Deckung eines 3mal Noch-Wahlkaufes und zweier Stellagenverkäufe durch Wahlkäufe und durch Wahlverkäufe. Da hier das Nochgeschäft à $B + N$ geschieht, so sind bekanntlich auch alle anderen Prämiengeschäfte zu diesem Kurse abgeschlossen gemeint; in Anwendung kommt das System (5), wobei für u, s, m und l beziehungsweise die Werte $+1, -2$, 3 und Null einzusetzen sind. Wir erhalten somit die Gleichungen

$$h + k - 4 + 3 = 0$$
$$k - 2 - 1 = 0,$$

deren Auflösung zum Resultat

$$k = 3 \text{ und } h = -2,$$

d. h. zu drei Wahlverkäufen und zu zwei Zwangsverkäufen führt. Daß wirklich die Geschäftskombination „ein 3mal Noch-Wahlkauf, zwei Stellagenverkäufe, drei Wahlkäufe und zwei Zwangskäufe" ein gedecktes System bildet, erproben wir an einem numerischen Beispiel.

Es handle sich um eine Aktie, deren Tageskurs etwa 681 ist; die Prämie für das 3mal Noch sei 12·6; die naturgemäße Prämie für den Wahlkauf à 693·6 ist alsdann gleich dem dritten Teile von 12·6, d. h. 4·2, und somit jene für den Wahlverkauf à 693·6 gleich der Summe 4·2 + 12·6, d. h. 16·8; hieraus ergibt sich für die Stellage à 693·6 die Prämie 21.

Dies festgesetzt, nehmen wir am Liquidationstermin den Kurs 701·5 an und ermitteln wir den aus der gesamten Operation resultierenden Gewinn:

α) Gewinn beim Nochgeschäfte. Der hiemit verbundene feste Kauf ergibt den Gewinn 20·5, und da wir hier von unserem Rechte die Aktie à 693·5 drei mal verlangen zu dürfen Gebrauch machen, so gewinnen wir weitere 3×8, d. h. 24. Ziehen wir hievon die gezahlte Prämie 12·5 ab, so erhalten wir beim Nochgeschäft einen effektiven Gewinn von 32.

β) Gewinn bei zwei Stellagenverkäufen à 693·5. Da hier die Wahl unserem Kontrahenten freisteht, so wird er kaufen, und zwar 2mal die genannte Aktie, so daß wir hiebei 2×8, d. h. 16 verlieren; wir haben aber zweimal die Prämie 21 einkassiert, so daß wir auch hier einen Schlußgewinn von 26 zu registrieren haben.

γ) Gewinn bei drei Wahlverkäufen. Hier verkaufen wir offenbar nichts und verlieren daher 3mal die Verkaufsprämie 16·8, d. h. im ganzen 50·4.

δ) Resultat der zwei Zwangsverkäufe. Unser Kontrahent wird hier offenbar kaufen, so daß wir 2×8, d. h. 16 verlieren; da wir aber 2mal die Prämie 4·2 erhalten haben, so schließen wir mit einem Verluste von bloß 7·6.

Das Endresultat ist somit Gewinn $32 + 26$, d. h. 58, Verlust hingegen $50{\cdot}4 + 7{\cdot}6$, d. h. 58, somit im ganzen weder Gewinn noch Verlust, wie es eben bei einem gedeckten Systeme sein muß. Auf gleiche Weise ließe sich dasselbe für einen beliebigen Kurs unter 681 nachweisen.

Zum Schlusse wollen wir noch die Ableitung eines m-mal Noch-Wahlkaufes aus irgend zwei anderen der behandelten Geschäfte vollständig ausführen. Zu diesem Behufe brauchen wir bloß im System (5) aus schon öfters dargelegten Gründen für u den Wert -1 zu substituieren, die nicht vorkommenden Geschäfte ganz einfach zu unterdrücken und die so erhaltenen Gleichungen nach den zwei übrig gebliebenen Größen aufzulösen; so finden wir:

α) Ableitung eines m-mal Nochkaufes aus Wahlkäufen und aus Wahlverkäufen. Wir setzen in den Gleichungen (5) $u = -1$, $l = 0$, $s = 0$ und erhalten

$$\begin{aligned} h + k - m &= 0 \\ k + 1 &= 0, \end{aligned}$$

somit $k = -1$ und $h = m + 1$, d. h. der Wahlkauf eines m-mal Nochs ist einem einfachen Zwangskaufe und „$m + 1$" einfachen Wahlkäufen desselben Objekts äquivalent.

β) Dasselbe aus Wahlkäufen und Stellagen. Setzt man in das erwähnte Gleichungssystem (5) $u = -1, l = 0$ und $k = 0$ ein, so findet sich

$$h + 2s - m = 0$$
$$s + 1 = 0$$

oder aufgelöst, $s = -1$ und $h = m + 2$, d. h. ein Stellagenverkauf und „$m + 2$" einfache Wahlkäufe.

γ) Dasselbe aus Wahlkäufen und festen Geschäften. Wir setzen $u = -l$, $s = 0$, $h = 0$ und erhalten durch Auflösung der Gleichungen

$$h - m = 0$$
$$-l + 1 = 0,$$

die laut Definition des Nochgeschäftes unmittelbar verständlichen Werte $h = m$ und $l = 1$, d. h. einen festen Kauf und m einfache Wahlkäufe.

δ) Die Ableitung aus Wahlkäufen und Stellagen führt durch Substitution von $u = -1$, $h = 0$ und $l = 0$ zu den Gleichungen

$$k + 2s - m = 0$$
$$k + s + 1 = 0,$$

somit zu den Werten $s = m + 1$ und $k = -(m + 2)$, welche „$m + 1$" Stellagenkäufen und „$m + 2$" Zwangskäufen entsprechen.

ε) So liefert die Ableitung des Nochgeschäftes aus Wahlverkäufen und festen Geschäften infolge Substitution von $u = -1$, $h = 0$ und $s = 0$ das System

$$k - m = 0$$
$$k - l + 1 = 0,$$

woraus $k = m$ und $l = m + 1$, d. h. m Wahlverkäufe und „$m + 1$" feste Verkäufe resultieren.

ζ) Schließlich erhält man die Ableitung des Nochgeschäftes aus Stellagen und festen Geschäften, indem man die Werte $u = -1$, $h = 0$ und $k = 0$ substituiert und so die Gleichungen

$$2s - m = 0$$
$$s - l + 1 = 0$$

auflöst; es ergibt sich $s = {}^{m}/_{2}$ und $l = {}^{m}/_{2} + 1$, was zu ${}^{m}/_{2}$ Stellagenkäufen und zu „${}^{m}/_{2} + 1$" festen Käufen führt.

Die Ableitungen des Noch-Wahlverkaufes würde durch Benützung des Systems (5_a) auf ganz gleiche Weise durchzuführen sein.

Bevor wir den ersten Teil der vorliegenden Arbeit schließen, wollen wir noch folgendes bemerken: Will man sich beim Börsenspiel der Gefahr allzu großer Verluste nicht aussetzen, so trachte man bloß solche Geschäftskombinationen abzuschließen, welche gedeckt sind und nach den in den vorhergehenden Kapiteln dargelegten Prinzipien bestimmt werden; gelingt es nun, bei diesen Operationen den Abschluß der einzelnen Geschäfte zu günstigeren Bedingungen zu bewerkstelligen, als es in unseren Gleichungen vorausgesetzt ist, so wird offenbar alles in dieser Richtung Erreichte einen sicheren Gewinn herbeizuführen im stande sein.

II. Teil.

Untersuchungen höherer Ordnung.

I. Kapitel.

Ableitung allgemeiner Gleichungen.

1. Einleitung. Im ersten Teile der vorliegenden Arbeit wurden die Prämiengeschäfte bloß in ihrer Abhängigkeit von einander untersucht, ohne hiebei auf die fundamentale Frage über die rechtmäßige Größe der bei den verschiedenen Geschäften zu zahlenden Prämien näher einzugehen; diese von den bisher angestellten Untersuchungen scharf getrennte Aufgabe wurde eben dem II. Teile dieses Werkchens reserviert.

Die Hilfsmittel, welche zum Angriffe dieses Problems notwendig sind, gehen leider über die Grenzen der elementaren Mathematik hinaus; nur die Anwendung der Wahrscheinlichkeits- und der Integralrechnung wird im stande sein, etwas Licht über diese für Theorie und Praxis höchst wichtige Frage zu werfen und Resultate an den Tag zu legen, die vielleicht verläßliche Anhaltspunkte beim Abschlusse der in Betracht kommenden Geschäfte liefern können werden.

2. Wahrscheinlichkeit der Marktschwankungen. Es liegt wohl nahe, daß der Kurs am Liquidationstermin mit dem Tageskurse B im allgemeinen nicht übereinstimmen, sondern mehr oder weniger bedeutenden Schwankungen über oder unter diesem Werte unterworfen sein wird; ebenso klar ist es aber auch, daß sich die Ursachen dieser Schwankungen und somit die Gesetze, denen sie folgen sollten, jeder Rechnung entziehen. Bei dieser Lage der Dinge werden wir also höchstens von der Wahrscheinlichkeit einer bestimmten Schwankung x sprechen können, und zwar ohne hiefür einen näher definierten, begründeten mathematischen Ausdruck zu besitzen; wir werden uns vielmehr mit der Einführung einer unbekannten Funktion $f(x)$ begnügen müssen, über welche zunächst nur die bescheidene Annahme, sie sei eine endliche und stetige Funktion der Schwankungen im ganzen in Betracht kommenden Intervalle, gemacht werden soll.

Dies vorausgeschickt, drücken wir die Wahrscheinlichkeit, daß sich der Kurs am Liquidationstermin zwischen $B+x$ und $B+x+dx$ befinde, mit anderen Worten, daß die Schwankung über B einen zwischen x und $x+dx$ liegenden Wert erreiche, durch das Produkt

$$f(x)\,dx \tag{1}$$

aus; für Schwankungen unter B nehmen wir der Allgemeinheit halber eine verschiedene Funktion $f_1(x)$ an, so daß die Wahrscheinlichkeit, mit welcher eine zwischen x und $x+dx$ befindliche Schwankung unter B zu erwarten ist, durch das Produkt

$$f_1(x)\,dx \tag{1$_a$}$$

gegeben sein wird; jedenfalls müssen die Funktionswerte bei der Schwankung Null für beide Funktionen gleich ausfallen, was eben durch die Gleichung

$$f(0)=f_1(0) \tag{2}$$

charakterisiert ist.

Aus den so definierten elementaren Wahrscheinlichkeiten lassen sich sodann für die endlichen Probabilitäten, daß die Schwankung zwischen a und b über resp. unter B falle, d. h., daß sich der Marktpreis am Liquidationstermin zwischen $B+a$ und $B+a+b$ resp. $B-a$ und $B-a-b$ befinde, die Integrale

$$w=\int_a^b f(x)\,dx \text{ resp. } w_1=\int_a^b f_1(x)\,dx \tag{3}$$

ableiten; führen wir weiter für die größten mutmaßlichen Schwankungen über und unter B beziehungsweise die Werte ω und ω_1 ein, so erhalten wir als gesamte Wahrscheinlichkeit, daß der Kurs überhaupt über B steige, das Integral

$$W=\int_0^\omega f(x)\,dx,$$

während für eine Kurserniedrigung eine Gesamtwahrscheinlichkeit

$$W_1=\int_0^{\omega_1} f_1(x)\,dx$$

resultiert. Da nun die Wahrscheinlichkeiten W und W_1 zusammen die Gewißheit liefern müssen, so wird zwischen letzteren Integralen die Relation

$$\int_0^{\omega} f(x)\,dx + \int_0^{\omega_1} f(x)\,dx = 1 \tag{4}$$

bestehen. Auf gleiche Weise stellen die Funktionen

$$F(x) = \int_x^{\omega} f(x)\,dx \text{ resp. } F_1(x) = \int_x^{\omega_1} f_1(x)\,dx \tag{5}$$

die Gesamtprobabilitäten dar, daß die Schwankungen über resp. unter B am Liquidationstermin die Größe x übersteigen; wir werden bald erfahren, welche bedeutende Rolle gerade diese Funktionen in den späteren Betrachtungen spielen werden.

Tragen wir auf einer horizontalen Geraden rechts von einem Punkte 0 die Marktschwankungen über B, links davon hingegen die Schwankungen unter B auf und errichten wir in den jeweiligen Endpunkten Senkrechte, welche die entsprechenden Funktionswerte $f(x)$ bezw. $f_1(x)$ darstellen sollen, so entstehen zwei kontinuierliche Kurven C und C_1, die wir füglich Schwankungswahrscheinlichkeitskurven nennen werden (siehe Fig. 23); die zwischen irgend zwei Ordinaten

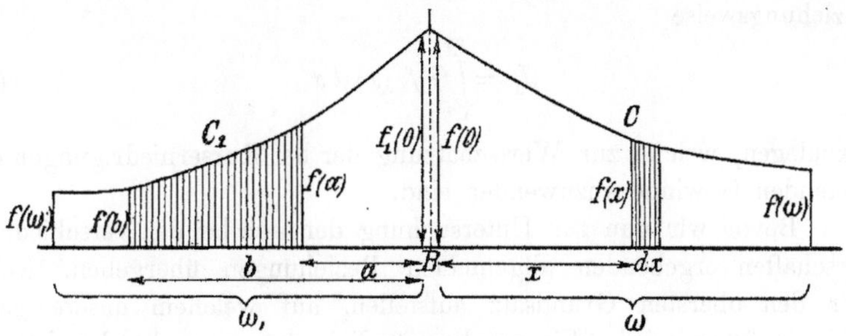

Fig. 23.

$f(a)$ und $f(b)$, zwischen dem entsprechenden Stücke der Kurve und der Geraden befindliche Fläche stellt offenbar den Wert der Integrale (3), d. h. die gesamte Wahrscheinlichkeit, daß die Schwankung am Liquidationstermin zwischen den angenommenen Grenzen a und b falle, dar.

3. Mathematische Erwartungen infolge von Kursschwankungen. Haben wir bei der Marktlage zwischen $B + x$ und $B + x + dx$, wofür eben die Wahrscheinlichkeit $f(x)\,dx$ besteht, einen Gewinn vom Betrage G zu erwarten, so stellt bekanntlich das Produkt

$$G\,f(x)\,dx$$

den sogenannten mathematischen Hoffnungswert des Gewinnes dar, d. h. jenen Wert, der unter diesen Umständen am plausibelsten als tatsächlicher Gewinn in Rechnung zu stellen ist. Alsdann liefert das Integral

$$i = \int_a^b G\,f(x)\,dx \tag{6}$$

den gesamten Hoffnungswert des Gewinnes für die angenommenen Grenzen, während das Integral

$$J = \int_0^\omega G\,f(x)\,dx, \tag{7}$$

erstreckt vom Kurse B bis zum höchsten erreichbaren Werte $B + \omega$, eben zur Bestimmung des Gesamtwertes der bei einer Kurserhöhung zu gewärtigenden Gewinne dient. Ganz analoge Bedeutung ist den Ausdrücken

$$i_1 = \int_a^b G\,f_1(x)\,dx, \tag{6$_a$}$$

beziehungsweise

$$J_1 = \int_0^{\omega_1} G\,f_1(x)\,dx \tag{7$_a$}$$

beizulegen, welche zur Wertschätzung der bei Kurserniedrigungen eintretenden Gewinne anzuwenden sind.

Bevor wir nun zur Untersuchung der sich bei den verschiedenen Geschäften ergebenden allgemeinen Beziehungen übergehen, wollen wir den obersten Grundsatz aufstellen, auf welchem unsere ganze Theorie fußen wird. Wir werden nämlich stets vom Standpunkte ausgehen, daß im Moment des Abschlusses eines jeden Geschäftes beide Kontrahenten mit ganz gleichen Chancen dastehen, so daß für keinen derselben im voraus weder Gewinn noch Verlust anzunehmen ist; wir stellen uns also jedes Geschäft unter solchen Bedingungen abgeschlossen vor, daß die gesamten Hoffnungswerte des Gewinnes und des Verlustes im Moment des Kontrakts einander gleich seien, oder, den Verlust als negativen Gewinn auffassend, daß der gesamte Hoffnungswert des Gewinnes für beide Kontrahenten der Null gleichkommen müsse.

Von einem so abgeschlossenen Geschäfte werden wir dann sagen, daß es der Bedingung der Rechtmäßigkeit entspricht.

4. Feste Geschäfte. Wurde zum Kurse B ein fester Kauf abgeschlossen, so ist bekanntlich beim Markte $B+x$ der Gewinn x, bei der Marktlage $B-x$ hingegen ein ebenso großer Verlust zu erwarten; es ergeben sich hieraus die elementaren Hoffnungswerte

$$x f(x)\,dx \text{ resp. } -x f_1(x)\,dx,$$

welche, von 0 bis zu den extremen Werten ω und ω_1 integriert, den Gesamtgewinn

$$G=\int_0^\omega x f(x)\,dx,$$

beziehungsweise den Gesamtverlust

$$V=\int_0^{\omega_1} x f_1(x)\,dx$$

liefern; dem Rechtmäßigkeitsprinzip entsprechend, sind diese Werte einander gleich zu betrachten, was zur Relation

$$\int_0^\omega x f(x)\,dx=\int_0^{\omega_1} x f_1(x)\,dx \tag{8}$$

führt. Selbstverständlich hätte sich das gleiche Resultat aus der Betrachtung eines festen Verkaufes ergeben.

5. Normale Prämiengeschäfte. Liegt ein zum Kurse B mittels einer Prämie P abgeschlossener Wahlkauf vor, so wissen wir daß beim Markte $B+x$ ein Gewinn $x-P$, beim Markte $B-x$ hingegen ein Verlust P entsteht; es ergeben sich hieraus für die betrachteten Marktlagen beziehungsweise die elementaren Hoffnungswerte

$$(x-P) f(x)\,dx \text{ und } -P f_1(x)\,dx,$$

und somit bei diesem Geschäfte ein Gesamtgewinn

$$G=\int_0^\omega (x-P) f(x)\,dx-\int_0^{\omega_1} P f_1(x)\,dx,$$

welcher nach unserem Grundsatze der Null gleichzusetzen ist. Es findet sich zunächst

$$0=\int_0^\omega x f(x)\,dx-P\int_0^\omega f(x)\,dx-P\int_0^{\omega_1} f_1(x)\,dx$$

und weiter, der Gleichung (5) zufolge,

$$P = \int_0^{\omega} x f(x)\, dx. \tag{9}$$

Diese Relation ist unmittelbar verständlich; sie spricht nämlich das Prinzip aus, daß die einzuzahlende Prämie der mathematischen Erwartung aller Vorteile gleichkommen muß, welche mit einer Kurserhöhung verbunden sind; in der Tat erlangt man ja durch Ableistung dieser Prämie nichts anderes als die Fakultät, jedes Steigen des Kurses über B zum eigenen Gewinne ausnützen zu dürfen.

Die Betrachtung des Wahlverkaufes hätte zur analogen Gleichung

$$P' = \int_0^{\omega_1} x f_1(x)\, dx \tag{9$_a$}$$

geführt; es folgt nun wegen (8)

$$P = P', \tag{10}$$

welche Gleichung sich schon im I. Teile als unerläßliche Bedingung für die Möglichkeit der Deckung normaler Geschäfte aufgedrängt hatte.

6. **Schiefe Geschäfte.** Betrachten wir einen à $B + M$ mittels Prämie P_1 abgeschlossenen Wahlkauf, so geht aus nachstehendem Schema

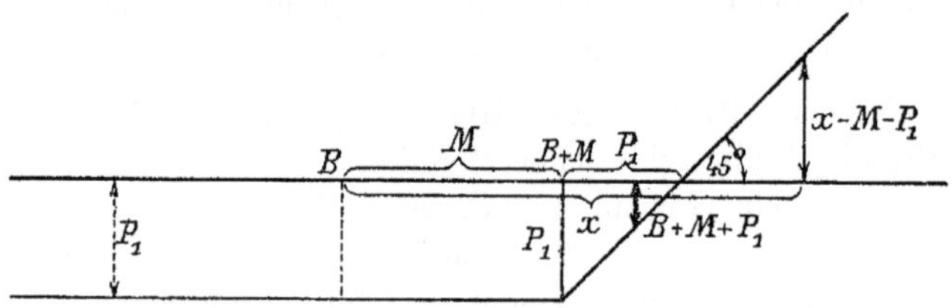

Fig. 24.

unmittelbar hervor, daß wir nur bei Marktschwankungen über B, die größer als $M + P_1$ sind, einen Gewinn, und zwar im Betrage $x - M - P_1$, zu erwarten haben, wobei wie immer die Schwankung x von B aus gerechnet wurde; solch einer Schwankung x entspricht ein elementarer Hoffnungswert

$$(x - M - P_1) f(x)\, dx,$$

mithin ist die gesamte bei diesem Geschäfte auftretende Gewinnhoffnung durch das Integral

$$G = \int_{M+P_1}^{\omega} (x - M - P_1) f(x)\, dx$$

dargestellt. Für Kurse unter $B + M + P_1$ haben wir dagegen Verlust und zwar: im Gebiete von $B + M$ bis $B + M + P_1$, wo also zwischen M und $M + P_1$ liegende Schwankungen in Betracht kommen, ist bei einer Schwankung x die Größe des Verlustes durch $M + P_1 - x$ gegeben, so daß ihr eine elementare mathematische Erwartung

$$(M + P_1 - x) f(x)\, dx$$

zukommt; der Gesamtwert des Verlustes in diesem ersten Gebiete ist somit

$$V_1 = \int_{M}^{M+P_1} (M + P_1 - x) f(x)\, dx.$$

Im zweiten Gebiete von B bis $B + M$ haben wir für jede Schwankung x einen Verlust P_1, somit einen elementaren Verlust

$$P_1 f(x)\, dx$$

und einen Gesamtverlust vom Betrage

$$V_2 = \int_0^M P_1 f(x)\, dx.$$

Im dritten Gebiete, d. h. für Schwankungen unter B, haben wir ebenfalls bei einer beliebigen Schwankung x den Verlust P_1, hier aber mit der Wahrscheinlichkeit $f_1(x)\, dx$; der elementare Hoffnungswert dieses Verlustes ist alsdann

$$P_1 f_1(x)\, dx,$$

somit der gesamte in diesem Gebiete erwachsende Verlust

$$V_3 = \int_0^{\omega_1} P_1 f_1(x)\, dx.$$

Nach unserem Grundsatze muß nun die Relation

$$G = V_1 + V_2 + V_3$$

stattfinden; eine einfache Reduktion der vorkommenden Integrale ergibt zunächst

$$\int_M^{\omega} (x - M - P_1) f(x)\, dx = P_1 \int_0^{\omega} f(x)\, dx - P_1 \int_M^{\omega} f(x)\, dx + P_1 \int_0^{\omega_1} f_1(x)\, dx,$$

und weiter

$$\int_M^{\omega}(x-M)f(x)\,dx - P_1\int_M^{\omega}f(x)\,dx = P_1\left[\int_0^{\omega}f(x)\,dx + \int_0^{\omega_1}f_1(x)\,dx\right] -$$

$$- P_1\int_M^{\omega}f(x)\,dx$$

und schließlich, der Gleichung (5) zufolge,

$$P_1 = \int_M^{\omega}(x-M)f(x)\,dx. \tag{11}$$

Dieser Ausdruck für P_1 ist auch a priori klar; endlich und schließlich erlangt man ja durch Einzahlung der Prämie P_1 nichts anderes als die Fakultät, jedes Steigen des Kurses über $B+M$ auszunützen; entspricht somit die Prämie P_1 dem aufgestellten Rechtmäßigkeitsprinzip, so muß sie dem Hoffnungswerte aller bei den genannten Kurserhöhungen eintretenden Gewinne gleichkommen, was eben den Inhalt der Formel (11) bildet.

Für $M=0$ geht der Ausdruck (11) in jenen der normalen Prämie P über, für $M=\omega$ hingegen ergibt sich, wie es sonst unmittelbar verständlich ist,

$$P_1 = 0. \tag{12}$$

Um einen Ausdruck für die beim Wahlverkaufe à $B+M$ abzuleistende Prämie P_2 zu gewinnen, lassen wir uns sofort von dem Gedanken leiten, daß letztere der mathematischen Erwartung der sich beim Geschäfte ergebenden möglichen Gewinne gleichzuhalten ist; ein Blick auf nachstehendes Schema

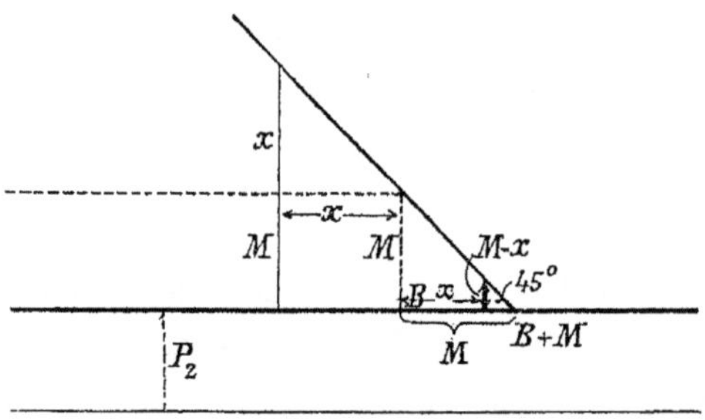

Fig. 25.

zeigt sofort, daß das Gewinngebiet in zwei Teile zu zerlegen ist, und zwar in einen von B bis $B+M$ und in einen anderen von B bis

$B - \omega_1$; im ersteren Teile entspricht einer Schwankung x ein Gewinn $M - x$ mit der Wahrscheinlichkeit $f(x)\,d\,x$, mithin ein elementarer Hoffnungswert

$$(M - x) f(x)\,d\,x,$$

welcher, von 0 bis M integriert, die gesamte mathematische Gewinnerwartung in diesem Teilgebiete, d. h.

$$G_1 = \int_0^M (M - x) f(x)\,d\,x$$

liefert. Im anderen Teile entspricht einer Schwankung x unter B ein Gewinn $M + x$ mit der Wahrscheinlichkeit $f_1(x)\,d\,x$, d. h. eine elementare mathematische Erwartung

$$(M + x) f_1(x)\,d\,x;$$

das von 0 bis ω_1 genommene Integral stellt alsdann den ganzen Hoffnungswert des Gewinnes in dem zweiten Gebiete dar, so daß wir zunächst zur Relation

$$P_2 = \int_0^M (M - x) f(x)\,d\,x + \int_0^{\omega_1} (M + x) f_1(x)\,d\,x$$

gelangen; die rechte Seite bringen wir sodann in die Form

$$P_2 = \int_0^{\omega} (M - x) f(x)\,d\,x - \int_M^{\omega} (M - x) f(x)\,d\,x + \int_0^{\omega_1} M f_1(x)\,d\,x +$$
$$+ \int_0^{\omega_1} x f_1(x)\,d\,x,$$

das heißt

$$P_2 = M \int_0^{\omega} f(x)\,d\,x - \int_0^{\omega} x f(x)\,d\,x + P_1 + M \int_0^{\omega_1} f_1(x)\,d\,x +$$
$$+ \int_0^{\omega_1} x f_1(x)\,d\,x,$$

woraus unmittelbar infolge bekannter Gleichungen die bemerkenswerte Formel

$$P_2 = P_1 + M \tag{13}$$

folgt. Hiemit erlangt diese schon im I. Teile dieses Werkchens als unerläßliche Bedingung für die Möglichkeit der Deckung schiefer Geschäfte gefundene Gleichung erst jetzt ihre volle Berechtigung und große Bedeutung, da sie jetzt nicht mehr den bloßen Charakter einer künstlichen Bedingung in sich trägt, sondern dem unanfechtbaren Prinzip der Gleichheit von Leistung und Gegenleistung entsprungen ist.

Für $M = 0$ erhält man wieder $P_2 = P_1 = P$, für $M = \omega$ hingegen, der Gleichung (12) zufolge,

$$P_2 = \omega. \tag{14}$$

Wie sich endlich die Stellagenprämien, die bekanntlich der Summe von P_1 und P_2 gleich sind, in beliebigen und in speziellen Fällen gestalten, brauchen wir nicht näher zu erörtern.

Ganz denselben Ideengang befolgend hätte man für die beim Wahlverkaufe à $B - M$ zu entrichtende Prämie den Ausdruck

$$P_1' = \int_M^{\omega_1} (x - M) f_1(x) \, d\, x,$$

und zwischen den Prämien des Wahlkaufes und des Wahlverkaufes die Relation

$$P_2' = P_1' + M$$

gefunden.

7. Nochgeschäfte. Fassen wir den Wahlkauf eines m-mal Nochs mit Prämie N ins Auge, so wissen wir aus früheren Auseinandersetzungen, daß der Gewinn durch $(m + 1)\,\varepsilon$, der Verlust hingegen durch das einfache η dargestellt ist, wobei die Größen ε und η beziehungsweise die Marktschwankungen über und unter $B + N$ bedeuten; die graphische Darstellung dieser Verhältnisse ist aus nachstehendem Schema

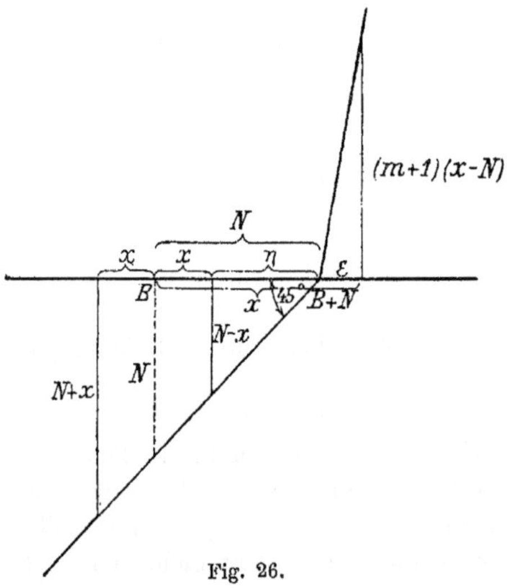

Fig. 26.

zu entnehmen. Das Gebiet des Gewinnes erstreckt sich von $B+N$ bis $B+\omega$; letzterem kommt in diesem Gebiete der elementare Hoffnungswert

$$(m+1)(x-N)f(x)\,dx$$

zu, woraus eine gesamte mathematische Erwartung

$$G=\int_N^\omega (m+1)(x-N)f(x)\,dx$$

resultiert. Der Verlust verteilt sich seinerseits auf zwei Gebiete; von B bis $B+N$ haben wir einen elementaren Hoffnungswert

$$(N-x)f(x)\,dx,$$

somit im ganzen einen Verlust

$$V_1=\int_0^N (N-x)f(x)\,dx;$$

von B bis $B-\omega_1$ hingegen ergibt sich

$$(N+x)f_1(x)\,dx$$

als elementarer Hoffnungswert, mithin

$$V_2=\int_0^{\omega_1} (N+x)f_1(x)\,dx$$

als gesamter in diesem Gebiete auftretender Verlust. Die Behandlung der Gleichung

$$G=V_1+V_2$$

liefert zunächst

$$m\int_N^\omega (x-N)f(x)\,dx+\int_N^\omega (x-N)f(x)\,dx=\int_0^\omega (N-x)f(x)\,dx-$$
$$-\int_N^\omega (N-x)f(x)\,dx+\int_0^{\omega_1} (N+x)f_1(x)\,dx,$$

und weiter

$$m\int_N^\omega (x-N)f(x)\,dx=N\left[\int_0^\omega f(x)\,dx+\int_0^{\omega_1} f_1(x)\,dx\right]-\int_0^\omega xf(x)\,dx+$$
$$+\int_0^{\omega_1} xf_1(x)\,dx$$

oder, wegen bekannter Gleichungen,

$$N = m\int_{N}^{\omega}(x - N) f(x)\, d\, x, \tag{15}$$

wodurch die im I. Teile a priori aufgestellte Relation

$$N = m\, P_1$$

wiedergefunden ist. Auf gleiche Weise hätte sich bei Betrachtung des Wahlverkaufes eines m-mal Nochs die analoge Beziehung

$$N' = m\int_{N'}^{\omega_1}(x - N')\, f_1(x)\, d\, x \tag{15$_a$}$$

ergeben. Was übrigens die weiteren Beziehungen zu den Stellagenprämien etc. betrifft, so wird auf das III. Kapitel des I. Teiles verwiesen.

8. **Differentialgleichungen zwischen den Prämien P_1 resp. P_2 und der Funktion f (x).** Das Integral

$$P_1 = \int_{M}^{\omega}(x - M) f(x)\, d\, x$$

stellt bekanntlich, wegen der Voraussetzung über $f(x)$, eine stetige Funktion der einzigen Veränderlichen M dar, so daß wir dasselbe nach M differenzieren können. Indem wir hier die allgemeinen Formeln

$$U = \int_{x_0}^{X} f(x\, \alpha)\, d\, x, \quad \frac{\delta\, U}{\delta\, X} = f(X\, \alpha), \quad \frac{\delta\, U}{\delta\, x_0} = -f(x_0\, \alpha),$$

beziehungsweise

$$\frac{\delta\, U}{\delta\, \alpha} = \int_{x_0}^{X} \frac{\delta\, f(x_1\, \alpha)}{\delta\, \alpha}\, d\, x,$$

welche bei der Differentiation nach den Grenzen, beziehungsweise nach Parametern unter dem Integralzeichen anzuwenden sind, in das Gedächtnis zurückrufen, erhalten wir bei einer ersten Differentiation unseres Integrals nach M, da letzteres sowohl an der unteren Grenze als auch in der Funktion unter dem Integralzeichen explizite vorkommt, offenbar

$$\frac{\delta\, P_1}{\delta\, M} = -(M - M) f(M) + \int_{M}^{\omega} - f(x)\, d\, x,$$

d. h. die bemerkenswerte Relation

$$\frac{\delta\, P_1}{\delta\, M} = -\int_{M}^{\omega} f(x)\, d\, x = -F(M), \tag{16}$$

während aus einer zweiten Differentiation die von Integralen ganz freie Differentialgleichung

$$\frac{\delta^2 P_1}{\delta M^2} = f(M), \tag{17}$$

resultiert. Umgekehrt folgt aus

$$\frac{\delta P_1}{\delta M} = -F(M) \tag{18}$$

durch Integration

$$P_1 = -\int F(M)\, d\, M + C, \tag{19}$$

wodurch die Bestimmung von P_1 in Funktion von M auf ganz andere Weise als durch direkte Auswertung seines Integrals vor sich gehen kann, was je nach der Form der Funktion $f(x)$ von sehr großem Vorteile sein könnte. Die Konstante C läßt sich leicht aus der Bedingung ermitteln, daß für $M = \omega$ auch die Prämie P_1, wie es die Gleichung (12) lehrt, verschwinden muß.

So ergibt sich für P_2, wenn man von der Gleichung

$$P_2 = M + P_1$$

ausgeht, aus einer ersten Differentiation

$$\frac{\delta P_2}{\delta M} = 1 - \int_M^\omega f(x)\, d\, x, \tag{16$_a$}$$

aus einer zweiten Differentiation hingegen

$$\frac{\delta^2 P_2}{\delta M^2} = f(M) = \frac{\delta^2 P_1}{\delta M^2}. \tag{17$_a$}$$

Wollen wir die Prämien P_1 und P_2, an der Hand der jetzt gewonnenen allgemeinen Resultate als Funktionen der unabhängigen Veränderlichen M auf graphische Weise darstellen, so erhalten wir zwei Kurven C_1 resp. C_2,

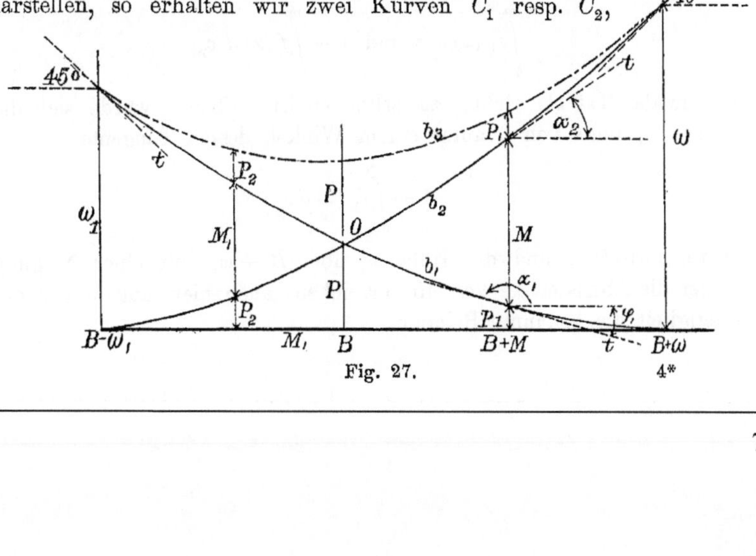

Fig. 27.

4*

deren erstere mit wachsendem M immer kleinere, die andere hingegen immer größere Ordinaten erlangt; ferner besitzen sie die besondere Eigenschaft, daß die Tangenten der Winkel φ_1 und α_2, welche eben den Differentialquotienten $\frac{-\delta P_1}{\delta M}$ und $\frac{\delta P_2}{\delta M}$ gleich sind, beziehungsweise die gesamten Wahrscheinlichkeiten darstellen, daß der Kurs am Liquidationstermin über $B + M$ steige oder unter diesen Wert falle. Die Kurve C_2 ist in A um 45^0 gegen die Abszissenaxe geneigt, während C_1 im Punkte $B + \omega$ die trigonometrische Tangente Null besitzt. Im Punkte 0 treffen die Kurven C_1 und C_2 zusammen, und zwar in einer Höhe, welche der normalen Prämie P gleich ist; die trigonometrischen Tangenten der für uns maßgebenden Winkel haben in diesem Punkte die Werte

$$\int_0^\omega f(x)\,dx \text{ resp. } 1 - \int_0^\omega f(x)\,dx,$$

welche offenbar die für eine Kurserhöhung resp. für eine Kurserniedrigung bestehenden Gesamtprobabilitäten sind.

Analoge Betrachtungen ließen sich für Geschäfte anstellen, die à $B - M$ abgeschlossen sind. Links von B würde P_2 die Rolle von P_1 spielen; die Kurve C_2 würde links von 0 unter einem Winkel ziehen, dessen Tangente

$$\int_0^{\omega_1} f_1(x)\,dx$$

betrüge, und sich langsam der Abszissenaxe anschmiegen, um den Punkt $B - \omega_1$ mit der Neigung Null zu erreichen; die Stetigkeit erfordert die Gleichheit von

$$\int_0^{\omega_1} f_1(x)\,dx \text{ und } 1 - \int_0^\omega f(x)\,dx,$$

was in der Tat als richtig zu erkennen ist. Ebenso würde sich die Kurve C_1 links von 0 unter einem Winkel, dessen Tangente

$$1 - \int_0^{\omega_1} f_1(x)\,dx$$

wäre, fortsetzen und die Höhe ω_1 über $B - \omega_1$ mit einer Neigung gegen die Abszissenaxe von 45^0 erreichen; auch hier muß wegen der Stetigkeit die bekannte Relation

— 53 —

$$\int_0^{\omega} f(x)\, d\, x = 1 - \int_0^{\omega_1} f_1(x)\, d\, x$$

bestehen.

Aus den Kurven C_1 und C_2 wäre sehr leicht die Kurve C_3 für die Stellagenprämien in ihrer Abhängigkeit von der Größe M darzustellen: man brauchte ja nur, wegen der bekannten Gleichung

$$S_1 = P_1 + P_2,$$

beliebig viele Ordinaten über die Kurve C_2 um die Ordinate von C_1 weiter zu verlängern, um beliebig viele Punkte der Kurve C_3 zu erhalten; als erste Ableitung von S_1 nach M ergäbe sich

$$\frac{\delta\, S_1}{\delta\, M} = \frac{\delta\, P_1}{\delta\, M} + \frac{\delta\, P_2}{\delta\, M},$$

d. h. infolge von (16) und (16_a),

$$\frac{\delta\, S_1}{\delta\, M} = 1 - 2\int_M^{\omega} f(x)\, d\, x, \tag{20}$$

als zweite Ableitung aber

$$\frac{\delta^2\, S_1}{\delta\, M^2} = 2\, f(M). \tag{21}$$

Aus (20) erfahren wir, daß die Stellagenprämie mit wachsendem M zu-, beziehungsweise abnehmen kann, je nachdem die Größe

$$1 - 2\int_M^{\omega} f(x)\, d\, x$$

positiv oder negativ ist; wird sie Null, was für solche Werte des M, welche der Gleichung

$$\int_M^{\omega} f(x)\, d\, x = {}^1/_2 \tag{22}$$

genügen, eintritt, so findet ein Extremum, und zwar ein Minimum statt, da der zweite Differentialquotient nach (21) positiv ist. Dieses Minimum kann freilich nur in der Nähe von B stattfinden, weil das Integral $\int_M^{\omega} f(x)\, d\, x$ mit wachsendem M rasch abnimmt und anderseits sein größter Wert sich sehr wenig von der halben Einheit unterscheiden kann.

Im ersten Teil dieses Werkchens hatten wir aus einer graphischen Darstellung den Schluß gezogen, daß eine schiefe Stellage immer teurer als eine gleich große normale Stellage zu bezahlen sei; das obige Ergebnis zeigt nun, daß dieser Schluß mindestens als voreilig zu bezeichnen ist. Es fällt in der Tat die Stelle des Minimums von S_1 nur dann mit dem Tageskurse B zusammen, wenn das Integral

$$\int_0^\infty f(x)\, d\, x$$

der halben Einheit gleich angenommen wird, d. h. wenn für eine Kurserhöhung die ganz gleiche Gesamtwahrscheinlichkeit wie für eine Kurserniedrigung herrschen würde. Da dies aber mit großer Annäherung in Wirklichkeit auch der Fall sein wird, da ja für Kurserhöhung und Kurserniedrigung im voraus gleiche Chancen anzunehmen sind, so bleiben wir bei jenem praktischen Schluß bestehen, daß die Prämie der normalen Stellage stets niedriger als jene für eine beliebige schiefe Stellage zu bemessen ist.

Es wird nicht uninteressant sein, wenn diese Resultate noch aus anderen, direkten Betrachtungen gewonnen werden. Die Prämie für eine normale Stellage ist offenbar

$$S = 2\int_0^\infty x\, f(x)\, d\, x,$$

jene für eine schiefe Stellage hingegen

$$S_1 = M + 2\int_M^\infty (x - M)\, f(x)\, d\, x.$$

Alsdann ist ihre Differenz

$$\delta = M + 2\int_0^\infty (x - M)\, f(x)\, d\, x - 2\int_0^M (x - M)\, f(x)\, d\, x - 2\int_0^\infty x\, f(x)\, d\, x,$$

oder noch

$$\delta = M + 2\int_0^\infty x\, f(x)\, d\, x - 2\, M\int_0^\infty f(x)\, d\, x + 2\int_0^M (M - x)\, f(x)\, d\, x -$$

$$- 2\int_0^\infty x\, f(x)\, d\, x,$$

und schließlich

$$\delta = M\left[1 - 2\int_0^\infty f(x)\, d\, x\right] + 2\int_0^M (M - x)\, f(x)\, d\, x. \tag{23}$$

Der zweite Teil der rechten Seite ist in dieser Gleichung wesentlich positiv, da für die in Betracht kommenden Grenzen die Funktion unter dem Integralzeichen positiv ist; da aber der erste Teil negativ und möglicherweise auch größer als der zweite Teil ausfallen könnte, so darf man sogar auf negative δ gefaßt sein, was schiefe Stellagen billiger als normale Stellagen charakterisieren würde. Nur bei der Voraussetzung

$$\int_0^\omega f(x)\,d\,x = {}^1/_2,$$

welche mit der früher erwähnten übereinstimmt, erhält man für δ einen wesentlich positiven Wert, d. h.

$$\delta = 2\int_0^M (M - x) f(x)\,d\,x, \tag{23$_a$}$$

so daß sich wirklich in diesem Falle für eine schiefe Stellage stets eine höhere Prämie als für eine normale ergeben würde.

II. Kapitel.

Anwendung der allgemeinen Gleichungen auf bestimmte Annahmen über die Funktion f (x).

1. Einleitung. In den folgenden Untersuchungen werden wir überall eine und dieselbe Funktion sowohl für Schwankungen über als auch für solche unter B, d. h.

$$f(x) = f_1(x)$$

annehmen; eine erste Folge davon ist die, daß wegen der Gleichung

$$\int_0^\omega x\,f(x)\,d\,x = \int_0^{\omega_1} x\,f_1(x)\,d\,x,$$

auch die Gleichheit der größten über und unter B erreichbaren Werte, d. h.

$$\omega = \omega_1$$

resultiert. Es ergibt sich ferner, daß die Integrale

$$\int_0^\omega f(x)\,d\,x \text{ und} \int_0^{\omega_1} f_1(x)\,d\,x$$

einander gleich werden, so daß, da ihre Summe gleich der Einheit ist, beständig die Relation

$$\int_0^\omega f(x)\,d\,x = {}^1/_2$$

erfüllt sein wird; auf diese Weise stellt B die wahrscheinlichste Marktlage am Liquidationstermin dar, was übrigens als a priori einleuchtend zu betrachten ist. Wir erfahren schließlich aus früheren Formeln, daß die Prämien des Wahlkaufes über B und des Wahlverkaufes unter B und umgekehrt bei gleicher Schiefe der Geschäfte einander gleichzuhalten sind, was offenbar auch für Nochgeschäfte, sobald sie dasselbe Multiplum betreffen, volle Geltung hat.

Die gemachte Annahme trifft in Wirklichkeit nicht zu; es könnte ja eine Kurserhöhung in unbeschränktem Maße stattfinden, während offenbar eine Kurserniedrigung höchstens bis zur Wertlosigkeit des Objektes vor sich gehen kann, was einer Schwankung unter B eben von der Größe B entsprechen würde. Da aber diese Fälle wohl auszuschließen und die Schwankungen als mehr oder weniger regelmäßige und im allgemeinen nicht erhebliche Oszillazionen um den Wert B aufzufassen sind, so darf man die gemachte Voraussetzung getrost akzeptieren und ihren Resultaten mit Zuversicht entgegensehen.

Was nun die Form der Funktion $f(x)$ selbst anlangt, so stoßen wir auf sehr große Schwierigkeiten. Allgemeine Anhaltspunkte, um die regellosen Schwankungen der Marktlage bei den verschiedenen Wertobjekten rechnerisch verfolgen zu können, gehen uns vollständig ab; wir könnten höchstens für jedes einzelne Wertobjekt aus statistischen Beobachtungsdaten die Wahrscheinlichkeit bestimmen, mit welcher der Kurs, sagen wir einen Monat später, eine ins Auge gefaßte Schwankung x erreicht oder auch übertrifft; geschieht dies g-mal unter m betrachteten Fällen, so wäre die erwähnte Wahrscheinlichkeit offenbar gleich g dividiert durch m.

Führen wir diese Rechnungen für die Reihe

$$x_1, x_2, \cdots x_{n-1}, x_n$$

von Schwankungen aus, so erhalten wir die korrespondierende Reihe

$$\frac{g_1}{m_1}, \frac{g_2}{m_2}, \cdots \frac{g_{n-1}}{m_{n-1}}, \frac{g_n}{m_n}$$

von Wahrscheinlichkeiten; nun stellen diese Gesamtwahrscheinlichkeiten offenbar nichts anderes als die entsprechenden Werte des Integrals

$$F(x) = \int_x^\infty f(x)\,dx = \frac{g}{m}$$

dar, so daß man durch die angeführten Rechnungen eine Reihe von Werten

$$F(x_1), F(x_2), \cdots F(x_{n-1}), F(x_n)$$

für die Funktion $F(x)$ gewinnen würde. Man könnte nun dieses ganze Beobachtungsmaterial durch Annahme einer empirischen, analytischen Gleichung für $F(x)$ darzustellen suchen, indem man durch die Methode der kleinsten Quadrate jene Werte der vorkommenden Konstanten bestimmen würde, die möglichst genau bei der Substitution von x_1, $x_2, \cdots x_n$ die Werte $F(x_1)$, $F(x_2), \cdots F(x_n)$ wiederzugeben im stande wären. Durch dieses Verfahren könnte für jedes beliebige Wertobjekt seine Funktion $F(x)$ ermittelt werden, die recht brauchbar wäre und, an die Relation

$$\frac{\delta P_1}{\delta M} = -F(M)$$

anknüpfend, die Beantwortung jeder Frage auf leichte und verläßliche Weise gestatten würde. Selbstverständlich sind auch die größten zu erwartenden Schwankungen ω aus Erfahrungsdaten zu entnehmen.

Diese mühsame Arbeit werden wir nicht ausführen, sondern uns im folgenden mit der Wahl einer bestimmten Form der Funktion $f(x)$ begnügen, bei welcher die etwa vorkommenden Konstanten durch Formulierung besonderer Bedingungen zu ermitteln sein werden.

2. Die Funktion f(x) sei durch eine konstante Größe dargestellt. Wir nehmen

$$f(x) = a$$

an, wodurch eben ausgedrückt ist, daß für jede beliebige Schwankung dieselbe Wahrscheinlichkeit besteht; bei Kursen, welche keinen starken Oszillationen unterworfen sind, dürfte diese Annahme ziemlich nahe liegend sein. Die immer zu erfüllende Bedingung

$$\int_0^\omega f(x)\,dx = 1/_2$$

liefert in diesem Falle

$$\int_0^\omega a\,dx = a\,\omega = 1/_2,$$

so daß für die Konstante a und für die Funktion $f(x)$ selbst der Ausdruck

$$f(x) = \frac{1}{2\,\omega} \tag{1}$$

resultiert. Die für die ganze Theorie höchst wichtige Funktion $F(x)$ ist hier durch das Integral

$$\int_x^\omega \frac{d\,x}{2\,\omega}$$

dargestellt, somit haben wir

$$F(x) = \frac{\omega - x}{2\,\omega}. \tag{2}$$

Hier ist die Schwankungswahrscheinlichkeitskurve durch eine Gerade repräsentiert, welche in der Höhe $\frac{1}{2\,\omega}$ parallel zur Abszissenachse läuft; die Funktion $F(x)$ stellt bekanntlich die schraffierte Fläche des nachstehenden Schema

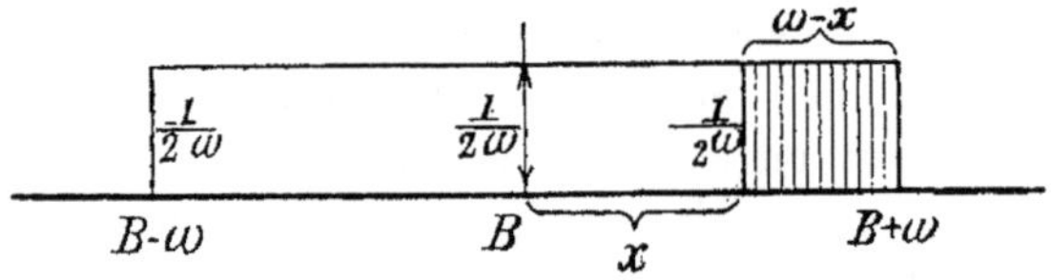

Fig. 28.

dar, wie es in der Tat durch Formel (2) bestätigt ist.

Die Anwendung der Gleichung

$$\frac{\delta P_1}{\delta M} = - F(M)$$

liefert in diesem Falle

$$\frac{\delta P_1}{\delta M} = - \frac{\omega - M}{2\,\omega},$$

nämlich

$$P_1 = -\int \frac{\omega - M}{2\,\omega}\, d\,M + C$$

oder ausgewertet,

$$P_1 = \frac{(\omega - M)^2}{4\,\omega}, \tag{3}$$

da die Konstante C, wegen $P_1 = 0$ für $M = \omega$, selbst verschwinden muß.

Es ergibt sich hieraus, wegen $P_2 = P_1 + M$, unmittelbar

$$P_2 = \frac{(\omega + M)^2}{4\,\omega}, \tag{3$_a$}$$

mithin für die schiefe Stellage die Prämie

$$S_1 = \frac{\omega^2 + M^2}{2\,\omega} = \frac{\omega}{2} + \frac{M^2}{2\,\omega}. \tag{4}$$

Für $M = 0$ leiten sich hieraus die für normale Geschäfte gültigen Größen, d. h.

$$P = \frac{\omega}{4} \text{ resp. } S = \frac{\omega}{2} \tag{5}$$

ab; die Prämiendifferenz zwischen schiefer und normaler Stellage ist

$$\delta = \frac{M^2}{2\,\omega},$$

wie es durch direkte Auswertung des Integrals

$$\delta = 2 \int_0^M (M - x) f(x)\, d\,x$$

bestätigt werden könnte.

Die allgemeine Gleichung für das Nochgeschäft, d. h.

$$N = m \int_N^\omega (x - N) f(x)\, d\,x = m\, P_1,$$

wird nach (3)

$$N = \frac{m\,(\omega - N)^2}{4\,\omega}, \tag{6}$$

welche Gleichung vom 2. Grade ist und auf sehr leichte Weise die Bestimmung von N in Funktion von ω und m gestattet; man erhält

$$N^2 - \frac{2\,\omega\,(m + 2)}{m}\, N = -\,\omega^2,$$

und hieraus

$$N = \frac{\omega}{m}\left(m + 2 - 2\sqrt{m + 1}\right); \tag{7}$$

das Radikand mußten wir hiebei bloß mit negativem Vorzeichen nehmen, da es sich sonst für N ein größerer Wert als ω, und zwar für ein beliebiges m ergeben hätte. Wollen wir das N durch die Prämie des einfachen normalen Geschäftes ausdrücken, so erhalten wir, wegen $\omega = 4\,P$,

$$N = \frac{4}{m}\left(m + 2 - 2\sqrt{m + 1}\right) P. \tag{7_a}$$

Das Verhältnis $\frac{N}{P}$ können wir aus der Gleichung (6) auch auf folgende Weise bestimmen: Es ist zunächst

$$N = \frac{m(4P - N)^2}{16P} = \frac{mP(4P - N)^2}{(4P)^2},$$

und hieraus

$$\frac{N}{P} = m\left(1 - \frac{N}{4P}\right)^2; \tag{8}$$

setzen wir nun

$$1 - \frac{N}{4P} = \rho,$$

so daß

$$\frac{N}{P} = 4(1 - \rho) \tag{9}$$

wird, so erhalten wir die Gleichung

$$m\rho^2 + 4\rho - 4 = 0, \tag{10}$$

mithin

$$\rho = \frac{-2}{m} \pm \sqrt{\frac{4 + 4m}{m^2}}$$

oder, da nur positive Werte von ρ einen Sinn haben,

$$\rho = \frac{2}{m}\left(\sqrt{m+1} - 1\right). \tag{11}$$

Für $m = 1$ ergibt sich $\rho_1 = 0{\cdot}8284$, somit

$$N_1 = 0{\cdot}6864\,P;$$

für $m = 2$ ist $\rho_2 = 0{\cdot}732$, folglich

$$N_2 = 1{\cdot}072\,P;$$

für $m = 3$ gehen rationale Werte hervor, nämlich

$$\rho_3 = {}^2/_3 \text{ resp. } N_3 = {}^4/_3\,P$$

und so weiter fort. So findet man zwischen den Nochprämien die Beziehungen

$$N_2 = 1{\cdot}562\ N_1,\ N_3 = 1{\cdot}942\ N_1 \text{ etc.}$$

Im Besitze dieser allgemeinen Formeln können wir auch die mannigfaltigsten Aufgaben lösen. Wollten wir z. B. erfahren, bei welchem Noch die betreffende Prämie gleich P ausfällt, so würden wir in (8) $\frac{N}{P} = 1$ setzen und die Gleichung nach m auflösen; es ergäbe sich

$$m = 1^7/_9 = 1{\cdot}7777.$$

Wollten wir noch wissen, bei welcher Schiefe die Differenz zwischen der normalen und der schiefen Stellage der Prämie P_1 gleichkommt, so hätten wir die Gleichung

$$\frac{M^2}{2\,\omega} = \frac{(\omega - M)^2}{4\,\omega}$$

nach M aufzulösen; wir erhielten

$$M = \omega\,(\sqrt{2} - 1), \text{ d. h. } 4\,P\;(\sqrt{2} - 1) = 1{\cdot}6168\,P$$

und so weiter fort.

3. Die Funktion f (x) sei durch eine lineare Gleichung dargestellt. Es sei

$$f(x) = a + b\,x;$$

zur Bestimmung der Koeffizienten a und b fügen wir zur gewöhnlichen Bedingung

$$\int_0^\omega f(x)\,d\,x = {}^1/_2$$

die weitere hinzu, daß die extremen Werte ω mit der Wahrscheinlichkeit Null erreicht werden, was durch die Relation

$$f(\omega) = 0$$

ausgedrückt ist.

Bei Wertobjekten, deren Kurse ziemlich bedeutenden Schwankungen unterliegen, dürften die hier gemachten Annahmen der Wirklichkeit besser entsprechen, als jene die den Rechnungen der vorigen Nummer zu Grunde gelegt wurden.

Aus der ersten Bedingung folgt nun

$$\int_0^\omega (a + b\,x)\,d\,x = \frac{(a + b\,\omega)^2 - a^2}{2\,b} = {}^1/_2,$$

aus der zweiten hingegen

$$a + b\,\omega = 0.$$

Die Auflösung dieser Gleichungen nach a und b liefert die Werte

$$a = \frac{1}{\omega} \text{ resp. } b = \frac{-1}{\omega^2},$$

so daß unsere Funktion durch den Ausdruck

$$f(x) = \frac{\omega - x}{\omega^2} \tag{12}$$

definiert ist.

Hier ist wieder die Schwankungswahrscheinlichkeitskurve eine Gerade, welche diesmal von der Ordinatenachse die Strecke $\frac{1}{\omega}$ abschneidet und die Abszissenachse in $B + \omega$ trifft (siehe Fig. 29); aus den zwei ähnlichen

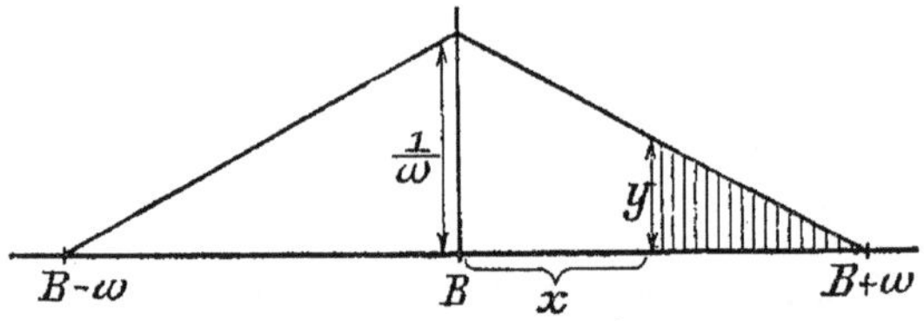

Fig. 29.

Dreiecken folgt die Proportion

$$y : \frac{1}{\omega} = (\omega - x) : \omega,$$

die in der Tat für y den in (12) enthaltenen Ausdruck wiedergibt.

Das zwischen x und ω genommene Integral wird in diesem Falle

$$\int_x^\omega \frac{\omega - x}{\omega^2} d\,x = \frac{(\omega - x)^2}{2\,\omega^2} \tag{13}$$

und stellt bekanntlich die in Figur 29 schraffierte Fläche dar; durch direkte Bestimmung dieser Fläche erhalten wir in der Tat

$$\frac{y}{2}(\omega - x), \text{ d. h. } \frac{(\omega - x)^2}{2\,\omega^2}.$$

Dieser Ausdruck ist aber auch dem negativ genommenen Differentialquotienten von P_1 gleich zu setzen; es ist nämlich, wenn wir der Gleichmäßigkeit halber auch die veränderliche Größe mit M bezeichnen,

$$\frac{\delta P_1}{\delta M} = - \frac{(\omega - M)^2}{2\,\omega^2},$$

mithin

$$P_1 = - \int \frac{(\omega - M)^2}{2\,\omega^2} d\,M + C.$$

Es ergibt sich hieraus unmittelbar

$$P_1 = \frac{(\omega - M)^3}{6\,\omega^2}; \tag{14}$$

die Konstante C ist der Nulle gleich, da P_1 für $M = \omega$ verschwinden muß. Hieraus leitet sich die normale Prämie P, indem man $M = 0$ setzt, im Betrage

$$P = \frac{\omega}{6} \tag{15}$$

ab; die Prämie für die normale Stellage ist alsdann

$$S = \frac{\omega}{3},$$

während sie für die schiefe Stellage die Größe

$$S_1 = \frac{(\omega - M)^3}{3\,\omega^2} + M = \frac{\omega}{3} + \frac{M^2}{\omega}\left(1 - \frac{M}{3\,\omega}\right)$$

erreicht; es folgt eine Prämiendifferenz

$$\delta = \frac{M^2}{\omega}\left(1 - \frac{M}{3\,\omega}\right), \tag{16}$$

die offenbar stets positiv ist, wie es eben sein muß.

Durch Benützung der Gleichung (15) läßt sich aus (14) eine Beziehung zwischen den schiefen und den normalen Prämien herstellen, und zwar: wir bringen die Formel (14) zunächst in die Form

$$P_1 = \frac{(6\,P - M)^3}{6^3\,P^2}, \text{ d. h. } \frac{P\,(6\,P - M)^3}{(6\,P)^3},$$

so daß schließlich die Gleichung

$$P_1 = \left(1 - \frac{M}{6\,P}\right)^3 P \tag{17}$$

resultiert.

Von dieser Gleichung gehen wir nun aus, um die Prämie N des Nochgeschäftes zu untersuchen; es ist nämlich

$$N = m\,P_1,$$

wobei P_1 selbst die Schiefe N besitzt, somit auch, nach (17),

$$N = m\left(1 - \frac{N}{6\,P}\right)^3 P;$$

es folgt weiter

$$\frac{N}{P} = m\left(1 - \frac{N}{6\,P}\right)^3 \tag{18}$$

oder, durch Einführung der Hilfsgröße

$$\rho = 1 - \frac{N}{6\,P},$$

welche die weitere Relation

$$\frac{N}{P} = 6(1 - \rho) \tag{19}$$

nach sich zieht, die einfache Gleichung 3. Grades

$$m \rho^3 + 6 \rho - 6 = 0, \tag{20}$$

welche mit der entsprechenden, in der vorigen Nummer abgeleiteten Gleichung 2. Grades sehr große Analogie zeigt.

Da in der Gleichung (19) ein Glied zwischen zwei gleichbezeichneten Gliedern fehlt, so schließen wir auf die Gegenwart von zwei imaginären Wurzeln, so daß eine einzige reelle Wurzel notwendig existieren muß, und zwar eine positive, weil das absolute Glied negativ ist. Für letztere Wurzel liefert nun die unmittelbare Anwendung der kardanischen Formel

$$\rho = \sqrt[3]{\frac{3}{m} + \sqrt{\frac{9}{m^2} + \frac{8}{m^3}}} + \sqrt[3]{\frac{3}{m} - \sqrt{\frac{9}{m^2} + \frac{8}{m^3}}}$$

oder etwas reduziert,

$$\rho = \sqrt[3]{\frac{1}{m}}\left[\sqrt[3]{3 + \sqrt{9 + \frac{8}{m}}} + \sqrt[3]{3 - \sqrt{9 + \frac{8}{m}}}\right]. \tag{21}$$

Hieraus berechnet sich für das einmal Noch, also für $m = 1$,

$$\rho_1 = 0{\cdot}88462$$

und sodann, vermöge (19),

$$N_1 = 0{\cdot}69288\, P;$$

für das zweimal Noch, d. h. für $m = 2$, ergibt sich

$$\rho_2 = 0{\cdot}81773,$$

woraus dann

$$N_2 = 1{\cdot}09362\, P$$

und so weiter folgt. So erhielte man

$$N_2 = 1{\cdot}578\ N_1 \text{ etc.}$$

Die Vergleichung dieser Resultate mit den entsprechenden, unter der Annahme der vorigen Nummer abgeleiteten Werten zeigt allerdings eine bemerkenswerte nahe Übereinstimmung.

Um auch hier zu erfahren, bei wieviel mal Noch die Prämie N der normalen Prämie gleich sein sollte, setzen wir in (18) $\frac{N}{P} = 1$ und lösen nach m auf; wir finden

$$m = 1{\cdot}728,$$

somit wieder ein mit dem entsprechenden der vorigen Nummer ziemlich gut übereinstimmendes Resultat.

Die Bestimmung der Schiefe, bei welcher die Prämie P_1 genau der Stellagendifferenz gleichkommt, geschieht folgendermaßen: Die Gleichsetzung von (14) und (16) liefert zunächst

$$\frac{(\omega - M)^3}{6\,\omega^2} = \frac{M^2}{\omega}\left(1 - \frac{M}{3\,\omega}\right),$$

und geordnet

$$M^3 - 3\,\omega\,M^2 - 3\,\omega^2\,M + \omega^3 = 0;$$

das liefert weiter

$$(M + \omega)\,(M^2 - \omega\,M + \omega^2) - 3\,\omega\,M\,(M + \omega) = 0$$

oder, da $M + \omega$ von Null verschieden ist,

$$M^2 - 4\,\omega\,M = -\,\omega^2.$$

Die Auflösung nach M ergibt

$$M = 2\,\omega \pm \sqrt{3\,\omega^2}$$

oder, da nur das negative Vorzeichen zu einem praktisch brauchbaren Resultat führt,

$$M = \omega\,(2 - \sqrt{3});$$

drücken wir ω durch P nach Gleichung (15) aus, so ergibt sich schließlich

$$M = 1{\cdot}608\ P,$$

also fast genau dasselbe Resultat, wie in der entsprechenden Aufgabe der vorigen Nummer.

Es dürfte nicht unzweckmäßig erscheinen, wenn wir einmal die Prämien P und P_1 durch direkte Auswertung der betreffenden Integrale bestimmen wollen. Es ist nämlich

$$P = \int_0^{\omega} x\,f(x)\,d\,x,$$

somit nach der angenommenen Form der Funktion $f(x)$,

$$P = \int_0^{\omega} \frac{x\,(\omega - x)}{\omega^2}\,d\,x;$$

wir erhalten

$$P = \int_0^{\omega} \frac{x\,d\,x}{\omega} - \int_0^{\omega} \frac{x^2\,d\,x}{\omega^2} = \left(\frac{x^2}{2\,\omega}\right)_0^{\omega} - \left(\frac{x^3}{3\,\omega^2}\right)_0^{\omega} = \frac{\omega}{2} - \frac{\omega}{3},$$

also wirklich

$$P = \frac{\omega}{6}.$$

Die Ermittlung von P_1 kommt auf die Auswertung des Integrals

$$P_1 = \int_M^\omega (x - M) f(x)\, dx$$

zurück; es ist in unserem Falle

$$P_1 = \int_M^\omega \frac{(x-M)(\omega - x)}{\omega^2}\, dx = \frac{1}{\omega^2} \int_M^\omega (\omega x - \omega M - x^2 + M x)\, dx,$$

somit also

$$P_1 = \frac{\omega + M}{\omega^2} \int_M^\omega x\, dx - \frac{M}{\omega} \int_M^\omega dx - \frac{1}{\omega^2} \int_M^\omega x^2\, dx,$$

oder integriert,

$$P_1 = \frac{\omega + M}{\omega^2} \frac{\omega^2 - M^2}{2} - \frac{M(\omega - M)}{\omega} - \frac{\omega^3 - M^3}{3\,\omega^2};$$

die Reduktion liefert

$$P_1 = \frac{\omega - M}{\omega^2} \left(\frac{\omega^2 + 2\,\omega M + M^2}{2} - M\omega - \frac{\omega^2 + \omega M + M^2}{3} \right),$$

$$\text{d. h. } \frac{\omega - M}{6\,\omega^2} (\omega^2 - 2\,\omega M + M^2),$$

also in der Tat

$$P_1 = \frac{(\omega - M)^3}{6\,\omega^2}.$$

Haben wir so einerseits die Richtigkeit der früheren Rechnung bestätigt, so haben wir auch anderseits die Gelegenheit gefunden, die Vortrefflichkeit der Gleichungen (16) und (19) des vorigen Kapitels zu erproben.

Eine erste Differentiation von P_1 nach M liefert

$$\frac{\partial P_1}{\partial M} = - \frac{(\omega - M)^2}{2\,\omega^2},$$

eine zweite hingegen

$$\frac{\partial^2 P_1}{\partial M^2} = \frac{\omega - M}{\omega^2};$$

wir sehen also in der Tat das erstemal die negative Funktion $F(M)$, das zweitemal hingegen die Funktion $f\ (M)$ selbst reproduziert, wie es eben durch die allgemeinen Formeln des vorigen Kapiltes erfordert wird.

4. Die Funktion f (x) sei durch eine ganze rationale Funktion 2. Grades dargestellt. Wir nehmen für $f(x)$ einen Ausdruck von der Form

$$f(x) = a + b x + c x^2$$

an, wobei die Koeffizienten a, b und c aus den Bedingungen

$$\int_0^\omega f(x)\, d x = {}^1/_2, f(\omega) = 0 \text{ und } \frac{\partial f(x)}{\partial x}\bigg|_{x = \omega} = 0$$

zu bestimmen seien. Die dritte hinzugekommene Bedingung hat nämlich den Sinn, daß die Schwankungswahrscheinlichkeitskurve im Punkte ω ein wirkliches Minimum besitzt, so daß sie sich also ziemlich langsam der Abszissenachse anschmiegt, wodurch die Erreichung des extremen Wertes ω viel schwerer als bei den in den vorigen Nummern gemachten Annahmen geschehen kann; die jetzige Voraussetzung dürfte somit in jenen Fällen gut anzuwenden sein, wo erhebliche Schwankungen zu erwarten und deswegen die extremen Werte groß genug anzunehmen sind. Die erste Bedingung liefert nun die Gleichung

$$\int_0^\omega (a + b x + c x^2)\, d x = a \omega + \frac{b \omega^2}{2} + \frac{c \omega^3}{3} = {}^1/_2,$$

die zweite aber

$$a + b \omega + c \omega^2 = 0,$$

die dritte endlich

$$b + 2 c \omega = 0,$$

da ja offenbar

$$\frac{\partial f(x)}{\partial x} = b + 2 c x$$

ist. Aus der letzten Bedingungsgleichung folgt zunächst

$$b = - 2 c \omega,$$

mithin aus der zweiten

$$a = c \omega^2,$$

welche Werte in die erste eingesetzt,

$$c = \frac{3}{2 \omega^3}$$

liefern; alsdann ist

$$a = \frac{3}{2 \omega} \text{ und } b = \frac{-3}{\omega^2},$$

so daß sich unsere Funktion in die einfache Form

$$f(x) = \frac{3 (\omega - x)^2}{2 \omega^3} \tag{22}$$

bringen läßt; die entsprechende Schwankungswahrscheinlichkeitskurve wäre also durch einen Parabelast dargestellt, welcher die Ordinatenachse in der Höhe $\frac{3}{2\omega}$ treffen und im Punkte $B+\omega$ die Abszissenachse selbst zur Tangente haben würde.

Die Funktion $F(x)$ wird in diesem Falle

$$F(x)=\int_x^\omega \frac{3(\omega-x)^2}{2\omega^3}\,dx=\frac{(\omega-x)^3}{2\omega^3},$$

so daß zur Bestimmung von P_1 die Gleichung

$$\frac{\partial P_1}{\partial M}=-\frac{(\omega-M)^3}{2\omega^3}$$

weiter zu behandeln ist. Es folgt

$$P_1=-\int\frac{(\omega-M)^3}{2\omega^3}\,dM+C,$$

also unmittelbar

$$P_1=\frac{(\omega-M)^4}{8\omega^3}; \tag{23}$$

die Konstante C ergab sich hiebei gleich Null. Alsdann ist die normale Prämie, die offenbar dem Werte $M=0$ entspricht,

$$P=\frac{\omega}{8}, \tag{24}$$

so daß sich eine Relation zwischen P_1 und P in der Form

$$P_1=\frac{(8P-M)^4}{8^4P^3}, \text{ d. h. } P_1=P\left(1-\frac{M}{8P}\right)^4 \tag{25}$$

aufstellen läßt. Dieses Resultat auf das Nochgeschäft angewendet, ergibt

$$N=mP\left(1-\frac{N}{8P}\right)^4,$$

da ja bekanntlich $N=mP_1$ ist, wenn P_1 der Schiefe N entsprechend angenommen ist. Es folgt nun aus letzterer Gleichung

$$\frac{N}{P}=m\left(1-\frac{N}{8P}\right)^4, \tag{26}$$

oder auch

$$m\rho^4+8\rho-8=0, \tag{27}$$

wenn der Kürze wegen

$$\rho=1-\frac{N}{8P}$$

oder, was auf dasselbe hinauskommt,

$$\frac{N}{P}=8(1-\rho) \tag{28}$$

gesetzt wird. Der Gleichung (27), welche ein negatives absolutes Glied und überdies zwischen gleichbezeichneten Gliedern ein fehlendes Glied besitzt, kommen nun zwei reelle Wurzeln, deren eine positiv, deren andere negativ ist und überdies zwei imaginäre Wurzeln zu; von den reellen ist offenbar nur die positive in Betracht zu ziehen.

Ohne die bezüglichen allgemeinen, sehr komplizierten Formeln zu entwickeln, welche die den verschiedenen m entsprechenden ρ zu berechnen gestatten würden, teilen wir die für $m=1$ und $m=2$ ausgeführten Rechnungen mit, und zwar: im ersteren Falle ergab sich ein Wert

$$\rho_1 = 0{\cdot}9131,$$

im anderen aber ein solcher

$$\rho_2 = 0{\cdot}862,$$

aus denen sich nach (28) die Beziehungen

$$N_1 = 0{\cdot}6952\ P$$

respektive

$$N_2 = 1{\cdot}104\ P$$

ableiten lassen. Es folgt hieraus zwischen N_1 und N_2 die Beziehung

$$N_2 = 1{\cdot}588\, N_1.$$

Die merkwürdige Übereinstimmung dieser Resultate mit den Ergebnissen der früheren Annahmen fällt sofort auf und zeigt also wie diese Beziehungen von der Art und Weise, nach welcher die Marktschwankungen auch vor sich gehen mögen, fast ganz unabhängig sind.

So findet man, daß, damit die Nochprämie der normalen Prämie P gleichkomme, ein solches Noch notwendig ist, für welches

$$m = 1{\cdot}7059\ \ldots$$

ist, was in recht guter Übereinstimmung mit den Ergebnissen der analogen Aufgabe unter anderen Annahmen steht.

5. Die Funktion $f(x)$ sei durch eine Exponentielle dargestellt. Wir setzen

$$f(x) = k\,a^{-hx}$$

und stellen an diese Funktion die einzige Bedingung, daß

$$\int_0^\omega f(x)\,dx = {}^1\!/_2$$

sei; bei dieser Form der Funktion können wir ungeniert die obere Grenze ω geradezu unendlich groß annehmen, da ja bei wachsendem x die Funktion außerordentlich rasch abnimmt, daher sie in diesem

Gebiete nur Glieder von untergeordneter Bedeutung liefern kann; wir schreiben somit

$$\int_0^\infty k\, a^{-h x} = {}^1/_2$$

oder ausgewertet,

$$k\left(\frac{a^{-h x}}{-h\, l\, a}\right)_0^\infty = \tfrac{1}{2} = \frac{k}{h\, l\, a};$$

es folgt zunächst

$$l\, a = \frac{2\, k}{h}, \text{ d. h. } a = e^{\frac{2 k}{h}},$$

so daß unsere Funktion die Form

$$f(x) = k\, e^{-2 k x} \tag{29}$$

annimmt. Die Funktion $F(x)$ wird alsdann

$$F(x) = k \int_x^\infty e^{-2 k x}\, d\, x = k\left(\frac{e^{-2 k x}}{-2\, k}\right)_x^\infty,$$

mithin

$$F(x) = \frac{e^{-2 k x}}{2}; \tag{30}$$

diese Funktion stellt bekanntlich die Wahrscheinlichkeit dar, mit der eine gegebene Schwankung x erreicht oder überstiegen wird; von dieser würde man auch ausgehen, um für die einzelnen Wertobjekte die Konstante k nach den im Anfange dieses Kapitels dargelegten Prinzipien zu bestimmen.

Aus (30) leiten wir zur Ermittlung von P_1 die Gleichung

$$\frac{\partial P_1}{\partial M} = -\frac{e^{-2 k M}}{2}$$

ab, somit

$$P_1 = -\tfrac{1}{2} \int e^{-2 k M}\, d\, M + C;$$

es resultiert

$$P_1 = \frac{e^{-2 k M}}{4\, k}, \tag{31}$$

wobei die Konstante C wegen der Bedingung $P_1 = 0$ für $M = \infty$, der Null gleich gesetzt wurde. Aus dieser Formel ergibt sich für $M = 0$ die normale Prämie

$$P = \frac{1}{4\, k}, \tag{32}$$

somit zwischen P_1 und P die einfache Beziehung

$$P_1 = P e^{-\frac{M}{2P}}. \tag{33}$$

Wenden wir das aufs Nochgeschäft an, so finden wir

$$N = m P e^{-\frac{N}{2P}},$$

mithin für das Verhältnis $\frac{N}{P} = R$ die Gleichung

$$R = m e^{\frac{-R}{2}}. \tag{34}$$

Um diese Gleichung näherungsweise zu lösen, denken wir uns in der rechten Seite ein Näherungswert

$$\rho = R + \delta \tag{35}$$

substituiert, wodurch dann für die linke Seite ein im allgemeinen von R verschiedener Wert

$$\rho_1 = R + \delta_1 \tag{36}$$

resultieren wird; sobald die Abweichungen vom wahren Werte unerheblich sind, wird zwischen ihnen die Relation

$$\delta_1 = \frac{-m}{2} e^{\frac{-R}{2}} \delta \tag{37}$$

bestehen, da ja δ_1 nahezu als Differential der rechts stehenden Funktion angesehen werden darf. Aus (35) und (36) folgt einerseits durch Addition

$$R = \frac{\rho + \rho_1}{2} - \frac{\delta + \delta_1}{2}, \tag{38}$$

anderseits aber durch Subtraktion

$$\delta - \delta_1 = \rho - \rho_1.$$

Aus letzterer Gleichung folgt nun mit Hilfe von (37)

$$\delta = \frac{\rho - \rho_1}{1 + \frac{m}{2} e^{-R/2}}$$

beziehungsweise

$$\delta_1 = \frac{-(\rho - \rho_1)\frac{m}{2} e^{-R/2}}{1 + \frac{m}{2} e^{-R/2}},$$

somit für die an das arithmetische Mittel $\frac{\rho+\rho_1}{2}$ anzubringende Korrektion

$$\frac{\delta+\delta_1}{2}=\frac{\rho-\rho_1}{2}\cdot\frac{1-\frac{m}{2}e^{\frac{-R}{2}}}{1+\frac{m}{2}e^{\frac{-R}{2}}}. \tag{39}$$

Diesen Vorgang wollen wir an den Fällen $m=1$ und $m=2$ erläutern.

Im ersten Falle ist also die Gleichung

$$R=e^{-\frac{R}{2}}$$

aufzulösen und

$$-\frac{\rho-\rho_1}{2}\,\frac{1-0{\cdot}5\,e^{\frac{-R}{2}}}{1+0{\cdot}5\,e^{\frac{-R}{2}}},\ \text{d. h.}\ -\frac{\rho-\rho_1}{2}\,\frac{e^{\frac{R}{2}}-0{\cdot}5}{e^{\frac{R}{2}}+0{\cdot}5}$$

als Korrektionsglied anzuwenden. Substituieren wir z. B. $\rho=0{\cdot}6$, so erhalten wir

$$\rho_1=e^{-0{\cdot}3}=0{\cdot}74082.$$

Alsdann ist

$$R=0{\cdot}67041+0{\cdot}07041\,\frac{e^{\frac{R}{2}}-0{\cdot}5}{e^{\frac{R}{2}}+0{\cdot}5},$$

da ja $\frac{\rho+\rho_1}{2}$ und $\frac{\rho-\rho_1}{2}$ eben die Werte

$$0{\cdot}67041 \text{ respektive } -0{\cdot}07041$$

besitzen. In Ermangelung eines besseren Wertes des R, substituieren wir im Korrektionsgliede für R den Wert

$$\frac{\rho+\rho_1}{2}=0{\cdot}67041,$$

wodurch das genannte Glied

$$0{\cdot}07041\,\frac{0{\cdot}89823}{1{\cdot}89823},\ \text{d. h.}\ 0{\cdot}033317$$

wird; es ist somit in erster Annäherung

$$R=0{\cdot}70373.$$

Um R in zweiter Annäherung zu bekommen, setzen wir den gefundenen Näherungswert in die aufzulösende Gleichung ein; wir finden

$$\rho_2 = e^{-0{\cdot}351866} = 0{\cdot}703375,$$

welcher Wert kleiner als der richtige ist, weil er kleiner als der substituierte Wert ausfiel. Hier könnten wir eine weitere Korrektion anbringen und hiemit die Annäherung so weit treiben als wir wollten; wir begnügen uns mit dem arithmetischen Mittel von 0·70373 und ρ_2, wir nehmen also

$$R = 0{\cdot}70355$$

an, so daß zwischen den Prämien des Einmal-Nochs und des einfachen normalen Geschäftes die Beziehung

$$N_1 = 0{\cdot}70355\, P$$

resultiert.

Für $m = 2$ gestaltet sich die Rechnung folgendermaßen: die aufzulösende Gleichung ist

$$R = 2\, e^{-\frac{R}{2}}$$

und das Korrektionsglied

$$-\frac{\rho - \rho_1}{2} \frac{e^{\frac{R}{2}} - 1}{e^{\frac{R}{2}} + 1}.$$

Wir setzen z. B. $\rho = 1$ ein und erhalten

$$\rho_1 = 2\, e^{-1/2}, \text{ d. h. } 1{\cdot}2131.$$

Es ist also

$$\frac{\rho + \rho_1}{2} = 1{\cdot}10655 \text{ und } \frac{\rho - \rho_1}{2} = -0{\cdot}10655,$$

mithin

$$R = 1{\cdot}10655 + 0{\cdot}10655 \frac{e^{\frac{R}{2}} - 1}{e^{\frac{R}{2}} + 1}.$$

Die Substitution von 1·10655 statt R im Korrektionsgliede liefert für letzteres den Betrag

$$0{\cdot}10655 \frac{0{\cdot}738939}{2{\cdot}738939}, \text{ d. h. } 0{\cdot}028746;$$

es ist also in erster Annäherung

$$R = 1{\cdot}1353.$$

Mit diesem Werte ergibt die aufzulösende Gleichung

$$\rho_2 = 2e^{-0{\cdot}56765}, \text{ d. h. } 1{\cdot}13371,$$

welcher Wert kleiner als der richtige ist. Wir nehmen das Mittel von 1·1353 und ρ_2 als genau genug an und schreiben

$$R = 1{\cdot}1345;$$

es wäre somit

$$N_2 = 1{\cdot}1345\ P.$$

Es leitet sich hieraus für N_2 und N_1 die Relation

$$N_2 = 1{\cdot}612\, N_1$$

ab. Wollten wir in Erfahrung bringen, bei welchem Noch die betreffende Prämie die Höhe der normalen Prämie erreicht, so fänden wir aus

$$1 = m\, e^{-1/2},$$

für m den Wert

$$\sqrt{e}, \text{ d. h. } 1{\cdot}6487\ \ldots$$

Es ist allerdings auffallend die beinahe vollkommene Übereinstimmung dieser numerischen Resultate mit jenen, die bei Voraussetzungen ganz anderer Natur in den vorhergehenden Nummern erhalten wurden.

6. Annahme des Fehlergesetzes für die Funktion $f(x)$. Beim Abschlusse des Kontraktes ist offenbar der Tageskurs B als jener Wert zu betrachten, für welchen am Liquidationstermine unter allen anderen Kursen die größte Wahrscheinlichkeit besteht; es könnten ja sonst nicht Käufe und Verkäufe, d. h. entgegengesetzte Geschäfte, mit gleichen Chancen abgeschlossen gedacht werden, wenn triftige Gründe da wären, die mit aller Entschiedenheit entweder das Steigen oder das Fallen des Kurses mit größerer Wahrscheinlichkeit voraussehen ließen. Indem wir uns also die Marktschwankungen über oder unter B gleichsam als Abweichungen von einem vorteilhaftesten Werte vorstellen, werden wir versuchen, denselben die Befolgung des Fehlergesetzes

$$\frac{h}{\sqrt{\pi}}\, e^{-h^2\lambda^2}\, d\lambda$$

vorzuschreiben, welches sich zur Darstellung der Fehlerwahrscheinlichkeiten sehr gut bewährt hat; obiger Ausdruck stellt nämlich die Wahrscheinlichkeit eines im Interval λ und $\lambda + d\lambda$ liegenden Fehlers dar, wobei h eine von der Genauigkeit der Beobachtung abhängige konstante Größe bedeutet. Auf unseren Fall übertragen, werden wir als Wahrscheinlichkeit einer zwischen x und $x + dx$ fallenden Schwankung den Ausdruck

$$\frac{h}{\sqrt{\pi}} e^{-h^2 x^2} dx$$

annehmen, so daß für unsere Funktion $f(x)$ die endgültige Form

$$f(x) = \frac{h}{\sqrt{\pi}} e^{-h^2 x^2} \tag{40}$$

folgt; die Größe h wird für die verschiedenen Objekte verschiedener Werte fähig sein, die in jedem besonderen Falle empirisch auf schon dargelegte Weise zu bestimmen sein werden.

Aus der so angenommenen Form unserer Funktion ergibt sich als Wahrscheinlichkeit, daß die Schwankung einen zwischen 0 und x befindlichen Wert erreiche, das Integral

$$w = \int_0^x \frac{h}{\sqrt{\pi}} e^{-h^2 x^2} dx$$

oder, durch Einführung der neuen Variablen $t = hx$,

$$w = \frac{1}{\sqrt{\pi}} \int_0^{hx} e^{-t^2} dt = \varphi(hx); \tag{41}$$

wegen der raschen Abnahme der Funktion $f(x)$ mit wachsendem x werden wir den extremen Wert ω unendlich groß annehmen dürfen; es ergibt sich

$$W = \frac{1}{\sqrt{\pi}} \int_0^{\infty} e^{-t^2} dt = \frac{1}{\sqrt{\pi}} \frac{\sqrt{\pi}}{2} = \frac{1}{2},$$

wodurch unsere Bedingung

$$\int_0^{\omega} f(x)\, dx = 1/2$$

an und für sich erfüllt ist.

Die Funktion $F(x)$, welche für die Wahrscheinlichkeit einer über x befindlichen Schwankung besteht, d. h.

$$F(x) = \int_x^{\omega} f(x)\, dx,$$

wird in diesem Falle

$$F(x) = \frac{1}{\sqrt{\pi}} \int_{hx}^{\infty} e^{-t^2}\, dt = \tfrac{1}{2} - \varphi(hx) = \psi(hx). \tag{42}$$

Die Prämie P_1 berechnen wir diesmal lieber aus seinem Integral

$$P_1 = \int_M^{\infty} (x - M) \frac{h}{\sqrt{\pi}} e^{-h^2 x^2}\, dx,$$

nämlich

$$P_1 = \int_M^{\infty} \frac{h}{\sqrt{\pi}} x e^{-h^2 x^2}\, dx - M \int_M^{\infty} \frac{h}{\sqrt{\pi}} e^{-h^2 x^2}\, dx;$$

das erste Integral läßt sich unmittelbar auswerten, das zweite aber durch die Funktion ψ ausdrücken; es ergibt sich

$$P_1 = \frac{e^{-M^2 h^2}}{2h\sqrt{\pi}} - M\psi(hM). \tag{43}$$

Aus diesem Ausdruck berechnen wir durch Nullsetzung von M die normale Prämie in der Form

$$P = \frac{1}{2h\sqrt{\pi}}. \tag{44}$$

Wir hätten allerdings die Prämie P_1 aus der gewöhnlichen Formel

$$\frac{\partial P_1}{\partial M} = -F(M)$$

ableiten können; es wäre dann nämlich

$$P_1 = -\int \psi(hM)\, dM + C,$$

oder durch teilweise Integration

$$P_1 = -M\psi(hM) + \int M \frac{\delta \psi(hM)}{\delta M}\, dM + C;$$

es ist aber offenbar

$$\frac{\partial \psi(hM)}{\partial M} = \frac{-e^{-h^2 M^2}}{\sqrt{\pi}} h,$$

so daß für P_1, da die Konstante C verschwindet, genau der Ausdruck (43) resultiert.

Die Einführung der Nochgeschäftsprämie liefert die Gleichung

$$N = m\left[\frac{e^{-N^2 h^2}}{2\sqrt{\pi}\,h} - N\psi(hN)\right],$$

— 77 —

die, wegen der aus (44) entspringenden Relation

$$h = \frac{1}{2\sqrt{\pi}P},$$

zunächst in die Form

$$\frac{N}{m} = Pe^{-\frac{N^2}{4\pi P^2}} - N\psi\left(\frac{N}{2\sqrt{\pi}P}\right),$$

oder durch Anwendung des Verhältnisses

$$R = \frac{N}{P},$$

in die endgiltige

$$R\left[\frac{1}{m} + \psi\left(\frac{R}{2\sqrt{\pi}}\right)\right] = e^{-\frac{R^2}{4\pi}} \tag{45}$$

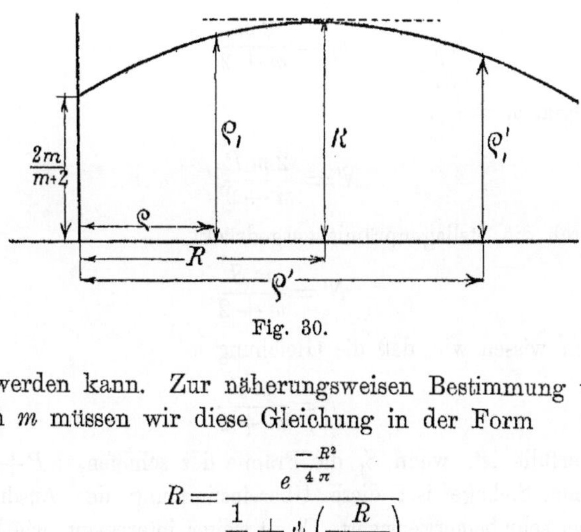

Fig. 30.

gebracht werden kann. Zur näherungsweisen Bestimmung von R bei gegebenem m müssen wir diese Gleichung in der Form

$$R = \frac{e^{-\frac{R^2}{4\pi}}}{\frac{1}{m} + \psi\left(\frac{R}{2\sqrt{\pi}}\right)} \tag{46}$$

anwenden; aus dem ersten Differentialquotienten, welcher sich nach einfacher Reduktion in die Form

$$\frac{e^{-\frac{R^2}{4\pi}}}{2\pi} \frac{e^{-\frac{R^2}{4\pi}} - \frac{R}{m} - R\psi\left(\frac{R}{2\sqrt{\pi}}\right)}{\left[\frac{1}{m} + \psi\left(\frac{R}{2\sqrt{\pi}}\right)\right]^2}$$

bringen läßt, erfahren wir, daß für kleine Werte von R die rechte Seite in (46) zunimmt, bis sie an der durch die Gleichung

$$e^{-\frac{R^2}{4\pi}} - \frac{R}{m} - R\,\psi\left(\frac{R}{2\sqrt{\pi}}\right) = 0$$

charakterisierten Stelle einen Maximalwert erlangt; dieser Wert ist aber, wie es die Gleichung (45) lehrt, kein anderer als der genaue Wert von R; aus dieser Betrachtung folgt nun, wie es die Figur 30 veranschaulicht, daß, wenn die Substitution einen Wert ergibt, der größer als der substituierte Wert ist, dieser letztere jedenfalls kleiner als der genaue Wert sein muß. Erhält man hingegen als Resultat der Substitution einen kleineren Wert, so ist dies ein Kennzeichen, daß der substituierte Wert den genauen schon überschritten hat: so hat man alle Mittel in der Hand, um die Gleichung (46) näherungsweise aufzulösen. Ganz besonders hervorzuheben ist das Ergebnis der Substitution $R = o$ in den transzendenten Gliedern; es wird nämlich

$$\rho_1 = \frac{2\,m}{m+2},$$

d. h. wegen $\rho_1 = \frac{N'}{P}$,

$$N' = \frac{2\,m\,P}{m+2},$$

oder durch die Stellagenprämie ausgedrückt,

$$N' = \frac{m\,S}{m+2}.$$

Nun wissen wir, daß die Gleichung

$$N = \frac{m\,S_1}{m+2}$$

streng erfüllt ist, wenn S_1 die Prämie der schiefen, à $P+N$ abgeschlossenen Stellage ist; diese Übereinstimmung der Ausdrücke ist allerdings sehr bemerkenswert. Es ist weiter interessant, wie hier wieder, und zwar auf so indirektem Wege sich die Prämie der schiefen Stellage höher als jene der normalen Stellage stellt, da ja, wie erwähnt, ρ_1 kleiner als der genaue Wert R, d. h. $\frac{N}{P}$, ist, so daß N' kleiner als der genaue Wert N, mithin auch S kleiner als S_1 ausfallen muß.

Wir wollen nun die Auflösung der Gleichung (46) für die speziellen Fälle $m = 1$ und $m = 2$ ausführen. Zu diesem Behufe sind Tabellen anzuwenden, welche die Werte der Funktion $\psi(\varepsilon)$, wobei ε

eine beliebige partikuläre Zahl ist, zu entnehmen gestatten: solch eine Tabelle haben wir am Schlusse des Werkes mitgeteilt.

Fangen wir mit der Substitution $\rho = 0{\cdot}5$ an, so erhalten wir für ρ_1 zunächst den Ausdruck

$$\rho_1 = \frac{e^{\frac{-0{\cdot}25}{4\pi}}}{1 + \psi\left(\frac{0{\cdot}25}{\sqrt{\pi}}\right)}, \text{ d. h. } \frac{e^{-0{\cdot}0199}}{1 + \psi\,(0{\cdot}141)}.$$

Nun ist $\psi\,(0{\cdot}141) = 0{\cdot}42097$, mithin

$\log \rho_1 = -0{\cdot}0199 \log e - \log 1{\cdot}42097 = 0{\cdot}8387676 - 1;$

es folgt

$$\rho_1 = 0{\cdot}68987,$$

welcher Wert sicherlich kleiner als der genaue ist. Substituieren wir nun etwa

$$\rho' = 0{\cdot}69,$$

so ergibt sich

$$\rho'_1 = \frac{e^{-0{\cdot}03788}}{1 + \psi\,(0{\cdot}19465)} = \frac{e^{-0{\cdot}03788}}{1{\cdot}391554} = 0{\cdot}691903,$$

ein Wert, der zwar kleiner als R ist, ihm aber sehr nahe liegen muß; wir begnügen uns mit diesem Werte und gewinnen so zwischen den Prämien des Einmal-Nochs und des einfachen normalen Geschäftes die Relation

$$N_1 = 0{\cdot}6919\,P.$$

Die Rechnung für den Fall $m = 2$ gestaltet sich folgendermaßen: Wir beginnen etwa mit

$$\rho = 1$$

und erhalten

$$\rho_1 = \frac{e^{\frac{-1}{4\pi}}}{0{\cdot}5 + \psi\left(\frac{1}{2\sqrt{\pi}}\right)} = 1{\cdot}0865,$$

so daß sowohl ρ als auch ρ_1 kleiner als R sind. Die Substitution

$$\rho' = 1{\cdot}09$$

liefert

$$\rho'_1 = \frac{e^{\frac{-1{\cdot}09^2}{4\pi}}}{0{\cdot}5 + \psi\left(\frac{1{\cdot}09}{2\sqrt{\pi}}\right)} = 1{\cdot}09371,$$

welcher Wert etwas kleiner als der genaue Wert sein muß; ohne die Annäherung weiter zu treiben, können wir die gesuchte Beziehung in der Form

$$N_2 = 1{\cdot}0938\ P$$

hinschreiben. Es ergibt sich weiter zwischen N_2 und N_1 die Relation

$$N_2 = 1{\cdot}581\ N_1.$$

Wollen wir endlich auch in diesem Falle das Problem lösen, bei welchem Noch die Gleichheit zwischen N und P eintreten würde, so haben wir in (45) $R = 1$ zu setzen und m aus der Gleichung

$$m = \frac{1}{e^{\frac{-1}{4\pi}} - \psi\left(\frac{1}{2\sqrt{\pi}}\right)}$$

zu bestimmen; es findet sich

$$m = 1{\cdot}7435.$$

Die merkwürdige Übereinstimmung dieser Resultate mit allen jenen, die sich in den vorhergehenden Nummern ergaben, fällt unwillkürlich auf und verleiht ihnen einen hohen praktischen Wert.

7. Anwendung des Bernoullischen Theorems. Ist über zwei entgegengesetzte Ereignisse, deren Wahrscheinlichkeiten p resp. q sind, eine Reihe von s Versuchen angestellt worden, so stellen $p\,s$ resp. $q\,s$ die wahrscheinlichsten Wiederholungszahlen der betrachteten Ereignisse dar; es werden nun offenbar in Wirklichkeit Abweichungen von diesen wahrscheinlichsten Werten stattfinden, denen nach dem Bernoullischen Theorem bestimmte Probabilitäten zugeschrieben werden können. Es ist nämlich nach dem erwähnten Satze die Wahrscheinlichkeit, daß eine Abweichung von der Größe

$$\gamma \sqrt{2\,s\,p\,q}$$

in einem oder im anderen Sinne erfolge, durch die Formel

$$w_1 = \frac{2}{\sqrt{\pi}} \int_0^{\gamma} e^{-t^2}\, dt + \frac{e^{-\gamma^2}}{\sqrt{2\,\pi\,s\,p\,q}} \tag{47}$$

ausgedrückt.

Um jetzt, von diesem Theorem ausgehend, einen mathematischen Ausdruck für die Wahrscheinlichkeit der Marktschwankungen zu gewinnen, verfahren wir auf folgende Weise: wir betrachten die Marktschwankungen als Abweichungen von einem wahrscheinlichsten Werte, und B ist in der Tat ein solcher, so daß die Wahrscheinlichkeiten ihres Auftretens durch das angeführte Theorem geregelt anzunehmen sind; nur haben wir in unserem Falle einen der Werte $p\,s$ oder $q\,s$, sagen wir den ersteren, durch B zu ersetzen, wodurch die Schwankung x durch

$$x = \gamma \sqrt{2\,q\,B}, \tag{48}$$

die Größe γ hingegen durch

$$\gamma = \frac{x}{\sqrt{2\,q\,B}} \tag{49}$$

repräsentiert ist; alsdann erhalten wir für die Wahrscheinlichkeit, mit welcher eine von o bis x in einem oder im anderen Sinne befindliche Schwankung zu erwarten ist, den Ausdruck

$$w_1 = \frac{2}{\sqrt{\pi}} \int_0^{\frac{x}{\sqrt{2\,q\,B}}} e^{-t^2}\,d\,t + \frac{e^{\frac{-x^2}{2\,q\,B}}}{\sqrt{2\,\pi\,q\,B}}.$$

Sehen wir nun vom zweiten Gliede auf der rechten Seite, welches nur von sekundärem Einfluß sein kann, vollständig ab und ziehen wir schließlich, wie es immer auch sonst geschehen, nur die Wahrscheinlichkeit in Betracht, daß die Schwankung x in einem einzigen Sinne zu erfolgen habe, so erhalten wir

$$w_1 = \frac{1}{\sqrt{\pi}} \int_0^{\frac{x}{\sqrt{2\,q\,B}}} e^{-t^2}\,d\,t = \varphi\left(\frac{x}{\sqrt{2\,q\,B}}\right). \tag{50}$$

Vergleichen wir dieses Ergebnis mit dem Ausdrucke (41) der vorigen Nummer, so ersehen wir aus der vollkommenen hier herrschenden Analogie, daß uns die Anwendung des Bernoullischen Theorems auf die Marktschwankungen zu demselben Resultate, wie die Annahme der Befolgung des Fehlergesetzes, führt. Die Konstante h des Fehlergesetzes sehen wir in diesem Falle durch

$$h = \frac{1}{\sqrt{2\,q\,B}} \tag{51}$$

dargestellt; sie erlangt zwar eine nähere Deutung, indem sie sich der Quadratwurzel von B verkehrt proportional zeigt, sie bleibt nichtsdestoweniger infolge der Gegenwart von q, worüber wir im voraus gar nichts behaupten können, noch immer ganz unbestimmt und könnte nur aus Erfahrungsdaten für jedes einzelne der in Betracht kommenden Wertobjekte auf empirische Weise ermittelt werden.

Setzten wir für alle Wertobjekte die Erfüllung der Bedingung

$$p = q = 1/2$$

voraus, so erhielten wir einfach

$$h = \frac{1}{\sqrt{B}}, \tag{51a}$$

so daß aus unseren Formeln jede Unbestimmtheit wegfallen würde und die numerischen Resultate sofort bei bloßer Angabe des Tageskurses gegeben werden könnten. Da aber die Größe der Schwankungen offenbar nicht allein von der Kurshöhe, sondern von mannigfachen äußeren Einflüssen abhängt, werden freilich die obiger Annahme entspringenden Resultate bloß als eine erste, mehr oder weniger grobe Annäherung aufgefaßt werden können; in jedem Falle werden sie aber eine sichere und feste Grundlage abgeben und zur ungefähren Orientierung vorzüglich dienen können. Nach dieser Annahme wäre also

$$P_1 = \frac{\sqrt{B}\, e^{-\frac{M^2}{B}}}{2\sqrt{\pi}} - M\psi\left(\frac{M}{\sqrt{B}}\right), \tag{52}$$

mithin die normale Prämie

$$P = \frac{\sqrt{B}}{2\sqrt{\pi}}$$

und die normale Stellage

$$S = \sqrt{\frac{B}{\pi}}; \tag{53}$$

die Untersuchungen über die Nochprämien erfahren durch diese besondere Annahme keine Vereinfachung und sind jenen der vorigen Nummer vollständig identisch.

Es handle sich z. B. um eine Aktie, deren Tageskurs etwa 615·25 K beträgt. Es ergäbe sich als Prämie für eine zu diesem Kurse abgeschlossene Stellage der Betrag

$$S = \sqrt{\frac{615 \cdot 25}{3 \cdot 14159}}, \text{ d. h. } 13 \cdot 99\ K,$$

und die Hälfte davon für die Prämie des einfachen normalen Geschäftes. So würde z. B. die Prämie für einen à 620 gehandelten Wahlkauf aus der Formel

$$P_1 = \frac{\sqrt{615 \cdot 25}}{2\sqrt{3 \cdot 14159}}\, e^{-\frac{4 \cdot 75^2}{615 \cdot 25}} - 4 \cdot 75\, \psi\left(\frac{4 \cdot 75}{\sqrt{615 \cdot 25}}\right)$$

zu berechnen sein; man fände

$$P_1 = 5{\cdot}734\ K.$$

Wegen der Gleichung

$$P_2 = P_1 + M,$$

wäre dann für den Wahlverkauf à 620 die Prämie

$$P_2 = 10{\cdot}484\ K,$$

für die à 620 abgeschlossene Stellage hingegen die Summe

$$S_1 = P_1 + P_2,\ \text{d. h. } 16{\cdot}218\ K$$

zu entrichten. Zwischen der normalen und der betrachteten schiefen Stellage würde sonach eine Differenz

$$\Delta = 2{\cdot}228\ K$$

resultieren. Die Prämie des Einmal-Nochs wäre

$$N_1 = 0{\cdot}6919\,.\,7 = 4{\cdot}8433\ K,$$

die des Zweimal-Nochs hingegen

$$N_2 = 1{\cdot}0938 \times 7 = 7{\cdot}7466\ K$$

und so weiter.

Tafel I.

Werte der Funktion $\psi(\varepsilon) = \frac{1}{\sqrt{\pi}} \int_{\varepsilon}^{\infty} e^{-t^2} dt.$

ε	ψ (ε)	Diff.	ε	ψ (ε)	Diff.	ε	ψ (ε)	Diff.
0·00	0·5000000	56417	0·29	0·3408582	51715	0·58	0·2060386	40069
0·01	0·4943583	56405	0·30	0·3356867	51408	0·59	0·2020317	39598
0·02	0·4887178	56383	0·31	0·3305459	51088	0·60	0·1980719	39125
0·03	0·4830795	56349	0·32	0·3254371	50764	0·61	0·1941594	38651
0·04	0·4774446	56305	0·33	0·3203607	50429	0·62	0·1902943	38174
0·05	0·4718141	56249	0·34	0·3153178	50087	0·63	0·1864769	37698
0·06	0·4661892	56180	0·35	0·3103091	49739	0·64	0·1827071	37217
0·07	0·4605712	56102	0·36	0·3053352	49382	0·65	0·1789854	36736
0·08	0·4549610	56013	0·37	0·3003970	49011	0·66	0·1753118	36256
0·09	0·4493957	55912	0·38	0·2954959	48652	0·67	0·1716862	35777
0·10	0·4437685	55800	0·39	0·2906307	48268	0·68	0·1681085	35284
0·11	0·4381885	55677	0·40	0·2858039	47884	0·69	0·1645801	34806
0·12	0·4326208	55544	0·41	0·2810155	47493	0·70	0·1610995	34322
0·13	0·4270664	55399	0·42	0·2762662	47095	0·71	0·1576673	33838
0·14	0·4215265	55244	0·43	0·2715567	46693	0·72	0·1542835	33354
0·15	0·4160021	55079	0·44	0·2668874	46283	0·73	0·1509481	32871
0·16	0·4104942	54903	0·45	0·2622591	45849	0·74	0·1476610	32388
0·17	0·4050039	54998	0·46	0·2576742	45468	0·75	0·1444222	31906
0·18	0·3995441	54640	0·47	0·2531274	45023	0·76	0·1412316	31424
0·19	0·3940801	54313	0·48	0·2486251	44592	0·77	0·1380892	30944
0·20	0·3886488	54097	0·49	0·2441659	44159	0·78	0·1349948	30465
0·21	0·3832391	53870	0·50	0·2397500	43719	0·79	0·1319483	29993
0·22	0·3778521	53634	0·51	0·2353781	43274	0·80	0·1289490	29507
0·23	0·3724887	53387	0·52	0·2310507	42828	0·81	0·1259983	29037
0·24	0·3671500	53131	0·53	0·2267679	42375	0·82	0·1230496	28565
0·25	0·3618369	52868	0·54	0·2225304	41920	0·83	0·1202381	28094
0·26	0·3565501	52592	0·55	0·2183384	41463	0·84	0·1174287	27627
0·27	0·3512909	52309	0·56	0·2141921	40983	0·85	0·1146660	27171
0·28	0·3460600	52018	0·57	0·2100941	40555	0·86	0·1119489	26688

— 85 —

Tafel I.

ε	ψ (ε)	Diff.	ε	ψ (ε)	Diff.	ε	ψ (ε	Diff.
0·87	0·1092801	26237	1·15	0·0519381	14862	1·43	0·0215713	7196
0·88	0·1066564	25780	1·16	0·0504519	14521	1·44	0·0208517	6992
0·89	0·1040784	25325	1·17	0·0489998	14185	1·45	0·0201525	6792
0·90	0·1015459	24873	1·18	0·0475873	13855	1·46	0·0194733	6598
0·91	0·0990586	24424	1·19	0·0461958	13528	1·47	0·0188135	6406
0·92	0·0966162	23980	1·20	0·0448430	13207	1·48	0·0181729	6218
0·93	0·0942182	23537	1·21	0·0435223	12893	1·49	0·0175511	6037
0·94	0·0918645	23099	1·22	0·0422330	12581	1·50	0·0169474	5858
0·95	0·0895546	22664	1·23	0·0409749	12275	1·51	0·0163616	5683
0·96	0·0872882	22233	1·24	0·0397474	11978	1·52	0·0157933	5514
0·97	0·0850649	21807	1·25	0·0385496	11675	1·53	0·0152419	5348
0·98	0·0828842	21383	1·26	0·0373821	11389	1·54	0·0147071	5185
0·99	0·0807459	21963	1·27	0·0362432	11103	1·55	0·0141886	5027
1·00	0·0786496	20548	1·28	0·0351329	10823	1·56	0·0136859	4872
1·01	0·0765948	20138	1·29	0·0340506	10546	1·57	0·0131987	4722
1·02	0·0745810	19731	1·30	0·0329960	10276	1·58	0·0127265	4575
1·03	0·0726079	19329	1·31	0·0319684	10010	1·59	0·0122690	4432
1·04	0·0706750	18930	1·32	0·0309674	9749	1·60	0·0118258	4292
1·05	0·0687820	18537	1·33	0·0299925	9493	1·61	0·0113966	4157
1·06	0·0669283	18149	1·34	0·0290432	9243	1·62	0·0109809	4023
1·07	0·0651134	17765	1·35	0·0281189	8996	1·63	0·0105786	3894
1·08	0·0633369	17384	1·36	0·0272193	8755	1·64	0·0101892	3770
1·09	0·0615985	17010	1·37	0·0263438	8518	1·65	0·0098122	3651
1·10	0·0598975	16640	1·38	0·0254920	8287	1·66	0·0094471	3523
1·11	0·0582335	16274	1·39	0·0246633	8058	1·67	0·0090948	3412
1·12	0·0566061	15915	1·40	0·0238575	7837	1·68	0·0087536	3299
1·13	0·0550146	15557	1·41	0·0230738	7619	1·69	0·0084237	3189
1·14	0·0534589	15208	1·42	0·0223119	7406	1·70	0·0081048	3080

Part B
Theory of Premium Contracts

Vinzenz Bronzin

Table of Contents

Part I.
Different Types and Inter-relationships of Contracts for Future Delivery.

Chapter I.
Normal Premium Contracts.

1. Introduction. Stock exchange transactions may be divided into spot and future contracts, depending upon whether delivery of the traded objects is to be effected instantly upon conclusion of the contract or at some date in the future. Contracts for future delivery may consist of two distinct types: unconditional forward contracts and premium contracts, as is customary to call the latter kind. Concerning the former, the traded objects[29] must be delivered or delivery of these must be taken, respectively; regarding the latter, one of the contracting parties, by making a payment upon conclusion of the deal, acquires the right to demand discharge of the contract or to cancel it (either in part or in its entirety) on the delivery date.

2. Unconditional Forward Contracts. Assuming an unconditional purchase or an unconditional sale, respectively, to have been effected at price B[30], which quite naturally will correspond or be close to the current market price, if we obtain a price $B + \varepsilon$ on the delivery date, evidently we will be faced with a gain or a loss, respectively, in the amount of ε, while a price of $B - \eta$ will yield a loss or a gain, respectively, in the amount of η. By way of graphical representation, we obtain the following self-explanatory diagrams; Figure 1 relating to an unconditional purchase, while Figure 2 depicts an unconditional sale[31].

We need hardly mention that the triangular areas in the diagrams to the right and the left of B must be assumed to be equivalent[32], since otherwise either a purchase or a sale would naturally be more advantageous.

Supposing n purchases of identical kind, it is apparent that the envisaged market outcomes on the delivery date yield gains of the form

$$n\varepsilon \quad \text{resp.} \quad -n\eta$$

[29] In modern terminology, this is the "underlying" (security, commodity, or object) of the derivative contract.

[30] In modern terminology, this is the forward (or futures) price.

[31] In modern terminology, Figure 1 represents a forward purchase (or a long position in a forward contract), while Figure 2 is a forward sale (or short position in a forward contract).

[32] This equivalence is analytically specificed later in this Treatise; see Part II, Chapter I, equation 8.

whereby we treat loss as a negative gain; likewise, supposing n sales of identical size, gains are represented by

$$-n\varepsilon \quad \text{resp.} \quad n\eta$$

From this we see that the effect of n sales is entirely equivalent to the effect of $-n$ purchases, so that

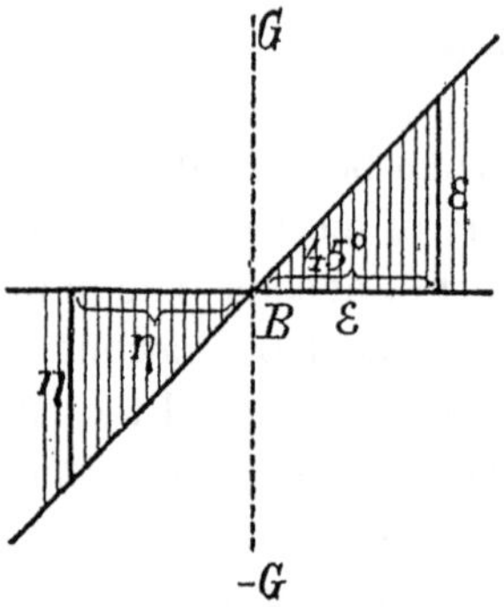

Fig. 1.

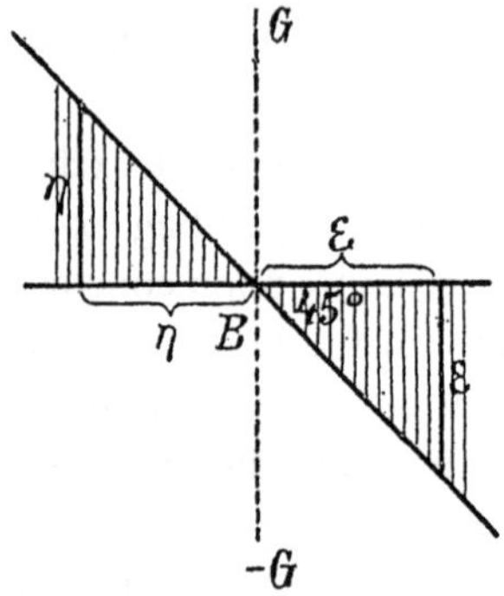

Fig. 2.

for analytical purposes we need to introduce only one concept, either purchase or sale: subsequently, we shall use the positive value to indicate purchase, throughout this treatise. Thus, e.g. the letter z represents a certain number of purchases, while $-z$ represents an equal number of sales; a result of the form $z = b$ will be taken to stand for e.g. 5 purchases, whereas $z = -7$ shall be construed to indicate 7 sales.

3. Simple Premium Contracts (Dont Contracts). If a purchase has been effected at price[33] B_1 while at the same time a certain premium (dont premium)[34] P_1 has been paid in order to be granted the choice between delivery or non-delivery of the traded object on the delivery date, we shall use the term conditional purchase[35]; the counterparty, being obliged to execute delivery or to refrain from it according to the course elected by the purchaser, is engaged in a constrained sale[36]. Had we concluded a purchase at price B_1 and paid a premium P_2 to be entitled to execute delivery or refrain from it at our discretion on the delivery date, we would be involved in what we shall term a conditional sale[37]: the counterparty, in

[33] In modern terminology, this is the exercise (or strike) price of the option contract.

[34] In modern terminology, this is simply called the option "price"; the notion "premium" is still used occasionally, primarily in the context of warrants, convertibles, or structured products.

[35] In modern usage, this represents a long call position, i.e. the purchase of a call option.

[36] In modern usage, this represents a short call position, i.e. the sale of a call option.

[37] In modern terminology, this represents a long put position, i.e. the purchase of a put option.

this case being required either to take or not to take delivery of the traded object depending on which choice we make, is concluding a constrained purchase[38]. The transactions dealt with here we shall refer to as simple premium contracts; they represent the building blocks, as it were, of which all other premium contracts are composed.*

A conditional purchase as well as a constrained sale, if in actuality effected, would have been concluded, it appears, at price $B_1 + P_1$ to which (the dont premium) P_1 has been added[39]; equally, a conditional sale and a constrained purchase would have been concluded, it appears, at price $B_1 - P_2$ from which the premium (the dont premium) P_2 has been deducted.

In order to represent gains and losses as they emerge from the different market outcomes conceivably present at the delivery date, we proceed thus:

In the case of a conditional purchase, we make a payment of P_1, which amount evidently obtains as a loss in the presence of any conceivable market outcome; however, owing to the acquired right to make the purchase or to refrain from it, we will be able to benefit from any market fluctuations exceeding B_1, whilst being protected against losses in the face of market fluctuations below B_1; hence, in the presence of market outcomes described by $B_1 + \varepsilon$ and $B_1 - \eta$, respectively, our gains will be of the form

$$\varepsilon - P_1 \quad \text{and} \quad -P_1$$

respectively. Regarding a conditional sale, P_2 will obtain as a loss irrespective of the market outcome; on the other hand, any decline of the price below B_1 would produce a commensurate gain, whilst any increase of the price above B_1 would not bring about a further loss; therefore, market prices of $B_1 + \varepsilon$ and $B_1 - \eta$, respectively, yield gains

$$-P_2 \quad \text{and} \quad \eta - P_2 \quad \text{respectively.}$$

Thus, n conditional purchases of the same quantity yield gains

$$n(\varepsilon - P_1) \quad \text{and} \quad -nP_1 \quad \text{respectively}$$

[38] In modern terminology, this represents a short put position, i.e. the sale of a put option.

*) In practice, one encounters the following terms describing the simple premium contracts presently in question: What we refer to as a conditional purchase is called a purchase involving a buyer's premium; a constrained sale is called a sale involving a buyer's premium; a conditional sale is called a sale involving a seller's premium; a constrained purchase is called a purchase involving a seller's premium. We have resolved to introduce our terms on account of their being briefer or at least better capable of characterising the nature of the contracts. [This is a footnote in the original Text]

[39] Adding (and subtracting) the option price to (from) the exercise price without compounding is justified because in the old days, the option premium was typically paid at the expiration of the contract. This contrasts the current practice.

whereas n conditional sales yield gains

$$-nP_2 \quad \text{and} \quad n(\eta - P_2) \quad \text{respectively.}$$

Since our gains present the counterparties with losses of the same size, and vice versa, n constrained sales yield gains of the form

$$-n(\varepsilon - P_1) \quad \text{and} \quad nP_1 \quad \text{respectively,}$$

whereas n constrained purchases yield gains of the form

$$nP_2 \quad \text{and} \quad -n(\eta - P_2) \quad \text{respectively.}$$

Once again, it is evident that the effects of n constrained sales and constrained purchases, respectively, are perfectly equivalent to those of $-n$ conditional purchases and conditional sales, respectively; hence, for the purposes of algebraic inspection, it will suffice to rely exclusively on the concepts of conditional purchase and conditional sale, provided that negative values are construed to represent constrained sales and constrained purchases, respectively.

Thus, if we take x and y, respectively, to denote a certain number of conditional purchases and conditional sales, respectively, then $-x$ and $-y$, respectively, represent as many constrained sales and constrained purchases, respectively. Accordingly, we will look upon $x = 4$ as indicating 4 conditional purchases, whilst $y = -6$ will be regarded to represent 6 constrained purchases.

The relationship of gains and losses may be presented graphically in the manner below:

α) Conditional purchase:

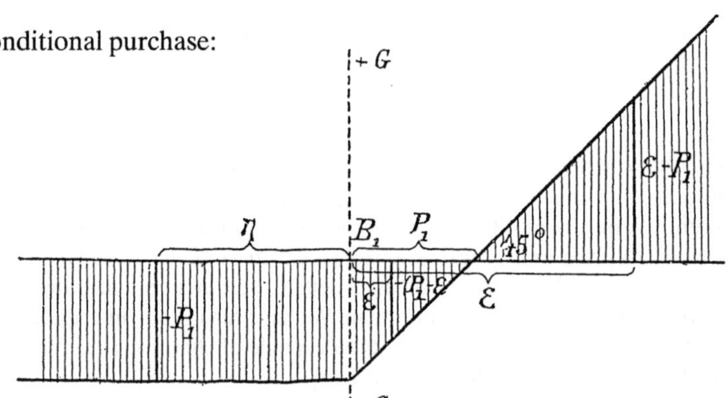

Fig. 3.

β) Constrained sale:

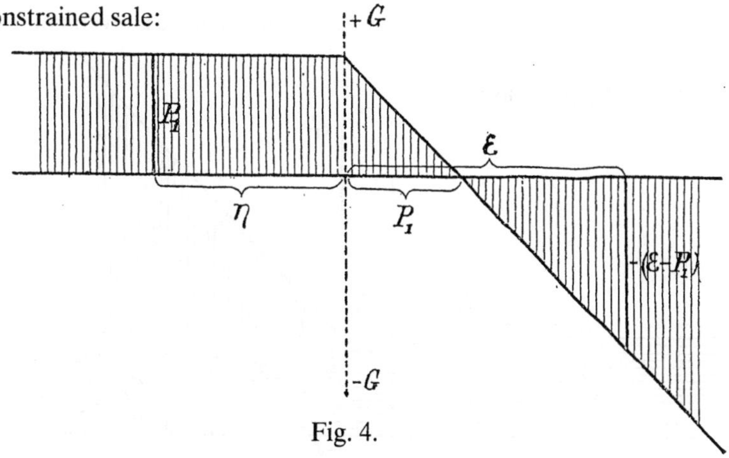

Fig. 4.

γ) Conditional sale:

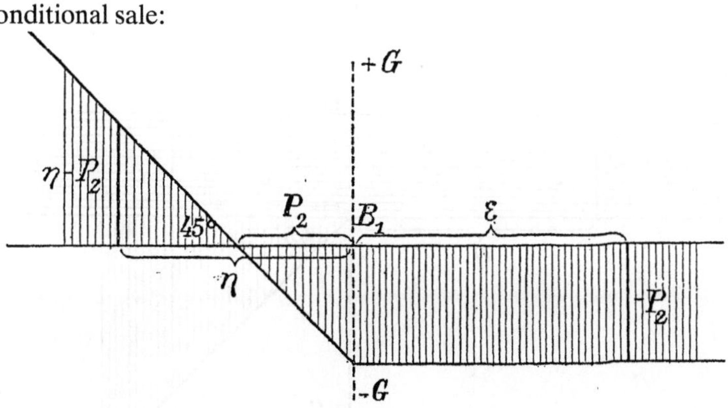

Fig. 5.

δ) Constrained purchase:

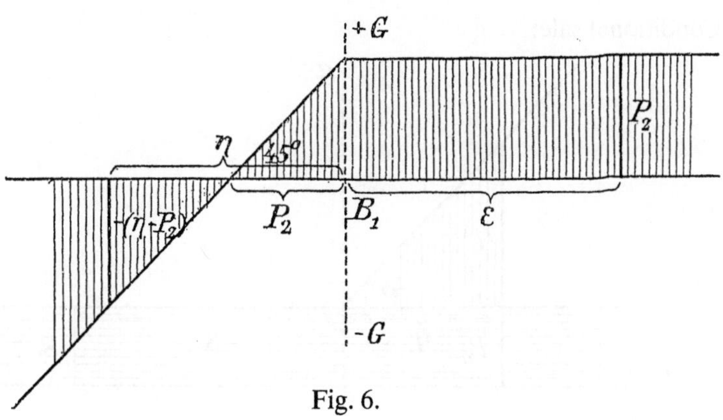

Fig. 6.

Obviously, the above diagrams may be laid out in more convenient fashion (see below):

α) Conditional purchase:

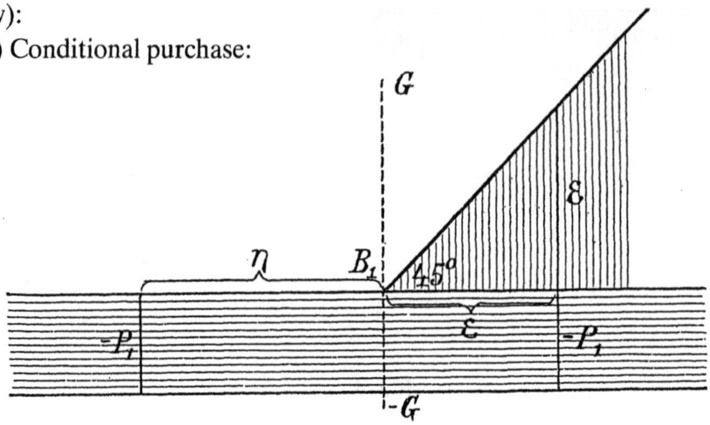

Fig. 7.

β) Constrained sale:

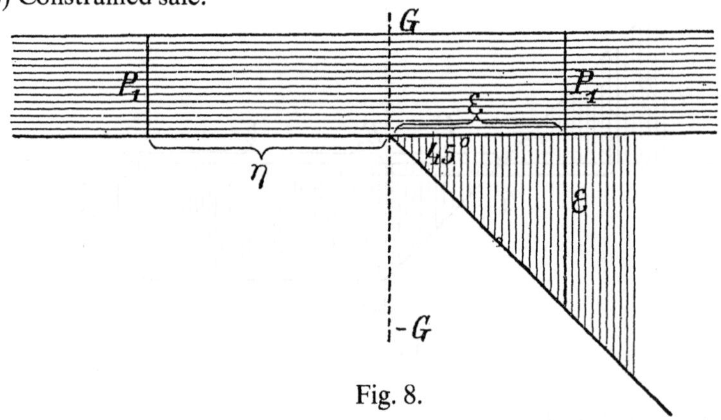

Fig. 8.

γ) Conditional sale:

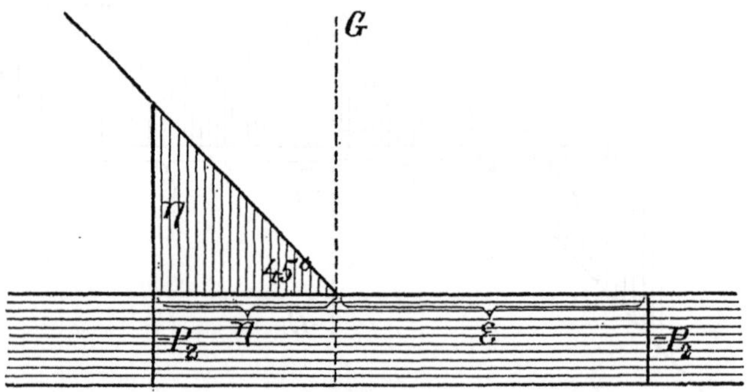

Fig. 9.

δ) Constrained purchase:

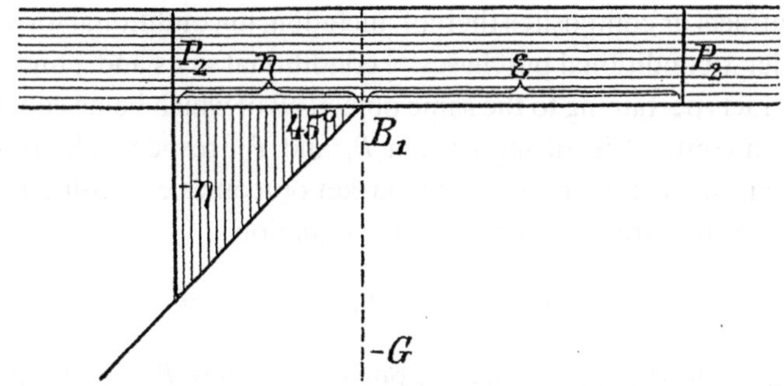

Fig. 10.

Hitherto, we have assumed that the contracts were entered into at price B_1, but we have not revealed any conditions upon which the price may be predicated; at this juncture, it is important to establish whether or not the price at which the premium contract was concluded coincides with the (current) price B of the unconditional forward contracts. It is from this vantage point that we elect to divide simple premium contracts into normal and skewed contracts, depending upon whether they are entered into at price B applying to the unconditional forward contracts or at a different price, say, $B + M$. We shall refer to the term M as the skewedness of the contract[40].

4. Coverage of Normal Contracts. Both from the mathematical expressions and the diagrams depicting gains and losses, it is immediately clear that gains from conditional contracts and losses from constrained contracts can be unlimited, whereas losses from the former and gains from the latter cannot exceed a determinate limit, viz. the amount of the premium to be paid[41]. At this point, it is evident that the conclusion of large numbers of constrained contracts holds the prospect of severe danger and may indeed bring about financial ruin. Hence, a prudent speculator will seek to combine his premium contracts in such a manner as to ensure that he will never be threatened by inordinate losses, irrespective of the prevailing market outcomes; in other words, he will strive for coverage of some kind. We shall look upon

[40] M is the difference between the forward price and the exercise price, and is what we may call "moneyness" of the option, depending whether it is a call option ($M < 0$) or a put option ($M > 0$). Notice that the exercise price itself exhibits no specific abbreviation throughout this Text, with one exception (Part I, Chapter II, Section 3).

[41] Trivially, the author assumes that the underlying cannot take negative values, which is a reasonable assumption in the case of market prices.

a composite of contracts as being covered, if in the presence of any conceivable market outcome neither gains are to be expected nor losses to be feared[42].

In order to determine the general laws of coverage as they apply to normal premium contracts or composites thereof, including unconditional forward contracts, we consider x conditional purchases, y conditional sales and z unconditional forward contracts pertaining to the same object, all of which being concluded at price B and each contract involving premia P_1 and P_2, respectively. Based upon this supposition, gains in the presence of market outcomes exceeding B, viz. if a price of $B + \varepsilon$ prevails, are represented by the equation

$$G_1 = x(\varepsilon - P_1) - yP_2 + z\varepsilon$$

whereas gains in the face of market outcomes below B, viz. if a price of $B - \eta$ prevails, are represented by the equation

$$G_2 = -xP_1 + y(\eta - P_2) - z\eta$$

These representations are rearranged to yield the respective forms

$$\left.\begin{array}{l} G_1 = (x + z)\varepsilon - xP_1 - yP_2 \\ G_2 = (y - z)\eta - xP_1 - yP_2 \end{array}\right\}, \tag{1}$$

in which condition they are instrumental in advancing the investigation.

It appears that complete coverage, as previously defined, can only be accomplished if for any value of ε and η, respectively, the expressions G_1 and G_2 are equal to zero, viz. the following equations being consistently satisfied

$$\left.\begin{array}{l} (x + z)\varepsilon - xP_1 - yP_2 = 0 \\ (y - z)\eta - xP_1 - yP_2 = 0 \end{array}\right\}, \tag{2}$$

Owing to the arbitrariness of ε and of η[43], the requirement will be fulfilled only if their coefficients equal zero, for which reason we arrive at the indispensable condition expressed by equations

$$\left.\begin{array}{l} x + z = 0 \\ y - z = 0 \\ x + y = 0 \end{array}\right\}, \tag{3}$$

the last equation having been added as an immediate corollary derived from the other two. The remainder of equation (2), viz.

$$xP_1 + yP_2 = 0$$

[42] This can be understood as a perfect hedging condition, in a normative sense.

[43] Apparently, no distributional assumptions about the price deviations from the forward price are necessary for the following analysis, i.e. the derived results are "distribution free".

assumes, on account of condition (3), the form

$$x(P_1 - P_2) = 0$$

yielding the relation,

$$P_1 = P_2 = P \tag{4}$$

since in general x will be unequal to zero[44]. Therefore, examination of the conditions of coverage as applicable to normal contracts evinces the subsequent principle: Due to $x + y = 0$, the sum of the conditional contracts must be equal to zero, as is required of the sum of all purchases or all sales, owing to $x + z = 0$ or $y + (-z) = 0$. In other words, there must be an equal number of conditional contracts and constrained contracts; at the same time, on account of $z = -x$, it is requisite that the number of unconditional forward sales pertaining to a certain object must be equal to the number of conditional purchases of the same object; or what amounts to the same, owing to $z = y$, the number of unconditional forward purchases to be concluded must be equal to the number of conditional sales. Moreover, in accordance with equation (4), the premia involved in the conditional purchase, the so-called buyer's premia, need to be equal to the premia involved in the conditional sale, the so-called seller's premia.

These results can be confirmed and made plain to see very easily by way of graphical representation. In point of fact, for our x, depending upon x assuming positive or negative values, there corresponds a certain number of diagrams as depicted by Figure 7 and Figure 8, respectively; of course, generally x will be taken to represent the difference between conditional purchases and their antipodal contracts, viz. constrained sales, which cancel each other out in their entirety; regarding the final result, it is apparent that only that difference needs to be taken account of. By the same token, y yields a certain number of diagrams as depicted by Figure 9 and Figure 10, respectively, depending upon y assuming positive or negative values (that is, depending upon whether or not conditional sales outweigh constrained purchases). If these x- and y-diagrams, allowing for the contingent involvement of unconditional forward contracts, are to cancel each other out, it is indispensible that the rectangular areas of the diagrams cancel each other out, and that the triangular areas of the diagrams cancel each other out; considering the rectangular parts in their own right, mutual cancellation requires an equal number of diagrams as depicted in Figure 7 and Figure 10, respectively, in addition to which heights P_1 and P_2 must be equal. Considering these prerequisites, obviously we discern, contained in them, the condition of an equal number of conditional and constrained contracts as well as the condition that the buyer's premia and the seller's premia be of equal size. Upon cancellation of the rectangles, there still

[44] The equality of call and put prices for "symmetric" contracts is a special case of the "put-call-parity"; the general parity is derived in Chapter II, Section 1, equation 4.

remain $2x$ or, amounting to the same, $2y$ triangular areas, whose conjunction provides x- or y-diagrams in the form of Figure 11, if x is positive, and in the form of Figure 12, if x is negative. In order to achieve coverage of the residual diagrams, it is apparent that either an equal number of unconditional forward purchases or an equal number of unconditional forward sales will be required, to which exactly converse diagrams correspond; herein lies the meaning of equations $z = -x$ and $z = y$, respectively.

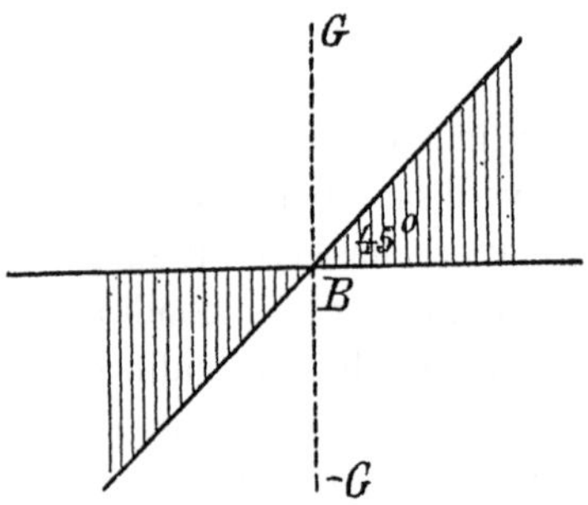

Fig. 11.

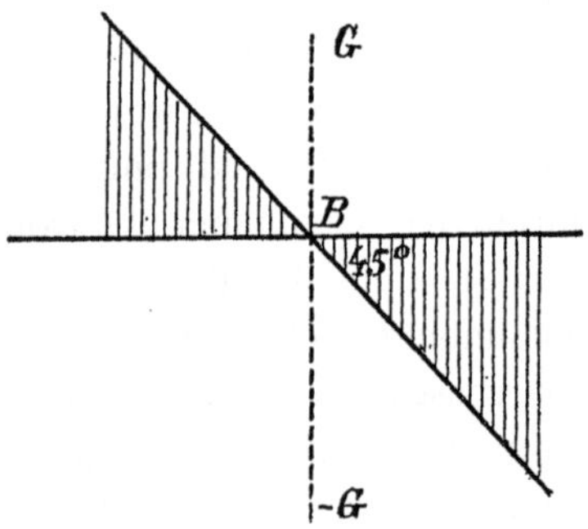

Fig. 12.

5. Equivalence of Normal Contracts. Having solved the problem of coverage, we have also solved the problem of equivalence. Two systems of contracts shall be regarded as equivalent, if one may be derived from the other; in other words, if, in the presence of any conceivable market outcome, the systems in question yield exactly the same gains and losses, respectively[45]. In light of this definition, we recognise immediately that two systems of equivalent contracts are obtained, if, in only one composite of covered contracts, some of the latter carry the converse algebraic signs. The system obtained in this manner is entirely equivalent to the system formed by the remaining contracts, for this reason: suppose coverage is achieved e.g. amongst contracts x, y, z, u etc; let us consider, say, contracts $-x$ and $-z$, which evidently form a covered composite in conjunction with x and z; hence, $-x$ and $-z$ bring about the same effect produced by the residual contracts y, u etc; consequentially, the system $-x$ and $-y$ must be equivalent to the system y, u . . .. From this result it is possible to derive a simple method of finding for a given system of contracts the equivalent system or the equivalent systems, respectively;

[45] In the terminology of modern option pricing, this is the principle of replication, or the replicating portfolio approach. It is an essential tool in financial engineering, and forms the basis for establishing arbitrage-free pricing restrictions for derivative contracts. Notice that the first sentence of this paragraph is a precise statement about the correspondence between the principle of replication ("the problem of equivalence") and the creation of a perfect hedge ("the problem of coverage").

all that is required is a procedure of substitution, whereby in the equations of coverage the contracts of the given system are replaced by contracts carrying opposite algebraic signs, while the former are solved for the residual terms, in which fashion the equivalent systems are obtained immediately. If the number of residual terms and the number of equations of condition are equal, there will be only one system which is equivalent to the given system, as the equations in question are of the first degree[46]; however, if the number of unknowns exceeds the number of equations, then, in general, there may be an infinite number of systems equivalent to the system under consideration. Finally, if the number of equations exceeded the number of unknown terms, then, in general, the given system could not be derived from the residual contracts.

We shall now proceed to apply these general considerations to the normal simple contracts examined hitherto, which are governed by the below equations of coverage

$$x + y = 0$$
$$x + z = 0$$

In view of these conditions, it appears that an infinite number of covered systems (and, hence, an infinite number of equivalent systems) exists, whose determination requires that one kind of contract be chosen, while the other two can be determined by solving for the two equations of condition.

Suppose, we are dealing with coverage of e.g. 200 conditional sales. We substitute y = 200 and solve for the equations

$$x + 200 = 0$$
$$x + z = 0$$

hence $x = -200$ and $z = 200$, viz. 200 constrained sales and 200 unconditional forward purchases. Thus, by necessity, we obtain a covered system consisting of 200 conditional sales, 200 constrained sales and 200 unconditional forward purchases, provided that the premia associated with the conditional and the constrained contracts are set to be equal. We shall take a numerical test to probe the finding. Let the traded objects be shares priced at 425 K, involving a premium of 6 K per share. If the price has increased to e.g. 468 K on the date when the trades are unwound, we suffer a loss of 1200 K concerning the 200 conditional sales, for evidently we will not elect to sell and, therefore, lose the deposited premium; similarly, we incur a loss of 6400 K concerning the 200 constrained sales, as our counterparties are likely to effect purchase, making a gain of 27 K per share (namely, 33 K owing to the increase in the share price, minus 6 K premium). Thus, our total loss amounts to

46 With some laxity, this condition is related to an Arrow-Debreu “complete market”, which is characterized by a unique replication strategy for derivative contracts.

6600 K, which is exactly offset by (a gain of 33 × 200 K from) the 200 unconditional forward purchases[47].

If we intend to derive a contract from two other contracts, we shall substitute the positive or the negative unit into one of the terms x, y or z in the equations, depending upon the nature of the contract to be derived, and determine by subsequent solution of the equations the contracts from which the one under consideration can be derived.

We might be interested e.g. in finding out how an unconditional forward contract may be derived from simple normal premium contracts. In place of z, we substitute the value -1, in which manner equations

$$x + y = 0 \quad \text{and} \quad x - 1 = 0$$

yield the values $x = 1$ and $y = -1$, viz. a conditional purchase and a constrained purchase as the system of contracts which is equivalent to an unconditional forward purchase[48]. For the derivation of a conditional sale we are required to substitute the value -1 into y, thus yielding $x = 1$ and $z = -1$, viz. a conditional purchase and an unconditional forward sale. Thus, in order to determine the system which corresponds to a constrained sale, we need to substitute the value $+1$ into x, which yields $y = -1$ and $z = -1$, viz. a constrained sale and an unconditional forward sale, and so forth.

6. Double Premium Contracts or Stellage Contracts. As for stellage contracts, by paying a premium upon conclusion of the contract, the so-called buyer of the stellage contract acquires the right to either purchase or sell the object underlying the trade at a fixed price B on the date of delivery; obviously, he will undertake a purchase if the price has increased above B, and he will choose to sell if the price has fallen below B; the counterparty, who is obligated to either make or take delivery of the object, assumes the position of seller of the stellage contract. It is apparent that the seller's gains and losses are the converse of those facing the buyer; hence, if we denote a determinate number of purchases of stellage contracts (stellage purchases) of the same object by σ, then $-\sigma$ represents the same number of sales of stellage contracts (stellage sales); therefore, $\sigma = 3$ e.g. represents a threefold stellage purchase, while $\sigma = -5$ represents a fivefold stellage sale.

From the definition of the stellage contract it is evident at once that this new type of contract is composed of two normal premium contracts, to wit: the stellage purchase consisting of a conditional purchase and a conditional sale; on the other

[47] The example illustrates that combining a short call with a long put is equivalent to a forward sale (short forward position), and can thus be fully hedged with a forward purchase (long forward).

[48] The example highlights how a forward purchase (long forward) can be replicated by combining a short put with a long call.

hand, a stellage sale consists of a constrained sale and a constrained purchase of the same object. Consequentially, the premium involved in a normal stellage contract will correspond to the double (of the) premium of the simple normal contract. Furthermore, it is plain to see that in the normal stellage the purchase of the object is effected at price $B + 2P$, while the sale is concluded at price $B - 2P$. The difference between these prices is referred to as the stellage's tension, which in a normal stellage amounts to 4 P; the arithmetic mean of which is referred to as the midpoint of the stellage, coinciding in the case of a normal stellage with the price B of the unconditional forward contracts. Finally, note that in the case of this type of contract, the buyer begins to enjoy gains only when market fluctuations occur which exceed or fall below $2P$, beyond which threshold gains may grow infinitely. If market fluctuations yield prices smaller than $2P$, the buyer incurs a loss; the latter increasing as fluctuations decrease, reaching a maximum value of $2P$ in the face of zero fluctuations, viz. when the price prevailing on the date of delivery is equal to the fixed price B.

Without having recourse to more specific considerations, we are now in a position to generalise our equations of coverage (3) to include stellage contracts in explicit form. Adding σ stellage purchases to x conditional purchases, $y$conditional sales, and $z$unconditional forward purchases, we obtain all in all $x + \sigma$ conditional purchases, $y + \sigma$ conditional sales and z unconditional forward purchases, which of necessity achieve coverage; immediate application of conditions (3) thus produces at once the following system of simultaneous equations

$$\left.\begin{aligned} x + y + 2\sigma &= 0 \\ x + z + \ \sigma &= 0 \\ y - z + \ \sigma &= 0 \end{aligned}\right\} \tag{5}$$

which firstly provides us with the conditions ensuring coverage, and, in accordance with the deliberations contained in section 5, also allows for the derivation of arbitrary equivalent systems of contracts.

In equations (5), of which one is immediately derived from the other two, we encounter four unknown terms, wherefore it is always possible to choose any two of them; consequentially, from the contracts in question, we may obtain doubly infinite composites which are perfectly covered. In addition, we observe that the problem of equivalent systems turns out to be more extensive than it may previously have appeared. Namely, if we wish to derive one type of contract from the other three, we need to substitute a determinate given numerical value for one of the terms appearing in equations (5) and hereupon solve two equations comprising three unknowns to determine the equivalent system of contracts; in this manner, we obtain an infinite number of systems equivalent to the type of contract in question, for which reason one type of contract cannot be derived in a determinate fashion from the other three. Only a system of any two types of contracts can be derived uniquely from the other two; for, once we choose the system comprising two contracts that we wish to derive, we are then required to perform the substitution of two of the four terms contained in equations (5) so that the remaining terms are completely determined by the equations.

If it is our intention to derive e.g. the arbitrary system "1 stellage sale and 3 conditional sales" from the two other contracts, we are required to substitute into (5) +1 and −3 and the converse values, respectively, for α and y, and then proceed to solve equations

$$x - 3 + 2 = 0$$
$$x + z + 1 = 0$$

We obtain

$$x = 1 \quad \text{and} \quad z = -2$$

viz. a conditional purchase and two unconditional forward sales, representing the system which is entirely equivalent to the system in question.

On another note, if we wish to derive e.g. a stellage purchase from the other three types of contract, we are required to substitute for α in (5) the converse value −1, and, in order to ascertain the equivalent systems, we need to solve equations

$$x + y - 2 = 0$$
$$x + z - 1 = 0$$

It is apparent, however, that this can be accomplished in an infinite number of ways, so that the stellage purchase in question yields an infinite number of equivalent combinations of contracts, one of which is e.g. $x = 3$, $y = -1$ and $z = -2$, viz. three conditional purchases, one constrained sale and two unconditional forward sales, and so on.

However, if the problem posed embraces the restriction demanding that one contract be derived from two other contracts, determinateness prevails, for the restriction gives expression to the circumstance that one of the three terms, which remain subsequent to the substitution of the contracts to be derived, is required to be equal to zero, owing to which there evidently are, in the presence of two equations, two unknowns available for further manipulations.

Hence, we are able to derive in a unique manner e.g. a stellage purchase either α) from conditional purchases and conditional sales, or β) from conditional purchases and unconditional forward purchases, or, finally, γ) from conditional sales and unconditional forward purchases. In all three cases, it is required that in (5) we substitute into σ the value −1, and further assume for α) $z = 0$, for β) $y = 0$, and for γ) $x = 0$. Thereupon, we obtain with respect to α)

$$x + y - 2 = 0$$
$$x - 1 = 0$$

and hence $x = 1$ and $y = 1$, viz. a conditional purchase and a conditional sale, which result is by definition evident a priori. Regarding β) we obtain

$$\begin{aligned} x - 2 &= 0 \\ x + z - 1 &= 0 \end{aligned}$$

namely $x = 2$ and $z = -1$, viz. two conditional purchases and one unconditional forward sale. Finally, with respect to γ) we have

$$\begin{aligned} y - 2 &= 0 \\ z - 1 &= 0 \end{aligned}$$

thus $y = 2$ and $z = 1$, viz. two conditional sales and an unconditional forward purchase. Apparently, the converse of these systems corresponds to a stellage sale.

If we wish to derive a constrained sale from stellage contracts and a constrained purchase, we are required to substitute in (5) the value +1 for y, and, as conditional purchases are precluded, also substitute zero into x, which yields

$$\begin{aligned} 1 + 2\sigma &= 0 \\ z + \sigma &= 0 \end{aligned}$$

hence $\sigma = -{}^1\!/_2$ and $z = {}^1\!/_2$ viz. a stellage sale and an unconditional forward purchase of half of the quantity in question, respectively.

Let us confirm the result by way of numerical example. Instead of only one contract, we suppose 100 constrained purchases, the equivalent of which should consist of 50 stellage sales and 50 unconditional forward purchases: we assume to be dealing with a stock whose price is 682; the premium of the simple contracts is 14 K, and hence 28 K for the stellage. If the price is 645 K on the day the transaction is unwound, 100 constrained purchases, on account of the counterparties being likely to sell, apparently result in a loss of

$$(37 - 14) \cdot 100 = 2300 \text{ K}$$

Note: 50 stellage sales result in a loss of

$$(37 - 28) \cdot 50 = 450 \text{ K}$$

whilst 50 unconditional forward purchases produce a loss of

$$37 \times 50 = 1850 \text{ K}$$

wherefore complete equivalence prevails.

Should the price increase by 68 K, 100 constrained purchases evidently result in a gain of

$$14 \times 100 = 1400 \text{ K}$$

while the remainder of contracts yield:

50 stellage sales . . . . $(68 - 28) \times 50 = 2000$ K loss
50 unconditional forward purchases . . . . $68 \times 50 = 3400$ K gain

producing overall, therefore, the same result.

It is perspicuous that there are 12 derivations of a contract from two other contracts of the types considered hitherto, that is, disregarding the converse contracts.

Chapter II.

Skewed Premium Contracts.

1. Coverage and Equivalence of Simple Skewed Premium Contracts. We examine h conditional purchases, k conditional sales, all of which being concluded at a price $B + M$ and involving premia P_1 and P_2,[49] respectively, as well as l unconditional forward purchase effected at the current price B. Recalling the considerations in section 3 of the previous chapter, examination of gains and losses in the face of arbitrary maket outcomes $B + M + \varepsilon$ and $B + M - \eta$, respectively, yield the respective equations

$$\left.\begin{aligned} G_1 &= h(\varepsilon - P_1) - kP_2 + l(M + \varepsilon) \\ G_2 &= -hP_1 + k(\eta - P_2) + l(M - \eta) \end{aligned}\right\} \qquad (1)$$

In order to achieve complete coverage, it is necessary and sufficient that in the face of any conceivable market outcome neither a gain nor a loss occur, or in other words, that equations

$$\begin{aligned} h(\varepsilon - P_1) - kP_2 + l(M + \varepsilon) &= 0 \\ -hP_1 + k(\eta - P_2) + l(M - \eta) &= 0 \end{aligned}$$

be persistently satisfied. Rearranging the equations to obtain the form

$$\left.\begin{aligned} \varepsilon(h + l) - hP_1 - kP_2 + lM &= 0 \\ \eta(k - l) - hP_1 - kP_2 + lM &= 0 \end{aligned}\right\} \qquad (2)$$

we learn at once that, due to the arbitrariness of ε and η, the first indispensable condition ensuring the persistent satisfaction of equations (2) consists in the elimination of the coefficients

$$h + l \quad \text{and} \quad k - l.$$

As analogous to normal contracts, we arrive at the system of simultaneous equations

$$\left.\begin{aligned} h + l &= 0 \\ k - l &= 0 \\ h + k &= 0 \end{aligned}\right\} \qquad (3)$$

[49] Call prices are (mostly) denoted by P_1, put prices by P_2.

whereby presently only two equations are independent of each other; hence, one of the three terms appearing in the equations may be chosen arbitrarily, so that an infinite number of covered systems can be derived from these simple contracts. In consequence of condition (3), equations (2) contract to form the single relation

$$-hP_1 - kP_2 + lM = 0$$

which due to (3) can be given the form

$$k(P_1 - P_2 + M) = 0$$

Since one of the terms in (3) may be chosen arbitrarily, as mentioned previously, we are free to assume that k is not equal to zero; therefore we obtain from the latter equation another remarkable condition in the form of

$$P_2 = P_1 + M \tag{4}$$

The premium of the conditional sale is larger than the premium of the conditional purchase by the extent of the contract's skewedness. If a premium contract is concluded at price $B - M$, and if P_1 represents the premium involved in a conditional purchase, it is apparent that we have the relation[50]

$$P_2 = P_1 - M \tag{4a}$$

Therefore, skewed contracts give rise to equations of coverage quite analogous to those associated with normal contracts; again, the number of conditional contracts is required to be equal to the number of constrained contracts, to which must be added as many unconditional forward sales as there are conditional purchases, or (amounting to the same) as many unconditional purchases as there are conditional sales. Further, as a prerequisite for coverage to be possible at all, the relationship between premia involved in conditional purchases and conditional sales must satisfy the conditions affirmed in (4) and (4a), respectively, which latter are self-evident, at least in a qualitative way.

The laws that we have arrived at may be represented graphically in the following manner: Let h, being the difference between the number of conditional purchases and their converse (constrained sales) be positive; thus h represents a

[50] Equation (4) (as well as 4a) is the general relation between put and call prices, known as put-call-parity. Compared to the parity used in the modern option pricing literature, the time-value of money does not show up in the equation, because – as stated earlier – the option prices were typically paid at expiration in the old days, which is assumed throughout the text.

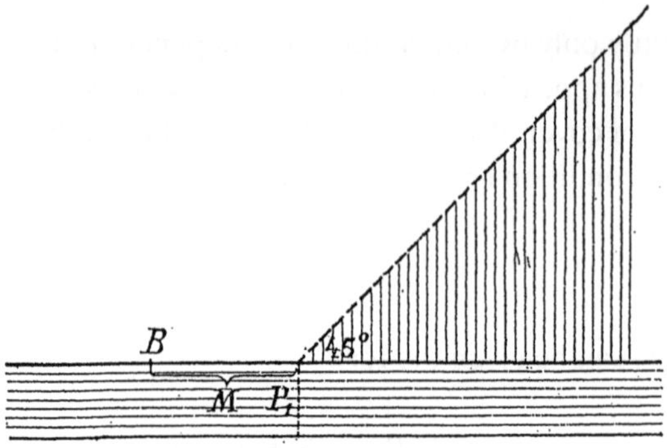

Fig. 13.

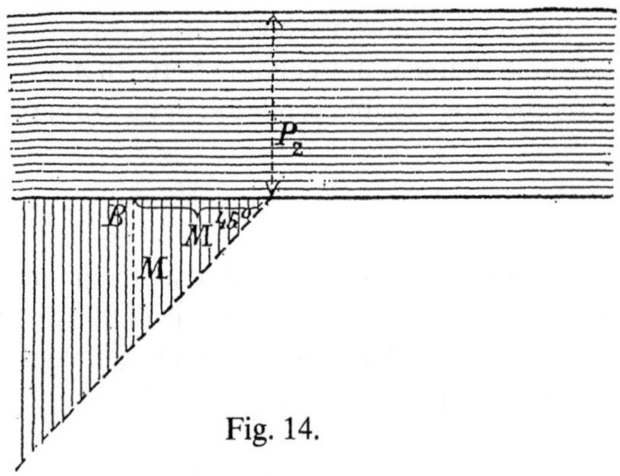

Fig. 14.

certain number of conditional purchases, to which corresponds an equal number of diagrams of the following form.

If these diagrams are to cancel each other out, we apparently require some of them to be of a kind whose rectangular parts represent gains. However, given the meaning of h, diagrams of this kind can be produced only by constrained purchases, viz. if k is negative; therefore, their form will be as follows.

In order to confirm the laws that we have arrived at analytically, we now apply suitable transformations to the above diagrams. We shall replace the diagram depicted in Fig. 13 by the following one, which may be derived from the former by adding the conversely equal shaded trapezoidal parts. Likewise, from a diagram contained in Figure 14, we may derive one in the form of (Figure) 16 to wit, by elimination of the corresponding unshaded trapezoidal pieces, both in the area of gains as well as in the area of losses. From the diagrams thus transformed, it is immediately evident that if condition

$$P_2 = P_1 + M$$

is satisfied, the polygonal parts in each diagram forming a pair cancel out each other; therefore, in order to achieve total elimination, it is required that diagrams

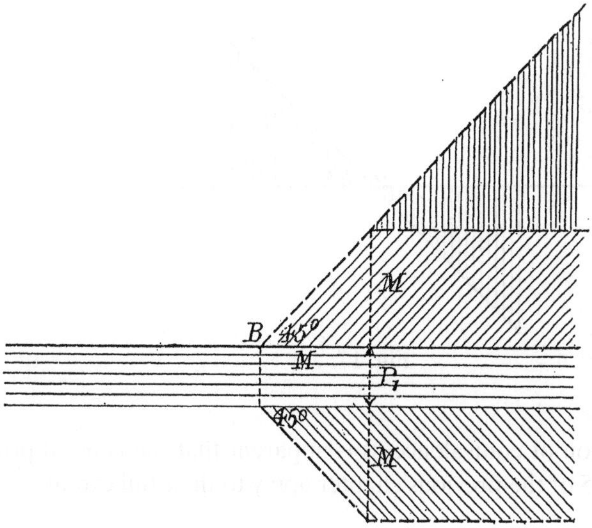

Fig. 15.

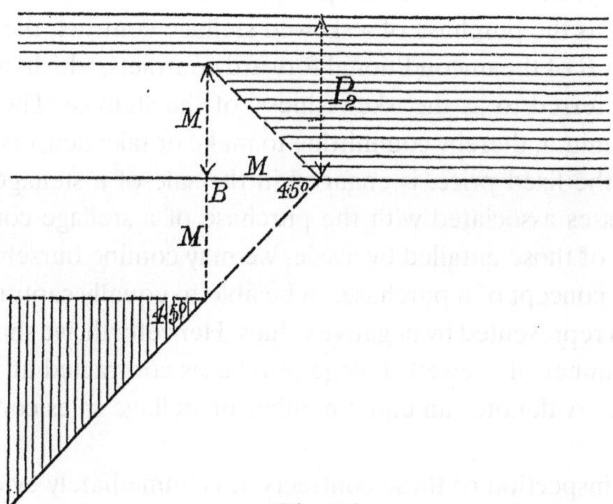

Fig. 16.

15 and 16 are of equal number, which takes us back to an earlier finding: that is to say, equation $h = -k$, viz. $h + k = 0$. Upon elimination of the polygonal parts, there remain only $2h$ triangular parts, whose conjunction yields h self-contained diagrams of the form depicted in Figure 17, to which corresponds an equal number of unconditional forward sales; in this way, we have corroborated the remaining law, namely $1 = -h$.

The same considerations apply if h is negative; in which instance, we obtain, in persistent consonance with the analytic results, k positive and unconditional forward purchases instead of unconditional forward sales.

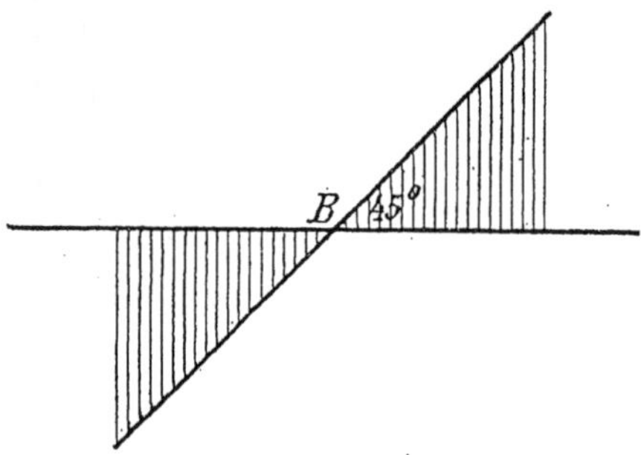

Fig. 17.

As for the question of equivalence, it is apparent that the general principles laid down in section 5 of the previous chapter apply to their full extent.

2. Skewed Stellage Contracts. If we pay a certain premium S_1 in order to be granted the right to either purchase or sell the traded object at our discretion on the date of delivery, and if this is based upon price $B + M$, we have concluded what one may refer to as the purchase of a skewed stellage contract; the difference M vis-à-vis the price B of the unconditional forward contracts, which may be positive or negative, is referred to as the 'skewedness' of the stellage. The counterparty receiving the premium, thereby committing to make or take delivery, respectively, of the object at the fixed price, is engaged in the sale of a stellage contract. As the gains and losses associated with the purchase of a stellage contract are the perfect converse of those entailed by a sale, we may confine ourselves to just one concept, say, the concept of a purchase, to be able to equally capture the concept of a sale, which is represented by negative values. Henceforth, we shall thus denote by s a certain number of skewed stellage purchases contracted at price $B + M$. Consequentially, $-s$ denotes an equal number of stellage sales concluded under the same terms.

Upon closer inspection of these contracts, it is immediately evident that they are composed of two simple skewed premium contracts, whereby the stellage purchase consists of a conditional purchase and a conditional sale, and the stellage sale consists of a constrained sale and a constrained purchase – all contracts being concluded at the same price $B + M$. For this reason, the premium S_1 paid to purchase a stellage contract will be equal to the sum of the premia involved in the conditional purchase and the conditional sale, where the contingent purchase of the object will be effected at price $B + M + P_1 + P_2$, and the contingent sale effected at price $B + M - P_1 - P_2$. The difference between the purchase and sale prices, namely

$$2S_1, \quad \text{or} \quad 2(P_1 + P_2)$$

is referred to as the tension T_1 of the skewed stellage, while its arithmetic mean, evidently coinciding with the underlying price $B + M$, is referred to as the midpoint of the stellage.

Graphically, it is easy to show that in the case of a skewed stellage gains and losses are larger than those evinced by a normal stellage of the same size; hence, we may expect the former to command a larger premium than the latter.

The diagram depicting gains and losses entailed by normal stellage contracts is shown in the figure below,

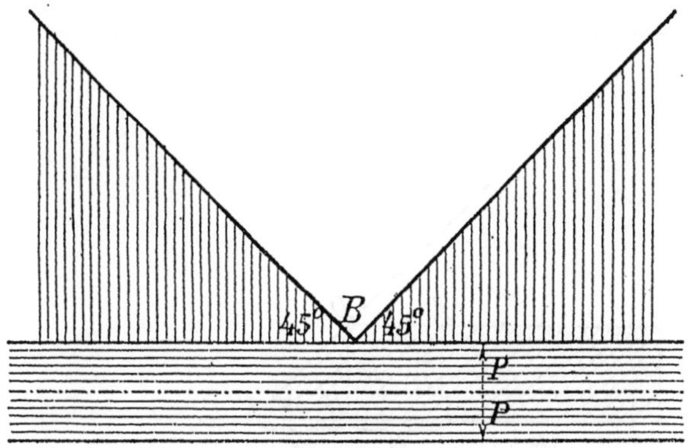

Fig. 18.

while gains and losses entailed by skewed stellage contracts are presented in the following figure.

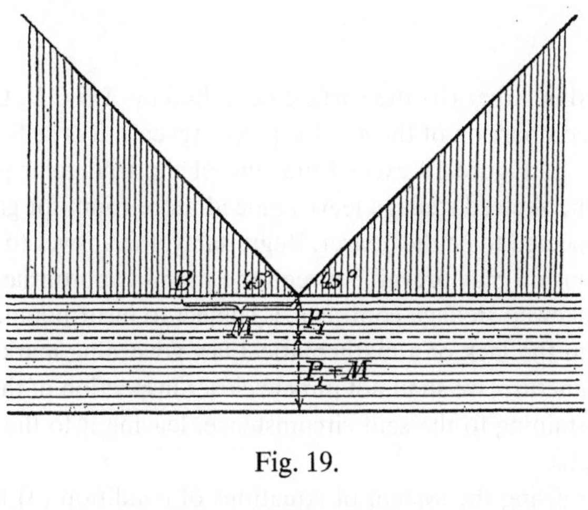

Fig. 19.

Concerning the previous diagram, if we wish to shift the triangular area to the right toward B, we are required, as is immediately evident from the below schema, to add the shaded area, whereas repositioning of the triangular area requires elimination of the shaded part, as can be seen from the following figure. Since the part

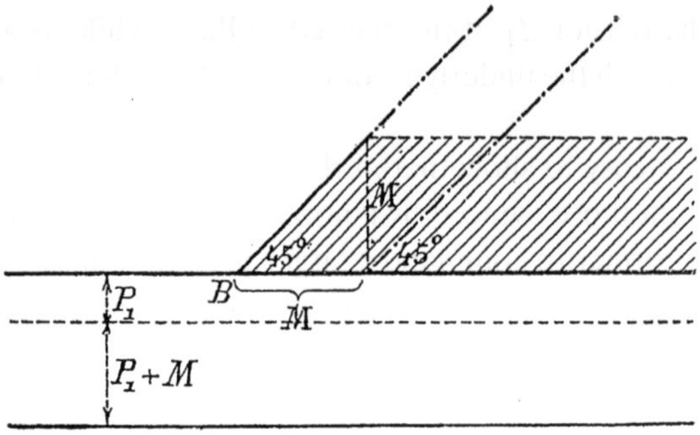

Fig. 20.

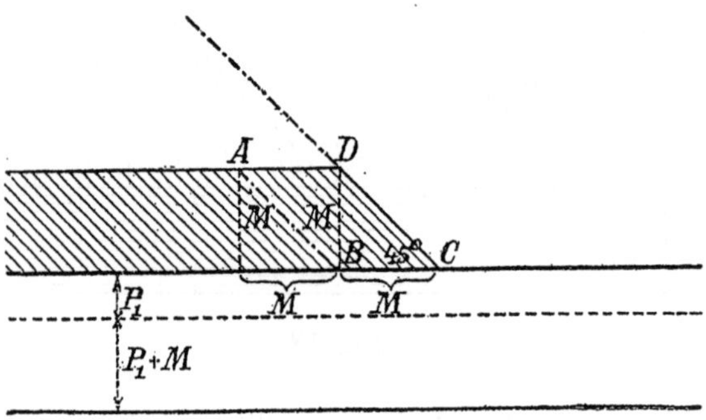

Fig. 21.

to be eliminated is larger (by the surface delimited by $A\ B\ C\ D$, than the part to be added, as a comparison of the shaded pieces reveals, it is self-evident that the triangular areas of Figure 19 exceed the sum of the triangular parts in schema 18, wherefore the skewed stellage leaves indeed more room for gains and, therefore, may be expected to be the dearer. Regrettably, the answer to the question as to which relationship may prevail between the premia appropriate to the nature of normal and skewed stellage contracts, is subject to insurmountable difficulties which arise from the lack of a mathematical law governing market fluctuations; at the present juncture, we shall not pursue closer inspection of this question and other issues pertaining to the said circumstance, leaving it to the second part of the present treatise.

When generalising the system of equations of condition (3) to encompass s stellage contracts, we need to be mindful of the fact discussed earlier, that s stellage contracts introduce an equal number of conditional purchases and conditional sales (we need hardly mention that all of these premium contracts are assumed to have been concluded at a price $B + M$), so that substituting $h + s$ and $k + s$ into

h and k yields the generalised system

$$\left.\begin{aligned} h + k + 2s &= 0 \\ h + l + \ \ s &= 0 \\ k - l + \ \ s &= 0 \end{aligned}\right\} \tag{5}$$

which is entirely analogous to the system (5) in the previous chapter, for which reason we may once again rely upon all considerations presented therein regarding covered and equivalent composites of contracts.

The following example will be instrumental in elucidating the general results. Consider a stock whose current price is 548 K. Further, consider a certain party who has sold 200 stellage contracts at a price of 654 and entered into 150 conditional purchases, also at a price of 654; how can coverage be achieved using the rest of the types of contract examined hitherto?

If we substitute in the above system of equations $s = -200$ and $h = 150$, then

$$\begin{aligned} 150 + k - 400 &= 0 \\ 150 + l - 200 &= 0 \end{aligned}$$

viz. $k = 250$ and $l = 50$. Hence, coverage is accomplished by means of 200 conditional sales to be concluded at a price of 654, and 50 unconditional forward purchases concluded at the current price; the size of the premia must, of course, satisfy the relation (4).

For numerical confirmation, let us assume the premium of the conditional purchase to be 7 K, while the current price on the date of delivery be e.g. 680. Since the premium of the conditional sales must be equal to $7 + 6 = 13$ K, in this particular instance, whereas the premium of the stellage contracts must be equal to $13 + 7 = 20$ K, we arrive at the following result:

α) 200 stellage sales:	$200\,(26 - 20) = 1200$ K loss
β) 150 conditional purchases:	$150\,(26 - 7) = 2850$ K gain
γ) 250 conditional sales:	$250 \times 13 = 3250$ K loss
δ) 50 unconditional purchases:	$50 \times 32 = 1600$ K gain.

The overall outcome involves neither a gain nor a loss, as was desired.

3. Composites of Simple Contracts of Different Prices. We turn to the important question as to whether and how contracts which do not have the same base[51] might achieve coverage. To this purpose we assume conclusion at prices B_1, B_2, $\ldots B_r, B_{r+1} = B, B_{r+2}, \ldots$ and B_{n+1}, respectively, of simple premium contracts h_1 and k_1, h_2 and k_2, $\ldots$ h_r and k_r, $h_{r+1} = x$ and $k_{r+1} = y$, h_{r+2} and k_{r+2}, $\ldots$ h and k_{n+1}, whereby, as before and without exception, the differing h relate

[51] i.e. contracts with different exercise prices, subsequently denoted by B_1, B_2, etc.

to conditional purchases, whereas the differing k relate to conditional sales; the former commanding premia $p_1, p_2, \dots p_r, p_{r+1} = p, p_{r+2}, \dots p_{n+1}$, the latter commanding premia $P_1, P_2, \dots P_r, P_{r+1} = P, P_{r+2}, \dots P_{n+1}$.[52] The premium contracts having been thus characterised, we add to them the unconditional forward contracts $l_1, l_2, \dots l_r, l_{r+1} = z, l_{r+2}, \dots l_{n+1}$, all of which we assume to have been concluded at the current price $B_{r+1} = B$. The schema below may render the matter more graphic.

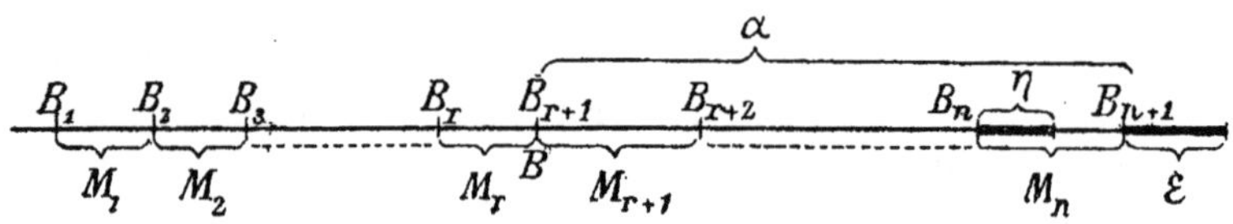

Fig. 22.

Let us look more closely at gains and losses as they ensue, depending upon the various market outcomes which may conceivably occur. In the presence of a market outcome defined by $B_{n+1} + \varepsilon$, the total gain would evidently be equal to the sum of the below partial gains

$$
\begin{aligned}
G_{n+1} &= h_{n+1}(\varepsilon - p_{n+1}) - k_{n+1}P_{n+1} + l_{n+1}(\overbrace{M_{r+1} + M_{r+2} + \cdots + M_n}^{\alpha} + \varepsilon) \\
G_n &= h_n(\varepsilon + M_n - p_n) - k_n P_n + l_n(\alpha + \varepsilon) \\
G_{n-1} &= h_{n-1}(\varepsilon + M_n + M_{n-1} - p_{n-1}) - k_{n-1}P_{n+1} + l_{n-1}(\alpha + \varepsilon) \\
&\vdots \\
G_{r+2} &= h_{r+2}(\varepsilon + M_n + \cdots + M_{r+2} - p_{r+2}) - k_{r+2}P_{r+2} + l_{r+2}(\alpha + \varepsilon) \\
G_{r+1} &= G = h_{r+1}(\varepsilon + M_n + \cdots + M_{r+1} - p_{r+1}) - k_{r+1}P_{r+1} + l_{r+1}(\alpha + \varepsilon) \\
G_r &= h_r(\varepsilon + M_n + \cdots + M_r - p_r) - k_r P_r + l_r(\alpha + \varepsilon) \\
&\vdots \\
G_2 &= h_2(\varepsilon + M_n + \cdots + M_2 - p_2) - k_2 P_2 + l_2(\alpha + \varepsilon) \\
G_1 &= h_1(\varepsilon + M_n + \cdots + M_1 - p_1) - k_1 P_1 + l_1(\alpha + \varepsilon)
\end{aligned}
$$

[52] To clarify, the p_j denote call option prices and P_j put option prices in the following derivation (up to equation 10), with j referring to the exercise price of the contract.

Likewise, in the presence of a market outcome defined by $B_n + \eta$, the total gain is equal to the sum of the following partial gains

$$
\begin{aligned}
g_{n+1} &= -h_{n+1}p_{n+1} + k_{n+1}(M_n - \eta - P_{n+1}) + l_{n+1}(\alpha - M_n + \eta)\\
g_n &= h_n(\eta - p_n) - k_n P_n + l_n(\alpha - M_n + \eta)\\
g_{n-1} &= h_{n-1}(\eta + M_{n-1} - p_{n-1}) - k_{n-1}P_{n-1} + l_{n-1}(\alpha - M_n + \eta)\\
&\vdots\\
g_{r+1} &= g = h_{r+1}(\eta + M_{n-1} + \cdots + M_{r+1} - p_{r+1}) - k_{r+1}P_{r+1}\\
&\qquad + l_{r+1}(\alpha - M_n + \eta)\\
&\vdots\\
g_1 &= h_1(\eta + M_{n-1} + M_n + \cdots + M_1 - p_1) - k_1 P_1 + l_1(\alpha - M_n + \eta)
\end{aligned}
$$

Proceeding in this manner, we will obtain, for any conceivable market outcome between the differing B_λ and below B_1, a similar system of partial gains, whose sum represents the total gain from the assumed market outcomes; apparently, it is possible to derive $n + 2$ systems of this kind.

If the contracts in question are to provide a completely covered composite, the indispensable condition must be satisfied whereby total gains be equal to zero for any conceivable market outcome, by dint of which we obtain $n + 2$ equations. Of these, as follows immediately from the two systems developed, the first two can be given the form

$$
\left.\begin{aligned}
\varepsilon(\Sigma h + \Sigma l) - \Sigma hp - \Sigma kP + \alpha\Sigma l + Q = 0\\
\eta(\Sigma h - h_{n+1} - k_{n+1} + \Sigma l) - \Sigma hp - \Sigma kP + (\alpha - M_n)\Sigma l + Q_1 = 0
\end{aligned}\right\} \tag{6}
$$

whereby Q and Q_1, respectively, are given by the expressions

$$
\begin{aligned}
Q &= h_n M_n + h_{n-1}(M_n + M_{n-1}) + \cdots + h_1(M_n + M_{n-1} + \cdots + M_1)\\
Q_1 &= k_{n+1}M_n + h_{n-1}M_{n-1} + h_{n-2}(M_{n-1} + M_{n-2}) + \cdots + h_1(M_{n-1}\\
&\qquad + \cdots + M_1)
\end{aligned}
$$

Analogously, we obtain

$$
\left.\begin{aligned}
\xi(\Sigma h - h_{n+1} - h_n - k_{n+1} - k_n + \Sigma l) - \Sigma hp - \Sigma kP +\\
+(\alpha - M_n - M_{n-1})\Sigma l + Q_2 = 0
\end{aligned}\right\} \tag{7}
$$

whereby

$$
\begin{aligned}
Q_2 &= k_{n+1}(M_n + M_{n-1}) + k_n M_{n-1} + h_{n-2}M_{n-2} + h_{n-3}(M_{n-2} + M_{n-3})\\
&\qquad + \cdots + h_1(M_{n-2} + \cdots + M_1)
\end{aligned}
$$

and so forth.

In view of the arbitrariness of terms ε, η, ξ[53] etc. it is requisite, if equations (6) and (7) are to be satisfied, that their coefficients be equal to zero; first, we obtain

$$\Sigma h + \Sigma l = 0$$

and, hence, upon elimination of the coefficient of η

$$h_{n+1} + k_{n+1} = 0$$

and further, upon elimination of the coefficient of ξ

$$h_n + k_n = 0$$

and so forth, so that we successively arrive at the remarkable system of equations of condition below

$$\left.\begin{array}{l} h_{n+1} + k_{n+1} = 0 \\ h_n + k_n = 0 \\ h_{n-1} + k_{n-1} = 0 \\ \quad\dots \\ h_2 + k_2 = 0 \\ h_1 + k_1 = 0 \\ \Sigma h + \Sigma l = 0 \end{array}\right\} \qquad (8)$$

to which we add, as an immediate corollary, equation

$$\Sigma k - \Sigma l = 0$$

From this system of equations we gather the remarkable fact that the premium contracts which have been concluded at different prices[54] form by themselves of necessity a covered system, so that combination of skewed contracts of this kind can be achieved by mere supraposition of composites that by themselves are covered. This is tantamount to proving the impossibility of deriving premium contracts of a specific class from other contracts concluded at different prices, or to cover them using the latter[55]. In the pursuit of the aforementioned combination of composites of contracts which are covered in accordance with established rules for the achievement of coverage, however, a reduction of the unconditional forward contracts is brought about, which under certain circumstances may cancel each other

[53] Again, together with equation (6) and (7), this assumption suggests a system of distribution-free arbitrage conditions.

[54] i.e. “exercise” prices.

[55] i.e. a system of “skewed” options cannot be hedged without using forward contracts. From this, the author assigns a key role to forward contrats in the overall system of coverage (hedging) relations.

out completely. Therefore, unconditional forward contracts represent the powerful mediators which are capable of tying together premium contracts concluded upon different bases, whilst however always grouping the latter in such a manner that for a given basis there is an equal number of conditional and constrained contracts.

Developing equations (6) and (7) further, once the terms associated with the arbitrary variables ε, η, ξ ..., have been eliminated, we find a series of equations of the form below:

$$\left.\begin{aligned} -\Sigma hp - \Sigma kP + \alpha\Sigma l + Q &= 0 \\ -\Sigma hp - \Sigma kP + (\alpha - M_n)\Sigma l + Q_1 &= 0 \\ -\Sigma hp - \Sigma kP + (\alpha - M_n - M_{n-1})\Sigma l + Q_2 &= 0 \\ &\vdots \\ -\Sigma hp - \Sigma kP + (\alpha - M_n - M_{n-1} - \cdots - M_1))\Sigma l + Q_n &= 0 \end{aligned}\right\} \quad (9)$$

whose satisfaction requires relations

$$\left.\begin{aligned} Q &= Q_1 - M_n \ \ \Sigma l \\ Q_1 &= Q_2 - M_{n-1}\Sigma l \\ Q_2 &= Q_3 - M_{n-2}\Sigma l \text{ etc.} \end{aligned}\right\}$$

to prevail. A glance at the expressions corresponding to the different Q reveals that the latter relations are identically satisfied; in other words, the equations of system (9) are all equivalent. For the purpose of deriving further conclusions, it is therefore entirely a matter of indifference as to which of these equations shall be used. If we choose the first of these, being aware that with respect to the final result the distribution of the unconditional forward contracts is a matter of indifference, provided that their sums, viz. Σh resp. Σk, are equal, we suppose the following distribution

$$\begin{aligned} l_{n+1} &= -h_{n+1} = k_{n+1} \\ l_n &= -h_n \ \ = k_n \\ &\vdots \\ l_1 &= -h_1 \ \ = k_1 \end{aligned}$$

wherefore the said first equation of system (9) can be given the form

$$-h_{n+1}p_{n+1} - h_n p_n - \cdots - h_1 p_1 + h_{n*1}P_{n+1} + h_n P_n + \cdots h_1 P_1 - \alpha h_{n+1} - \alpha h_n - \cdots \alpha h_1 + h_n M_n + h_{n-1}(M_n + M_{n-1}) + \cdots + h_1(M_n + M_{n-1} + \cdots + M_1) = 0$$

which produces

$$h_{n+1}(-p_{n+1} + P_{n+1} - \alpha) + h_n(-p_n + P_n - \alpha + M_n) + h_{n+1}(-p_{n-1} + P_{n-1} - \alpha + M_n + M_{n-1}) + h_1(-p_1 + P_1 - \alpha + M_n + M_{n-1} + \cdots + M_1) = 0$$

Since the different h may be looked upon as being arbitrary terms, owing to our being able to choose arbitrarily a term in each of the covered systems, and that therefore their coefficients must disappear, the latter equation becomes decomposed to form the system

$$\left.\begin{aligned} P_{n+1} &= p_{n+1} + \alpha \\ P_n &= p_n + \alpha - M_n \\ P_{n-1} &= p_{n-1} + \alpha - M_n - M_{n-1} \\ &\vdots \\ P_1 &= p_1 + \alpha - M_n - M_{n-1} - \cdots - M_1 \end{aligned}\right\} \quad (10)$$

which renders a general expression for relation (4), which had been derived initially from a special case[56].

If additionally we elect to explicitly represent stellage contracts in the system of equations (8), we evidently obtain

$$\left.\begin{aligned} h_{n+1} + k_{n+1} + 2s_{n+1} &= 0 \\ h_n + k_n + 2s_n &= 0 \\ &\vdots \\ h_1 + k_1 + 2s_1 &= 0 \\ \Sigma h_1 + \Sigma l + \Sigma s &= 0 \\ \Sigma k - \Sigma l + \Sigma s &= 0 \end{aligned}\right\} \quad (11)$$

The principles thus derived shall prove to be of the greatest importance when we come to the types of contracts examined in the subsequent chapter.

If we wish to achieve coverage in as straightforward a manner as feasible, for e.g. two conditional purchases concluded at price B_1 and three constrained purchases concluded at price B_2, possibly availing ourselves of unconditional forward contracts and simple premium contracts, we are required to substitute in the system

$$\left.\begin{aligned} h_1 + k_1 &= 0 \\ h_2 + k_2 &= 0 \\ \Sigma l + h_1 + h_2 &= 0 \end{aligned}\right\} \quad (12)$$

2 into h_1, -3 into k_2, and to solve for h_1, k_1 and $\Sigma 1$; in this instance, we arrive at a unique solution given by

$$h_2 = 3, \; k_1 = -2, \; \Sigma l = -5,$$

viz. 3 conditional purchases at price B_2, 2 constrained purchases at B_1, and 5 unconditional forward sales at the current price, implying that the premia satisfy conditions (10).

56 Equation (10) is a general version of the put-call parity relation (4), and could be directly derived from it after appropriately defining α and M_j.

In the earlier example, in addition to the contracts we assumed to have been entered into, we could have made the decision to choose in arbitrary fashion some unconditional forward contracts, say, four unconditional forward purchases. This would give us the system (12) in the form

$$\begin{aligned} 2 + k_1 &= 0 \\ h_2 - 3 &= 0 \\ 4 + l + 2 + h_2 &= 0 \end{aligned}$$

yielding

$$h_2 = 3,\ k_1 = -2,\ l = -9$$

viz. the same overall composite as above.

Concerning the complemented system (11), we would proceed in similar manner, if, in addition, we desired to deal with stellage contracts.

Chapter III.

Repeat Contracts.

1. The Nature of Repeat Contracts[57]**.** We may speak of a conditional n-repeat purchase of a certain object, if the object is bought in the manner of an unconditional forward contract at the current price B, and it is bought only once, and, if the buyer has also made payment of a premium to be granted the right to demand the object n times at price $B + N$ on the date of delivery. Likewise, we may speak of a conditional n-repeat sale, if the quantity in question is sold in the manner of an unconditional forward contract only once at the current price B, and, if the seller has also made payment of a certain premium to be granted the right to make m times delivery of the same quantity at price $B - N$, or to refrain from delivery; it is clear that holders of such contracts will exercise their right, if, in the former case, the price exceeds $B + N$ on the day the contract is unwound, and in the latter case, if the price has declined below $B - N$.[58]

Furthermore, it is clear that the counterparties are faced with the exact converse of gains and losses to be expected by their opposites; therefore, constrained repeat contracts may be considered to be negative conditional repeat contracts; if u and v, respectively, represent certain quantities of conditional m-repeat purchases

[57] These contracts are also called options "to double", "to triple" etc. or just options "of more".

[58] Notice the following feature: the repeat premium N not only represents the price of the contract, but also determines the exercise price of the repeat-call $(B + N)$ and the repeat-put $(B - N)$, respectively. Bachelier (1900), pp. 55–57, also prices repeat-options ("options d'ordre n").

and conditional sales, respectively, then $-u$ and $-v$, respectively, represent an equal number of constrained repeat sales and constrained purchases of the same type.

Upon taking a closer look at the types of contracts described above, we learn at once that m-repeat purchases consist of an unconditional forward purchase entered into at price B, and m skewed conditional purchases effected at price $B + N$; likewise, m-repeat sales consist of an unconditional sale concluded at price B, and m skewed conditional sales commanding a price of $B - N$. Therefore, it may be expected that the premia N to be paid ensue from the relation

$$N = mP_1 \tag{1}$$

where P_1 represents the premia required for the simple skewed conditional purchase concluded at price $B + N$, and the simple skewed conditional sale effected at price $B - N$, respectively. Reminding ourselves of the relation

$$P_2 = P_1 + N$$

which, in this case, must hold with respect to the premia to be paid for the conditional sale concluded at price $B + N$, and the conditional purchase entered into at price $B - N$, we further arrive at

$$N = \frac{m}{m+1} P_2 \tag{2}$$

Introduction of the stellage premium

$$S_1 = P_1 + P_2$$

yields by dint of (1) and (2)

$$N = \frac{m}{m+2} S_1 \tag{3}$$

or, expressed by their tension T_1,

$$N = \frac{m}{2m+4} T_1 \tag{4}$$

Having developed these important relations which must prevail between the premia commanded by repeat contracts and skewed premium contracts, we would like to present some preliminary considerations of a very general nature regarding the transformations and combinations which may be expected to be prevalent among repeat contracts and contracts examined in earlier chapters.

Applying the principles derived in the previous chapter, it is immediately evident that coverage and equivalence, respectively, in regard of repeat contracts, which effectively are simple skewed premium contracts, are possible only upon incorporation of skewed contracts concluded upon the same basis; thus, coverage and derivation, respectively, of conditional repeat purchases can be effectuated only on the basis of premium contracts concluded at price $B + N$, while conditional repeat sales can be effectuated only on the basis of premium contracts entered into at price $B - N$. Hence, we recognise the impossibility of deriving especially conditional repeat purchases from two types of contracts, of which e.g. one consists of conditional repeat sales (so called notified contracts), while the other consists of any arbitrary contracts, notwithstanding the fact that textbooks, which are still recommended today, teach (and represent by means of horridly bowdlerised formulae) the very opposite.

Having said this, we shall endeavour to derive the equations which are necessary and sufficient for the purpose of engendering covered and equivalent systems, respectively, comprising the entirety of contracts introduced hitherto. It appears advisable to attempt to generalise the system of equations (5) encountered in the previous chapter in such a manner as to incorporate repeat contracts, thereby resolving the posed problem in its full generality.

In a first step, we shall consider conditional repeat purchases, that is, u in number. If we have u conditional repeat purchases, it is apparent that we will further require u unconditional forward purchases at price B and mu simple conditional purchases at price $B + N$; in order that the system of equations (5) explicitly represent these contracts too, we are merely required to substitute $h + mu$ into h, and $l + u$ into l, whereas k remains unchanged. Thus, we obtain

$$\left.\begin{aligned} h + k + 2s + mu &= 0 \\ k + s - l - u &= 0 \end{aligned}\right\} \tag{5}$$

However, in order to allow for v conditional repeat sales, we proceed thus: In the face of v conditional repeat sales, it is apparent that we require v unconditional forward sales at price B, and mv simple conditional sales at price $B - N$, hence we substitute into system (5) $k + m$ for k, and $l - v$ for l, while h remains unchanged; we obtain

$$\left.\begin{aligned} h + k + 2s + mv &= 0 \\ h + s + l - v &= 0 \end{aligned}\right\} \tag{5a}$$

In order to derive systems (5) and (5a), we have retained only two equations, namely those which are distinct for their simplicity. Thus, system (5) relates to those composites containing conditional repeat purchases, and it incorporates premium contracts, all of which having been concluded at price $B + N$; on the other hand, system (5a) relates to composites containing conditional repeat sales, and it consists of premium contracts traded at a price of $B - N$. The design of these separate systems is readily recognised and easy to remember. There is a recurrence in them of the law that permeates the entire theory, namely, that the sum of the conditional contracts must be equal to zero, as is required of the sum of conditional purchases and unconditional forward purchases, and as is required of the sum of conditional sales and unconditional forward sales.

These systems of simultaneous equations, each consisting of two equations in two unknowns, contain an infinite number of the composites and transformations which can be achieved by dint of the premium contracts hitherto made available on the stock exchange; it is always possible to choose any three types of contracts from which the remaining two types of contracts may be derived by an exceedingly easy calculation, the latter contracts (in conjunction with the arbitrarily chosen contracts) forming a perfectly covered system of contracts. In like manner, the derivation of equivalent systems may be continued ad infinitum. Thus, a certain type of contract may be derived in an infinite number of ways from the other four or, indeed from three of the other four; also, a composite of two contracts may be derived in an infinite number of ways from the remaining contracts. However, the task of deriving a composite of contracts from two other contracts allows for a unique solution; as is apparent, here we are dealing with the determination of two terms alone which evidently ensue in a unique way from the two equations given by systems (5) and (5a); the three remaining terms may either be given or some of them may be set to equal zero.

We shall proceed with the derivation of one contract from two other contracts. Each of the systems (5) and (5a) yields 30 derivations, respectively, since each of the five types of contracts

$$h,\ k,\ s,\ l,\ u \quad \text{resp.} \quad h,\ k,\ s,\ l,\ v$$

may be derived in six-fold manner by two of the four remaining terms. Considering the circumstance that the derivations which do not include repeat contracts may be looked upon as entirely homogenous, irrespective of whether they result from system (5) or system (5a), we do not obtain a total of 60 separate derivations, but only 48, since, in the absence of repeat contracts, the said composites may be arrived at in twelve-fold manner.

2. Direct Derivation of the Results Obtained in the Previous Section. It may be expedient to derive once again the systems of equations (5) and (5a) as well as the relations between the premia associated with repeat contracts and those associated with skewed premium contracts, applying to this purpose the method of arbitrary coefficients. If we are dealing with a conditional purchase involving an m-repeat contract with a premium equal to N, it is apparent that, if the price rises to $B + N + \varepsilon$ on the date when the contract is unwound, the gain is

$$N + \varepsilon + m\varepsilon - N \quad \text{viz.} \quad \varepsilon + m\varepsilon$$

since the right to demand m repetitions of delivery of the traded object at price $B + N$ will be exercised. However, if the price declines to $B + N - \eta$, the gain is equal to

$$N - \eta - N \quad \text{viz.} \quad - \eta$$

since what matters here is only the gain from the unconditional forward purchase and the loss of the paid premium N. If we have u contracts of this kind, the market outcomes under consideration would evidently result in gains

$$u(\varepsilon + m\varepsilon), \quad \text{resp.} \quad - u\eta$$

Proceeding in the same manner, regarding v conditional repeat contracts, in the presence of market outcomes $B - N + \varepsilon$, resp. $B - N - \eta$ on the date when the contracts are unwound, we would obtain successful results of the form

$$-v\varepsilon, \quad \text{resp.} \quad v(\eta + m\eta)$$

It is apparent that for the respective counterparties, gains would be the converse of the above results.

Considering u conditional purchases of m-repeat contracts, l unconditional forward pruchases at price B, h conditional purchases and k conditional sales at price $B + N$, a market outcome defined by $B + N + \varepsilon$ yields an overall gain of

$$G_1 = h(\varepsilon - P_1) - kP_2 + l(N + \varepsilon) + u(\varepsilon + m\varepsilon)$$

whereas a market outcome defined by $B + N - \eta$ yields an overall gain amounting to

$$G_2 = -hP_1 + k(\eta - P_2) + l(N - \eta) - u\eta$$

Simple rearrangement yields

$$\begin{aligned} G_1 &= \varepsilon(h + l + u + mu) - hP_1 - kP_2 + lN \\ G_2 &= \eta(k - l - u) - hP_1 - kP_2 + lN \end{aligned}$$

For the contracts in question to be fully covered, it is required, firstly, that the coefficients of ε and η be equal to zero, viz. equations

$$\left.\begin{aligned} h + l + u + mu &= 0 \\ h - l - u &= 0 \\ h + k + mu &= 0 \end{aligned}\right\} \tag{6}$$

must be satisfied, whereby the third equation results as the sum of the former two. In these equations, we encounter system (5), provided that we introduce stellage contracts into the system and retain only the last two equations.

Secondly, it is evident that the relation

$$-hP_1 - hP_2 + lN = 0$$

must be persistently satisfied; if we substitute the value resulting from (6) into h und l, we obtain

$$(k + mu)P_1 - kP_2 + N(k - u) = 0$$

or in reduced form,

$$k(P_1 - P_2 + N) + u(mP_1 - N) = 0$$

However, since regarding h, l, k and u there are only two equations independent of one another, two of the former variables are arbitrary; if we take k and u to be arbitrary, the coefficients associated with them must be equal to zero in the last equation, for which reason the relations

$$N = mP_1 \quad \text{resp.} \quad P_2 = P_1 + N$$

which we had posited a priori elsewhere, are encountered once again.

In a similar manner, we obtain system (5a), if we take v conditional repeat sales as our point of departure.

3. Examples. Consider coverage of a conditional 3-repeat purchase and two stellage sales by means of conditional purchases and conditional sales. As the repeat contract is concluded at price $B + N$, we know that the remainder of the premium contracts is supposed to have been entered into at that same price; we apply system (5), whereby we are required to substitute +1, −2, 3, and zero into u, s, m and−1, respectively. Thus, we obtain equations

$$\begin{aligned} h + k - 4 + 3 &= 0 \\ k - 2 - 1 &= 0 \end{aligned}$$

whose solution results in

$$k = 3 \quad \text{and} \quad h = -2$$

viz. three conditional sales and two constrained sales. Regarding the composite of contracts consisting of a conditional 3-repeat purchase, two stellage sales, three conditional purchases and two constrained purchases, we shall offer a numerical example to prove that the composite actually represents a covered system.

Consider a stock trading at a current price of 681; the premium of the 3-repeat contract is $12 \cdot 6$; the proper premium of the conditional purchase concluded at price $693 \cdot 6$ would be equal to the third part of $12 \cdot 6$, viz. $4 \cdot 2$, thus, the premium commanded by the conditional purchase concluded at price $693 \cdot 6$ would be equal to the sum $4 \cdot 2 + 12 \cdot 6$, viz. $16 \cdot 8$; therefore, the premium of the stellage contract concluded at the price $693 \cdot 6$ would be 21.

This having been established, we suppose a current price of price of $701 \cdot 5$ to prevail on the date the transaction is unwound and derive the gain from the entire operation:

α) Gain from repeat contracts. The adherent unconditional forward purchase yields a gain of 20 · 5, and since we exercise our right to demand threefold delivery of the stock at a price of 693 · 5: we enjoy an additional gain of 3 × 8, viz. 24. Subtracting the disbursed premium of 12 · 5, the repeat contract provides us with an effective gain of 32.

β) Gain from two stellage sales at a price of 693 · 5. As the counterparty is free to choose, he will proceed to effect the purchase, that is, he will purchase the stock twice. Hence, we shall incur a loss of 2 × 8, viz. 16; however, we have received the premium of 21 twice, for which reason we register a final gain of 26.

γ) Gain from three conditional sales. In this case, it is evident, we do not proceed to effect a sale. Hence, we incur a loss to the tune of three times the sales premium of 16 · 8, viz. 50 · 4 in total.

δ) Outcome of two constrained sales. Evidently, our counterparty will decide to make a purchase, for which reason, we incur a loss to the tune of 2 × 8, viz. 16; however, since we have twice received the premium of 4 · 2, we end up with a loss of 7 · 6.

The final result thus comprises a gain of 32 + 26, viz. 58, and a loss of 50·4 + 7·6, viz. 58; hence, in total, there is neither a gain nor a loss, just as it ought to be in a covered system. In the same manner, we could demonstrate the same result for any price below 681.

In conclusion, we shall fully spell out the derivation of a conditional m-repeat purchase from any other two of the contracts that we have examined. To this purpose, in system (5), we are merely required to substitute −1 into u, the rationale of which having been already explained repeatedly, simply suppress the contracts that do not apply, and solve the equations thus obtained for the two remaining terms; in this way, we find:

α) Derivation of a m-repeat contract from conditional purchases and conditional sales. In equations (5) we sustitute $u = -1, l = 0, s = 0$, and obtain

$$\begin{aligned} h + k - m &= 0 \\ k + 1 &= 0 \end{aligned}$$

hence, $k = -1$ and $h = m + 1$, viz. the conditional purchase of an m-repeat contract is equivalent to a simple constrained sale and "$m + 1$" simple conditional purchases of the same objects.

β) Ditto – conditional purchases and stellage contracts. Substituting in the system of equations (5) $u = -1, l = 0$ and $k = 0$, we find

$$\begin{aligned} h + 2s - m &= 0 \\ s + 1 &= 0 \end{aligned}$$

or in solved form, $s = -1$ and $h = m + 2$, viz. a stellage sale and "$m + 2$" simple conditional purchases.

γ) Ditto – conditional purchases and unconditional forward contracts. Substituting $u = -l, s = 0, h = 0$ and solving the equations

$$h - m = 0$$
$$-l + 1 = 0$$

we obtain, in accordance with the definition of a repeat contract, and therefore self-evidently $h = m$ and $l = 1$, viz. an unconditional forward contract and m simple conditional purchases.

δ) The derivation from conditional purchases and stellage contracts entails substitutions $u = -1, h = 0$ and $l = 0$ and, thus, equations

$$k + 2s - m = 0$$
$$k + s + 1 = 0$$

and, thus, $s = m+1$ and $k = -(m+2)$, which represent "$m+1$" stellage purchases and "$m + 2$" constrained purchases.

ε) Derivation of the repeat contract from conditional sales and unconditional forward contracts entails substitutions $u = -1, h = 0$ and $s = 0$ the system

$$k - m = 0$$
$$k - l + 1 = 0$$

from which result $k = m$ and $l = m + 1$, viz. m conditional sales and "$m + 1$" unconditional forward sales.

ζ) Finally, derivation of the repeat contract from stellage contracts and unconditional forward contracts is accomplished by substituting $u = -1, h = 0$ and $k = 0$ and solving equations

$$2s - m = 0$$
$$s - l + 1 = 0$$

which yields $s = m/2$ and $l = m/2 + 1$, giving us $m/2$ stellage purchases and "$m/2 + 1$" unconditional purchases.

Derivation of the conditional repeat sale is accomplished in quite similar vein by using system (5a).

Before concluding the first part of the present work, we would like to offer the following remark: He who plays for a stake at the stock exchange, yet wishes not to be in danger of inordinate loss, should endeavour conclusion of only such contracts as are covered and will be found in accordance with the principles laid down in the preceding chapters. If in the pursuit of these transactions we succeed in concluding contracts at prices more favourable than the prices supposed in our equations, anything accomplished in that way will evidently bring about unendangered gains.[59]

[59] This is an explicit statement about the feasibiliy of riskless return opportunities if contracts can be purchased at better terms than those derived from "covered" positions. Combining this insight with the fact that such a position requires no initial capital directly leads to the notion of arbitrage gains.

Part II.

Higher Order Analyses.

Chapter I.

Derivation of General Equations.

1. Introduction. In the first part of the present treatise, we examined the interdependence of premium contracts exclusively, that is to say, we did not pay attention to the fundamental issue of the appropriate size of the premia paid in connection with the disparate contracts; this latter task, which is distinctly set apart from the inquiry pursued hitherto[60], has been left to the second part of this modest work.

The tools which are needed to tackle the problem extend beyond the limits of elementary mathematics, unfortunately; only by applying the theory of probability and the integral calculus will it be possible to cast light upon the question that is so important both from a theoretical and a practical point of view, and to arrive at conclusions which perhaps yield reliable points of reference for those closing deals predicated upon the contracts in question.

2. Probability of Market Fluctuations. It is reasonable to suppose that the price prevailing on the date the deals are unwound will generally not coincide with the current price B, rather being likely to be subject to more or less significant fluctuations above or below that value; it is equally evident that the causes of these fluctuations, and hence the laws governing them, elude reckoning[61]. Under the circumstances, we shall at best be entitled to refer to the likelihood of a certain fluctuation x, in the absence of a clearly defined and reasoned mathematical expression; instead, we shall have to be content with the introduction of an unknown function $f(x)$, concerning which we initially rely upon the modest assumption that it represents a finite and continuous function of the fluctuations enclosed within the interval under inspection.

---

[60] The separation between the derivation of "relative" pricing relations whithout distributional assumptions about the underlying (e.g. the put-call-parity) and "absolute" pricing results which are based on specific stochastic assumptions is a major methodological feature of this Treatise; it is typically credited to Merton's (1973) classic paper.

[61] The statement that the "causes" of the future price flucuations (i.e. their deviations from the current forward price) and the "laws governing them" is closely related to a similar statement in Bachelier's (1900) text, p. 1. However, Bachelier's achievement is to uncover the specific probability distribution (i.e. the Normal) implied by his assumption that the market price is governed by a random walk process in continuous time. Bronzin does not make assumptions about the dynamics of the underlying market price anywhere.

That said, we express the probability that the price prevailing on the date the transaction is unwound will be between $B + x$ and $B + x + dx$, or put differently, that fluctuations above B will assume a value between x und $x + dx$, by the product

$$f(x)\,dx \tag{1}$$

regarding fluctuations below B, we suppose, in order to accommodate the highest level of generality, a different function $f_1(x)$, so that the likelihood, with which fluctuations between x and $x + dx$ may be expected to be below B, will be given by the product

$$f_1(x)\,dx \tag{1a}$$

at any rate, in the presence of zero fluctuation, the values of the function must be equal for both functions, which is captured by the equation

$$f(0) = f_1(0) \tag{2}$$

From the elementary probabilities thus defined, we can derive integrals for the finite probabilities that fluctuations between a and b occur above resp. below B, viz. that the market price on the date when the deals are unwound will be between $B + a$ and $B + a + b$ resp. $B - a$ and $B - a - b$, namely

$$w = \int_a^b f(x)\,dx \quad \text{resp.} \quad w_1 = \int_a^b f_1(x)\,dx \tag{3}$$

introducing ω and ω_1 to denote the largest conjectured fluctuations above resp. below B, we obtain, as the total probability that the price will rise above B, the integral

$$W = \int_0^\omega f(x)\,dx$$

whereas the total probability of a price decline is given by

$$W_1 = \int_0^{\omega_1} f_1(x)\,dx$$

Since probabilities W and W_1 must add up to denote certainty, there will prevail a relation between the latter integrals in the form of

$$\int_0^\omega f(x)\,dx + \int_0^{\omega_1} f(x)\,dx = 1 \tag{4}$$

In the same manner, functions

$$F(x) = \int_x^\omega f(x)\,dx \quad \text{resp.} \quad F_1(x) = \int_x^{\omega_1} f_1(x)\,dx \tag{5}$$

represent the total probability that fluctuations above resp. below B on the date when the deals are unwound will exceed x; shortly, we shall learn just what an important role these very functions assume in subsequent considerations.

Consider a horizontal line, upon which we plot to the right of point 0 market fluctuations above B, and to the left of point 0 fluctuations below B. Further, at the respective endpoints, we draw perpendicular lines which represent the values of the functions $f(x)$ resp. $f_1(x)$; in this fashion, we engender two continuous curves, C and C_1, which we shall suitably term 'curves of fluctuation probabilities' (see Fig. 23); the surface, between the corresponding parts of the curve and the horizontal line, enclosed within any two ordinates

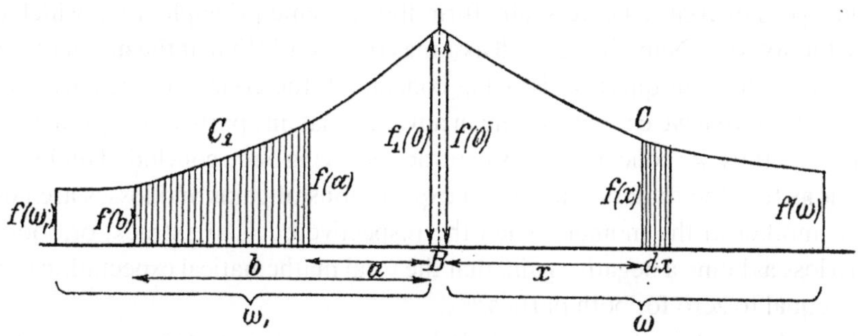

Fig. 23.

$f(a)$ and $f(b)$, evidently represents the value of the integral (3), viz. the total probability that fluctuations at the date when the deals are unwound will lie within the supposed limits a and b.

3. Mathematical Expectations Due to Price Fluctuations. In the presence of the market outcomes lying between $B + x$ and $B + x + dx$ whose probability is expressed by $f(x)\,dx$, if we may expect a gain in the amount of G, then the product

$$Gf(x)\,dx$$

represents the so-called mathematical expectation of the gain, viz. that value which under the prevailing conditions it is most plausible to consider the actual gain. Further, the integral

$$i = \int_a^b Gf(x)\,dx \tag{6}$$

provides the total mathematical expectation of the gain with respect to the supposed limits, whereas the integral

$$J = \int_0^\omega Gf(x)\,dx \tag{7}$$

ranging from price B to the highest attainable value $B + \omega$, serves to determine the total value of the gain to be expected in the face of an increase in price. Analogous meaning can be attached to the expressions

$$i_1 = \int_a^b G f_1(x)\, dx \tag{6a}$$

respectively

$$J_1 = \int_0^{\omega_1} G f_1(x)\, dx \tag{7a}$$

which are applicable for the purpose of gauging gains in the face of declining prices.

Prior to examining the general relationships which prevail with regard to the various types of contracts, we shall affirm the supreme principle upon which our entire theory rests. Namely, we shall assume consistently that at the moment when any contract here in question is being concluded, the counterparties are facing equal odds, so that we cannot assume in advance that any party will enjoy a gain or incur a loss; thus, we conceive of any contract as having been concluded under such conditions that the total mathematical expectations of gains and losses are equal to one another at the moment when the respective deals are struck, or, looking upon a loss as being a negative gain, that the total mathematical expectation of the gain is equal to zero for both parties.[62]

We shall refer to a contract concluded under these circumstances as complying with the condition of fairness.

4. Unconditional Forward Contracts. If an unconditional forward purchase has been concluded at price B, then, as we know, in the presence of a market outcome defined by $B + x$, a gain of x is to be expected, while in the presence of a market outcome defined by $B - x$, a loss of equal size may be expected; thus, we have the elementary mathematical expectations

$$x f(x)\, dx \quad \text{resp.} \quad - x f_1(x)\, dx$$

which, integrated over the range from 0 to the extreme values ω und ω_1, yields the total gain

$$G = \int_0^{\omega} x f(x)\, dx$$

and the total loss, respectively,

$$V = \int_0^{\omega_1} x f_1(x)\, dx$$

[62] This "zero expected profit" condition is weaker than the no-arbitrage condition. Interestingly, it is the same condition which is also imposed by Bachelier (1900), pp. 32–34. Notice that B. is well aware of the importance of this general valuation principle – he calls it the "supreme principle upon which our entire theory rests".

in accordance with the principle of fairness, these values are to be considered equal, providing us with the relation

$$\int_0^{\omega} xf(x)\,dx = \int_0^{\omega_1} xf_1(x)\,dx \tag{8}$$

Needless to say, we would arrive at the same result when considering an unconditional forward sale.

5. Normal Premium Contracts. In the presence of a conditional purchase concluded at price B and involving a premium P, we know that a market outcome defined by $B + x$ yields a gain of $x - P$, whereas a market outcome defined by $B - x$ yields a loss P; thus, concerning the market outcomes under consideration and the elementary mathematical expectations, respectively, we obtain

$$(x - P)f(x)\,dx \quad \text{and} \quad -Pf_1(x)\,dx$$

and hence, concerning the contract, a total gain of

$$G = \int_0^{\omega} (x - P)f(x)\,dx - \int_0^{\omega_1} Pf_1(x)\,dx$$

which in accordance with our principle, is to be equated to zero. Initially, we find

$$0 = \int_0^{\omega} xf(x)\,dx - P\int_0^{\omega} f(x)\,dx - P\int_0^{\omega_1} Pf_1(x)\,dx$$

and further, according to equation (5),

$$P = \int_0^{\omega} xf(x)\,dx \tag{9}$$

This relation is immediately evident, giving expression to the principle according to which the premium to be paid must be equal to the mathematical expectation of all favourable outcomes resulting from an increase in price[63]; after all, it is by disbursing the premium that one acquires the right to take advantage of gains from any increase of the price above B.

Examination of the conditional sale would provide us with the analogous equation

$$P' = \int_0^{\omega_1} xf_1(x)\,dx \tag{9a}$$

[63] Equation (9) is a conditional or truncated expectation. In modern usage $f(x)$ would be interpreted as pricing function representing state (or Arrow-Debreu) prices assigned to the continuum of market states (prices).

it follows, according to (8)

$$P = P' \tag{10}$$

the equation which asserted itself already in Part One as being an indispensable prerequisite for the possibility of accomplishing coverage in normal contracts.

6. Skewed Premium Contracts. Considering a conditional purchase concluded at price $B + M$ and involving premium P_1, it is apparent from the subsequent schema

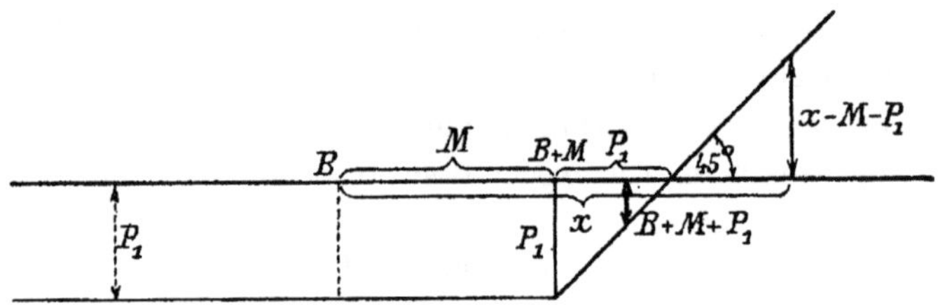

Fig. 24.

that we may expect a gain only in the presence of market fluctuations above B and larger than $M + P_1$, and that gain will amount to $x - M - P_1$, whereby, as always, fluctuation x is determined relative to B; corresponding to fluctuation x is the value of an elementary mathematical expectation

$$(x - M - P_1)f(x)\,dx$$

consequently, the entire expectation of a gain associated with this contract is represented by the integral

$$G = \int_{M+P_1}^{\omega} (x - M - P_1)f(x)\,dx$$

By contrast, prices below $B + M + P_1$ result in a loss, namely: given fluctuation x, in the area ranging from $B + M$ to $B + M + P_1$, where fluctuations enclosed within M and $M + P_1$ may occur, the size of the loss is defined by $M + P_1 - x$, so that its corresponding elementary mathematical expectation is

$$(M + P_1 - x)f(x)\,dx$$

The total loss in this first area is thus

$$V_1 = \int_{M}^{M+P_1} (M + P_1 - x)f(x)\,dx$$

In the second area, ranging from B to $B + M$, we have, for any fluctuation x, a loss P_1, hence an elementary loss

$$P_1 f(x)\,dx$$

and a total loss in the amount of

$$V_2 = \int_0^M P_1 f(x)\,dx$$

In the third area, viz. pertaining to fluctuations below B, we also have, for any arbitrary fluctuation x, a loss P_1, however, the probability here being $f_1(x)dx$; therefore, the elementary mathematical expectation of this loss is

$$P_1 f_1(x)\,dx$$

and thus, the total loss arising within this area is

$$V_3 = \int_0^{\omega_1} P_1 f_1(x)\,dx$$

According to our principle, the relation

$$G = V_1 + V_2 + V_3$$

must prevail; a simple reduction of the relevant integrals initially yields

$$\int_M^{\omega} (x - M - P_1) f(x)\,dx = P_1 \int_0^{\omega} f(x)\,dx - P_1 \int_M^{\omega} f(x)\,dx + P_1 \int_0^{\omega_1} f_1(x)\,dx$$

and further

$$\int_M^{\omega} (x - M) f(x)\,dx - P_1 \int_M^{\omega} f(x)\,dx = P_1 \left[\int_0^{\omega} f(x)\,dx + \int_0^{\omega_1} f_1(x)\,dx \right] - \\ - P_1 \int_M^{\omega} f(x)\,dx$$

and finally, in accordance with equation (5),

$$P_1 = \int_M^{\omega} (x - M) f(x)\,dx \tag{11}$$

It is evident a priori that this expression corresponds to P_1; after all, it is by disbursement of premium P_1 that one acquires the right to take advantage of any price increase above $B + M$; premium P_1 being in conformance with the principle of fairness, that premium then must be equal to the mathematical expectation of any gains associated with the range of price increases under consideration, which is precisely the purport of formula (11)[64]

For $M = 0$, expression (11) approaches the expression corresponding to the normal premium, for $M = \omega$, however, we evidently obtain,

$$P_1 = 0 \tag{12}$$

In order to derive an expression corresponding to premium P_2 specifically associated with a conditional sale at price $B + M$, we are immediately inspired by the conception that the latter must be equated to the mathematical expectation of the gains that may arise from the contract; a look at the below schema

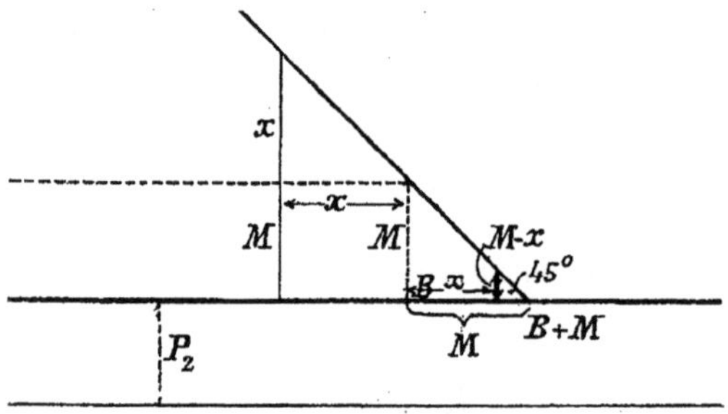

Fig. 25.

reveals at once that the area of gains must be divided into two parts, namely one ranging from B to $B + M$, and another ranging from B to $B - \omega_1$; concerning the former part, gain $M - x$, having probability $f(x)dx$, corresponds to fluctuation x, and hence to an elementary mathematical expectation defined thus

$$(M - x) f(x)\, dx$$

which, integrated over the values ranging from 0 to M, yields the total mathematical expectation of gains in this part of the area, viz.

$$G_1 = \int_0^M (M - x) f(x)\, dx$$

In the second part, gain $M + x$, having probability $f_1(x)dx$, corresponds to fluctuation x below B, viz. we have an elementary expectation defined by

$$(M + x) f_1(x)\, dx$$

Taking the integral over the values ranging from 0 to ω_1, we obtain the total mathematical expectation of the gain in the second part, in which manner we arrive at the relation

$$P_2 = \int_0^M (M - x) f(x)\, dx + \int_0^{\omega_1} (M + x) f_1(x)\, dx$$

64 Equation (11), a generalization of equation (6), is the key option valuation equation of this Chapter.

We then alter the right-hand side to assume the form

$$P_2 = \int_0^{\omega} (M-x)f(x)\,dx - \int_M^{\omega} (M-x)f(x)\,dx + \int_0^{\omega_1} Mf_1(x)\,dx + \int_0^{\omega_1} xf_1(x)\,dx$$

that is

$$P_2 = M\int_0^{\omega} f(x)\,dx - \int_0^{\omega} xf(x)\,dx + P_1 + M\int_0^{\omega_1} f_1(x)\,dx + \int_0^{\omega_1} xf_1(x)\,dx$$

from which, applying familiar equations, follows immediately the remarkable formula

$$P_2 = P_1 + M \tag{13}$$

In this fashion we have finally established the full justification and exceptional importance of this equation, which we had already arrived at in Part One of our treatise, where it had been discovered to represent an indispensable precondition for efforts to accomplish coverage with regard to skewed contracts; for now the equation no longer appears to have the mere character of an artificial condition, but proves to originate in the unassailable principle of the reciprocity of equivalent services[65].

For $M = 0$ one obtains once again $P_2 = P_1 = P$, however, for $M = \omega$, according to eqation (12), we have

$$P_2 = \omega \tag{14}$$

Finally, it is not necessary to examine at greater length the manner in which stellage premia, being the sum of P_1 and P_2, as we know, are formed in arbitrary and special cases.

Pursuing much the same train of thought, we find the premium of a conditional sale at price $B - M$ to be represented by the expression

$$P_1' = \int_M^{\omega_1} (x - M)f_1(x)\,dx$$

and the relation between the premia of the conditional purchase and the conditional sale

$$P_2' = P_1' + M$$

7. Repeat Contracts. Revisiting a conditional m-repeat purchase, we know from earlier considerations that gain is represented by $(m + 1)\,\varepsilon$, while loss is represented by the simple η, whereby ε and η denote market fluctuations above and

[65] Apparently, Bronzin perceives the restatement of the put-call parity in equation (13) to be more rigorously founded than the derivation in Part I, Chapter I (equation 4). In fact, both derivations are equivalent.

below $B + N$, respectively; the graphical representation is given in the below schema

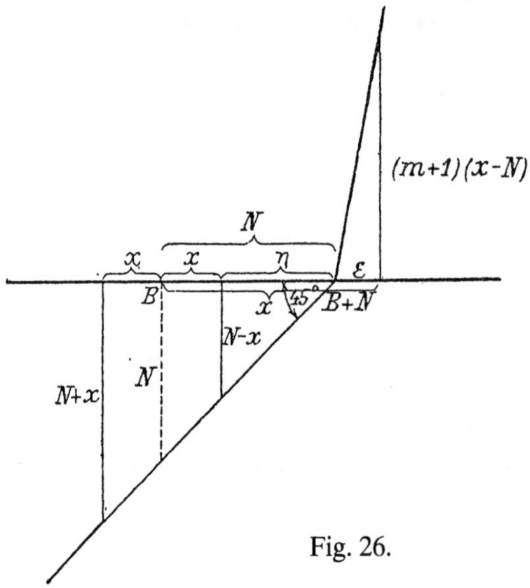

Fig. 26.

The area of gain extends from $B + N$ to $B + \omega$; the latter, in this area, corresponding to the elementary mathematical expectation

$$(m + 1)(x - N)f(x)\,dx$$

resulting in a total mathematical expectation of the form

$$G = \int_N^{\omega} (m + 1)(x - N)f(x)\,dx$$

Loss is divided into two areas; from B to $B + N$ we have an elementary mathematical expectation of

$$(N - x)f(x)\,dx$$

thus, in total a loss given by

$$V_1 = \int_0^N (N - x)f(x)\,dx$$

from B to $B - \omega_1$ on the other hand, we have

$$(N + x)f_1(x)\,dx$$

representing the elementary mathematical expectation, and hence

$$V_2 = \int_0^{\omega_1} (N + x)f_1(x)\,dx$$

representing the total loss occurring in the area. Manipulation of equation

$$G = V_1 + V_2$$

initially yields

$$m \int_N^\omega (x - N) f(x)\, dx + \int_N^\omega (x - N) f(x)\, dx = \int_0^\omega (N - x) f(x)\, dx - \\ - \int_N^\omega (N - x) f(x)\, dx + \int_0^{\omega_1} (N + x) f_1(x)\, dx$$

and further

$$m \int_N^\omega (x - N) f(x)\, dx = N \left[\int_0^\omega f(x)\, dx + \int_0^{\omega_1} f_1(x)\, dx \right] - \int_0^\omega x f(x)\, dx + \\ + \int_0^{\omega_1} x f_1(x)\, dx$$

or, due to familiar equations,

$$N = m \int_N^\omega (x - N) f(x)\, dx \tag{15}$$

in which fashion we arrive once again at the relationship affirmed in Part I

$$N = m P_1$$

In a similar vein, treatment of a conditonal m-repeat sale evinces the analogous relationship

$$N' = m \int_{N'}^{\omega_1} (x - N') f_1(x)\, dx \tag{15a}$$

As regards further relationships pertaining to stellage premia etc., refer to Chapter III of Part I.

8. Differential Equations Pertaining to Premia P_1 and P_2, resp., and Function $f(x)$. The integral

$$P_1 = \int_M^\omega (x - M) f(x)\, dx$$

as we know, represents, on account of the assumption pertaining to $f(x)$, a continuous function of the sole variable M, so that we can differentiate the integral with respect to M. Recalling the general formulae

$$U = \int_{x_0}^X f(x\alpha)\, dx, \quad \frac{\delta U}{\delta X} = f(X\alpha), \quad \frac{\delta U}{\delta x_0} = -f(x_0\alpha)$$

and

$$\frac{\delta U}{\delta \alpha} \int_{x_0}^{X} \frac{\delta f(x_1 \alpha)}{\delta \alpha} dx$$

respectively, which are to be applied when differentiating with respect to the limits[66] or the parameters under the integral sign, differentiation of our integral with respect to M (as the latter appears both in the lower limit and the function under the integral sign) evidently yields

$$\frac{\delta P_1}{\delta M} = -(M - M) f(M) + \int_{M}^{\omega} -f(x)\, dx$$

viz. the remarkable relationship

$$\frac{\delta P_1}{\delta M} = -\int_{M}^{\omega} f(x)\, dx = -F(M) \tag{16}$$

whereas a second differentiation yields a differential equation which does not contain any integrals at all[67]:

$$\frac{\delta^2 P_1}{\delta M^2} = f(M) \tag{17}$$

Conversely, given

$$\frac{\delta P_1}{\delta M} = -F(M) \tag{18}$$

integration yields

$$P_1 = -\int F(M)\, dM + C \tag{19}$$

in which way the determination of P_1 as a function of M can be accomplished in a fashion quite different compared to the direct evaluation of its integral, which in turn may be of great advantage, depending upon which form function $f(x)$ takes[68]. The constant C can be readily derived due to the condition requiring that for $M = \omega$ the premium P_1 must disappear, as equation (12) suggests.

Thus, with respect to P_2 we find, based upon equation

$$P_2 = M + P_1$$

66 This is typically known as the Leibniz Rule.

67 Since $f(M)$ is a probability density and positive by definition, it follows from equation (17) that the relationship between the moneyness M (and thus, the exercise price) and the option price P_1 is convex; see Figure 27 below.

68 The restatement of option prices in terms of an indefinite integral with respect to the moneyness (or exercise price) is indeed a remarkable finding. The applications, and simplifications, derived from it are shown in Chapter II of this Treatise: see e.g. the derivation at the end of section 3, or the alternative derivation of (43) subsequent to equation (44).

and an initial differentiation

$$\frac{\delta P_2}{\delta M} = 1 - \int_M^\omega f(x)\,dx \tag{16a}$$

while, based on a second differentiation, we obtain

$$\frac{\delta^2 P_2}{\delta M^2} = f(M) = \frac{\delta^2 P_1}{\delta M^2}$$

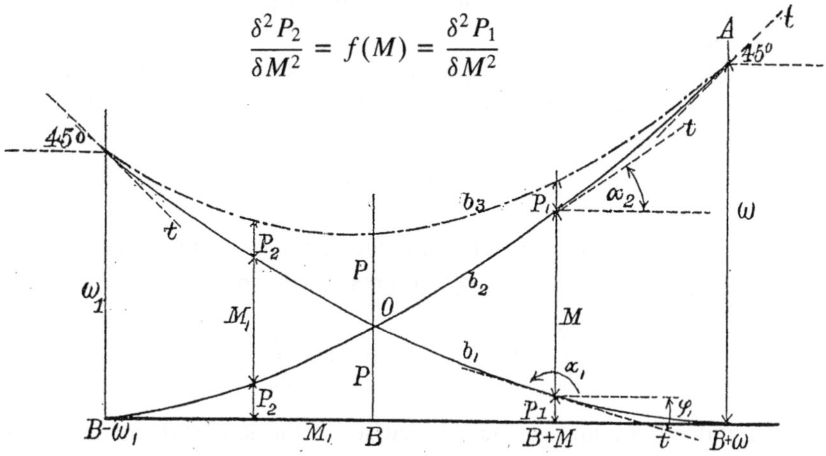

Fig. 27.

Using the general results established hitherto[69], if we attempt to design a graphical representation of premia P_1 and P_2 as functions of the independent variable M, we obtain two curves C_1 and C_2, respectively[70]; the former being characterised by ordinates which become smaller as M increases, the latter, by contrast, featuring ordinates which become larger as M increases. There is another attribute salient to the curves, in that the tangents of the angles φ_1 and α_2, which are equal to the differential quotients $\frac{-\delta P_1}{\delta M}$ and $\frac{\delta P_2}{\delta M}$, represent the entire range of probabilities that the price on the date when the contracts are unwound will rise above or fall below $B + M$. At point A, the curve C_2 is at an angle of 45° relative to the abscissa, while at point $B + \omega$, C_1 evinces a trigonometric tangent equal to zero. Curves C_1 and C_2 intersect at point 0, that is, at a height equal to the normal premium P;

[69] The insight that the function $f(x = M)$ can be recovered from second derivatives (the convexity) of call and put option prices with respect to the moneyness M, is fundamental. It can also be found in Bachelier (1900), p. 51, however, without an interpretation or discussion. This insight is particularly interesting if, as stated in an earlier footnote, the probability function is interpreted as "pricing" density. This relationship has been made explicit in an unpublished paper by Black (1974) and later, by Banz / Miller (1978) and Breeden / Litzenberger (1978).

[70] Unfortunately, the shortcuts C_1, C_2 (and C_3) are erreoneously denoted by b_1, b_2 (and b_3) in Figure 27. The downward sloping curve b_1 (respectively, the upward sloping curve b_2) refers to the call (put) price.

at which point, the trigonometric tangents of the angles which we are concerned with assume values

$$\int_0^{\omega} f(x)\,dx \quad \text{resp.} \quad 1 - \int_0^{\omega} f(x)\,dx$$

representing, quite evidently, the total probabilities of an increase or a decline in price, respectively.

Analogous considerations apply to contracts concluded at $B - M$. To the left of B, we find that P_2 assumes the role of P_1: To the left of 0, curve C_2 forms an angle with the tangent

$$\int_0^{\omega_1} f_1(x)\,dx$$

gradually approximating the abscissa, eventually to result, at point $B - \omega_1$, in a gradient equal to zero; continuity requires equality of

$$\int_0^{\omega_1} f_1(x)\,dx \quad \text{and} \quad 1 - \int_0^{\omega} f(x)\,dx$$

which, indeed, we find verified. Likewise, to the left of 0, curve C_1 continues, forming angles with tangents

$$1 - \int_0^{\omega_1} f_1(x)\,dx$$

until reaching height ω_1 above $B - \omega_1$ at a slope of 45° relative to the abscissa; again, the requirement of continuity demands the familiar relation

$$\int_0^{\omega} f(x)\,dx = 1 - \int_0^{\omega_1} f_1(x)\,dx$$

Using curves C_1 and C_2, we can readily construct curve C_3 which represents stellage premia as a function of M; on account of the familiar equation

$$S_1 = P_1 + P_2$$

we extend, by the ordinate of C_1, an arbitrary number of ordinates above curve C_2 to obtain an arbitrary number of points on curve C_3; the first derivative of S_1 with respect to M being

$$\frac{\delta S_1}{\delta M} = \frac{\delta P_1}{\delta M} + \frac{\delta P_2}{\delta M}$$

viz. owing to (16) and (16a),

$$\frac{\delta S_1}{\delta M} = 1 - 2\int_M^{\omega} f(x)\,dx \tag{20}$$

the second derivative, however, being

$$\frac{\delta^2 S_1}{\delta M^2} = 2f(M) \tag{21}$$

From (20) we learn that, as M becomes larger, the stellage premium increases or decreases, respectively, depending upon the term

$$1 - 2\int_M^\omega f(x)\,dx$$

being positive or negative; if the term is equal to zero, which holds true for values of M which satisfy equation

$$\int_M^\omega f(x)\,dx = {}^1/_2 \tag{22}$$

an extremum occurs, that is, a minimum, as the second differential quotient is positive according to (21). Of course, this minimum can occur only in the vicinity of B, because the integral $\int_M^\omega f(x)\,dx$ gets smaller as M increases, whilst on the other hand its largest value will differ very little from one half of unity.

In the first part of the treatise, we had drawn the conclusion from a graphical representation that a skewed stellage contract will always be more expensive than a normal stellage contract of the same size: the above result, however, reveals that this conclusion should be regarded as being somewhat premature. Indeed, the minimum of S_1 coincides with the current price B only, if the integral

$$\int_0^\omega f(x)\,dx$$

is supposed to correspond to one half of unity, viz. if increases and decreases in price, respectively, were subject to the same total probability. Since, however, in reality this is likely to be the case in large measure, for we may suppose equal chances for rising and declining prices, we therefore uphold the practical conclusion that the premium adhering to the normal stellage contract should always be deemed lower than the one associated with an arbitrary skewed stellage contract.

It will be interesting to see whether these results can be drawn from alternative, more immediate considerations. Evidently, the premium adhering to a normal stellage contract is given by

$$S = 2\int_0^\omega x f(x)\,dx,$$

whereas, the premium associated with a skewed stellage contract takes the form

$$S_1 = M + 2\int_M^\omega (x - M) f(x)\,dx$$

Therefore, their difference is

$$\delta = M + 2\int_0^{\omega} (x - M) f(x)\,dx - 2\int_0^{M} (x - M) f(x)\,dx - 2\int_0^{\omega} x f(x)\,dx$$

or

$$\delta = M + 2\int_0^{\omega} x f(x)\,dx - 2M\int_0^{M} f(x)\,dx + 2\int_0^{M} (M - x) f(x)\,dx - \\ - 2\int_0^{\omega} x f(x)\,dx$$

and finally

$$\delta = M\left[1 - 2\int_0^{\omega} f(x)\,dx\right] + 2\int_0^{M} (M - x) f(x)\,dx \tag{23}$$

The second part on the right-hand side of this equation is essentially positive, since the function under the integral sign is positive as regards the limits envisaged; however, as the first part may turn out to be negative and possibly also larger than the second part, we may have to expect negative δ, which characterises skewed stellage contracts as less expensive than normal stellage contracts. Only under the condition that

$$\int_0^{\omega} f(x)\,dx = {}^1\!/_2$$

which concurs with the condition earlier mentioned, do we have an essentially positive value for δ, viz.

$$\delta = 2\int_0^{M} (M - x) f(x)\,dx \tag{23a}$$

on which specific grounds a skewed stellage contract in actual fact always commands a higher premium than a normal stellage contract.

Chapter II.

Application of General Equations to Satisfy Certain Assumptions Relating to Function $f(x)$.

1. Introduction. In the course of the subsequent examination, we shall always suppose one and the same function to apply to fluctuations both above and below B, viz.

$$f(x) = f_1(x)$$

implying firstly the corollary whereby due to equation

$$\int_0^{\omega} xf(x)\,dx = \int_0^{\omega_1} xf_1(x)\,dx$$

equality prevails among the largest values to be obtained above and below B, viz.

$$\omega = \omega_1$$

Moreover, it follows that the integrals

$$\int_0^{\omega} f(x)\,dx \quad \text{and} \quad \int_0^{\omega_1} f_1(x)\,dx$$

become equal, so that, their sum being equal to unity, the relationship

$$\int_0^{\omega} f(x)\,dx = {}^1/_2$$

will be satisfied consistently; in this manner, B represents the most probable market outcome on the date when the contract is unwound[71], which, incidentally, is plausible on a priori grounds. After all, we learn from earlier formulae that the premia of the conditional purchase above B and the conditional sale below B (and, conversely, when these contracts display equal skewedness) must be equal, which apparently holds perfectly true regarding repeat contracts, if these refer to the same multiple.

[71] Interpreting the forward price as the "most likely" market price, plus the assumption of symmetry $f(x) = f_1(x)$, implies that the forward price B is the expected market price. In the languague of modern option pricing, this is only true under the risk-neutral probability density. In terms of the true (or statistical) probability density, this would define risk premia away. Notice however that this implication, i.e. the association between the forward price and the expected future market price, is irrelevant for Bronzin's subsequent analysis. All that matters is that the expected value of the densities is substituted by a preference-free "market" parameter (the forward price) – independent of subjective expectations.

The supposition is not met in reality; after all, an unlimited price increase is conceivable, while it is apparent that a price decrease can proceed only to the point where the object has lost its entire value, which corresponds to a fluctuation below B not larger than B[72]. However, since such instances may be ruled out, and fluctuations can be thought of as following a more or less regular pattern, oscillating rather moderately around B in general, we may confidently feel entitled to accept the supposition and look forward with assurance to the results derived from it.

As concerns the form which function $f(x)$ takes, we are confronted with formidable difficulties. We simply do not possess general leads helping us to calculate the irregular fluctuations of market outcomes for the variegated objects of value; at best, we can determine from statistical observations[73] the probability for any given object of value, that is, the probability with which the price, say, in a month's time, will achieve or even exceed a fluctuation x which we might care to single out; if this is accomplished g times in m instances, the said probability is evidently obtained by dividing g by m.

If we perform these calculations for the series of fluctuations

$$x_1, x_2, \ldots x_{n-1}, x_n$$

we obtain the corresponding series of probabilities

$$\frac{g_1}{m_1}, \frac{g_2}{m_2}, \ldots \frac{g_{n-1}}{m_{n-1}}, \frac{g_n}{m_n}$$

apparently, these total probabilities represent nothing more than the respective values of the integral

$$F(x) = \int_x^{\omega} f(x)\,dx = \frac{g}{m}$$

hence, by performing the calculations referred to above, we may arrive at a series of values

$$F(x_1), F(x_2), \ldots F(x_{n-1}), F(x_n)$$

relating to the function $F(x)$. We are free to represent this entire observational material by applying an empirical analytical equation for $F(x)$, namely by using the least squares method to determine those values of the constants which, upon

[72] Unlike Bachelier, Bronzin recognizes that market prices can typically not take negative values and hence, the probability density should be modelled asymmetrically. This was originally accomplished in the option pricing literature in Sprenkle's thesis (reprinted in Cootner 1964), where a lognormal density is assumed. Of course, Bronzin's subsequent justification by trivializing the problem is not very convincing.

[73] The subsequent analysis is particularly interesting, because it is the only empirical part of this Treatise. The author describes a least-squares approach in determining the functional form of $F(M)$ to be used in the modified valuation equation (19).

substitution of $x_1, x_2, \ldots x_n$, are suited to reproducing most faithfully the values $F(x_1)$, $F(x_2)$, $\ldots$ $F(x_n)$. By this procedure, it would be possible to determine for any arbitrary object of value its function $F(x)$ the latter being quite useful, and tying in with relation

$$\frac{\delta P_1}{\delta M} = -F(M)$$

it would allow us to answer any question in a convenient and reliable manner. Of course, ω, the largest fluctuations to be expected, must equally be inferred from observational data.

We shall not perform this laborious task; instead we will content ourselves with the selection of a specific form of the function $f(x)$ whereby the constants that may exist will be determined by specifying special conditions.

2. Function $f(x)$ Being Represented by a Constant Term. We suppose

$$f(x) = a$$

expressing thus that the same probability prevails for any arbitrary fluctuation; regarding prices which are not subject to substantial oscillations, the supposition may be considered rather appropriate. The inviolable condition

$$\int_0^{\omega} f(x)\,dx = {}^1\!/_2$$

yields in this case

$$\int_0^{\omega} a\,dx = a\omega = {}^1\!/_2$$

such that for the constant a and for the function $f(x)$ itself we obtain the expression

$$f(x) = \frac{1}{2\omega} \tag{1}$$

The function $F(x)$, which is pivotal to the entire theory, is represented by the integral

$$\int_0^{\omega} \frac{dx}{2\omega}$$

therefore, we have

$$F(x) = \frac{\omega - x}{2\omega} \tag{2}$$

The curve denoting the probability of fluctuations is represented by a straight line, which is parallel to and above the abscissa; as we know, the shaded area in the below schema represents the function $F(x)$,

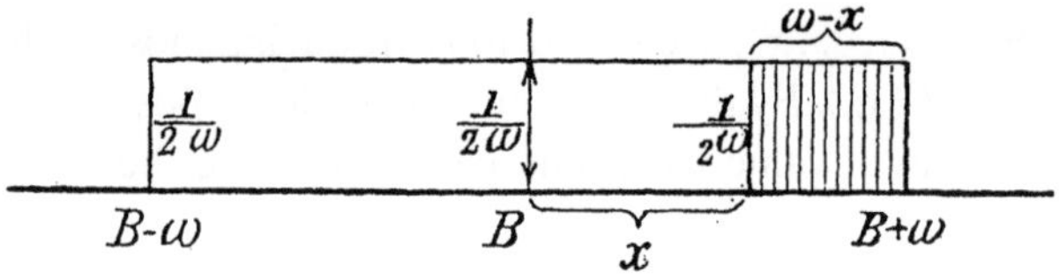

Fig. 28.

as is, indeed, confirmed by formula (2).

Application of equation

$$\frac{\delta P_1}{\delta M} = -F(M)$$

yields in this case

$$\frac{\delta P_1}{\delta M} = -\frac{\omega - M}{2\omega}$$

namely[74]

$$P_1 = -\int \frac{\omega - M}{2\omega}\, dM + C$$

or in evaluated form,

$$P_1 = \frac{(\omega - M)^2}{4\omega} \tag{3}$$

whereby, due to $P_1 = 0$ for $M = \omega$, the constant C itself must disappear. On account of $P_2 = P_1 + M$, it follows immediately that

$$P_2 = \frac{(\omega + M)^2}{4\omega} \tag{3a}$$

and, hence, for the skewed stellage contract, we obtain premium

$$S_1 = \frac{\omega^2 + M^2}{2\omega} = \frac{\omega}{2} + \frac{M^2}{2\omega} \tag{4}$$

From this we derive for $M = 0$ the terms applicable to the normal contracts, viz.

$$P = \frac{\omega}{4} \quad \text{resp.} \quad S = \frac{\omega}{2} \tag{5}$$

the difference in the premia for skewed and normal stellage contracts is

$$\delta = \frac{M^2}{2\omega}$$

as can be confirmed by direct evaluation of the integral

$$\delta = 2\int_0^M (M - x) f(x)\, dx$$

[74] A summary table of the option prices derived from the different functional (or distributional) specifications of $f(x)$ can be found in Chapter II.2 of this Book.

The general equation for the repeat contract, viz.

$$N = m \int_N^\omega (x - N) f(x)\, dx = m P_1$$

becomes, according to (3),

$$N = \frac{m(\omega - N)^2}{4\omega} \tag{6}$$

which provides us with a second-order equation, allowing us to determine (in a very convenient manner) N as a function of ω und m; one obtains

$$N^2 - \frac{2\omega(m+2)}{m} N = -\omega^2$$

and from there

$$N = \frac{\omega}{m}(m + 2 - 2\sqrt{m+1}) \tag{7}$$

we were required to use a radicand with negative algebraic sign, as otherwise we would obtain a value for N larger than the value for ω, that is, for any arbitrary m. If we express N by the premium of the simple normal contract, we obtain, due to $\omega = 4P$,

$$N = \frac{4}{m}(m + 2 - 2\sqrt{m+1})P \tag{7a}$$

Using equation (6), the ratio $\frac{N}{P}$ can also be determined in the following manner: Initially, we have

$$N = \frac{m(4P - N)^2}{16P} = \frac{mP(4P - N)^2}{(4P)^2}$$

and from there

$$\frac{N}{P} = M\left(1 - \frac{N}{4P}\right)^2 \tag{8}$$

determining

$$1 - \frac{N}{4P} = \rho$$

so that we get

$$\frac{N}{P} = 4(1 - \rho) \tag{9}$$

we obtain equation

$$m\rho^2 + 4\rho - 4 = 0 \tag{10}$$

therefore

$$\rho = \frac{-2}{m} \pm \sqrt{\frac{4 + 4m}{m^2}}$$

alternatively, as only positive values for ρ make sense,

$$\rho = \frac{2}{m}(\sqrt{m+1} - 1) \tag{11}$$

For $m = 1$ we obtain $\rho_1 = 0.8284$, hence

$$N_1 = 0.6864P$$

For $m = 2$ we obtain $\rho_2 = 0.732$, hence

$$N_2 = 1.072P$$

for $m = 3$ we arrive at rational values, namely

$$\rho_3 = {}^2/_3 \quad \text{resp.} \quad N_3 = {}^4/_3 P$$

and so forth.[75] In this way, we find these relationships among premia for repeat contracts etc.

$$N_2 = 1.562N_1, \quad N_3 = 1.942N_1 \quad \text{etc.}$$

These general formulae enable us to solve problems of the most varied kind. For instance, if we wished to learn what type of repeat contract would require a premium equal to P, we would substitute in (8) $\frac{N}{P} = 1$ and solve the equation for m, yielding

$$m = 1\,{}^7/_9 = 1.777$$

Further, if we wished to determine the skewedness which makes the difference between the normal and the skewed stellage equal to premium P_1 we would have to solve equation

$$\frac{M^2}{2\omega} = \frac{(\omega - M)^2}{4\omega}$$

for M; we would obtain

$$M = \omega(\sqrt{2} - 1), \quad \text{viz.} \quad 4P(\sqrt{2} - 1) = 1.6168P$$

and so forth.

3. Function $f(x)$ Being Represented by a Linear Equation. Suppose

$$f(x) = a + bx$$

[75] An analysis of the repeat-premia and a comparison with the prices derived by Bachelier (p. 56) can be found in Chapter 5.7 of this Book.

In order to determine the coefficients a and b, we augment the ordinary condition

$$\int_0^{\omega} f(x)\,dx = {}^1\!/_2$$

by another condition, whereby the extreme values ω have a probability of zero, which is expressed by the relationship

$$f(\omega) = 0$$

The proposed suppositions are likely to better approximate reality in the case of objects of value whose price is subject to significant fluctuations, as opposed to those underlying the calculations performed in the previous section.

Following from the first condition, we have

$$\int_0^{\omega} (a + bx)\,dx = \frac{(a + b\omega)^2 - a^2}{2b} = {}^1\!/_2$$

following from the second condition, however, we have

$$a + b\omega = 0$$

Solving these equations for a und b provides values

$$a = \frac{1}{\omega} \quad \text{resp.} \quad b = \frac{-1}{\omega^2}$$

so that our function is defined by the expression

$$f(x) = \frac{\omega - x}{\omega^2} \tag{12}$$

Here, once again, the curve denoting the probability of fluctuations is represented by a straight line, which in this instance cuts off the stretch $\frac{1}{\omega}$ from the ordinate, meeting the abscissa at $B + \omega$ (see Fig. 29); from the two similar

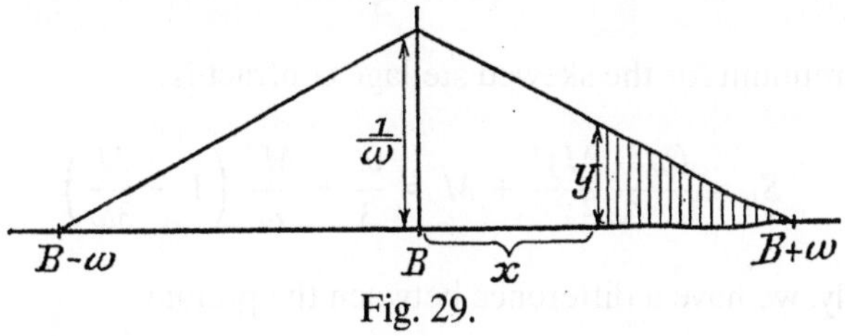

Fig. 29.

triangles, we derive the proportion

$$y : \frac{1}{\omega} = (\omega - x) : \omega,$$

which, indeed, reproduces for y the expression contained in (12).

In this case, the integral taken over x und ω yields

$$\int_x^\omega \frac{\omega - x}{\omega^2} dx = \frac{(\omega - x)^2}{2\omega^2} \tag{13}$$

and represents, as we know, the shaded area in Figure 29; and indeed, by direct determination of this area we obtain

$$\frac{y}{2}(\omega - x), \quad \text{viz.} \quad \frac{(\omega - x)^2}{2\omega^2}$$

This expression is to be equated with the negative of the differential quotient of P_1; for we have, if in order to preserve uniformity we denote the variable term by M,

$$\frac{\delta P_1}{\delta M} = -\frac{(\omega - M)^2}{2\omega^2}$$

and hence

$$P_1 = -\int \frac{(\omega - M)^2}{2\omega^2} dM + C$$

It follows immediately that

$$P_1 = \frac{(\omega - M)^3}{6\omega^2} \tag{14}$$

The constant C is equal to zero, since P_1 must disappear for $M = \omega$. From this we derive, by substituting $M = 0$, the normal premium P in the amount of

$$P = \frac{\omega}{6} \tag{15}$$

the premium for the normal stellage contract is then

$$S = \frac{\omega}{3}$$

whereas the premium for the skewed stellage contract is

$$S_1 = \frac{(\omega - M)^3}{3\omega^2} + M = \frac{\omega}{3} + \frac{M^2}{\omega}\left(1 - \frac{M}{3\omega}\right)$$

consequentially, we have a difference between the premia

$$\delta = \frac{M^2}{\omega}\left(1 - \frac{M}{3\omega}\right) \tag{16}$$

the difference evidently always being positive, as it should be.

Applying equation (15), we can derive from (14) a relationship between the skewed and the normal premia by giving formula (14) the form

$$P_1 = \frac{(6P - M)^3}{6^3 P^2}, \quad \text{viz.} \quad \frac{P(6P - M)^3}{(6P)^3},$$

thus finally arriving at equation

$$P_1 = \left(1 - \frac{M}{6P}\right)^3 P \tag{17}$$

We take this equation as our starting point in order to examine the premium of the repeat contract; for we have

$$N = mP_1$$

whereby P_1 itself possesses skewedness N, and hence, on a account of (17),

$$N = m\left(1 - \frac{N}{6P}\right)^3 P$$

It follows further that

$$\frac{N}{P} = m\left(1 - \frac{N}{6P}\right)^3 \tag{18}$$

or, introducing the auxiliary term

$$\rho = 1 - \frac{N}{6P}$$

entailing the additional relationship

$$\frac{N}{P} = 6(1 - \rho) \tag{19}$$

the simple third-order equation

$$m\rho^3 + 6\rho - 6 = 0 \tag{20}$$

is arrived at, which is highly analogous to the pertinent second-order equation arrived at in the previous section.

Since in equation (19) a term is missing between two identical terms, we infer the presence of two imaginary roots, for which reason there must exist a single real root, in fact, a positive one, because the absolute term is negative. Concerning the latter root, direct application of the cardanic formula yields

$$\rho = \sqrt[3]{\frac{3}{m} + \sqrt{\frac{9}{m^2} + \frac{8}{m^3}}} + \sqrt[3]{\frac{3}{m} - \sqrt{\frac{9}{m^2} + \frac{8}{m^3}}}$$

and in somewhat reduced form,

$$\rho = \sqrt[3]{\frac{1}{m}}\left[\sqrt[3]{3+\sqrt{9+\frac{8}{m}}}+\sqrt[3]{3-\sqrt{9+\frac{8}{m}}}\right] \tag{21}$$

From this, we calculate with respect to the 1-repeat contract, that is, for $m =$ 1,

$$\rho_1 = 0.88462$$

and further, due to (19),

$$N_1 = 0.69288P$$

For the 2-repeat contract, viz. $m = 2$, we obtain

$$\rho_2 = 0.81773$$

from which follows

$$N_2 = 1.09362P$$

and so forth. In this way, one obtains

$$N_2 = 1.578N_1 \quad \text{etc.}$$

Comparison of these results with the pertinent values obtained under the assumption made in the previous section does indeed reveal a remarkably high degree of concordance.

In order to establish the number of m in a repeat contract which results in premium N being equal to the normal premium, we substitute in (18) $\frac{N}{P} = 1$ and solve for m; we find

$$m = 1.728$$

once again, arriving at a result that shows rather a high degree of concordance vis-à-vis the result obtained in the previous section.

Determination of the skewedness for which premium P_1 is equal to the stellage difference, is accomplished as follows: Equating (14) and (16) yields

$$\frac{(\omega - M)^3}{6\omega^2} = \frac{M^2}{\omega}\left(1 - \frac{M}{3\omega}\right)$$

and in ordered form

$$M^3 - 3\omega M^2 - 3\omega^2 M + \omega^3 = 0$$

yielding further

$$(M + \omega)(M^2 - \omega M + \omega^2) - 3\omega M(M + \omega) = 0$$

or, in view of $M + \omega$ being unequal to zero,

$$M^2 - 4\omega M = -\omega^2$$

Solving for M yields

$$M = 2\omega \pm \sqrt{3\omega^2}$$

or, considering that only a negative algebraic sign brings about a result of practical value,

$$M = \omega(2 - \sqrt{3})$$

if we express ω by P in accordance with equation (15), we obtain eventually

$$M = 1.608P$$

that is, almost exactly the same result as the one arrived at in the pertinent exercise in the previous section.

It would appear expedient to attempt determination of the premia P and P_1 by direct evaluation of the relevant integrals. For we have

$$P = \int_0^{\omega} xf(x)\,dx$$

and hence, according to the supposed form of function $f(x)$

$$P = \int_0^{\omega} \frac{x(\omega - x)}{\omega^2}\,dx$$

we obtain

$$P = \int_0^{\omega} \frac{x\,dx}{\omega} - \int_0^{\omega} \frac{x^2\,dx}{\omega^2} = \left(\frac{x^2}{2\omega}\right)_0^{\omega} \left(\frac{x^3}{3\omega^2}\right)_0^{\omega} = \frac{\omega}{2} - \frac{\omega}{3}$$

thus, actually

$$P = \frac{\omega}{6}$$

Determination of P_1 brings us back to the evaluation of the integral

$$P_1 = \int_M^{\omega} (x - M)f(x)\,dx$$

in the present case

$$P_1 = \int_M^{\omega} \frac{(x - M)(\omega - x)}{\omega^2}\,dx = \frac{1}{\omega^2}\int_M^{\omega} (\omega x - \omega M - x^2 + Mx)\,dx$$

and hence

$$P_1 = \frac{\omega + M}{\omega^2} \int_M^\omega x\,dx - \frac{M}{\omega} \int_M^\omega dx - \frac{1}{\omega^2} \int_M^\omega x^2\,dx$$

or in integrated form,

$$P_1 = \frac{\omega + M}{\omega^2} \frac{\omega^2 - M^2}{2} - \frac{M(\omega - M)}{\omega} - \frac{\omega^3 - M^3}{3\omega^2}$$

reduction yields

$$P_1 = \frac{\omega - M}{\omega^2} \left(\frac{\omega^2 + 2\omega M + M^2}{2} - M\omega - \frac{\omega^2 + \omega M + M^2}{3} \right)$$

$$\frac{\omega - M}{6\omega^2} (\omega^2 - 2\omega M + M^2)$$

and, therefore, indeed

$$P_1 = \frac{(\omega - M)^3}{6\omega^2}$$

In confirming the correctness of the earlier calculation, we have also had occasion to assay the excellence of equations (16) and (19) from the previous section.

Initial differentiation of P_1 with respect to M yields

$$\frac{\partial P_1}{\partial M} = -\frac{(\omega - M)^2}{2\omega^2}$$

further differentiation, however, yields

$$\frac{\partial^2 P_1}{\partial M^2} = \frac{\omega - M}{\omega^2}$$

In the first instance, we actually witness the negative function $F(M)$; in the second instance, however, we see the function $f(M)$ itself being reproduced, as is required by the general formulae introduced in the previous chapter.

4. Function $f(x)$ Being Represented by a Second-Order Polynomial Function. With regard to $f(x)$, we suppose an expression of the form

$$f(x) = a + bx + cx^2$$

whereby the coefficients a, b and c are determined with the following conditions in mind

$$\int_0^\omega f(x)\,dx = {}^1\!/_2, \quad f(\omega) = 0 \quad \text{and} \quad \left.\frac{\partial f(x)}{\partial x}\right|_{x=\omega} = 0$$

The third, additional condition implies that the curve denoting the probability of fluctuation has indeed a minimum at point ω, so that the curve will approach and finally merge with the abscissa rather slowly, wherefore it is a great deal more difficult to actually reach the extreme value ω compared to the circumstances defined by the suppositions made in previous sections. The present suppositions should be usefully applicable in those cases where significant fluctuations are to be expected, and where, therefore, one must suppose sufficiently large extreme values. The first condition is provided by equation

$$\int_0^{\omega}(a + bx + cx^2)\,dx = a\omega + \frac{b\omega^2}{2} + \frac{c\omega^3}{3} = {}^1/_2,$$

the second condition is provided by

$$a + b\omega + c\omega^2 = 0$$

and finally, the third condition is provided by

$$b + 2c\omega = 0$$

since evidently we have

$$\frac{\partial f(x)}{\partial x} = b + 2cx$$

From the last equation of condition follows

$$b = -2c\omega$$

hence, from the second follows

$$a = c\omega^2$$

substituting these values into the first equation, we obtain,

$$c = \frac{3}{2\omega^3}$$

We thus have

$$a = \frac{3}{2\omega} \quad \text{and} \quad b = \frac{-3}{\omega^2}$$

so that our function can be given the simple form

$$f(x) = \frac{3(\omega - x)^2}{2\omega^3} \tag{22}$$

thus, the pertinent curve of fluctuation probabilities is represented by the branch of a parabola touching the ordinate at height $\frac{3}{2\omega}$ and having the abscissa itself as a tangent at point $B + \omega$.

In this instance, function $F(x)$ becomes

$$F(x) = \int_x^\omega \frac{3(\omega - x)^2}{2\omega^3}\, dx = \frac{(\omega - x)^3}{2\omega^3}$$

and hence, in order to determine P_1, we must further manipulate equation

$$\frac{\partial P_1}{\partial M} = -\frac{(\omega - M)^3}{2\omega^3}$$

It follows that

$$P_1 = -\int \frac{(\omega - M)^3}{2\omega^3}\, dM + C$$

and therefore

$$P_1 = \frac{(\omega - M)^4}{8\omega^3} \tag{23}$$

where the constant C equals zero. Thus, the normal premium, which obviously corresponds to $M = 0$, is equal to,

$$P = \frac{\omega}{8} \tag{24}$$

so that we have a relationship between P_1 and P of the form

$$P_1 = \frac{(8P - M)^4}{8^4 P^3} \quad \text{viz.} \quad P_1 = P\left(1 - \frac{M}{8P}\right)^4 \tag{25}$$

Applying this result to the repeat contract, we obtain

$$N = mP\left(1 - \frac{N}{8P}\right)^4$$

since, as we know, $N = mP_1$, if P_1, is supposed to be in accordance with skewedness N. From the latter equation it follows that

$$\frac{N}{P} = m\left(1 - \frac{N}{8P}\right)^4 \tag{26}$$

or

$$m\rho^4 + 8\rho - 8 = 0 \tag{27}$$

if, for the sake of brevity

$$\rho = 1 - \frac{N}{8P}$$

or, which amounts to the same,

$$\frac{N}{P} = 8(1 - \rho) \tag{28}$$

is substituted. Associated with equation (27), which reveals a negative absolute term as well as a missing term between two identical terms, we find two real roots, of which one is positive, while the other is negative, as well as two imaginary roots; concerning the real roots, it is evident that only the positive one is of relevance.

Instead of developing the pertinent general and highly complicated formulae, which allow us to calculate the ρ corresponding to the various m, we report the calculations performed for $m = 1$ and $m = 2$, namely: in the first instance, we obtain

$$\rho_1 = 0.9131$$

however, in the second instance, we have

$$\rho_2 = 0.862$$

from which we may derive, according to (28), the relationships

$$N_1 = 0.6952P$$

and

$$N_2 = 1.104P$$

respectively. This entails the relationship between N_1 and N_2 such that

$$N_2 = 1.588N_1$$

The noteworthy correspondence of these results with those obtained from earlier suppositions is striking, demonstrating that these relationships are almost entirely unrelated to the manner in which market fluctuations may be brought about.

Thus, we find that in order for the repeat premium to be equal to the normal premium P, we require a repeat contract satisfying

$$m = 1.7059\ldots$$

which is in rather close agreement with the results from the analogous problem posed under different assumptions.

5. Function $f(x)$ Being Represented by an Exponential Function. We substitute

$$f(x) = ka^{-hx}$$

and require the function to satisfy the sole condition that

$$\int_0^{\omega} f(x)\,dx = {}^1\!/_2$$

Since the function is taking this form, we are unrestrained in assuming the upper boundary ω to be infinitely large, since as x increases, the function decreases at an exceedingly high rate, because in this area the function produces only terms of subordinate significance; hence, we write

$$\int_0^\infty ka^{-hx} = {}^1\!/_2$$

or in evaluated form,

$$k\left(\frac{a^{-hx}}{-hla}\right)_0^\infty = \tfrac{1}{2} = \frac{k}{hla}$$

Next, it follows that

$$la = \frac{2k}{h}, \quad \text{viz.} \quad a = e^{\frac{2k}{h}},$$

so that our function assumes the form

$$f(x) = ke^{-2kx} \tag{29}$$

Therefore, function $F(x)$ assumes the form

$$F(x) = k\int_x^\infty e^{-2kx}\,dx = k\left(\frac{e^{-2kx}}{-2k}\right)_x^\infty$$

and thus

$$F(x) = \frac{e^{-2kx}}{2} \tag{30}$$

As we know, this function represents the probability with which a given fluctuation x will be attained or surpassed; which we would also assume to be applicable in order to determine the constant k for the several objects of value, that is, of course, subject to the principles laid down at the beginning of the present chapter.

In order to determine P_1, we derive from (30) the equation

$$\frac{\partial P_1}{\partial M} = -\frac{e^{-2kM}}{2}$$

and hence

$$P_1 = -\tfrac{1}{2}\int e^{-2kM}\,dM + C$$

resulting in

$$P_1 = \frac{e^{-2kM}}{4k} \tag{31}$$

whereby the constant C is equal to zero, on account of the condition $P_1 = 0$ for $M = \infty$. From this formula we obtain for $M = 0$ the normal premium

$$P = \frac{1}{4k} \tag{32}$$

and thus the simple relationship between P_1 and P

$$P_1 = Pe^{-\frac{M}{2P}} \tag{33}$$

Applying the result to the repeat contract, we find

$$N = mPe^{-\frac{N}{2P}}$$

and hence, regarding the relationship $\frac{N}{P} = R$, the equation

$$R = me^{\frac{-R}{2}} \tag{34}$$

In order to solve this equation approximatively, we suppose an approximate value on the right-hand side such that

$$\rho = R + \delta \tag{35}$$

Consequentially, we shall have on the left-hand side a value, in general, unequal to R

$$\rho_1 = R + \delta_1 \tag{36}$$

if the deviations from the true value become insignificant, we obtain the relationship

$$\delta_1 = \frac{-m}{2} e^{\frac{-R}{2}} \delta \tag{37}$$

since δ_1 may be looked upon as being almost the differential of the function on the right-hand side. From (35) and (36) follows by dint of addition

$$R = \frac{\rho + \rho_1}{2} - \frac{\delta + \delta_1}{2} \tag{38}$$

and, on the other hand, by dint of subtraction

$$\delta - \delta_1 = \rho - \rho_1$$

From the latter equation we derive with the help of (37)

$$\delta = \frac{\rho - \rho_1}{1 + \frac{m}{2} e^{-R/2}}$$

and

$$\delta_1 = -\frac{-(\rho - \rho_1)\frac{m}{2} e^{-R/2}}{1 + \frac{m}{2} e^{-R/2}}$$

respectively, and thus the requirement to apply to the arithmetic mean $\frac{\rho+\rho_1}{2}$ the following correction

$$\frac{\delta + \delta_1}{2} = \frac{\rho - \rho_1}{2} \frac{1 - \frac{m}{2} e^{\frac{-R}{2}}}{1 - \frac{m}{2} e^{\frac{-R}{2}}} \tag{39}$$

We shall elucidate the operation with respect to $m = 1$ and $m = 2$.

Firstly, the equation

$$R = e^{-\frac{R}{2}}$$

is to be solved, and the term of correction

$$-\frac{\rho - \rho_1}{2} \frac{1 - 0.5e^{\frac{-R}{2}}}{1 + 0.5e^{\frac{-R}{2}}} \quad \text{viz.} \quad -\frac{\rho - \rho_1}{2} \frac{e^{\frac{R}{2}} - 0.5}{e^{\frac{R}{2}} + 0.5}$$

is to be applied. Substituting e.g. $\rho = 0.6$, we obtain

$$\rho_1 = e^{-0.3} = 0.74082$$

Hence

$$R = 0.67041 + 0.07041 \frac{e^{\frac{R}{2}} - 0.5}{e^{\frac{R}{2}} + 0.5}$$

since $\frac{\rho+\rho_1}{2}$ and $\frac{\rho-\rho_1}{2}$ take the values

$$0.67041 \quad \text{and} \quad -0.07041$$

respectively. For want of a better value than R, we substitute for R in the term of correction the value

$$\frac{\rho + \rho_1}{2} = 0.67041$$

in which manner the said term becomes

$$0.07041 \frac{0.89823}{1.89823} \quad \text{viz.} \quad 0.033317$$

thus, in a first approximation, we have

$$R = 0.70373$$

In order to obtain R by means of a second approximation, we substitute the resultant approximate value in the equation to be solved; we find

$$\rho_2 = e^{-0.351865} = 0.703375$$

which value being smaller than the correct one, as it had turned out to be smaller than the substituted value. We are free to apply further corrections, thus advancing the appproximation to any degree deemed desirable; we content ourselves with the arithmetic means of 0.70373 and ρ_2, that is, we suppose

$$R = 0.70355$$

so that the following relationships prevail between the premia of the 1-repeat contract and the simple normal contract

$$N_1 = 0.70355P$$

For $m = 2$ the calculation is as follows: The equation to be solved is

$$R = 2e^{-\frac{R}{2}}$$

and the pertinent term of correction is

$$-\frac{\rho - \rho_1}{2} \frac{e^{\frac{R}{2}} - 1}{e^{\frac{R}{2}} + 1}$$

Substituting e.g. $\rho = 1$, we obtain

$$\rho_1 = 2e^{-1/2} \quad \text{viz.} \quad 1.2131$$

Hence

$$\frac{\rho + \rho_1}{2} = 1.10655 \quad \text{and} \quad \frac{\rho - \rho_1}{2} = -0.10655$$

and therefore

$$R = 1.10655 + 0.10655 \frac{e^{\frac{R}{2}} - 1}{e^{\frac{R}{2}} + 1}$$

Substituting 1.10655 instead of R in the term of correction yields with respect to the latter

$$0.10655 \frac{0.738939}{2.738939} \quad \text{viz.} \quad 0.028746$$

as a matter of first approximation, we therefore have

$$R = 1.1353$$

Given this value, the equation to be solved yields

$$\rho_2 = 2e^{-0.56765} \quad \text{viz.} \quad 1.13371$$

which value being smaller than the correct one. We suppose the mean of 1.1353 and ρ_2 to be sufficiently precise, and write

$$R = 1.1345$$

therefore

$$N_2 = 1.1345P$$

From this we derive for N_1 and N_2 the relationship

$$N_2 = 1.612N_1$$

If we wished to learn what kind of repeat contract involves a premium equal to the normal premium, we would gather from

$$1 = me^{-1/2}$$

for m the value

$$\sqrt{e} \quad \text{viz.} \quad 1.6487\ldots$$

The almost complete concordance of these numerical results with those arrived at under very different assumptions in the previous sections is indeed remarkable.

6. Application of the Law of Error to $f(x)$. When concluding a contract, it seems evident that the current price B ought to be regarded amongst all prices as the value associated with the highest probability of holding on the date when the deal is unwound; after all, we could not conceive of purchases and sales, that is to say, opposite contracts, as being concluded with a view to having equally likely prospects, if we had cogent reasons which led us to anticipate most assertively the greater likelihood of an increase or a decline in price, as the case may be.[76] While looking upon market fluctuations above or below B as being deviations from a most felicitously chosen value, as it were, we shall at the same time attempt to subject them to the law of error[77]

$$\frac{h}{\sqrt{\pi}} e^{-h^2\lambda^2}\, d\lambda$$

which has proven tried and true concerning the representation of probabilities of error; in point of fact, the above expression represents the probability of an error lying within the interval λ and $\lambda + d\lambda$, whereby h is a constant term which depends upon the exactitude of the underlying observations. Applying this to the case at

[76] The same reasoning is used by Bachelier (1900), pp. 31–32, to motivate the Martingale property of spot prices.

[77] "Law of error" was the prevailing characterization of what was later called Normal or Gaussian distribution. Specifically, the law of error referred to a Normal distribution with zero mean and standard deviation $(h\sqrt{2})^{-1}$; h measures the precision of the observations and is typically called "precision modulus".

hand, we shall suppose that the probability of a fluctuation lying between x and $x + dx$ is given by the expression

$$\frac{h}{\sqrt{\pi}} e^{-h^2 x^2}\, dx$$

consequentially, our function $f(x)$ takes the final form

$$f(x) = \frac{h}{\sqrt{\pi}} e^{-h^2 x^2} \tag{40}$$

the term h assuming different values for different objects, in every specific case these values need to be determined empirically in the way already described.

Our function taking the supposed form, the probability that the fluctuation assumes a value between 0 and x is given by the integral

$$w = \int_0^x \frac{h}{\sqrt{\pi}} e^{-h^2 x^2}\, dx$$

or, introducing the new variable $t = hx$,

$$w = \frac{1}{\sqrt{\pi}} \int_0^{hx} e^{-t^2} dt = \varphi(hx) \tag{41}$$

Function $f(x)$ decreasing rapidly as x grows, it appears fair to suppose the extreme value ω infinitely large; thus, we have

$$W = \frac{1}{\sqrt{\pi}} \int_0^{\infty} e^{-t^2} dt = \frac{1}{\sqrt{\pi}} \frac{\sqrt{\pi}}{2} = \frac{1}{2}$$

therefore our condition

$$\int_0^{\omega} f(x)\, dx = {}^1\!/_2$$

is satisfied in principle.

Function $F(x)$, representing the probability of fluctuations above x, viz.

$$F(x) = \int_x^{\omega} f(x)\, dx$$

becomes in this instance

$$F(x) = \frac{1}{\sqrt{\pi}} \int_{hx}^{\infty} e^{-t^2} dt = \tfrac{1}{2} - \varphi(hx) = \psi(hx) \tag{42}$$

In this case, we prefer to calculate premium P_1 on the basis of its integral

$$P_1 = \int_M^{\infty} (x - M) \frac{h}{\sqrt{\pi}} e^{-h^2 x^2}\, dx$$

namely

$$P_1 = \int_M^\infty \frac{h}{\sqrt{\pi}} x e^{-h^2x^2}\, dx - M \int_M^\infty \frac{h}{\sqrt{\pi}} e^{-h^2x^2}\, dx$$

the former integral can be directly evaluated, the second one may be expressed by function ψ; hence we obtain[78]

$$P_1 = \frac{e^{-M^2h^2}}{2h\sqrt{\pi}} - M\psi(hM) \tag{43}$$

Applying this expression, we substitute zero into M to calculate the normal premium in the form of

$$P = \frac{1}{2h\sqrt{\pi}} \tag{44}$$

We could have derived premium P_1 from the ordinary formula

$$\frac{\partial P_1}{\partial M} = -F(M)$$

in which case, we would have

$$P_1 = -\int \psi(hM)\, dM + C$$

or by dint of partial integration

$$P_1 = -M\psi(hM) + \int M \frac{\delta\psi(hM)}{\delta M}\, dM + C$$

however, it is apparent that

$$\frac{\partial\psi(hM)}{\partial M} = \frac{-e^{-h^2M^2}}{\sqrt{\pi}} h$$

and therefore, as the constant C disappears, we obtain expression (43) for P_1.

Introducing the premium of the repeat contract, we have equation

$$N = m\left[\frac{e^{-N^2h^2}}{2\sqrt{\pi}h} - N\psi(hN)\right]$$

which, due to (44) giving rise to the relationship

$$h = \frac{1}{2\sqrt{\pi}P}$$

[78] This (or the preceding) expression is the closest resemblance of Bronzin's formulas with the celebrated Black-Scholes-Merton model. A detailed discussion is provided in Chapter 5.5 of this Book.

must be rearranged so as to take the form

$$\frac{N}{m} = Pe^{-\frac{N^2}{4\pi P^2}} - N\psi\left(\frac{N}{2\sqrt{\pi}P}\right)$$

or, by applying the ratio

$$R = \frac{N}{P}$$

can be given the final form

$$R\left[\frac{1}{m} + \psi\left(\frac{R}{2\sqrt{\pi}}\right)\right] = e^{-\frac{R^2}{4\pi}} \tag{45}$$

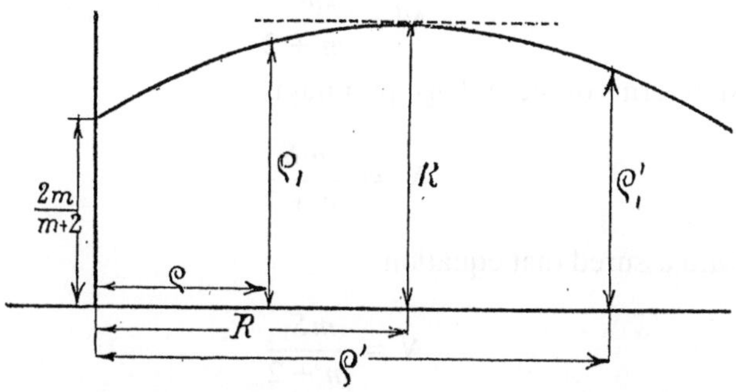

Fig. 30.

M given, in order to determine R by way of approximation, we are required to apply this equation in the form

$$R = \frac{e^{\frac{-R^2}{4\pi}}}{\frac{1}{m} + \psi\left(\frac{R}{2\sqrt{\pi}}\right)} \tag{46}$$

the first differential quotient, which upon simple reduction is given the form

$$\frac{e^{\frac{-R^2}{4\pi}}}{2\pi} \frac{e^{\frac{-R^2}{4\pi}} - \frac{R}{m} - R\psi\left(\frac{R}{2\sqrt{\pi}}\right)}{\left[1 + \psi\left(\frac{R}{2\sqrt{\pi}}\right)\right]^2}$$

and reveals that the right-hand side of (46) increases for small values of R, that is, up to the point described by equation

$$e^{\frac{-R^2}{4\pi}} - \frac{R}{m} - R\psi\left(\frac{R}{2\sqrt{\pi}}\right) = 0$$

where a maximum value is attained; however, it proves to be precisely the value of R, as we can see from equation (45). From this consideration it follows, as is graphically demonstrated in Figure 30, that, if substitution yields a value larger than the substituted value, the latter must be smaller than the exact value. However, if as a result of the substitution one obtains a smaller value, this is indicative of the substituted value having exceeded the exact value: Thus, all means are now available to us in order to solve equation (46) by approximation. Notice especially the result of substituting $R = 0$ into the transcendental terms; hence we have

$$\rho_1 = \frac{2m}{m+2}$$

viz. owing to $\rho_1 = \frac{N'}{P}$

$$N' = \frac{2mP}{m+2}$$

or expressed in terms of the stellage premium,

$$N' = \frac{mS}{m+2}$$

Now we are assured that equation

$$N = \frac{mS_1}{m+2}$$

is strictly satisfied, if S_1 is the premium of the skewed stellage contract concluded at price $P + N$; the concordance of the expressions is remarkable indeed. Further, it is interesting to note once again, and by such roundabout demonstration this time, that the premium of the skewed stellage contract exceeds the premium of the normal stellage contract, for, as mentioned previously, ρ_1 is smaller than the exact value R, viz. $\frac{N}{P}$, so that N' must be smaller than the exact value N, and hence it is also true that S is bound to be smaller than S_1.

We shall now solve equation (46) with respect to the special cases where $m = 1$ and $m = 2$. To this purpose, we avail ourselves of tables which allow us to find the values for the function $\psi(\varepsilon)$, where ε is any particulate number: we have appended such tables to the final part of this treatise.

Commencing by substitution of $\rho = 0.5$, we obtain for ρ_1 the expression

$$\rho_1 = \frac{e^{\frac{-0.25}{4\pi}}}{1 + \psi\left(\frac{0.25}{\sqrt{\pi}}\right)} \quad \text{viz.} \quad \frac{e^{-0.0199}}{1 + \psi(0.141)}$$

We have $\psi(0.141) = 0.42097$, hence

$$\log \rho_1 = -0.0199 \log e - \log 1.42097 = 0.8387676 - 1;$$

thus

$$\rho_1 = 0.68987$$

which value being evidently smaller than the exact one. Substituting

$$\rho' = 0.69$$

yields

$$\rho_1' = \frac{e^{-0.03788}}{1 + \psi(0.19465)} = \frac{e^{-0.03788}}{1.391554} = 0.691903$$

a value which is smaller than R, though very close to it; being satisfied with this value, we thus arrive at a relationship between the premia of the 1-repeat contract and the simple normal contract such that

$$N_1 = 0.6919P$$

For $m = 2$ the calculation is as follows: We commence by substituting

$$\rho = 1$$

and obtain

$$\rho_1 = \frac{e^{\frac{-1}{4\pi}}}{0.5 + \psi\left(\frac{1}{2\sqrt{\pi}}\right)} = 1.0865$$

so that both ρ and ρ_1 are smaller than R. Substituting

$$\rho' = 1.09$$

we have

$$\rho_1' = \frac{e^{\frac{-1.09^2}{4\pi}}}{0.5 + \psi\left(\frac{1.09}{2\sqrt{\pi}}\right)} = 1.09371$$

which value must be somewhat smaller than the exact one; discontinuing the process of approximation at this stage, we may define the quested relationship in this form[79]

$$N_2 = 1.0938P$$

Further, we have a relationship between N_2 and N_1 such that

$$N_2 = 1.581N_1$$

[79] Compared to the numerical value derived by Bachelier (1900) under a Normal distribution (1.096), the correspondance is almost perfect.

Finally, in the present case, if once again we wish to solve the problem which requires us to determine the kind of repeat contract characterised by N being equal to P, we have to substitute in (45) $R = 1$ and determine m from equation

$$m = \frac{1}{e^{\frac{-1}{4\pi}} - \psi\left(\frac{1}{2\sqrt{\pi}}\right)}$$

In this manner we find

$$m = 1.7435$$

It is inevitable to notice the remarkable concordance of these results with those arrived at in the previous sections; such agreement lending considerable practical value to the findings.

7. Application of Bernoulli's Theorem.[80] Concerning two opposite events, whose probabilities are p and q respectively, if a series of trials has been conducted with respect to the occurrence of these events, ps and qs, respectively, these represent the most likely numbers of repetitive occurrences of the events under investigation. It is apparent that in reality deviations from these most likely values will occur, which deviations, according to Bernoulli's theorem, can be assigned determinate probabilities. According to the theorem, the probability that a deviation in the magnitude of

$$\gamma\sqrt{2spq}$$

occurs, in this direction or the other, is expressed by the formula

$$w_1 = \frac{1}{\sqrt{\pi}}\int_0^{\gamma} e^{-t^2}dt + \frac{e^{-\gamma^2}}{\sqrt{2\pi spq}} \tag{47}$$

In order to find a mathematical expression of the probability of market fluctuations, based on this theorem, we proceed in the following manner: We regard the market fluctuations as being deviations from a most likely value, and indeed, B represents such a value, for which reason we suppose the probability of its occurrence to be governed by the said theorem; in our specific case, we are required to substitute B for one of the two values ps or qs: let us say the former, so that now the fluctuation x is represented by

$$x = \gamma\sqrt{2qB} \tag{48}$$

80 The subsequent derivation assumes a binomial distribution of the underlying market price changes ("fluctuations"). Given the popularity of the binomial model in option pricing, after being developed by Cox / Ross / Rubinstein (1979) and others, this final distributional specification in Bronzin's text is amazing. Of course, the author addresses the issue from a purely statistical perspective without focusing on dynamic replication and the like.

wheareas γ is represented by

$$\gamma = \frac{x}{\sqrt{2qB}} \tag{49}$$

Thus, with regard to the probability that, within the range of 0 to x, we may expect a fluctuation in this direction or the other, we obtain the expression

$$w_1 = \frac{2}{\sqrt{\pi}} \int_0^{\frac{x}{\sqrt{2qB}}} e^{-t^2} dt + \frac{e^{\frac{-x^2}{2qB}}}{\sqrt{2\pi q B}}$$

If we completely disregard the second term on the right-hand side, which can only be of secondary moment, and then, as has been our consistent procedure previously, take into account only the probability that fluctuation x follows one particular direction, we arrive at

$$w_1 = \frac{1}{\sqrt{\pi}} \int_0^{\frac{x}{\sqrt{2qB}}} e^{-t^2} dt = \varphi\left(\frac{x}{\sqrt{2qB}}\right) \tag{50}$$

Comparing this result with expression (41) obtained in the previous section, we learn (from the perfect analogy which prevails between the findings) that applying Bernoulli's theorem to market fluctuations leads to the same result that we had arrived at when supposing the applicability of the law of error. The constant h of the law of error we find represented in the present case by

$$h = \frac{1}{\sqrt{2qB}} \tag{51}$$

While the constant acquires a more precise meaning – in that it is seen to be inversely proportional to the square root of B – it is nonetheless still entirely indeterminate due to the presence of q, regarding which we can offer no proposition in advance whatsoever, and thus the constant can be ascertained only from empirical data pertaining to any of the particular objects of value at hand.

Regarding all objects of value, if we suppose that condition

$$p = q = {}^1/_2$$

is satisfied, we simply obtain

$$h = \frac{1}{\sqrt{B}} \tag{51a}$$

in which manner any indeterminateness disappears from our formulae, and we arrive at the numerical results immediately upon mere specification of the current price. However, since the size of the fluctuations is evidently not dependent upon the price alone, instead hinging upon multifarious external influences, we can, of course, treat the results emerging from the above suppositions merely as a first and more or less crude approximation; at any rate, the results do however provide a safe and firm scaffolding and serve with exquisite effect as a means of rough orientation. According to this supposition, we have thus

$$P_1 = \frac{\sqrt{B}e^{-\frac{M^2}{B}}}{2\sqrt{\pi}} - M\psi\left(\frac{M}{\sqrt{B}}\right) \tag{52}$$

hence, the normal premium is given by

$$P = \frac{\sqrt{B}}{2\sqrt{\pi}}$$

and the normal stellage contract is given by

$$S = \sqrt{\frac{B}{\pi}} \tag{53}$$

the investigations into repeat premia do not undergo simplification on the grounds of this special supposition, and are perfectly identical to the ones derived in the previous section.

Let us suppose we are dealing with a stock whose current price is 615.25 K. A stellage contract concluded at this price would command a premium of

$$S = \sqrt{\frac{615.25}{3.14159}} \quad \text{viz.} \quad 13.99 \text{ K}$$

and a simple normal contract would command a premium to the tune of one half of this amount. Thus, e.g. the premium of a conditional purchase concluded at price 620 is calculated based on the formula

$$P_1 = \frac{\sqrt{615.25}}{2\sqrt{3.14159}} e^{-\frac{4.75^2}{615.25}} - 4.75\psi\left(\frac{4.75}{\sqrt{615.25}}\right)$$

one obtains

$$P_1 = 5.734 \text{ K}$$

On account of equation

$$P_2 = P_1 + M$$

the premium of the conditional purchase conducted at a price of 620 is

$$P_2 = 10.484 \text{ K}$$

whereas, the premium for the stellage contract concluded at price 620 is

$$S_1 = P_1 + P_2 \quad \text{viz.} \quad 16.218 \text{ K}$$

Between the normal stellage contract and the skewed contract there is a difference

$$\Delta = 2.28 \text{ K}$$

The premium of the 1-repeat contract is

$$N_1 = 0.6919 \cdot 7 = 4.8433 \text{ K}$$

whereas the premium of the 2-repeat contract is

$$N_2 = 1.0938 \times 7 = 7.7466 \text{ K}$$

and so forth.

Table I.

Values of the function $\psi(\varepsilon) = \dfrac{1}{\sqrt{\pi}} \displaystyle\int_{\varepsilon}^{\infty} e^{-t^2} dt.$

ε	ψ (ε)	Diff.	ε	ψ (ε)	Diff.	ε	ψ (ε)	Diff.
0·00	0·5000000	56417	0·29	0·3408582	51715	0·58	0·2060386	40069
0·01	0·4943583	56405	0·30	0·3356867	51408	0·59	0·2020317	39598
0·02	0·4887178	56383	0·31	0·3305459	51088	0·60	0·1980719	39125
0·03	0·4830795	56349	0·32	0·3254371	50764	0·61	0·1941594	38651
0·04	0·4774446	56305	0·33	0·3203607	50429	0·62	0·1902943	38174
0·05	0·4718141	56249	0·34	0·3153178	50087	0·63	0·1864769	37698
0·06	0·4661892	56180	0·35	0·3103091	49739	0·64	0·1827071	37217
0·07	0·4605712	56102	0·36	0·3053352	49382	0·65	0·1789854	36736
0·08	0·4549610	56013	0·37	0·3003970	49011	0·66	0·1753118	36256
0·09	0·4493957	55912	0·38	0·2954959	48652	0·67	0·1716862	35777
0·10	0·4437685	55800	0·39	0·2906307	48268	0·68	0·1681085	35284
0·11	0·4381885	55677	0·40	0·2858039	47884	0·69	0·1645801	34806
0·12	0·4326208	55544	0·41	0·2810155	47493	0·70	0·1610995	34322
0·13	0·4270664	55399	0·42	0·2762662	47095	0·71	0·1576673	33838
0·14	0·4215265	55244	0·43	0·2715567	46693	0·72	0·1542835	33354
0·15	0·4160021	55079	0·44	0·2668874	46283	0·73	0·1509481	32871
0·16	0·4104942	54903	0·45	0·2622591	45849	0·74	0·1476610	32388
0·17	0·4050039	54998	0·46	0·2576742	45468	0·75	0·1444222	31906
0·18	0·3995441	54640	0·47	0·2531274	45023	0·76	0·1412316	31424
0·19	0·3940801	54313	0·48	0·2486251	44592	0·77	0·1380892	30944
0·20	0·3886488	54097	0·49	0·2441659	44159	0·78	0·1349948	30465
0·21	0·3832391	53870	0·50	0·2397500	43719	0·79	0·1319483	29993
0·22	0·3778521	53634	0·51	0·2353781	43274	0·80	0·1289490	29507
0·23	0·3724887	53387	0·52	0·2310507	42828	0·81	0·1259983	29037
0·24	0·3671500	53131	0·53	0·2267679	42375	0·82	0·1230496	28565
0·25	0·3618369	52868	0·54	0·2225304	41920	0·83	0·1202381	28094
0·26	0·3565501	52592	0·55	0·2183384	41463	0·84	0·1174287	27627
0·27	0·3512909	52309	0·56	0·2141921	40983	0·85	0·1146660	27171
0·28	0·3460600	52018	0·57	0·2100941	40555	0·86	0·1119489	26688

Table I. (continued)

ε	ψ (ε)	Diff.	ε	ψ (ε)	Diff.	ε	ψ (ε	Diff.
0·87	0·1092801	26237	1·15	0·0519381	14862	1·43	0·0215713	7196
0·88	0·1066564	25780	1·16	0·0504519	14521	1·44	0·0208517	6992
0·89	0·1040784	25325	1·17	0·0489998	14185	1·45	0·0201525	6792
0·90	0·1015459	24873	1·18	0·0475873	13855	1·46	0·0194733	6598
0·91	0·0990586	24424	1·19	0·0461958	13528	1·47	0·0188135	6406
0·92	0·0966162	23980	1·20	0·0448430	13207	1·48	0·0181729	6218
0·93	0·0942182	23537	1·21	0·0435223	12893	1·49	0·0175511	6037
0·94	0·0918645	23099	1·22	0·0422330	12581	1·50	0·0169474	5858
0·95	0·0895546	22664	1·23	0·0409749	12275	1·51	0·0163616	5683
0·96	0·0872882	22233	1·24	0·0397474	11978	1·52	0·0157933	5514
0·97	0·0850649	21807	1·25	0·0385496	11675	1·53	0·0152419	5348
0·98	0·0828842	21383	1·26	0·0373821	11389	1·54	0·0147071	5185
0·99	0·0807459	21963	1·27	0·0362432	11103	1·55	0·0141886	5027
1·00	0·0786496	20548	1·28	0·0351329	10823	1·56	0·0136859	4872
1·01	0·0765948	20138	1·29	0·0340506	10546	1·57	0·0131987	4722
1·02	0·0745810	19731	1·30	0·0329960	10276	1·58	0·0127265	4575
1·03	0·0726079	19329	1·31	0·0319684	10010	1·59	0·0122690	4432
1·04	0·0706750	18930	1·32	0·0309674	9749	1·60	0·0118258	4292
1·05	0·0687820	18537	1·33	0·0299925	9493	1·61	0·0113966	4157
1·06	0·0669283	18149	1·34	0·0290432	9243	1·62	0·0109809	4023
1·07	0·0651134	17765	1·35	0·0281189	8996	1·63	0·0105786	3894
1·08	0·0633369	17384	1·36	0·0272193	8755	1·64	0·0101892	3770
1·09	0·0615985	17010	1·37	0·0263438	8518	1·65	0·0098122	3651
1·10	0·0598975	16640	1·38	0·0254920	8287	1·66	0·0094471	3523
1·11	0·0582335	16274	1·39	0·0246633	8058	1·67	0·0090948	3412
1·12	0·0566061	15915	1·40	0·0238575	7837	1·68	0·0087536	3299
1·13	0·0550146	15557	1·41	0·0230738	7619	1·69	0·0084237	3189
1·14	0·0534589	15208	1·42	0·0223119	7406	1·70	0·0081048	3080

References

The original text contains no references. The following references are cited in the complementary footnotes added by the Editors.

Bachelier L (1900, 1964) Théorie de la spéculation. Annales Scientifiques de l' Ecole Normale Supérieure, Paris, Ser. 3, 17, pp. 21–88. English translation in: The random character of stock market prices (ed. Paul Cootner), MIT-Press (1964), pp. 17–79

Banz R, Miller M (1978) Prices for state-contingent claims: Some estimates and applications. Journal of Business 51, pp. 653–672

Black F (1974) The pricing of complex options and corporate liabilities. Unpublished manuscript, University of Chicago

Breeden D, Litzenberger R (1978) Prices of state-contingent claims implicit in option prices. Journal of Business 51, pp. 621–651

Cootner P (1964) The random character of stock market prices. MIT-Press

Cox J, Ross S, Rubinstein M (1979) Option pricing: A simplified approach. Journal of Financial Economics 7, pp. 229–263

Merton RC (1973) Theory of rational option pricing. Bell Journal of Economics and Management Science 4, pp. 141–183

Stoll H (1969) The relationship between call and put option prices. Journal of Finance 23, pp. 801–824

Part C
Background and Appraisal of Bronzin's Work

Introduction

In this part of the book, we discuss the background of Bronzin's scientific work (chapters 6 and 7), and start with a review and evaluation of his *Theorie der Prämiengeschäfte* from the perspective of modern option pricing (chapter 5). It is interesting to observe how many elements of modern finance theory can be found in his Treatise – such as the unpredictability of security prices, the fair pricing principle – and although most of them are motivated intuitively rather than derived from an economic model, how many major insights into the structure of option pricing can be derived thereof. The notion of arbitrage as a key pricing principle is clearly present in his work, although the author only devotes a single explicit statement to it:

> "if in the pursuit of these transactions we succeed in concluding contracts at prices more favorable than the prices supposed in our equations, anything accomplished in that way will evidently bring about unendangered gains" (Bronzin 1908, p. 38)

This is not the modern notion of arbitrage in the sense of a dynamically adjusted hedge position, simply because Bronzin develops no stochastic process for the underlying security price but rather suggests alternatives for the terminal price distribution. Even the term "arbitrage" does not show up in his book; the term was used at this time predominantly for exploiting price inconsistencies between international trading places and instruments traded at different locations due to frictions, conventions and trading practices. In other aspects, Bronzin's work contains analytical insights which are even remarkable from a modern perspective; e.g. he derives a mathematical relationship between a second derivative of option prices and the pricing density which can be exploited to derive closed form solution for option values in a very simple way.

It is somehow problematic to evaluate academic work from a later perspective, biased by linguistic priors (e.g. terminology) and views shaped – or distorted – by established scientific tradition. Things could always have developed differently, and if Bachelier would not have laid the continuous time stochastic foundations for financial modelling, or more trivially, the work would not have been rediscovered in the 50s, a different and perhaps even more successful analytical framework for derivatives would have evolved eventually. From an evolutionary scientific perspective it seems appropriate to understand and judge scientific progress out of the tradition of the time. We therefore include a review of the history of probabilistic modelling in the context of financial applications (chapter 6). Statistical and probabilistic models shaped the evolution of actuarial science and its applications to modern life insurance during the 17th and 18th centuries. Following the historian Lorraine Daston, the creation and propagation of a mathematical theory of risk played an essential role in disconnecting gambling and speculation from the new (life) insurance business, which underpinned widely accepted moral values such as foresight, prudence, and responsibility.

Unfortunately, a similar transformation did not occur in the case of speculation on financial markets. It remained in the shadow of games and lotteries until the 1950s, and only Markowitz's portfolio theory and Bachelier's rediscovered work laid the foundations of a systematic, statistically based investment science. Why took it so long to apply statistical and probabilistic models to financial markets? As chapter 6 sets out, a possible reason is that "probabilistic determinism" survived extremely long in the natural and social science, an attitude which deeply routed in a mechanical – and not genuinely probabilistic – understanding of natural and social processes. This contradiction was most obvious in statistical physics, and even Einstein's Brownian motion model could apparently coexist with a deterministic view of the world by its originator! This background made it difficult to understand the random character – not to mention the random nature – of financial markets. In addition to being complex and inaccessible for most researchers by lack of experience, financial markets were perceived to be located somewhere between a natural phenomenon, like tide and weather, and a sophisticated gambling casino and as such governed by the laws of chance like dice or lotteries. Probabilistic thinking however experienced a fundamental shift in the second decade after the turn of the century when Richard von Mises, among others, removed the dichotomy between natural laws and randomness, and forcefully argued that natural phenomena cannot be separated from intervening human action, measurement, or perception. He formulated the irregularity principle as a general doctrine of probability, and stressed its affinity to what we would call "fair game" assumption in modern finance. But the potential of this insight for modeling financial markets remained unrecognized.

It took surprisingly long to recognize that the maximizing behavior of people creates unpredictability, randomness, and can be expressed by statistical laws. This was intuitively recognized by Jules Regnault and Bronzin, and explicitly rationalized by Bachelier's claim that the expected change of speculative prices must be zero at any instant in order to equate the number of buyers and sellers of securities. While still intuitively, the statement perfectly demonstrates how a basic notion of capital market equilibrium is related to the stochastic properties of speculative price. However, the formal mathematical proof of the Martingale property of anticipatory prices had to wait more than six decades until Paul A. Samuelson's seminal paper.

Both, Bachelier's and Bronzin's achievements provide interesting, but unusual insights into the production process of scientific research: the selection of the subject largely remains in the dark, and there is no obvious connection to earlier work. Their contribution, although known and occasionally quoted in the years after it got published, was not much explored by other researchers and got finally forgotten. No practical application of their models is known either. Both authors paid their price for selecting a somehow "strange" topic (to use Henri Poincaré's wording about Bachelier's thesis) and unusual methodological approach: Bronzin got seriously sick during writing his book, and Bachelier got only a satisfactory grade for his dissertation which prevented an academic career at one of the prestigious *Hautes Écoles* in Paris. But their fate also demonstrates that pioneering work can occasionally grow in isolation from the mainstream, detached from the scientific community or concrete applications. What seems to be much more important is a liberal working atmosphere which tolerates and accelerates new ideas. The analysis of the socio-economic environment of Bronzin's life in chapter 7 reveals that Trieste featured an extremely open minded socio-cultural climate at the beginning of the 20th century, attracting an international, broad-minded audience of researchers, writers, and thinkers. This contrasted with the situation in Vienna where anti-Semitism was growing and the business climate was adverse; for instance, forward trades were treated as gambles after 1901, which was tantamount to interdiction. Not so in Trieste where the stock exchange was flourishing and even maintained strong ties to the Academy. Professors, practitioners and students equally benefited from the apparently relaxed atmosphere between the academic and business world; Bronzin's interest in option theory most probably originated from courses which the Academia offered to practitioners from the insurance, banking and economic community in Trieste. But interestingly, at the time when Bronzin wrote his treatise, no option or forward contracts were traded at the stock exchange of Trieste! His motivation for writing the book was educational and aimed at, as good education always intends, outlining an innovative path of future development. But apparently, he was too optimistic about the reception of his work.

5 A Review and Evaluation of Bronzin's Contribution from a Financial Economics Perspective

Heinz Zimmermann*

In this chapter,[1] Bronzin's Treatise (1908) is analyzed from the perspective of modern financial economics. In the first two sections, we shortly characterize the general approach and institutional background of Bronzin's analysis (5.1 and 5.2). The key valuation elements, such as the notion of "coverage", "equivalence", "fair pricing" and other fundamental insights about the properties of option prices are discussed in Section 5.3; it's amazing to see how closely these valuation principles are related to the major principles of modern finance. Sections 5.4 to 5.6 deal with the major part of Bronzin's analysis, the impact of alternative probability distributions on option prices. Among them, the Normal law of error (*Fehlergesetz*) is of particular interest because it allows a direct comparison to the celebrated Black-Scholes model; this relationship is explicitly addressed in Section 5.5. In Section 5.7, "repeat contracts" are analyzed which were a special type of option contract issued as extensions of forward contracts. Finally, Section 5.8 tries to summarize Bronzin's contribution and to put it in perspective of the history of option pricing in the 20th century.

5.1 General Characterization

Bronzin's book contains two major parts. The first part is more descriptive and contains a characterization and classification of basic derivative contracts, their profit and loss diagrams, and basic hedging conditions and (arbitrage) relationships. The second and more interesting part is on option pricing and starts with a general valuation framework, which is then applied to a variety of distributions for the price of the underlying security in order to get closed form solutions for calls and puts. Among these distributions is the "law of error" (*Fehlergesetz*) which is an old wording for the normal distribution.[2] It is interesting to notice that the separation of topics between "distribution-free" and "distribution-related" results is in perfect line with the modern classification of option pricing topics, following Merton (1973).

* Universität Basel, Switzerland. *heinz.zimmermann@unibas.ch*

[1] This chapter is an extension of sections 2–4 of Zimmermann and Hafner (2007), and includes material from Sections 2–5 from Hafner and Zimmermann (2006) and from unpublished notes (Zimmermann and Hafner 2004).

[2] For the sake of clarity, we refer to this distribution as the "Nornal law of error" in this chapter. A characterization is provided in section 5.4.5.

Bronzin's methodological setup is completely different from Bachelier's, at least in terms of the underlying stochastic framework. He develops no stochastic process for the underlying asset price and uses no stochastic calculus, but directly makes different assumptions on the share price distribution at maturity and derives a rich set of closed form solutions for the value of options. This simplified procedure is justified insofar as his work is entirely focused on European style contracts, so intertemporal issues (e.g. optimal early exercise) are not of interest.

5.2 Institutional Setting

The analysis of Bronzin covers forward contracts as well as options, but his main focus is on the latter. The term "option" does not show up. Instead, his analysis is on "premium contracts" which is an old type of option contract used in many European countries up to the seventies, before warrants and traded options became popular; see e.g. Courtadon (1982) for an analysis of the French premium market, and Barone and Cuoco (1989) for the Italian market.

In contrast to modern options, premium contracts were mostly written on forward contracts, rather than on the spot. The premium gives the buyer the right to withdraw from a fixed (e.g. forward) contract, or to enter a respective contract. This characterization can also be found in Bronzin: A long call option (*Wahlkauf*) is a forward purchase plus the right to "actually accept" the underlying object at delivery; a long put option (*Wahlverkauf*) is a forward sale plus our "reserved right to actually deliver or not, at our discretion" (p. 2). A further institutional difference to modern options is that the premium was typically paid at (or a few days before) delivery, not at settlement (deferred-premium options). However, Bronzin is not specific about this point.[3] Throughout the book, the time value of money does not enter his analysis explicitly, which either means that the premium is paid at delivery, or he assumes an interest rate of zero. Also, most premium contracts were American style – but Bronzin does not address the question of early exercise in his analysis. It is a general difficulty of Bronzin's analysis that it is not related to specific institutional characteristics, contracts, or underlying securities.[4] The underlying is often just called "object" and its price is referred to as "market" price.

[3] E.g., his wording "if we buy forward at B_1 and pay a specific premium P_1" (p. 3) enables both interpretations. In fact, both practices seem to have been prevalent at that time; according to e.g. Siegfried (1892) the practice to pay the premium a few days before maturity was common at the Berlin stock exchange, unlike the practice elsewhere.

[4] Except in the final numerical example on the second-last page, where he refers to "shares" (*Aktien*).

Throughout the analysis, he distinguishes between "normal" and "skewed" contracts: A normal option contract exhibits an exercise price (denoted by K in this paper[5]) equal to the forward price B, while skewed contracts exhibit exercise prices deviating by the absolute amount $M > 0$ from the forward price, $K = B \pm M$.

In addition to these standard (or simple) options, Bronzin analyses two special contracts: options where the buyer has the right to determine whether he wants to buy or sell the underlying at maturity (called *Stella-Geschäfte*)[6]; and "repeat contracts" (called *Noch-Geschäfte*) which entitle the buyer to deliver a pre-defined multiple of the original contract size at expiration.

5.3 Key Valuation Elements

5.3.1 Coverage and Equivalence

Two key concepts, "coverage" and "equivalence" play an important role in the first part of Bronzin's book (sections 4 and 5 in chapter I, section 3 in chapter II). Bronzin defines a "covered" position as a combination of transactions (options and forward contracts) which is immune against profits and losses.[7] Two systems of positions are called "equivalent" if one can be "derived" from the other, or stated differently, if they provide exactly the same profit and loss for all possible "states of the market".[8] From a linguistic point of view, it is interesting to notice that Bronzin explicitly uses the word "derived" in this context. He explicitly notes the equivalence between hedging and replication by observing that one can always get two systems of equivalent transactions by taking a subset of contracts within a complex of covered transactions and reversing signs.[9] A concrete example of this insight can be found in section 5, where he stresses that a combination of a short call with a long put is equivalent to a forward sale (short forward), and can thus be fully hedged with a forward purchase (long forward).

[5] The exercise price of the option exhibits no specific symbol in Bronzin's book – it is directly denoted by $B \pm M$ or other parameters where needed.

[6] They are also shortly addressed by Bachelier; see (p. 53) on "double primes".

[7] Original text: „*Wir werden einen Komplex von Geschäften dann als gedeckt betrachten, wenn bei jeder nur denkbaren Marktlage weder Gewinn zu erwarten noch Verlust zu befürchten ist*" (p. 8).

[8] Original text: „*Zwei Systeme von Geschäften nennen wir nämlich dann einander äquivalent, wenn sich das eine aus dem anderen ableiten lässt, in anderen Worten, wenn dieselben bei jeder nur dankbaren Lage des Marktes einen ganz gleichen Gewinn resp. Verlust ergeben*" (p. 10).

[9] Original text: „*[...] dass wir sofort zwei Systeme äquivalenter Geschäfte erhalten, wenn wir nur in einem Komplexe gedeckter Geschäfte einige derselben mit entgegengesetzten Vorzeichen betrachten*" (p. 10).

Bronzin derives an immediate application of these insights: the put-call-parity, first for the special case of symmetric, i.e., ATM call and put positions (chapter 1, section 4, p. 9), and subsequently for skewed positions, i.e., calls and puts with arbitrary but equal exercise price (chapter 2, section 1) which he calls a "remarkable condition" (p. 17). Denoting the call (put) option price by P_1 (P_2), he writes the parity for exercise price $B+M$, $M>0$, as

$$P_2 = P_1 + M \qquad \text{(equation 4, p. 17)}, \qquad (5.1a)$$

and for exercise price $B-M$ the parity is correspondingly

$$P_2 = P_1 - M \qquad \text{(equation 4a, p. 17)}. \qquad (5.1b)$$

This reflects the important insight that the difference between call and put prices is equal to the "moneyness" of the call (if $M = K - B > 0$) or the put option (if $M = B - K > 0$), defined relative to the forward price respectively. If the option price is paid at contract settlement, or alternatively if the time value of money is taken into account, the relationship to the standard put-call-parity can be derived by replacing $M = K - B$ by $\hat{M} \equiv Ke^{-rT} - S_0$ in equation (5.1a) and allowing for positive and negative values; r denotes the riskless interest rate, T the time to maturity, and S_0 the current value of the underlying asset. This leads to the well-known relationship $P_2 = P_1 \pm Ke^{-rT} - S_0$ typically credited to Stoll (1969) for the original derivation.[10] It is important to notice that Bronzin derives this parity relationship as a necessary condition for the feasibility of a perfect hedge (p. 18).[11] It is apparently obvious for him that a position which is fully hedged against all states of the market cannot exhibit a positive price – but the term "arbitrage" does not show up in Bronzin's text.[12] But Bronzin even delivers an explicit statement about the feasibiliy of *riskless* return opportunities, if contracts can be purchased at better terms than those derived from "covered" positions (p. 38): "if in the pursuit of these transactions we succeed in concluding contracts at prices more favourable than the prices supposed in our equations, anything accomplished in that way will evidently bring about *unendangered* gains"

[10] An earlier analysis of the put-call parity is the unpublished thesis by Kruizenga (1956); Haug (2008) refers to even earlier, and more detailed, derivations of the parity.

[11] See e.g. his remark: "*Es müssen überdies zwischen den Prämien der Wahlkäufe und Wahlverkäufe, damit überhaupt eine Deckung möglich ist, die aufgestellten Bedingungen [...] eingehalten werden [...]*" (p. 18).

[12] Interestingly, Bronzin (1904) published a paper entitled "Arbitrage" a few years before. But the term was apparently applied to a more specific type of transactions at this time.

(editor's emphasis).[13] Combining this insight with the fact that such a position requires no initial capital, directly leads to the modern notion of arbitrage gains.

A further insight of Bronzin is related to the hedging of calls and puts with different exercise prices (chapter 2, section 3)[14]; he derives the "strange fact" that a perfect hedge requires a separate coverage of all option series, i.e. that there are no hedging effects between different series[15]. It should be noticed that Bronzin does not allow for "delta" hedges (which are not "perfect" in his terminology) because they would require a pricing model, which are not discussed before part II of his text. At the same time, Bonzin recognizes indirect hedging effects between different series through forward contracts: Because full coverage of individual series requires short or long forward contracts – they may now partially or fully cancel out each other. In a very euphuistic wording, Bronzin characterizes forward contracts as the "powerful intermediaries" (*mächtigen Vermittler*[16]), by which the different option series can be linked to each other.

5.3.2 Forward Price

From the beginning of his analysis, Bronzin's focus is on the future variability (volatility) and the current state of the market, not the trend and price expectations. Although he clearly recognizes the random character of market fluctuations,[17] he does not develop a stochastic process for these fluctuations (which is the key element of Bachelier's derivation), but directly characterizes the deviation of the future market price around the expected value – for which he considers the forward price a natural choice.[18] Thus, the distribution of market

[13] Quoted from the translation in chapter 4. Original text: "*gelingt es nun, bei diesen Operationen den Abschluss der einzelnen Geschäfte zu günstigeren Bedingungen zu bewerkstelligen, als es in unseren Gleichungen vorausgesetzt ist, so wird offenbar alles in dieser Richtung Erreichte einen* sicheren *Gewinn herbeizuführen im stande sein*" (p. 38); editor's emphasis.

[14] We will subsequently refer to options with different exercise prices (and maturities, which are not considered here) as "series".

[15] Unfortunately, this part of the text (p. 27) is difficult to read, even in German: "*[...] dass die zu verschiedenen Kursen abgeschloseenen Prämiengeschäfte für sich selbst gedeckte Systeme bilden müssen, [...], wodurch die Unmöglichkeit nachgewiesen wird, Prämiengeschäfte einer einzelnen Gattung durch andere auf Grund verschiedener Kurse abgeschlossener Geschäfte zu decken resp. abzuleiten*".

[16] From a linguistic point of view it may just be interesting to notice that a different translation of the German „*Vermittler*" is "arbitrator", which is fairly close to "arbitrage".

[17] He argues that he does not know any general criteria to characterize the random (in the German original: *regellos*) market movements for the various underlyings analytically. Original text: "*Allgemeine Anhaltspunkte, um die regellosen Schwankungen der Marktlage bei den verschiedenen Wertobjekten rechnerisch verfolgen zu können, gehen uns vollständig ab*" (p. 56).

[18] He also assumes that the forward price is "naturally" close or even identical to the current spot price; the original text: "*[...] zum Kurse B, welcher natürlicherweise mit dem Tageskurse nahe oder vollkommen übereinstimmen wird [...]*" (p. 1). Since there is no mention about interest rates, the time value of money, or discounting anywhere in his book, this also implies a basic notion of efficient markets.

prices at maturity is characterized by deviations from the forward price, $\tilde{x} \equiv \tilde{S}_T - B$, where S_T denotes the stock price at maturity (in the notation of our paper).

Bronzin gives several justifications why to use the forward price as the mean of the probability distribution at maturity. He repeatedly argues that the forward price is the most likely among all possible future market prices (p. 56, p. 74, p. 80), i.e. the forward price is an unbiased predictor of the future spot price. Otherwise, he argues, that one could not imagine sales and purchases (i.e. opposite transactions) with equal chances if strong reasons would exist leading people to ultimately predict either a rising or falling market price with higher probability.[19] Thus, the forward price is regarded as the most "advantageous" price for both parties in a forward transaction.[20]

A slightly different reasoning is used when discussing the payoff diagram of a forward contract, where he states that the forward price B must be such that the two "triangle parts" to the left and the right of B, i.e. to the profit and loss of the contract, must be "equivalent" because otherwise, selling or buying forward should be more profitable[21]. This does not necessarily imply an unbiased forward price, although there is little doubt that he wants to claim this.

While the issue of price expectations seems to be important for Bronzin, it is not relevant for the development of his model. The important point is that the mean of the price distribution is based on observable market price (spot or forward price), not price expectation or other preference-based measures.[22] These would be relevant if statements about risk premiums or risk preferences should be made, which is not the intention of the author. Instead, his focus is on consistent (or in his wording, "fair") pricing relationships between spot, forward, and option contracts – which qualifies his probability density as a risk neutral density.

[19] Original text: "*Es könnten ja sonst nicht Käufe und Verkäufe, d.h. entgegengesetzte Geschäfte, mit gleichen Chancen abgeschlossen gedacht werden, wenn triftige Gründe da wären, die mit aller Entschiedenheit entweder das Steigen oder das Fallen des Kurses mit grösserer Wahrscheinlichkeit voraussehen liessen*" (p. 74).

[20] On p. 56, the reasoning for this insight is justified by the fact that the call and put prices coincide if the exercise price is equal to the forward price.

[21] Original text: "*Es braucht kaum der Erwähnung, dass die dreieckigen Diagrammteile rechts und links von B als äquivalent anzunehmen sind, da sonst entweder der Kauf oder der Verkauf von Haus aus vorteilhafter sein sollte*" (p. 1). The wording "*von Haus aus*" is no longer used in the German language, but the meaning in this context is "naturally".

[22] The same is true for Bachelier's analysis. In contrast to Bronzin, he does not argue with the forward price, but he apparently assumes that the price at which a forward contract (*opération ferme*) is executed is equal to the current spot price (see his characterization on p. 26; notice that his x is the deviation of the stock price at expiration from the current value).

5.3.3 Fair Pricing

Bronzin extends the characterization of market prices to the definition of expected profits and losses from financial contracts. He considers a valuation principle as "fair" if the expected value[23] of profits and losses is zero for both parties when the contract is written (pp. 41-42). For this purpose, the conditions of each transaction must be determined in a way that the sum of expected profits of both parties (taking losses as negative profits) is zero[24]. Bronzin calls this the "fair pricing condition" (*Bedingung der Rechtmässigkeit*). Obviously, it is a zero profit condition assuming that there is no time value of money and no compensation for risk. It is the same assumption Bachelier makes to justify the martingale assumption of stock prices[25].

Based on the discussion in the previous section, he therefore considers a pricing rule as fair if expected profits and losses of a contract are derived from a "pricing" density of the underlying which is centered at the forward price. The general pricing equation he derives from this principle is

$$P_1 = \int_M^{\omega} (\tilde{x} - M) f(x) dx \qquad \text{(equation 11, p. 46)} \qquad (5.2)$$

where again, P_1 denotes the call option price and ω is the upper bound of the probability density, which may be finite or infinite. $\tilde{x}$ is the deviation of the market price from forward price B, $\tilde{x} \equiv \tilde{S}_T - B$ (in the notation of this paper), and M is the deviation of the exercise price from the forward price, $M = K - B$ (in the notation of this paper). Apparently, $\tilde{x} - M = \tilde{S}_T - B$. Of course, (5.2) is a risk-neutral (and specifically, preference-free) valuation equation because no expectations, risk premia or preferences show up in the parameters. The forward price makes it all. This interpretation is reinforced by an additional observation of the author, which is discussed in the subsequent section.

[23] It is important to notice that the statement, in the literal sense, is about expected, not current (riskless), profits. It is therefore not a no-arbitrage condition. Original text: "*[...] dass im Moment des Abschlusses eines jeden Geschäfts beide Kontrahenten mit ganz gleichen Chancen dastehen, so dass für keinen derselben* im voraus *weder Gewinn noch Verlust anzunehmen ist*" (p. 42); editor's emphasis.

[24] Original text: "*wir stellen uns also jedes Geschäft unter solchen Bedingungen abgeschlossen vor, [...] dass der gesamte Hoffnungswert des Gewinns für beide Kontrahenten der Null gleichkommen müsse*" (p. 42).

[25] For example: "*L'espérance mathématique du spéculateur est nulle*" (p. 18); "*Il semble que le marché, c'est-à-dire l'ensemble des spéculateurs, ne doit croire à un instant donné ni à la hausse, ni à la baisse, puisque, pour chaque cours coté, il y a autant d'acheteurs que de vendeurs*" (pp. 31–32); "*L'espérance mathématique de l'acheteur de prime est nulle*" (p. 33).

The "fair pricing principle" is illustrated with a simple ATM call: The expected profit if the market exceeds the forward price B is $G = \int_0^{\omega}(x-P)f(x)dx$, where P is the price of the call option. Notice that because there is no time value of money, the option premiums can be added and subtracted from the terminal payoff. The expected loss in the down market is respectively $V = \int_0^{\omega_1} Pf_1(x)\,dx$, and the "fair pricing condition" implies

$$G - V = \int_0^{\omega}(x-P)\,f(x)\,dx - \int_0^{\omega_1} Pf_1(x)\,dx = 0$$

which can be solved for the option price

$$P = \int_0^{\omega} xf(x)dx.$$

For out-of-the-money calls ($X = B + M$), the profit and loss function is defined over four consecutive market price intervals bounded by $[\omega_1; B, B+M; B+M+P_1; \omega]$, and thus generalizes to

$$\underbrace{-\int_0^{\omega_1} P_1 f_1(x)\,dx}_{V_3} \underbrace{- \int_0^{M} P_1 f(x)\,dx}_{V_2} \underbrace{- \int_M^{M+P_1}(M+P_1-x)\,f(x)\,dx}_{V_1} + \underbrace{\int_{M+P_1}^{\omega}(x-M-P_1)\,f(x)\,dx}_{G} = 0$$

where three loss components must be taken into account. This yields after some manipulations

$$P_1 = \int_M^{\omega}(x-M)\,f(x)\,dx$$

The price of the equivalent in-the-money put option is derived as

$$P_2 = \int_0^{\omega_1}(M+x)\,f_1(x)\,dx + \int_0^{M}(M-x)\,f(x)\,dx$$

which after some manipulations (p. 47) leads to the put-call-parity

$$P_2 = P_1 + M$$

as discussed earlier.

5.3.4 Substituting Probabilities by Prices: A Prologue to Risk Neutral Pricing

The most amazing part of Bronzin's Treatise is in section 8 of the first chapter in part II, where he relates the probability function $f(x)$ to option prices. In modern option pricing, this was explicitly done in an unpublished and hardly known paper by Black (1974),[26] and a few years later by Breeden and Litzenberger (1978). By referring to the rules of differentiation with respect to boundaries of integrals, and expressions within the integral (generally known as Leibniz rules), he derives the "remarkable" expression

$$\frac{\partial P_1}{\partial M} = -\int_M^{\omega} f(x)\,dx = -F(M) \qquad \text{(equation 16, p. 50),} \qquad (5.3)$$

where $F(x) \equiv \int_x^{\omega} f(x)\,dx$, and $F(M)$ is the exercise probability of the option; apparently the sign of $\frac{\partial F(x)}{\partial x}$ is negative. Equation (5.3) postulates that the negative of the exercise probability is equal to the first derivative of the option price with respect to the exercise price (respectively, M). He notes this expression makes it much easier to solve for the option price P_1 than in the standard valuation approach, namely by evaluating the indefinite integral

$$P_1 = -\int F(M)\,dM + c \qquad \text{(equation 19, p. 51)} \qquad (5.4)$$

where c is a constant which is not difficult to compute (it will be zero or negligible in most cases). This is a powerful result: Option prices can be computed by integrating $F(M)$ over M. Depending on the functional form of $f(x)$, this drastically simplifies the computation of option prices. From there, it is straightforward to show that the second derivative

[26] Many years ago, William Margrabe made me aware of this paper. Not many people seem to know this tiny piece; e.g. it is also missing in the Merton and Scholes *Journal of Finance* tribute after Fischer Black's death, where a list of his published and unpublished papers is included (Merton and Scholes 1995).

$$\frac{\partial^2 P_1}{\partial M^2} = f(M) \qquad \text{(equation 17, p. 51)} \qquad (5.5)$$

directly gives the value of the (probability density) function at $x = M$.[27] As Breeden and Litzenberger (1978) have shown, this derivative multiplied by the increment dM can be interpreted as the implicit state price in the limit of a continuous state space. Absence of arbitrage requires that state prices are strictly positive, which implies $\frac{\partial^2 P_1}{\partial M^2} > 0$, i.e. option prices must be convex with respect to exercise prices. If this is condition is not satisfied, a butterfly spread[28] would generate an arbitrage profit. Bronzin also shows that equation (5.5) can be applied without adjustments to put options.

Bronzin thus recognized the key relationship between security prices and probability densities; he was fully aware that information on the unknown function $f(x)$ is impounded in observed (or theoretical) option prices, and just need to be extracted. This establishes $f(x)$ as a true pricing function (or density). Bronzin discusses both, the empirical and analytical implications of his finding.

Empirical implications: Although Bronzin's interest is clearly on the analytical side of his models, he is well aware of the empirical implications. As already noted earlier in this chapter, he claims the difficulties in specifying the function $f(x)$ on a priori grounds (p. 56)[29] and suggests to fit the function $F(x)$ with empirical data[30]: For different predetermined values of x, compute the relative frequency $\frac{g}{m}$ by which the market price exceeded x in the past:

$$F(x_j) = \int_{x_j}^{\omega} f(x_j)\, dx_j = \frac{g_j}{m_j} \; \forall j$$

[27] Bachelier (1900) on p. 51 also shows this expression, but without motivation, comments, or potential use.

[28] This is a strategy where three options contracts (on the same underlying) with different exercise prices are bought and sold. If the exercise prices are $K - \Delta K$, K and $K + \Delta K$, the strategy is to sell two contracts at K and buy one contract at $K - \Delta K$ and one at $K + \Delta K$. Any non-convexities in the corresponding option prices $P_1(K - \Delta K)$, $P_1(K)$ and $P_1(K + \Delta K)$ can be exploited by this strategy.

[29] Original text: „*Was nun die Form der Funktion $f(x)$ selbst anlangt, so stossen wir auf sehr grosse Schwierigkeiten. Allgemeine Anhaltspunkte, um die regellosen Schwankungen der Marktlage bei den verschiedenen Wertobjekten rechnerisch verfolgen zu können, gehen uns vollständig ab*“ (p. 56).

[30] $F(x)$ denotes the probability that the market price exceeds a predetermined value x.

He then suggests that to determine the functional form of $F(x=M)$ by running a least-square regression of the empirical $F(x_1),...,F(x_n)$ values on $x_1,...,x_n$. He claims, quite correctly, that this procedure generates a specific function $F(x)$ for every possible underlying, which would be very handy, and by relating the result to $\frac{\partial P_1}{\partial M}=-F(M)$ could answer any question in a simple and reliable way ... (p. 57). However, being a mathematician, he then says that he does not want to do this troublesome job, but is satisfied with specific functional specifications of $f(x)$. This will be discussed in section 5.4.

The *analytical* implications of equations (5.3)–(5.5) play a key role in his derivation of option prices in the second part of his book. We provide a brief illustration using the "triangle distribution" which he uses later in his analysis. $f(x)$ is specified as a linear function $f(x)=a+bx$, defined over the interval $[0;+\omega]$; and respectively $f_1(x)=a+b|x|$ if x is in the negative range $[-\omega; 0]$. For $f(\omega)=f_1(\omega)=0$ to hold, the parameters must be specified as $a=\frac{1}{\omega}$, $b=-\frac{1}{\omega^2}$, which implies $f(x)=\frac{\omega-x}{\omega^2}$.

The standard pricing approach requires the solution of the integral

$$P_1=\int_M^\omega (x-M)f(x)dx=\int_M^\omega (x-M)\frac{\omega-x}{\omega^2}dx$$

which is a quite complicated task (see p. 66). In contrast, the procedure suggested by Bronzin is much simpler:

- First, compute $F(M)$, i.e. the probability that $\tilde{x}$ exceeds $x=M$. This given by $\frac{(\omega-M)^2}{2\omega^2}$.
- Second, solve $\frac{\partial P_1}{\partial M}=-F(M)=-\frac{(\omega-M)^2}{2\omega^2}$ for P_1, which is given by the integral $P_1=-\int F(M)dM+c=-\int\frac{(\omega-M)^2}{2\omega^2}dM+c$. The solution is $P_1=\frac{(\omega-M)^3}{6\omega^2}$. Notice that the constant is zero because $P_1(M=\omega)=0$ (see p. 62).

A graphical illustration is provided in Figures 5.1a–c. We assume $\omega=10$ and an exercise price of $M=5$. The resulting (call) option price is 0.208.

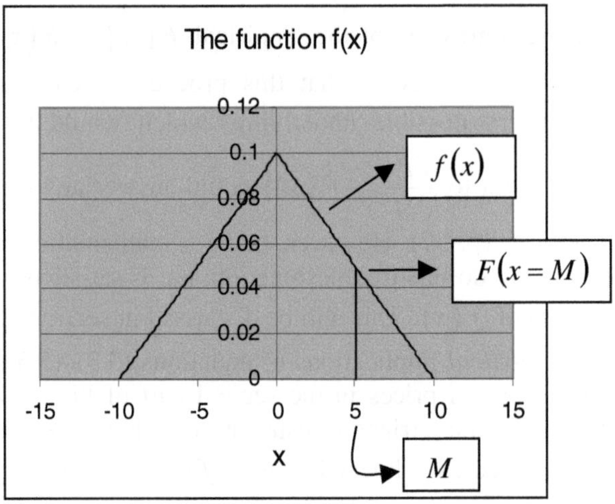

Fig. 5.1a

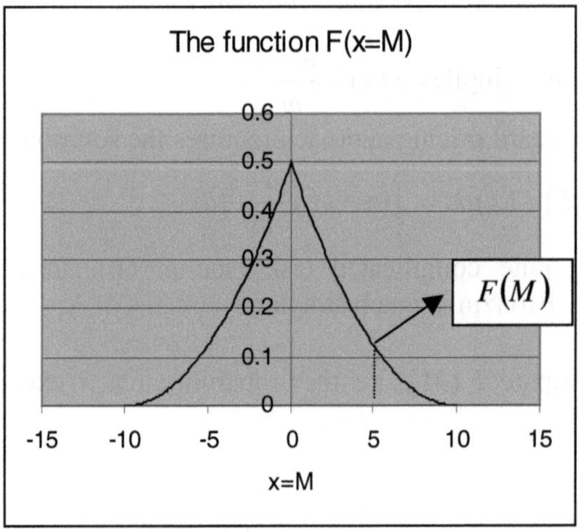

Fig. 5.1b

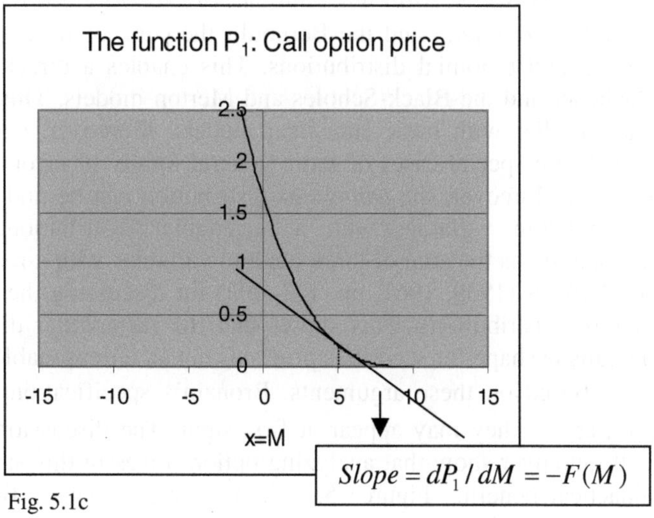

Fig. 5.1c

Figs. 5.1a–c. The Bronzin approach to option pricing – or: three ways to represent the exercise probability $F(M)$ of an option: illustration with the triangle pricing density.

5.4 Option Pricing with Specific Functional or Distributional Assumptions

The specification of the pricing density $f(x)$ and the derivation of closed form solutions for option prices is the objective of the second chapter in part II. Bronzin discusses six different functional specifications of $f(x)$ and the implied shape of the density for a given range of x. From a probabilistic point of view, this part of the book seems to be slightly outdated, because the first four "distributions" lack any obvious stochastic foundation. The function $f(x)$ seems to be specified rather ad-hoc, just to produce simple probability shapes for the price deviations from the forward price: a rectangular distribution, a triangular distribution, a parabolic distribution, and an exponential distribution.

This impression particularly emerges if Bachelier's thesis is taken as benchmark, where major attention is given to the modeling of the probability law governing the dynamics of the underlying asset value. This was an extraordinary achievement on its own. In order to be fair about Bronzin's approach, one should be aware of the state of probability theory at the beginning of the last century. As Bernard Bru mentioned in his interview with Murad Taqqu (see Taqqu 2001, p. 5), "probability did not start to gain recognition in France until the 1930's. This was also the case in Germany".

However, the fifth and sixth specification of $f(x)$ are the normal law of error (*Fehlergesetz*) and the Bernoulli theorem, or in modern terminology, the normal and binomial distributions. This enables a direct comparison with the Bachelier and the Black-Scholes and Merton models. This implies that Bronzin was familiar with basic statistical models. Moreover, even the four "ad-hoc" models are special cases of more general family of error laws, called "Pearson laws"[31]. Moreover, the *triangular* distribution can be understood as the sum of two random variables with a rectangular distribution; and the *parabolic* distribution as the sum of three random variables with a rectangular distribution; see Jeffreys (1939, 1961, pp. 101–103) for discussing the convergence of sums of error distributions. This shows that the rectangular distribution, despite its unrealistic shape for securities prices, is not an unreasonable choice to start with.

Based on these arguments, Bronzin's specifications of $f(x)$ are not so arbitrary as they may appear at first sight. The discussion in the next sections will moreover show that analyzing option prices in this simple setting has great didactical benefits. Figures 5.2a-5.2d illustrate four of Bronzin's six distributional assumptions.

For the subsequent discussion it is useful to recall that x denotes the market price of the underlying asset at maturity *minus the forward price*. Bronzin now makes the simplifying assumption that functions $f(x)$ and $f_1(x)$ are symmetric around B, i.e. that $f(x) = f_1(x)$. This implies[32] $\omega = \omega_1$, and consequently, $\int_0^{\omega} f(x)dx = 0.5$ (p. 55). This assumption makes the expected market price equal to the forward price; as discussed earlier, Bronzin considers this a straightforward (*a priori einleuchtend*, p. 56) economic assumption. At the same time, he is entirely aware that a symmetric probability density is not consistent with the limited liability nature of the underlying "objects": while price increases are potentially unbounded, prices cannot fall below zero[33]. However, he plays this argument down by saying that these (extreme) cases are fairly unlikely, and price variations can be regarded as more or less uniform (*regelmässige*) and generally not substantial (*nicht erhebliche*) oscillations around B. Based on this reasoning,

[31] See e.g. Jeffreys (1939, 1961), pp. 74-78. This book is very helpful in understanding the terminology on the normal distribution, called the normal law of error, as used at the beginning of the past century.

[32] Notice that $\int_0^{\omega} xf(x)dx = \int_0^{\omega_1} xf_1(x)dx$ must hold.

[33] Original text: "*[...] es könnte ja eine Kurserhöhung in unbeschränktem Masse stattfinden, während offenbar eine Kursemiedrigung höchstens bis zur Wertlosigkeit des Objekts vor sich gehen kann*" (p. 56).

he seems to be very confident about the results being derived from this assumption...[34]

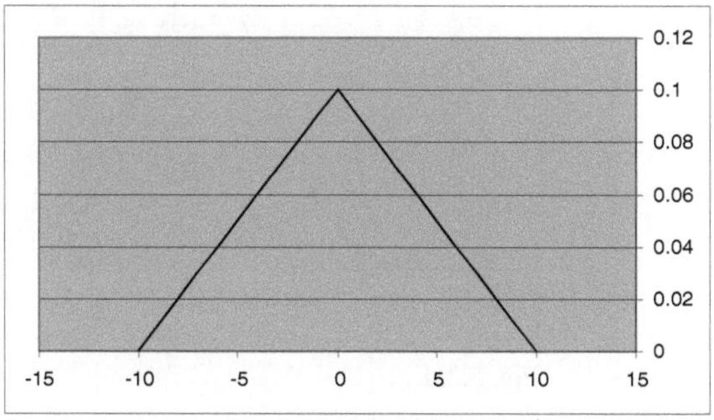

Fig. 5.2a

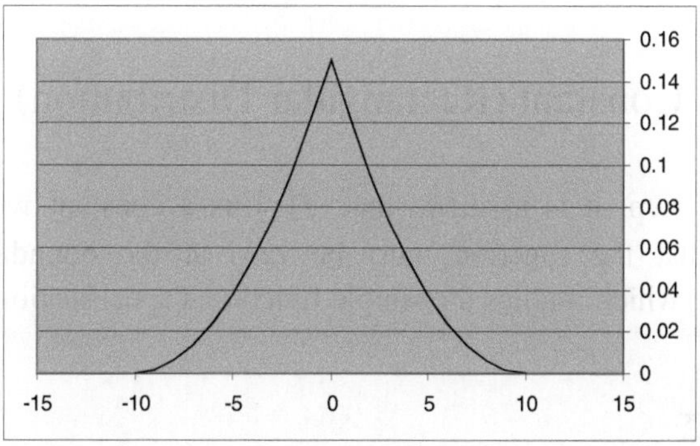

Fig. 5.2b

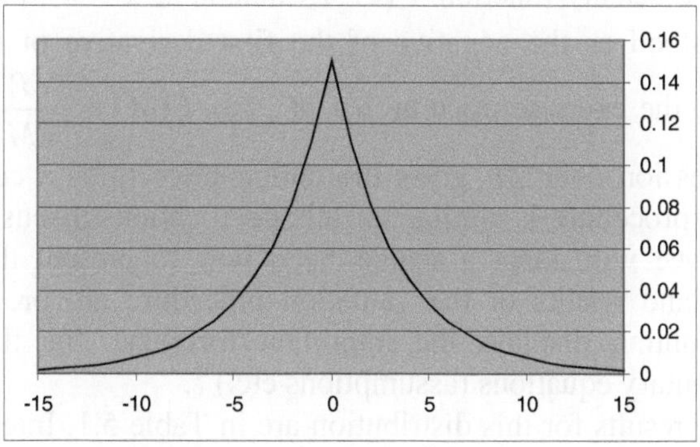

Fig. 5.2.c

[34] Original text: "*[...] so darf man die gemachte Voraussetzung getrost akzeptieren und ihren Resultaten mit Zuversicht entgegensehen*" (p. 56).

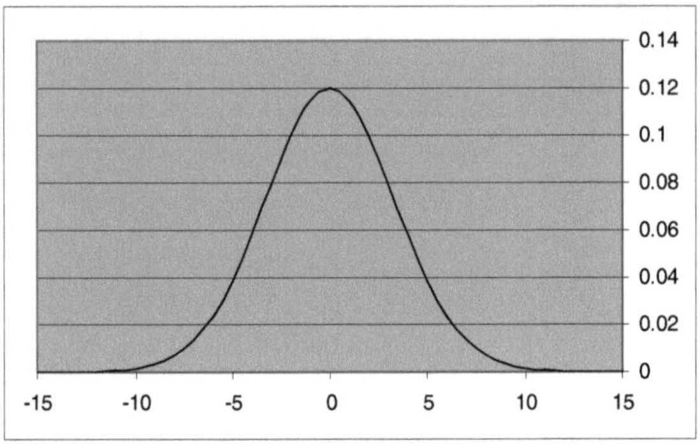

Fig. 5.2.d

Figs. 5.2a–d. Four of Bronzin's 6 Specifications of the Pricing Density Function (linear, quadratic, exponential, normal law of error and the associated densities).

5.4.1 A Constant (Rectangular Distribution)

In a first step, it is assumed that $f(x)$ is a constant within $[-\omega;+\omega]$. This implies that the function must be zero at the boundaries of the integral, $f(\omega)=0$, which implies the simple functional specification

$$f(x)=\frac{1}{2\omega}$$

for the pricing density. Based on this function, we are able to derive the cumulative density function $F(x)$. Evaluated at $x=M$, this function which can be understood as the negative of the first derivative of the option price with respect to the exercise price at $B+M$, i.e. $F(M)=-\frac{\partial P_1}{\partial M}$. Simply integrating this expression over M gives the option price (plus a constant). Because this valuation procedure is similar for all specifications discussed in the subsequent sections, we will adapt a standardized way to present the results. The major elements and results of the valuation procedure are presented in Tables; the second column displays the important formulae, the third column contains complimentary equations (assumptions etc.)[35].

The results for this distribution are in Table 5.1. Interpreting ω as volatility of the underlying, the formula neatly separates the impact of intrinsic value

[35] If not mentioned otherwise, the results in the Tables are those derived by Bronzin, while the interpretation in the text is our's.

M and volatility on option price. As done for other specifications, the relationship between the ATM call price P and general call price P_1 is given by

$$P_1 = \left(1 - \frac{M}{4P}\right)^2 P$$

Also, the symmetry between put and call prices with respect to the forward price is easily recognized. Of course, the distribution is unrealistic for most practical applications, but the pedagogical merits are straightforward.

Table 5.1 The function $f(x)$ is a constant (rectangular distribution).

Function $f(x)$	$f(x) = a$	$f(\omega) = 0$
Density $f(x)$	$f(x) = \frac{1}{2\omega}$	
Exercise probability $F(x = M)$	$F(M) = \frac{\omega - M}{2\omega}$	
Pricing kernel	$\frac{\partial P_1}{\partial M} = -F(M) = -\frac{\omega - M}{2\omega}$	
Call	$P_1 = \frac{(\omega - M)^2}{4\omega}$	
ATM Call/Put	$P = \frac{\omega}{4}$	
Put	$P_2 = \frac{(\omega + M)^2}{4\omega}$	

5.4.2 A Linear Function (Triangular Distribution)

Next, the function $f(x)$ is assumed being linear within the subintervals $[-\omega;0]$ and $[0;+\omega]$. The implied density function is then a symmetric triangle with its vertex equal to $1/\omega$ at the forward price; see Figure 5.2a. The rest of the pricing equations is displayed in Table 5.2. Assuming the same boundaries ω as in the previous section[36], it is interesting to notice that the ATM option prices decrease from one fourth of ω (as for the uniform distribution) to one sixth. This nicely shows the impact of shifting part of the probability mass (i.e. one eighth on each side of the distribution) from the "tails" to the center of the distribution, or the

[36] This does not keep the standard deviation of the distribution the same, of course.

reverse. To put it differently, the "riskier" uniform density implies an ATM option price which is $\omega/4 \div \omega/6 = 1.5$ times, or respectively 50%, higher than the price implied by the triangular distribution – although only 25% of the probability mass is shifted from the tails to the center.

Again, as in the previous section, the non-ATM call price can be easily decomposed to an intrinsic and volatility part.

Table 5.2 The function $f(x)$ is linear (triangular distribution).

Function $f(x)$	$f(x) = a + bx$	$f(\omega) = 0$
Density $f(x)$	$f(x) = \dfrac{\omega - x}{\omega^2}$	$a = \dfrac{1}{\omega},\ b = \dfrac{-1}{\omega^2}$
Exercise probability $F(x = M)$	$F(M) = \dfrac{(\omega - M)^2}{2\omega^2}$	
Pricing kernel	$\dfrac{\partial P_1}{\partial M} = -F(M) = -\dfrac{(\omega - M)^2}{2\omega^2}$	$P_1(M = \omega) = 0 \Rightarrow c = 0$
Call	$P_1 = \dfrac{(\omega - M)^3}{6\omega^2}$	
ATM Call/Put	$P = \dfrac{\omega}{6}$	
Relation between ATM Call and general Call	$P_1 = \left(1 - \dfrac{M}{6P}\right)^3 P$	

5.4.3 A Quadratic Function (Parabolic Distribution)

In the next step, Bronzin assumes a quadratic function for $f(x)$ within the interval $[-\omega;0]$ and $[0;+\omega]$. Notice the conditions under which the parameters $\{a, b, c\}$ are derived. Note that $f'(x = \omega) = 0$ ensures that the function has its minimum at $x = \omega$ where it asymptotically approaches the abscissa. Compared to the triangular distribution discussed before, the probability of reaching ω is (again) smaller; see Figure 5.2b. Bronzin suggests to use this distribution for modeling extreme values with small probabilities by setting ω sufficiently large (p. 67). Nevertheless, we now assume that ω is the same as in the previous two sections in order to facilitate comparisons.

Since extreme value have again become less likely compared to the triangular distribution, it is not surprising that the value of ATM options is again lower, i.e. it decreases from one sixth of ω to one eighth. The other results are similar and need no further comment.

Table 5.3 The function $f(x)$ is quadratic (parabolic distribution)

Function $f(x)$	$f(x)=a+bx+cx^2$	$f(\omega)=0,\ f'(x=\omega)=0$
Density $f(x)$	$f(x)=\dfrac{3(\omega-x)^2}{2\omega^3}$	$a=\dfrac{3}{2\omega},\ b=\dfrac{-3}{\omega^2},$ $c=\dfrac{3}{2\omega^3}$
Exercise probability $F(x=M)$	$F(M)=\dfrac{(\omega-M)^3}{2\omega^3}$	
Pricing kernel	$\dfrac{\partial P_1}{\partial M}=-F(M)=-\dfrac{(\omega-M)^3}{2\omega^3}$	$P_1(M=\omega)=0 \Rightarrow c=0$
Call	$P_1=\dfrac{(8\omega-M)^4}{8\omega^3}$	
ATM Call/Put	$P=\dfrac{\omega}{8}$	
Relation between ATM Call and general Call	$P_1=\left(1-\dfrac{M}{8P}\right)^4 P$	

5.4.4 An Exponential Function (Negative Exponential Distribution)

Finally, an exponential distribution is assumed for $f(x)$; in contrast to the functions assumed before, the range of x over which the function is defined, needs no arbitrary restriction. The function asymptotically converges to zero for large x; see Figure 5.2c. The range of x values is unbounded, and rare events with small probabilities can even be handled much easier by this functional specification. The parameter k determines the variability of x – a bigger k reduces the variability. As shown in the next section, the standard deviation (volatility) of the distribution is given by $\sigma = 1/2k$. Then the price of ATM option is straight *half* the volatility! Again, the general option prices separate the impact of the volatility and moneyness in an extremely nice way.

The comparison with the option price derived from the previous distribution (quadratic) is not straightforward. First, we should know the probability by which the exponential distribution exceeds the maximum value of the parabolic distribution ω; this is given by the function $F(x=\omega)=\dfrac{e^{-2k\omega}}{2}$ (see Bronzin p. 70, equation 30). We then calibrate k such that the exponential function is identical to the quadratic at $x=0$. The quadratic function is $f_q(x=0)=\frac{3}{2\omega}$, and setting it equal to the exponential at $x=0$, $f_{\exp}(x=0)=k$, we get $k=\frac{3}{2\omega}$. The probability that realizations from the exponential density exceed the maximum of the parabolic, ω, is therefore

$$F(x=\omega)=\frac{e^{-2\frac{3}{2\omega}\omega}}{2}=\frac{e^{-3}}{2}=0.02489$$

which is approximately 2.5%, or on a two sided basis, 5%. So it is easy to find how the "extra" risk is rewarded. The ATM option price under our calibration for k is

$$P\left(k=\frac{3}{2\omega}\right)=\frac{1}{4k}=\frac{1}{4\times\frac{3}{2\omega}}=\frac{1}{\frac{6}{\omega}}=\frac{\omega}{6}$$

which exceeds the respective option price from the parabolic distribution by $\frac{\omega/6}{\omega/8}-1=\frac{1}{3}$, i.e. one third.

Table 5.4 The function $f(x)$ is exponential (negative exponential distribution).

Function $f(x)$	$f(x)=ka^{-hx}$	$\omega=\infty$
Density $f(x)$	$f(x)=ke^{-2kx}$	$a=e^{2k/h}$
Exercise probability $F(x=M)$	$F(M)=\frac{e^{-2kM}}{2}$	
Pricing kernel	$\frac{\partial P_1}{\partial M}=-F(M)=-\frac{e^{-2kM}}{2}$	$P_1(M=\omega)=0 \Rightarrow c=0$
Call	$P_1=\frac{e^{-2kM}}{4k}$	
ATM Call/Put	$P=\frac{1}{4k}$	
Relation between ATM Call and general Call	$P_1=e^{-\frac{1}{2}\frac{M}{P}}P$	

5.4.5 The Normal Law of Error

The most exciting specification of $f(x)$ is the law of error (*Fehlergesetz*) defined by $f(x)=\frac{h}{\sqrt{\pi}}e^{-h^2x^2}$ [37]. Unlike the previous specifications of $f(x)$, this is now a direct specification of the probability density. Reasoning that market variations above and below the forward price B can be regarded as deviations from the markets' most favorable outcome, Bronzin suggest to use the law of error as a very reliable law to represent error probabilities[38]. Of course, the density corresponds to a normal distribution with zero mean and a standard deviation of $\sigma_{err}=\frac{1}{h\sqrt{2}}$. Or alternatively, setting $h=\frac{1}{\sigma\sqrt{2}}$ gives us the normal $N\{0,\sigma^2\}$.[39] With respect to terminology, we subsequently use the wording "normal law of error" or "error distribution".

In order to compare the ATM option price with the previous section, it is necessary to have equal variances. The variance of the exponential distribution is given by

$$Var_{\exp}(x)=\int_0^\infty x^2 f(x)\,dx=\int_0^\infty x^2 k e^{-2kx}dx$$

Applying the formula $\int_0^\infty x^n e^{-ax}dx=n!a^{-n-1}$ gives

$$Var_{\exp}(x)=k\int_0^\infty x^2 e^{-2kx}dx=k\times\left\{2\times(2k)^{-2-1}\right\}=\frac{2k}{(2k)^3}=\frac{1}{(2k)^2}$$

---

[37] The (normal) law of error should not be confused with error *function* which is an integral defined by $erf(x)=2\int_0^x\frac{1}{\sqrt{\pi}}e^{-t^2}dt$, related to the cumulative standard normal $N\{.\}$ by $erf(x)=2\left[N\{x\sqrt{2}\}-0.5\right]$.

[38] Original text: „*Indem wir uns also die Marktschwankungen über oder unter* B *gleichsam als Abweichungen von einem vorteilhaftesten Werte vorstellen, werden wir versuchen, denselben die Befolgung des Fehlergesetzes [...] vorzuschreiben, welches sich zur Darstellung der Fehlerwahrscheinlichkeiten sehr gut bewährt hat; [...]*" (p. 74).

[39] As a historical remark, the analytical characterization as well as the terminology related to the "normal" distribution was very mixed until the end of the 19th century; while statisticians like Galton, Lexis, Venn, Edgeworth, and Pearson have occasionally used the expression in the late 19th century, it was adopted by the probabilistic community not earlier than in the 1920s. Stigler (1999), pp. 404–415, provides a detailed analysis of this subject.

so that the volatility is

$$\sigma_{\exp}(x)=\frac{1}{2k} \tag{5.6}$$

The variance of the error distribution can be computed by the same procedure; alternatively one can easily substitute the parameter $h=\frac{1}{\sigma\sqrt{2}}$ in the function to get

$$f(x)=\frac{h}{\sqrt{\pi}}e^{-h^2x^2}=\frac{\frac{1}{\sigma\sqrt{2}}}{\sqrt{\pi}}e^{-\frac{1}{2\sigma^2}x^2}=\frac{1}{\sigma\sqrt{2\pi}}e^{-\frac{1}{2}\left(\frac{x}{\sigma}\right)^2}$$

which is the density function of a normally distributed variable with zero mean and standard deviation σ. Solving $h=\frac{1}{\sigma\sqrt{2}}$ for σ gives

$$\sigma_{err}(x)=\frac{1}{h\sqrt{2}} \tag{5.7}$$

which shows the standard deviation of the error distribution implied by a specific choice of parameter h. Since h is inversely related to the standard deviation of the distribution, it measures the precision of the observations, and is called *precision modulus;* see Johnson et al. (1994), p. 81.

The relationship between the volatility of the exponential and the error distribution is then given by the equality $2k=h\sqrt{2}$ or

$$h=k\sqrt{2}\,. \tag{5.8}$$

The implied ATM option price is therefore

$$P_{err}\left(h=k\sqrt{2}\right)=\frac{1}{2k\sqrt{2}\sqrt{\pi}}=\frac{1}{k\sqrt{8\pi}}=\frac{1}{5.013\times k}$$

which is only about 80% of the exponential ATM option price $P_{\exp}=\frac{1}{4k}$. This is not surprising: compared to the exponential distribution, the error (or normal) distribution has more weight around the mean and less around the tails – given the same standard deviation.

It is also interesting to compare the ATM option price with the quadratic case examined two sections before. For this purpose we need to know the relationship between the parameters h and ω; combining $h=k\sqrt{2}$ with

$k = \frac{3}{2\omega}$ which was used as condition of consistency between the quadratic and exponential function (in the previous section), this gives $h = \frac{3}{2\omega}\sqrt{2} = \frac{\sqrt{4.5}}{\omega}$.

Inserting this in $P = \frac{1}{2h\sqrt{\pi}}$ yields

$$P_{err} = \frac{1}{2\frac{\sqrt{4.5}}{\omega}\sqrt{\pi}} = \frac{\omega}{7.51988482}$$

which is only approx. 6% more than the price of the respective option priced with the quadratic function, $P_q = \frac{\omega}{8}$. The similarity of the option prices is not surprising given the similarity of the two densities; see Figures 5.2b and 5.2d.

The impact of the moneyness is less obvious than in the former cases. This will be discussed below when we compare the formula with the Black-Scholes case.

Table 5.5 The function $f(x)$ is the normal law of error

Density $f(x)$	$f(x) = \frac{h}{\sqrt{\pi}} e^{-h^2x^2}$	$\omega = \infty$
Exercise probability $F(x = M)$	$F(M) = \psi(hM)$ $\psi(\varepsilon) = \frac{1}{\sqrt{\pi}} \int_{\varepsilon}^{\infty} e^{-t^2} dt$	
Pricing kernel	$\frac{\partial P_1}{\partial M} = -F(M) = \ldots$	$P_1(M = \omega) = 0 \Rightarrow c = 0$
Call	$P_1 = \frac{e^{-M^2h^2}}{2h\sqrt{\pi}} - M\,\psi(hM)$	
ATM Call/Put	$P = \frac{1}{2h\sqrt{\pi}}$	

5.4.6 The Binomial Distribution ("Bernoulli Theorem")

While sections 2 through 6 in the 2nd chapter of part II in Bronzin's book are direct specifications of the pricing density $f(x)$, the approach taken in his final section 7 is slightly different. It can be understood as a concrete specification of the (inverse) volatility factor h in the previous (i.e. the error) distribution. The reasoning of the author to motivate this distribution is very similar to the binomial model of Cox et al. (1979). Assuming that s (consecutive) price movements[40] are governed by "two opposite events" (e.g. market ups and downs) with probability p and q, which can be thought as Bernoulli trials. The expected value of the distribution is sp (or alternatively, sq)[41]. Of course, the events can be scaled arbitrarily by choosing the parameter s appropriately. Therefore, one of the expected values (which one is arbitrary) can be set equal to the forward price, e.g. $B = sp$. The price distribution can then be understood as being generated by cumulative deviations of market events from their most likely outcome, the forward price. The standard deviation of this distribution is $\sqrt{spq} = \sqrt{Bq}$. The option prices can then be derived as follows:

If $\tilde{x}$ denotes the price deviations between the market price and the forward price, Bronzin uses the following expression to describe the probability that $\tilde{x}$ is in the interval $[0; x^*]$ [42]

$$\frac{1}{\sqrt{2\pi}} \int_0^{z^*} e^{-\frac{1}{2}z^2} dz + \frac{e^{-z^2}}{\sqrt{2\pi}\sqrt{Bq}}, \text{ with } z^* = \frac{x^*}{\sqrt{Bq}}, \ \tilde{z} = \frac{\tilde{x}}{\sqrt{Bq}} \tag{5.9}$$

and neglects the second expression in his subsequent analysis (the term being "of secondary importance", which is of course not exactly true). He then notices that for $h = \frac{1}{\sqrt{2qB}}$, or in our own notation, for

$$\sigma(x) = \frac{1}{h\sqrt{2}} = \sqrt{qB}; \tag{5.10}$$

this is the same integral as in the previous section where $f(x)$ was specified by the normal density. He concludes that the application of the Bernoulli theorem to

[40] Again, there is no reference to a time dimension in Bronzin's approach. In the Cox et al. (1979) setting, these would be interpreted as consecutive market movements. In the Bronzin setting, the binomial approach is just used to characterize the deviations from the expected (i.e. forward) price.

[41] Original text: "*[...] so stellen ps resp. qs die wahrscheinlichsten Wiederholungszahlen der betrachteten Ereignisse dar*" (p. 80).

[42] We use a simpler notation than Bronzin, who operates with the error function; see his equations (47) and (50).

market movements leads to the same results as the application of the error law[43]. Given the asymptotic properties of the binomial distribution, this is of course not a surprising result. It is, however, interesting to notice that he treats the Bernoulli model as a way to motivate the "limiting" case of the error function in the same way as Cox et al. (1979) demonstrate that their binomial model converges to the Black-Scholes model in the limiting case. Finally it is interesting to notice that Bachelier (on p. 38ff) also uses a binomial tree to retrieve the properties of the Wiener process developed before.

Bronzin also recognizes that the volatility, respectively his h, is not a variable which can be directly observed. He repeatedly stresses this point by arguing that this parameter needs to be empirically estimated for each underlying – again on p. 81. However, he recognizes that by specifying the expected value of his binomial distribution by $sp = B$, then the only part which remains unspecified in his volatility expression is the q parameter; see equation (21). If the "preference based" q parameter would be known, then the volatility could be directly inferred from the forward price B. E.g. if $q = \frac{1}{2}$, then the volatility would be the square root of half the forward price, $\sigma(x) = \sqrt{\frac{B}{2}}$: see Bronzin's equation (51a). He is surprised, or puzzled, about this finding (p. 82) and notices that the volatility of market prices is likely to depend on many other factors than the observed forward price. However, it may be useful to read the result of equation (21) in a different way, namely by understanding q as the endogenous variable. It then implies that $q = \frac{\sigma^2(x)}{B}$, i.e. increasing the variance of the underlying while leaving B increases probability q. This is by no means a surprising result. We just have to re-interpret Bronzin's probabilities as risk-neutral probabilities, which is legitimate as discussed earlier (Section 4.3). Increasing the variance while leaving the stock price and interest rate (and thus, the forward price) constant, implies a shift of the risk-neutral density to the left (the risk-neutral mean of the distribution falls), which means a higher probability for bad states. This is exactly what a higher probability q means; remember that the forward price was matched with the expected value of the distribution sp, so that p are the probabilities of the "good" states (market event) by definition.

[43] Original text: "*[...] so ersehen wir aus der vollkommenen hier herrschenden Analogie, dass uns die Anwendung des Bernoullischen Theorems auf die Marktschwankungen zu demselben Resultate, wie die Annahme der Befolgung des Fehlergesetzes, führt*" (p. 81).

5.5 A Comparison of Bronzin's Law-of-Error Based Option Formula with the Black-Scholes Formula

Obviously, Bronzin's specification of the pricing density as "normal law of error", as described in the previous Section 5.4.5, is particularly interesting, because it promises a direct link to the celebrated Black-Scholes model[44] which is also based on a normal distribution.[45] As seen before, setting $h = \frac{1}{\sigma\sqrt{2}}$ in the error function generates a normal distribution with standard deviation σ. The problem is, however, that the Black-Scholes model assumes a normal distribution for the *log*-prices, while Bronzin makes this assumption for the price *level* itself. Extending this difference to the underlying stochastic processes, Bronzin's distribution can be interpreted[46] as the result of an arithmetic Wiener process, while the Black-Scholes model relies on a geometric Wiener process.

Since there is an immediate link between the two processes, why not interpreting Bronzin's price levels as log-prices? This is, however, not adequate in the option pricing framework because the value of options is a function of the payoff emerging from the (positive) difference between settlement *price* and exercise *price* of the option, not their logarithms. In this respect, the approach of Bronzin is the same as the one of Bachelier. It was only Sprenkle (1961, 1964) and later Samuelson (1973) who corrected the possibility of negative prices in the Bachelier model by modeling the Wiener process of speculative price in logs instead of levels[47].

More precisely, the analytical complication comes from the following point. The pricing function for a call option with exercise price $B+M$ in the Bronzin setting is

$$P_1 = \int_M^{\infty} (\tilde{x} - M) f(x) dx, \quad f(x) = \frac{h}{\sqrt{\pi}} e^{-h^2 x^2} = \frac{1}{\sigma(x)\sqrt{2\pi}} e^{-\frac{1}{2}\left(\frac{x}{\sigma(x)}\right)^2} \tag{5.11}$$

where $\tilde{x}$ is the deviation of the market price at maturity from the forward price, described by the error distribution, or the normal, with zero mean and standard

[44] We adopt the common terminology in using „Black-Scholes" for the models developed by Black and Scholes (1973) and Merton (1973).

[45] Notice that the comparison between the Bronzin and Black-Scholes models in this section is limited by the fact that Bronzin's analysis is not based on a stochastic *process* of the underlying asset price, but simply on its distribution. Therefore, the "equivalence" of the formulas cannot account for the time-proportionality of the variance emerging from the Random Walk assumption in the Black-Scholes model.

[46] As noted before, there is no reference to a specific stochastic process in Bronzin's text.

[47] To clarify the terminology: either the log (more precisely: the natural logarithm) of the stock price follows an arithmetic Wiener process and is normally distributed, or the stock price itself follows a geometric Wiener process and is *log*normally distributed.

deviation $\sigma(x)=\frac{1}{h\sqrt{2}}$. In contrast, the Black-Scholes solution assumes a lognormal distribution for $\tilde{x}$. How does this change the shape of the option formula?

Before we are able to address this question, we have to examine Bronzin's general option formula first, which has not yet been derived in Section 5.4.5 before. Based on this derivation, we are then able to address the explicit relation between Bronzin's formula with Black-Scholes in Sections 5.4.2 and 5.4.3.

5.5.1 Derivation of Bronzin's Formula (43)

Under the normal law of error, the option price is the solution to the following expression:

$$P_1 = \int_M^\infty (\tilde{x}-M) f(x) dx = \int_M^\infty \tilde{x}\, f(x) dx - M \int_M^\infty f(x) dx, \tag{5.12}$$

with $f(x)=\frac{h}{\sqrt{\pi}}e^{-h^2x^2}$

The first integral is the conditionally expected market price at maturity (corrected by the forward price) – conditional upon option exercise. The second integral is the exercise probability. No explicit solution is available for the second integral, but Bronzin provides a table for alternative values for $\psi(\varepsilon)=\frac{1}{\sqrt{\pi}}\int_\varepsilon^\infty e^{-t^2}dt$ in an Appendix (pp. 84–85). As a side remark, notice that t exhibits a standard deviation of $\frac{1}{\sqrt{2}}$, and it is related to the standard normal by

$$\frac{h}{\sqrt{\pi}}\int_M^\infty e^{-h^2x^2}dx = \underbrace{\frac{1}{\sqrt{\pi}}\int_{hM}^\infty e^{-t^2}dt}_{\equiv\psi(hM)} = \frac{1}{\sqrt{2\pi}}\int_{hM\sqrt{2}}^\infty e^{-\frac{1}{2}z^2}dz = \frac{1}{\sqrt{2\pi}}\int_{M/\sigma(x)}^\infty e^{-\frac{1}{2}z^2}dz = N\left(-\frac{M}{\sigma(x)}\right)$$

$$. \tag{5.13a}$$

This relationship will be useful below. In contrast to the second integral, the first integral $\frac{h}{\sqrt{\pi}}\int_M^\infty \tilde{x}\, e^{-h^2x^2}dx$ has an explicit solution. Notice that the solution of the integral $\int x\, e^{ax^2} dx$ is $\frac{1}{2a} e^{ax^2}$. Setting $a = -h^2$ and evaluating the integral at the boundaries $[M, \infty]$, we find

$$\int_M^\infty x\, e^{-h^2x^2} dx = \left[\frac{1}{-2h^2} e^{-h^2x^2} \right]_M^\infty = -\frac{1}{-2h^2} e^{-h^2M^2},$$

and the first integral becomes

$$\frac{h}{\sqrt{\pi}} \int_M^\infty \tilde{x}\, e^{-h^2x^2} dx = \frac{h}{\sqrt{\pi}} \left\{ \frac{1}{2h^2} e^{-M^2h^2} \right\} = \frac{1}{2h\sqrt{\pi}} e^{-M^2h^2}. \quad \text{5.13b)}$$

Bronzin's pricing formula for call options is then

$$P_1 = \frac{1}{2h\sqrt{\pi}} e^{-M^2h^2} - M\, \psi(hM), \qquad \psi(\varepsilon) = \frac{1}{\sqrt{\pi}} \int_\varepsilon^\infty e^{-t^2} dt \quad \text{(equation 43, p. 76).} \quad (5.14)$$

This formula enables to separate between the impact of volatility ($M = 0$) and intrinsic value on option price. Notice that the first term adds the same positive amount to the option value irrespective whether the option is in- or out-of-the money ($M \neq 0$).

Based on this derivation, we are now able to analyze the relationship between equation (5.14), Bronzin's "normal law-of-error" based option formula, and the Black-Scholes formula. We do this under two different perspectives: First, we show how we have to rewrite the Bronzin formula to get Black-Scholes, after adjusting for the different distributional assumption (Section 5.5.2); second, we adapt Bronzin's solution procedure outlined in this section to derive a "Bronzin style" Black-Scholes formula (Section 5.5.3).

5.5.2 Deriving the Black-Scholes Formula from Bronzin (43)

After adjusting for the specific distributional assumptions, it is easy to show that Bronzin's formula (43), i.e. our equation (5.14), is formally consistent with the Black-Scholes and Merton, and, respectively, the Black (1976) forward price based valuation models. Notice that the subsequent notation is ours, not Bronzin's. Specifically, we introduce the following variables: the time to maturity T, the underlying asset price today S_0 and at expiration S_T, the exercise price K, the mean and volatility of the log price change of the underlying per unit time, μ and σ, the standard normal $\tilde{z}$ with density $N'(z)$.

We start with equation (5.12) and have to re-interpret the variables: we replace $\tilde{x} - M = \left[\tilde{S}_T - B\right] - \left[K - B\right] = \tilde{S}_T - K$, where we assume that $\tilde{S}_T$ is the lognormally distributed stock price whereas $\tilde{x}$ is the deviation from the forward price, and assumed normal in the specification of equation (5.12). In terms of the standard normal $\tilde{z}$, we get

$$\tilde{S}_T = S_0 e^{\mu T + \sigma \tilde{z}\sqrt{T}}, \text{ with } \mu = \frac{E\left[\ln\left(\frac{S_T}{S_0}\right)\right]}{T}, \sigma^2 = \frac{Var\left[\ln\left(\frac{S_T}{S_0}\right)\right]}{T}. \tag{5.15}$$

Adapting the risk-neutral valuation approach, the drift of the log stock price changes can be replaced by $\mu = r - \frac{1}{2}\sigma^2$. In order to be consistent with Bronzin's equation, we assume an interest rate of zero and one time unit to maturity, $T = 1$ (e.g. one year if volatility is measured in annual terms). The forward price is then equal to the current stock price, $B = S_0$, implying $\tilde{S}_T = Be^{-\frac{1}{2}\sigma^2 + \sigma\tilde{z}}$. The Black-Scholes valuation equation can then be written as

$$P_1 = \int_{-z_2}^{\infty} \left(Be^{-\frac{1}{2}\sigma^2 + \sigma\tilde{z}} - K\right) N'(z)dz. \tag{5.16}$$

The remaining task is to investigate how the lower integration boundary of the lognormal integral (5.16), denoted by $-z_2$, is related to M in (5.12), respectively hM in (5.14). We have from (5.13a)

$$\psi(hM) = \frac{1}{\sqrt{\pi}} \int_{hM}^{\infty} e^{-t^2} dt = \frac{1}{\sqrt{2\pi}} \int_{-z_2 = M/\sigma(x)}^{\infty} e^{-\frac{1}{2}z^2} dz = \frac{1}{\sqrt{2\pi}} \int_{-\infty}^{z_2 = -M/\sigma(x)} e^{-\frac{1}{2}z^2} dz = N(z_2)$$

where the integration boundary can be approximated by

$$z_2 = -\frac{M}{\sigma(x)} = -\frac{K-B}{B\sigma} = -\frac{\frac{K}{B} - 1}{\sigma} \approx -\frac{\ln\frac{K}{B} + \frac{1}{2}\sigma^2}{\sigma} = \frac{\ln\frac{B}{K} - \frac{1}{2}\sigma^2}{\sigma} = \frac{\ln\frac{S_0}{K} - \frac{1}{2}\sigma^2}{\sigma}$$

which is exactly the Black-Scholes boundary. The derivation shows the equivalence of Bronzin's valution equation (5.14) with the lognormal models of Black-Scholes, Merton, Black, etc. if the stock price $B + \tilde{x} = \tilde{S}_T$ is specified as a lognormal instead of a normal variable and the integration boundary is adjusted correspondingly.

5.5.3 The "Bronzin-Style" Black-Scholes Formula

Based on the derivation of Bronzin's "normal law-of-error" option formula (43) (our equation (5.14) in Section 5.5.1), we can also try to write the Black-Scholes formula in the "Bronzin style". We rewrite (5.16) as

$$P_1 = \int_{-z_2}^{\infty} \left(B\left(e^{-\frac{1}{2}\sigma^2 + \sigma \tilde{z}} - 1\right) - \underbrace{(K - B)}_{M} \right) N'(z)dz$$

where the exponential expression is approximated by

$$e^{-\frac{1}{2}\sigma^2 + \sigma \tilde{z}} \approx 1 + \left(-\frac{1}{2}\sigma^2 + \sigma \tilde{z}\right) + \frac{1}{2}\left(-\frac{1}{2}\sigma^2 + \sigma \tilde{z}\right)^2 + - \ldots = 1 + \sigma \tilde{z} + - \ldots$$

where we neglect asymptotically vanishing terms. We then get

$$P_1 = B\sigma \int_{-z_2}^{\infty} \tilde{z} \left(\frac{1}{\sqrt{2\pi}} e^{-\frac{1}{2}z^2} \right) dz - M\ N\{z_2\}$$

or written in a slightly more complicated way

$$P_1 = B\sigma \int_{-z_2}^{\infty} \tilde{z} \left(\frac{\frac{1}{\sqrt{2}}}{\sqrt{\pi}} e^{-\left(\frac{1}{\sqrt{2}}\right)^2 z^2} \right) dz - M\ N\{z_2\}$$

which is the same as setting $h = \frac{1}{\sqrt{2}}$ in the Bronzin solution (5.13b). The option price is thus

$$P_1 = B\sigma \frac{e^{-(-z_2)^2\left(\frac{1}{\sqrt{2}}\right)^2}}{2\left(\frac{1}{\sqrt{2}}\right)\sqrt{\pi}} - M\ N\{z_2\} = B\sigma \frac{1}{\sqrt{2\pi}} e^{-\frac{1}{2}(z_2)^2} - M\ N\{z_2\}$$

which can also be written as

$$P_1 = B\sigma\, N'\{z_2\} - M\, N\{z_2\}, \quad z_2 = \frac{\ln\frac{B}{K} - \frac{1}{2}\sigma^2}{\sigma} \tag{5.17a}$$

This can be considered the "Bronzin-style" Black-Scholes formula. The value of the put option is then simply

$$P_2 = P_1 + M = B\sigma\, N'\{z_2\} - M\, N\{z_2\} - (-M) = B\sigma\, N'\{z_2\} - M\left[N\{z_2\} - 1\right] \tag{5.17b}$$

Notice that these expressions are approximations – but they highlight some interesting aspects of the Black-Scholes formula. The exact relation to the Bronzin model (5.14) is straightforward. First, approximate

$$z_2 = \frac{\ln\frac{B}{K} - \frac{1}{2}\sigma^2}{\sigma} = \frac{-\ln\frac{M+B}{B} - \frac{1}{2}\sigma^2}{\sigma} = \frac{-\ln\left(1 + \frac{M}{B}\right) - \frac{1}{2}\sigma^2}{\sigma} \approx \frac{-M/B}{\sigma} = -\frac{M}{B\sigma}$$

and replace $B\sigma = \sigma(x)$. It was shown in equation (5.13a) that $N(z_2) = N\left(-\frac{M}{\sigma(x)}\right) = \psi(hM)$ which shows the equivalence of the second term in the pricing equation. The equivalence of the first term requires exactly the same substitutions and approximations, i.e.

$$B\sigma \frac{1}{\sqrt{2\pi}} e^{-\frac{1}{2}(z_2)^2} = \frac{\sigma(x)}{\sqrt{2\pi}} e^{-\frac{1}{2}\left(-\frac{M}{\sigma(x)}\right)^2} = \frac{1}{2h\sqrt{\pi}} e^{-h^2 M^2}$$

just by recognizing $h = \frac{1}{\sigma(x)\sqrt{2}}$. This completes the formal equivalence between the Bronzin and Black-Scholes model: The two models just differ with respect to the distributional assumption of the underlying market price; Bronzin assumes a normal distribution for the price level (respectively, its deviation from the forward price), while Black-Scholes assume a normal distribution for the *log* price (in addition, with time-proportional moments). But the rest of the two models is *identical,* including the risk-neutral valuation approach (a preference-free mean of the pricing density) – which is an amazing observation.

5.5.4 A Simple Expression (Approximation) for At-The-Money Options

The approximation of equation (5.17a) can also be used to get a "back on the envelope" formula for ATM Black-Scholes prices. We set $M = 0$ and $z_2 = -\frac{1}{2}\sigma$ to get $P_1 = B\sigma \frac{1}{\sqrt{2\pi}} e^{-\frac{1}{8}\sigma^2}$. For conventional volatilities, the exponent is extremely small, so that the exponential expression is close to unity (e.g. if the volatility is 20%, the expression is 0.995). So we get

$$P_1 \approx \frac{B\sigma}{\sqrt{2\pi}} = 0.399 \times B\sigma \tag{5.18}$$

which corresponds to Bronzin's ATM option value; substituting $h = \frac{1}{\sigma(x)\sqrt{2}}$ in his equation (44) gives

$$P_1 = \frac{1}{2h\sqrt{\pi}} = \frac{1}{2\left(\frac{1}{\sigma(x)\sqrt{2}}\right)\sqrt{\pi}} = \frac{\sigma(x)}{\sqrt{2\pi}}$$

Notice, however, that Bronzin's expression is exact, while ours (equation 5.18) is an approximation. The same expression can be found in Bachelier (1900), after appropriate adjustments[48].

Thus, the (relative) price of an ATM option is 39.9% or 40% of the absolute price volatility. If the forward rate has a volatility of 20%, then the value of an ATM call or put option with 1 year to maturity is approximately 8% of the forward price, the price of a respective 3 month option is 4%.

---

[48] See his 2nd equation on p. 51, $a = k\sqrt{t}$, where a is the price of an ATM option (in French: *prime simple*) and t is the time to maturity. Denoting the standard deviation of the normally distributed stock price changes over the time period t by $\sigma(x)\sqrt{t}$, it follows immediately that k must be specified by $k = \frac{\sigma(x)}{\sqrt{2\pi}}$ in his probability density function (e.g. see his 5th equation on p. 38). It then follows that $a = \frac{\sigma(x)\sqrt{t}}{\sqrt{2\pi}}$, which is our expression, except that the volatility has an explicit time dimension in Bachelier's distribution.

5.6 Summary of the Formulas, and Flusser's Extensions

Table 5.6 displays the densities derived from the various (six) functional specifications of the terminal price, occasionally the implied standard deviation, and resulting call option prices (P_1).

Table 5.6 Overview on Bronzin's option formulas for alternative distributional assumptions.

	Density function	*Standard deviation*	*Bronzin's call option price*
Uniform distribution	$f(x)=\frac{1}{2\omega},\ x\in[-\omega;+\omega]$		$P_1=\frac{(\omega-M)^2}{4\omega}$
Triangular distribution	$f(x)=\frac{\omega-x}{\omega^2},\ x\in[-\omega;+\omega]$		$P_1=\frac{(\omega-M)^3}{6\omega^2}$
Parabolic distribution	$f(x)=\frac{3(\omega-x)^2}{2\omega^3},\ x\in[-\omega;+\omega]$		$P_1=\frac{(8\omega-M)^4}{8\omega^3}$
Exponential distribution	$f(x)=ke^{-2kx}$	$\sigma_{\exp}(x)=\frac{1}{2k}$	$P_1=\frac{e^{-2kM}}{4k}$
Error (normal) distribution	$f(x)=\frac{h}{\sqrt{\pi}}e^{-h^2x^2}$	$\sigma_{err}(x)=\frac{1}{h\sqrt{2}}$	$P_1=\frac{e^{-M^2h^2}}{2h\sqrt{\pi}}-M\,\psi(hM)$
Bernoulli (binomial) distribution	$\frac{1}{\sqrt{2\pi}}\int_0^{z^*}e^{-\frac{1}{2}z^2}dz+\frac{e^{-z^2}}{\sqrt{2\pi}\sqrt{Bq}}$ $z^*=\frac{x^*}{\sqrt{Bq}},\ \tilde{z}=\frac{\tilde{x}}{\sqrt{Bq}}$	$\sigma_{bin}(x)=\sqrt{qB}$	

There is only one explicit reference and extension to Bronzin's work, which is an article by Gustav Flusser[49] published in the Annual (*Jahresbericht*) of the Trade Academy in Prague; see Flusser (1911)[50]. While highly mathematical, the author merely extends and generalizes the second part of Bronzin's option pricing

[49] Gustav Flusser studied mathematics and physics, and was a professor at the German and Czech University of Prague. He was also a member of the social-democratic party in the parliament. He starved in the concentration camp of Buchenwald in 1940.

[50] We are grateful to Ernst Juerg Weber who called our attention to this paper and made it available to us.

formulas for alternative distributions for the underlying price[51]:

- polynomial funtions of n-th degree
- rational algebraic functions
- Irrational functions
- goniometric (periodic) functions
- logarithmic functions
- exponential functions.

However, the author does not add original contributions to Bronzin's work, in the sense of general pricing principles or extensions thereof, so there is no need to discuss or reproduce the derived formulas here.

5.7 Valuation of Repeat Contracts ("*Noch*"-*Geschäfte*)

This section reviews the valuation of a specific type of combined forward-option contract which had apparently some importance in the days of Bronzin. In brief terms, the holder of a forward contract acquires an option, by paying a premium N_m (the *Noch*-premium), to repeat the transaction m times at maturity. In case of a long forward contract, the holder acquires the right to increase the original contract size by the multiple m of the original contract size, i.e. to buy additional shares at maturity of the forward contract. The exercise price is set above the forward price, namely at $B+N_m$. Equivalently, the holder of a short forward contract acquires an option to sell an additional quantity of m times the original contract size at maturity; the exercise price is fixed below the forward price, at $B-N_m$. We will call the first option contract a repeat-call option, the second contract a repeat-put option.

Unlike in a standard option contract, the premium N_m serves a double function: It is the option price paid in advance, but also stands for the premium added to (or subtracted from) the forward price in fixing the exercise price of the option. This double function complicates the determination of the fair premium[52]. A fundamental restriction in computing the premium is $N_m = mP_1$, where P_1 is the price of a simple "skewed" (non-ATM) call option. Bronzin

[51] The author motivaties the paper as follows (original text): "*Die vorliegende Arbeit will auf Grund der Untersuchungen Bronzin's die Höhe der Prämie bei den verschiedenen Formen, welche die Börsenlage annehmen kann, bestimmen, die von ihm gewählte endliche und stetige Funktion der Kursschwankungen* $f(x)$ *auf allgemeine Basis stellen und derselben die Form der [...] Funktion erteilen.*" (p. 1)

[52] Obviously, it is fairly arbitrary that the premium of the option has to be identical to the "markup" to be paid at exercise. But it seems that this was a business standard.

shows that this condition must hold by arbitrage (pp. 48-50, equation 15). More specifically, the valuation problem for a repeat-call option can be stated as[53]

$$N_m = mP_1 = m\int_{N_m}^{\infty}(\tilde{x} - N_m)f(x)dx, \tag{5.19}$$

where $f(x)$ is the pricing density, as discussed in Section 5.5. The following remark on $(\tilde{x} - N_m)$ could be useful: Remember that $\tilde{x}$ denotes the deviation of the market price at maturity from the forward price; according to our contractual characterization of the repeat-option, the exercise price consists of the forward price plus (minus) the premium, $K = B \pm N_m$. So, the skewness of the contract, characterized by M, is entirely determined by the premium. Hence, the payoff of the contract is given by

$$x - M = [S_T - B] - [K - B] = [S_T - B] - [(B + N_m) - B] = x - N_m$$

which is the expression in our equation (5.19).

Repeat contracts are analyzed throughout Bronzin's book. A description of the contracts and some fundamental hedging relationships can be found on pp. 30–37; general pricing relationship are derived on pp. 48–50; and concrete pricing solutions for the various specifications of $f(x)$ are provided throughout his second chapter of part II.

Pure inspection of our equation (5.19) suggests that finding explicit solutions for the premium N_m is not an easy task: It shows up on the left hand side of the equation, and twice on the right hand side – within the payoff function and on the integration boundary. For very simple specifications of the pricing density, explicit solutions can be easily derived, but approximations or numerical solutions are inevitable for even slightly more complicated choices. An extremely elegant solution is provided by Bachelier (1900) for the case of normal distributions; we will discuss this shortly.

For illustrative purposes, we only briefly outline the solution for the simplest case, when $f(x)$ is assumed to be constant within the interval $[-\omega;+\omega]$. According to Table 5.1, the option price for the constant case is $P_1 = \frac{(\omega - M)^2}{4\omega}$. In order to get the repeat-option premium N_m, the skewness of the option must be adjusted to $M = N_m$, and by equation (5.20) the expression must be multiplied by m:

[53] In the following, we adapt the notation of Bronzin, except that we add the subscript m to the repeat-option premium N.

$$N_m = mP_1 = m\frac{(\omega - N_m)^2}{4\omega}$$

This is a quadratic equation in our unknown N_m, which can be easily solved; however, ω would remain unspecified in this setting. It will be useful to substitute this parameter by the (possibly observable) ATM option price given by $P = \frac{\omega}{4}$, which results in

$$\frac{N_m}{P} = m\left(1 - \frac{1}{4}\frac{N_m}{P}\right)^2 \tag{5.20}$$

It turns out that the structure of this expression (relating the premium to the ATM option price) is very useful throughout the analysis, particularly for computational purposes. In our simple setting here, the solution is given by

$$\frac{N_m}{P} = \frac{4\left(m + 2 - 2\sqrt{1+m}\right)}{m}$$

which is Bronzin's equation (7a) on p. 59. Alternative integer values for m can now be plugged in this expression to get the fair premium for 1-time, 2-times, 3-times etc. repeat-options, e.g.

$$N_1 = \frac{4 \times \left(1 + 2 - 2 \times \sqrt{1+1}\right)}{1} = 4 \times \left(3 - 2 \times \sqrt{2}\right) = 0.6863\,P$$

$$N_2 = \frac{4 \times \left(2 + 2 - 2 \times \sqrt{1+2}\right)}{2} = 2 \times \left(4 - 2 \times \sqrt{3}\right) = 1.072\,P$$

and so on. It is, of course, interesting to notice that the premium does not increase proportionally with the number of repeats. Specifically, the relation between N_2 and N_1 is

$$N_2 = 1.562\,N_1$$

which is a figure that attracts a lot of attention in Bronzin's analysis. Alternatively, one could also be interested in finding the number of repeats which are necessary[54] to equate the premium to the price of an ATM option, i.e. $\frac{N_m}{P}=1$; we just have to insert this ratio in equation (5.20) and solve for m:

$$m=\frac{\frac{N_m}{P}}{\left(1-\frac{1}{4}\frac{N_m}{P}\right)^2}=\frac{1}{\left(1-\frac{1}{4}\right)^2}=\frac{1}{9/16}=1.777$$

An overview on the solutions for the other specifications of the pricing density can be found in Table 5.6. The amazing observation is how similar the numerical values are (see the bold figures) given the different shape of the distributions. Bronzin shows repeatedly puzzled about this "remarkable", "strange" coincidence.

It is interesting to notice that Bachelier analyzes the same contracts, called *options d'ordre n* (in contrast to *primes* analyzed otherwise)[55]. He provides a particularly elegant solution to the pricing problem. Throughout his analysis he assumes that the (absolute) stock price changes are characterized by a normal (with mean zero and annualized volatility[56] $k\sqrt{2\pi}$). He then uses an extremely useful approximation of the normal integral which results in

$$N_m=P\left(\frac{m+2}{m}\pi-\sqrt{\left(\frac{m+2}{m}\pi\right)^2-4\pi}\right)$$

(see his 5th equation of p. 56); we have changed the symbols to match our notation. Plugging in the desired parameters m, gives the following values:

m	*1*	*2*	*3*	*4*	*5*	*10*
Bachelier	0.6921	1.0955	1.3825	1.6075	1.7948	2.4870
Bronzin	0.6919	1.0938				

which shows that the values for $m=1,2$ are virtually identical. Obviously, the Bachelier solution is much more elegant and allows to directly compute the premium for an arbitrary number of multiples. It is obvious that the increase of the premium is degressive with respect to m.

[54] This is somehow unrealistically from a practical point of view, because the solution will not be an integer in general.
[55] See Bachelier (1900), pp. 55–57.
[56] Notice that this is not "our" k from the exponential function.

Table 5.6 Valuation characteristics of repeat-options (*Noch-Geschäfte*).

	constant	linear	quadratic	exponential	law of error
Reference	pp. 59–61	pp. 63–65	pp. 68–69	pp. 71–74	pp. 76–80
$\frac{N_m}{P}$	$m\left(1-\frac{N_m}{4P}\right)^2$	$m\left(1-\frac{N_m}{6P}\right)^3$	$m\left(1-\frac{N_m}{8P}\right)^4$	$me^{-\frac{1}{2}\frac{N_m}{P}}$	$m\left(e^{-\frac{1}{2}\left(\frac{N_m}{\sqrt{2\pi}P}\right)^2}-\frac{N_m}{P}\varphi\left\{\frac{N_m}{2P\sqrt{\pi}}\right\}\right)$
N_1	0.6864 P	0.6928 P	0.6952 P	0.70355 P	0.6919 P
N_2	1.672 P	1.0936 P	1.104 P	1.1345 P	1.0938 P
$\frac{N_2}{N_1}$	**1.562**	**1.578**	**1.588**	**1.612**	**1.581**
$m\left(\frac{N_m}{P}=1\right)$	**1.777**	**1.728**	**1.7059**	**1.6487**	**1.7435**

All figures are adapted from Bronzin, no own computations.

5.8 Bronzin's Contribution in Historical Perspective

When comparing Bronzin's contribution to Bachelier's thesis, which should be regarded as the historical benchmark, then without any doubt, Bachelier was not only earlier, but his analysis is more rigorous from a mathematical point of view. Bronzin can not be credited for having developed a new mathematical field, as Bachelier did with his theory on diffusions. Bronzin did no stochastic modeling, applied no stochastic calculus, derived no differential equations (except in the context of our equation 5.4), he was not interested in stochastic processes, and hence his notion of volatility has no time dimension. But apart from that, every element of modern option pricing is there:

- He noticed the unpredictability of speculative prices, and the need to use probability laws to the pricing of derivatives.
- He recognized the informational role of market prices, specifically the forward price, to price other derivatives. No expected values show up in the pricing formulas. His probability densities can be easily re-interpreted as risk-neutral pricing densities.
- He understood the key role of hedging and arbitrage for valuation purposes; he derives the put-call parity condition, and uses a zero-profit condition to price forward contracts and options.
- He develops a simplified procedure to find analytical solutions for option prices by exploiting a key relationship between their derivatives (with respect

to their exercise prices) and the underlying pricing density. He also stresses the empirical advantages of this approach.

- He extensively discusses the impact of different distributional assumptions on option prices.

Besides of pricing simple calls and puts, he develops formulas for chooser options and, more important, repeat-contracts. All this is a remarkable achievement, and it is done with a minimum of analytics.

On the expository side, Bronzin developed for the first time a consistent and modern terminology for forward and option contracts (in German, obviously), by dropping most of the heterogeneous and cumbersome wording prevalent in the literature at that time. Moreover, his consequent mathematical approach was a breakthrough in the textbook literature because he thereby avoids endless numerical examples and complicated diagrams in the characterization of derivative contracts (see Fürst 1908, which was a popular textbook in these days).

There are few things on the less elegant side: the discussion and the large systems of hedging conditions in the first part belongs to it, and some numerical procedures to solve for the repeat-option premiums also. But nevertheless, Bronzin's contribution is important, not only in historical retro-perspective. He definitively deserves his place in the history of option pricing, as other researchers as well.[57]

It is difficult to evaluate how Bronzin judged the scientific originality of his booklet, and whether this is a fair criterion to apply at all – because he had apparently written it for educational purposes. Given that he published it as a "professor", and that he has published a textbook on actuarial theory for beginners two years before (Bronzin 1906), it may well be that he regarded his option theory as a simple textbook, or a mixture between textbook and scientific monograph. Bronzin did not overstate his own contribution – he even understates it by regularly talking about his "booklet" (in German: *Werkchen*) when referring to it.[58]

The originality in the field of option pricing is difficult to assess anyway. Who deserves proper credit for the Black-Scholes model? The early Samuelson (1965) paper contains the essential equation[59]. Even more puzzling is a footnote in the Black-Scholes paper (p. 461) where the authors acknowledge a comment

[57] The paper by Girlich (2002) review some of the pre-Bachelier advances in option pricing and concludes: "In the case of Louis Bachelier and his area of activity the dominant French point of view is the most natural thing in the world and every body is convinced by the results. The aim of the present paper is to add a few tesseras from other countries to the picture which is known about the birth of mathematical finance and its probabilistic environment". The work by Espen Haug on the history of option pricing is also revealing; see Haug (2008) in this volume.

[58] The German word is actually a funny combination of *Work* which means, in an academic setting, a substantial contribution, while the ending ...*chen* is a strong diminutive.

[59] Or to use Samuelson's own wording: "Yes, I had the equation, but 'they' got the formula [...]"; see Geman (2002).

by Robert Merton suggesting that if the option hedge is maintained continuously over time, the return on the hedged position becomes certain. But it is the notion of the riskless hedge which makes the essential difference between Black-Scholes and the earlier Samuelson and Merton-Samuelson models[60,61]! Surprisingly enough that Merton was kind enough to delay publication of his (accepted) 1973 paper until Black and Scholes got theirs accepted[62].

An open question is to what other publications Bronzin is referring to: He surely knew the most important publications in German about probability and options. Options were well known instruments at this time at the stock exchanges in the German spoken part of Europe, and the many different forms of contracts were described in most textbooks. Moreover, several books treated legal issues related to options. But the mathematical modeling of options didn't seem to be an issue in the literature. In this context, the natural question arises, whether Bronzin knew about Bachelier's work. *Honni soit qui mal y pense …* – but extensive quoting was not the game at the time anyway. Bachelier did not quote any of the earlier (but admittedly, non mathematical) books on option valuation either. For example, the book of Regnault (1863) was widely used and contains the notion of random walk, the Gaussian distribution, the role of volatility in pricing options, including the square-root formula[63]. According to Whelan (2002) who refers to a paper by Émile Dormoy published in 1873, French actuaries had a reasonable idea to price options well before Bachelier's thesis, although a clear mathematical framework was missing. Einstein in his Brownian motion paper (1905) did not quote Bachelier's thesis as well; it is an open issue

[60] To be precise, the notion of a "near" risk-less hedge strategy can also be found in the Samuelson and Samuelson and Merton papers. Samuelson (1965) analyses the relationship between the expected return on the option (warrant), β, and the underlying stock, α, and argued that the difference "cannot become too large. If $\beta > \alpha$ […] hedging will stand to yield a sure-thing positive net capital gain (commissions and interest charges on capital aside!)" (p. 31). Samuelson and Merton (1969) extend the earlier model and derive a "probability-cum-utility" function Q (see p. 19), which serves as a new probability measure (in today's terminology) to compute option prices. They show that under this new measure (or utility function), all securities earn the riskless rate; they explicitly write $\alpha_Q = \beta_Q = r$ to stress this point (see p. 26, equations 20 and 21 and the subsequent comments). Although Merton and Samuelson recognized the possibility of a (near) risk-less hedge and a risk-neutral valuation approach, they were not fully aware of the consequences of their findings.

[61] Black (1988) gives proper credit to Robert Merton: "Bob gave us that [arbitrage] argument. It should probably be called the Black-Merton-Scholes paper".

[62] Bernstein (1992) and Black (1989) provide interesting details about the birth of the Black-Scholes formula.

[63] The argument is derived from a funny analogy: He considers the mean (or fair) value of an asset as the *center of a circle*, and every point within the circle represents a possible future price. The radius describes the standard deviation. He then assumes that, as time elapses, the range of possible stock prices as represented by the area within the circle increases proportionally. This implies that the radius (i.e. the standard deviation) increases with the square root of time. A detailed analysis of Regnault's contribution is given in several papers by Jovanovic and Le Gall; see e.g. Jovanovic and Le Gall (2001).

whether he knew the piece at all. Distribution of knowledge seems to have been pretty slow at this time, particularly between different fields of research, and across different languages. And again, extensive references were simply not common in natural sciences (e.g. Einstein's paper contains a single reference to another author).

Thus, it remains an open question whether Bronzin was aware of Bachelier's thesis. At least, based on his training in mathematics and physics at the University of Vienna (see Section 6 below), he would have been perfectly able to understand and recognize the Bachelier's seminal work.[64] After all, the question is not so relevant, because the approach is fundamentally different, and there are sufficiently many innovative elements in his treatise. It is also surprising that (almost) no references are found on his work. Although it is generally claimed that Bachelier's thesis was lost until the Savage-Samuelson rediscovery (as reflected in Samuelson 1965) it was at least quoted since 1908 in several editions of a French actuarial textbook by Alfred Barriol.

Bronzin's book had a similar recognition. It was mentioned in a textbook about German banking by Friedrich Leitner, a professor at the *Handels-Hochschule* in Berlin; see Leitner (1920). And with Bronzin's more pragmatic pricing approach, it is difficult to understand why the seeds for another, more scientific understanding of option pricing did not develop, or the formulas did not get immediate practical attention. At least, Bronzin was not a doctoral candidate as Bachelier, but a distinguished professor mentioned in the Scientists' Annual (*Jahrbuch der gelehrten Welt*). Moreover, the flourishing insurance industry in Trieste should have had an active commercial interest in his research. It however might be evidence for Hans Bühlmann's and Shane Whelan's[65] claim that the contribution of actuaries to financial economics is generally underestimated (see Whelan 2002 for detailed references). While Poincaré's reservation on Bachelier's thesis is, at least, limited to his "queer" subject (see Taqqu 2001) and can, somehow, be understood from a purely academic point of view, it is more difficult to understand why a reviewer of Bronzin's book[66] commented that "it can hardly be assumed that the results will attain a particularly practical value". Indeed, it took long for financial models do gain adequate recognition in those days.

---

[64] According to Granger and Morgenstern (1970), the work of Louis Bachelier was well known in Italy shortly after being published: "The only economist to our knowledge who has paid repeated attention to Bachelier was Alfonso De Pietri-Tonelli, a student and exposer of Pareto who, in his work 'La Speculazione di Borsa' (1912), repeatedly quoted Bachelier approvingly. [...] His references to Bachelier were repeated in his later, more popular book 'La Borsa' (1923). [...] De Pietri-Tonelli, in turn, was completely neglected in Anglo-American literature" (Granger and Morgenstern 1970, p. 76). Apparently, the year of the first publication should be 1919 instead of 1912 (see, e.g. Barone 1990).

[65] See Whelan (2002) for detailed references.

[66] See the review in the *Monatshefte für Mathematik und Physik* in 1910 (Volume 21), most probably written by its editor, Gustav von Escherich.

Table 5.3 Overview on early option pricing models up to Black-Scholes

Bachelier (1900)	Characteristics: Arithmetic Wiener process (negative prices possible); Drift of the process is zero. $P_1 = S\,N\{z_2\} + \sigma(S)\sqrt{T}\,N'\{z_2\} - K\,N\{z_2\},\quad z_2 \equiv \frac{S-K}{\sigma\sqrt{T}}$
Bronzin (1908)	Characteristics: Normal distribution for price levels (negative prices possible); forward price used as expected value. $P_1 = B\,N\{z_2+\sigma\} - (K-B)\,N\{z_2\},\quad z_2 = -\frac{K-B}{\sigma(x)}$
Sprenkle (1961) (1964)	Characteristics: Lognormal distribution of price levels; positive drift of stock returns (α); risk aversion recognized, but no discounting (i.e. interest rate of zero). $P_1 = Se^{\alpha T}\,N\{z_2+\sigma\} - K(1-\eta)\,N\{z_2\},\ z_2 = \frac{\ln\frac{S}{K} + \left(\alpha - \frac{1}{2}\sigma^2\right)T}{\sigma\sqrt{T}}$
Boness (1964)	Characteristics: Lognormal distribution; nonzero interest rate and risk premium, and positive expected stock return (α) used for discounting the expected option payoff. $P_1 = S\,N\{z_2+\sigma\} - Ke^{-\alpha T}\,N\{z_2\},\ z_2 = \frac{\ln\frac{S}{K} + \left(\alpha - \frac{1}{2}\sigma^2\right)T}{\sigma\sqrt{T}}$
Samuelson (1965)	Characteristics: Lognormal distribution; nonzero interest rate and risk premium; expected return on the underlying stock (α) is different from the expected return on the option (β), and in general $\beta > \alpha$. $P_1 = Se^{(\alpha-\beta)T}\,N\{z_2+\sigma\} - Ke^{-\beta T}\,N\{z_2\},\ z_2 = \frac{\ln\frac{S}{K} + \left(\alpha - \frac{1}{2}\sigma^2\right)T}{\sigma\sqrt{T}}$ And since the difference $\beta - \alpha$ „cannot be too large" (p. 31), specifically if $\alpha = \beta$, the formula would become (in analogy to Boness) $P_1 = S\,N\{z_2+\sigma\} - Ke^{-\alpha T}\,N\{z_2\},\ z_2 = \frac{\ln\frac{S}{K} + \left(\alpha - \frac{1}{2}\sigma^2\right)T}{\sigma\sqrt{T}}$
Samuelson/ Merton (1969)	Under a „probability-cum-utility" density *Q* (as opposed to the effective probability function *P*) we have: $\alpha = \beta = r$ (p. 26), implying the equivalence between Samuelson (1965) and the Black-Scholes model.
Black/ Scholes (1973) *Merton* (1973)	$P_1 = S\,N\{z_2+\sigma\} - Ke^{-rT}\,N\{z_2\},\ z_2 = \frac{\ln\frac{S}{K} + \left(r - \frac{1}{2}\sigma^2\right)T}{\sigma\sqrt{T}}$
Definitions	P_1 : Call option price; K : Exercise price; η : Relative risk aversion; α : Expected growth rate of the stock price (the underlying) resp. expected stock return; β : Expected growth rate of the warrant or option price; r riskless interest rate.

Other overviews on early option pricing models are provided by Haug (2008) and Smith (1976). The table is adapted from Hafner and Zimmermann (2006).

References

Bachelier L (1900, 1964) Théorie de la spéculation. Annales Scientifiques de l' Ecole Normale Supérieure, Ser. 3, 17, Paris, pp. 21–88. English translation in: Cootner P (ed) (1964) The random character of stock market prices. MIT Press, Cambridge (Massachusetts), pp. 17–79

Barone E (1990) The Italian stock market: efficiency and calendar anomalies. Journal of Banking and Finance 14, pp. 483–510

Barone E, Cuoco D (1989) The Italian market for 'premium' contracts. An application of option pricing theory. Journal of Banking and Finance 13, pp. 709–745

Bernstein P (1992) Capital ideas. The Free Press, New York

Black F (1974) The pricing of complex options and corporate liabilities. Unpublished manuscript, University of Chicago, Chicago

Black F (1976) The pricing of commodity contracts. Journal of Financial Economics 3, pp. 167–179

Black F (1988) On Robert C. Merton. MIT Sloan Management Review 28 (Fall)

Black F (1989) How we came up with the option formula. Journal of Portfolio Management 15, pp. 4–8

Black F, Scholes M (1973) The pricing of options and corporate liabilities. Journal of Political Economy 81, pp. 637–654

Boness J (1964) Elements of a theory of stock-option value. Journal of Political Economy 72, pp. 163–175

Breeden D, Litzenberger R (1978) Prices of state-contingent claims implicit in option prices. Journal of Business 51, pp. 621–651

Bronzin V (1904) Arbitrage. Monatsschrift für Handels- und Sozialwissenschaft 12, pp. 356–360

Bronzin V (1906) Lehrbuch der politischen Arithmetik. Franz Deuticke, Leipzig/Vienna

Bronzin V (1908) Theorie der Prämiengeschäfte. Franz Deuticke, Leipzig/Vienna

Cootner P (ed) (1964) The random character of stock market prices. MIT Press, Cambridge (Massachusetts)

Courtadon G (1982) A note on the premium market of the Paris Stock Exchange. Journal of Banking and Finance 6, pp. 561–565

Cox J, Ross S, Rubinstein M (1979) Option pricing: a simplified approach. Journal of Financial Economics 7, pp. 229–263

De Pietri-Tonelli A (1919) La Speculazione di Borsa. Industrie Grafiche Italiane

De Pietri-Tonelli A (1923) La borsa. L'ambiente, le operazioni, la teoria, la regolamentazione. Ulrico Hoepli, Milan

Einstein A (1905) Über die von der molekular-kinetischen Theorie der Wärme geforderte Bewegung von in ruhenden Flüssigkeiten suspendierten Teilchen. Annalen der Physik 17, pp. 549–560

Flusser G (1911) Über die Prämiengrösse bei den Prämien- und Stellagegeschäften. Jahresbericht der Prager Handelsakademie, pp. 1–30

Fürst M (1908) Prämien-, Stellage- und Nochgeschäfte. Verlag der Haude- & Spenerschen Buchhandlung, Berlin

Geman H (2002) Foreword, mathematical finance – Bachelier Congress 2000. Springer, Berlin

Girlich H-J (2002) Bachelier's predecessors. Working Paper, Universität Leipzig, Leipzig

Granger C, Morgenstern O (1970) Predictability of stock market prices. Heath Lexington Books, Lexington (Massachusetts)

Hafner W, Zimmermann H (2006) Vinzenz Bronzin's Optionspreismodelle in theoretischer und historischer Perspektive. In: Bessler W (ed) Banken, Börsen und Kapitalmärkte. Festschrift für Hartmut Schmidt zum 65. Geburtstag. Duncker & Humblot, Berlin, pp. 733–758

Haug E (2008) The history of option pricing and hedging. This Volume

Jeffreys H (1939, 1961) Theory of probability, 1st and 3rd edn. Clarendon Press, Oxford (UK)

Johnson N, Kotz S, Balakrishnan N (1994) Continuous univariate distributions, 2nd edn. J. Wiley & Sons, New York

Jovanovic F, Le Gall P (2001) Does God pratice a random walk? The "financial physics" of a 19th century forerunner, Jules Regnault. European Journal for the History of Economic Thought 8, pp. 332–362

Kruizenga R (1956) Put and call options: a theoretical and market analysis. Unpublished doctoral dissertation, Massachusetts Institute of Technology, Cambridge (Massachusetts)

Leitner F (1920) Das Bankgeschäft und seine Technik, 4th edn. Sauerländer

Merton R C (1973) Theory of rational option pricing. Bell Journal of Economics and Management Science 4, pp. 141–183

Merton R C, Scholes M (1995) Fischer Black. Journal of Finance 50, pp. 1359–1370

Regnault J (1863) Calcul des chances et philosophie de la bourse. Mallet-Bachelier et Castel, Paris (an electronic version of the book is available online)

Samuelson P A (1965) Rational theory of warrant pricing. Industrial Management Review 6, pp. 13–32

Samuelson P A (1973) Mathematics of speculative price. SIAM Review (Society of Industrial and Applied Mathematics) 15, pp. 1–42

Samuelson P A, Merton R C (1969) A complete model of warrant pricing that maximizes utility; with P.A. Samuelson. Industrial Management Review 10, pp. 17–46

Siegfried R (ed) (1892) Die Börse und die Börsengeschäfte. Sahlings' Börsen-Papiere, 6th edn, 1st Part. Haude- & Spener'sche Buchhaltung, Berlin

Smith C (1976) Option pricing. A review. Journal of Financial Economics 3, pp. 3–52

Sprenkle C M (1961, 1964) Warrant prices as indicators of expectations and preferences. Yale Economic Essays 1, pp. 178-231. Also published in: Cootner P (ed) (1964) The random character of stock market prices. MIT Press, Cambridge (Massachusetts), pp. 412–474

Stigler S (1999) Statistics on the table. The history of statistical concepts and methods. Harvard University Press, Cambridge (Massachusetts)

Stoll H (1969) The relationship between call and put option prices. Journal of Finance 23, pp. 801–824

Taqqu M S (2001) Bachelier and his times: a conversation with Bernard Bru. Finance and Stochastics 5, pp. 3–32

Whelan S (2002) Actuaries' contributions. The Actuary, pp. 34–35

Zimmermann H, Hafner W (2004) Professor Bronzin's option pricing models (1908). Unpublished manuscript, Universität Basel, Basle

Zimmermann H, Hafner W (2006) Vincenz Bronzin's option pricing theory: contents, contribution, and background. In: Poitras G (ed) Pioneers of financial economics: contributions prior to Irving Fisher, Vol. 1. Edward Elgar, Cheltenham, pp. 238–264

Zimmermann H, Hafner W (2007) Amazing discovery: Vincenz Bronzin's option pricing models. Journal of Banking and Finance 31, pp. 531–546

6 Probabilistic Roots of Financial Modelling: A Historical Perspective

Heinz Zimmermann*

This chapter explores possible probabilistic roots of Bachelier's and Bronzin's work. Why did they choose their specific probabilistic setting? Are there parallels to the early development of life insurance two centuries earlier, when the emerging statistical probabilism, advanced by major mathematicians of that time, was explicitly used to "domesticate" speculation and to transform it to a morally acceptable business model? Perhaps, the models of Bachelier and Bronzin grew out of the same attempt, namely transforming speculation to an ethical sound investment science. However, things were much more complicated at the turn of the 20th century: the public opinion about speculation and financial markets was very negative, and the probabilistic understanding was in a fundamental transition, from determinism to a genuine notion of uncertainty. This is best illustrated in the probabilistic modelling of thermodynamic processes, most notably in the work of Boltzmann (one of Bronzin's teachers), and the emerging field of social physics. From this perspective, it is not surprising that financial markets were not a natural topic for probabilistic modelling, and the achievement of Bachelier, Bronzin and their possible predecessors is all the more remarkable.

6.1 Introduction: Mathematics and the Taming of Speculation

The birth and growth of modern financial markets, in particular derivatives and risk management, would not have been possible without the enormous progress achieved in probabilistic and statistical modelling during the 20th century. Actuarial science, mathematical finance, and financial economics were not only quick in adapting this knowledge, but played also an active role in the development in several fields, such as stochastic processes (Martingales), risk theory (premium principles), time series econometrics (GARCH modelling), and others. What is self-evident in our days was far from obvious in the late 19th or early 20th century when Bachelier, Bronzin[1] and possibly other authors undertook the first steps in modelling financial market prices in order to obtain a rational, scientific basis for pricing derivative contracts. While it is not easy to

* Universität Basel, Switzerland. *heinz.zimmermann@unibas.ch.* I am grateful for many discussions with Wolfgang Hafner, who shaped my understanding of many issues covered in this chapter. Yvonne Seiler provided helpful comments.

[1] To simplify quoting, "Bachelier" refers to Bachelier (1900), and "Bronzin" to Bronzin (1908) in this chapter.

identify the intellectual foundations of Bachelier's and Bronzin's work – aside from their very different approach – this chapter nevertheless tries to review the tradition of probabilistic modelling in two related disciplines: actuarial science (in particular life insurance) and physics (in particular thermodynamics). We thereby hope getting possible answers to some of the following questions from this analysis: Did Bachelier's and Bronzin's work build on a probabilistic tradition in financial modelling? Why did they choose their specific probabilistic setting? Is there a relationship between their works, i.e. are there common theoretical, or intellectual, grounds?

In this context, it may regarded as an amazing parallel between the two lives and achievements in that they were both students in an environment of theoreticians in search of new analytical tools for getting a deeper and new understanding of the intrinsic structure of the world: entropy and probability. As noted elsewhere in this volume, Bachelier submitted his thesis to Henri Poincaré, and Bronzin took courses and seminars with Ludwig Boltzmann at the Technical University of Vienna[2]. Both, Poincaré and Boltzmann, building on the foundations laid by Maxwell, laid the mathematical foundations of modern physics – although their approach and cognitive understanding was different[3].

But unfortunately, there are otherwise not many common grounds for their respective work, and we know little about their motivation to choose their topic, their approach, and why they did not put more effort to propagate their work. However, an examination of the history of probabilistic thinking, particularly in the areas of insurance and physics, will perhaps help to understand why their work did not get the adequate recognition at the time when it was published, in the scientific community as well as in business practice. It is for example interesting to notice that Bachelier's mathematical treatment of games (Bachelier 1914) was widely appreciated, quoted and re-published, while his *Théorie de la Spéculation* was largely ignored and underrated[4]. Why had mathematics such a difficult standing in the context of financial markets and speculation?

---

[2] Based on our communication with his son, Andrea Bronzin, who also showed us testimonies signed by L. Boltzmann.

[3] An excellent description of this topic can be found in Chapter 14 in Krüger et al. (1987b), contributed by Jan von Plato. For a more complete treatment see von Plato (1994).

[4] As noted elsewhere, the thesis advisor Henri Poincaré was not overwhelmed by the thesis and its topic. However, Bachelier's thesis was not completely ignored; for example, the work was well known in Italy shortly after being published. See Chapter 5, Section 5.8, for some respective references related to Granger and Morgenstern (1970) and De Pietri-Tonelli (1919). Also, Bachelier's thesis was highly appreciated in a book review published in the famous *Monatshefte für Mahtematik und Physik*; see Chapter 10 by W. Hafner in this volume for a discussion.

Speculation

A possible answer may be found in the terrible reputation which speculation, and the stock exchange in particular, had during the late 19th and early 20th centuries[5]. Stäheli (2007) gives instructive examples and a detailed discussion of this point. A well-known example which illustrates that this attitude was not idiosyncratic to some critics, but shared wide public acceptance, is a speech of the Prussian Minister of Traffics, Albert von Maybach, before the parliament in November 1879. Puzzled by the stock price boom of the railway companies, he straightforwardly called the stock exchange a "poison tree" (*Giftbaum*) casting its harmful cloud on the life of the entire nation, whose roots and branches must be destroyed by the government (Stillich 1909, p. 8).[6] In other examples, anti-Semitic feelings were mobilized by stories about price manipulation, conspirative activities and expropriation of Jewish speculators; the book of Solano (1893) is a unique example of this dismal strand of literature.

Was the *zeitgeist* responsible why the mathematical treatment of speculative subjects was not accepted or recognized at the turn of the century? Yes and no – because the mathematical approach can as well be considered as an attempt to *change* that perception. Three levels are worth investigating in this context: an educational (the "uneducated" speculator), emotional (the "irrational" speculator), and ethical (the "immoral" speculator).

Rationalizing speculation?

It was widely believed at this time that the masses of unsuccessful, badly educated and irrationally acting speculators bear a particular responsibility in destabilizing markets. Stäheli (2007) gives many examples illustrating that perception. The following quote draws on a book by J. Ross published in 1937:

> "[T]he group [of speculators] is relatively able and well informed on its main activity in life such as business, yachting, or dentistry, but the same cannot be said regarding the evaluation of securities or the

[5] A detailed analysis of the many faces of "speculation" from a social sciences perspective, with many references to the 19th and early 20th century literature, can be found in Stäheli (2007). Chapters 2 and 3 cover the distinction between games and speculation. See also Preda (2005), p. 149ff, for an analysis of the investor in the 18th century from a sociological perspective.

[6] The original German wording is much more colorful: "*Die Börse hat natürlich ein Interesse daran, eine Menge Papiere zu haben, an diesen sie verdient. Meine Herren! Ich rechne es mir gerade als Verdienst an, in dieser Beziehung die Tätigkeit der Börse zu schränken. Ich glaube, dass die Börse hier als ein Giftbaum wirkt, der auf das Leben der Nation seinen verderblichen Schatten wirft, und dem die Wurzeln zu beschneiden und seine Äste zu nehmen, halte ich für ein Verdienst der Regierung*" Quoted from Stillich (1909).

> art of speculation. In fact, as regards the stock market the public is amateurish in all the respects except in speech".[7]

A mathematically based approach to speculation would apparently be a perfect educational device to improve (and signal) competence – but far more yet: it gives speculative activity a rational, theoretical basis, free from irrational emotions, uncontrollable passions (Daston 1988, p. 161) and animal spirits. The quest for an "ideal" speculator (Stäheli 2007, p. 247) whose "mind has been cleared of the delusions of hope and the visions of sudden wealth" (Gibson 1923, p. 13) was over-due, and a mathematical approach, call it "investment science", could be well suited to "domesticate" or "tame" speculators in their risky, emotion driven behaviour.[8] The fears from the masses destabilizing financial markets had a lot to do with the democratization of financial markets in the 19th century. It was important to develop a scientific framework by which an elite of rational investors can be separated from the incompetent and irrationally acting mass.[9]

Whether the works of Bachelier, Bronzin and maybe other yet unknown authors were indeed intended to domesticate and rationalize speculation to give it a scientific, unemotional flair is a hypothesis for which we have little direct evidence.[10] At least, it has a historically parallel in the 18th century when "statistical probabilism" was explicitly exploited in the insurance sector to separate insurance from gambling, and to transform old fashioned life insurance, characterized by speculative aleatory contracts, to a sound business model matching the moral standards of the time. Thus, the mathematical treatment of a subject (life insurance) played an active role in rationalizing business practices and shaping moral values. This important insight is elaborated by Lorraine Daston in her treatise (Daston 1988).

It could help to explain why Bronzin, Bachelier and their predecessors (such as Jules Reganult in France[11]) *failed* to be successful in their scientific attempts: Mathematics is an insufficient means to rationalize the handling of risk if it is not coupled with attempts to affect social values. So, the turn of the century was probably a bad time for it – speculation was heavily in the public

[7] Detailed references can be found in Stäheli (2007), p. 90, from where the quote originates.

[8] "Taming" refers to the title of the book on the rise of probabilistic thinking by Hacking (1990), and the term "domestication" originates from the title of Daston (1987). Both expressions perfectly reflect the issue to be discussed here in the context of speculation.

[9] Stäheli (2007), p. 149ff, provides an in-depth discussion of this point from a social inclusion-exclusion perspective.

[10] Bachelier's thesis, although it is a doctoral dissertation and addresses a rather specific topic (option pricing), was very broadly entitled "Theory of Speculation", and Bronzin's treatise bears the character of an educational textbook. Therefore, both publications undoubtedly aimed at addressing a broader audience.

[11] As discussed in Section 6.4, Regnault *explicitly* intended to affect moral values, i.e. the bad public perception, against speculation on financial markets with his remarkable contribution. Unfortunately, neither Bachelier nor Bronzin offer any motivation for their respective methodological approach.

criticism, was condemned, and derivative contracts were forbidden shortly afterwards.

Times were more supportive after the Second World War when the application of mathematics to a wide range of social and economic problems was legitimated by their success during wartime: operations research applied to business and economic planning (pioneered by Dantzig's *Linear Programming* or Markowitz's *Portfolio Selection*), comparative static and dynamic analysis of economic systems (pioneered by Samuelson's groundbreaking *Foundations* in 1947), or game theory (with von Neumann and Morgenstern's monumental work in 1944) are just the most visible milestones of this emerging trend after the war. Not surprisingly, it was Samuelson to promote Bachelier's forgotten thesis (after Savage brought it to his attention) and to make the first systematic steps in the modelling of stochastic speculative price. Unfortunately, the work of Bronzin did not get discovered and had no mentor.

The rest of this chapter covers the following topics: In the next section, we shortly address the roots of probability as scientific discipline, and in the subsequent section (6.3), we discuss the beginnings of statistical probabilism and the birth of actuarial science in the 18th century. Here, the dual role of mathematics is highlighted – the separation of insurance from speculation and as a secondary effect, the shaping moral values. Section 6.4 provides a discussion of the deterministic, mechanical view of the world prevailing in the probabilistic thinking until the late 19th century, best reflected in Boltzmann's probabilistic interpretation of the second law of thermodynamics and the controversies which it provoked. The quest for finding stable statistical regularities in aggregates, averages, measurement errors etc., culminating in the Normal distribution (error law), was a major cognitive trend of the time and reflects the desire for stability, order, and predictability in an increasingly uncertain world. This belief also swept over to social sciences (called social physics), and even stimulated the work of Jules Reganult to postulate major insights into the statistical behaviour of stock market prices – decades before Bachelier and Bronzin, and unrecognized by both (as far as what is known). However, time was overdue to replace the mechanical view by a deeper, genuine understanding of uncertainty; this transition is addressed in Section 6.5. Two specific topics are addressed in the remaining part of the chapter: in Section 6.6 the probabilistic controversy carried out in the context of Boltzmann's statistical physics is analysed, and possible parallels to the modelling of stock prices are discussed, in particular with respect to the modelling of diffusions (Brownian motions) where Bachelier's model preceded Einstein's famous paper. In contrast, Bronzin's distributional approach is much simpler; however, as shown in Section 6.7, the statistical (actuarial) literature around 1900 was not a great help for his effort because it apparently lacked any interest in modelling financial market risks. Some short remarks conclude this chapter.

6.2 Mathematics and Probability: The Beginnings

The emergence of probability as a scientific mathematical field dates back to the 17th century; before, in the Renaissance, probabilistic thinking had no cognitive power, and as such, probability

> "is a child of low sciences, such as alchemy or medicine, which had to deal in opinion, whereas the high sciences, such as astronomy or mechanics, aimed at demonstrable knowledge" (Hacking 2006, Contents).

The steps towards a mathematical treatment of probability were therefore far from immediate and required an intellectual tour-de-force, a synthesis of two detached mental traditions – the "high" mathematics on the one side, and the "low" probabilistic reasoning – perceived as entertainment (*Gesellschaftsspiel*) (Bonss 1995, p. 277) rather than science – on the other. It is important to recognize this difficulty, because it is a key structural element in the application of probability theory to financial issues, in particular, related to speculation and financial markets.

The roots of probability theory are typically seen in the famous exchange of letters between Blaise Pascal and Pierre Fermat, or in the first published treatise on mathematical probability by Christiaan Huygens and Johann de Witt in 1657. However, the new discipline which recognized and emphasized the general relevance of probabilistic and statistical reasoning was shaped in the 18th and 19th century by the leading mathematicians of the time, such as Jakob Bernoulli, Abraham de Moivre, Thomas Bayes, Marquis de Laplace, Daniel Bernoulli, Jean D'Alembert, Friedrich Gauss, Francis Galton, Adolphe Quetelet and many others.[12] Still, the development and application probabilistic models to other fields than games of chance (lotteries), astronomy, population statistics and mortality tables used in actuarial practice remained relatively rare up to the second part of the 19th century, when a "probabilistic revolution"[13] emerged in many disciplines, particularly in physics, biology, psychology, and to some extent economics. Applying probabilistic models to financial problems was common in actuarial science, particularly life insurance, at the end of the 19th century, but in fields related to speculation, banking, security markets, or derivative contracts, the number of attempts in statistical or probabilistic modelling was limited to a number of isolated and hardly appreciated

[12] Excellent reviews of the early history of probability are: Stigler (1986) and Daston (1988).
[13] The term is borrowed from Krüger et al. (1987) which contains a collection of essays covering the diffusion and application of probabilistic and statistical thinking in the 19th and 20th centuries.

contributions[14]. In the reviews about the history of probabilistic thinking (e.g. Porter's 1986 extensive work on the rise of statistical thinking from 1820 to 1900), financial markets are simply inexistent. Therefore, the work of Bronzin as well as of Bachelier marked a unique – yet unappreciated – breakthrough.

It would however be too optimistic to believe that the application of probabilistic methods in areas such as actuarial science and physics would have been a natural and immediate process. In this chapter, we show that this is not actually the case. The probabilistic models in these fields remained for long in a "deterministic" view of the world, and the breakthrough was remarkably slow. In physics, for instance, Boltzmann – one of the protagonists of statistical physics – did not believe in a probabilistic world (but instead in a mechanical modelling of molecules) until the end of his days, and so did Einstein. Only quantum theory should fundamentally challenge this view. Therefore, the random-walk model in continuous time suggested by Bachelier, or the error-law distribution suggested by Bronzin, can be regarded, together with their rationalization, as true early attempts for a probabilistic modelling of stock prices and the derivation of fair pricing in the *modern* sense. Surprisingly, also in insurance it took a long period of time towards a systematic application of probability theory to the pricing of insurance contracts. The next section shortly reviews this amazing development which is characterized by a remarkable shift in the perception of insurance as a business model: from a speculative gamble towards a moral duty, and mathematics supported this shift by providing the tools to transform the business model from judgements to rules.

6.3 A Long Way from Gambling to Morals: Statistical Probabilism and the Birth of Actuarial Science in the 18th Century

The computation of the fair price of financial contracts under condition of risk has always been a subject of interest of insurers, jurists, gamblers, economists and mathematicians – long before insurance companies, banks and brokers started to professionally manage and trade risks using probabilistic and statistical tools. Nevertheless, a shift occurred during the second part of the 17th and 18th century when mathematical probabilists such as Jakob and Nicholas Bernoulli, Ludwig and Christiaan Huygens or Abraham de Moivre became increasingly interested in applying statistics to probabilistic modelling, especially in areas such as gambling, insurance and annuities. Lorraine Daston characterizes this shift as follows:

[14] Among these contributions in the pre-1900 period are: Edgeworth (1888), Levèvre (1870) and Regnault (1863); see Girlich (2002) and Chapter 18 in this volume. A volume edited by Geoffrey Poitras (2006) contains original contributions reviewing many of the pre-20th century contributions to finance, including those of Jules Regnault, Henri Lefèvre, and Louis Bachelier.

> "Whereas earlier writers on insurance, annuities, and other risky ventures had emphasized prudent judgment based on the particulars of the individual case, the probabilists proposed general rules to determine the fair price of risk" (Daston 1988, p. 112).

Specifically:

> "The jurists and their clients had looked to experience and judgment; the mathematicians looked to tables and calculation. This was the theoretical legacy of mathematical probability to institutionalized risk taking in the eighteenth century; [...]" (Daston 1988, p. 138).

A prominent institutionalized form of risk taking in that century was life insurance, and most applications of the probabilists were in the area of mortality statistics and its application to the modelling of life expectancy and fair life insurance premiums. It is however interesting to notice that the practical implications of this new "mathematical theory of risk"[15] were apparently extremely limited – or in the words of Daston (continuing upon the preceding quote): "nil" (Daston 1988, p. 138). And more specifically:

> "It should be noted that not only businessmen but also jurists took almost no account of how the theory of aleatory contracts had been modified by mathematical probability" (Daston 1988, pp. 171–172).

> "Why did the practitioners of risk fail to avail themselves of a mathematical technology custom-made for them?" (Daston 1988, p. 139).

The author of these quotes provides a long list of different perceptions about risk between old insurers and probabilists (Daston 1988, p. 115), and ironically, many of the examples remind to current controversial issues in the debate over risk measurement (such as where or not there is time diversification of risk). This is an interesting observation, because it contradicts today's widespread perception that life insurance (or actuarial science at large) is – and ever was – the classic and immediate field of application of mathematical statistics; but the adaptation was not so quick as one might think, in spite of the theoretical progress which was made. Therefore, in the 1760s, *The Equitable* was still the first and only company in applying probability mathematics as a business standard for its life insurance business.

[15] This wording is adapted from Daston (1988), p. 125.

Why did the insurance sector resist so long in making use of the new techniques? Daston (1988), Chapter 3, Zelizer (1979)[16] and Clark (1999) provide detailed analyses of this rather long process and the driving forces behind. There is no doubt that the progress in mathematics (probability theory and statistics), the availability of new statistical data (mortality tables[17]) and the emergence of a new profession (actuaries) played a key role in this transformation. However, Daston (1988) argues that the breakthrough of the new mathematical theory of risk in the insurance practice required a more fundamental change, specifically a transformation of moral values. It should be noticed that speculation was extremely popular at that time, in particular in the middle classes (the bourgeoisie) of the society. Even life insurance was widely regarded – and used – as a speculative activity in the first part of the 18th century. The key argument of Daston is that the practical implications of the new probability mathematics was limited until it was explicitly used to separate gambling from (traditional) insurance, i.e. socially "unnecessary" from "necessary" risk taking.[18] This distinction was of prime importance for the subsequent development of the (in particular: life) insurance business.

Separating insurance from gambling

The previous point is moreover essential because it highlights the role which formal scientific methods (as well as the way in which this is orchestrated and cultivated) play in the public acceptance and legitimation of new business practices. Unfortunately, as argued below, financial speculation never made the step from gambling to a sound "investment science" before the turn of the 20th century, albeit numerous attempts towards formalization exist.

The probabilistic foundation of insurance affected the public perception of life insurance both on an intellectual (or technical) and moral level. The new techniques promised a higher certainty to the insured persons, and created a new attitude towards risk and thereby underpinned widely-accepted social values such as foresight, prudence, and responsibility.
The safety from the new techniques relied on

- the exploitation of statistical regularities (mortality statistics)

[16] Unlike the work of Daston, which focuses on Europe (continental and UK) and the period between 1650 to 1840, and to which we extensively reference in this chapter, Zelizer's (1979) work more narrowly focuses the public debate about the morals of the US life-insurance market and its practices in the 19th and 20th century.

[17] The first mortality table was published in 1693 by Edmond Halley, which provided a link between the life insurance premium and the average life span (life expectancy).

[18] This view is challenged by a more recent study by Clark (1999). Based on evidence about the risk-taking behaviour of people *before* the "breakthrough" of the new actuarial-based insurance companies, he finds that a clear distinction between "insurance" and "gambling" was not so clear-cut.

- trust into the (mathematical, probabilistic) scheme to fix adequate premiums.

It is interesting that these two aspects were regularly and explicitly stressed in the advertisement brochures of many major life insurance companies.[19] This contrasted the early 18th century life insurance business which was widely regarded – and practiced – as a speculative activity[20], and in most jurisdictions the resemblance of insurance to gambling was reinforced by the legal treatment of insurance policies as aleatory contracts. As such, they not only relied on but explicitly emphasized uncertainty, they did not promise safety or financial planning to the customer, but emphasized risk; they consequently left the impression of a gamble and were increasingly criticized in the public discussion. Daston even argues that quantifying uncertainty by means of probability theory "seemed to presume too much certainty" for the life contracts to be sufficiently risky (Daston 1988, pp. 171–172). The paradigm shift is obvious.

More importantly, the new "safety" derived from the new mathematical theory of risk created

> "[...] an image of life insurance diametrically opposed to that of gambling. The prospectuses of the Equitable and the companies that later imitated it made the regularity of the statistics and the certainty of the mathematics emblematic for the orderly, thrifty, prudent, far-sighted père de famille, in contrast to the wastrel, improvident, selfish gambler" (Daston 1988, p. 175).

Fortuna was replaced by paterfamilias, and mathematics was an indispensable servant in the process of "domestication of risk": it replaced the "portrait of the gambler as one racked by uncontrollable passions" (Daston 1988, p. 161) by a rationally acting agent, prudent, socially responsible, equipped with actuarial models, and guarantor for a rational handling of risks.

Moral effects were always used as an explicitly part of the marketing of the new contracts. The famous mathematician and probabilist Pierre-Simon Laplace, himself author of a famous treatise on probability (Laplace 1812), considered insurance as "advantageous to morals, in favoring the gentlest tendencies of nature" (quote based on Daston 1988, p. 182). Propagandizing the moral of the business model and underpinning it with sound mathematical principles, based on the best available statistics, was indeed a remarkable break in the history of

[19] An example is given by Daston from the prospectus of *The Equitable*, which "stressed the certainty of the underlying principle of the new scheme, which was 'grounded upon the expectancy of the continuance of life; which, although the lives of men separately taken, are uncertain, yet in an aggregate of lives is reducible to a certainty' " (quote based on Daston 1988, p. 178).

[20] In England, such bets were sold by insurance offices like The Amicable Society or The Royal Exchange Assurance Corporation.

financial contracting, and the emerging life insurance industry worked hard to reinforce this perception from its very beginning.

Institutions and regulation

An important step in this development was the establishment of an institution which pioneered the new approach: The Equitable Society for the Assurance of Life, short *The Equitable* in the UK, in 1762[21]; the new actuarial foundations allowed the company to abandon the tradition of flat rates by charging adequate premiums against insurers' benefits with respect to their life expectancy. Similar companies were founded elsewhere, e.g. the *Compagnie Royal d'Assurance* in France (founded 1789), or the *Corporation for Relief of Poor and Distressed Widows and Children of Presbyterian Ministers* in the US (founded 1759). Other countries joined the trend much later, e.g. Switzerland with the *Schweizerische Rentenanstalt* (today: Swiss Life) in 1857 or *De Nationale Levensverzekering Bank* in the Netherlands (founded 1863).

This process of innovation was accelerated by major regulatory actions, such as the Life Assurance Act of 1774 (also known as the Gambling Act) in England, which prohibited insurance on lives in which the policyholder did not have a real and documented financial "interest". This implied a clear separation between "insurance" (i.e. financial contracting based on insurable interest) and "gambling" where anybody could place a bet on the life or death of any other person. Life insurance was now considered a prudential institution aimed at underwriting personal and family security. Therefore, regulatory action reinforced the distinction between necessary and unnecessary risk and risk taking – a distinction which has always been hard to justify economically, now and then. Amazingly enough, economists did not seem to contribute to this discussion in these days. This should however become different towards the end of the 19th century.[22]

The result of this process was amazing, and is summarized by Daston:

> "Since roughly the beginning of the 19th century, gambling has come to be seen as irrational as well as immoral, and insurance, particularly life insurance, as both prudent and tantamount to a moral duty" (Daston 1988, p. 140).

[21] The name of the company also represents its program: "equitable" means "commensurate with risk" (the German wording is more precise: *risikogerecht*).

[22] Cohn (1868), Weber (1894, 1896) or Stillich (1909) are just a few examples for this literature.

The case of financial markets

This shift was never done, or did never succeed, for speculation as related to financial markets. Speculation with stocks or commodities always remained in the orbit of games and lotteries, for reasons yet to be investigated. Even at the end of the 19th century, financial markets did not even get the attention of mathematicians and probabilists. However, the conflict between the growth of financial markets, the need for risk capital to finance public and private investment during the *Gründerjahre*, and moral issues related to speculative activities accentuated in the second part of the 19th century. The attempts were numerous, particularly in the German speaking part of Europe, to outline the economic role and benefits of stock exchange trading and speculation; an excellent example is Cohn (1868). However, the public opinion against speculation accelerated after the 1873 stock exchange crashes in Vienna and Berlin, which plunged the economies into a long-lasting recession. This nourished strong anti-Semitism in German speaking Europe because Jews were made responsible for the speculative activities, greed, the exploitation of the working class, and the coming crisis. The anti-Semitic, anti-speculation literature published in these decades reveals the emotionality of this conflict. Nevertheless, several authors and in particular, a Committee of Inquiry (*Börsen-Enquete-Kommission*), tried to put things into an objective, economically well-founded perspective, among others the sociologist Max Weber who devoted an entire treatise to the operation and economic functions of stock exchanges (Weber 1894, 1896). However, public values were hard to be affected by these writings, and at the turn of the century, public opinion about speculation and banking was so negative that public pressure and regulatory measures increasingly confined these activities. Derivatives, aimed at exploiting price differences without physical delivery of securities or commodities, were often treated as gambles (*Differenzeinwand*) or simply forbidden, so from 1931 to 1970, at German exchanges.

Was mathematics also commissioned to rationalize the perception about speculation, to brighten the public opinion about financial markets and investments – like statistical probabilism was exploited to improve the morals of the life insurance business two centuries before? The work of Bachelier and Bronzin may be regarded as such an attempt; but it may have been too late, too difficult, or simply the wrong time. In addition, at the end of the 19th century, the spirit of probabilism was not yet ready for the modelling of complexities like financial markets. This may sound surprising, but "probability" was long framed in a rather deterministic view (or construction) of natural and social processes. The next section will clarify this argument.

6.4 "Rien ne serait incertain ...": Probability Without Uncertainty from Laplace to Social Physics

Although probability theory and statistics reveals an impressive progress since its birth in the 17th century, both in terms of analytical results and applications, a closer analysis of the underlying cognitive pattern leaves a puzzling picture about the perception of uncertainty.[23] From the perspective of our time, decades after our view of the word has been shaped by dynamical systems, chaos theory, cybernetics, not to mention quantum physics, it is hard to reconcile probabilistic models with a deterministic structure – or view – of the world (nature, society). However, this was not regarded as a contradiction over long periods of time: "We associate statistical laws with indeterminism, but for much of the 19th century they were synonymous with determinism of the strictest sort" (Daston, 1988, p. 183). We argue below that this cognitive mindset, and its transition towards a more genuine understanding of uncertainty at the end of that century, was an additional obstacle in the emergence of a probabilistic understanding (and specifically: the probabilistic modelling) of financial markets.

The balancing act between determinism and probabilism was seen in the difference between an objective, or genuine uncertainty governing the structure and processes of the world, and the limited information or knowledge individuals have to perceive the inner structure of the world. A frequently quoted example illustrating this attitude is a passage from the famous treatise on probability by Pierre-Simon Laplace:

> "*Nous devons donc envisager l'état présent de l'univers comme l'effet de son état antérieur et comme la cause de celui qui va suivre. Une intelligence qui, pour un instant donné, connaitrait toutes les forces dont la nature est animée et la situation respective des êtres qui la composent, si d'ailleurs elle était assez vaste pour soumettre ces données à l'Analyse, embrasserait dans la même formule les mouvements des plus grands corps de l'univers et ceux du plus léger atome: rien ne serait incertain pour elle, et l'avenir, comme le passé, serait présent à ses yeux*" (Laplace 1812)[24].

[23] The "emergence of probability" as a scientific field is described in several outstanding texts: In addition to Daston (1988), typical references are Porter (1986), Hacking (1990, 2006), and von Plato (1994). The two volumes edited by Krüger et al. (1987a, 1987b) have become a standard reference.

[24] The quote is not from the original source, but from the Collected Works of Laplace (1886), Section "De la probabilité", pp. vi–vii. An English translation can be found in Lindley (2007), p. 22: "We may regard the present state of the universe as the effect of its past and the cause of its future. An intellect which at any given moment knew all of the forces that animate nature and the mutual positions of the beings that compose it, if this intellect were vast enough to submit the data to analysis, could condense into a single formula the movement of the greatest bodies of the universe and that of lightest atom; for such an intellect nothing could be uncertain and the future just like the past would be present before its eyes".

This characterization is illuminating in its clarity; it demonstrates that knowledge ("[...] knew all of the forces [...]") and information processing capacity ("[...] if this intellect were vast enough to submit the data to analysis [...]") were regarded as constitutive or constructive features of probability. The idea of an omniscient "intelligence" was to survive many more decades – at least until Einstein's well-known verdict that God does not play dice.[25]

Statistical physics

Laplace's final wording that "the future just like the past would be present before its eyes" can also be read as an allusion to the time-symmetry of Newtonian mechanics, and in any case discloses the same perception of the world. It is therefore not surprising that the biggest challenge for this probabilistic perception occurred in physics, specifically in thermodynamics, towards the end of the 19th century, when the inconsistence between a Newtonian determinism and obvious empirical facts in the behaviour of gases – that heat always flows from hot to cold bodies, which violates time symmetry – became obvious. It was James Clerk Maxwell's achievement to declare the second law of thermodynamics as only *probable* – which represented a revolution in the tradition of natural laws.[26]

In contrast to Maxwell, Ludwig Boltzmann, although "the language and concepts of probability theory were central to his research in this field from the beginning" (Porter 1986, p. 208) was never comfortable with probabilism in thermodynamics. How interchangeable probabilities, averages, determinism and classical mechanics were for him is reflected in the introduction of his famous 1872 paper:

> "*Die Bestimmung von Durchschnittswerten ist Aufgabe der Wahrscheinlichkeitsrechnung. Die Probleme der mechanischen Wärmetheorie sind daher Probleme der Wahrscheinlichkeitsrechnung. Es wäre aber ein Irrtum, zu glauben, dass der Wärmetheorie deshalb eine Unsicherheit anhafte, weil daselbst die Lehrsätze der Wahrscheinlichkeitsrechnung in Anwendung kommen*" (Boltzmann 1872, 2000, pp. 1–2).[27]

[25] As discussed in Section 6.6, this picture is all the more surprising as Einstein suggested the first formal stochastic model, together with Bachelier, for what is known as the Brownian motion (Einstein 1905).

[26] According to Porter (1986), p. 20, the first explicit connection between "the indeterminacy of certain thermodynamic principles and their statistical character" occurred in 1868.

[27] The page numbers refer to the German text reprinted in Boltzmann (2000), Chapter 1. Translation adapted (and extended) from Porter (1986), p. 113: "The determination of averages is the task of the calculus of probability. The problems of the mechanical theory heat are therefore problems of the calculus of probability. It would be a mistake, however, to believe that the theory of heat involves uncertainty because the principles of probability come into application here."

And even in one of his late talks, in 1899, he maintained:

> "A precondition of all scientific knowledge is the principle of the complete [*eindeutig*] determination of all natural processes [...] This principle declares, that the movement of a body does not occur purely accidentally [...] but that they are completely determined by the circumstances to which the body is subject" (Boltzmann 1899, 1905).[28]

Like many other of the 19th century probabilists, he assumed a deterministic system *in principle*, but as being so complex due to the immense number of objects (molecules) and causing influences that only a statistical approach is able to characterize its behaviour.

Although the implicit or explicit determinism of Boltzmann's work, depending of the reading or interpretation, is not undisputed in the literature[29], the struggle and inner conflict of the founder of statistical physics to adopt a probabilistic understanding of nature as opposed to mechanical laws, "never comfortable with the dependence of science on probabilities, except in terms of stable frequencies" (Porter 1986, pp. 216–217), is indeed striking.[30] Section 6.6 provides a more detailed discussion of this topic.

Averages, Error Law, and the Desire for Stability

This was however not Boltzmann's idiosyncratic view of the word; it reflects much more the perception inherent in the probabilistic and statistical literature up to the 19th century. The derivation of predictable implications, i.e. stable statistical regularities, for aggregates – or averages – of individual, possibly unobservable particles or objects represented a cognitive trend not only in natural science, but corresponded to the probabilistic spirit of statistical thinking in many other disciplines as well: it reflects the desire for stability, order, and predictability. A whole battery of statistical insights such as Poisson's Law of Large Numbers, de Moivre's Law of Errors (also called Normal Law), Gauss' and Legendre's Least Squares Method, Laplace's Central Limit Theorem and concepts such as Quetelet's Average Man, Boltzmanns' Time Averages, replaced a good part of the certainty which had to be sacrificed with the rise of probabilistic thinking over time.

[28] The quote is taken from Porter (1986), p. 208. The original German text can be found in Boltzmann (1899, 1905), pp. 276–277. The first year refers to the talk delivered at Clark University, the second year to the first German publication of the talk.

[29] See von Plato (1994), p. 78ff, for a contradiction of this view.

[30] Throughout his work, Boltzmann treats (logical) probabilities as completely interchangeable with relative frequencies, which is somehow confusing. "Logical" probabilities are ratios between the specific and total number of possible events, while "statistical" (or empirical) probabilities are relative frequencies of events over repeated outcomes, i.e. limiting values; see Bonss (1995), p. 282ff, for a detailed discussion.

With respect to the theory of risk, Daston concludes:

> "The mathematical theory of risk has triumphed, and with it the belief that whole classes of phenomena previously taken to be the very model of the unpredictable, from hail storms to suicides, were in fact governed by statistical regularities. These regularities took the form of distributions rather than functional relationships, but they were hailed as regularities all the same ..." [...] "Order was to be found in the mass and over the long run, in large numbers, no longer in the individual case" (Daston 1899, p. 183).

While the picture of stable laws as related to masses, or averages, was strongly shaped in natural science (physics, astronomy) and actuarial statistics, it was quickly adapted to broader social issues: Adolphe Quetelet, an astronomer and statistician, with a particular interest in measurement errors in astronomy, advocated in his work the universality of the Normal law of error for social phenomena such as crime, marriage or suicide rates. He invented the concept of the "average person" (*l'homme moyen*), a statistical construct characterized by the average of measured variables that follow a normal distribution. He called this research program "social physics" (*physique sociale*)[31], and it was quickly taken up by other researchers and applied to a broad range of social phenomena.[32] Among these was Jules Regnault.

The Financial Physics of Jules Regnault

Regnault's achievement, documented in a single published work (Regnault 1863), was indeed surprising, both for its content and its emergence. Armed with the intellectual background and theoretical instruments from social physics, he was the first (and based on our current knowledge: for several decades the only) researcher interested in the modelling of financial market prices and to advocate the random walk model with normally distributed prices.[33] He empirically tested this distributional assumption and observed that (standard) deviations are "in

[31] The major work about social physics is Quetelet (1835); Porter (1986), pp. 41–55, gives an overview of his work.

[32] The "representative" firm, introduced in Alfred Marshall's *Principles* (Book IV, Chapter XIII, Section 9) and popularized (as well as generalized to the representative individual) by John Hicks *Value and Capital*, grew out of a similar perception – although not explicitly related to a probabilistic framework or a distributional assumption. See Brodbeck (1998), Chapter 2, for a critical appraisal of the adaptation of social physics to economic analysis. Notably, the representative investor, the Robin Crusoe economy, etc. are still alive and well in economic modelling today.

[33] A full appraisal of Regnault's unique achievement is given by a series of papers by Franck Jovanovic and coauthors, see e.g. Jovanovic and Le Gall (2001), Jovanovic (2001), Jovanovic (2006).

direct proportion to the square root of time" (Regnault 1863, p. 50). He moreover, for the first time, addressed the particularities of an economic system to explain the statistical properties of price fluctuations: new information and zero-expected gains from security trades (proposition of "equal chances"). These are remarkable insights derived from a researcher who was entirely detached from any scientific tradition or scientific community[34]. But even more interesting than his statistical findings is the moral claim motivating his work, as discussed by Jovanovic (2001, 2006). The objective of his analysis was to rationalize arguments in the ongoing public debate about the dangers and harmful effects of speculation. His approach

> "was not based on moral presumptions per se but on a rational demonstration of the consequences of immoral behavior of individuals – driven by their sole 'personal interest' – on society as a whole as well as on individuals, proving that such behavior led to their inexorable ruin. He indeed believed that unlike morals as such, a 'scientific proof' was definitively convincing. [...] His aim was thus, from a scientific perspective, to separate two kinds of speculation: short-term speculation [gambling] and long-term speculation [speculation]" (Jovanovic 2006, p. 195).

A more direct moral claim was derived from the symmetrical nature of his random walk specification[35] which for him was

> "a means to show that stock markets are moral, in the sense that they based on equal chances for all participants" (Jovanovic 2006, p. 201).

Of course, the argument is quite fragile viewed from modern asset pricing theory assuming positive expected stock returns. What is the meaning of "fair" in this setting? Moreover, Regnault makes extensive use of averaging and law-of-large-number arguments to provoke the view that short-term components "inexorably cancel each other out", while the long-term components are "admirably regular".[36] This was exactly in the spirit of Laplace's and Quetelet's statistical determinism and was aimed at scientifically proofing that, although the market mechanism produces biases and error over short horizons, these are averaged out

[34] Regnault was a money market trader managing his own business with his brother.
[35] Regnault, like Bachelier, assumed a random walk without drift, i.e. a price increase occurs with the same probability as a price decrease.
[36] Both quotes are translated in Jovanovic (2006), p. 205.

– "corrected" – over a long horizon;[37] the market can consequently be regarded as a stable, predictable, trustful system governed by unobservable, deterministic laws – in spite of speculation. Therefore, the role of statistics "was for him a way to discover and to approximate deterministic laws" (Jovanovic 2006, p. 205) in the behavior of stock market prices. This was in perfect line with the tradition of the 19th century determinism of social physics.

Did Regnault's intensions materialize? According to the analyses of Jovanovic (2006), pp. 210–211 and 213–214, the impact was not substantial; the book was hardly quoted outside France and was not mentioned in Bachelier. He used state-of-the art statistics, studied a highly relevant and original topic, derived practically important results, tried to emphasize the moral consequences of his analysis aimed at separating gambling from sound speculation and thereby legitimizing financial markets – very much as the mathematical probabilists did in the 18th century, but without achieving their success. Was it because he was an outsider of the scientific community, or because no community supporting a financial science existed which was receptive and eager for innovation (as argued by Jovanovic)?

Preliminary insights

At least, several differences to the case of actuarial mathematics can be identified:

1. Being part of a scientific community is important to launch and disseminate original ideas, but the opinion leaders in the field must be on-stage. Remember the enthusiasm of Laplace in favor of the new life insurance contracts. Financial science failed having strong advocates – until the 50s of the 20th century when Leonard Savage and Paul A. Samuelson discovered the relevance of Bachelier's work.
2. With the rise of the actuarial-based life insurance business, a new profession was formed, the actuary, with strict professional standards, and supported by the leading mathematicians of the time. In the course of time, substantial supervisory responsibility was assigned to the associations of actuaries. The chief actuary of an insurance company is an academically trained authority, and holds a key position (occasionally even going along with a cult of personality). Similar professional associations and standards which could

[37] It should be mentioned that although the random walk model still deserves much sympathy today, Regnault's statistical implications (with respect to time diversification, law of large numbers, stability over long time horizons) are highly questionable; Paul A. Samuelson has written extensively on this subject and warned from treating small probabilities as zero; see e.g. Samuelson (1994). Samuelson's analysis also highlights the crucial difference between subdividing and adding (independent) risks (originally in Samuelson 1963), which points to a fundamental confusion in the early discussion about "aggregates" (ensembles) and "averages" which were occasionally treated equal. See also footnote 71 for a further discussion.

have shaped the confidence towards financial markets were inexistent in these days – they developed only after the 2nd World War (e.g. the US Financial Analysts Association) or in the 90s (e.g. risk management professionals).

3. The case for developing an *investment* (and financing) science, a scientific understanding of financial markets, is much more difficult than developing a scientific approach to the pricing of concrete, e.g. life insurance, contracts.[38] This has to do with the fact that the functioning of financial markets was, and still is, a mystery to many people. Changing the public attitude towards speculation is much easier if related to a specific financial product than in the context of abstract markets, their pricing behavior, etc.
4. Institutions (firms, exchanges, bureaus, agencies, sometimes even publicly respected investment professionals) play an important role in the public transition of attitudes. Without insurance companies like *The Equitable*, the success story of actuarial science and modern insurance would not have been possible. In finance and investing, such stories are more difficult to find. An example is the emergence of modern derivatives exchanges after 1973, without which standardized derivative contracts and technologies such as the Black-Scholes model would not have gained broad public attention and acceptance.

A word of caution

Summing up: Understanding statistical regularities, and probability laws, as approximations or means to discover deterministic natural laws in the Newtonian sense, made it for many decades possible to view probabilism as being compatible with determinism. As discussed in the context of Laplace's (1812) quote at the beginning of this section, it is useful to separate an "objective", intrinsic uncertainty of natural or social processes from randomness arising from limited knowledge, information processing capacity, or inability. The latter is well compatible with a deterministic view of the world, as discussed in this section.

Viewed from today, this cognitive understanding appears somehow strange, and even dangerous. As discussed by Bonss, if probabilities

> "are associated too closely with a natural [law] and are understood as a purely mathematical problem [...], then they represent a modernized instrument for the construction of uniqueness, necessity and control-

[38] Not surprisingly, Bachelier and Bronzin developed their models for the pricing of concrete contracts (options), and the modelling of the underlying stock market was a necessity, but not the primary focus.

> lability, and this is exactly a trend which prevails until today" (Bonss 1995, p. 287).[39]

The certainty about individual phenomena was substituted by certainty in statistical laws – a dangerous deal, as evidenced by the failures of modern risk management systems in our days. With respect to controllability, Bonss' criticism corresponds very much to the reasoning of the sociologist Ulrich Beck claiming that in many cases the "dimensionality of risk is constricted to technical controllability from its very conception" (Beck 1986, p. 39).[40]

From a social sciences perspective, the major shortcoming of the deterministic position has to be seen in the neglect of the feedback mechanisms originating from individual and collective action from learning, error correction, strategic behavior and the like, which changes the structure of the probability laws itself and makes the underlying probabilistic structure of system to be unstable – and unpredictable, but not only because of lack of information or knowledge.[41] The question is whether the inherent deterministic structure of nature and society was ever questioned *before* the quantum-chaos-cybernetics revolution, which constructed a new perception of the dynamic behavior and intrinsic operation of complex systems in the 20th century. We are far from being able to address this question here, but the thinking of two personalities plays a key role in this context: Charles Peirce and Richard von Mises.

6.5 Towards the End of Deterministic Probabilism: Peirce and von Mises

Peirce's life[42] was devoted to measurement and measurement errors, their distribution, and much more: he ultimately advocated a view of nature that is fundamentally stochastic. He wrote about the emergence of his own cognitive perception:

> "It was recognizing that chance does play a part in the real world, apart from what we may know or be ignorant of. But it was a transitional belief which I have passed through" (Peirce 1893a, p. 535).

[39] The original German text: "*Denn wer Wahrscheinlichkeiten zu einem Natur[problem] macht und sie [...] als ein mathematisches Problem begreift, für den sind sie letztlich ein modernisiertes Mittel zur Herstellung von Eindeutigkeit, Notwendigkeit und Beherrschbarkeit, und genau dies ist ein Trend, der bis heute anhält*". We have translated the German "*Naturproblem*" with natural *law* because the author is using this more adequate wording in the preceding sentence.

[40] The original German quote is: "*[dass] die Dimensionalität des Risikos vom Ansatz her bereits auf technische Handhabbarkeit eingeschränkt [wird]*".

[41] In economics, this effect is known as the Lucas-critique against activist policy action.

[42] See Hacking (1990), Chapter 23 and Porter (1986), pp. 219–230, for concise overviews on Peirce's probabilistic thinking.

This concise statement reveals an understanding which clearly separates a deeper "chance" governing the universe from cognitive inabilities such as limited knowledge, ignorance, or measurement. He always advocated a view that the universe can be understood as well as a product of "absolute chance". Quoting Peirce, Hacking writes about that rejection of epistemological tradition:

> "The ultimate 'reality' of our measurements and what they measure has the form of the Gaussian law of error. It is bank balances and credit ledgers that are exact, said Peirce, not the constants of nature. Stop trying to model the world, as we have done since the time of Descartes, on the transactions of shopkeepers. The 'constants' are only chance variables that have settled down in the course of the evolution of laws" (Hacking 1990, p. 214).[43]

Specifically and unlike his contemporary thinkers persisting in their deterministic-probabilism tradition, he denied that errors disappear if observations or research methods become arbitrarily sophisticated; he regarded error as part of the underlying probability laws: this was new. Interestingly he did not deduct this insight from a theoretical framework or any kind of scientific reasoning, but intuitively from everyday observation:

> "It is sufficient to go out into the air and open one's eyes to see that the world is not governed altogether by mechanism. [...] The endless variety in the world has not been created by law. When we gaze upon the multifariousness of nature, we are looking straight into the face of a living spontaneity" (Peirce 1887, p. 63).

Of course, Peirce's thinking was not idiosyncratic; Porter (1986), pp. 222–224, discusses how it was related to other French philosophers; but what makes his thinking unique is the clearness in which he recognized the moods of the time and in which he was able to anticipate the upcoming radical change of probabilistic thinking:

> "As well as I can read the sign of the times, the doom of necessitarian metaphysics is sealed" (Peirce 1887, p. 64).

He not only criticized the traditional epistemological approach, but also shaped an alternative cognitive model which contains many elements of the evolutionary thinking in the 20th century, which he straightforwardly called "evolutionary love" (see Peirce 1893b).

Is there anything else to be said about modern probability? Unfortunately, the implications for analyzing financial markets are not straightforward from

[43] The original source to which Hacking refers is Peirce (1892). A detailed quote from Peirce's original writing about this point can also be found in Porter (1986), pp. 220–221.

Peirce's work. For this purpose, we address our attention to a probabilistic thinker one generation after Peirce, Richard von Mises, who specifically argued against the mechanical (i.e. deterministic) structure of statistical physics. Drawing on work by Ernst Mach (Mach 1919), he stated "a deep contradiction [...] in physical statistics, one that has not been conquered yet" (von Mises 1920, p. 227)[44]. The criticism originates in Mach's insight that a statistical interpretation "in the large" (i.e. the observables of the macrosystem, the second law of thermodynamics) is inconsistent with the determinism "in the small" (i.e. in the microsystem of atoms and molecules); it is impossible to derive statistical implications from the differential equations of classical physics:

> "*Mit Recht wandte Ernst Mach dagegen ein, dass aus den mechanischen Gesetzen niemals ein Verhalten, wie es der zweite Hauptsatz der Thermodynamik fordert, gefolgert werden könne*" (von Mises 1936, p. 221).

And more precisely:

> "*[...] die statistische Auffassung im grossen ist nicht vereinbar mit Determinismus im kleinen, man kann statistische Aussagen nicht aus den Differentialgleichungen der klassischen Physik herleiten*" (von Mises 1936, p. 222).

The quote reveals the quest for a *genuinely* stochastic architecture of dynamical systems, not relying on deterministic roots such as Boltzmann's exact (but unobservable) microstates. Therefore, von Mises (1931) suggested terminating the mechanical interpretation of the ergodic hypothesis[45] in favor of an entirely probabilistic approach; he showed that in a probabilistic setting, ergodicity implies that the observable macrostates of a statistical system exhibit the Markov property[46]. In simple terms such a system (or process) lacks predictability. This forms the basis for von Mises' general principle of probability: the irregularity principle (*Prinzip der Regellosigkeit*). An infinite sequence of numbers is random or irregular (*regellos*) if the subsequent realization cannot be predicted with more than 50 percent probability at any stage in its sequence.[47] Interest-

[44] The quote is based on the translation in von Plato (1994), p. 191.

[45] The ergodic hypothesis assumes that a dynamical system evolves through all states over time if the time period is sufficiently long. In particular, there is a zero probability that any state will never recur. An implication is that the *time average* of a microscopic system is equal to the average *across systems* of a specific ensemble (i.e. systems with different microstates but the same observable macrostate).

[46] The Markov property states that the conditional probability distribution of the future states of a system, given all information about the current and past states, is only a function of the current state.

[47] More precisely, the axiom states that the limiting value of the relative frequencies of observations must be constant under repeated choices of subsequences.

ingly, von Mises was fully aware of the closeness of the irregularity principle to the "fair game" assumption of modern finance: he sees the principle as being fully equivalent to a gambling strategy where unlimited gains can be excluded, which he briefly called *Prinzip vom ausgeschlossenen Spielsystem* (principle of the excluded gambling system)[48]. A vivid description of the equivalence of the two principles can be found in the context of so called "foolproof" systems of gambling jerks in Monte Carlo and their sad experience:

> "*Dass sie nicht zum gewünschten Ziele führen, nämlich zu einer Verbesserung der Spielchancen, also zu einer Veränderung der relativen Häufigkeiten, mit der die einzelnen Spielausgänge innerhalb der systematisch ausgewählten Spielfolge auftreten, das ist die traurige Erfahrung, die über kurz oder lange alle Systemspieler machen müssen. Auf diese Erfahrungen stützen wir uns bei unserer Definition der Wahrscheinlichkeit*" (von Mises 1936, p. 30).

Notice that in the last sentence of this quote, von Mises restricts the definition of probability exclusively to cases where the principle applies. Among the concrete examples he uses to highlight his principle are lotteries and insurance, but unfortunately not financial markets, which would apparently be the ultimate starting point to investigate the irregularity, respectively, the excluded gamble principle. But unfortunately, the probabilistic thinkers (with the notable exceptions of Regnault, Bachelier and Bronzin) were not aware or interested in random phenomena related to financial markets or speculation. Unlike physical systems or natural events in general, there is a specific, *man-made* cause for randomness and non-predictability in financial markets: the attempt to process information as completely ("efficiently") as possible, to equalize profits between sellers and buyers, whatever approach is used. Financial markets would therefore be the perfect object of study in the attempt to escape from a deterministic-probabilistic setting. Why did this not occur?

Remember that the achievement of Maxwell and Boltzmann was to replace a deterministic natural law by a "probable" law. This was of course revolutionary. However, von Mises even went a step further and raised randomness itself, respectively his principle of excluded gambles (or irregularity), to a natural law like the energy conservation principle:

> "*Was das Energieprinzip für das elektrische Kraftwerk, das bedeutet unser Satz vom ausgeschlossenen Spielsystem für das Versicherungswesen: die unumstössliche Grundlage aller Berechnungen und aller Massnahmen. Wie von jedem weittragenden Naturgesetz können wir von diesen beiden Sätzen sagen: Es sind Einschränkungen,*

[48] For a popular version of his thoughts, see von Mises (1936), pp. 30–34, in particular point 3 in his summary.

> *die wir [...] unserer Erwartung über den künftigen Ablauf von Naturvorgängen auferlegen*" (von Mises 1936, p. 31).

This is a remarkable break in the probabilistic tradition: natural laws are regarded as restrictions on *genuine* probability laws governing all natural and man-made processes!

For him, randomness was an inherent property of all natural phenomena; he argued that even the most exact, fully automated mechanical processes generate randomly varying results (von Mises 1936, pp. 212–213), and the best measurement techniques do not avoid error and randomness (p. 213). Consequently, he saw no fundamental difference between the randomness of "physical", mechanical processes of the lifeless nature, without intervening human actions, and typical "games of chance" (pp. 210–211):

> "*Hat man nun einmal erkannt, dass ein automatischer Mechanismus zufallsartig schwankende Resultate ergeben kann, so liegt kein Grund mehr vor, die analoge Annahme für die Gasmolekel abzulehnen*" (von Mises 1936, p. 212).

For him, the distinction between a purely mechanical system (of atoms or molecules in an isolated bin) and the mechanism of games of chance relies purely on a cognitive bias (*Vorurteil*), which cannot be defended under any circumstances (p. 211).

Ascribing a probabilistic structure to the lifeless nature, to processes unaffected by human action ("*Prozesse, in die keine Menschenhand eingreift*", p. 210) was indeed revolutionary in the thinking of this time. According to our earlier remarks on the principle of excluded gambles, it not surprising that he regarded "games of chance" (*Glücksspiele*) such as dice, coin tossing, lotteries, or the then popular *Bajazzo* game all the same as natural phenomena being governed by intrinsic probability laws. However, it is important to notice that von Mises was equally interested in the impact of human action in causing, perceiving and measuring random events. He repeatedly stresses the importance of the "free will" of people as an ultimate source of randomness. Most interesting in our context are, again, his remarks about the "games of chance" which he regarded by no means as independent of human action[49]:

[49] An interesting side-aspect of this notion is von Mises' discussion about "pure" games of chance – where the personal characteristics of the player (including her skill) has no effect on the relative frequencies of profits after (infinitely) many repetitions. He moreover argued that games where the skill of the individual players has no or only a marginal effect on the relative frequencies of profits should be forbidden or require authorization (von Mises 1936, pp. 165–166). It must be noted that the distinction between "pure luck" and "skill" played an important role in the public debate about gambling and speculation in the first decades of the 20th century, and von Mises apparently wanted to advocate a simple statistical criterion in that emotional debate. It would have been interesting to extend this discussion to speculation on financial markets.

> "*Auch bei den Glücksspielen, deren Ablauf doch den Vorgängen in der unbelebten Natur viel näher steht, ist das Dazwischentreten einer freien Willenshandlung erkennbar*" (von Mises, 1936, p. 210).

From this insight, it would have only been a small step to financial markets, where the probability law is almost entirely determined by the optimizing behaviour of the market participants. If, in contrast, the ups and downs of financial markets are regarded as a natural phenomenon, driven by a probability law disconnected from human action – like dice or tides – then it is indeed hard to develop a probabilistic understanding of financial processes. The tension between these two "views" (natural versus man-made uncertainty), which is well reflected in von Mises' quote, might well be one of the reasons why researchers have long hesitated to analyse financial markets as a research object: the nature of randomness was probably too obscure. As far as financial markets are perceived as "games of chance" or gambles, it was definitively more difficult to identify the underlying probability law than in the case of dice or lotteries – where at least under ideal conditions the probability law is given by construction. If on the other hand financial markets are regarded as a social institution with interacting individuals, it was hard to see how a probability law could emerge from the "free will" (von Mises' *Dazwischentreten einer freien Willenshandlung)* of a mad crowd of speculating individuals as well.

Nevertheless, von Mises' approach would have been the perfect setting to analyse financial markets where the probability law (irregularity) emerges from human action – however: collective action! The latter point is important: in the case of financial markets, it is not the behaviour (i.e. the free will) of an *individual* which determines the probability law of the observed phenomena (e.g. stock prices), but the actions and interaction of a large number of market participants. Without a minimum understanding of economic principles which have not yet been developed in the early 20th century, it was indeed difficult to derive statistical implications from a complex market mechanism. But it was possible! Bachelier derived the random walk property from a simple market clearing condition (the number of buyers and sellers must be equal), and Regnault from a fair pricing condition (equal chance for both parties).[50] Whether correct or not, the achievement of these authors was to recognize the probabilistic consequences of basic economic conditions or restrictions imposed by the market clearing mechanism. Later in the century, with the progress of modern finance, the stochastic implications of market equilibrium, no arbitrage pricing, informational efficiency, herding etc. was extensively studied.

[50] Bronzin uses a similar argument to justify the Normal distribution centred at the forward price.

Conclusions

Bachelier and Bronzin have both chosen a conventional probabilistic setting for their respective work: Bachelier's approach derives from statistical physics, but he extended Boltzmann's equations to a complete continuous-time characterization of stochastic processes. He derived the diffusion equation independently before Einstein. In contrast, Bronzin's approach directly draws – in the relevant part of his work – on the Normal law of error. He recognized that this law can be applied to the modelling of deviations of stock prices from the prevailing forward price. Both authors were apparently not aware of Reganult's pioneering work. We shall address their work as related to statistical physics, which seemed to be the state-of-the art modelling of dynamical systems around the turn of the century, in Section 6.6.

We conclude from this analysis that the deterministic view of probabilism still prevalent that the end of the 19th century was not a fruitful basis on which a genuine probabilistic modelling of financial market could have emerged: consider the difficulties of the transition in physics, where at least the cognitive process takes place under laboratory conditions. Given the fundamental questions which were debated in this ideal setting, it was simply far from obvious how to extend these thoughts from the dynamical behaviour of gases to the behavior of financial market prices. Therefore, a "science of investing", supported by major scientists of the time, could not develop – and the seminal contributions of Regnault, Bachelier, Bronzin and possible others remained individual achievements lacking broad recognition. From this perspective it even seems that a pragmatic approach – i.e. the ultimate *need* for a simple stochastic setting – emerging from the valuation of option contracts was the natural starting point for a probabilistic modelling of financial markets. The achievement of Bachelier, Bronzin and their possible predecessors is all the more remarkable.

6.6 Motion and Predictibility: Probabilistic Modelling in Physics and Finance

Maxwell's achievement was a statistical formulation of the kinetic theory of gas in the 60s of the 19th century. According to kinetic theory, heat is due to the random movement of atoms and molecules, so it looks much like kinetic energy. In contrast to other forms of energy, however, these movements cannot be observed or predicted, while other energies result from orderly movements of particles. Maxwell argued, although random in nature, the velocity of molecules can be described by mathematical functions derived from the laws of probability, specifically, as a normal distribution.

It is the same reasoning which is found in the introductory sections of Bachelier's and Bronzin's writings: They both argue that although speculative markets (prices) behave in a completely random and unpredictable way, this does not prevent, but rather motivate, the use of mathematical – probabilistic – tools. This is reflected by the following quotes:

> "*Si le marché, en effet, ne prévoit pas les mouvements, il les considère comme étant plus ou moins probables, et cette probabilité peut s'évaluer mathématiquement*" (Bachelier 1900, pp. 21–22).[51]

> "*ebenso klar ist es aber auch, dass sich die Ursachen dieser Schwankungen und somit die Gesetze, denen sie folgen sollten, jeder Rechnung entziehen. Bei dieser Lage der Dinge werden wir also höchstens von der Wahrscheinlichkeit einer bestimmten Schwankung* x *sprechen können, und zwar ohne hiefür einen näher definierten, begründeten mathematischen Ausdruck zu besitzen; wir werden uns vielmehr mit der Einführung einer unbekannten Funktion* $f(x)$ *begnügen müssen [...]*" (Bronzin 1908, pp. 39–40).[52]

This marked a fundamental change in the perception of risk in the context of financial securities.

Back to Poincaré and Boltzmann – things become slightly more complicated. Their approach to model the unpredictability, irreversibility, or chaotic behavior of dynamical systems was quite different and created much controversy. It was not clear how to reconcile probabilistic and statistical laws with the mechanical laws of Newtonian physics.

Boltzmann addressed the problem by proofing the irreversibility of macroscopic systems through kinetic gas theory – which is, after all, a purely mechanic, deterministic point of view: While any *single* molecule obeys the classical rules of reversible mechanics, for a large *collection* of particles, he claimed, that the "laws of statistics" imply irreversibility and force the second Law to hold. From any arbitrary initial distribution of molecular velocities, molecular collisions always bring the gas to an equilibrium distribution (as characterized by Maxwell). In a series of famous papers included as Chapter 2 and 3 in Boltzmann (2000) he showed that, for non-equilibrium states, the entropy is proportional to the logarithm of the probability of the specific state. The system is stable, or in thermal equilibrium, if entropy reaches its maximum – and hence, the associated probability. So, maximum entropy (disorder) is the most likely – and hence: equilibrium – state in a thermodynamic system. In

[51] Translation from Cootner: "If the market, in effect, does not predict its fluctuations, it does assess them as being more or less likely, and this likelihood can be evaluated mathematically" (Cootner 1964, p. 17).

[52] Translation from Chapter 4 in this volume: "[...] it is equally evident that the causes of these fluctuations, and hence the laws governing them, elude reckoning. Under the circumstances, we shall at best be entitled to refer to the likelihood of a certain fluctuation x, in the absence of a clearly defined and reasoned mathematical expression; instead, we shall have to be content with the introduction of an unknown function $f(x)$ [...]".

short: Boltzmann recognized "how intimately the second Law is connected to the theory of probability and that the impossibility of an uncompensated decrease of entropy seems to be reduced to an improbability" (Klein 1973, p. 73).

This theorem is widely regarded as the foundation of statistical mechanics, by describing a thermodynamic system using the statistical behavior of its constituents: It relates a *microscopic property* of the system (the number or probabilities of states) to one of its *thermodynamic properties* (the entropy).[53]

In an earlier paper (reprinted as chapter 1 in Boltzmann 2000), he derived a differential equation (his equation 16) characterizing the state of a physical system by a time-dependent probability distribution. The equation is moreover able to explain why the normal distribution appears in Maxwell's theory[54]; together with his theorem this gives "entropy" – previously simply understood as a measure of disorder of a thermodynamic process – a well-founded probabilistic interpretation. According to von Plato (1994), p. 78, Boltzmann's differential equation can be regarded as the "first example of a probabilistically described physical process" – in continuous time, notably. However, he was heavily criticized, because, after all, it was a purely *meachanical* proof of the second law of Thermodynamics: he claimed using "laws of probability"[55] to bridge the conflict between *macroscopic* (thermodynamic) irreversibility and *microscopic* (mechanical) *reversibility* of molecular motions – which is an obvious methodological conflict.

It is therefore not surprising that Boltzmann's probabilistic interpretation of entropy was not accepted by all researchers at that time without reservation, and created much quarrel, controversy, and polemic. While Boltzmann (and Clausius) insisted on a strictly mechanical interpretation of the second Law, Maxwell still claimed the statistical character of the Law. A major objection came in 1896 from one of Planck's assistants in Berlin, E. Zermelo, which is particularly interesting in our context because it is the place where Poincaré enters the scene. Zermelo referred to a mathematical theorem published by Poincaré in 1893 (the "recurrency theorem") which implies that any spatially bounded, mechanical system ultimately returns to a state sufficiently close to its initial state after a sufficiently long time interval. This was inconsistent with Boltzmann's theorem and a kinetic theory of gas in general. If the validity of mechanical laws is assumed for thermodynamic processes on a microscopic level, entropy cannot increase monotonically, and irreversible processes are impossible: hence, the world is not a mechanical system!

Boltzmann's reaction to this criticism is enlighting: While accepting the probabilistic character of the second law of thermodynamics, he claims that the recurrence of a system to its original state is so infinitely improbable that there is

[53] See Fischer (1990), p. 167.

[54] See Boltzmann (2000), p. 30, the second equation, and the remarks afterwards.

[55] It should be noted that Boltzmann used probabilities are fully interchangeable with relative frequencies.

a chance over only an unrealistically long time horizon to *observe* such an occurrence.[56] He con-cludes:

> "*[...] wie zweifellos [solche] Sätze, welche theoretisch nur den Charakter von Wahrscheinlichkeitssätzen haben, praktisch mit Naturgesetzen gleichbedeutend sind*" (Boltzmann 1896, 2000, p. 242).[57]

Equating a probabilistic system with Newtonian type natural laws as "practically useful approximation" to reality (he uses this wording elsewhere in the same paper, p. 238) does of course not resolve the inherently conflicting views: Defending a statistical model based on mechanical rules applied to unobservable microstates by reasoning that the molecules in their immense quantity affect the observables (the macrostates) of the system in a highly probable, for practical purposes essentially deterministic way (flow from low to high entropy, from cold to heat, from low to high probability states), reflects an inconsistent picture of nature. It was particularly flawed after the turn of the century when researches became interested in the modelling of the random behaviour of phenomena over infinitesimally short time intervals, such as Brownian motion and speculative prices. Among the critics was Ernst Mach, who – as already discussed in Section 6.5 – explicitly addressed the inconsistency of deriving statistical propositions "in the large" from determinism "in the small" (see e.g. Mach 1919). Or as von Plato (1994, p. 123) puts it, the contradiction that „behind the irreversible macroscopic world, there exists an unobservable, reversible microworld." But it is amazing to see how notable scientists resisted to "swap the solid ground of the laws of thermodynamics – the product of a century of careful experimental verification – for the ephemeral world of statistics and chance" (Haw 2005). Boltzmann himself considered kinetic theory as a purely mechanical analogy; after all, nobody had ever physically observed the particles kinetic theory was all about.

The situation however changed quickly with the work by Marian von Smoluchowski and Albert Einstein on the "Brownian motion"[58], i.e. the old observation from Robert Brown in the early 19th century that small particles in a liquid were in constant motion, carrying out a chaotic "dance" – not being caused by any external influence. Was this a violation of the second Law on the level of single particles? Einstein was able to prove that liquids are *really* made of atoms, and experiments moreover demonstrated that the movements of the Brownian particles were perfectly in line with Boltzmann's kinetic gas theory! The study of

[56] He compares the case with throwing a fair dice, where it is not impossible that the same eye turns up 1000 times in sequence. He compares Zermelo's conclusion with a player who rejects the fairness of the dice because he did not (yet) observe this (see Boltzmann 1896, 2000, p. 237).

[57] The page numbers refer to the German text reprinted in Boltzmann (2000), Chapter 6. Translated: "[...] how, undoubtedly, propositions which have theoretically the character of propositions in probability only, are practically equivalent to natural laws".

[58] From the many relevant papers on this issue, Einstein (1905) and von Smoluchowski (1906) are the most important references.

Brownian motion changed the old observability issue – a major criticism of Maxwell and Boltzmann's theory – dramatically: the missing piece between assuming an immense number of *unobservable* individual molecules and an *observable* equilibrium resulting from an immense number of erratically colliding molecules, had a solution: The observed Brownian motion *is* the direct consequence of molecular collisions. Notice, that what one sees under the microscope are not the molecules or the "true" (continuous) motion of the Brownian process per se, but the average (precisely, the root mean square) displacement or velocity over a finite interval of observation.[59]

Einstein's achievement was to compute whether such thermal motion induced from molecular collision is observable. It was – and the results corresponded exactly to the observed behaviour of the Brownian particles averaged over a discrete interval. It is interesting to notice that the probabilistic basics of Einstein's fundamental insight are very modest:

> "He accepted the molecular theory and its inherently statistical character, with probabilities referring to the behaviour of a single system in time. This interpretation of probability gives immediate reality to fluctuations as physical phenomena occurring in time whose conditions of observability can be determined" (von Plato 1994, p.121).

In short, the molecular structure of matter combined with Boltzmann's interpretation of probability as a limit of time average is all what was needed to relate discrete observations (the Brownian fluctuations) to a probabilistic law operating in continuous-time. Thus, Einstein successfully integrated the thermodynamics of liquids with Boltzmann's interpretation of the second Law with statistical mechanics. But this was exactly Boltzmanns' vision at the end of his 1877-paper! He claimed, that it is very likely that his theory is not limited to gases, but represents a natural law applicable to e.g. liquids as well, although the mathematical difficulties of this generalization appeared "extraordinary" to him:

> "*Es kann daher als wahrscheinlich bezeichnet warden, dass die Gültigkeit der von mir entwickelten Sätze nicht bloss auf Gase beschränkt ist, sondern dass dieselben ein allgemeines, auch auf [...] und tropfbar-flüssige Körper anwendbares Naturgesetz darstellen, wenngleich eine exakte mathematische Behandlung aller dieser Fälle*

[59] From a constructivist cognitive perspective, this is an important insight: The theoretical model of the Brownian motion determines (creates) the relevant magnitude to observe in the experiment (see von Plato 1994, pp. 128–129 for an interesting discussion of this point). In this case, it is the mean displacement of the observed particles, which is proportional to the square root of the diffusion coefficient of the Brownian model. In the language of statistics, the diffusion coefficient is half the variance of the process. Hence, the mean displacement is proportional to the standard deviation, or "volatility", of the process. An analogy to option pricing is immediate: The assumption of Brownian motion, implying the Black-Scholes model, determines the relevant magnitude to "observe" from the market: implied volatility.

dermalen noch auf aussergewöhnliche Schwierigkeiten zu stossen scheint" (Boltzmann 1877, 2000, p. 196).

Einstein formulated a theory of Brownian motion in terms of a differential equation – the celebrated diffusion equation (Einstein 1905). But again – while he could easily live with statistical concepts in the context of atoms and molecules, he was never comfortable with probabilistic consequences of quantum mechanics ("God does not play dice"). Today, much of the controversy whether a deterministic or a stochastic system is needed to cause the irreversibility of macroscopic processes is alleviated – chaos theory has established as a powerful mathematical intermediary. Poincaré was one of the pioneers in this field – but nevertheless, Boltzmann was aware as well that the dynamic properties of a thermodynamic system depend crucially on the initial state of the system, and prediction becomes impossible.[60]

What has all this to do with finance? A lot – because it is well known that Einstein's mathematical treatment of the Brownian motion was pioneered by Bachelier. The surprising fact is, however, that Bachelier wrote his thesis under supervision of Henri Poincaré, whose sympathy with the probabilistic modelling of dynamic systems was, as discussed before, limited. It is in fact amazing how strong Bachelier's belief was in the power of probability theory – Delbean and Schachermayer (2001) even call it "mystic". This is best reflected in the concluding statement of his thesis:

> "*Si, à l'égard de plusieurs questions traitées dans cette étude, j'ai comparé les résultats de l'observation à ceux de la théorie, ce n'était pas pour vérifier des formules établies par les méthodes mathématiques, mais pour montrer seulement que le marché, à son insu, obéit à une loi qui le domine: la loi de la probabilité*" (Bachelier 1900, p. 86).[61]

Maybe, this exuberant commitment to probability was not too beneficial for the overall evaluation of the thesis by his advisor, Poincaré! After all, "it must be said that Poincaré was very doubtful that probability could be applied to anything

[60] This statement originates from a reply to one of Zermelo's criticisms; see Fischer (1990), p. 174.

[61] Translation from Cootner (1964), p. 75: "If, with respect to several questions treated in this study, I have compared the results of observations with those of theory, it was not to verify formulas established by mathematical methods, but only to show that the market, unwittingly, obeys a law which governs it, the law of probability".

in real life [...]" (Taqqu 2001, p. 9) which was fundamentally different from Bachelier's view and ambition.[62]

In any case, Bacheliers' approach would have emerged more naturally from Boltzmann's statistical mechanics. The similarity of the theoretical reasoning is most evident if one compares the first page of Bachelier's thesis, where he describes the motivation and adequacy of probability theory for characterizing stock price movements, with the setup of Boltzmann's (1877) kinetic gas theory. The uncountable determinants of stock prices, their interaction and expectation seem to have a similar (or even the same) role with respect to the unpredictability (or maximum chaos) of the system as the collision of innumerable small molecules and the second law of thermodynamics.

And although Bachelier went a substantial step further by developing the first mathematical model of a stochastic process operating in continuous time, his probabilistic reasoning (as reflected in his 1912 probability theory monograph) remains extremely "cautious", as illustrated by the followings examples:[63]

- On the origins of randomness and chance: Not a genuine uncertainty governing stock prices, but rather "the 'infinity of influences' is responsible for things occurring as if guided by chance":

  "*[...] un tel marché soumis constamment à une infinité d'influences variables et qui agissent dans divers sens doit finalement se comporter comme si aucune cause n'était en jeu et comme si le hasard agissait seul. [...] en fait, la diversité des causes permet leur élimination; l'incohérence même du marché est sa méthode*" (Bachelier 1912, p. 277).

- On the independence of price increments: this is due "to the complexity of causes, that makes all things happen as if they were independent":

  "*[...] il est évident qu'en réalité l'indépendance n'existe pas, mais, par suite de l'excessive complexité des causes qui entrent en jeu, tout se passe comme s'il y avait indépendance*" (Bachelier 1912, p. 279).

- On continuous time processes: Because a discrete number of sequential observations (or events, experiments) leads to complicated expressions, he assumes such a large number of observations that "the succession of experiments can be considered continuous", and respectively, "that makes us conceive the transformation of probabilities in a sequence as a continuous phenomenon".

[62] However, contrary to Taqqu's view is the fact that Poincaré's probabilistic expertise played an important role in the famous "Dreyfus affair". Based on his some 100 pages long report written on behalf of the Court in 1904, Poincaré (and his two coauthors) concluded that the memorandum based on which Dreyfus was formerly declared guilty applied probability theory, and the rules of probability, in an illegitimate and incorrect way.

[63] The examples and original French quotes are all taken from Bachelier (1912), the English wordings (in parentheses) from von Plato (1994), pp. 134–136.

> "*Pour satisfaire à cette dernière condition, nous supposerons une suite d'épreuves en nombre très grand, de telle sorte que la succession de ces épreuves puisse être considérée comme continue et que chaque épreuve puisse être considérée comme un élément*" (Bachelier 1912, p. 153).
>
> And even more explicitly:
>
> "*Cette assimilation fournit une image précieuse qui fait concevoir la transformation des probabilités dans une suite d'épreuves comme un phénomène continu*" (Bachelier 1912, p. 153).

Apparently, the limit of continuous time is regarded as a valid approximation to a random process effectively operating over discrete intervals (i.e. a finite number of random events); this is in line with the classical (frequentistic) perception of probabilities, which by no means surprising because continuous processes were associated with mechanical, not random phenomena.[64]

Overall, Bachelier's wording is remarkable: the market operates "as if by chance" *(comme si le hazard...)*, price increments occur "as if independent" (*comme s'il y avait independence...)* and "as a continuous phenomenon" *(comme un phénomène continu...)*. But what *is* effectively, in Bachelier's perception, the intrinsic nature (or cause) of randomness, independence and continuity? Whether this cautious probabilistic wording suggests a genuine deterministic view of the world, as interpreted by von Plato (1994, p. 135), is questionable. It could equally well reflect a modern epistemological thinking: Perhaps, Bachelier's interest was not too much concerned about the constitution of the reality as it *is,* but rather how it is perceived or how it can be constructed in order to get viable results[65]. This pragmatic or constructivist interpretation is not so far-fetched as it may appear. Hans Vaihinger published his famous epistemology of "As If" (*Philosophie des Als-Ob*) in 1911 at about the same time as Bachelier's treatise (1912). According to this philosophical position, "useful fictions" are fully legitimate mental constructions (his examples include: atoms, infinity, soul, etc.) as long as they serve a "viable purpose" (*lebens-praktischen Zweck*).

Was thermodynamics ever applied to economic modelling? While not in a probabilistic setting, Vilfredo Pareto (1900) made an analogy with the second

[64] The association of random events with discrete, rather than continuous, phenomena was clearly a consequence of the frequentistical interpretation of probabilities. Reichenbach (1929) provides an in-depth discussion of this point, and particularly addresses the "paradox" that the states of the Brownian motion are treated independent over infinitesimally short time intervals, "even though one knows that there obtains a continuous causal chaining of these states, which excludes probability" (Quote from von Plato, 1994, p. 136). According to Reichenbach, what has to be done to resolve the paradox is to transform "the strict causal determination of the continuous evolution into a probabilistic one" (von Plato, p. 136). This was accomplished by the well-known axiomatic, measure-theoretic foundation of probability theory in Kolmogorov's *Grundbegriffe* just a few years later.

[65] The term "viability" is borrowed from the radical constructivism of Ernst von Glasersfeld; since Vaihinger's approach contains many elements of constructivism, the term seems to be adequate here.

Law in discussing the redistribution of wealth between individuals by changing the conditions of free competition.[66] He claims that this process necessarily leads to a corrosion of welath – and attributes to this "theorem" the same (or "analogeous") role as the second Law in physics:

> "*Man kann den Reichtum von bestimmten Individuen auf andere übertragen, indem man die Bedingungen der freien Konkurrenz abändert, sei es in Bezug auf die Produktionskoeffizienten, sei es in Bezug auf die Umwandlung der Ersparnisse in Kapitalien. Diese Übertragung von Reichtum ist notwendigerweise mit einer Zerstörung von Reichtum verbunden. [...] Dieses Theorem spielt in der Wirtschaftslehre eine analoge Rolle wie das zweite Prinzip der Thermodynamik*" (Pareto 1900, p. 1119).

But we are not aware of entropy-based foundations of economic systems or financial markets around the turn of the century. Was there a probabilistic revolution in economics at all? This is not the place to discuss this fundamental issue.[67]

Unfortunately, Bronzin being an admiring student of Boltzmann and having attended his lecture on the theory of gases (*Gastheorie*), did not use any element of statistical mechanics for modelling price processes or their distribution – which is a surprising fact indeed. Rather, his approach was more in the probabilistic tradition of actuarial science.

6.7 Actuarial Science and the Treating of Market Risks at the Turn of the Century

As noted in Section 6.3, the path from applying probabilistic models to "gambling" to the management and pricing "insurance" risks was by no means straightforward. It has been argued that this step required (a) the measurement and quantification of risks (e.g. based on mortality tables), and (b) the creation of a business model which emphasized the separation of insurance from gambling and thereby capitalized (and to a certain extent determined) the changing moral perception about responsibility and risk bearing. Since these early days, actuarial science played a pivotal role for the expansion of the insurance sector as the driving force behind the economic growth and industrialization, particularly in

[66] In the 20th century, references to thermodynamics in economic modelling, although not explicitly in a probabilistic setting, can be found in Samuelson's *Foundations*.
[67] See Krüger et al. (1987b), Chapter 6, about this point.

the 19th century.[68] By reading actuarial textbooks and monographs published in German, towards the end of the 19th century, three features are apparent:

First, we observe a more rigorous probabilistic treatment of the key concepts of insurance mathematics – the emergence of elements of a formal "risk theory". A good example is an encyclopaedia article on "insurance mathematics" by Georg Bohlmann (1900) which is an axiomatic treatment of probability containing many elements of Kolmogorov's famous treatment 33 years later. This attempt resulted from the insight that the insurance business needed a more solid, *scientific basis* for calculating risks, covering potential losses and determining adequate premiums[69]. Also, there was an increasing demand for a precise, probability-based terminology of the key actuarial terms; this is reflected in the following statement (related to a book review):

> "*Die Begriffe: Nettoprämie, Jahresrisico, Prämienreserve u.s.w. sind uns geläufig, wie sie sie erlernt, wir operiren mit ihnen, ohne zu untersuchen, ob sie ausreichend oder gar präcise definirt sind. Werden diese Begriffe [...] vor der eingehenden Kritik Stand halten können? [...] ich glaube es aber mit nichten*" (Altenburger 1898).

A *second* observation is the increasing analogy between the nature of insurance contracts and "games of chance" (*Zufallsspiele*). An early although non-mathematical characterization of this kind is Herrmann (1869), and a rigorous mathematical treatment is Hausdorff (1897); both authors characterize insurance contracts as special forms of games of chance[70]. Hausdorff's treatise is particularly revealing; he analyzes different types of (what we would call nowadays) financial contracts, their expected loss and profit for the involved parties. He also analyzes the impact of various amortization or redemption

---

[68] It is interesting to see how nation-building and the development of the old-age-pension-system paralleled each other. For example, Bismarck installed the state-sponsored old-age-pension-system with the intention to create a conservative attitude by the workers. Loth (1996), p. 68, quotes Bismarck: The pension system was created "*[um] in der grossen Masse der Besitzlosen die konservative Gesinnung [zu] erzeugen, welche das Gefühl der Pensionsberechtigung mit sich bringt*".

[69] *Assicurazioni Generali* (in Trieste) was apparently very proud to publish the actuarial foundations of its life business in 1905, elaborated by Vitale Laudi and Wilhelm Lazarus over many years, as an opulent monograph. But ironically, in 1907, *Generali* changed their foundations of its life business and re-adopted the generally used formula of Gompertz-Makeham (see Assicurazioni Generali 1931, p. 99).

[70] The term "games of chance" (*Zufallsspiele*) is already used by the physiologist, logician, philosopher and mathematician Johannes von Kries (1886), Chapter 3 and 7, although not in a rigorous mathematical setting.

schedules on optimal call policies and bond prices (such as for callable bonds, lottery bonds, premium bonds).[71]

This directly leads to the *third* observation, namely the increasing – although still quite limited – perception of market risk as opposed to the (traditional) actuarial risk.[72] The growing perception of market risk was caused, among other things, by substantial and permanent deviations of market interest rates from their actuarial (fixed) level, as well as by the substantial losses insurance companies suffered during the stock market crash in the 70s. Companies were forced to hold special reserves[73] (*Kursschwankungsreserven*). Although the analytical methods were quite advanced, the treatment and economic understanding of market risk was quite limited. Even Emanuel Czuber, a renowned Professor at the *Technische Hochschule* in Vienna, spezializing in insurance mathematics, was pessimistic whether a formal "risk theory" could be helpful for managing market risk:

> "*Als wesentlichste dieser Aufgaben [der Risikotheorie] wird [...] die rechnungsmässige Bestimmung desjenigen Fonds hingestellt, der [...] notwendig ist, um das Unternehmen gegen die Folgen eines eventuellen Verlustes aus Abweichungen von den Rechnungselementen mit einem vorgegebenen Wahrscheinlichkeitsgrade zu schützen*" (Czuber 1910).

In simple terms: risk theory is about computing VaR- (value-at-risk) based reserves to cover the risks from inadequate actuarial assumptions (e.g. interest rates). But Czuber claims that risk theory is not applicable to interest rate risk, because

> "*[...] [die Risikotheorie] ruht auf dem Boden der zufälligen Ereignisse[...]. Die Änderungen des Zinsfusses [...] tragen aber nicht den*

[71] The treatise also contains a lucid discussion on the distinction between aggregate and average risk of games, i.e. the distinction between adding and sub-dividing risks. Samuelson (1963) is typically credited for this clarification. Interestingly, the argument is similar to von Smoluchowski's (1906) criticised *Denkfehler* in the molecular theory of the Brownian motion: before Einstein's and von Smoluchowski's theory, it was argued that the immense number of collisions of Brownian particles by molecules would average out any net effect. Interestingly, von Smoluchowski's illustrates this *Denkfehle*r by an analogy to gambling: "The mean deviation of gain or loss is on the order of the square root of the number of trials" (quote from von Plato 1994, p. 130).

[72] The insignificant perception of market risk before the 70s is, for instance, reflected in Herrmann's (1869) treatise of insurance companies, devoting four (!) lines to interest rate uncertainty, by stating that the problem can be handled simply by choosing a sufficiently low actuarial rate in the computation of premiums.

[73] Between 1878 and 1884, *Assicurazioni Generali* increased these newly created reserves (*Reserve für die Coursschwankungen der Werthpapiere*) from 43'000 to 845'000 Kronen, or in relation to the book value of equity, from 1% to 16% (Assicurazioni Generali 1885, p. 6).

> *Charakter des Zufälligen an sich, das Systematische waltet hier vor*" (Czuber 1910, p. 411).

i.e. interest rates do not behave randomly! Even if this would be correct – what about other market risks? Indeed, the same author argues elsewhere[74], that past asset returns (*Verzinsung*) behave so randomly (*unregelmässig*) that they cannot be used to predict future returns:

> "*Aus den Erfahrungen kann wohl ein Bild darüber gewonnen werden, wie sich die Verzinsung der verschiedenen Anlagewerte in der Vergangenheit gestaltet hat; bei dem unregelmässigen Charakter der Variationen, die oft durch lange Zeiträume unmerklich vor sich gehen, um dann plötzlich ein starkes Tempo einzuschlagen, lässt sich ein begründeter Schluss auf die Zukunft schwer ziehen*" (Czuber 1910, p. 233).

Obviously, there was no consistent picture about market risks and their probabilistic (stochastic) modelling – which is representative for the actuarial literature at this time. Therefore, Bronzin's (1908) contribution constituted a substantial step forward.

6.8 Concluding Remarks

"Mathematics is a language" – this saying attributed to the physicist J. Willard Gibbs is mostly used in the attempt of attributing a fairly innocent role to formal systems in the scientific process – the mathematical language as representing just a distinct formalism by which images about the real world are processed and communicated. However, the statement appears less innocuous if one takes a (radical) constructivist epistemological perspective, where language does not barely transmit, but *creates* knowledge, and *shapes* the perceptions about the world, instead of just passively reflecting it. The world is adapted to the cognitive needs of the individuals, and mathematics, mathematical statistics, like any other formal system, is an essential part of this cognitive process. Importantly, the very nature, depth and breath of the analytical repertoire determine appearance and scope of phenomena.

In the case of probability theory, a constructivist understanding has particularly dramatic consequences because the object of study – uncertainty, risk, error, fear – is an abstract category, away from direct observation[75], and a

[74] By discussing the difficulties in determining an adequate, long-term actuarial interest rate (or average return level).

[75] Notice that unlike the realization of risk and uncertainty (e.g. a burning house, a crashing stock market) the risk itself and the related categories (e.g. risk aversion, fear) are not directly observable.

probabilistic model, whether mathematical or not, first and foremost aims at *representing* the relevant object in a particular framework. In this regard, the deterministic view of nature which characterized the probabilistic thinking until the end of the 19th century, did much more than merely *reflect* a certain view of the world or determine a specific kind of formalism, but it also narrowed – or framed – the range of probabilistic phenomena to be studied, or considered to be eligible for rigorous scientific study. The nature of social or economic processes was framed within the probabilistic framework of social physics, a stereotype copy of the determinism underlying statistical physics. But not even this framework allowed it to consider financial markets as a relevant, interesting and revealing object of study – a mixture of skepticism, insignificance and moral disregard did not even support the early attempts in this direction. Methodology and language shape reality: this is all-too true for the perception of financial markets. Compared to other disciplines, it took extremely long until financial market showed up on the agenda of scientific research. Whether the probabilistic approach under which the success stories of option pricing, risk management and portfolio theory have emerged is *viable* or not, is another issue. There is little doubt that the current financial market crisis is not caused by the probabilistic foundations of the prevalent risk management models and practices. Therefore, an examination of the history and foundations of probabilistic modelling in financial markets (from stochastic modelling to statistics and financial econometrics) would be a revealing field of study, in particular from a constructivist perspective. There are not many attempts to accomplish this challenge. Elena Esposito argues that probability theory creates the fiction of a probable reality and draws largely on financial markets and risk theory to underpin this hypothesis (see Esposito 2007 and Chapter 11 in this volume), and motivates an interesting constructivist research program.

References

Altenburger J (1898) Das Problem vom Risico in der Lebensversicherung. Oesterreichische Revue. Organ für Assecuranz und Volkswirthschaft 23, No. 38. Jena

Assicurazioni Generali (1885) Jahresbericht der Generali-Versicherungsgesellschaft für 1884. Trieste

Assicurazioni Generali (1931) Die Jahrhundertfeier der Assicurazioni Generali. Trieste

Bachelier L (1900, 1964) Théorie de la spéculation. Annales de l'École Normale Supérieure 17, pp. 21–86. English translation in: Cootner P (ed) (1964) The random character of the stock market prices. MIT Press, Cambridge (Massachusetts), pp. 17–79

Bachelier L (1912) Calcus des probabilités. Gauthier-Villars, Paris

Bachelier L (1914) Le jeu, la chance et le hazard. Flammarion, Paris (Reprinted in 1993: Editions Gabay, Paris)

Beck U (1986) Risikogesellschaft. Auf dem Weg in eine andere Gesellschaft. Suhrkamp, Frankfurt on the Main

Bohlmann G (1900) Lebensversicherungs-Mathematik. Enzyklopädie der mathematischen Wissenschaften, Vol. I, Part II, D4b. Teubner, Leipzig

Boltzmann L (1872) Weitere Studien über das Wärmegleichgewicht unter Gasmolekülen. Wiener Berichte 66, pp. 275–370. Reprinted as Chapter 1 in: Boltzmann L (2000) Entropie und Wahrscheinlichkeit. Harri Deutsch, Frankfurt on the Main, pp. 1–87

Boltzmann L (1877) Über die Beziehung zwischen dem zweiten Hauptsatz der mechanischen Wärmetheorie und der Wahrscheinlichkeitsrechnung resp. den Sätzen über das Wärmegleichgewicht. Wiener Berichte 76, pp. 373–435. Reprinted as Chapter 3 in: Boltzmann L (2000) Entropie und Wahrscheinlichkeit. Harri Deutsch, Frankfurt on the Main, pp. 137–196

Boltzmann L (1899, 1905) Über die Grundprinzipien und Grundgleichungen der Mechanik. Lecture at Clark University. Published in: Populäre Schriften 253 (1905), pp. 253–307. English translation: Theories as representations. In: Danto A, Morgenbesser S (eds) (1960) Philosophy of Science. Meridian Books, New York

Boltzmann L (1986) Entgegnung auf die wärmetheoretischen Betrachtungen des Hrn. E. Zermelo. Wied. Ann. 57, pp. 773–784. Reprinted as Chapter 6 in: Boltzmann L (2000) Entropie und Wahrscheinlichkeit. Harri Deutsch, Frankfurt on the Main, pp. 231–242

Boltzmann L (2000) Entropie und Wahrscheinlichkeit. Harri Deutsch, Frankfurt on the Main (Ostwalds Klassiker der exakten Wissenschaften, Vol. 286).

Bonss W (1995) Vom Risiko. Unsicherheit und Ungewissheit in der Moderne. Hamburger Edition, Hamburg

Brodbeck K (1998) Die fragwürdigen Grundlagen der Ökonomie. Wissenschaftliche Buchgesellschaft, Darmstadt

Bronzin V (1908) Theorie der Prämiengeschäfte. Franz Deuticke, Leipzig/ Vienna

Clark G (1999) Betting on lives: the culture of life insurance in England, 1695–1775. Manchester University Press, Manchester/ New York

Cohn G (1868) Die Börse und die Spekulation. Lüderitz'sche Verlagsbuchhandlung, Berlin

Cootner P (ed) (1964) The random character of stock market prices. MIT Press, Cambridge (Massachusetts)

Czuber E (1910) Wahrscheinlichkeitsrechnung und ihre Anwendung auf Fehlerausgleichung, Statistik und Lebensversicherung, 2nd edn, Vol. 2. Teubner, Leipzig/ Berlin

Daston L (1987) The domestication of risk: mathematical probability and insurance 1650-1830: from gambling to insurance. In: Krüger L, Daston L and Heidelberger M (eds) (1987) The probabilistic revolution, Vol. 1. MIT Press, Cambridge (Massachusetts), pp. 237–260

Daston L (1988) Classical probability in the enlightenment. Princeton University Press, Princeton

Delbean F, Schachermayer W (2001) Applications to mathematical finance. Working Paper, Eidgenössische Technische Hochschule Zürich, Zurich

De Pietri-Tonelli A (1919) La speculazione di borsa. Industrie Grafiche Italiane-Rovigo, Belluno

Edgeworth F Y (1888) Mathematical theory of banking. Journal of the Royal Statistical Society 51, pp. 113–127

Einstein A (1905) Über die von der molekular-kinetischen Theorie der Wärme geforderte Bewegung von in ruhenden Flüssigkeiten suspendierten Teilchen. Annalen der Physik 17, pp. 549–560

Esposito E (2007) Die Fiktion der wahrscheinlichen Realität. Suhrkamp, Frankfurt on the Main

Fischer P (1990) Ordnung und Chaos. Physik in Wien an der Wende zum 19. Jahrhundert. In: Bachmaier H (ed) Paradigmen der Moderne. John Benjamins Publishing Company, Amsterdam

Gibson T (1923) The facts about speculation. Originally published by Thomas Gibson, reprinted in 2005 by Cosimo Classics, New York

Gigerenzer G, Swijtink Z, Porter T et al (1989) The empire of chance. Cambridge University Press, Cambridge

Girlich H (2002) Bachelier's predecessors. Revised version presented at the 2nd World Congress of the Bachelier Finance Society in 2002, June 12–15. Crete

Granger C, Morgenstern O (1970) Predictability of stock market prices. Heath Lexington Books, Lexington (Massachusetts)

Hacking I (1990) The taming of chance. Cambridge University Press, Cambridge
Hacking I (2006) The emergence of probability, 2nd edn. Cambridge University Press, Cambridge
Hausdorff F (1897) Das Risico bei Zufallsspielen. Berichte über die Verhandlungen der Königl. Sächs. Gesellschaft der Wissenschaften zu Leipzig. Math.-phys. Classe 49, pp. 497–548. Re-printed in: Bemelmans J, Binder C, Chatterji S et al (eds) (2006) Felix Hausdorff, Gesammelte Werke, Vol. V. Springer, Berlin/ Heidelberg, pp. 445-496
Haw M (2005) Einstein's random walk. Physics World (January), pp. 19–22
Herrmann E (1869) Die Theorie der Versicherung vom wirthschaftlichen Standpunkte, 2nd edn. Graz
Jovanovic F (2001) Pourquoi l'hypothèse de marche aléatoire en théorie financière? Les raisons historiques d'un choix éthique. Revue d'Economie Financière 61, pp. 203–211
Jovanovic F (2006) A 19th century random walk: Jules Regnault and the origins of scientific financial economics. In: Poitras G (ed) (2006) Pioneers of financial economics: contributions prior to Irving Fisher, Vol. 1. Edward Elgar Publishing, Cheltenham (UK), pp. 191–222
Jovanovic F, Le Gall P (2001) Does God pratice a random walk? The "financial physics" of a 19th century forerunner, Jules Regnault. European Journal for the History of Economic Thought 8, pp. 332–362
Klein M J (1973) The development of Boltzmannn's statistical ideas. In: Cohen E G D, Thirring W (eds) The Boltzmann Equation. Springer, Berlin/ Heidelberg, pp. 53–106
Knorr Cetina K, Preda A (eds) (2005) The sociology of financial markets. Oxford University Press, Oxford/ New York
Krüger L, Daston L, Heidelberger M (eds) (1987a) The probabilistic revolution, Vol. 1: Ideas in history. MIT Press, Cambridge (Massachusetts)
Krüger L, Gigerenzer G, Morgan M (eds) (1987b). The probabilistic revolution, Vol. 2: Ideas in the sciences. MIT Press, Cambridge (Massachusetts)
Laplace P S (1812) Théorie analytique des probabilités. Courgier, Paris. Also reprinted in 1886: Oeuvres Complètes de Laplace. Gauthier-Villars, Paris (and available online)
Levèvre H (1870) Théorie elémentaire des opérations de bourse. Bureau du Journal des Placements Financiers Paris
Lindley D (2007) Uncertainty. Anchor Books, New York
Loth W (1996) Das Kaiserreich. Obrigkeitsstaat und politische Mobilisierung. Deutscher Taschenbuch Verlag, Munich
Mach E (1919) Die Leitgedanken meiner naturwissenschaftlichen Erkenntnislehre und ihre Aufnahme durch die Zeitgenossen. Sinnliche Elemente und naturwissenschaftliche Begriffe. Zwei Aufsätze. Barth, Leipzig
Pareto V (1900) Anwendung der Mathematik auf Nationalökonomie. In: Encyklopädie der Mathematischen Wissenschaften, Vol. 1, Part 2. Leipzig
Peirce C (1887) Science and immortality. Boston. Reprinted in: Peirce Edition Project (2000) Writings of Charles S. Peirce. A Chronological Edition, Vol. 6. Indiana University Press, Bloomington, pp. 61–64
Peirce C (1892) The doctrine of necessity examined. The Monist 2, pp. 321–337. Reprinted in: Peirce C (1965) Collected papers of Charles Sanders Peirce, 3rd edn, Vol. 6 (Scientific Metaphysics). Harvard University Press, Cambridge (Massachusetts), pp. 35–65
Peirce C (1893a) Reply to the necessitarians. The Monist 3, pp. 526-570. Reprinted in: Peirce C (1965) Collected papers of Charles Sanders Peirce, 3rd edn, Vol. 6 (Scientific Metaphysics). Harvard University Press, Cambridge (Massachusetts), pp. 588–618
Peirce C (1893b) Evolutionary love. The Monist 3, pp. 176-200. Reprinted in: Peirce C (1965) Collected papers of Charles Sanders Peirce, 3rd edn, Vol. 6 (Scientific Metaphysics). Harvard University Press, Cambridge (Massachusetts), pp. 287–317
Peirce C (1965) Collected papers of Charles Sanders Peirce, 3rd edn, Vol. 6 (Scientific Metaphysics). Harvard University Press, Cambridge (Massachusetts)

Poitras G (ed) (2006) Pioneers of financial economics: contributions prior to Irving Fischer. Edward Elgar Publishing, Cheltenham (UK)
Porter T (1986) The rise of statistical thinking 1820–1900. Princeton University Press, Princeton
Preda A (2005) The investor as cultural figure of global capitalism. Chapter 7 in: Knorr Cetina K, Preda A (eds) (2005) The sociology of financial markets. Oxford University Press, Oxford/ New York, pp.141–162
Quetelet A (1835) Sur l'homme et le développement de ses facultés, ou Essai de physique sociale, Vol. 2. Bachelier, Paris
Regnault J (1863) Calcul des chances et philosophie de la bourse. Mallet-Bachelier, Paris
Reichenbach H (1929) Stetige Wahrscheinlichkeitsfolgen. Zeitschrift für Physik 53, pp. 274–307
Samuelson P A (1963) Risk and uncertainty: a fallacy of large numbers. Scientia 98, pp. 108–113
Samuelson P A (1994) The long-term case for equities: and how it can be oversold. Journal of Portfolio Management 21, pp. 15–24
Solano A (1893) Der Geheimbund der Börse. Hermann Beyer, Leipzig
Stäheli U (2007) Spektakuläre Spekulation. Suhrkamp, Frankfurt on the Main
Stigler S (1986) The history of statistics. The measurement of uncertainty before 1900. Harvard University Press, Cambridge (Massachusetts)
Stillich O (1909) Die Börse und ihre Geschäfte. Karl Curtius, Berlin
Taqqu M (2001) Bachelier and his times: a conversation with Bernard Bru. Finance and Stochastics 5, pp. 3–32
Vaihinger H (1911) Philosophie des Als Ob. Meiner-Verlag, Leipzig
von Kries J (1886) Die Principien der Wahrscheinlichkeitsrechnung. Akademische Verlagsbuchhandlung J.C.B. Mohr, Freiburg i.Br.
von Mises R (1920) Ausschaltung der Ergodenhypothese in der physikalischen Statistik. Physikalische Statistik 21, pp. 225–232, pp. 256–262
von Mises R (1931) Wahrscheinlichkeitsrechnung und ihre Anwendung in der Statistik und theoretischen Physik. Franz Deuticke, Leipzig/ Vienna
von Mises R (1936) Wahrscheinlichkeit, Statistik und Wahrheit, 2nd edn. Springer, Vienna
von Plato J (1994) Creating modern probability. Cambridge University Press, Cambridge (Cambridge Studies in Probability, Induction and Decision Theory)
von Smoluchowski M (1906) Zur kinetischen Theorie der Brownschen Molekularbewegung und der Suspensionen. Annalen der Physik 21, pp. 756–780
Weber M (1894) Die Börse. I. Zweck und äußere Organisation der Börsen, Vol. 1, Booklet 2 and 3. Friedrich Naumann (ed). Göttinger Arbeiterbibliothek. Vandenhoeck & Ruprecht, Göttingen, pp. 17–48
Weber M (1896) Die Börse. II. Der Börsenverkehr, Vol. 2, Booklet 4 and 5. Friedrich Naumann (ed). Göttinger Arbeiterbibliothek. Vandenhoeck & Ruprecht, Göttingen, pp. 49–80
Zelizer V (1979) Morals and markets: the development of life insurance in the United States. Columbia University Press, New York

In addition, to the following classics is informally referred to:

Dantzig G (1959) Linear programming and extensions. Princeton University Press, Princeton
Hicks J (1939) Value and capital. Clarendon, Oxford
Kolmogorov A (1933) Grundbegriffe der Wahrscheinlichkeitsrechnung. Springer, Berlin
Markowitz H (1959) Portfolio Selection: efficient diversification of investments. J. Wiley & Sons, New York
Marshall A (1890) Principles of economics. Macmillan, London
Samuelson P A (1947) Foundations of economic analysis. Harvard University Press, Cambridge (Massachusetts)
von Neumann J, Morgenstern O (1944) Theory of games and economic behavior. Princeton University Press, Princeton

7 The Contribution of the Social-Economic Environment to the Creation of Bronzin's "Theory of Premium Contracts"

Wolfgang Hafner*

The present chapter argues that Bronzin's life, during the period of his most active academic work and up until its climax with the publication of his treatise "Theory of Premium Contracts" was biographically typical of his day. Both his personal and psychological development and the specific cultural, social and political biotope in which he lived complemented each other optimally. At the time, the political and socio-cultural climate of Trieste was fundamentally more liberal and open than that of Vienna. This broad-minded and enlightened climate made room for scientific considerations which did not correspond to the usual established patterns and social norms of the day.

7.1 Introduction

The culturally flourishing city of Vienna around 1900 was – in the eyes of one of its chroniclers – the greatest achievement of the Austrian bourgeoisie. Numerous writers, composers and musicians sprang from its fertile soil. The concept of psychoanalysis, too, evolved in this social environment, characterized as it was by such contradictory developments. On the one hand, for example, the bourgeoisie, with its belief in progress, promoted the capitalistic industrialization process; on the other hand, it turned its back on the future in endeavouring to preserve feudal structures such as the monarchy. Within the Austrian Empire the feudalization of entrepreneurship was stronger and more radical than in other countries. In the context of attempts to establish a critical position within the Viennese bourgeoisie in opposition to the bourgeois leaning towards feudalism and to distance this from its notions of liberalism, certain contradictions arose which helped to thrive the features and developments of Vienna described above (Erdheim 1982, p. 47ff).

Bronzin spent some years in Vienna when this thriving city was in high bloom. Bronzin, according to his nephew Angelo Bronzin, participated ardently in the social and political student life of Vienna while pursuing his university studies: He was recognized as an adept card player and also acted as the

* *whafner@wolfgang-hafner.ch*

secretary for Italian students studying in Vienna. (Bronzin A),[1] However, we do not know much about his activities in Vienna or about the contacts that he kept, since, apart from the article mentioned above, no written testimonies such as letters have been traced. However, it is certain that Bronzin was very closely affiliated with the Austro-Hungarian cultural context throughout his life and that he assumed an intermediating role in this connection. Thus, the Austrian federal chancellor Josef Klaus congratulated him on his 95th birthday with the words: "It is not only your long-standing service as a respected director of the former Imperial and Royal Commercial Academy for which I recognized you, but also for the very special attention you have given to promoting social cohesion amongst the diverse nationalities residing within this city".[2] Certain influences on his scientific work can be traced to his university studies and educational training.[3] The question as to what other contemporary factors may possibly have influenced his career and scientific activities remains unanswered.

7.2 Anxiety as a Characteristic of the Socio-Cultural Climate

Though factors arising from socio-economic and cultural circumstances ("*Zeitgeist*") are diffuse in the effects they cause, they may nonetheless have had a strong influence on Bronzin's "world view" and guided his interest in knowledge. One psychological symptom that was a striking characteristic of the epoche was the phenomenon of anxiety.

Discussions about the phenomenon of anxiety and why it was prevalent at the time became an important topic of intellectual talks.[4] According to Freud – and he is by no means alone in this matter – the society of the day, as characterized in his essay, "Cultural Sexual Morality and Modern Nervosity", was being swept by a tide of "swiftly spreading nervosity" (Freud 1908, p. 14)[5].

---

[1] Angelo Bronzin wrote: "*Era conosciuto in tutta Vienna come famoso giocatore di carte [...]*" ("was know throughout Vienna as a famous card player [...]").

[2] Letter from March 30th 1967. Klaus wrote: "*Es sind mir nicht nur Ihre Verdienste als langjähriger angesehener Direktor der ehemaligen k.k. österreichischen Handelsakademie bekannt, sondern auch Ihre besonderen Bemühungen um das Zusammenleben der verschiedenen Nationen in dieser Stadt*".

[3] Bronzin was a student of Ludwig Boltzmann, a leading physicist around the turn of the century. From 1894 to 1896 he attended lectures and seminars in thermodynamics, analytical mechanics and the kinetic theory of gasses. Boltzmann was – though not a single-minded, but yet an acknowledged – devotee of the determinate structure of the processes in nature (see Chaper 6 of this book).

[4] Glaser (1979), p. 53ff, names various contemporary authors who wrote on the topic of 'anxiety': among others, Thomas Mann and Hugo von Hofmannsthal.

[5] Freud's book appeared in Franz Deuticke Verlag in Vienna, which also published Bronzin's book, "Theory of Premium Contracts".

Illustrating this, Freud cited the writing of W. Erb from 1893 ("Concerning the Current Increase in Anxiety"):

> "The original question posed now enquired whether the causes explaining anxiety in modern-day life were present to such a degree as to explain the dramatic increase in the frequency of its occurrence – and this question is to be answered affirmatively and without reservation, and can be quickly substantiated with a glance at our modern lifestyle".

Following Erb, Freud now established that rapid economic and cultural change were decisive in contributing to a general state of agitation:

> "The demands on the individual to perform in the fight for survival have increased considerably and can only be satisfied by mobilizing all an individual's available resources; at the same time the individual's needs, the urgency to enjoy life in times of crisis had grown [...], and the harsh political, industrial and financial crises were having an effect on a much wider spectrum of the population than had previously been the case [...], political, religious and social conflicts, the hustle and bustle of party politics, election commotion and excessive partisanship to associations encouraged inflamed viewpoints and pushed people ever harder to enforced efforts, robbing them of time for recovery, sleep and rest" (Freud 1908, p. 15).

The effect that this tension had on the individual expressed itself in all the different roles they assumed. Musil, who studied mathematics, as Bronzin had done, wrote in his masterpiece "Man without Qualities":

> "The individual had a professional, a national, a civic, a class, a geographic, a sexual, a conscious and an unconscious identity – and perhaps even a private one [...]" (Musil 1999, p. 35).

Anxiety was the recurrent theme which ran like a leitmotiv through Vienna's cultural life at its zenith; but not only there. The German sociologist and philosopher, Georg Simmel (1858–1918), postulated in his work "The Philosophy of Money" that an internal connection existed between anxiety, stimuli, hyper-excitement, and the value of money. He referred to the analogy between nerves and stimulus response in order to explain the function of money and the contradiction between quality and quantity: Quantity is measurable and comparable: Quality, in contrast, is volatile and emotionally charged. Emotionally-driven speculation, with its capriciousness, contradicts the nature of money which is based on comparability:

> "[...] External stimuli that affect our nerves are not at all noticeable beneath a certain level; once a certain level is reached, the stimuli suddenly provoke feelings, a simple quantitative increment causing them to produce a marked qualitative experience; in certain cases the effect progresses and reaches an upper limit causing the sensibility to diminish again [...] Because money is associated with an anticipation of the pleasurable sensation derived from the items it will purchase, it then produces this sensation in its own right. It thus becomes the sole object offering a measure of comparison, representing the threshold values of the individual pleasure sensations" (Simmel 1991, p. 344ff).

The value of money assumes so a mediating role enabling comparison between states which are otherwise difficult to compare.

With the homogenization created by the mediating function of money, on the one hand a 'depersonalization' takes place, an equalization and levelling of different qualities; on the other hand, a 'reification' occurs, a process that requires all things to be conceptualized.[6] At the same time it is also possible to capture and express social processes in terms of mathematical formulae. Nerves, money and the market were seen to be components of a long-term converging process at the time – where disruptions could lead to illness as exemplified in Freud's analyses of "anxiety".[7]

It is easier for some groups of individuals to tolerate the demands of adapting to cultural change; for others this is more difficult. According to Freud – discoveries he made in his research investigations and psychoanalytical sessions – certain groups of people with specific patterns of socialization are particularly subject to nervous ailments: These are people whose parents come from simple, rural environments. It is difficult for children and adolescents from such backgrounds to meet the demands of rapid integration into new cultural environments – such as Vienna. They would therefore often react with nervous disturbances (Freud 1908, p. 14f).

These patterns described by Freud are evident in Bronzin's curriculum vitae. A few signposts in Bronzin's life indicate this: He grew up in Rovignjo, a small picturesque seaport on the peninsula Istria. His father was a shipping commander, who wished his son to enter the same career. However, teachers soon recognized Bronzin's talent and entreated his parents to allow him to study.

[6] See Glaser (1979), p. 66; on the economic significance of stimuli, creating new needs and which could thus be considered as setting the foundation of an independent system (see the article by Yvan Lengwiler, "The Origins of Expected Utility Theory" with the section on Weber-Fechner (20.3. Decreasing Marginal Utility).

[7] The extent to which illness may serve as a metaphor for an epoche is debateable. The physician and founder of the branch of Psychosomatics, Georg Walther Groddeck (1866–1934), who laid the foundation for the psychosomatic approach, is seen as the defender of this thesis, while Susan Sontag in her book, entitled "Illness as Metaphor", sees the interpretation of specific illness profiles as metaphors for prevailing circumstances as being used in order to attribute blame.

Bronzin went to the gymnasium of Capodistria where he graduated. In 1892 he left the sleepy island of Istria to continue his studies at the technical high school and subsequently went on to study at the University of Vienna where he acquired his mathematical training. During this period he completed military training courses in Graz and in 1897 took up a teaching appointment at the Scuola Superiore, followed by an appointment at the Academy in Trieste. Presumably during the years between 1906 and 1907 or when Bronzin was 34- or 35-years of age, he composed his treatise, "Theory of Premium Contracts", which appeared in 1908.

In 1909 Bronzin succumbed to the kind of nervous breakdown that Freud described as being typical for people with similar biographies (Accademia di commercio e nautica in Trieste, 31.7.1909)[8] – and this in spite of the fact that Angelo Bronzin described him as being an extraordinarily strong and capable individual, a superb fencer and runner.

After this breakdown in his health Bronzin dedicated himself virtually exclusively to school and family. He largely gave up his scientific activities.[9] In 1917 a book was published in honour of the centenary jubilee celebrating commercial training at the Academy. In it, the curricula and publications of all previous and acting professors of the Academy were mentioned with the exception of Bronzin's book on "Theory of Premium Contracts".[10] In the following years, Bronzin committed himself so intensively to the school's interests that Dario De Tuoni dedicated a paper of his on the history of the Academy and the *Istituto Commerciale*, which sprung from it, to Bronzin, celebrating him as a "brave hero" (De Tuoni 1925).[11]

When Bronzin returned to Trieste in 1897 and began teaching at a gymnasium, the situation in the city had become fraught with tension as in Vienna and underwent radical changes. But the conflicts evolved more on ethnical problems than on the contradiction of feudalism contra liberalism as it was the case in Vienna: The population had risen in Trieste between 1890 and 1900 by almost 14 percent; in the following 10 years it increased by approximately 24 percent.

[8] Bronzin's nervous breakdown is explained in a file note on declining his election to the office of Academy Director as being due to intensive publishing activities and ill health within the family: "*[...] di salute della propria famiglia e dai suoi studi [...] per la compliazione e publicazione di libri matematici*" ([...] suffering extreme anxiety about wellfare of his own family and his studies [...] owing to the compilation and publication of the books on mathematics). Also, in August 1909, one of his beloved daughters died.

[9] Only in 1911 he wrote a paper entitled, "*Sul Calcolo della Pasqua nel Calendario Gregoriano*" (On the calculation of Easter according to the Gregorian calendar). Surprisingly in 1911 Karl Flusser, Professor of Mathematics at the Prague Karl's University, published an analytical paper on further distribution probabilities for option prices (Flusser 1911).

[10] Subak (1917) previous publications by Bronzin are mentioned, as are his calculations determining the date of Easter (see footnote 9).

[11] De Tuoni dedicated his work to Bronzin: "*A Vincenzo Bronzin * Della antica Istria * Dotta Eroica * Puro Figlio * Ultimo Direttore * Nei Tempi del duro Servaggio * Dell'Accademia di Commercio * E * Giustamente Primo * Per chiare Virtù * Alto Valore nelle matematiche Discipline * Purezza di Patrio Amore * Del Regio Istituto Commerciale*".

By 1910, of the 221,000 inhabitants living there, approximately 120,000 were Italian, 52,000 were Slovenian, 12,000 were Austro-German, 2,000 Croatian and a further 35,000 came from other nations. At the same time the tensions between the different ethnic groups were exacerbated, and social skirmishes were on the increase. From 1902 there were various strikes, and in 1906 the socialists gained a surprising victory in the elections.

Nevertheless the phenomenon of anxiety and reflection on this and related topics (self-reflection, the intensive analysis of personal needs and desires) as well as discussions on the individual's perceptions of self and others were not alien concepts to Trieste's citizens. Freud's teaching fell of fertile ground here. The founder of the Italian psychoanalytical school, Edoardo Weiss, was a Triestian and the most famous novel of the period, *La coscienza di Zeno* by Italo Svevo, was based on an imaginary report written by a patient for his psychoanalyst. In addition to this, in 1918 Svevo translated Freud's "Interpretation of Dreams" into Italian (Di Salvo 1990). Bronzin's move from his research activities to more schoolish, pedagogic pursuits fitted in completely with the contemporary withdrawal into narrower circles.

7.3 The Social, Political and Cultural Difference Between Trieste and Vienna

In spite of the similar prevailing mood of 'anxiety' in both of these cities, there were some significant differences between Vienna and Trieste: In the Vienna of the 1890's a strong anti-Semitism was growing which allowed Karl Lueger (1844–1910), a declared anti-Semite, to become mayor in 1897. In 1890 Lueger voiced the opinion in the course of a parliamentary speech:

> "I ask you what are Christian farmers to do when the corn market is solely in the hands of the Jews? What are Christian bakers to do? What are Christians to do when more than 50-percent of Vienna's attorneys and the preponderant part of its doctors are Jewish? [...] The Jews [...] have invented their own form of German, one that we do not even understand, so-called Yiddish [...] and they use it so that they are not understood when talking among themselves" (Cited according to Fuchs 1949, p. 60).

The anti-Semitism widely prevalent in Vienna did not exist in Trieste. Quite the contrary: Trieste flourished in the eighteenth and nineteenth century as the crucible city of the Habsburgs and favoured the integration of immigrants. Immigrants of Jewish origin were also able to profit from the climate, rising relatively quickly to assume prestigious political functions – an exceptional case, unique in the Habsburg Empire – as noted by the female historian, Tullia

Catalan, in her analysis of the situation of Jews in Trieste (Catalan 2001, p. 511). This freedom not only existed for people of Jewish origin, but in general for all foreigners. In a letter of December 7th, 1901, the management of the Trieste's stock exchange opposed a proposal put forward by the government of Vienna to prohibit foreigners from becoming members of the exchange regulation board (Board of the Stock Exchange 1901a).

Thus Trieste offered much scope for social manoeuvre, in no small part due to the special function of the city in linking Austro-Hungaria with the Mediterranean and its emerging role as a crucible city. This gave several single-minded Triestians the freedom to realize their vision of how to shape their lives, even if it clashed with normality. Guido Voghera was a talented mathematician, socialist and Jew who had a common-law marriage with his wife that was based on conviction. This prompted the protest from the bourgeois society, lead to his ostracism, and cost him his position as a mathematics teacher at the state gymnasium. As a consequence, Voghera had to work for a short period as mechanic and man-Friday for a brother-in-law of his. In spite of this, he was appointed professor to the Academy by Bronzin in 1910. Since the Academy was directly dependent on Austro-Hungarian administration, the Triestians were not able to impede Voghera's appointment. (Voghera 1967, p. 63f and Leiprecht 1994)[12] The contradiction between the political administration in the hands of Royal and Imperial Monarchy on the one hand, and the cultural-ethnic dominance of the Italianità on the other hand, created an independence in Trieste, which – as seen in Voghera's case – could be fully exploited, as long as the responsible parties, in this case Bronzin, took advantage of the liberal freedom as a matter of course.

7.4 Trieste and Its Attitude Towards Speculation

Trieste developed differently from the rest of the Austro-Hungarian area in other fields as well. Thus it was in Vienna in 1892 that Karl Lueger, already mentioned above, demanded in a parliamentary discussion concerning taxation of stock exchange turnovers and share profits that stockbrokers should be disenfranchised of their voting rights: He considered that the "taxation of the exchange trades would be no different than reclaiming some part the theft that the gaming hell had taken from the public good". During this discussion a parliamentary member shouted out: "Just hang the stock-exchange Jews, and you will see the price of bread tumble". Consequent to this political tirade, forward trading on the Vienna stock exchange – a central but also risk-laden side of exchange dealings – was practically brought to a standstill. In 1901 the Viennese court accepted the objection that forward trades were contracts based on

[12] Patrick Karlsen indicated Voghera's book to us.

gambling and gaming principles, whereupon they were divested of their legal basis (Schmit 2003, p. 143ff).

This stood in stark contrast to the situation in Trieste and the attitudes prevailing amongst professors at the Academy who were secure in their relationship to trade and stock exchange dealings. The number of students increased continually. In the short period before World War I, there was a sharp increase in the number of students.[13] During this period – despite the decrease in forward-trading on the Viennese stock exchange – professors and students remained loyal to the Trieste stock exchange. A visitor from Trieste's Chamber of Commerce reported in 1908:

> "Thanks to the kindness of some experienced stock-jobbers, the students received an introduction to the functioning of bank operations, futures contracts, and other important trade operations".[14]

This relaxed relationship with the stock exchange and respective speculative instruments was all more easy in Trieste as hardly any mentionable forward trading was conducted there. In 1901 the responsible ministry of the Austro-Hungarian Empire carried out a survey on stock exchanges for the purpose of obtaining stronger control over stock-exchange trading. The director wrote in a letter to the High r.r. Commissions and to the High Imperial Council:

> "It only need be a question of corn or milled products, the Director of the Triestian Stock Exchange must recognize and stress the undeniable fact that objectives have been and are always aimed at real consignment deliveries and were not simply being exploited to dissimulate some gamble". (Board of the Stock Exchange 1901b)

This allowed students to discuss possible speculative trades with stock-exchange agents in an all the more unstrained manner, as everything took place in a virtual context and in no way had any connection with reality. Additionally, there was little difference in the attitudes adopted by students and practitioners. The academy did offer further education courses for financial specialists – and this was one of the issues that Bronzin contested. The virtual debate must have been resumed there again.

[13] I.R. Accademia di Commercio e di Nautica in Trieste, Sezione Commerciale, diversi anni scolastici, Trieste, 1909–1914.

[14] See: The Triestian Newspaper ("*Triester Zeitung*"), 20th January, 1909.

References

Accademia di commercio e nautica in Trieste (1909) Archive of the state of Trieste, b. 101 e regg 273, 31.07.1909, AA 345/09. Trieste

Board of the Stock Exchange (1901a) Letter of December 7th, 1901, Archive of the state of Trieste, sub Borsa. Trieste

Board of the Stock Exchange (1901b) Presentation of the Triestian Board of the Stock Exchange to the Imperial and Royal Ministry (hohen k.k. Ministerien) and the High Imperial Council of December 7th, 1901, Archive of the state of Trieste, sub Borsa. Trieste

Bronzin (n.d.) A Rovignesi Illustri. In: La Voce della Famia Ruvignisa. Trieste

Catalan T (2001) Presenza sociale ed ecomomica degli ebrei nella Trieste absburgica tra Settecento e primo Novecento. In: Storia economica e sociale di Trieste, Vol. 1, La città dei gruppi, a cura di Roberto Finzi e Giovanni Panjek. Edizioni Lint, Trieste, p. 483ff

De Tuoni D (1925) Il Regio Istituto Commerciale di Trieste, Saggio Storico. Trieste

Di Salvo T (1990) Italo Svevo: la sua vita, le sue idee, le sue opere. In: Svevo I (1990) La Conscienza di Zeno, a cura di Tommaso Di Salvo. Zanichelli, Bologna, pp. V–XLIV

Erdheim M (1982) Die gesellschaftliche Produktion von Unbewusstheit – Eine Einführung in den ethnopsychoanalytischen Prozess. Suhrkamp, Frankfurt on the Main

Flusser G (1911) Ueber die Prämiengrösse bei den Prämien- und Stellagegeschäften. In: Jahresbericht der Prager Handelsakademie. Prague, pp. 1–30

Freud S (1908) Die 'kulturelle' Sexualmoral und die moderne Nervosität. In: Freud S (1908) Fragen der Gesellschaft – Ursprünge der Religion, Studienausgabe Vol. IX, published in 1974 by Alexander Mitscherlich et al. Fischer Verlag, Frankfurt on the Main

Fuchs A (1949) Geistige Strömungen in Oesterreich 1867–1918. Globus Verlag, Vienna

Glaser H (1979) Sigmund Freuds Zwanzigstes Jahrhundert – Seelenbilder einer Epoche, Materialien und Analysen. Fischer Taschenbuch Verlag, Frankfurt on the Main

Groddeck G W (1974) Das Buch vom Es (Geist und Psyche). Kindler Taschenbücher, Munich

Leiprecht H (1994) Das Gedächtnis in Person – fast ein Jahrhundert lebte Giorgio Voghera in Triest. Du 10, pp. 67–71

Musil R (1999) Mann ohne Eigenschaften, Vol 1. Rowohlt, Reinbek

Schmit J (2003) Die Geschichte der Wiener Börse, Frühwirth Bibliophile Edition

Simmel G (1989) Philosophie des Geldes. Suhrkamp, Frankfurt on the Main (published by Frisby D P and Köhnke K C)

Sontag S (1979) Illness as metaphor. Allan Lane, London

Subak G (1917) Cent'Anni d'Insegnamento Commerciale – La Sezione Commerciale della I.R. Accademia di Commercio e Nautica di Trieste. Presso la Sezione Commerciale della I.R. Accademia di Commercio e Nautica, Trieste

Vorghera G (1967) Pamphlet Postumo – Biografia di Guido Voghera, contenuta in una lettera del figlio al dott. Carlo Levi, Edizioni Umana, Trieste

Part D
Cultural and Socio-Historical Background

Introduction

How was the economic, cultural and social atmosphere in the late Habsburg monarchy? Why did Bronzin's contribution not get a broader recognition by economists and mathematicians in the socio-economic setting of that time?

These are the guiding questions of the articles in this part of the book. Josef Schiffer's first contribution is about the economic development at the time of the late Habsburg monarchy. He has a complete different view of the traditional perception of the economic situation in the Austro-Hungarian empire: The Austro-Hungarian empire was not at all a sick state, dominated by sociability, as often described. He writes that two or three decades before World War I "the Habsburg monarchy not only had become a common economic area but was also quite able to compete at least in its key industries with the other important European nations". Therefore, not the economic development was to be held responsible for the collapse of the Austro-Hungarian State, the predominant reason was the conflict between the different nationalities. Trieste's political transformation after the turn of the century is a perfect object of study for this development. Before World War I ethnical and political struggles dominated the economically prospering town.

The great economic spurt of the empire was also backed by the development of sciences, but there was still a gap between application and theory, especially in mathematics and physics. But nevertheless, at the end of the 19th century discussions were established on a remarkable higher scientific level than a quarter century before. In physics, Austria with the physicist Ludwig Boltzmann was one of the leading nations in developing new models and theories for a better understanding of the different states of matter (*Gastheorie*). And in mathematics the Austrians were also capable to catch up to the leading European nations (France, Germany) before World War I, thanks to their open-minded attitude towards the development in other, more advanced centers of mathematical research in Germany and France. This attitude can be observed for example in the famous *Monatshefte für Mathematik und Physik*, a journal and review edited by the Institute for Mathematics of the University of Vienna, the flagship of Austrian mathematics, as Wolfgang Hafner shows in his chapter. But nevertheless, a deterministic social structure without much opportunities for the gifted to work their way up still prevailed. All happened by coincidence. Although the editors of the *Monatshefte* tried to maintain a strict conservative guideline, there was still space for new ideas, featured by scientists working on the borderline between practice and theory.

Behind the efforts to develop new scientific approaches was the forward-pressing forces of the economic interests. In order to maintain the desired economic progress it was necessary to support broader research and education in mathematics. For example, in order to accelerate mass production in the emerging industries, new capacities and new equipment had to be developed, which were based on industrial sciences and engineering which obviously relied on the scientific basis of the exact sciences, notably mathematics. This development did not occur without conflicts between the traditional and more economically orientated mathematicians. A similar development could be observed with the prevalence of statistical and probabilistic thinking. In Austria-Hungaria old-age pension-funds were not established by public institutions, but by private insurance companies and local corporations, so there was the need for specific specialist know-how even in remote places. In this respect, the fragmentation of the empire helped to establish and diffuse knowledge. But the general attitude of the leading mathematicians was to keep mathematics as a philosophical, well-protected discipline remote from practical applications, which would eventually accelerate the danger of devaluation of science's most prestigious discipline. In the forefront of World War I and on the background of the evolution of the different ethnical conflicts it also became more and more difficult to keep control over the scientific mainstream.

But nevertheless, the question remains why Bronzin's work did not find adequate recognition and application if both – economic development and the broad diffusion of probabilistic thinking – was so widespread in Austria-Hungaria. The sociologist Elena Esposito takes a constructivist perspective on this issue in her contribution and argues that there was no need to produce security in these days: "The calculation of implied volatility convincingly suggests that risk is controllable, even if the future is unknowable – a much more congent requirement today than in Bronzin's day." Was it, because at the time of Bronzin, risk was associated with external causes, a feature of an outer world, and not as an inherent part of a complex structure of social or natural systems as it is done today?

8 The Late Habsburg Monarchy – Economic Spurt or Delayed Modernization?

Josef Schiffer*

In historical perspective the Austro-Hungarian Monarchy around 1900 was over a long period of time perceived as a state which chiefly flourished in cultural fields. However at the same time it was viewed as persisting in the state of hopeless economical backwardness. This paper attempts to revise the rather distorted picture and to replace it by a more differentiated consideration which is based on the research results achieved by economic historians in the past decades.

In some regions of the Austrian Monarchy industrialization in the strict sense had begun to spread later than in most of Western Europe. This meant the Habsburg Empire as a whole did not develop along the ideal-typical model-cases of modernization postulated in economic theory. But in the two or three decades preceding World War I Austria-Hungary not only had become a common economic area but was also quite able to compete at least in its key industries with the other major European powers. The regional differences and infrastructural weak points, especially at the periphery of the empire, do not seem to have hampered economic modernisation in such a massive way as was often proposed. The development of the urban society and its specific melting-pot mentality, which formed the fertile ground for the rich cultural output of Fin-de-siècle Austria, were massively induced by the transformation- and migration-processes caused by the Industrial modernization. The ethnic conflicts between the different nationalities finally led to the dissolution of the Austro-Hungarian State in the aftermath of World War I, but there is little evidence that it was caused by economic backwardness. Nowadays, as one of the results of the common past, the Republic of Austria once again takes an important role in the economic and social integration of the East- and Southeast-European countries into the European Union.

8.1 The Cliché of the "Merry Old" Habsburg Monarchy

It is a common known fact, that for the last decades the cultural sciences have taken a keen interest in the fascinating aura attached to the Habsburg monarchy. By the late nineteenth century this multi-national empire had grown into a vast political structure in the heart of Europe. It is also widely acknowledged by historians that it experienced spectacular peaks of cultural and scientific achievements in the very last decades of its existence, yet was destined to disappear virtually overnight from the political map and disintegrate into a number of smaller states

* *josef.schiffer@uni-graz.at*

in the aftermath of World War I. Since the 1960s at least, researchers dealing with the *Wiener Moderne* (Viennese modernism modernity) and Austria-Hungary's remarkable accomplishments around 1900 for a long time preferred to concentrate primarily on artistic, cultural and philosophical phenomena. These are represented by distinguished and influential personalities such as Klimt, Mahler, Musil, Freud, Kraus and Wittgenstein amongst many others[1].

By contrast, the socio-economic environment of the Central European region around 1900 would tend to receive less attention. However, emerging prior to and in parallel with "artistic" modernism, the modernisation and acceleration of life – induced by industrialisation, urbanisation and novel means of transport – was not at all inconsequential with regard to the cultural development of the Habsburg monarchy and the multiethnic identity of its inhabitants. The ethnic and cultural diversity of the thriving metropolises in Central Europe was not least a result of widespread migratory processes taking place within the Habsburg monarchy.[2] In combination with the economic and technological revolutions at the close of the 19th century this frequently caused crises and conflicts, yet at the same time these elements formed the indispensable fertile ground for the "creative milieu" of the *Wiener Moderne*.[3]

The supposed economic backwardness of the Habsburg monarchy in the 19th century, and the seeming failure of its political agencies to effectively cope with the problems of economic development have for a long time been looked upon as simple enough facts. This opinion formed the basis for a rather simplistic explanation concerning the final collapse of the multi-ethnic state. The unresolved conflicts between the different national groups formed the core of this argument, because they were regarded as the decisive factor constraining economic prosperity and thus creating an injust and therefore instable society. The suppression or discrimination of ethnic groups was considered the key reason why there was achieved neither sustained economic growth nor a levelling of the enormous differences in economic development amongst the various regions of the Dual Monarchy.[4]

The caricature depicting "Kakanien" – hopelessly backward in terms of technology and kept together only by the paternal authority of the old emperor Franz Joseph I as well as a sophisticated and repressive bureaucracy – is thus quite frequently found both in scientific literature dealing with the history of Austria-Hungary[5] as well as in memoirs or work of fiction[6] of the interwar period.

[1] Cf. Johnston (1972), Schorske (1980), Janik and Toulmin (1973).
[2] Cf. Steidl and Stockhammer (2007).
[3] Cf. Csáky (1998), p. 140.
[4] Cf. Eigner (1997), pp. 112–122 and Good (1992).
[5] Cf. Nyíri (1988), pp. 68–70, 83–86.

8.2 Survey of the Research on the Austro-Hungarian Economy

While there is copious literature on the political and cultural facets of the Habsburg Empire, research papers concerning economic aspects are few and far between. In the period between World Wars I and II, the economic historians' perspective was largely confined to anecdotal and polemical treatises that dealt with the inevitable decline and disintegration of the monarchy. The Hungarian social scientist Oskar Jászi was a particularly adamant proponent of the view stressing the state's economic failure. His central hypothesis suggests that Austria-Hungary's inability to generate sustained economic growth, and its lagging behind the German empire, were also the reasons for its demise as a political union.[7] In his *The Dissolution of the Habsburg Monarchy*, published in 1929, he contends "While the German empire [...] created a powerful and technologically advanced industrial system, [...] Austria-Hungary emerged unsuccessful from the fierce competitive race" and he summarises: "From an economic point of view, the Austrian-Hungarian monarchy was already a vanquished empire by 1913, and in this way it entered the First World War in 1914" (Jászi 1929).[8]

The foundations of a more objective view were created when in the mid-1960s American economic historians started to look at the economic development in Central and Eastern Europe in the light of new analytic-quantitative methods. In the post-war period, the stage model developed by Walt W. Rostow and presented in his *The Stages of Economic Growth* had been widely received amongst economists. His theory is based on the assumption that the transition to a modern, self-sustained and far-reaching pattern of growth can be recognised by a conspicuous discontinuity in a country's economic development. Rostow calls this stage the "take-off phase", which is characterised by a sudden increase in the rate of investment, lasting two or three decades, and the emergence of a leading sector. This stage presupposes a number of societal preconditions. Following up

---

[6] Stefan Zweig writes in his memoirs: "Our Austrian indolence in political matters, and our backwardness in economics as compared with our resolute German neighbour, may actually be ascribed in part to our Epicurean excesses. But culturally this exaggeration of artistic events brought something unique to maturity – first of all an uncommon respect for every artistic presentation, then, through centuries of practice, a connoisseurship without equal, and finally, thanks to that connoisseurship, a predominant high level in all cultural fields. [...] One lived well and easily and without cares in that old Vienna, and the Germans to the North looked with some annoyance and scorn upon their neighbours on the Danube, who instead of being 'proficient' and maintaining rigid order, permitted themselves to enjoy life, ate well, took pleasure in feasts and theatre and, besides, made excellent music" (Zweig 1964, pp. 18, 24). In a similar vein, recurrent themes of this kind, depicting the placid way of going about things in Cacania to contrast it against the ways of the German empire are also found in the writings of Robert Musil, Joseph Roth, Max Brod and numerous other authors.

[7] Cf. Good (1986), Jászi (1918), p. 75.

[8] Quoted according to Good (1986), p. 14.

on Rostow, several economic historians, embarking on case studies involving a number of European countries, endeavoured to determine this brief phases when the level of production accelerated thus causing a higher rate of growth (Rostow 1960).[9]

Alexander Gerschenkron, having worked with the Vienna *Institut für Konjunkturforschung*[10] prior to his emigration to the US, emphasised in his theoretical work on industrialisation the discontinuous character of economic improvement in the countries of the Central European region. In a reference to Rostow, his approach is also based on the concept of a short phase of acceleration, the "great spurt" as he preferred to call it (Gerschenkron 1965). After 1900, he suggests, a leap forward of this kind had generated a strong growth momentum subsequent to a lengthy period of stagnation. However, this thesis does not give sufficient consideration to the great geographical differences in the economic development of the crown lands under the rule of the Danubian monarchy. The western provinces of the monarchy had attained a relatively high level of industrialisation quite early, whereas the regions in the East and the South-East belonged to the most backward areas in Europe.[11]

From the early 1970s however, the theories of Rostow and Gerschenkron were challenged by more differentiating and statistically supported results which pointed to a longer period of sustained growth since the middle of the 19th century in the Central European region. In their path-breaking studies, Nachum T. Gross, Richard Rudolph and John Komlos, supported by extensive statistical material from Austrian archives, produced evidence of continuity in the industrial development of Central Europe. A substantial part of the findings, whose validity remains largely unchallenged to date, has been made available to the German-speaking regions with the publication of the first volume in the series entitled *Die Habsburgermonarchie 1848-1918* in 1973[12]. At the same time Austrian historians, still tending towards a more descriptive approach, were focussing mainly on business cycle policies, corporate bodies and theoretical concepts, rather than actual ongoing economic activities (Matis 1972, März 1968).

Research interest in the economic conditions of Austria-Hungary has been on the wane since the mid-1990s, the Austrian monarchy being covered peripherally or not at all in comprehensive treatises on European economic history.[13] At the same time, there has been a growing preponderance of analyses devoted to specific industries. This applies e.g. to the profound study *Engineering and Eco-*

[9] Cf. Good (1986), p. 16.
[10] Cf. Feichtinger (1999), p. 302.
[11] Cf. Eigner (1997), p. 112.
[12] Cf. Brusatti (1973).
[13] Cf. e.g. Treue (1966). Although representing the second-largest country in Europe in terms of area, in this book the monarchy is given no consideration with regard to the period following the end of Josephism (1790). The same is the case with regard to Pierenkemper (1996).

nomic Growth by Max-Stephan Schulze[14], who in his investigation of the mechanical engineering industry in Austria-Hungary finds the hypothesis of an even and sustainable development confirmed for this particular segment. Teaching at the London School of Economics, Schulze is currently one of the few contemporary economists who devote attention to a comprehensive examination of the economic development and growth processes in the dual monarchy.[15]

Ökonomie und Politik by Roman Sandgruber[16] may be regarded as representative of the more recent publications by Austrian historians. In a broad survey ranging from the Middle Ages to the present, Sandgruber devotes himself to many different issues such as the demographic development and urbanisation, thus linking up traditional themes of economic history with social and cultural history. However, and regrettably, in his presentation – placing the emphasis for the bigger part on popular high-lights such as the Viennese stock market crash of 1873 – he largely confines himself to the boundaries of the contemporary Austrian state, thus capturing only part of the monarchy's impressing economic rise. This shortcoming is also found in other accounts[17] which focus on the territory of today's Republic of Austria thus failing to take the full historical nexus into consideration, possibly to sidestep allegations of clinging to an sentimental imperial attitude.

8.3 Early Industrialisation, "*Gründerzeit*" and Stock Market Crash

In the closing decades of the 18th century, the industrial revolution which originated in Western Europe had begun to show its effects in various parts of the Habsburg monarchy. During the reign of Maria Theresa, the state developed a lively interest in the establishment of manufactories to strengthen external trade. However, the centres of industrial production remained confined to the more convenient locations in Bohemia, the Austrian part of Silesia, and the Alpine provinces.[18]

During the Napoleonic Wars – which saw continental Europe cut off from continuing technological advances in Great Britain – industrial expansion slowed down considerably in the years after 1800. A number of reasons account for this development: the economic effects of the continental system on foreign trade, an inadequate infrastructure owing to difficult geographic conditions, the cost of

[14] Cf. Schulze (1996), p. 161 and Schulze (1997a), pp. 282–304.
[15] Cf. Schulze (1997b), p. 293ff and Schulze (2007), p. 189ff.
[16] Cf. Sandgruber (1995).
[17] Cf. e.g. Jetschgo et al. (2004) and Bruckmüller (2001).
[18] Cf. Good (1986), p. 27. Thus, Austria was one of Europe's leading producers of iron ore in the 18th century; in 1767, Styria alone produced as much pig-iron as England.

war, and – related to it – a lack of capital available for the establishment of innovative industries. Furthermore, political reforms inspired by economic liberalism were adopted at a relatively late stage, compared to other countries. Not until the agrarian reform of 1848 were sufficient numbers of rural workers available for industrial employment, while the enactment of the *Gewerbefreiheit* (the freedom to conduct commercial activities) in 1848 finally created one of the most important preconditions for the growth of the monarchy's industrial base.[19]

By about the middle of the century, the economic integration of the Habsburg monarchy was given further significant impetus: after completion of the first railway line, the removal of the customs barrier between Austria and Hungary exerted a very strong effect on goods traffic. The results of this act of trade liberalisation as such were negligible in terms of money since tariffs had been rather low; what mattered hugely were the consequences of the transport revolution. Trains and cargo steam-ships were carrying coal, wood and agrarian products in large quantities to the industrial centres, thus creating the basis for an emerging common market.[20] However, proving to be an inhibiting factor, the relative cost of commodities was rather high compared to England and Germany as domestic production of coal and iron was insufficient until gaining momentum only toward the end of the century. Similarly, steam-engines had to be imported at a high cost until the middle of the century, which made their deployment appear uneconomic in wide areas.[21]

To satisfy the growing need for capital, it became vital to establish joint-stock banks modelled on the French *Crédit Mobilier*. In 1853, the first bank of this type was founded with the help of private bankers Eskeles and Brandeis-Weikersheimer: the *Niederösterreichische Escompte-Gesellschaft*. In response to efforts by the Pereire brothers to set up a subsidiary of *Crédit Mobiliere* in Austria, the house of Rothschild, supported by a number of aristocrats, including Prince Schwarzenberg – created the *Credit-Anstalt für Handel und Gewerbe* in 1855, whose equity capital – at 100 million Gulden – was astronomical at that time. This enormous capital base enabled *Credit-Anstalt* to extend its activities beyond the regular business of a merchant bank, such as offering long-term loans and acquiring industrial enterprises on a large scale.[22]

In subsequent years, a number of financial institutions funded by foreign investors enhanced the Austrian banking community. In the early 1860s, two of these startup projects involving joint-stock banks were completed: in 1863 *Bodencreditanstalt* was set up backed by French capital, and a year later, the *Anglo-Österreichische Bank*, as the name suggests supported mostly by English capital, was established.[23]

[19] Cf. Sandgruber (1995), p. 233.
[20] Cf. Eigner and Helige (1999), pp. 58, 64.
[21] Cf. Gross (1980).
[22] Cf. März (1968), p. 37.
[23] Cf. Good (1986), p. 181.

Like in most European countries, railway construction was the crucial agent for the economic upturn. Subsequent to the privatisation of most railway lines, a process beginning in 1854, substantial progress was made in railway construction until the late 1860s. The development of the railroad network was beneficial not only to the construction industry and the iron industry: newly emerging sectors like mechanical engineering and coal mining benefited as well. Attesting to the rapid spread of the industrial revolution was an increase both in freight and passenger rail transport. Between 1848 and 1873, the volume of cargo rose from 1.5 million to 41 million tons, while the number of passengers soared from 3 million to 43 million.[24] Equally impressive were the capacity increases regarding the use of steam engines; since the middle of the 19th century, steam engines came to be looked upon as an indicator of economic growth in the new era of technological-industrial progress. Within a quarter of a century, the number of stationary steam engines installed within the borders of the monarchy increased fifteen fold from 671 (1852) to 9,160 (1875).[25]

In the 1860s, the Habsburg Empire got increasingly entangled in foreign policy conflicts, especially regarding its rivalry with Prussia over dominance in the German Confederation (*Deutscher Bund*). The resulting wars ended in severe military defeat, as a consequence of which economically highly developed areas like the provinces Lombardy and Venetia were lost. Moreover, this had a disastrous effect upon the empire's renown which was already marred as it had become discredited as a *Völkerkerker* (a prison of peoples) in an era characterised by liberation movements fighting for national independence. Additional negative effects were brought about by a number of poor grain-harvests and the unavailability of cotton imports from North America due to the US Civil War (1861-1865) which severely hurt Bohemia's emergent textile industry. These factors had adverse effects on the growth of the Austrian economy, at least temporarily, giving rise to crisis-ridden set backs.[26]

Notwithstanding the unfortunate outcome of conflicts in the arena of foreign policy, and even though the *Ausgleich* (compromise) achieved with Hungary in 1867 would weaken the influence of Austrian enterprises in the Transleithian half of the empire, economic development was making good progress in the years thereafter. Along with the extension of the railway network, the Austrian iron industry experienced a significant upturn in spite of strong foreign competition. The introduction of new steel production techniques (e.g. the Siemens-Martin and the Gilchrist-Thomas methods) elicited not only notable increases in output, but also a number of proprietary product developments and improvements.[27]

[24] Cf. Sandgruber (1995), p. 236. For instance, the "cotton crisis" during the period 1861 to 1864 resulted, according to Sandgruber, in a cutback of 80% of jobs in the Cisleithanian cotton industry, which is tantamount to 280,000 jobs.

[25] Cf. Hobsbawm (1998), p. 55.

[26] Cf. Sandgruber (1995), p. 243.

[27] Cf. Matis and Bachinger (1973).

At the Vienna stock exchange, a massive speculative bubble concerning stocks and bonds was heating up more and more thanks to innumerable corporate start-ups[28] and the influx of capital triggered by the investment of French reparations paid to the German empire. The exaggerated boom of the *Gründerzeit* (Period of Promoterism) was epitomised by the financial failure of the world exhibition held in Vienna, ultimately leading to the stock exchange crash of 1873. Despite its devastating magnitude, the crash would impede economic expansion only temporarily. However, it produced far-reaching psychological, not to say traumatic, repercussions affecting attitudes: it heralded the end of the short heyday of liberalism in Austria. Not least due to the economic depression and the decline of liberalism, new political mass movements emerged – the Christian Social Movement (*Christlichsoziale*), the Social Democrats (*Sozialdemokraten*) and the German Nationals (*Deutschnationale*). Anti-Capitalism and anti-Semitism found a rich breeding ground in this atmosphere. Government policy was now preoccupied with the pursuit for more homeland security and dominated by the worries and narrow outlook of small trade; the nationalisation of the railways, the introduction of protective tariffs and a renewed curtailment of economic freedom were considered panaceas in dealing with the crisis.[29]

8.4 Stagnation and Economic Expansion

During the 1880s, the industrial structures of Austria-Hungary were undergoing rapid and profound changes: corporate mergers and the concentration of businesses to form large firms advanced rapidly in various industries; the iron industry saw the formation of cartels (price-rigging)[30], a practice that was to spread to other industries, including the leading sugar refineries. At the same time, direct intervention by the state's "visible hand" (as opposed to the "invisible hand" of market forces) was intensified by the use of subsidies, policies intended to achieve stabilisation, nationalisation and municipalisation specifically targeting infrastructure.[31] In the wake of the stock exchange crash, investment activity suffered a palpable downturn which was reflected most pronouncedly in a drastic production cutback in the area of mechanical engineering. Between 1870 and

[28] Cf. Matis (1972), p. 423. According to Matis, in the brief boom period from 1866 to 1873, approx. 1,011 million Gulden were invested in newly established companies; by contrast, in the period from 1874 to 1900 similar investments amounted to only 374.4 million Gulden.

[29] Cf. Sandgruber (1995), p. 248ff.

[30] Cf. Bundesministerium für Handel und Wiederaufbau (1961), p. 157. It is instructive to note that the industrialist Karl Wittgenstein (the rather less-known father of the philosopher Ludwig Wittgenstein) had been able, between 1878 and 1889, to bring large parts of Austria's iron and steel industry under his control, thus creating the monarchy's foremost corporate empire at the turn of the century. Cf. Schiffer (2001), Bramann and Moran (1979, 1980).

[31] Cf. Eigner and Helige (1999), p. 79f.

1874, 334 locomotives were built per year, while in subsequent years the annual number fell to an average of 118.[32]

The temporary slowdown of growth in the Cisleithianian[33] economy can be explained by intensive efforts to relocate production, especially mining, to the Hungarian part of the empire. The investment activities of the Hungarian state played an important role; the Hungarian government, not least for chauvinistic reasons, getting far more involved in industrial policy than the authorities in the Austrian half of the empire. At any rate, from 1885 onward, Transleithania witnessed an increase in manufacturing capacities and productivity so strong that it is fair to speak of a take-off phase.[34] These investment programs induced by the Hungarian government were made possible in no small measure due to the steady flow of Austrian capital into Hungarian public bonds.[35] Nonetheless, in the Austrian half of the empire, many industries registered robust growth rates, which by the end of the 19th century ensured "the definitive step leading from an agrarian to an industrial state"[36]. The new techniques for processing iron required the use of bituminous coal, while at the same time making possible the smelting of low-grade Bohemian iron ore, for which purpose the centres of production were relocated increasingly to the north of the monarchy, which also had better transport access to the German empire.[37] Numerous industries, for example textiles and food production, increasingly settled in the periphery of large cities like Vienna, Prague, Budapest, Brünn (Brno) and Trieste. The division of labour between the two halves of the empire created a common economic sphere with a high degree of autarchy. But this strategy also proved short-sighted insofar as it neglected to address problems of international competitiveness, and as a result, in a number of sectors, the gap in terms of innovativeness vis-à-vis other industrial nations grew larger.[38] Therefore, economic development lagged behind compared to Western Europe, though not by that degree as was occasionally proposed in the more dated literature: relative growth rates actually proved very robust during the decades before World War I. Austria-Hungary's low per capita averages in terms of income and productivity are due largely to the predominantly agrarian regions in the East (Galizien/Galicia[39], Bukowina/Bukovina) and the South

[32] Cf. Schulze (1997a), p. 289.
[33] Cisleithania and Transleithania refer to the Austrian and the Hungarian parts of Austria-Hungary, divided by the River Leitha (Lajta).
[34] Cf. Pacher (1996), p. 108.
[35] Cf. Schulze (1997a), p. 280f.
[36] Pacher (1996), p. 135.
[37] Cf. Brousek (1987), p. 120ff.
[38] Cf. Eigner and Helige (1999), p. 95.
[39] A historical region of East Central Europe currently divided between Poland and the Ukraine. The nucleus of historic Galicia is formed of three western Ukrainian regions: Lemberg/Lviv, Tarnopol/Ternopil and Stanislau/Ivano-Frankivsk.

(Dalmatien/Dalmatia, Krain/Carniola, Küstenland/Austrian Littoral), which were barely industrialised even on the eve of World War I.[40]

By European standards, the banks of Austria-Hungary were rather unique in that they participated actively in the transformation of large firms into joint-stock companies and provided a large amount of the loans demanded by the big groups. Related to this was the growing influence of the banks in matters concerning the fate of these companies. This was as a result of close personal ties, since the banks preferrably assigned directors and other high-level executives to act as members of the board of management or the supervisory board in these companies.[41]

Closely related to this trend was the expansion of stock markets, especially in Budapest, that were given additional impetus by numerous corporate start-ups. A little less than a decade after the stock exchange crash of 1873, the year 1882 saw another massive market slide in connection with speculative machinations involving Paul-Eugène Bontoux and *Société de l'Union Général* which put the Vienna stock exchange in the doldrums for another ten years. Trading remained largely confined to bonds and bond-like railway stocks. Along with the general economic upturn from 1888/89 onwards, there was a considerable pick-up of turnover at the Vienna stock exchange, the industrial index increasing by 60% during the next few years, until the international financial crisis of 1895 (with its epicentre in London) led to another massive slide.[42]

8.5 Dawn of the Modern Era

According to the research reviewed here, the transition towards industrial society seems to have accelerated significantly from the mid 1890s. Finally, a marked and enduring upswing set in, which would later be referred to as "the second *Gründerzeit*". Whilst small and mid-sized firms remained the predominant corporate form, concentration processes in many sectors gave rise to industrial centres like Ostrau (Ostrava), Kattowitz (Katowice), Steyr and Kapfenberg which the influx of immigrants from all parts of the monarchy turned into major urban agglomerations. Due to improvements in the infrastructure, education and vocational skills, new manufacturing sectors – such as the large-scale chemical industry, the electrical industry and vehicle manufacturing – took root in Austria-Hungary rather quickly, stimulating the establishment of fairly large corporations. At the beginning of the 20th century, the capital city of Vienna was home to eight electrical industry corporations, each of which numbered one thousand or more employees. However, most of these firms had been established or were directly

[40] Cf. Good (1986), pp. 211, 239.
[41] Cf. Good (1986), p. 185.
[42] Cf. Pacher (1996), p. 133.

controlled by foreign (most notably German) concerns such as *Siemens-Schuckert* or *AEG*.[43]

As the steadily growing power demand of industry could no longer be covered by wood and coal, the exploration of new resources became a major issue. Unlike coal deposits, which were confined to certain regions, conditions for accessing new resources proved favourable, especially regarding electricity generated by hydropower from the Danube and the Alpine regions, as well as oil from Galicia.[44] Thanks to ample deposits, the oil industry experienced a boom that catapulted Austria-Hungary to third place among the oil producing countries, behind the US and Russia. In 1909, at the peak, 14,933,000 barrels, the equivalent of approximately five percent of world production at that time, were extracted from Galicia's oil wells. For once, there was a lack of government influence, since the political agents did not champion nationalisation but free enterprise. The large oil producers failed to form enduring cartels, the large Polish landowners proved indifferent, and the American competitors resorted to dumping which rendered the export of Galician oil unprofitable.[45]

Novel forms of mobility caused dramatic changes in the urban areas: as early as 1883/84, horse-powered tramways were superseded by steam traction in Vienna and Brünn (Brno). By the turn of the century, the electric tramway was standard, even in urban areas of secondary importance, such as Graz and Lemberg (Lviv). In Budapest, the opening of the first underground railway in continental Europe took place in 1896: a line connecting the city centre with the fairgrounds at Hero's Square (Hősök tere) on the occasion of festivities commemorating the Hungarian millennium.[46]

The system of communications, with its rapidly-growing service density, provides another graphic indicator of change. By the turn of the century, the entire monarchy was covered with a close-meshed network of telephone and telegraph lines. After the turn of the century, the number of telephone extensions increased rapidly, especially in urban centres. This resulted not only in a very significant acceleration of information flows, a hallmark of the modern era, but also generated entirely new types of jobs and, in particular, increasingly women were offered popular avenues of employment in factories and offices.[47]

Along with this and the emergence of department stores, the spread of electrical and gas connections in private households, and the increasing demand for luxury goods, the picture of a society emerges that has caught up with western

[43] Cf. Banik-Schweitzer (1993), p. 231.
[44] Cf. Eigner and Helige (1999), p. 98.
[45] Cf. Hochadel (2007), p. 15 and Fleig Frank (2005).
[46] Cf. Dienes (1996); concerning Lemberg (Lviv) see http://de.wikipedia.org/wiki/Straßenbahn_Lemberg (accessed 4 September 2008); concerning Budapest see http://de.wikipedia.org/wiki/Metro_Budapest.
[47] Cf. Sandgruber (1995), p. 277. Austria (together with the US) was the first country to see the keypunching machine, developed by Otto Schäffler in 1891, being used for the analysis of large mounds of data.

Europe in all areas of urban life. In a single period spanning less than ten years, the number of households consuming electrical energy in Vienna increased fourfold from 29,800 (1904) to 160,168 (1914).[48] However, the blessings of civilisation remained confined to a minority, and the glamour of the modern world should not hide the fact that living conditions for the working classes were bleak. Whilst a lack of opportunities for employment induced migration away from rural areas, life in the industrial districts was often still characterised by inhumane working conditions, low wages, and crowded housing conditions in mass accommodation. Due to mass migration bound for the rapidly growing urban centres, the proportion of the rural population continued to decrease, by 1910 falling below 40% in the developed parts of Cisleithania.[49]

While the favourable economic climate of the years after 1900 reflects this development, prosperity was increasingly overshadowed by conflicts between national groups. Growth rates considerably exceeded those of most other Europeans countries, while Austria-Hungary benefited to an above-average degree from the international economic boom in the years 1904 to 1908. The Vienna stock exchange though recovered only slowly from the setback suffered in November 1895 and remained a "side show" in Europe's financial arena. Industrial and railway stocks comprised just 2.3 percent of all securities, banking stocks represented 18 percent, while the vast remainder related to fixed income securities. Similarly, price gains and turnover remained modest. Only mining stocks registered appreciable gains.[50]

During the tenure of the cabinet led by *Ministerpräsident* (prime minister) Ernest von Koerber (1900–1904) a modernisation program was passed – not least as a reaction to conflicts among national groups – that addressed infrastructure improvements and contained specific plans to upgrade the transport infrastructure. The "Koerber plan" was passed in 1901 under the title "*Investitionsgesetz*" (investment law), providing for the construction of new railway routes in the Austrian hinterland, and, at the core of the plan, a direct north-south railway connection through the mountain ranges of Tauern and Karawanken linking Prague and Trieste. In addition, the plan provided for canals and other waterways, especially the link between the Danube and Oder rivers, which had been envisaged for a long time.[51] Some of the projects never materialised, partly because the treasury department under Eugen von Böhm-Bawerk proved exceedingly reluctant to release funds, and partly because of resistance from special interests fearing competitive pressure from improved transport routes.[52]

Nevertheless, the interventionist policies of the Koerber cabinet exerted a positive influence on the overall economic climate and contributed to the fact that

[48] Cf. Pacher (1996), p. 157.
[49] Cf. Eigner and Helige (1999), p. 121.
[50] Cf. Pacher (1996), p. 183.
[51] Cf. Gerschenkron (1977), p. 24.
[52] Cf. Sandgruber (1995), p. 306.

Austria-Hungary, in spite of her still very large agrarian component, was able to come very close to the satisfactory economic key average figures achieved by Europe's industrial nations.[53] In this regard, the monarchy's orientation towards exporting played a momentous role: for example, textiles, sugar and industrial products met with strong demand in the Balkan countries and in the Middle East, crucially contributing to a relatively even balance of trade.[54] However, the upturn did not necessarily bring about better living conditions for all segments of the population. In spite of the growing economic integration of the various regions of the monarchy, above-average economic growth rather amplified income differences amongst the working population, thus as one side-effect causing massive overseas emigration to the United States.[55]

8.6 Summary and Outlook

Promoted for diverse reasons, and adamantly advocated, the hypothesis according to which the Austro-Hungarian monarchy was an economically backward empire has been definitely refuted by research findings in the past decades. This hypothesis relied in no small part on equating political instability, caused by numerous national conflicts and government crises, with an alleged economic failure of the dual monarchy, which was frequently characterised by pejorative terms like "Europe's China" or "the sick man at the Danube".[56]

Only to a limited extent did the economic prosperity and thriving economic situation during the final two decades prior to World War I have a stabilising effect on the crisis-ridden multi-national state. In the eastern regions of the monarchy, lagging behind economically, there was a sense of being discriminated against in economic and social terms, whilst in the industrial centres of Bohemia-Moravia, a feeling spread that one would continue to be barred from having any say in political matters. Although the Habsburg state deviated (thanks to these regional differences) in some respects from the "ideal type" case of economic modernisation, there can be no doubt that it had advanced to a considerable extent on one of the many conceivable paths toward becoming a modern industrial society. For these reasons, the disintegration of the dual monarchy after the end of World War I cannot be explained primarily in terms of economic causes. In retrospect it appears that structural disparities, and the attendant anachronistic injustices of the political system, had more to do with it.[57]

[53] Cf. Eigner and Helige (1999), p. 121. For instance, in 1913, Austria's per capita income was only 11% lower than that of Germany, and already equal to that of France.
[54] Cf. Palotás (1991), p. 65.
[55] Cf. Sandgruber (1995), p. 311.
[56] Cf. Sandgruber (1995), p. 310.
[57] Cf. Eigner (1997), p. 122.

In contrast to the view held by Oskar Jászi (quoted above) and despite the amazing regional differences in the degree of industrial development, the Austro-Hungarian monarchy was nonetheless a functioning economic sphere on the eve of World War I; it was less oriented toward exporting than Germany, but it was still the largest domestic market in Europe. In his *The Economic Problem of the Danubian States*, published in 1947, Friedrich Hertz, the notable sociologist and economic historian, speaks of "the great economic achievement" of Austria-Hungary, "which was never adequately recognised"; and he expresses regret in view of the break-up of this historically grown unit, since "the advantages of the economic community were stunning" (Hertz 1947, p. 51).

The disintegration – more adequately put: the smashing up, facilitated by the victorious powers – of this common economic area (and significant domestic market) in the wake of World War I, dealt a severe blow not only to *Restösterreich* (residual Austria) and its further economic development but also to the countries of Central Europe, from which they were not able to recuperate for decades.[58] Especially the nascent Republic of Austria was seriously afflicted with economic stagnation. Until 1938, her economy's performance was one of the worst in Europe; in fact, only Spain was worse off.[59] Alternative concepts pursued during the inter-war period, such as the short-lived *Donauföderation* (Danube federation), and subsequent decades of communist rule, turned out to be failures.

Only towards the end of the 20th century would the countries of Central and Eastern Europe that had emerged from the Habsburg monarchy once again embark on a route towards the realisation of common economic concepts. Finally, with the 2004 European Union enlargement by the joining of Slovenia, Hungary, Czech Republic, Slovakia and Poland (and the subsequent 2007 accession of Romania and Bulgaria), that in their entirety or in parts used to belong to the sphere of power or influence of the Habsburg monarchy were restored to economic and political unity under the auspices of equality – after almost an entire century had passed. For the purpose of analysing these new integrative movements, the economic history of the Habsburg state represents not only an instructive historic model of a common economic area but also provides clues that may be used in assessing progress.[60] The integrative role that Austria is playing in these regions is nowadays also evident in the economic sphere; well-known and tradition-steeped company names, especially those of banks and insurance companies, are ubiquitous in the streets of Central and Eastern European cities.

[58] Cf. Komlos (1989), p. 224.
[59] Cf. Jetschgo et al. (2004), p. 304.
[60] Cf. Schall (2001), p. 19.

References

Banik-Schweitzer R (1993) Metropolen des 19. Jahrhunderts (mit einigen Ausblicken auf ihre Weiterentwicklung). In: Bericht über den neunzehnten Österreichischen Historikertag in Graz in der Zeit vom 18. bis 23. Mai 1992. Veröffentlichungen des Verbandes Österreichischer Historiker und Geschichtsvereine 28, pp. 230–236

Bramann J K, Moran J (1979, 1980) Karl Wittgenstein, Business Tycoon and Art Patron. Austrian History Yearbook 15/16, pp. 107–124

Brousek K M (1987) Die Großindustrie Böhmens 1848–1918. Oldenbourg, Munich

Bruckmüller E (2001) Sozialgeschichte Österreichs. Verlag für Geschichte und Politik, Vienna

Brusatti A (ed) (1973) Die Habsburgermonarchie 1848–1918, Vol. 1. Die wirtschaftliche Entwicklung. Verlag Akademie der Wissenschaften, Vienna

Bundesministerium für Handel und Wiederaufbau (ed) (1961) 100 Jahre im Dienste der Wirtschaft, Bd. 1. Vienna

Csáky M (1998) Ideologie der Operette und Wiener Moderne. Ein kulturhistorischer Essay, 2nd revised edn. Böhlau, Vienna/ Cologne/ Weimar

Dienes G M (1996) Verkehrsgeschichte Graz. In: Ausstellungskatalog Stadtmuseum Graz (1996) Translokal. 9 Städte im Netz 1848–1918. Graz

Eigner P (1997) Die wirtschaftliche Entwicklung der Habsburgermonarchie im 19. Jahrhundert: Ein Modellfall verzögerter Industrialisierung? In: Beiträge zur historischen Sozialkunde 27, pp. 112–122

Eigner P, Helige A (eds) (1999) Österreichische Wirtschafts- und Sozialgeschichte im 19. und 20. Jahrhundert. 175 Jahre Wiener Städtische Versicherung. Brandstätter, Vienna/ Munich

Feichtinger J (1999) With a little help from my friends. Die österreichische Wissenschaftsemigration in den dreißiger Jahren dargestellt am Beispiel der Sozial- und Wirtschaftswissenschaften, der Jurisprudenz und der Kunstgeschichte. Ein sozial-, und disziplingeschichtlicher Versuch. Doctoral dissertation, Universität Graz, Graz

Fleig Frank A (2005) Oil empire. Visions of Prosperity in Austrian Galicia. Harvard University Press, Cambridge (Massachusetts)/ London

Gerschenkron A (1965) Economic Backwardness in Historical Perspective. Harvard University Press, Cambridge (Massachusetts)

Gerschenkorn A (1977) An economic spurt that failed. Four lectures in Austria history. Princeton University Press, Princeton

Good D F (1986) Der wirtschaftliche Aufstieg des Habsburgerreiches 1750–1914. Böhlau, Vienna/ Cologne/ Graz

Good D F (1993) The economic lag of Central and Eastern Europe: evidence from the late nineteenth-century Habsburg Empire. Working Papers in Austrian Studies 7/93, Center for Austrian Studies, University of Minneapolis, Minneapolis

Gross N T (1980) The Habsburg Monarchy 1750–1914. In: Cipolla C M (ed) The emergence of industrial societies, 6th edn, Part 1. Fontana, London

Hertz F (1947) The economic problem of the Danubian States. A Study in Economic Nationalism. London

Hobsbawn E (1998) The age of capital 1848–1875. Weidenfeld & Nicolson, London

Hochadel O (2007) Kakanien im Ölrausch. "Der Standard", 14 and 15 August 2007, p. 15

Janik A, Toulmin S (1973) Wittgenstein's Vienna. Simon and Schuster, New York

Jászi O (1918) Der Zusammenbruch des Dualismus und die Zukunft der Donaustaaten. Vienna

Jászi O (1929) The dissolution of the Habsburg Monarchy. Chicago

Jetschgo J, Lacina F, Pammer M et al (2004) Österreichische Industriegeschichte 1848 bis 1955. Die verpasste Chance. Ueberreuther, Vienna

Johnston W M (1972) The Austrian mind: an intellectual and social history, 1848-1938. University of California Press, Berkeley (California)

Komlos J (1989) Eine Theorie der industriellen Revolution. In: Katalog der Niederösterr. Landesausstellung (1989) Magie der Industrie. Leben und Arbeiten im Fabrikszeitalter. Oldenbourg, Munich

März E (1968) Österreichische Industrie- und Bankenpolitik in der Zeit Franz Joseph I. Am Beispiel der k. k. priv. Credit-Anstalt für Handel und Gewerbe. Europa Verlag, Vienna

Matis H (1972) Österreichs Wirtschaft 1848–1913. Konjunkturelle Dynamik und gesellschaftlicher Wandel im Zeitalter Franz Josephs I. Duncker & Humblot, Berlin

Matis H, Bachinger K (1973) Österreichs industrielle Entwicklung. In: Brusatti A (ed) Die Habsburgermonarchie 1848–1918, Vol. 1. Die wirtschaftliche Entwicklung. Verlag Akademie der Wissenschaften, Vienna, pp. 105–232

Nyíri J C (1988) Am Rande Europas. Studien zur österreichisch-ungarischen Philosophiegeschichte. Böhlau, Vienna/ Graz.

Pacher S (1996) Die Wirtschaftsentwicklung Österreich-Ungarns von 1867 bis 1914. Eine quantitativ-konjunkturzyklische Analyse. Doctoral dissertation, Universität Graz, Graz

Palotás E (1991) Die Rolle der Wirtschaftsbeziehungen zwischen Österreich-Ungarn und den Balkanländern in den letzten Jahrzehnten des 19. Jahrhunderts. In: Haselsteiner H (ed) Wirtschafts- und Kulturbeziehungen zwischen dem Donau- und dem Balkanraum seit dem Wiener Kongress. Institut für Geschichte, Graz, pp. 65–81

Pierenkemper T (1996) Umstrittene Revolutionen. Die Industrialisierung im 19. Jahrhundert. Fischer, Frankfurt on the Main

Rostow W W (1960) The stages of economic growth. A non-communist manifesto. Cambridge (Massachusetts)

Sandgruber R (1995) Ökonomie und Politik. Österreichische Wirtschaftsgeschichte vom Mittelalter bis zur Gegenwart. Ueberreuther, Vienna

Schall G (2001) Der österreichisch-ungarische Dualismus als Integrationskonzept. Verlag Dr. Kovac, Hamburg

Schiffer J (2001) Karl Wittgenstein und die "Fackel". Eine Kontroverse zwischen literarischer Moderne und ökonomischer Modernisierung. In: Feichtinger J, Stachel P (eds) Das Gewebe der Kultur. Kulturwissenschaftliche Analysen zur Geschichte und Identität Österreichs in der Moderne. Studienverlag, Innsbruck, pp. 269–288

Schorske C E (1980) Fin-de-siècle Vienna: politics and culture. Alfred A. Knopf, New York

Schulze M-S (1996) Engineering and economic growth. The development of Austria-Hungary's machine-building industry in the late nineteenth century. Peter Lang, Frankfurt on the Main

Schulze M-S (1997a) The machine-building industry and Austria's great depression after 1873. Economic History Review 50, pp. 282–304

Schulze M-S (1997b) Economic development in the nineteenth-century Habsburg Empire. Austrian History Yearbook 28, pp. 293–307

Schulze M-S (2007) Origins of catch-up failure: comparative productivity growth in the Habsburg Empire, 1870–1910. European Review of Economic History 11, pp. 189–218.
Online also: http://www.lse.ac.uk/collections/economicHistory/workingPapers.htm.
Accessed 13 August 2008

Steidl A, Stockhammer E (2007) Coming and leaving. Internal mobility in late imperial Austria. Working Paper Series No. 107, Vienna University of Economics, Department of Economics, Vienna

Treue W (1966) Wirtschaftsgeschichte der Neuzeit. Das Zeitalter der technisch-industriellen Revolution 1700 bis 1966, 2nd edn. Alfred Kroener Verlag, Stuttgart

Zweig S (1964) The World of Yesterday ("Die Welt von gestern"). University of Nebraska Press, Omaha (trans. E. a. C. Paul)

9 A Change in the Paradigm for Teaching Mathematics

Wolfgang Hafner*

In the following article we shall be tracing the international socio-economic influences, particularly those specific to Trieste, which laid the foundations for the development of Bronzin's work on premium contracts. The educational system played a central role in institutionalizing certain concepts and ideas. Most notably, there was a change of paradigm in the teaching methodology for mathematics education that was the outcome of a national and international collaborative effort, which culminated in a campaign for improved education. However, significant differences existed not only with regard to how training objectives in teaching were to be implemented, but also with regard to the possibilities for integrating research results into the subject matter – such as, for example, probability theory.

9.1 Economic Development Demands a Change of Paradigm in the Teaching of Mathematics

Towards the end of the nineteenth century there was a strong upsurge in mathematics education all across Europe, owing to the increase demand for technically trained personnel. The cause of this development was the economic transformation taking place in Europe, based on the transition from a more trade-oriented structure of production to industrialized structures of mass production. This structural change required that technical specialists such as engineers gained new skills, since new methods of production had to be developed: During the handcraft production stage of manufacturing, traditional processes that were handed down from master to apprentice predominated; whereas, in the industrial production stage, it became necessary for mathematical and on mathematical models based design ideas to be developed and realized independently (Czuber 1910, p. 1).

This necessitated a fundamentally different approach to education that had to be much more closely oriented to the requirements of the changes taking place in production processes. Consequently, Felix Klein (1849–1925), one of the leading mathematicians of the time, pressed for change in his inaugural lecture for his professorship in mathematics in Erlangen in 1872:

* *whafner@wolfgang-hafner.ch*

> “We urge that more interest be placed in mathematics, more life in your lectures, more intelligence in your treatment of the subject! It is a judgement often heard in student circles that mathematics does not matter. The worst about this is that is it is not far from the truth, as the mathematics taught seldom transmits anything of educational importance. Instead of developing an understanding of mathematical operations, instead of training active observation skills in geometry, time is spent in adopting an empty formalism or in practicing mechanical stunts. Here, one is taught to become a virtuoso at reducing long lines of ciphered expressions, where not one student is able to imagine what they represent [...] However, if one were to expect a student who had been trained in this fashion to be capable of developing his own ideas, [...] not a spur of independent initiative could to be found” (Lorey 1938, p. 20).

Klein was not alone in demanding comprehensive changes in mathematics education, as well as in the associated didactics. The Frenchman, Henri Poincaré (1854–1912), who was, like Felix Klein, one of the most outstanding mathematicians of his day, postulated a programme of didactics that would be more strongly aligned to the personality of the students, laying weight on an organic structural content, suited to the age of the student:

> “The task of the educator is to make the child's spirit pass again where its forefathers have gone, moving rapidly through certain stages but suppressing none of them. In this regard, the history of science must be our guide”.

At the same time, Poincaré emphasized how important it was to promote intuitive understanding in maths lessons:

> “The principal aim of mathematics education is to develop specific intellectual faculties, intuition not being the least precious of these. It is thanks to intuition that the world of mathematics is in touch with the real world [...]” (both excerpts translated from: L’enseignement Mathématique 1899, p. 160).[1]

[1] “*La tâche de l'éducateur est de faire repasser l'esprit de l'enfant par où a passé celui de ses pères, en passant rapidement par certaines étapes mais en n'en supprimant aucune. À ce compte, l'histoire de la science doit être notre guide*” and “*Le but principal de l’enseignement mathématique est de développer certaines facultés de l’esprit, et parmi elles l’intuition n’est pas la moins précieuse. C’est par elle que le monde mathématique reste an contact avec le monde réel* [...]”.

9.2 Internationalization of Mathematics Education

This demand for a new approach to didactics in maths education was well received and supported internationally. In order to spread and implement the new educational ideas, Henri Fehr of Geneva and Charles Ange Laisant of Paris founded the journal "*L'Enseignement Mathématique*" (Mathematics Teaching). Their prime objective here was to strengthen the exchange of information on maths education between different international countries (L'enseignement Mathématique 1899, p. 1). This petition produced a sustained echo. In the following years, inventories of the educational objectives and teaching bodies responsible for different higher levels of education (from gymnasiums to universities) were published in almost all European countries.

The patronage of the journal "*L'Enseignement Mathématique*" was international and listed the names of the most influential international mathematicians. The journal discussed in equal measure both new scientific discoveries and the optimal approaches for training mathematical abilities. Leading mathematicians did not shy away from taking issue on very practical questions regarding instruction.[2] Furthermore, they reported on the contents of the most important foreign mathematics journals and discussed the most significant recent textbooks and reference books.

In 1908 the "International Commission on Mathematical Instruction" (ICMI) was established by members from this circle of mathematicians in Rome, with Felix Klein as its president. Other members were the Swiss Henri Fehr as Secretary General and publisher of the journal "Mathematics Education", as well as the Englishman Alfred George Greenhill.

Already in 1904, on Klein's instigation, a commission of natural scientists and physicians was founded to promote mathematics education, with the sponsorship for it spreading rapidly. While the national commission had the principle aim of improving mathematics at all levels of education within Germany, an international commission had first to carry out a survey on mathematics education in the most influential countries – as had already been petitioned in the journal "*L'enseignement Mathématique*". Furthermore, members of the international commission, the American David Eugene Smith; the Austrian Emanuel Czuber; and the Italian Guido Castelnuovo were selected. Czuber and Castelnuovo were both intensely occupied with probability theory.

[2] See, for example, Henri Poincaré (Paris) and W. Franz Meyer (Königsberg). Poincaré wrote on the topic "La Notation différentielle et l'enseignement" (L'enseignement Mathématique 1899, p. 106ff); Meyer on the topic "Sur l'économie de la pensée dans les mathématiques élémentaires" (L'enseignement Mathématique 1899, p. 261ff).

9.3 Collaboration with Commerce

Whether and how rapidly the growth in industry's new needs could be satisfied or needed to be satisfied was argued adamantly. Felix Klein, who was appointed professor at Göttingen wanted to align Prussia to the French model of the *Ecole Polytechnique* and promote the unification of universities and technical colleges ("*Technische Hochschulen*"). He met with immense resistance. Above all, it were the universities that rejected his postulate, as they saw "*pure mathematics*" at risk of being contaminated by the utilitarian considerations associated with the applied research carried out by the technical colleges. An amalgamation of universities and technical colleges could not be enforced. Technical colleges were thus set up as a system of advanced learning facilities on a level parallel with universities.

Discussions on facilitating the integration and participation of industrial interests in the system of higher education still continued. Once again, it was Felix Klein, at the vanguard of the changes, who forced closer collaboration. He founded a society to promote industry's support for applied physics research. In 1923 Klein said:

> "Picking up on suggestions made in America, it has always been my aim to attract the interest of industrial circles to these ideas in general, and to our Göttinger institute in particular. Although I, for one, am attracted to the thought of bringing ideas to fruition through private initiative, where the public around me expects the intercession of state welfare everywhere, I, nevertheless, found myself drawn more towards the idea of a fruitful mutual liaison and collaborative effort between the quiet scholar and the active, creative, real-world industrialist" (Klein 1923, p. 27).[3]

Representatives from the most prestigious industries became members of "*The Society for the Promotion of Applied Physics*".[4] The question as to how far a "pure" education should be venerated or how closely industry's needs were to be pursued had become an issue of central importance to both to the technical colleges as well as the universities.

[3] "*Den amerikanischen Anregungen folgend, war es von vornherein meine Absicht, industrielle Kreise für diese Gedankengänge im allgemeinen und für unser Göttinger Institut im besonderen zu interessieren. Obwohl mich hierbei der Gedanke reizte, in unserem überall auf Staatshilfe wartenden Volke einmal aus privater Initiative Ideen zur Verwirklichung zu bringen, lag mir dennoch bedeutend mehr an der befruchtenden gegenseitigen Einwirkung, welche ich mir von der Zusammenarbeit des stillen Gelehrten und des im praktischen Leben stehenden schöpferisch tätigen Großindustriellen versprach*".

[4] Among others Krupp, Krauss (Krauss-Maffey), Siemens.

9.4 Specific Specialist Know-How

From the beginning of the nineteenth century, mathematicians had started trying to define the social landscape with the help of statistical methods and to record deviations from the norm more adequately (Gingerenzer 1989, p. 68). With increasing industrialization and the associated erosion of familiar structures, a need grew for new non-family-oriented forms of social security. The Reich Chancellor, Otto von Bismarck, implemented a pension reform for a state pension and invalidity insurance plan in the last quarter of the nineteenth century, which failed its initial trial owing to the lack of supporting statistical data (Pflanze 1998, p. 407). Political interests underlay Bismarck's state insurance system. The pension reform was to forge a strong tie between the working masses and the German state. The reform had the goal of "fostering conservative feelings amongst the large mass of have-nots, generated by the sense of entitlement that pension eligibility was to produce" (Loth 1996, p. 68).[5] The appeal to the need for long-term security in a world which had become more insecure could only be exploited in the interests of political objectives if the necessary statistical and actuarial know-how was available for constructing the models required to guarantee that security. This was why scientific analysis aimed at preparing fundamental data for the insurance industry gained in importance (Czuber 1899, p. 2).

Increasingly towards the end of the eighteen-nineties, forward-looking politicians and university scientists – particularly in German-speaking Europe – set up chairs and lectureships for Insurance Science. In 1895, for example, a seminar for Insurance Economics was opened in Göttingen on the instigation of Felix Klein. As early as 1860, lectures were already held on "Political Arithmetic" for capital and pension insurance at the Vienna Commercial Academy; in 1890 a second private lectureship was established with E. Blaschke posted to it. In 1895 the first course on actuarial practice was held, an example soon followed by the University of Vienna and other universities (Czuber 1910, p. 17).

The French Journal "*L'Enseignement Mathématique*" featured an article entitled, "Actuarial Mathematics", which gave an account of actuarial training in Vienna and of its two educational institutions, its university and technical colleges, which were presented as role models for the whole of Europe. It also praised the fact that the Austrian Federal Ministry of the Interior had introduced the first diploma for actuaries in 1895 (Fehr 1899, p. 450). In contrast to this, just before the end of the century for example, France was noted as having insufficient technical know-how in insurance matters:

[5] "[...] *in der grossen Masse der Besitzlosen die konservative Gesinnung (zu) erzeugen, welche das Gefühl der Pensionsberechtigung mit sich bringt*".

"A few lectures on actuarial science at the *Ecole Polytechnique* would have helped avoid the catastrophes we have seen recently [...]" (L'enseignement Mathématique 1899, p. 148).[6]

9.5 Teaching Probability Theory and Actuarial Techniques

The great demand for mathematicians trained in the technical aspects of insuring was driven primarily by the need that pension insurances had for technical know-how, "even in small places" (Fehr 1899, pp. 447). Nevertheless, actuarial training remained a second choice, and was seen as an escape-hatch for those mathematicians who were unable to take up a position in teaching (Fehr 1899, p. 448). In places densely populated with insurance firms, as was the case in Trieste, which boasted the *RAS* (*Riunione Adriatica Sicurta*) and the *Generali* ("the pride of Austrian assurance"[7]), there was a strong demand for insurance specialist know-how, before the advent of training courses at universities and commercial academies. This knowledge was, not surprisingly, acquired on the job.

The preparatory work which paved the way for the future application of mathematics to insurance techniques had already been accomplished – particularly in physics. The use of models based on probability theory and statistics had a major role to play in the development of new ideas for the future. Maxwell and Boltzmann formulated their Gas Theory, the Maxwell-Boltzmann Distribution, with the help of probability distributions of the speed of individual gas particles.

However, mathematics was not only promoted at university level and expanded with various applied sub-disciplines: The driving idea was to embed mathematics in different levels of the educational system and assign it with specific aims. The priorities set by different countries can also be seen in the syllabi of the preparatory educational levels below university and commercial academy. In countries with strong corporate and commercial structures – such as Austria-Hungary – probability theory and combinatorics were taught at gymnasium level – if to a somewhat limited extent in the normal gymnasiums, more comprehensively in the junior high schools (*Realschule*). Whereas, in countries that had centralistic tendencies, such as France and Germany, these subjects were practically absent.[8] Felix Klein only rudimentarily mentioned probability theory and combinatorics in his Meraner syllabus, which was conceived as an exemplary syllabus for mathematic lessons at gymnasiums. In 1892 this area of mathematics was even taken off the syllabus in Germany and

---

[6] "*Quelques leçons professées à l'école Polytechnique sur la science de l'actuaire auraient évité bien des catastrophes qui se sont produites dans ces dernier temps* [...]".

[7] For more, see: "Der Versicherungsfreund und Volkswirtschaftliche Post", Januar 1903, No.11, p. 2f.

[8] On France, see for example, the commentary on Cantor's book on "*Politische Arithmetik*" in L'Enseignement Mathématique (1899), Vol. 1, p. 147.

only later reintroduced in 1901 (Inhetveen 1976, p. 206f). This was in contrast to the Austro-Hungarian empire where probability calculations were offered at this school level.[9] A broadening of thought and ideas associated with probability concepts must have, therefore, primarily taken place in the Austro-Hungarian area.

Austro-Hungarian commercial academies played a special role in instituting these courses of study, which mainly served to train business specialists; however, following the increasing presence of insurance and pension institutions, the syllabi began to deal with probability and combinatoric calculations.[10] The subject called "Political Arithmetic", which, in addition to the basic principles of probability calculations and compound interest also covered insurance calculations and analysis of mortality tables and the like, enhanced the diffusion of fundamental mathematics-based probability concepts in the classroom. This specialization was facilitated by the spread of commercial academies in the second half of the nineteenth century. Viennese businessmen joined together at this time and founded a private "*Handelsakademie*" (commercial academy), followed by around twenty other commercial academies (Prague, Pest, Vienna, Graz, Linz, Krakow), also mostly initiated by businessmen. At these schools "Political Arithmetic" was taught around 1900 with the same complement of lessons as for common algebra (Dolinsik 1910, p. 20ff).

The reforms of the commercial educational institutions followed a course similar to that of mathematics. There was the same ambition amongst the commercial institutions to communicate information on syllabi and training courses on an international basis as there was with the universities for mathematics. The leading figurehead for commercial education was the Slowene Eugenio Gelcich, who as predecessor to Bronzin, held the directorship of the "*k.u.k. Handels- und Nautische Akademie*" (Imperial and Royal Commercial and Nautical Academy) (Subak 1917, p. 269). Already during his directorship in Trieste, he was simultaneously the central inspector for commercial education for the whole of the Habsburg empire, until he became privy counsellor and senior civil servant to the empire in 1904. Under his aegis, a set of volumes giving a global overview of the training syllabi for the commercial profession appeared (Subak 1917, p. 269ff). He organized international conferences for teachers of commerce; he strove to standardize education in the higher commercial educational institutions; and he introduced a still stronger form of centralization for quality control in education. The nucleus of his efforts was Trieste, where the dissonances of the empire's different peoples were greatest. The motivation of his efforts was the attempt to promote the integration of the different groups through growing trade enhanced by better commercial

[9] For a discussion of the role of combinatorics and probability theory in Germany see: Inhetveen (1976), p. 206f, on Education in Austria: Freud (1910).
[10] In France and Germany, combinatoric, and the probability and insurance theory associated with it, were not part of the subject matter offered by commercial academies. See Gelcich (1908), p. 266ff.

education. For instance, although "*La Scuola Superiore di Commercio Revoltella*" was a commercial school of university stature, founded by a Triestian businessman with the aim of promoting the "*Italianità*" and adamantly supporting the alignment of Trieste to Italy, Gelcich had it funded with a substantial sum of money to ensure its existence (Dlabac and Gelcich 1910, p. 304). The plans to set up an Italian (Law) Faculty in Trieste just before the outbreak of the world war and to fulfil the desire to have an Italian university collapsed with the opposition of the heir apparent, Franz Ferdinand (Engelbrecht 1984, p. 319). A part of Gelcich's plan was to force the expansion of the commercial university in Vienna at which Bronzin was to have taken up a professorship.

9.6 Trieste as a Centre for the Teaching of Applied Probability Theory

That Trieste held a leading position in commercial education and thus also in the teaching of mathematics applied to insurance techniques and the concepts of probability theory can be traced back to certain historical facts. Already, from the time of its foundation in the year 1817, the "*k.u.k. Handels- und Nautischen Akademie*", established in Trieste by Vienna with the centralistic aim of securing its centre of trade, had taught the basics of insurance and probability calculations on its syllabus (Subak 1917, p. 55).[11] During the revision of the syllabus in the subsequent decades, this section was extended. In 1900 Vinzenz Bronzin was appointed to this school as professor for commercial and political arithmetic. Around 1903, the following aspects of probability calculation and insurance techniques were taught on the syllabus:

- absolute, relative and compound probability and mathematical expectancy
- time value and duration of insured capital for life insurance
- calculation of reserves for an insurance, balance sheets of insurance agencies and pensions (Subak 1917, p. 163)

Still – and this is what characterized Trieste as a nucleus for the development of new ideas in the field of probability calculations and their application – the academy was not the only school of higher learning in Trieste in which probability calculations were seriously studied in the last quarter of the nineteenth century: In 1876 the "*Revoltella*" started holding courses. This presented a challenge to the traditional Triestian "*k.u.k. Handels- und Nautische*

[11] The syllabus during the foundation stage provided for: "*delle combinazioni e del probabile per le sicurtà, le tontine, ed altre istituzioni*". "*Tontine*" was a form of life insurance which would accept receipts against payment under the obligation that the capital value be repaid with interest to those investors who should still live when the capital or pension was to be recovered.

Akademie" (Vinci 1997, p. 110ff). Up until 1889, the *Revoltella* was located in the same building as the old "*k.u.k. Handels- und Nautische Akademie*". In the first years of the *Revoltella*'s existence, the professors held lectures at both schools; later, as the ethnic conflicts worsened, the contact between the two schools weakened.[12]

The lessons of the newly founded *Revoltella* concentrated on probability theory. In 1879 the subject of statistics was already widely taught. For example, under the title "*Statistica*":

- statistics and the calculation of probability
- probability theory and social contingencies
- the average age of society, average age of lifespan, and expected longevity (Revoltella 1878).[13]

Three years later this was followed by: "The calculation of means, maximum and minimum values and variability measures, research in the law of statistical regularity, the law of steady-state, growth and causality" as well as the application of statistics: "statistics as a means for investigating the regularities of social life" (Revoltella 1881).[14] In 1889 even the issue of the poor scientific backing that statistics received was part of the curriculum (Revoltella 1888).[15] But the perception of probability as a field of investigation was much more searching than the pursuit of simple statistics.

So in 1882 Giorgio Piccoli, a lawyer and professor at the school, and later its director, published his lectures in a book with the title "*Elementi di Diritto sulle Borse e sulle operazioni di Borsa secondo la Legge Austriaca e le norme della Borsa Triestina, Lezione*" (The elements of governing the stock exchange and trading operations under Austrian law and the rules of the Triest Stock Exchange, Lessons) (Piccoli 1882). In this book, he also analysed the different instruments traded at the stock exchanges, in particular also 'contract for differences' (CFD) and options (Piccoli 1882, p. 35). For him, someone who writes an option is selling an insurance, thereby insuring the other side of the transaction against price fluctuation (Piccoli 1882, p. 38f).[16] Following his line

[12] For example the previous director of the Accademia, Pio Sandrinelli, who was pensioned in 1899, taught also at the Revoltella (Subak 1917, p. 269).

[13] "*La statistica ed il calcolo della probabilità; La teoria della probabilità ed i fatti sociali; L'età media delle popolazioni, la vita media, la vita probabile*".

[14] "*Il computo delle medie, il valore dei massimi, dei minimi e dei numeri di oscillazione, la ricerca delle leggi e regolarità statistiche, le leggi di stato, di sviluppo e di causalità*" and "*la statistica come mezzo di investigazione della regolarità della vita sociale*".

[15] "*Poi si passo ad esporre lo stato odierno della scienza statistica in Europa, e accennare ai principali scrittori ed alle principali opere che vi furono pubblicate; in specie esaminando quelle di Quetelet, di Czörnig, di Bodio, di Mayr-Salvioni, Gabaglio ed altri*".

[16] "*Economicamente il premio va considerato come un premio di assicurazione. Il datore del premio è l'assicurato; il prenditore è l'assicuratore; il danno effettivo ed incerto, che altrimenti in seguito a mutamenti nel prezzo di una merce pattuita a termine lo potrebbe colpire. Anche nel*

of reasoning, having a background in the insurance business, he implicitly relied on the application of mathematical models in analysing such contracts and viewed the price of an option in relation to a possible oscillation of the value of the underlying asset. As a consequence of this, Piccoli emphasised the possibililty of insuring aspects of commercial risks, even credit risk. This was a remarkable insight. In an annotation, he elaborated on this point and argued that both, the credit risk as well as market price risks could be part of a simple commercial insurance contract (Piccoli 1882, annotation 109).[17] This statement opened the possibility for a gifted mathematician to apply mathematics and statistics to the analysis of the risks and potential rewards of derivatives; i.e. forward ("time") and option ("premium") contracts. This is the theoretically background on which Vinzenco Bronzin developed thirty years later his remarkable option pricing theory. He derived solutions for the pricing of premium contracts based on probability theory.

The development of new mathematical models, diverging from the main stream, based on theoretical probability concepts flourished in a broad field scientific research activities and also benefited from mathematicians who worked outside the universities. Significantly, Gustav Flusser, who taught at the Prague commercial academy, as a mathematician and physicist, was the only person to endeavour to further develop Bronzin's model.[18]

The innovative new theoretical approaches to probability theory and insurance techniques at both commercial academies were only of limited interest to the major insurance corporations in Trieste: Graduates of the "*Scuola Superiore di Revoltella*" moved all over Europe, sponsored by different stipends, while the graduates of the Academy mostly remained in Trieste, where only a minority of them found positions of employment in the major insurance companies.[19] The precarious financial state in which the two schools found themselves was another reflection of their unfortunate circumstances and the lack of support from the Trieste administration and economy. According to a newspaper article in 1909, visitors to the Academy noticed that an old-fashioned urinal

> "inevitably flooded the terrace and caused an offensive smell [...]; sometimes windows were falling out of the rotten frames [...]; once

contratto a premio, come nel contratto di assicurazione, il premio limita i pericoli e le speranze del contratto per ambedue i contraenti".

[17] "*Nelle mie lezioni sul contratto di assicurazione rilevai come l'istituto dell' assicurazione sia ormai diretto anche a difendere dai danni che possono derivare dall'esercizio del commercio, sia pel (sic!) pericolo congiunto col credito (star del credere) sia per quello della oscillazione nel prezzo delle merci pattuite a termine (contratti a premio)*".

[18] See Flusser (1910, 1911)! (Juerg Weber pointed us to this article).

[19] In 1904/05 four of the alumni of the Academia got a job by *Generali*, the rest got jobs by banking and trading corporations (I.R. Accademia di Commercio e di Nautica in Trieste 1905). For the *Revoltella* see Vinci (1997), p. 124ff.

> half a frame fell down on the street, luckily without harming anyone".[20]

And concerning the *Revoltella*, Gelcich remarked:

> "The credit institutes, commercial networks and local conditions, such as the chamber of commerce and the borough were hardly interested in the school and were unwilling to make any effective sacrifice" (Dlabac and Gelcich 1910, p. 304f).[21]

The two schools were unable to convince business circles and, especially, the insurance firms in Trieste of the promising opportunities to be derived from good training and the benefits of introducing innovative finance concepts. Under these circumstances, it is not surprising that Bronzin's innovative research was not taken up by the insurance sector. Why it was that the insurance sector remained indifferent to Bronzin's new work is unclear. Possibly, the two insurance companies' orientation in view of the nationalities conflict was of such major consequence that other risks – like the market risks that Bronzin described in his work – remained subordinate.

9.7 Conclusion

Towards the end of the nineteenth century, the transmission of probability theory and its applications were tied up with the needs of the insurance and assurance sectors in their search to find models which could be employed to produce reliable groundwork for planning. The spread of this subbranch of mathematics and the applied research associated with it was unsteady. Particularly in countries which had strong corporative pension structures, there was a wide field of knowledge to draw on, and the training of (insurance) actuaries was promoted. The commercial academies were, for the most part, sponsors of the diffusion of such knowledge within the Austro-Hungarian empire, while Trieste played a central role as the centre of its insurance sector. However, the impetus to innovate that the Triestian commercial academies were pushing for was not supported by the local economy; i.e., the insurance sector.

[20] See: Triester Zeitung, 29th January, 1910.

[21] "*Die Kreditinstitute, die kommerziellen Kreise und die lokalen Faktoren, wie die Handelskammer und die Gemeinde nahmen an der Anstalt nur ein geringes Interesse und brachten für dieselbe keine ausreichenden materiellen Opfer*".

References

Czuber E (1899) In: Mitteilungen des Verbandes oestr. und ung. Versicherungs-Techniker, No. 1. Prochaska, Teschen, p. 22

Czuber E (1910) Der Mathematische Unterricht an den technischen Hochschulen. Vienna

Dlabac F, Gelcich E (1910) Das kommerzielle Bildungswesen in Oesterreich. Vienna

Dolinsik M (1910) Bericht über den mathematischen Unterricht in Oesterreich. Der mathematische und physikalische Unterricht an den höheren Handelsschulen, Vol. 2. Hölder, Vienna

Engelbrecht H (1984) Geschichte des österreichischen Bildungswesens, Erziehung und Unterricht auf dem Boden Oesterreichs, Vol 4. Von 1848 bis zum Ende der Monarchie. Oesterreichischer Bundesverlag, Vienna

Fehr H (1899) La préparation mathématique de l'actuaire. L'Enseignement Mathématique, Revue Internationale, Vol. 1, pp. 447–453

Flusser G (1910, 1911) Ueber die Prämiengrösse bei den Prämien- und Stellagegeschäften. In: Jahresbericht der Prager Handelsakademie, 1910/ 1911. Prague

Freud P (1910) Die mathematischen Schulbücher an den Mittelschulen und verwandten Anstalten: "Bericht über den mathematischen Unterricht in Oesterreich". Vol. 6. Hölder, Vienna

Gelcich E (1908) Das kommerzielle Bildungswesen in Frankreich, Griechenland, Peru, Uruguay, Paraguay und Costa Rica. Hölder, Vienna

Gigerenzer G, Swijtink Z, Porter T et al (1989) The empire of chance: how probability changed science and everyday life. Cambridge University Press, Cambridge

Inhetveen H (1976) Die Reform des gymnasialen Mathematikunterrichts zwischen 1890 und 1914 – eine sozioökonomische Analyse. Verlag Julius Klinkhardt, Bad Heilbronn

I.R. Accademia di Commercio e di Nautica in Trieste (1905) Anno scolastico 1904–1905. Sezione Commerciale. Trieste

Klein F (1923) Göttinger Professoren. Lebensbilder aus eigener Hand. Mitteilungen des Universitätsbundes Göttingen, Vol. 5, Booklet 1

L'enseignement Mathématique (1899) Revue Internationale, 1st Ser., Vol. 1. Geneva

Lorey W (1938) Der Deutsche Verein zur Förderung des mathematischen und naturwissenschaftlichen Unterrichts e.V., 1891–1938, ein Rückblick zugleich auch auf die mathematische und naturwissenschaftliche Erziehung und Bildung in den letzten fünfzig Jahren. Frankfurt on the Main

Loth W (1996) Das Kaiserreich. Obrigkeitsstaat und politische Mobilisierung. Deutscher Taschenbuch Verlag, Munich

Pflanze O (1998) Bismarck: Der Reichskanzler. Beck, Munich

Piccoli G (1882) Elementi di Diritto sulle Borse e sulle operazioni di Borsa secondo la Legge Austriaca e le norme della Borsa Triestina, Lezione. Trieste

Revoltella (1878) Publico corso Superiore d'insegnamento commerciale, Fondazione Rivoltella in Trieste, Anno Scolastico 1878–79. Trieste

Revoltella (1881) Programma di Statistica svolto nell'anno accademico 1881–1882 nella scuola Superiore di Commercio Revoltella. Trieste

Revoltella (1888) Scuola Superiore di Commercio, Fondazione Revoltella in Trieste, Anno Scolastico 1888–89. Trieste

Sedlak V (1948) Die Entwicklung des Kaufmännischen Bildungswesens in Oesterreich in den letzten hundert Jahren. In: Loebenstein E (ed) (1948) 100 Jahre Unterrichtsministerium 1848–1948. Festschrift des Bundesministeriums für Unterricht in Wien. Vienna

Subak G (1917) Cent'Anni d'Insegnamento Commerciale. La Sezione Commerciale della I.R. Accademia di Commercio e Nautica di Trieste. Trieste

Vinci A M (1997) Storia dell'Università di Trieste: Mito, Progetti, Realtà, Quaderni del Dipartimento di Storia. Università di Trieste. Edizioni Lint, Trieste

Review of Bronzin's Book in the „Monatshefte für Mathematik und Physik"

V. Bronzin, Theorie der Prämiengeschäfte. F. Deuticke, Wien, 1908

In zwei Teilen entwickelt der Verfasser die verschiedenen Formeln und die gegenwärtige Beziehung derselben in den börsenmäßigen Prämiengeschäften.

Der erste Teil ist der Aufzählung dieser Formeln gewidmet, während im zweiten Teile versucht wird, Anhaltspunkte für die mathematische Berechnung der Prämien zu geben. Zu diesem Zwecke werden die Prämien für die verschiedenen Börsengeschäfte als Funktionen der Wahrscheinlichkeit von Kursschwankungen dargestellt und für spezielle Gestalten dieser Wahrscheinlichkeitsfunktion ausgerechnet. Es ist kaum anzunehmen, dass die bezüglichen Resultate einen besonderen praktischen Wert erlangen können, wie ja übrigens auch der Verfasser selbst andeutet.

Translation:

V. Bronzin, Theory of Premium Contracts, F. Deuticke, Vienna, 1908

In two parts, the author derives a number of formulae and how they relate to premium contracts.

The first part is dedicated to the presentation of the formulae, while the second part attempts to establish approaches to the mathematical determination of the premia. To this purpose, the premia are represented as functions of the probability of price fluctuations, and calculated with respect to specific forms of this probability function. It is unlikely that the respective results will ever be of notable practical value, as the author himself seems to imply.

Reference

Monatshefte für Mathematik und Physik (1910) Vol. 21. Von Escherich G et al (eds). Universität Wien, Mathematisches Seminar, mit Unterstützung des Hohen K. K. Ministeriums für Kultus (Cultus) und Unterricht. Verlag des Mathematischen Seminars der Universität Wien, Leipzig/ Vienna, Literaturberichte, p 11

10 *Monatshefte für Mathematik und Physik* – A Showcase of the Culture of Mathematicians in the Habsburgian-Hungarian Empire During the Period from 1890 until 1914

Wolfgang Hafner*

When Vinzenz Bronzin published his book "Theorie der Prämiengeschäfte" ("Theory of Premium Contracts"), he received no support from the "Monatshefte für Mathematik und Physik" ("Monthly Bulletin of Mathematics and Physics"), the foremost publishing organ for mathematicians in the Austro-Hungarian empire. On the contrary, his ideas were judged to be of no practical use.[1] This raises questions about the values that guided the mathematicians responsible for the bulletin.

This chapter on the "Monatshefte für Mathematik und Physik" analyses the periodical in an effort to gain insight into the thinking, the working methods, as well as the values and the world view of the leading mathematicians of royal-imperial (i.e. "kaiserlich-königlich" or k. u. k.) Austria-Hungary at the beginning of the 20th century. Owing to the composition of the editorial board, the Monatshefte reflect the attitudes of the opinion leaders amongst the empire's community of mathematicians.[2] Created around 1890, the Monatshefte provided an organ that facilitated the process of identity and tradition building among k. u. k., i.e. Austrian-Hungarian mathematicians.

In this chapter, we argue that specific aspects characteristic of the Austro-Hungarian community of mathematicians supported a preoccupation of the Monatshefte with geometrical and theoretical issues; while on the other hand, emanating from academic disciplines such as actuarial mathematics, applied forms of mathematics began to take hold.

An analysis of the scientific orientation of the Monatshefte – as revealed in the published articles – forms the basis of our discussion. At the same time, by examining obituaries and reviews of recently issued books published in the Monatshefte, we endeavour to achieve a closer understanding of changes and developments in the attitudes and thinking of the mathematicians themselves. This approach rests on the hypothesis that obituaries and book reviews are to a lesser degree subject to constraints of form and content than the scientific papers published in the Monatshefte, and, therefore, may provide a better insight into the "Weltanschauung" (world view) of the authors. According to this assumption, statements contained in obituaries and book reviews may anticipate imminent debates and later developments. After all, formal requirements, the

* *whafner@wolfgang-hafner.ch*
I am grateful to Christa Binder (Vienna) and Tobias Straumann (Zurich) for their comments.

[1] Monatshefte (1910), Vol. 21, Literaturberichte, p. 11: "*Es ist kaum anzunehmen, dass die bezüglichen Resultate einen besonderen praktischen Wert erlangen können [...]*". Translation: "It is unlikely that the respective results will ever be of notable practical value [...]".

[2] Cf Chapter 2.

axiomatic approach and the presentation of arguments in strictly logical fashion typical of scientific papers are likely to be present to a far lesser extent in obituaries and book reviews. Scientific parameters, however, constrain an author's scope of expression – or make it more difficult to decode the cultural, social and philosophical background of an article. By contrast, reviews and obituaries are hardly constrained by similar formal provisions.[3]

Our analysis is inevitably of a restricted nature in that it covers only 24 years, i.e. the period from the founding of the *Monatshefte* until the onset of World War I. Moreover, the periodical represents an extract of the scientific discourse amongst *k. u. k.* mathematicians of the time.[4]

10.1 Internationalisation and the Advance of Science

As explained in a 1935 obituary for the founding member Gustav von Escherich, the *Monatshefte* had been established to provide Austrian mathematicians with an opportunity to publish articles, "because, considering the vibrant scientific activities in Germany, the work of Austrian mathematicians – situated in a remote position vis-à-vis the centres of mathematical research – could hope to be included in the German periodicals only as a secondary option".[5] Hence, the *Monatshefte* attempted to enable representatives of the Habsburgian-Hungarian scientific periphery to develop a position of their own vis-à-vis the centre of scientific activities in Germany, and to present themselves to an international audience.

During its initial phase from 1890 to 1899, a little over two thirds of the articles published in the *Monatshefte* were written by Austrian authors; from 1900 to 1909 the number fell to 57 percent. The share of articles by authors from other parts of the *k. u. k.* empire increased in the same period from approximately 15 to 20 percent, while the share of scientific contributions by German authors increased from 6 to 12 percent. Contributions by mathematicians from other nations (Swiss, French, Dutch etc.) remained largely unchanged at a level between 11 and 13 percent.[6] From about 1900 onwards, the periodical began to open itself up slightly, offering other mathematicians a platform for publication. Until World War I, a retained tendency toward a more international selection of authors continued. In the 1914 issue, six out of a total of twelve authors resided within the empire's core territory, i.e. today's Austria; two were from other parts of the Habsburg empire (Chernivtsi and Prague), two authors indicated German cities as place of residence (Bierstadt and Munich), while the Dane Niels Nielsen

[3] Cf explanatory note 25.

[4] Further areas that should be dealt with in a comprehensive analysis are the proceedings of the *Akademie der Wissenschaften* (Academy of Sciences) and other periodicals.

[5] Wirtinger, W.: Obituary on Gustav von Escherich, Monatshefte (1935), Vol. 42, p. 2ff.

[6] Monatshefte (1899), Vol. 10, index volume 1–10 and Monatshefte (1909), Vol. 20, alphabetical index for the volume 11–20.

from Copenhagen was able to publish two articles.[7] During this period, there was an increase in the number of authors residing outside of the Habsburgian-Hungarian empire.

This opening to accommodate international developments was part of a multi-faceted long-term program.[8] There were efforts to encourage a linguistic-cultural opening-up amongst mathematicians. For example, they were urged to study other important European languages, to be able to read foreign contributions in the original.[9] The *Monatshefte* reflect this trend. In growing numbers, foreign articles were published – albeit irregularly. However, shortly before World War I, the numbers increased.[10] In this way, a contribution was made to the intended international orientation of Austro-Hungarian mathematicians.[11]

During the course of the examined period until 1914, the *Monatshefte* reflect a surge of articles clearly striving to achieve higher standards in terms of the formal requirements of science. The articles reveal a growing apparatus of footnotes and references, while from 1896 onwards a new section was introduced – *"Literatur-Berichte"*, later *"Literaturberichte"*, (reviews of literature) – serving as a discursive forum to promote reflections on scientific publications. From this time onwards, increasingly, some authors would add initials or their full name to the review articles. It may be safely assumed that unsigned reviews were written by the *Monatshefte* editors.

These formal novelties are a sign of the alignment of the *Monatshefte* within international scientific context. Thus, the footnotes enabled readers to follow up on the sources and other pertinent information relating to an article.[12] Identifying the author gained currency which gave readers outside the Vienna circle of mathematicians an opportunity to get to know the author of a review, or even to contact him directly. At the time of the periodical's inauguration, the readership would have learned of the author in informal ways, but this changed with increased circulation. By signing a review, the authors gained a public profile outside the Vienna circle.

[7] Monatshefte (1914), Vol. 25.

[8] Until 1850, mathematics had virtually no significance at the University of Vienna. There were few foreign contacts. To deal with this shortcoming, upon completion of their doctoral thesis, students of outstanding talent were sent to the centres of mathematics in Berlin, Göttingen, Paris and Milan (Binder 2003, p. 2).

[9] Monatshefte (1901), Vol. 12, Literaturberichte, p. 12.

[10] Monatshefte (1909): Godeaux, Lucien, Liège, "Sur une coincidence bicubique", p. 269ff; Monatshefte (1910): W.H. Young, Cambridge, "On parametric integration", p. 125ff; Monatshefte (1913): Teixeira, F. Gomes, Porto, "Sur les courbes à développées intermédiares circulaire", p. 347ff and Dodd, Edward L., Austin, "The error-risk of certain functions of the measurements", p. 268ff.

[11] As early as 1891, in the second issue we find an article by Carvallo E., Paris, entitled "Sur les systèmes linéaires, le calcul des symboles differentiels et leur application à la physique mathématique" Monatshefte (1891), Vol. 2, p. 177ff.

[12] On footnotes cf: Burke (2002), p. 243f.

10.2 *Monatshefte* – Editors and Issuance

At any given time, the position of editor of the "*Monatshefte für Mathematik und Physik*" was held by two or three full professors at the University of Vienna, who would ordinarily also be members of the *Akademie der Wissenschaften.* The founders of the *Monatshefte* were the two mathematicians Gustav von Escherich and the emeritus professor Emil Weyr, who already in 1888 had envisaged the idea of publishing an Austrian mathematical periodical.[13] Escherich and Weyr were leading figures amongst the elite of mathematicians in Austria-Hungary. Born in Mantua in 1849 as the son of an officer, von Escherich was full professor of mathematics at Vienna university from 1884 to 1920; from 1892 he was "*wirkliches Mitglied der kaiserlichen und königlichen Akademie der Wissenschaften*", from 1904 he was "*Obmann*" of the newly established *Mathematische Gesellschaft* (Mathematical Society) in Vienna and the university's vice-chancellor ("*Rektor*") in 1903/04 (Binder 2003, p. 12ff). Born in Prague in 1848 as the son of a professor of mathematics, Emil Weyr hailed from Bohemia and experienced a phenomenal career. "Smooth and bright was his career, void of struggles and need", writes his chronicler Gustav Kohn. At the age of only 27, Weyr was appointed full professor at Vienna university: he published scientific papers in four languages, but died shortly after the inception of the *Monatshefte* in 1894.[14]

Leopold Gegenbauer assumed Weyr's position on the editorial board of the *Monatshefte.* Born in 1849, Gegenbauer was versatile and gifted in languages; having first studied history and Sanskrit, he then changed to mathematics, pursued later academic research under Weierstrass (Karl Theodor Wilhelm Weierstraß, 1815–1897) in Berlin, and after a short interlude in Chernivtsi, he was appointed full professor in Innsbruck. In 1893 he was appointed full professor at the University of Vienna. The obituary dedicated to him emphasises his activities relating to the insurance industry.[15]

In 1903, Franz Mertens joined the editorial board of the *Monatshefte*. Born in Poland, Mertens spent several years as professor of mathematics in Cracow and Graz: he received a professorship in Vienna in 1894, at the age of 54. He occupied himself with the number theory, the theory of invariants and the theory of elimination.

When Gegenbauer died in 1903, his editorial position was taken by von Escherich's student Wilhelm Wirtinger. The same year, aged 38, Wirtinger had been appointed full professor at University of Vienna (Binder 2003, p. 14). Until World War I, the editorial board was formed by the triumvirate consisting of von Escherich, Mertens and Wirtinger. It is likely that von Escherich, who acted as

[13] Wirtinger, W.: Obituary on Gustav von Escherich, Monatshefte (1935), Vol. 42, p. 3.
[14] Kohn, G.: Obituary on Emil Weyr, Monatshefte (1895), Vol. 6, p. 1ff.
[15] Stolz, O.: Obituary on Leopold Gegenbauer, Monatshefte (1904), Vol. 15, p. 2ff.

editor throughout the entire period, was the dominant figure. At any rate, he was an assertive and redoubtable lobbyist.[16]

Not long after the inception of the *Monatshefte*, the editors assumed responsibility for the publishing tasks. The first two volumes of the *Monatshefte* were published by *Manz'sche Hof-Verlags- und Universitäts-Buchhandlung* in Vienna, but in 1892 a new arrangement took effect: The *Verlag des Mathematischen Seminars* (the publishing house of the Department of Mathematics) of the University of Vienna took on the task; and from 1894 distribution was handled by the *Wiener Buchhandlung J. Eisenstein*. It is not clear – from reading the *Monatshefte* – why the Department of Mathematics would take care of the publishing tasks. The technical preparation of the *Monatshefte* for publication is likely to have been complex and costly, considering the large number of formulae and graphic representations that tend to accompany mathematical publications. Transferring the publishing tasks from a private publishing house to the Department of Mathematics increased the economic leeway of the editors.

The term "*Monatshefte*" is misleading, since it suggests a monthly publication. Perhaps it had been envisioned initially to produce monthly issues, a possibility suggested by the fact that in the first issues some of the contributions were published in sequels.[17] However, the ambition to publish in regular monthly intervals never came to fruition.

10.3 Identity Building in the Community of Mathematicians

Representing the most important means of written communication within the community of mathematicians in the *k u. k.* empire, the *Monatshefte* journals were strongly influenced by the various currents within the scientific discipline of mathematics. Mathematics is a generic term, but includes the sub-disciplines of arithmetic and geometry which in turn comprise different branches with their own specific approaches, depending on the number of axioms underlying the respective constructs of ideas. The followers of these constructs form "schools", as it were.[18] Characterised by social structures similar to those of clans or families, these schools cultivate and disseminate specific epistemic content based on generally accepted standards. The process of identifying the affiliation of a mathematician with a "school" seeks to establish his or her position within a branch network essentially akin to a genealogical tree, relying thereby on the

[16] See Meinong and Adler (1995), p. 17ff.

[17] For more on the contributions published in sequels see inter alia Haubner, J.: "Ueber Strombrechung in flächenförmigen Leitern", Monatshefte (1890), Vol. 1, p. 247ff and 357ff or by Carvallo, E.: "Sur les systèmes linéaires, le calcul des symboles différentiels et leur application à la physique mathématique", Monatshefte (1891), Vol. 2, p. 177ff, p. 225ff and 311ff.

[18] Note the debates conducted on the fundamentals of geometry around 1900 (Scriba and Schreiber 2001, p. 474).

course of studies followed and academic degrees achieved.[19] To this day, historical reviews register who was whose student, and therefore may be considered heir to a certain epistemic tradition.[20] As analogous to genealogical research of ancestors and relatives, so family trees of scientific-intellectual affiliations and influences are arrived at.

In these family trees, certain outstanding personalities are accorded the function of role models. Small wonder that around 1914 the *Monatshefte* favourably reviewed the third edition (1912) of a book entitled "*Gedenktagebuch für Mathematiker*" (Memorial Diary for Mathematicians). Facts surrounding the birth of great mathematicians are expanded in the book, to deliberate over their works. The author of the review in the *Monatshefte* comments on the book thus:

> "With affectionate care, the author has achieved completion of a treatise that provides mathematicians with a calendar of feast days commemorating the giants in their field".[21]

Ancestor worship of this kind is indicative of a paternalistically oriented memorial culture relying on "great names" and outstanding role models. The cult of memorial days for the great among mathematicians corresponds to the traditional feast days dedicated to Catholic saints and recorded in demotic calendars of saints, whose purpose is to accompany the faithful – through the course of the year – with reminders of the works and deeds of the holy. This memorial cult is part of an archaic mechanism known from traditional societies, being instrumental in preserving certain features characteristic of and formative to a social group. In this way, a common group identity is created under the auspices of a central figure, the obituaries representing another act of solemn commemoration. Mathematicians are not exempted from the practice.

However, in the *Monatshefte*, solemn commemoration is not the sole prerogative of the leading figures. To some extent, the obituaries are a means for the mathematicians – perceiving themselves as a community of common destiny – to collectively and publicly come to grips with grief and thus to strengthen their collective identity. As if to protest the hardships of life, Emil Müller, full professor of geometry at *Technische Hochschule Wien*, penned an obituary on the promising young geometer Ludwig Tuschel, who had been consumed by tuberculosis at the age of 27.[22] The obituary's emphasis on the young assistant's passion makes it an exemplary document:

---

[19] See for a modern variant of this mnemonic structure the "Mathematics Genealogy Project" at North Dakota State University: http://genealogy.math.ndsu.nodak.edu.

[20] See for an example Binder (2003), p. 13, where the students of von Escherich and Wirtinger are listed.

[21] Monatshefte (1914),Vol. 25, Literaturberichte, p. 15.

[22] Müller, E.: Obituary on Ludwig Tuschel, Monatshefte (1914), Vol. 25, p. 177ff.

> "Anyone who gained closer insight into this vibrant geometrical imagination is compelled, in the interest of science, to deeply deplore the most untimely annihilation of this talented young man – offspring of a healthy family – through the treacherous ailment of tuberculosis, and furthermore, precluding him for a long time beforehand from devoting himself to the fervent urge of scientific activity".

An obituary like this is no longer of the type that seeks to establish the historical significance of a leading figure's scientific work, serving much rather to enact an emotive, public farewell to a human being cut off in his prime. In this way, identity building is not so much a matter of dealing with factual issues; instead it is sought on the emotional level, as is characteristic of an emotionally involved, family-like group. It is not rare for obituaries published in the *Monatshefte* to reveal considerable emotive intensity. It would be instructive to examine whether the degree of sobriety of the obituaries is negatively correlated with the tendency of the main articles to increasingly incorporate the hallmarks of rigorous science. While the style of the early obituaries from 1890 was rather sober, those appearing later become more and more emotional.

10.4 Geometry and "Pure" Mathematics Dominate the Choice of Subject Matter in the *Monatshefte*

Towards the end of the 19th century, geometry held a dominant position in mathematics. In parallel with this, around the turn of the century a more applied approach to mathematics began slowly to take hold in the universities. Encouraged by Felix Klein, the first chair in Germany for applied mathematics was established in 1904 (Scriba and Schreiber 2001, p. 507). The new trend is reflected to some extent in the *Monatshefte*. In obituaries on some of the editors, Gegenbauer e.g., the new focus on applied mathematics is given emphasis. Gegenbauer is said to have stated:

> "The 20th century is the century of technology: we should orient ourselves toward technology, unless we intend to condemn ourselves to atrophy [...]"[23]

In the obituaries on both von Escherich and Gegenbauer, the point is prominently made that they had been decisively instrumental in establishing a chair of actuarial mathematics.[24]

[23] Stolz, O.: Obituary on Leopold Gegenbauer Monatshefte (1904), Vol. 15, p. 7.

The *Monatshefte* hardly reflect these developments in applied science which were based on arithmetic procedures and sought to achieve calculability. On the contrary: throughout the entire period examined here, the themes pursued in the scientific articles published in the *Monatshefte* reveal a largely unchanged course, aligned to the discussion of geometrical and other theoretical problems.

In fact, almost two thirds of the contributions contained in the early volumes of the *Monatshefte* dealt with geometrical issues. Aspects bearing on physics are presented only to the extent that they depend on mathematical considerations.[25] Thus, there is no article in the *Monatshefte* by Ludwig Boltzmann, the outstanding personality of Austria-Hungary's mathematical-physical republic of letters. This is surprising, since the first issue of the *Monatshefte*, containing an article "On the theory of ice-formation" by J. Stefan, the physicist and doctoral advisor to Boltzmann, could have created the basis for more extensive publishing activities by physicists.[26]

The *Monatshefte* were even less concerned with other problems of applied mathematics than with practical issues of physics. A few miscellaneous articles addressed issues such as ballistic problems.[27] Only one article deals with problems of demography (that is, mathematical statistics), and this was contributed by the same Prussian author who had written about ballistic problems.[28] It appears that the treatment of topics not squarely in line with the preferred issues of the *Monatshefte* was left to mathematicians from outside Austria-Hungary.

There were no contributions relating to actuarial mathematics, although some of the editors of the *Monatshefte*, e.g. Gustav von Escherich and Leopold Gegenbauer, actively encouraged the impartment of actuarial literacy.[29] During the period in question, only four articles on probability theory appeared, some of

[24] Karl Bobek; too, was "*wissenschaftlicher Beirat*" (scientific advisor) to an accident insurance company, Monatshefte (1900), Vol. 11, p. 98. The large number of advisory assignments of mathematicians in insurance companies is related to the fact that the *k. u. k.* empire relied on private-sector solutions to retirement provisions and disability insurance.

[25] Articles on physics problems mostly deal with subjects such as these: "Ueber Strombrechung in flächenförmigen Leitern" (Haubner J., in Monatshefte (1890), Vol. 1, p 247ff and 357ff) or "Ueber die Schwingungen von Saiten veränderlicher Dichte" (Radaković M., in Monatshefte (1894), Vol. 5, p. 193ff), "Zur mathematischen Theorie der Verzweigung von Wechselstromkreisen mit Inductanz" (Kobald E., in Monatshefte (1903), Vol. 14, p. 133ff).

[26] Stefan, J.: "Ueber die Theorie der Eisbildung" (On the theory of ice-formation), Monatshefte (1890), Vol. 1, p. 1ff.

[27] For instance: Oekinghaus, E., Königsberg in Pr.: "Die Rotationsbewegungen der Langgeschosse während des Fluges" (Rotary motion of long [high length to diameter ratio] projectiles in flight), Monatshefte (1907), Vol. 18, Part 1, p. 245ff and Monatshefte (1909), Vol. 20, Part 2, p. 55ff. And by the same author: "Das ballistische Problem auf hyperbolisch-lemniskatischer Grundlage" (The ballistic problem from a hyperbolic-lemniscatic perspective), Monatshefte (1904), Vol. 15, p. 11ff.

[28] Oekinghaus, E.: "Die mathematische Statistik in allgemeinerer Entwicklung und Ausdehnung auf die formale Bevölkerungstheorie", (Mathematical statistics, generalised and extended to deal with the formal theory of population) Monatshefte (1902), Vol. 13, p. 294ff.

[29] Wirtinger, W.: Obituary on Gustav von Escherich, Monatshefte (1935), Vol. 42, Part 1, p. 4.

them rather brief, one having been first published in English, one appearing in the first issue of the *Monatshefte* in 1890, and another two appearing in the second issue in 1891.[30] An amazing fact, considering that Ludwig Boltzmann's research based on statistics and probability considerations represented the cutting edge throughout the world. What is more, at the time there was a surge in probability reasoning which was reflected in a number of text books and publications on "political arithmetic".[31] The mathematical scholars of Austria-Hungary that were leading figures in the calculus of probability and kindred subjects such as actuarial mathematics proceeded with their publications by a detour that would take them to periodicals dedicated either to higher education or the insurance industry. Alternatively, their contributions appeared in German periodicals.[32]

In emphasising geometry very strongly, the *Monatshefte* gave exaggerated expression to a then-current trend. At the time when the *Monatshefte* was delving deeply into issues of geometry, the subject had already reached its zenith. During the first half of the 20th century, geometry increasingly lost its pre-eminent position within the science of mathematics (Scriba and Schreiber 2001, p. 2).

10.5 Forms of Geometry

The scientific articles published in the *Monatshefte* were very supportive of a specific number of schools of thought. Above all, the founders of the *Monatshefte*, Weyr and von Escherich, had their own preferred approaches to the study of mathematics, and handed these on to their students.[33] For example, Gustav von Escherich's thesis of habilitation (Graz, 1874) dealt with "*Die Geometrie auf den Flächen konstanter Krümmung*" (The geometry of surfaces of constant curvature). Later, he devoted himself to the infinitesimal calculus, and was a follower of the methods associated with Weierstrass.

Weyr was a representative of so-called "synthetic geometry", which relied on a restricted number of logically consistent and precisely defined tenets to expand heuristic and calculatory models. The methodology of "synthetic geometry" is described by Gustav Kohn in his obituary on Weyr:

---

30 Dodd, Erward L.: The Error Risk of Certain Functions of the Measurments, Monatshefte (1913), p. 268ff; the first article was written by Czuber and published in the first issue of the Monatshefte: "Zur Theorie der Beobachtungsfehler" (On the theory of observational errors), pp. 457–465, he published another article in 1891: "Zur Kritik einer Gauss'schen Formel" (Critique of a Gaussian formula), p. 459f, and he also published in the Monatshefte of 1891: Müller Fr.: "Zur Fehlertheorie (On the theory of errors). Ein Versuch zur strengeren Begründung derselben" (An attempt at a rigorous derivation), p. 61ff.

31 Bronzin (1906), too, authored a text book of this kind: "Lehrbuch der Politischen Arithmetik (Text book of political arithmetic)".

32 See for instance Czuber (1899), p. 279ff and Czuber (1898), p. 8ff.

33 Wirtinger, W.: Obituary on Gustav von Escherich, Monatshefte (1935), Vol. 42, p. 2f and Kohn, G.: Obituary on Emil Weyr, Monatshefte (1895), Vol. 6, p. 4.

> "From a known quality of a geometrical object, one derives a new (equivalent) quality that resides in a certain algebraic correspondence. In a certain way, that quality appears to have a more abstract form and to be detached from that particular object. It is thus amenable to a transformation into the qualities found in the most diverse objects, with regard to which we succeed in producing a correspondence by way of certain geometrical constructions".[34]

In addition, von Escherich and Weyr promoted the geometrical way of thinking also for didactic reasons, since they considered it paramount to advance the capacity for spatial visualisation in the new generation of natural scientists.[35] Another motivating aspect was provided by the observation that the teaching of differential geometry was seriously deficient in German-speaking regions.[36] Consequentially, in the first issues of the *Monatshefte* in 1890 and 1891, articles on geometry were published dealing with the following subjects:

- "*Grundzüge einer rein geometrischen Theorie der Collineation und Reciprocitäten*" (Basics of a purely geometrical theory of collineation and reciprocity) (Ameseder, A.)
- "*Ueber die Relationen, welche zwischen den verschiedenen Systemen von Berührungskegelschnitten einer allgemeinen Curve vierter Ordnung bestehen*" (On the relations prevailing between different systems of conic sections in a general curve of the fourth order) (Kohn, G.)
- "*Die Schraubenbewegung, das Nullsystem und der lineare Complex*" (The screw movement, the nullsystem and the linear complex) (Küpper, C.)
- "*Das Potential einer homogenen Ellipse*" (The potential of a homogenous ellipse) (Mertens, F.)
- "*Ueber orthocentrische Poltetraeder der Flächen zweiter Ordnung*" (On orthocentric poltetrahedra of second order surfaces) (Machovec, F.)
- "*Ueber die Beleuchtungscurven der windschiefen Helikoide*" (On the illuminated curves of skew helicoids) (Schmid, T.)

---

[34] Monatshefte (1895), Vol. 6, p. 2: "*Aus einer bekannten Eigenschaft eines geometrischen Gebildes wird eine neue (ihr äquivalente) Eigenschaft einer gewissen algebraischen Correspondenz abgeleitet. Jene Eigenschaft erscheint dadurch gewissermassen abstracter gefasst und von dem besonderen Gebilde losgelöst. Sie lässt sich jetzt in Eigenschaften der verschiedensten Gebilde umsetzen, an denen es gelingt, eine Correspondenz der betrachteten Art durch irgendwelche geometrischen Constructionen hervorzurufen*".

[35] Monatshefte (1905), Vol. 16, Literaturberichte, p. 53.

[36] Monatshefte (1903), Vol. 14, Literaturberichte, p. 4.

This attests to a trend, still prevalent toward the end of the 19th century, to accord geometry priority, whilst the subject had already begun to fan out into a diversity of sectors.[37]

It is interesting in how far specific cultural and social factors may encourage and shape a certain attitude toward specific mathematical disciplines. In their book "*5000 Jahre Geometrie*" (5000 years of geometry), mathematicians Scriba and Schreiber propose the idea that alongside a "professional, deductive mathematics", there is "a non-professional and subliminal mathematics which finds expression in the intuitive application of concepts, forms and procedures, that is, in forms of knowledge and skills not expressly couched in verbal terms, yet available as the material product of certain techniques, artisanry and art" (Scriba and Schreiber 2001, p. 3). Taking into consideration this idea, there seems to be a rather obvious affinity of geometrical thinking with the kind of *Jugendstil*, especially its ornamentation, moulded largely by Viennese artists, whose geometrical figures are less inspired by a rationalist style – as develeoped by M.C. Escher – than by "natural processes". Geometry's references to the graphical-artistic as well as the playful variants of the *Jugendstil* may be another explanation of the importance accorded to geometry in the Habsburgian-Hungarian empire.[38] At any rate, the border area between geometical and artistic drawing was blurred in the 19th century. Rudolf Staudigl, elected in 1875 to serve as full professor of descriptive geometry at the *Polytechnikum* of Vienna, taught both technical and freehand drawing during his earlier academic lecturing career. Upon concluding his studies, and prior to becoming a lecturer, he acted as an assistant teaching descriptive geometry, in which capacity he was required to give drawing lessons and offer lectures on ornamentation.[39]

The philosopher Edmund Husserl, probably one of the most famous students of Emil Weyr, refers in his late work to aspects that may represent further

[37] In their book "5000 years of geometry", Scriba and Schreier list the below aspects as essential topics in 19th century geometry:

- further development of descriptive geometry: inter alia, multiplane method, central perspective, illumination geometry
- projective geometry: including invariance of cross-ratios, points at infinity, straight lines, planes, "*Geometrie der Lage*"
- theory of geometrical constructions: inter alia, theory of the division of the circle, algebraic methods to prove the impossibility of doubling the cube and trisecting an angle with compass and straightedge.
- differential geometry: inter alia curvature and torsion of spatial curves, theory of curvilinear surfaces in space, spaces of constant curvature are homogenous and isotropic
- non-euclidian geometry: proof of the existence on "non-euclidean" geometries and refutation of the euclidean parallel postulate
- the vector concept and n-dimensional geometry: inter alia magnetic and electric "vector fields", rotation, divergence, calculation with complex numbers as vectors, *Anfänge der Topologie* (origins of topology) cf p. 448f; the enumeration is incomplete.

[38] On the close connection between the art of drawing and mathematics in the 19th century see also Scriba and Schreiber (2001), p. 521.

[39] N. N.: Obituary on Rudolf Staudigl, Monatshefte (1891), Vol. 2, p. 480.

reasons for the exceptional importance of geometry in Vienna. Husserl considers geometry the ideal embodiment, the most fundamental acme of science. Husserl's argument runs as follows: the scientific ideal of "precision" and that of lucid and open boundaries so central to geometry, is reflected in the corresponding phenomenological concept of *Reinheit* (purity), which is equally predicated on lucidity and demarcation (Scarfo 2006, p. 51). Geometry, or rather, the qualities of demarcation and lucidity ascribed to it, would appear an antagonism vis-à-vis the chiefly instinct-driven, playful, and emotionally charged Vienna *Jugendstil.*

Regarding the methodology of mathematical proofs, the counterpart to geometrical precision is the "*äusserste Strenge*" (utter rigor) in the Weierstrassian vein, which both von Escherich and Weyr are thought to have adhered to.[40] In his book "*Vorlesungen über die Entwicklung der Mathematik im 19. Jahrhundert*" (Lectures on the development of mathematics in the 19th century), Felix Klein considers that "[...] the contemporary generation is accustomed to looking at Weierstrass as a representative of pure mathematics alone" (Klein 1979, p. 282).[41] At the same time, in those days turf wars were being waged between the various mathematical schools. It is conceivable that this desire for *Reinheit* (purity) and demarcation is reflected in von Escherich's inaugural address delivered on the occasion of his assuming the position of Vice-Chairman *("Rektor")* of the university. In this speech, he opposes the usurpation of mathematics by the engineering sciences:

> "There is neither a royal nor an engineering road to mathematics; to try to advance mathematics as as mere appendage of applied science is to divest it of its general nature, thus destroying an inestimable means of deeper insight" (von Escherich 1903).[42]

This attitude is suggestive of an attempt to maintain mathematics as a discipline of *Reinheit* (purity), which may be expected to be associated with a negative posture vis-à-vis alternatives and other schools of thought.

While the bulk of scientific articles published in the *Monatshefte* dealt with geometrical issues and themes not too close to applied concerns, this is not to say that "geometrical problems" represented the sole subject matter and that,

[40] Weierstrass acquired an exceptional reputation especially by pursuing a logically sound reconstruction of mathematical analysis; cf also Binder (2003), p. 12.

[41] "*Die heutige Generation ist gewöhnt, in Weierstrass einen Vertreter ausschliesslich der reinen Mathematik zu sehen*". However, Klein qualifies his statement by making reference to a quote in which Weierstrass points out that he "is not entirely unwelcoming to the application of mathematics, and certainly does not oppose it" (*den Anwendungen der Mathematik doch nicht ganz fern steht und sie keineswegs ablehnt* (p. 283)). Klein conducted this lecture during World War I.

[42] "*So wenig als einen Königsweg gibt es in der Mathematik einen Ingenieursweg, und sie gleichsam als Anhängsel der Anwendung entwickeln, hiesse sie ihres allgemeinen Charakters entkleiden und damit ein unschätzbares Instrument unserer Erkenntnis unbrauchbar machen*".

therefore, a hard and fast demarcation vis-à-vis other disciplines reigned supreme. In fact, there was considerable overlap and problems of delineation with regard to an arithmetic versus a geometrical approach to mathematical problems, as can be seen from the widespread interest taken by Viennese mathematicians in "*geometrische Wahrscheinlichkeit*" (geometrical probability). Teaching in Vienna, in 1884 Emanuel Czuber was the first to write a book in German on geometrical probability, which established his renown as a mathematician (Scriba and Schreiber 2001, p. 447). Around 1900, Czuber published an article entitled "*Wahrscheinlichkeitsrechnung*" (calculus of probability) in "*Encyklopädie der Mathematik und ihrer Grenzgebiete*" (Encyclopaedia of mathematics and adjacent subjects), a well known encyclopaedia issued by leading German-speaking scientists.[43] Years later, another Viennese, W. Blaschke, coined the term "*Integralgeometrie*" (integral geometry) to denote this area of study (Scriba and Schreiber 2001, p. 447).

Thus, methodologically the path had been paved for the years later realized transition from geometrical to arithmetic subjects. Thus, Weierstrass' analysis was essentially predicated on the tenet that an evenly convergent series of functions will converge toward a continuous limit function. This is tantamount to the metric completeness of "the space of continuous functions on M" with respect to the maximum norm of this vector space (Scriba and Schreiber 2001, p. 489). In this way, metric mathematics becomes a key element for the transfer of geometrical concepts into other branches of mathematics.

10.6 Scientific Articles, Book Reviews, and Obituaries

It was five years after the establishment of the *Monatshefte*, i.e. beginning only in 1895, that reviews started to appear in the periodical of newly published books on mathematics, physics and the didactics of these subjects, under the heading "*Literatur-Berichte*" or "*Literaturberichte*" (reviews of literature). Before long, the reviews would prove very popular; by 1897, 55 new books were discussed. In 1902, the number of reviews increased to 105. In the following years, the number of reviews remained large, collaborators and editors of the *Monatshafte* reviewing up to one hundred or even more new publications every year. What induced the authors to write up a review can only be a matter of surmise. In certain cases material incentives may have played a role; the reviewer could keep the reviewed book. A momentous consideration for a reviewer was the prospect of using the book as a means to directly or indirectly present his own views and thoughts to the readership.

The number of obituaries is considerably lower than the number of book reviews. From 1890 to 1914, a total of 11 obituaries were published in the *Monatshefte* (Adolf Ameseder, Rudolf Staudigl and Josef Petzval in the *Monats-*

[43] Volume 1: Arithmetik und Algebra, Part 2, pp. 733–768.

hefte of 1891; Franz Machovec and Anton Winckler in the *Monatshefte* of 1892, Emil Weyr (1895), Karl Bobek (1900), Leopold Gegenbauer (1904), Wilhelm Weiss (1905), Otto Stolz (1906), Ludwig Boltzmann (1907), and Ludwig Tuschel (1914)).

While the scientific papers published in the *Monatshefte* primarily presented the (most recent) research results of Habsburgian-Hungarian mathematicians to other groups of researchers, the objective of the book reviews was to open a window for mathematicians from which to follow research conducted in the rest of Europe and thus to keep up with international developments. The book reviews served the mathematicians of the Habsburgian-Hungarian empire as a means of scientific communication, providing them with information on (and an interface with) worldwide developments in mathematics. At the same time, the reviews provided a platform for reflections and discussions on developments in one's own "sovereign territory".

The bulk of reviews dealt with publications from German-speaking regions; however, increasingly, French publications were discussed, and also, sporadically, papers written in English, Italian, even in Esperanto.[44] The linguistic focus reflects the topics emphasised in the *Monatshefte*: From a mathematician's point of view, France was one of the leading nations, not least thanks to the outstanding personality of Henri Poincaré, who became corresponding member (1903) and honorary member (1908) of the *kaiserliche und königliche Akademie der Wissenschaften* (the royal and imperial Academy of Science).[45] A little over 15% of all reviews from the period 1906 to 1914 dealt with French publications.[46]

Of course, at times, this average figure was considerably surpassed, for instance in 1903, when Poincaré became corresponding member of the academy of science. In the *Monatshefte* of 1903, roughly two-thirds of the book reviews were dedicated to French volumes. Since they remained unsigned by identification code or full name, they are likely to have been written mostly by the editors, including von Escherich. As early as 1895, the *Monatshefte*, in a review of an algebra textbook, drew attention to the French tradition whereby even the country's most famous mathematicians would contribute to the creation of textbooks addressing the general public.[47] These attempts at disseminating knowledge were characterised by the author of the paper as exemplary.

---

[44] Monatshefte (1910). Vol. 21, Literaturberichte, p. 26, dealing with the book entitled "La kontinuo. Elementa teorio starigita sur la ideo de ordo kun aldono pri transfinitaj nombroj" by E.V. Huntington, in German: Das Kontinuum; elementare Theorie, aufgebaut auf dem Begriff der Ordnung, mit einem Anhang über die transfiniten Zahlen. (The continuum; elementary theory based on the concept of order, including an appendix on transfinite numbers). The book was reviewed by Hans Hahn.

[45] According to an interview statement (18. July 2008) by Richard Sinell, head of the *Archiv der Akademie der Wissenschaften*, Vienna.

[46] Vinzenz Bronzin had a collection of numerous French books, as the author of this paper discovered on a visit to Bronzin's son Andrea.

[47] Monatshefte (1895), Vol. 6, Literatur-Berichte, p. 15.

The editors' admiration of French mathematicians went even further. In fact, they were fond of the French lifestyle at large. In the *Monatshefte* of 1899, an anonymous reviewer discussed a volume dealing with the making of liqueur. "*Les recettes du distillateur*" (The recipts of the distiller).[48] It remains an open question whether the emerging focus on developments in France represented an attempt at relativising the German influence.[49] Political aspects may have played a role. After all, Leopold Gegenbauer, one of the two publishers of the *Monatshefte*, was involved in educational policy issues and in local politics.[50]

10.7 Vocational Identity and Careers of Mathematicians

In the face of a society marked by relatively rigid rules and where the course of a life largely follows the same pattern, as described by Stefan Zweig in his book "*Die Welt von Gestern*" (The World of Yesterday), it is intriguing to query whether exceptional talents succeed in breaking the mould. The careers of mathematicians may provide pointers to a community's adaptability and power of integration, offering indications of a social, and hence ideational, propensity to assimilate the faculties and skills of its members. In the understanding of the time, the exceptional performance of mathematicians was thought to be due to the cumulation of mathematical talent in certain families and biological-physical attributes like the shape of the skull, or the brain structure of eminent mathematicians[51].

In this kind of analysis, there is no mention of social and other environmental factors, although a number of outstanding mathematicians of the Habsburgian empire honoured with obituaries in the *Monatshefte* came from the Weyr family of Prague, or were influenced by it, providing evidence that highly gifted mathematicians could be found amongst the poorer social strata. A case in point is Wihelm Weiss, who became a mathematician by "coincidence", as it was put in his obituary. His career advancement presents us with the ideal story of a social climber, whose industry and capability would make him ascend from humble origins to become a distinguished professor. The obituary dedicated to him gives this account: Wilhelm's father took him from the dull countryside to the city of Prague, where he asked a police officer to direct him to a nearby

[48] Monatshefte (1899), Vol. 10, Literatur-Berichte, p. 22.

[49] Note that von Escherich opposed the appointment of a lecturer (at the *Konservatorium*) who represented the *alldeutsche* (Pan-Germanic) cause. This was not in line with the general trend: Karl Lueger, Mayor of Vienna from 1897 until 1910 and an adherant of the *alldeutsche* cause, was conspicuous by aspersions which he cast upon "*die Professoren*" (the professors) (Hamann 1998, p. 134).

[50] Gegenbauer wrote a paper on the regulation of salaries for university professors, in which he requested the nationalisation of tuition fees. During 1889–1892, he acted as member of the municipal council of Innsbruck, Monatshefte (1904), Vol. 15, p. 6.

[51] Monatshefte, (1901), Vol. 12, Literatur-Berichte, p. 12.

German school. The police officer referred them to a *Realschule* (secondary modern school).

> "Owing to the humble circumstances of his father, the young boy could find accommodation only in the poorest quarters of the city, where he lived in the same room with beggars and other sad company, with his daily nourishment at times consisting of a cup of coffee in the morning and a bun".[52]

He became acquainted with the father of the Weyr brothers, the professor of mathematics Franz Weyr, who became his patron: eventually he was able to study in Leipzig under Felix Klein (1849–1920; corresponding member of the *k. u. k. Akademie der Wissenschaften*) and earn a doctorate from the university of Erlangen. Similarly, Karl Bobek, professor of mathematics in Prague, who died aged 44, received well-directed aid and encouragement from Franz Weyr, even though at times he lived in dire straits.[53] Being a mathematician was not by itself a safeguard against a financially precarious existence.[54] It is a striking fact that both mathematicians originating from a humble background were discovered by Franz Weyr. For the good of the cause, in individual cases, apparently forces of integration would become efficacious regardless of social origin. However, there was no understanding of the importance of socio-structural factors and the attendant need for proactive support. All was left to "coincidence".

Worth noting is the fact that the mathematicians honoured by obituaries in the *Monatshefte* tended to have a record of foreign experience. The first three obituaries appearing in 1891 list the following sojourns abroad: Leipzig and Erlangen in the case of Ameseder; Anton Winckler was originally from Germany, and studied or taught in Königsberg [today's Kaliningrad] (under Jacobi) and in Berlin.[55] Emil Weyr attended lectures by Luigi Cremona in Italy. Pursuing studies, Karl Bobek stayed a year in Leipzig (Felix Klein) and spent half a year in Paris. Leopold Gegenbauer did a two-year stint in Berlin, where he attended lectures by Weierstrass, Kronecker and Kummer. In 1878/79, he attended lectures by Cremona in Rome and studied in the Vatican Library.[56] Wilhelm Weiss studied from 1884 to 1887 under Felix Klein in Leipzig and later on in Erlangen. Similarly, beginning in 1869, Otto Stolz attended lectures by Weierstrass and Kummer in Berlin, and in Göttingen (F. Klein) in 1871.

[52] Waelsch, F.: Obituary on Wilhelm Weiss, Monatshefte (1905), Vol. 16, p. 3: "*Die kümmerlichen Verhältnisse des Vaters gestatteten den Knaben nur in dem elendsten Viertel der Stadt unterzubringen; dort lebte er im selben Zimmer mit Bettlern und anderer trauriger Nachbarschaft, seine Nahrung für den Tag beschränkte sich manchmal auf den Morgenkaffee und ein Semmel*".

[53] Pick, G.: Obituary on Karl Bobek, Monatshefte (1900), Vol. 11, p. 97.

[54] To eke out a living, Anton Winckler conducted private lectures in his apartment. Czuber, E: Obituary on Anton Winckler, Monatshefte (1892), Vol. 3, p. 403.

[55] Czuber, E.: Obituary on Anton Winckler, Monatshefte (1892), Vol 3, p. 403ff.

[56] Stolz, O.: Obituary on Leopold Gegenbauer, Monatshefte (1904), Vol. 15, p. 6.

According to his obituary, Ludwig Boltzmann did not do a longer stint abroad while still a student.[57] The Austrian mathematicians spent their "*Wanderjahre*" (years of travel) mostly in Germany, where they attended lectures most notably by Weierstrass and Klein. A small number spent appreciable time in Italy: only one attended lectures in Paris.

It is striking that in all obituaries the didactic abilities of the deceased are strongly emphasised. At the same time, books on didactics represent an important part of the literature reviewed. The reviews dealt both with books aimed at different grades in school, and with publications like "*Abhandlungen über den mathematischen Unterricht in Deutschland*" (treatises on mathematical instruction in Germany), a publication in several volumes, edited by Felix Klein. In his paper in the *Monatshefte*, one of the reviewers quotes from Felix Klein's conclusion, where the latter explains the need for broadly based instruction in mathematics:

> "Science, unguided in its course, tends by its very nature toward specialisation and an enhancement of the level of abstraction that makes it hard for the ordinary mind to access the subject. By contrast, the manner of looking at the educational system sought by the IMUK – International Commission of Mathematical Education – brings to the fore the wide extension of the whole subject and the natural mode of human thinking. And this countervailing force seems naturally required, even indispensable in our time".[58]

The conveyance of mathematical literacy was considered a matter of high priority. As for Wilhelm Weiss, his teaching activities are described as the very purpose of his life. Emil Weyr earned an excellent reputation for supporting the conveyance of geometrical literacy to Austria's *Mittelschullehrer* (teachers at the secondary school level).[59] Concerning Anton Winckler, his skills as an excellent teacher – sensitive to the needs of his students – are acknowledged, as well as his efforts at improving technical education in Austria.[60] In addition to a scientific career, education and the teaching profession offered further vistas for those seeking social recognition. Declining offers to switch to the private sector, and remaining faithful to his teaching position throughout his life, Bronzin too reveals the profile of an exceptionally gifted conveyor of mathematical skills.

---

[57] Jäger, G.: Obituary on Ludwig Boltzmann, Monatshefte (1907), Vol. 18, p. 3.

[58] Monatshefte (1914), Vol 25, p. 45: "*Die Wissenschaft, sich selbst überlassen, strebt ihrer Natur nach immer mehr dazu, sich zu spezialisieren und sich durch gesteigerte Abstraktion dem allgemeinen Verständnis zu entfremden. Dementgegen bringt eine Betrachtung des Unterrichtswesens, wie sie die IMUK (Internationale Mathematische Unterrichtskommission) anstrebt, die grosse Ausdehnung des Gesamtbereiches, auf den die Wissenschaft hinwirken soll, und die ursprüngliche Art des menschlichen Denkens in den Vordergrund. Und das scheint als Gegengewicht gerade in jetziger Zeit natürlich, ja unentbehrlich*".

[59] Kohn, G.: Obituary on Emil Weyr, Monatshefte (1895), Vol. 6, p. 4.

[60] Czuber, E: Obituary on Anton Winckler, Monatshefte (1892), Vol. 3, p. 405.

10.8 Changing Attitudes Towards Financial Mathematics

Moritz Benedikt Cantor (1829-1920) authored a large, multi-volume opus on the history of mathematics.[61] His work as a historian of mathematics earned him ample praise in the *Monatshefte*.[62] Only one of Cantor's publications did not meet with the full support of reviewers publishing in the *Monatshefte*: In 1898, he published his lecture on "Political arithmetic" which he had presented to cameralists (cameralism being a precursor of the modern science of public administration) at the University of Heidelberg.[63] In the preface, Cantor explains why he decided to publish the book, distancing himself strictly from speculative activities and the attendant "casino game" of the bourse:

> "Nowadays, it is necessary for almost everyone to have a certain grasp of the calculations underlying stock exchange transactions that are entirely confined to purchase and sale, however dispensable (even detrimental) a knowledge of these types of transactions unique to the games going on at the bourse may under certain circumstances turns out to be. In this humble little treatise, the reader obtains information on the one thing – to the purposeful exclusion of information on the other [...]" (Cantor 1898, p. IV).[64]

The reviewer of Cantor's book picks up the diminutive and goes on to depreciate 'the humble little treatise': "*Das vorliegende Schriftchen des Grossmeister* [...]" (The present smallish script by the grand master [...]), but then he adds appreciatively that the various aspects have been dealt with in "*zweckmässiger Ausführlichkeit*" (appropriate detail).[65] The review does not carry a code of

---

[61] Cantor (1894), 4 volumes (4 Bände).

[62] "*Bei der allgemein anerkannten grossen Bedeutung des fundamentalen Werkes Cantor's haben wir dieser Abtheilung nicht etwa durch ein Wort des Lobes oder der Empfehlung den Weg zu ebnen, sondern nur unserer grossen Freude über das Erscheinen derselben Ausdruck zu geben* [...]" Considering that the great importance of Cantor's fundamental opus has been widely recognised, we do not need to pave the way for this department with words of praise and recommendation; it is entirely sufficient for us to give expression to the exceptional delight that the publication of this work informs us with (Monatshefte (1895), Vol. 6, Literatur-Berichte, p. 21 and also Monatshefte (1896), Vol. 7, Literatur-Berichte, p. 21).

[63] Cantor (1898), the book comprises 145 pages.

[64] "*Heutzutage wird es fast für jedermann notwendig sein, etwas von den Rechnungsweisen des auf Kauf und Verkauf sich beschränkenden Börsengeschäftes zu verstehen, so entbehrlich, ja so schädlich unter Umständen die Kenntnis derjenigen Geschäftsformen sich erweisen kann, welche dem Börsenspiel eigentümlich sind. In diesem Büchlein findet der Leser Auskunft über das Eine unter absichtlicher Vermeidung des Anderen* [...]".

[65] Monatshefte (1899), Vol. 10, Literatur-Berichte, p. 13. In the "Bulletin of the American Mathematical Society" Cantor's treatise is presented much more positively: "I know of no work in which the theory of probabilities and the formation of life tables are more clearly and concisely developed". Bull. Amer. Math. Soc. (1899), p. 488.

identification, and is therefore likely to have been written by one of the *Monatshefte* editors (presumably, von Escherich).

Cantor's "Political arithmetic or the arithmetic of everyday life" was published in 1898. In 1908, Bronzin's book "Theory of premium contracts" was published, and was reviewed anonymously in the *Monatshefte* in 1910.[66] The reviewer's attitude toward the application of mathematical methods to issues relating to stock exchange activities remained unchanged. The issue of the *Monatshefte* in which Bronzin's book was discussed also contained a review of R. de Montessus' book entitled "Leçons élémentaires sur le calcul des probabilités". In his book, de Montessus refers explicitly to Bachelier, prominently mentioning the essential assumption made by the latter that "*die mathematische Hoffnung des Spekulanten null ist*" (the mathematical expectation [literally: hope] of the speculator is zero) and calling it the "Théorème de Bachelier" (de Montessus 1908, p.101).[67] However, the reviewer does not go into this financially important assumption underlying the calculation of mathematical expectations. Thus he criticises that

> "the mathematical part is less than satisfactory; for instance, the derivation of the law of probability with reference to stock exchange speculations is certainly not immaculate, and suffers from the error that the same function is used both for probability a priori and probability a posteriori. Indeed the result, according to which this law of probability is supposed to be simply a two-sided law of error, is certainly not very plausible [...]".[68]

No explication is being offered as to why this idea is not 'plausible'. This review does not carry a code of identification either. It is again likely to have been written by von Escherich.

Three years after the critical discussion of the work by Bronzin and R. de Montessus, an author using the identification code "Be" reviews – in the *Monatshefte* of 1913, and on almost five pages – the volume by Louis Bachelier entitled "*Calcul des Probabilités*" which had been published in 1912.[69] The length of the review is unusual for the *Monatshefte* and the discussion is of a benevolent kind: The reviewer refers to Bachelier's first book "*Théorie de la*

[66] It is almost certain that von Escherich authored the review, considering that Bronzin used to be one of his students.

[67] "L'espérance mathématique du spéculateur est nulle".

[68] Monatshefte (1910), Vol. 21, Literaturberichte, p. 13: "*der mathematische Teil einiges zu wünschen übrig (lässt); beispielsweise ist die Ableitung des Wahrscheinlichkeitsgesetzes für die börsenmässigen Spekulationen gewiss nicht einwandfrei und leidet an dem Fehler, dass für die Wahrscheinlichkeit a priori dieselbe Funktion benützt wird wie für jene a posteriori. In der Tat ist auch das Resultat, nach welchem dieses Wahrscheinlichkeitsgesetz einfach ein zweiseitiges Fehlergesetz sein sollte, gewiss nicht sehr plausibel* [...]"

[69] Bachelier (1912).

spéculation", which, he argues, introduced Bachelier to the public. He is sympathetic to Bachelier's self-willed pertinacity:

> "The author follows his own path [...]. It is characteristic of the book that even in parts dealing with problems belonging to the classical theory of probability, no references to the literature are found. The book opens wide vistas for detailed research [...]. Overall, a book whose content should prove fruitful: not only regarding the theory of probability, but also in view of its exceedingly numerous applications outside of that theory".[70]

There is a marked difference between these two reviews. The reviewer of Bachelier's work is likely to be Ernst Blaschke, born in 1856. Considering his career, he is likely to have been sympathetic to Bachelier's mathematical analysis: Blaschke attended lectures at the Vienna *Handelsschule* (College of Commerce), concluding his later studies with a doctoral thesis on the determination of a Riemann surface. From 1882 onward, he was permanently employed in the insurance sector, while at the same endeavouring to embark on an academic career. In 1890, he received the *venia legendi* for political arithmetic at the *Technische Hochschule* (the Institute of Technology, a university focusing on engineering sciences), and from 1894 onward he was authorised to teach the same subject at the university, too. In 1896, Blaschke became a civil servant acting as an insurance expert, in which capacity he was especially concerned with the standardisation of government regulations in all European countries. In 1899, on the recommendation of Czuber, he was appointed associate professor at the *Technische Hochschule*. He was corresponding member of a number of actuarial associations, including the *Institut des Actuaires français* (Einhorn 1983, pp. 374–386). His practical experience, academic career and activities as an insurance expert with a profound command of the theories of probability, made him the ideal conveyor of a school of thought that until then had been neglected. With the onset of World War I, however, these auspicious beginnings petered out. Excepting the review in question, the bibliography of E. Blaschke contains no indication that he would continue to occupy himself with the issue (Einhorn 1983, pp. 382–386).

[70] Monatshefte (1913), Vol. 24, Literaturberichte, p. 4–8: "*Der Verfasser wandelt ganz seine eigenen Bahnen* [...]. *Es ist für das Werk bezeichnend, dass sich in ihm auch dort, wo Probleme, welche der klassischen Wahrscheinlichkeitslehre angehören, behandelt werden, auch nicht ein Literaturhinweis findet... Das Werk eröffnet der Einzelforschung weite Gebiete* [...]. *Im ganzen ein Werk, dessen Inhalt nicht nur auf dem Gebiet der Theorie der Wahrscheinlichkeit, sondern in seinen überaus zahlreichen Anwendungsmöglichkeiten auch ausserhalb desselben reiche Früchte tragen dürfte*".

10.9 Conclusion

Throughout the entire period examined here, the themes pursued in the scientific articles published in the *Monatshefte* – from the periodical's inauguration until World War I – reveal a course aligned mainly to the discussion of geometrical and other theoretical problems. However, shortly before the war, editorial categories subsumed under "*Literatur-Berichte*" (reviews of literature) that were subject to less stringent formal criteria attest to an opening up vis-à-vis hitherto neglected, applied issues –such as the analysis of stock exchange transactions with the help of theories of probability. Characteristically, the protagonists of this change were not part of the traditional circle of mathematicians, but operated as actuarial mathematicians and statisticians on a side track within the scientific discipline of mathematics.

References

Bachelier L (1912) Calcul des probabilités. Gauthier-Villars, Paris

Binder C (2003) Vor 100 Jahren: Mathematik in Wien. In: Internationale Mathematische Nachrichten, No. 193, pp. 1–20

Bronzin V (1906) Lehrbuch der politischen Arithmetik. Franz Deuticke, Leipzig/ Vienna

Bulletin of the American Mathematical Society (1899) Vol. 5, No. 10

Burke P (2002) Papier und Marktgeschrei: Die Geburt der Wissensgesellschaft. Wagenbach, Berlin

Cantor M (1894) Vorlesungen über Geschichte der Mathematik. Teubner, Leipzig

Cantor M (1898) Politische Arithmetik oder die Arithmetik des täglichen Lebens. Teubner, Leipzig

Czuber E (1884) Geometrische Wahrscheinlichkeiten und Mittelwerthe. Leipzig

Czuber E (1898) Kritische Bemerkungen zu den Grundbegriffen der Wahrscheinlichkeitsrechnung. Zeitschrift für das Realschulwesen Number 23, pp. 8–17

Czuber E (1899) Die Entwicklung der Wahrscheinlichkeitstheorie und ihrer Anwendungen. Bericht erstattet der Deutschen Mathematiker-Vereinigung

Czuber E (1900–1904) Wahrscheinlichkeitsrechnung. In: Encyklopädie der mathematischen Wissenschaften, Vol. 1: Arithmetik und Algebra, Part 2. Teubner, Leipzig, pp. 733–768

de Montessus de Ballore R F (1908) Leçons élémentaires sur le calcul des probabilités. Gauthier-Villars, Paris

Einhorn R (1983) Vertreter der Mathematik und Geometrie an den Wiener Hochschulen 1900–1940. Doctoral dissertation, University of Technology, Vienna

Hamann B (1998) Hitlers Wien, Lehrjahre eines Diktators. Piper, Munich

Klein F (1979) Vorlesung über die Entwicklung der Mathematik im 19. Jahrhundert. Springer, Berlin/ Heidelberg/ New York

Meinong A, Adler G. (1995) Eine Freundschaft in Briefen. Rodopi, Amsterdam (Studien zur Oesterreichischen Philosophie, Vol. 24)

Monatshefte für Mathematik und Physik (1890–1914) Vol. 1–25. Von Escherich G et al. (eds). Universität Wien, Mathematisches Seminar, mit Unterstützung des Hohen K. K.

Ministeriums für Kultus (Cultus) und Unterricht. Verlag des Mathematischen Seminars der Universität Wien, Leipzig/ Vienna

Scarfò L (2006) Philosophie als Wissenschaft reiner Idealitäten: zur Spätphilosophie Husserls in besonderer Berücksichtigung der Beilage III zur Krisis-Schrift. Utz, Munich (Philosophie, Vol. 24)

Scriba C J, Schreiber P (2001) 5000 Jahre Geometrie: Geschichte, Kulturen, Menschen. Springer, Berlin

von Escherich G (1903) Reformfragen unserer Universitäten. Inaugural speech. Die Feierliche Inauguration des Rektors der Wiener Universität für das Studienjahr 1903/1904 am 16. Oktober 1903. Selbstverlag der k. u. k. Universität, Vienna

11 The Certainty of Risk in the Markets of Uncertainty

Elena Esposito*

The history and interpretation of the model for pricing options that Bronzin proposed delineates and explains the evolution of the concept and indicates how risk was perceived by the society of the day. Financial derivatives, which were developed specifically to address trading risks, are now of central importance to a society for which security has become an empty concept and risk has become inevitable. Any attempt to secure protection from risk has itself become a risky venture. We find ourselves faced with a condition of endemic risk in which our search for security ends, not in protecting ourselves from dangers, but rather in generating new ones. Formalised models for pricing options have been very successful over the last decades because they dress risk in terms of volatility, which offers the clinical illusion of neutralizing the unpredictability of a future overshadowed by unstable markets and destabilized by a heightened sensitivity to risk. The calculation of implied volatility convincingly suggests that risk is controllable, even if the future is inevitably unknowable – a much more cogent requirement today than in Bronzin's day: This also explains why his formula for pricing options met with only moderate applause back then compared to the strikingly similar models used today. But experience and theoretical reflection show that the very attempt to establish a prophylactic system against risk only generates yet further risks, thus reinforcing the impossibility of controlling the future.

11.1 A Premature Novelty

Apart from all the mathematical and formal aspects of Bronzin's treatise, we want to study the introduction which presents us with an apparent enigma: Why have his work and techniques on options-pricing, so similar in many respects to the Black-Scholes formula, been ignored for so many decades, while the Black-Scholes equation not only received the Nobel Prize but has had such a resonance as to be celebrated as "the most successful theory, not only in finance, but in all of economics"?[1] To attribute this simply to historical contingency; i.e., to chance, is particularly unsatisfactory in this case, because one cannot avoid suspecting that the different receptions of the two works are the result of deeper structural elements: This aspect is all the more problematic in view of the

* Università di Modena-Reggio Emilia, Italy. *elena.esposito@unimore.it*

[1] Quoted in McKenzie and Millo (2003), p. 108. The question is posed in Zimmermann and Hafner (2006a), p. 21; (2006b), pp. 238, 262; (2007), p. 532.

inscrutable role played by financial instruments (derivatives and options) in our society today, and by the obscurity of the world of finance in general. Also, a comparison of Bronzin's work with the slightly better appreciated text by Louis Bachelier[2] does not simplify the question; it makes it even more mysterious: Considered jointly, both papers seem to compensate each other's respective weaknesses (the lack of stochastic techniques in Bronzin: the use of subjective evaluations in Bachelier), and jointly offer all the necessary components of a sound methodology for future options pricing. And then one asks all the more why they were not better recognized earlier, and why Bronzin's innovation had to be discovered only much later when it was no longer novel.

The hypothesis I would like to discuss here is that, perhaps, one should reverse the terms of the question. Analogies with the celebrated Black-Scholes formula, rather than constituting the enigma, hold the key to explaining why Bronzin's work suffered from this absence of acclaim: That the two theoretical proposals were dealt with differently precisely because of their similarities; that the major difference between them was the epoch and social context in which they appeared. What later constituted the strength for the latter, was initially perceived as a weakness in the former.

In order to develop our line of reasoning, we start by looking at the differences between the society of Bronzin's time and the present day (Section 11.1). In particular, we look at the changes to the denotation and evaluation of risk (Section 11.2), and then consider the relevance of risk for financial markets and the strategies these markets use to deal with it (Section 11.3). Derivatives and, in particular, options seem to be specialized instruments for trading risk itself, rather than for simply trading an aspect of their real, physical underlying value. This is why they have had such an impact on a society in which uncertainty regarding the future is paramount. It also explains why options pricing reflects the difficulty of quantifying risk, which is equivocal and self-referential (Section 11.4). The current models are examined from this perspective and compared with Bronzin's proposal, emphasizing the advantages as well as the limitations of both (Section 11.5), in an environment where models developed for the purpose of controlling risks tend to elevate them (Section 11.6).

11.2 Risk Society and Trading with Risk

Financial markets and especially the function that options hold in them have changed substantially. It is true that similar instruments, in the general form of the "sale of promises" are very ancient and can be traced back to the Middle Ages, ancient Greece or even Mesopotamia, and such markets can be found in the East as early as the 18th century and in several European countries in the

[2] Cf. Bachelier (1900), Zimmermann and Hafner (2006b), p. 238.

course of the 19th century[3]. In spite of such historical records, many authors[4] see the beginning of the nineteen-seventies as introducing a revolutionary innovation in finance with the advent of first stock options exchange in Chicago in 1973, comparable in stature to the introduction of double-entry bookkeeping or paper currency[5]. And again, we face an enigma: continuity or discontinuity; tradition or revolution?

It seems that both interpretations are true: Derivatives have been known for millennia, but in the last three decades new hybrid products have been developed, both abstract and self-referential in application, complex and refined, which did not exist before. This new breed of engineered financial instrument is a conscious invention, addressing new needs and creating a completely unprecedented abstraction of the markets. Financial markets sell something very different from traditional commodities, something abstract and intangible, that is difficult to characterize – and becoming a new form of commodity, associated with an unfamiliar appraisal of certainty and risk (we will soon come back to this).

This explains, in part, the different social image of the stock exchange in Bronzin's times, when it stills looked suspiciously like a doubtful place for gambling, and where chance invited speculation to participate in an irresponsible and irrational bet, investment decisions being cast like dice. Securities dealings were not yet invested with terminology borrowed from serious scientific statistics. The term 'random' would later be used to alleviate the player's responsibility with assurances that the new, enlightened yet counterintuitive guarantor of the markets, 'rationality', was sovereign in determining outcomes[6].

Today the situation is very different. First of all, this is because the contemporary "risk society" has deeply modified the evaluation and the relevance of risk[7]: the problem of risk, that once concerned only specific groups of people exposing themselves to dangers (Luhmann mentions sailors and mushroom collectors), is now a ubiquitous concern that everyone shares. Risk refers to a decision that an individual makes to exchange something he actually possesses for the expectation of a potentially greater gain, on condition that he forfeit his possessions, should his wager fail: If the weather is good, sea trading brings great earnings, but if there is a storm, the merchant seaman loses all his wealth. The debate on ecological risks has extended this awareness to everyone who is involved in decisions that compare a very probable advantage (the production of energy at low cost from nuclear power stations) with extremely improbable losses, but which, should they occur, entail immeasurably disastrous conse-

[3] Cf. Swan (2000), Hull (1999), p. 2, Millman (1995), p. 26, Shiller (2003), p. 299f.

[4] Cf. for instance Strange (1986), p. 58, Mandelbrot and Hudson (2004), p. 75, Oldani (2004), p. 16.

[5] Cf. Millman (1995), p. 26. Also Brian and Rafferty (2007), p. 135, speak of derivatives as "a new kind of global money".

[6] Cf. Zimmermann and Hafner (2006a), p. 15; (2006b), p. 257.

[7] Cf. on this regard the lively debate in the social sciences around Beck (1986), Douglas and Wildawsky (1982) and Luhmann (1991).

quences (a possible accident) – for example, were one to reject the construction of nuclear power plants, the possible exhaustion of non-renewable energy sources and serious pollution problems would have to be taken into account. It does not suffice to avoid a risk in order to prevent or eradicate it. This does not provide security. In such a situation, it is very difficult to reach a decision, because there are no risk-free options; there is only a selection of risks on offer to be compared and from which to make a choice – a situation of endemic and unavoidable risk.

Beside risk perception, objective market conditions have also changed in the period that has seen the birth and explosive spread of financial derivatives. It has been observed repeatedly that the nineteen-seventies were also marked by the demise of the Bretton Woods agreements (1971); i.e., of the abandonment of every form of link, however indirect and mediated, trying to link the value of money to an external reference (e.g., the American gold reserves). This move precipitated a period of fluctuating exchange rates (continuing today), of oscillating financial prices and of great social instability – and the absence of any compensating stability, or guarantee for a parity of exchanged values. The private markets are now the ones that "sell stability"[8], but in the mediated and dynamic form of new financial instruments (i.e. paradoxically very unstable).

11.3 The Risks of Security

It is well known that derivatives were developed as hedging instruments; i.e., as a protection against risk – thinking first of all of risks already present. According to the standard definition[9], hedging aims at eliminating risks that one is exposed to owing to factors that cannot be controlled, such as weather conditions or variations in exchange rates and currencies. The purpose of hedging is to make commodity futures safe in face of all the unforeseeable contingencies that the market and the world present and the prospect of financial losses. Thus used, derivatives are not risky, irresponsible bets, because they do not generate risks that did not exist before, but simply offer certainty in more and more unstable and restless markets. Risk should be restricted to speculative purposes only, and speculation should be carried out under very different conditions: when the financial operation creates a risk that was not previously there; for example, betting on the variation in exchange rates or on the movements of stock indexes. Only then, would speculation be responsible for increasing the riskiness and unreliability of the markets.

The problem, however, is that the distinction between hedging and speculation is factually much less clear-cut than it appears to be theoretically. In practice, it is often very difficult to distinctly differentiate hedging and

[8] Cf. Millman (1995), p. 298.
[9] Cf. for instance Hull (1998), p. 11.

speculation. Market traders try to catch profit opportunities without distinguishing between a medium to long-term investment and a short-term trade (speculation); even those individuals who does not primarily have speculative intentions cannot avoid using instruments like financial leverage and short sales in practice. One also has to consider the distinction between specific (or individual) risk and systemic risk: Hedging can reduce or control a specific risk for a given operator, but tends to generate further risks for the financial system as a whole[10]. The very hedging operations that guarantee an operator protection from his individual risk, can destabilize the markets, making them volatile and restless: Portfolio insurance schemes tend to strengthen these tendencies, selling when the market goes down and buying when it goes up, and the transactions on the market for derivatives offer further transaction opportunities to dealers who speculate on the underlying assets without any regard for the original hedging purpose. As a matter of fact, it was discovered subsequently that hedging activities had a worse impact on the 1993 European monetary market crisis than did the openly speculative activities of operators like the renowned George Soros[11].

Speculation and hedging are two faces of the same coin, and are always found to be used together. Without speculators even hedging operations could not be transacted, or only with much greater reticence: On the one hand, speculation expands the available supply of potential buyers and sellers nearly indefinitely, making it easier for a hedging partner to be found; on the other hand, speculators are essential to dealers who are unwilling to bear risks because the former are ready to buy these risks.

The situation in the financial markets corresponds to the social sciences thesis that sees risk as a central feature of contemporary society – risk as irrefutable and solipsistic because it can never provide a "solution" that negates itself in establishing a condition of safety[12]. One cannot escape risk, because, analogous to Zeno's dichotomy paradox, the search for a safehouse from future damages (always possible because the future remains unknown) disappears endlessly into the future as each step of the search presents yet further hazards and any attempt to avert each hazard creates a pitfall of moral hazard, a mistaken sense of safety expressing itself in negligence. In negating risk, according to Luhmann, one does not access safety, an empty concept, but only danger – i.e., one is never certain of not suffering damage, but one can at the most be sure of not being responsible for this situation. Things can always go wrong, and the difference between risk and danger is a question of attribution: one speaks of risk when the potential damage is attributed to one's own behaviour (for example, as with wreckless driving or illnesses caused by smoking) and of danger when the

[10] In the language of financial operators one indicates often with α the individual risk, that depends on the ability of the operator and remains indeterminate, and with β, the systemic risk or market risk.

[11] Cf. Millman (1995), pp. 210–211.

[12] Cf. especially Luhmann (1991), Chapter 1.

damage is attributed to external factors (for example, natural catastrophes or passive smoking)[13]. The negation of risk does not nullify it, but only opens the door to an unspecified danger, not safety.

Looking closer, however, every danger can be seen as a risk: One might protect a community from earthquakes with anti-seismic buildings or better monitoring and warning systems; one might avoid passive smoking by changing one's office or trying to convince the smokers to give up smoking. The distinction between risk and danger is not located in the physical world but in the perspective of the observer, whose preference determines whether the responsibility of a negative outcome is to be attributed to the decision-maker or to the world. This duplicity of viewpoint is mirrored in the distinction between speculation and hedging, where hedging itself can have speculative effects and speculation can be carried out with the intention of protecting the agent against damages. The perspective must then move from a first-order observation (observation of the world and the objects in it) to a second-order observation (observation of the observers and the way in which they observe)[14], with different problems and much more complex solutions – especially because the perspectives of the observers always remain, at least partially, concealed and the observation remains unavoidably occluded (i.e., uncertain, i.e., risky).

Thus whether one speculates or hedges, the issue is not the autonomous creation of risk (there are no riskless operations in financial markets, as will be discussed further on) or the presence of speculative purposes. The issue rather concerns the current risk-burdened society, a different society from the one in which Bronzin operated. Risk has become endemic and unavoidable, thereby losing its negative connotations and becoming a fundamental social element to be faced. Attribution is an autocratic means of accepting or rejecting responsibility for events depending on the acceptability of their outcomes. From the point of view of observation theory this is the fundamental difference between the society of the beginning of the 20th century and the societies of the preceding few decades: Both have to face the spread of disorder and uncertainty, and both have looked for instruments with which to protect themselves, but in Bronzin's day insecurity, chaos and disorder were attributed to the world (for example, in the form of the relentless diffusion of entropy according with the second principle of thermodynamics)[15]. Disorder seemed to have become the fundamental law of the universe: For Knight, uncertainty had become the fundamental condition of economic behaviour. Here, disorder and uncertainty were still due to external factors which did not undermine the belief in the possibility of certainty and order (today the term used is danger). One spoke of negentropy in the sense of a creation of "islands" of order opposing the

[13] The distinction partly reproduces (but reversing the terms) the one of risk and uncertainty proposed by Knight in the nineteen-twenties and become by now a classic of economics, tormented by the problem of uncertainty (cf. Knight 1921).

[14] On the distinction of first-order and second-order observation (cf. Von Foerster 1981).

[15] Cf. Stengers (1995), among many others.

spreading of general disorder. Risk society radicalises this condition, turning to the observer and generalizing risk, so that it becomes something pervasive, inevitable and omnipresent affecting every behaviour and every decision. The individual then faces the security of risk and the risks of security – and this requires new conceptual and practical tools. The evolution of financial markets demonstrates this clearly.

11.4 Pricing Uncertainty

In the field of derivatives, the movements of financial markets, even if they refer to the transactions of goods with precise fixed characteristics (dates and delivery conditions), no longer have anything to do with the features of the products or with the conditions of the transaction. One of the advantages of the new financial products is that there is a very low correlation between the obtained results and the results of their "traditional" underlying activities: i.e., their value is independent of the market's performance, which enables them (if adequately managed) to achieve profits even when the markets are losing ground (and vice versa). One calls these products market-neutral – which means that they do not have to do with goods, but instead trade (sell and buy) something that is different from the assets exchanged on traditional markets. But what is this?

With derivatives, one can earn money even when the underlying assets are depreciated, hence the object of the transaction is evidently not the underlying asset, but something else that refers to the asset, but which does not coincide with it. One speaks of hedging, and in this case, it seems that the desired good, the one bought and sold on the derivatives market, is safety: contracts are stipulated in order to obtain safety, which, once secured makes the buyer independent of the unpredictable vacillations of the markets (and of the values of the assets). One then realizes that it is this safety that is actually bought and sold, and that one speculates on expectations and on their stability – hardly a safe solution. Safety disappears; the asset negotiated on derivatives markets is actually risk; once sold, risk circulates in the financial system, is distributed and decentralized, adjusting to the interests and the particular attitudes of the dealers (Luhmann 1991, p. 197). Risk, that once fell only on banks (credit risk) and on customers (entrepreneurial risk), is transferred today to the operators, objectified and generalized, losing the definitions of its former different modalities: the distinctions of interest-rate risk, volatility risk, credit risk, transaction risk have all become tokens of a universal type of risk, that is itself the object of transactions (LiPuma and Lee 2005, p. 414).

What is bought and sold is abstract risk, not safety. The general result of the various financial trades is not the elimination of risk, making transactions safer: Risk is simply reshaped, objectified and transferred to other interested parties (Pryke and Allen 2000, p. 268ff). This is the dream of an observer like Kenneth Arrow, who longed for a world that would be safe because every possible risk could be transferred to someone else (Stix 1998): It is a nightmare from another viewpoint, that sees the world as prey to an uncontrolled proliferation of risk: the view of our risk society. Even if a single operator can feel protected by a hedging operation (because he is no longer exposed to the possibility of an unfavourable movement in prices, having paid the price for a most-likely, unlikely probability[16]), at the level of the economy as a whole, the so-called systemic risk increases enormously, because the dynamism of markets and the level of exposure of investments increase: Since risk does not only apply to one subject or a small group of subjects, the risk is spread and one can risk more, speculating or engaging in adventurous enterprises. The management of risk, as we known, does not lead to a reduction but to a multiplication of risks[17].

This is "commodified risk"[18]. However, as all commodities must have a price, the question this prompts is how to find a non-arbitrary way to price an entity that has a value precisely because it is independent of the market's movements but that itself must be traded on specialized markets. How is it possible to price risk when the world has nothing to do with it, and risks can be worth little when things go well, and a great deal when things go wrong, or vice versa? This is the great issue to which the Black-Scholes formula (earlier addressed by Bronzin's proposal) gives an answer.

Let us look a little closer at the central issue. The buyer of an option stipulates a sort of insurance contract on the price range of the underlying asset expected at its expiration date. It is this bandwidth of values, and not the price itself, that is betted on the markets. Under the name of volatility, the markets trade this variability as an object in its own right that quotes its own value, and that is measured and employed as a reference for transactions: if volatility increases, options gain a higher value; if it sinks, they become cheaper – completely dissociated from the direction the market is taking. It does not matter whether the values rise or fall, but how much and how quickly they change. Also the "temporal value" of options depends on it; i.e., the fact that their price tends to decrease as the expiration date draws nearer: precisely because the possibility of variation decreases.

As a consequence of the use of mathematical models and of the formula for pricing options, in the "second order" market of derivatives, the complexity of the economic world is reduced to volatility; i.e., to the uncertainty of future expectations, such that the operators dealing with options buy and sell volatility in order to speculate or protect themselves from the contingencies of the market. Complex strategies are developed that are usually "neutral with respect to the underlying asset"; i.e., that is, they are not subject to the market trend, and allow profits to be made under all market conditions: rising, falling or even remaining

[16] And as a matter of fact it is not at all certain that it improves the overall result of the operation; there can be on the contrary even worse performances: the purchase of safety has itself costs. Cf. Colombo (2006), p. 79.

[17] Cf. Strange (1998), p. 44ff. Moral hazard is only one aspect of this general syndrome.

[18] According with the definition of Brian and Rafferty (2007), p. 136.

"flat". One can also devise strategies (with imaginative names like "straddle" or "strangle") that deal specifically with different types of volatility; i.e., the speed of the markets, where earnings are to be made by betting on the speed and spread of price movements (irrespective of market changes).

This form of volatility trading shows that expectations of price movements have superseded a direct market orientation to prices: where evaluations are formed by observations of how market observers respond to the market; not by an observation of market movements. This has produced a specialized second market. Uncertainty, which presents a problem and obstacle for traditional (first-order) markets, becomes a resource to be exploited in these abstract, "dematerialised" (second-order) markets. And this is also the reason for the enormous and rapid success of derivatives, linked, as they are, to the increase in uncertainty and instability associated with the break-up of the Bretton Woods agreements and the growing globalisation of the markets – and, finally, with the spread of risk. The real problem with the option pricing formulas, from this viewpoint, is the difficulty of finding a way to "put a price on uncertainty" (Stix 1998) in face of an increasingly indeterminable and unforeseeable future.

11.5 Foreseeing Uncertainty

How is it done? It is well known that it is very difficult to find an empirically plausible way to estimate derivatives and similar instruments, first because it is very difficult to isolate the relevant variables: If a hypothesis does not work, is it because the hypothesis is wrong or because the markets have not behaved efficiently? Or perhaps, they were not efficient precisely because they reacted to the hypotheses that were intended to foresee them? This solipsistic circularity is enclosed in the enigma of evaluating volatility, which has been recognized to be "one of the more complex concepts of the market", but which is apparently, nonetheless, handled with ease and competence in everyday practice by financial operators (Caranti 2003, p. 107).

The problem is that volatility is not directly observable and always presents an element of uncertainty. This makes it a factor of major importance for the options market. At least three kinds of volatility can be distinguished[19]: historical volatility, which measures the variability of past prices (ascertainable but no reliable indicator of the future); anticipated volatility (i.e. a measure of the subjective expectation that each operator has, but which obviously cannot be formalized); and implicit volatility, which should provide an approximation of operators' perceptions of what the market expects (distinguished from what everyone expects subjectively)[20]. It is implicit volatility that is the hinge on

[19] Cf. for instance Colombo (2006), p. 186.

[20] This is more or less the variable indicated in Keynes's famous "beauty contest": the observation of what the others think is the prevailing opinion: cf. Keynes (1936), p. 316.

which option pricing models depend – a very curious notion, intellectually akin to a kind of reckless objectification of subjectivity: Since one does not know what will happen in the future, and since one cannot even know with certainty what the operators expect, one replaces this uncertainty with an observation of what might reasonably be expected on the basis of the past experience, and of what everyone supposes everyone else might expect. This is not simply a repetition of the past, but also includes deviations and surprises, reminding us of the past that has taught us not to trust it – but it is also not simply what people expect: It is well known that rationality is often not reasonable at all in market psychology. Implicit volatility, a forward-looking measure, represents how the expectations of other players are observed, not expectations as such which remain inaccessible – but offers a measurable given, from which everyone then draws their own information upon which to build their expectations. Second-order observation is replaced with a kind of first-order observation of market observers.

The great advantage of the Black-Scholes formula lies precisely in its having found a way to estimate implicit volatility – a way that is as circular as the notion itself, and which perhaps works precisely because of this. The formula is calculated by running the Black-Scholes model backwards: Once the price of an option is known, it can be inserted in the formula which uses it to estimate a value for volatility, that will then be used for future calculations. The solution is extremely sophisticated on a mathematical level, using stochastic models drawn from the formulas used in the particle physics for calculating Brownian motion; but what is more significant, it uses the assumption that price movements, like the movement of particles, are random. The basic idea here is that the randomness of fluctuations in security prices paradoxically make the market calculable[21].

Beyond this formalism, the idea aims to neutralize uncertainty and eradicate the problem that had blocked students like Paul Samuelson in their attempt to formalize options pricing: the difficulty of calculating a "risk premium", a "discount" on the price of the option in order to compensate the risk present in purchasing it. The assumption is that all the important information (including the probability of future fluctuations of the price of the security) is already contained in the price itself. If the stock is risky, its price is already lower then the expected future value, and the price of the option does not need to adjust for this. In other words: Future uncertainty is already implicit in the present price, even if it is difficult to see this. The same neutralization can be found in Bronzin's proposal, which, from this point of view, appears to present the same advantages offered much later by the Black-Scholes formula (the lack of stochastic calculations

[21] Cf. Arnoldi (2004), p. 37. In this regard it is interesting to notice that Bronzin's model, in contrast to later ones, does not only use normal (Gaussian) distribution in order to describe the movements of prices, but confronts it with other possible probability distributions – showing thereby the contingency of the choice and the presence of alternative possibilities: an awareness that other formalizations lack. I am grateful to Heinz Zimmermann for this remark.

being non-essential here). Bronzin developed a model that only referred to forward prices and not to expected values; i.e., a model that does not account for preferences and does not need to account for subjective elements such as price expectations, risk propensity or a reward for risk (Zimmermann and Hafner 2006a, p. 4; 2007, p. 535; 2006b, p. 259). In Bronzin's model, volatility can be calculated "objectively" and corresponds to a "driftless random walk" (Zimmermann and Hafner 2006b, p. 239), precisely because time plays a less important role than dimension does. Actually, the whole construction corresponds to a world of "limited", prescribed uncertainty, as introduced with the 20th century, rather than to the recursive and intrinsically uncertain world of today's risk society, which faces endemic and ineradicable risk, escalating as soon as one tries to control it. It is paradoxical that the mathematical solution was to be found in a society confronted with a far higher degree of complexity.

Obviously, the application of the formula leaves many doubts often voiced, even by the authors of the formula themselves: and this, in addition to the practical difficulties it presents, such as the assumptions of fixed interest rates, uninterrupted negotiation, the lack of transaction costs, arbitrage opportunities and equity dividends, and especially the idea that volatility rates are statistically normally distributed (i.e., a "simple" exposure to chance) – while the market produces repeated crises that do not corroborate the model, and often uncontrolled forms of positive feedback, or non-random tendencies[22]. With the Black-Scholes mechanism, however, the unforeseeable elements of market uncertainty can be neutralized, and one is given a procedure that can be formalized and applied to mathematical models.

11.6 Producing Uncertainty

The apparent objectivity of the procedure and the availability of computer calculations makes trading with options appear more reliable, eliminating the aspects of improvisation and chance which at the time of Bronzin made it a suspect activity[23]. In a market afflicted with uncertainty but supported by the calculation capacity of computers, the Black-Scholes formula has had an enormous success – being itself self-referential like all the assumptions it rests upon. McKenzie and Millo[24] have pursued the reception of this formula across financial markets and over time, from the initial distrust based on poor empirical support in the nineteen-seventies (initially the model did not seem to accurately describe reality at all) to the confidence backed by empirical evidence in the mid-nineteen-eighties. Their hypothesis is that the formula succeeded in working so well, not because it accurately described the movements of the markets from

[22] The basic issue of Mandelbrot and Hudson (2004).

[23] But this is also, as we can observe today, the hidden (or repressed) weakness of the whole model, as Maurer (2007) maintains.

[24] Cf. McKenzie and Millo (2003); McKenzie (2006), Chapter 5.

the beginning, but because the markets themselves changed as a result of the formula's diffusion. It owes its success particularly to its computer compatibility. The model has been increasingly used as a trading guide, and has recommended itself as such – precisely because it is constructed to employ implicit volatility. The world of financial operators is shaped by the models they use for understanding it so as to orient themselves (a condition that McKenzie termed "performativity" which is increasingly helpful in explaining the dynamics of today's abstract and self-referential financial markets[25]).

The Black-Scholes formula has worked because the markets were ready to receive it and have subsequently changed so as to validate it. This did not happen with Bronzin's proposal, undoubtedly because communication problems hindered the diffusion of his work. The failure of Bronzin's work to establish itself was due to a different cause: More significantly, it was ahead of its time. In his day, markets were not as unstable and volatile as today, which meant that uncertainty was seen in very different terms. The financial markets were not then obsessed with the phenomenon of uncertainty and the need to evaluate it. Today, we have reified risk and created a new concept with the term "commodified risk" used in financial derivatives dealings. Bronzin's formula, which also draws its strength from its ability to transform uncertainty into an objectified datum which can be observed and traded, did not have equal application possibilities: His epoch provided neither high-powered computer technology nor the explosive opportunity to revolutionize markets that was available at the end of the nineteen-eighties to the Black-Scholes methodology. The different destinies of the two proposals cannot then be surprising, even in view of their great similarities.

From a different point of view, on the other hand, the power of both models depends on assumptions. Derivatives markets are markets of uncertainty that transform hunches about other individuals' expectations into profit opportunities: the fact that no individual knows for sure what the other individual expects from an unknown future. One employs derivatives because one cannot know the future, a future that is both indeterminate and yet prescribed by preparations that are put in place today in the attempt to ascertain what will be tomorrow. Under these conditions, every reliable forecast is destined to falsify itself, because the future reacts to the expectations imposed on it – where every additional reliable forecast contributes to an increased unpredictability of the future. But the circular model used in derivatives pricing reduces this indeterminate area to a technical problem, to an ability to competently manipulate available data, transforming past uncertainty in present certainty – thus losing track of the future it should align itself to.

More concretely: the world financial operators move in is a world in which the unpredictability of the future continuously renews itself: a financial world that "marks the market" daily and makes constants adjustments, a world in which

[25] Cf. McKenzie (2006, 2007).

the imitation of other individuals' strategies is the objective of many competing strategies – a world that is anything but random, a highly structured world, even though the structures are so adaptable as to escape every attempt to model them. The structure is conceived for the purpose of change, not stasis, and it is just this (and not the absence of structure) that makes the market incalculable. Under such conditions, the formalized models, widely used, with the intention of controlling market complexity and contingency, appear, on the contrary, to increase these problems – as has become evident recently. The formal correlate of the "volatility smile" is the "volatility skew", observed in the graphs corresponding to the model: a deviation from the expected movements that signals that the markets expect the unexpected; i.e., extreme movements like crashes, that contradict the forecasts formulated by the models. The markets react to expectations of expectations, and produce new unpredictability. One then speaks of a new form of "model risk", a result of the model's orientation – not because the models are inaccurate, but precisely because they are accurate[26]. This does not mean that models are inept, as today's extremely abstract financial markets could not function without them: but, more importantly, their task is to manage the lack of correspondence (mismatch) between their representation of the world and the world as it actually is, and not to foretell its destiny.

References

Arnoldi J (2004) Derivatives: virtual values and real risks. Theory, Culture & Society 21, pp. 23–42

Bachelier L (1900, 1964) Théorie de la speculation. Annales de l'École Normale Supérieure 17, pp. 21–86. English translation in: Cootner P (ed) (1964) The random character of the stock market prices. MIT Press, Cambridge (Massachusetts), pp. 17–79

Beck U (1986) Die Risikogesellschaft: Auf dem Weg in eine andere Moderne. Suhrkamp, Frankfurt on the Main

Bronzin V (1908) Theorie der Prämiengeschäfte. Franz Deuticke, Leipzig/ Vienna

Bryan D, Rafferty M (2007) Financial derivatives and the theory of money. Economy and Society 36, pp. 134–158

Caranti F (2003) Guida pratica al trading con le opzioni. Dominare i mercati controllando il rischio. Trading Library, Milan

Colombo A (2006) Investire con le opzioni. Il Sole 24 Ore, Milan

Douglas M, Wildawsky A (1982) Risk and culture: an essay on selection of technological and environmental dangers. University of California Press, Berkeley

Hull J C (1998) Introduction to Futures and Options Markets. Prentice-Hall, Upper Saddle River (New Jersey) (Italian translation: Introduzione ai mercati dei futures e delle opzioni. Il Sole 24 Ore, Milan, 1999)

Keynes J M (1936) The general theory of employment, interest and money. Macmillan, London (Italian translation: Teoria generale dell'occupazione, dell'interesse e della moneta e altri scritti. UTET, Turin, 1978)

Knight F H (1921) Risk, uncertainty and profit. The London School of Economics and Political Science, London

[26] Cf. Stix (1998).

LiPuma E, Lee B (2005) Financial derivatives and the rise of circulation. Economy and Society 34, pp. 404–427
Luhmann N (1991) Soziologie des Risikos. De Gruyter, Berlin/ New York
Mandelbrot B, Hudson R L (2004) The (mis)behavior of markets. A fractal view of risk, ruin, and reward. Einaudi, Turin (Italian translation: Il disordine dei mercati. Una visione frattale di rischio, rovina e redditività. Einaudi, Turin, 2005)
Maurer B (2007) Repressed futures: financial derivatives theological unconscious. Economy and Society 31, pp. 25–36
McKenzie D (2006) An engine, not a camera. How financial models shape markets. MIT Press, Cambridge (Massachusetts)
McKenzie D (2007) The material production of virtuality: innovation, cultural geography and facticity in derivative markets. Economy and Society 36, pp. 355–376
McKenzie D, Millo Y (2003) Constructing a market, performing theory: the historical sociology of a financial derivatives exchange. American Journal of Sociology 109, pp. 107–145
Millman G J (1995) The vandals' crown. Free Press, New York (Italian translation: Finanza barbara. Garzanti, Milan, 1996)
Oldani C (2004) I derivati finanziari. Dalla Bibbia alla Enron. F. Angeli, Milan
Pryke M, Allen J (2000) Monethized time-space: derivatives – money's 'new imaginary'? Economy and Society 29, pp. 264–284
Shiller R J (2003) The New Financial Order. Princeton University Press, Princeton (Italian translation: Il nuovo ordine finanziario. Il rischio nel XXI secolo. Il Sole 24 ore, Milan, 2003)
Stengers I (1995) Perché non può esserci un paradigma della complessità. In: G Bocchi, M Ceruti (eds) (1995) La sfida della complessità. Feltrinelli, Milan, pp. 61–83
Stix G (1998) A calculus of risk. Scientific American 278, pp. 86–90
Strange S (1986) Casino capitalism. Basil Blackwell, Oxford (Italian translation: Capitalismo d'azzardo. Laterza, Rome/ Bari, 1988)
Swan E J (2000) Building the global market. A 4000 year history of derivatives. Kluwer, The Hague/ London/ Boston
von Foerster H (1981) Observing systems. Intersystems Publications, Seaside (California)
Zimmermann H, Hafner W (2006a) Vinzenz Bronzin's Optionspreismodelle in theoretischer und historischer Perspektive. In: Bessler W (ed) Banken, Börsen und Kapitalmärkte. Festschrift für Hartmut Schmidt zum 65. Geburtstag. Duncker & Humblot, pp. 733–758
Zimmermann H, Hafner W (2006b) Vincenz Bronzin's option pricing theory: contents, contribution, and background. In: Poitras G (ed) (2006) Pioneers of financial economics: contributions prior to Irving Fisher, Vol. 1. Edward Elgar, Cheltenham, pp. 238–264
Zimmermann H, Hafner W (2007) Amazing discovery: Vincenz Bronzin's option pricing models. Journal of Banking and Finance 31, pp. 531–546

Part E
Trieste

Introduction

In Bronzin's days, Trieste was a town marked by contradictions: On the one hand there existed a strong business-orientated attitude, based on the important function of the port as the only access of Austria-Hungaria to the Mediterranean Sea. On the other hand there was as part of the evolution of a specific culture of the *italianità* a trend against a market-orientation of the town, because it was perceived that a market-oriented attitude or/and behaviour endangered the cultural identity. Those contradictory guidelines had developed within the town.

Trieste, "the first port of the Empire", also became more and more a part of the Austrian and Central European economy during the 19th century and this development undermined the special status of the town as a free port and turned into a port of transit. In this transition process towards a new economic stage the wheeler-dealer adventure-like merchant capitalism was replaced by a less speculative and more regulated form of capitalism. Also, the Stock Exchange of Trieste declined and the once important management of the Bourse lost its influence. Parallel to the decline of the stock exchange other functions became more important based on already existing and now prospering institutions: Insurance companies like *Assicurazione Generali* and *Riunione Adriatica di Sicurta* became the leading enterprises in the town. They had a formative impact on local politics through the Chamber of Commerce, where the leading families were reunited. In the following years the Chamber of Commerce became the real government of Trieste.

Parallel with the evolution of insurance companies was a shift in the risk culture in Trieste: During the commercial period in the 19th century, Trieste's businessmen acquired large fortunes generally over one generation, as Anna Millo writes, accompanied by cracks and bankruptcies; but afterwards, in the period of the predominance of the insurance enterprises, a more conservative risk behaviour was cultivated in accordance with the business-model of the insurance companies. That meant lower returns but greater security.

With the evolution of the insurance companies and the decline of the trade-orientated business, the culture of Trieste achieved its culmination with writers like Svevo, Saba and others, as Francesco Magris and Giorgio Gilibert notice in their essay about the cultural landscape. They describe the role of Trieste as an international melting-pot with strong influences from different cultures and so different political interests: The predominant Italian community wished to reunite with Italy. On the other hand the Slaves, the Germans, also the Greeks, the French and the Jewish were generally more affiliated with the culture of the Austro-Hungarian empire. The different interests influenced also the culture of Trieste. Magris and Gilibert remark on the difference between the Austro-Hungarian and the Italian culture: "The schools of the Empire were profoundly rooted in this study of 'realia', of reality in this healthy, vigorous, positive attention dedicated to things ...": So the Habsburgs put their attention more to real things – in contrast to the Triestinian attitude as expressed by Italo Svevo's irony. In the eyes of Magris and Gilibert Bronzin was an exponent of the Austro-Hungarian culture with their strong relation to reality. After World War I with the decline of the empire, the influence of the Austro-Hungarian culture on Trieste naturally diminished.

The success of the insurance ship-business in Trieste was based on a long-standing experience with the marine-trade insurance business, but – more important – on the development of new scientific methods to calculate specific risks in the field of life-insurance. Ermanno Pitacco shows in his article the role of Trieste as a centre of actuarial research. He analyses the period from 1800s to the early 1900s and notices that the actuarial community in Trieste only addressed life insurance topics. Within the insurance companies he also notices a strong concentration on statistical issues, for example on computational topics, formal tools and actuarial models. Issues related to investment risks were basically disregarded. The framework of insurance for the individual was the predominant issue. Pitacco argues, that during the last century a huge number of problems in the framework of individual insurance had to be resolved, and therefore there was no room or need to develop models for financial investments. The financial structure of life insurance products was rather simple and consisted mainly of profit participations and bonus schemes. There was no obvious need to adopt complex pricing models such as those developed by Bronzin. Therefore, it is not surprising why attempts towards a better and more systematic understanding of financial markets were overlooked or neglected. Pitacco describes the world of actuarial science in the 20th century as an essentially a self-contended world with no need to adopt methods developed in other fields of science.

12 Speculation and Security. The Financial World in Trieste in the Early Years of the Twentieth Century

Anna Millo*

The years coinciding with the publication of Vinzenz Bronzin's main work, which appeared in 1908, represent for Trieste a time of fast-paced and intense economic and social development, that put this Adriatic town, before the first World War, on the international map as a great industrial, port and financial centre.

More and more integrated in the economy of the Habsburg Empire, Trieste's financial landscape is still dominated by the merchant families that were the historical protagonists of the growing trading wealth between the 18th and 19th century. They have control of the Stock Exchange, the evolution of the powerful institution created in 1755 to regulate market exchanges and which has followed the decline of this trading centre, now turned into a port of transit. In spite of the limited number of listed companies and monetary exchanges, the Stock Exchange Committee, through its regulations, puts in place a strong self-management and self-regulating system, it issues strict surveillance provisions, and performs a screening function to shape the trading system, overseeing and defending it from the assaults of unrestrained speculation.

The decline of the Stock Exchange is accompanied by the rise of insurance companies. Established in the first half of the 19th century, in the early 20th century *Assicurazioni Generali* and *Riunione Adriatica di Sicurtà* were the main insurance companies of the Habsburg Empire, ready to conquer also the markets of Europe and the Far East. They were still in the hands of Trieste's great historical merchant families, who made up the most relevant and influential group of stakeholders. These were business enterprises aimed to collect private savings, with the need to set aside significant reserves to face unexpected risks, which leads the management to opt for investments that offer lower returns but greater security, mainly consisting in government stock and also in real estate.

Thus speculation and security coexist in a unique balance in Trieste's financial world.

12.1 From the Emporium to the "First Port of the Empire"

The first fourteen years of the twentieth century standing between Europe and the world war coincide for Trieste with the opening of an economic and social cycle of accelerated modernisation and intense development. In this short but intense period of time – that also sees the original and lively contribution of

* Università degli Studi di Bari, Italy. *anna.millo@libero.it*

Trieste's culture in forms not exclusively related to humanities and literature, as witnessed by Vinzenz Bronzin[1] and his mathematical theorization – the town undergoes an extensive transformation that would turn this Adriatic town into "the first port of the Empire" and one of the most important in the Mediterranean. The Emporium and its trading functions between Central Europe and the East, that gained fame between the eighteenth and nineteenth century but has now become outdated in the new era of worldwide trades, was replaced by a great international shipping, industrial and financial centre.

In terms of project scope and weight of investments, the engine of this change and of economic growth is – as in the past – the Austrian State, that takes upon itself the role of propelling force, now supported by Austrian and German capital. New railway connections and the enlargement of port facilities, the thrust to the shipping and ship-building industry propel Trieste towards unexpected achievements. In 1913 port activities hit their highest point, after growing from an average value of 1,903,000 tons in 1900 to 3,450,000 tons in the last year before the war. Demographic growth in that same year reaches its peak too, to remain unparalleled in the history of the town, counting 247,000 inhabitants that make it a "great European centre", the third largest urban settlement of the Empire after Vienna and Prague.

Technological developments, the construction of new infrastructures, the enhancement of transport means and exchange networks, the training of professionals possessing the skills necessary to promote and to guide development – the latter an aspect that is all but secondary to modernisation, where the scientific and didactic work of Vinzenz Bronzin acquires its true meaning – are pivotal for project that the government in Vienna has conceived for Trieste in the context of a bigger plan of industrialization for the economy of the country as a whole. Its champion is, in 1901, Minister Koerber, who intends to prevent the loss for Austria of the power struggle on the international scene and to reduce the contrasts among different nationalities inside the State, that are threatening the solidity of the ancient Empire[2].

Thus Trieste found itself more and more closely integrated in the Austrian and Central-European economy, while at the same time losing that distinctive trait that for two centuries in its history had made it a sort of island in Austrian territory, where the particularism of economic interests that had thrived in the shadow of the free port and the administrative autonomy granted by the State reigned supreme. The local middle-class elites had contributed to this evolution, by obtaining the full support of the State to drive commercial development and urban growth in the golden age of the emporium. The self-governing body of the town and at the same time the representative of the interests of the commercial class was the powerful Committee (*Deputazione*) at the helm of the Mercantile

[1] On the culture in Trieste a vast overview in Ara and Magris (1987). On the figure of Vinzenz Bronzin see Hafner and Zimmermann (2006).

[2] For a more detailed analysis see my previous work Millo (2003), also with reference to the listed bibliography.

Exchange. The institution in charge of the stock and commodities exchange, set up in 1755 under Maria Theresa's rule as Trieste blossomed as a free port, had consolidated its position over the decades through a process of internal selection of its members, recognized as the most reliable operators who were then called to preside over market itself. It was the expression of the great family-run or ethnic-religious commercial houses, that had come to settle down in the eighteenth century in the Adriatic emporium as brokers for trading and shipping activities (including insurance) that were part of the discount and exchange operations circuit, international in its scope just like the horizon of their sales[3].

When, in the early Nineteenth century, in the wake of the new thrust of industrialisation and technology, commerce, credit and insurance had split into separate and distinct activities, the Trieste markets were ready to make the most of existing potential for development, following however a rather peculiar path. Instead of adjusting their traditional brokerage function in commerce by shifting their focus from commodities to stock, according to the model of the merchant banks disseminated all over Europe and engaged exclusively in financial activities, operators in Trieste prefer to get together in associations, allocating the proceeds of their trades into modern enterprises with a large share base, first in shipping and insurance, and then in banking and the industry. This independent entrepreneurial path had been dictated by the peculiar characteristics of the Trieste marketplace, and yet it must not be forgotten that these alliances and cooperation efforts were made possible also by the integrated economic system that had arose under the supervision of the Stock Exchange Committee, with shared regulations to be complied with as an expression of shared underlying values. Cemented in the faithfulness to the original ethnic-cultural heritage in a climate that was open to coexistence and a firm footing in the new society that had grown around the port, a complex web of diverse interests started to diversify in various branches of activity, where however trading and financial capitals remained linked to family-run businesses (Millo 1998, pp. 17–73).

This peculiar scenario – if plunged into a completely different context – is still to be found in the early Twentieth century. At the head of the Stock Exchange "Management" (now called "*Direzione*") in 1913 is a group of economic operators (Borsa Valori di Trieste 1913a) whom we also find as shareholders of the *Banca Commerciale Triestina*, *Riunione Adriatica di Sicurtà* (*Ras*) and *Assicurazioni Generali*, the leading credit and insurance institutions active in Trieste. In some cases they are the heirs of the largest commercial enterprises from the time of the emporium, who were able to diversify and increase their interests (Giovanni Scaramangà, Demetrio Economo, Riccardo Albori, Gustavo Schütz, all directors of *Generali*, the former three having been bestowed by the Habsburgs with aristocratic titles in recognition of the honourable reputation that accompanied their business success); others are members of the same family (the economic structure repository of the good

[3] For more general aspects see Curtin (1988), pp. 237 ff. For the local dimension see De Antonellis Martini (1968) and Millo (2001), especially pp. 382–388.

name of the enterprise and of the trust it evokes on the markets), whose members hold similar positions of economic and social prestige (Carlo Escher, brother of Alfredo, *Ras* director and member of the *Herrenhaus*, the branch of the Austrian Parliament appointed by the Empire; Massimiliano Brunner, father of Arminio, a textile entrepreneur and *Ras* director, and cousin of Rodolfo, representative of the Executive board of *Generali*); others, while having come to settle down in Trieste at a later date, have become by now part of the economic elite of the town (Ernesto Nauen, coffee merchant and *Ras* director). Yet others express in themselves their connection to these various institutions (Gustavo Alberti, managing director of *Banca Commerciale Triestina* and *Ras* director). Only a few represent that lesser industry of transformation that recently, through local capital, has arisen around the intermediate port (Alfredo Pollitzer, soap industrialist). It is a business world (rather than a financial one, in the strictest sense of the term), closely intertwined by a close-knit network of shared interests that dates back to the now faded era of the emporium. The undisputed predominance on the local marketplace is now replaced by the control of interests that remain important, but are limited to well-defined sectors of the economy in Trieste.

12.2 The Decline of the Stock Exchange

The Stock Exchange list[4], while providing a partial depiction of the real economy, reflects the progressive retreat that local enterprises had to face, reclassifying their position according to a new balance of power. A sign of the new developments can be found in the quotation of the shares of the main Viennese banks which, having now penetrated the no-longer defended local marketplace, participate with heavy investments in the new port and industrial economy of Trieste: firstly the Union Bank that, having a share in the Austrian Lloyd, has always concentrated a large portion of its interests in the Adriatic port, but also *Creditanstalt* and *Wienerbankverein*. The latter, following a depression crisis that had led to a steep decrease of interest rates, in 1904 had even succeeded in getting a foot in the Banca Commerciale Triestina, the strongbox – so to speak – of local businesses. The presence of the industry is, instead, scarcely represented and limited to those marginally relevant factories that have recently sprung up thanks to indigenous capital to transform raw materials arrived by sea (*Jutificio Triestino*, *Raffineria di Oli Minerali*). Absent from the list are the much more important shipping and ship-building businesses, the symbol of the new era of integration of the Trieste capital in the Empire (*Cantiere Navale Triestino, Austro-Americana & Fratelli Cosulich*, established with decisive contributions of Austrian capital, like the *Vereinigte Österreichis-*

[4] See as an example Borsa Valori di Trieste (1908), envelope 4 (1), *Corsi di liquidazione stabiliti dalla Direzione di Borsa. Gennaio 1908.* Archivio di Stato di Trieste

che Textilindustrie that was set up in 1912 by Arminio Brunner, sponsored by the *Boden-Credit-Anstalt*), while still present are the Austrian Lloyd with its yard, the Technical Works ("*Stabilimento Tecnico*"). The character of the Trieste-based shipping company established in 1833 for connections between the Mediterranean and the Indian Ocean and the Far East was not put into question, but it was essentially kept afloat by state subsidies, so that the last rescue operation and debt settling dates to 1907.

Of much greater weight, exalted by their uniqueness in the overall modesty of the list, were the shares of the two main insurance companies, *Ras* and *Generali*, with their associates in the hail branch, *Meridionale di Trieste* and *Società Ungherese di Budapest*. At the time these two Trieste-based companies had taken on an international dimension, since their markets extended well beyond the boundaries of the Empire, to Northern Europe and the Mediterranean basin. Their stock, impermeable to Viennese banks, had remained solidly in the hands of the local economic class, bearing witness to their remarkable and enduring financial standing in spite of the blows suffered; see Michel (1976), pp. 213–215, Millo (1989), pp. 22–25 and Sapelli (1990a), pp. 25–29. The quotation of their shares exceeded their nominal value, a sign of the public's approval and perhaps also of a demand that likely surpassed market supply.

National debt circulation was ensured by the presence of the debt of the State (Austrian revenue, Hungarian revenue), of public loans and various bonds.

The decline of the Trieste Stock Exchange following the drying up of its function as trading centre is also made evident by another aspect. Foreign currencies and exchanges are scarcely represented, while currency forward operations had once been one of the most widespread activities at the time of the free port, but they did not survive the introduction in Austria in 1899 of the new convertible golden coin, the crown. Even earlier, in 1894, the establishment of the *Banca Commerciale Italiana* had made Trieste's mediation with Milan for foreign currency transactions superfluous, since from then on this operation could be performed directly from Berlin and Vienna. In this sector too it was precisely the banks, the institutions with the largest financial means, that become such valiant competitors in financial matters as to shut out the most ancient commercial establishments in Trieste that could no longer compete, particularly in the expansion of credit on personal property and in underwriting syndicates (Millo 2005, p. 285).

Also in the absence of a quantitative analysis on the overall business volumes and on the materials that were most often traded – which the currently available sources do not allow – it does not appear misleading to conclude that the Trieste Stock Exchange's role as provider of liquidity for the entire local economic system had been reduced in the early twentieth century to a rather small one.

It is relatively easier, instead, to examine the rules and regulations underpinning its operations, the practices that were adopted, the roles and powers that emerged in its context. Of particular relevance were its self-regulatory function, the surveillance procedures, the filtering action that the local economic operators put in place to deal with a market subject to constant fluctuations, that however would not be forsaken to uncontrollable swings.

When in 1850 and with the subsequent reforms of 1868-69 the Chambers of Commerce were established in Austria, the Chamber of Trieste, taking on the specific task of representing the interests that were entrusted with the new institution, had also taken over the functions and the management of the Stock Exchange, bringing in

> "[...] all the objects and deals concerning the exchange, the sale and the trade of commodities [...]; the exchange of money or of bills representing currencies, and the people who deal with them in their profession; particularly it includes anything related to the institute of exchange, the performance of the Stock Exchange, the brokers, any commercial association and organization of similar entities [...]"[5] (Millo 2005, pp. 274–275).

At that time the emporium had entered an irreversible crisis, a prelude to the abolition of the free port decreed in 1891, and the Stock Exchange had followed suit. Nevertheless, the local economic class was careful not to relinquish its predominance on what remained, still, the most important business regulating centre on a local scale. Therefore in the new system the Stock Exchange Committee became an executive body of the Chamber of Commerce. In Trieste the management of the Stock Exchange was not made up of and elected by the traders, as was the case elsewhere, but it was appointed by the Chamber itself, that chose among its members the eight representatives to be charged with running the institution, while the president and vice-president were the same who held these posts at the Chamber. This close-knit relation remained tight even when, following the crack that in 1873 had wrecked the Vienna Stock Exchange, in 1875 in Austria a new law came into force on the organisation of Stock Exchanges. It provided for its complete autonomy, while remaining compliant with other fundamental normative guarantees that were valid throughout the national territory to which local customs in use at the time had to adjust. In 1878 the Trieste Chamber of Commerce issued the new Statute, in which the Committee still depended for its essential tasks of surveillance and control on the Chamber itself (Camera di Commercio e d'Industria di Trieste 1878)[6]. In this phase regulations were issued on stock exchange activities, aimed to shape its main traits also for the future.

The Trieste Stock Exchange clearly distinguished – according to the Austrian law of 1875 – between commercial operations and others related to bills (i.e. bills of exchange, credit instruments), currencies and exchanges. As regards the latter, a regulation of 1880 remained in force that envisaged the possibility to

[5] The topic is also discussed by Filini (1921) and Fornasin (2003).
[6] For a juridical analysis see Piccoli (1882).

perform both spot and forward operations, including deals compensated through options defined as *dont, Noch* and *Stellage*[7] (Direzione di Borsa 1880, pp. 11–12). For commerce the "customs of the marketplace" were in force, those provisions of habit that can be referred to the updated regulation issued in 1901, that was interesting also because it points towards the special conditions created by Austrian State policies in favour of Trieste's trades, where art. 2 states:

> "In the absence of special agreements, any foreign good subject to duty is intended to be sold with duty charges to be paid by the purchaser.
>
> For national goods subject to an export premium or the restitution of the fiscal and consumption duty, said premiums shall be given to the seller" (Deputazione di Borsa 1901, p. 1 and p. 10).

From both regulations the will emerges clearly on the part of those in charge of the Stock Exchange to shape the system of transactions so as to make it function efficiently, circumscribing the competition field and translating any possible variant into corresponding rules, defined by custom and experience. This self-regulation of Stock Exchange activities is reflected concretely – having Austria embraced the example from Germany – in the establishment of arbitration, a sort of special panel of magistrates that responded to an ancient aspiration of the Trieste commercial class and its vocation for self-government. Operators whose technical expertise and moral standing were widely recognized were selected to act as arbitrators by virtue of their pragmatic knowledge, thus allowing the whole system to proceed swiftly and efficiently to the solution of any controversy arising in its context (Dorn 1873).

The Law of 1875 also set out the rules illustrating the functions to be performed by the brokers, or "licensed" middlemen. In order to be accepted to the post they were required to pass an examination held by the Management of the Stock Exchange and to be sworn in before the political authorities, in that they had acquired the status of public officials. They were in charge of setting the daily and mark-up prices. They had to comply with strict rules. They were forbidden to close deals when the suspicion existed that they were intended to be concluded only in appearance or to the detriment of third parties. Similarly they were forbidden to trade in securities not quoted on the official Stock Exchange list and to close deals on their own. Furthermore they were forbidden to be representatives or associates of traders, as well as to sit on the board of any company. Without prejudice to the validity of their contract, they were authorised to withhold the name of those who had appointed them, when they had received from this person an adequate coverage[8]. The technical knowledge they were expected to possess, which they had to prove in a competitive

[7] A modern theoretical point of view in Zappa (1994), pp. 25–89.

[8] Interesting information on the provisions of the Austrian law of 1875 can be found in Pfleger and Gschwindt (1899), p. 582.

examination (generally they were graduates of the Academy of Commerce, where Vinzenz Bronzin taught) and the strict ethical precepts that inspired their work, made them a genuine "professional corps", with a corresponding professional corporation (the "*Gremio*" or "Guild of licensed middlemen") to safeguard their interests. While belonging to a lower social class compared to the top businessmen, they represented an important expression of that diverse civil society in Trieste that had thrived in the shadow of the commercial middle-class. The "Guide of Trieste" in the first decade of the 1900s records around sixty members of the professional guild, but only eight specialised in "exchanges and securities", yet another indication of the reduced financial role of the Stock Exchange[9].

Only the Stock Exchange statutes of 1906 and 1912, in a completely different economic scenario, put in motion a progressive loosening of the bond between the Stock Exchange and the Chamber of Commerce, first through the dissolution of the administrative connections, then by opening the way to the Management to Stock traders. While in fact the top institutions remained firmly in the hands of the main representatives of the Trieste economy, as mentioned above, without the addition of any new members, it is significant that, fearing a loosening of the controls, the Management was given even more explicit disciplinary powers against "those who challenged the validity of a deal in a manner that is against good faith, by raising the exception of gambling"; see Borsa di Trieste (1906); Borsa di Trieste (1912).[10]

It is not known whether these restrictions were introduced also to respond to another need, namely to contrast a speculation that had become more intense. As is known, it was particularly forward operations that generated lengthy and controversial discussions, since they attracted those sham and unproductive maneuverings that for quite some time now had led to the bad reputation of the economy of monetary exchange among the general public. Among the operators the opinions were more nuanced. An official inquiry on Stock Exchanges in Germany carried out in 1889 recognised that deals compensated through options "are mainly closed in the periods when the market is in critical conditions, and serve the purpose of artificially containing risks" (Pfleger and Gschwindt 1899, p. 571) while an English economist, Arthur Crump, in 1874 had defined "option speculation [...] the most prudent way to speculate and also the most sensible for all the parties involved"[11] (Crump 1899, p. 349). Censures were pointed to gambling, intended as participation "in Stock Exchange negotiations without knowing anything about the conditions of the market of a certain article, or the

[9] See, as an example, *Guida di Trieste 1915*, Archivio di Stato di Trieste, Trieste, 1915, pp. 788–789. See also *Regolamento interno del Gremio dei sensali patentati*, Archivio di Stato di Trieste, Trieste, 1898. On civil society in Trieste see Millo (1998), pp. 101 ff.

[10] The text refers specifically to article 16 of the last statute, based on which, for example, in 1913 the following disciplinary procedure was undertaken: *Processo disciplinare contro Francesco Primc per eccezione di giuoco*, see the corresponding file in Trieste State Archives, Trieste Stock Exchange, ib. , envelope 12 (2).

[11] Penetrating insights on these issues are expressed in Berta (1990).

commitments undertaken [...] without any reference to the assets and liabilities of the interested party" (Pfleger and Gschwindt 1899, p. 580). Most feared was the interference of smaller speculators, who were believed to be more inclined to cheating and distant from that rational and savvy knowledge of the market that the largest investors claimed to possess. Unlike these opinions, the theory drawn up by Vinzenz Bronzin in 1908 (Bronzin 1908) appears as pure mathematical abstraction, devoid of misleading imprints and inspired by the observation of practical behaviour. But – this begs the question – could having established through a mathematical equation the value of an option have encouraged economic applications that were undesirable in an environment that shied away from external intrusion and reserved to itself the management of the delicate and fluid mechanisms lying at its very foundations?

Similar considerations as the ones put forth for the decline of the Stock Exchange can be formulated also for the trading of commodities (Borsa Valori di Trieste 1913b), limited in this period to a few items (citrus fruits, cottons, groceries and drugs) destined to a market that is no more than regional, outside of the main international shipping traffic that concerns most of the arrivals, replacing the trade of the emporium. The only novelty concerns the coffee futures market, that characterised for some time the largest European ports like Bremen, Antwerp and Le Havre, but started in Trieste only in 1907, after the revision of the Statute of the Stock Exchange with the inclusion of a specific provision for its introduction[12]. The reason for such a delay in the starting of trades for a commodity that, by its own nature, requires operations of this type, with purchases before harvest and sales for a later date, is probably to be found in the fact that in order to start this commercial activity the local operators called for the participation of the State and this is likely to have required quite a lengthy legislative and bureaucratic process. As the rapid rise of the port of Trieste in the early 1900s was the result of a particular customs and tariffs policy, set to offer conditions that would increase trading in the Adriatic port, also for coffee arriving to Trieste a differential duty was levied as well as special facilitations for re-export to the East. This specific case too documents how entrepreneurship in Trieste results from the happy marriage between innovative endogenous forces and the action of the State, ready to respond to its needs.

Elements of speculation are not, to be sure, completely foreign to this branch of trade ("Ah that coffee that in Brazil is badly blossoming this spring!", exclaims in 1912 Scipio Slataper in his most famous novel[13] (Slataper 1989, p. 102) referring to the hopes for a rise in its value), where large liquid capitals are invested, for which the difference in price, the carry-over, represents the interest on the capital invested. However here too the market was carefully guarded. In 1891, at the time when the free port status was abolished, an "Association of interested parties to the coffee trade" was set up, which brought together the

[12] The "customs of the marketplace" only envisaged "*a caricazione* or fixed delivery or by a set deadline": See Deputazione di Borsa (1901), p. 10.
[13] On the culture in Trieste see again Ara and Magris (1987).

main players on the Trieste economic scene, Adolf Escher, Tönnes Konow (also on the board of *Banca Commerciale Triestina*), the great commercial institution of Morpurgo&Parente (with a similar interest in the *Banca*). The "Settlement Bank", to enable associates to meet their deadlines and fulfill their obligations and to find coverage and extensions, was set up in 1907 with a guarantee fund that saw the participation of *Generali*, *Ras*, the Chamber of Commerce and the Austrian Lloyd, in other words the main players on the Trieste economic and Stock Exchange scene, joined together in that inextricable tangle of commerce and finance that has always been their distinctive trait right from the start[14]. Free bargaining on the market, price fluctuation are all elements that not only are not foreign, but that are intimately familiar and mastered by the operators themselves. Also the interaction between the State and the market – so typical of the economic history of Trieste in the Habsburg era – contributes to creating a market that is guarded and defended rather than inclined to welcome the assaults of speculation.

12.3 The Rise of Insurance Companies

In the nineteenth century, when activities in the Emporium reach their peak, the Stock Exchange, representing the meeting place for the supply and demand of goods and services, contributed to price setting and to trading credit instruments, and later to the circulation of the national debt. Buying and selling was done "within four months" or on the spot, in cash, with a two or three percent discount (Beltrami 1959, p. 2). Speculation was therefore mainly centred on price differentials, variations between marketplaces that were not integrated due to the vast distances that separated them at a time when communications were still backwards. The considerable profits derived however also from the almost exclusive monopoly of Trieste in the Adriatic trade, after the decline of Venice and Ancona, while Rijeka – which was to be awarded free port status only in 1867 – would specialise in business with Hungary.

The cases of Trieste traders who acquired a large wealth in short periods of time, generally over one generation, accompanied by cracks and bankruptcies that were just as numerous, were interpreted by the operators as a sign of the healthy condition of the market. The risk was not hidden, but conceived as an integral part of commercial activities, where uncertainty reigned supreme: uncertainty over the possible insolvency of a debtor, uncertainty in the difficult art of controlling information when faraway European and non-European markets were reached at a time of slow communication and without the support of the telegraph, but also uncertainty for the possible loss of ships and shipments for events that were utterly unforeseeable, a storm, a shipwreck, a fire. Controlling the risk – the insurance policies underwritten on the marketplace that

[14] Useful information, if partially inexact, in Associazione Caffe' Trieste (1991), pp. 29–32.

were offered from the 1700s by an association of Trieste dealers[15] – becomes first a business, and later a business enterprise proper. Risk speculation and entrepreneurship thus coexist on the Trieste marketplace since its origin and its peculiarity lies in making insurance activities thrive – building on the experience acquired after one century on the international foreign exchange and money market – until they become more structured into modern companies with a large share base. *Assicurazione Generali* (established in 1831) and *Riunione Adriatica di Sicurtà* (established in 1838) enlarged the field of risk, promoting new directions for expansion, towards Italy, the Danube area, the East and the Hanseatic towns. Around the middle of the century the marked economic and social development of the most advanced portion of the continent leads to the identification of the wealthy middle-class as the main target for the life branch. Between the 1870s and 1880s another decisive passage takes place for Trieste's insurance industry, the separation of the management from the control exerted by risk capital. Company managers and groups, possessing more and more refined technical knowledge, draw up new innovation strategies that bring the two Trieste-based companies in the early 1900s to become leaders in the Empire in terms of structure and size[16].

Two are the aspects on which this analysis will focus.

The first regards the special financial nature of the insurance companies, an instrument to collect and manage private saving. In this sense their investment policy is as far as possible from the concept of speculation, inspired instead by criteria of extreme prudence and caution. Indeed, they pursue an optimum balance between real estate investments and government stock, which has low returns but is more reliable. Commenting on the funds available in 1909 and the use to be made of said funds, the board of directors of *Generali* tellingly opted for "the principle of not increasing exceedingly the investments in stocks and shares, but investing instead significant sums of money in real estate purchases, also in the belief that owning great palaces [...] will prove an effective advertising opportunity" (Assicurazioni Generali 1909). If in some countries (like Italy, Spain, Germany, Greece) investments in state securities were dictated by precise provisions of law, this choice was nevertheless pursued with conviction by the top insurance management for its relative security. In 1914, right before the war, *Assicurazioni Generali* boasted a corporate capital of 12,600,000 crowns, while the guarantee funds they had collected amounted to 480,984,656 crowns. Without considering investments in real estate, the saving thus collected was invested for a total of 254,309,342 crowns in "bond paper", of which 226,814,563 crowns belonging to the life branch and 27,494,779 to elementary branches. Investments in the monetary circuit were divided into loans to the State (for example, Austrian revenue, Austrian war loan, Hungarian

[15] As early as 1770 a mercantile circular took note of the insurance competition in the emporium: the document is published in Basilio (1914), pp. 308–309.

[16] On the origins of insurance in Trieste see Sapelli (1990b). For subsequent developments see Millo (2004).

treasury bills), to cities (loan to the city of Vienna, Prague, Trieste, Leopoli), railways and public works.

More limited sums based on the smaller size of the enterprise, but the same choice of use characterised the *Riunione*, whose corporate capital in 1914 amounted to 10 million crowns with guarantee funds amounting overall to 180,678,102 crowns. Invested in Austrian public bills were 68,101,678 crowns from the life branch and 21,878,441 crowns from the elementary branches, divided into Austrian and Hungarian revenue at 4%, provincial loans (Galicia, Krain), railway bonds (in Upper Austria, Moravia, Galicia, Bosnia-Herzegovina). The two Trieste-based companies played a role that was therefore important in funding the development and the transformation of the economy of the Empire, to which they contributed also in another form, by underwriting "debentures" of savings banks and of mortgage banks, interested through the concession of mortgage credits to the modernisation of agriculture. Very rare are instead for the two companies the interests in the shares of banks engaged in credit for the industry and commerce. The latter is clearly viewed as too risky and too uncertain an investment compared to the aims of the insurance industry, that opts instead for full independence in their presence on the financial circuits[17] (see Assicurazioni Generali 1915, pp. 22–26 and Riunione Adriatica di Sicurta' in Trieste 1915, pp. 8–11).

The second remark focuses on the technical-actuarial aspects that are the foundations of the insurance activity. Since the image of an insurance that is fully trustworthy is closely intertwined with such knowledge, it did not remain exclusively in the hands of an inner circle of experts, but was presented to a larger audience as per the will of the management of the two companies.

The occasion presented itself for *Generali* in 1906, when it became necessary to acknowledge the fact that a downward trend was afoot internationally in capital rentability. Therefore the 4 percent rate of interest offered on insurance premium tariffs together with the one linked to the calculation of the mathematical reserves of premiums was lowered to 3.5 percent. Hence the need to undertake a complex operation to adjust to the new rate not only future reserves, but also those of existing portfolios, in order to prevent a non-homogeneous capitalisation that would continue for the duration of the policies under way. First *Generali* (1906) then, a few years later, *Riunione* who followed its sister company along the same route (1911), identified the most suitable instrument in an increase in their corporate capital, whose profit would be used to integrate reserves, all brought from 4 to 3.5 percent. The measure for both companies was carried out by the historical families, part of the body of shareholders in many instances since the very establishment, ruling out resorting to external forces, like Austrian and German banks for which Trieste's insurance companies thus remained off-limits. It was nevertheless necessary not to overlook possible negative consequence among the clients.

[17] For a more general overview see Feis (1977), especially pp. 163–168.

The operation proposed by the Management – wrote *Generali* to its shareholders – would bring to the Company great moral and material advantages. Indeed [...] its prestige will be enhanced before the public for the remarkable increase in the guarantees offered to the insured [...] (Assicurazioni Generali 1906a).

In such a delicate scenario the correct management and the healthy technical and commercial organisation could however prove not to be enough to appease the anxiety of the clients and it was therefore necessary to show maximum transparency to maintain their trust. Both *Generali* and *Ras* printed then between 1906 and 1908 two publications, characterised by great scientific rigour, but undoubtedly aimed at a non-specialist public. The volume by *Generali* presented with corporate pride the merits of the two technical experts who had most contributed to the drawing up of the probabilistic thought at the heart of the life branch, which would in the future prove to be indeed the true cornerstone of the entrepreneurial fortunes of both the Trieste-based companies. Vitale Laudi, born in Trieste in 1837, had graduated in mathematics in Padua in 1859, while the dealer Wilhelm Lazarus, born in Hamburg in 1825, regarded as the intellectual father of the complex calculations carried out by the pair, was a self-taught mathematician. Starting in the 1860s he participated with original contributions to discussions in the context of the German actuarial culture, the most advanced of the continent, a typical representative of a time when science and practice were still engaged in active dialogue. The mathematical part of the book was devoted to issues such as the equalisation of the "table" of *Generali*, the biological foundation of the "equalisation formula" according to Lazarus, continuous life annuities and their relations, the actuarial value of a capital payable at the death of one or more insured. The second part was entirely devoted to the technical values of insurance, in other words it presented the *Table of mortality* perfected by Laudi-Lazarus over the course of the 1870s-80s (see Assicurazione Generali 1906b).

But actuarial science at the time was a sort of "work in progress", constantly debated. *Generali* itself, a few years later, feeling that this model was inadequate, ended up adopting a revised version by Julius Graf. Among the most gifted talents of the new generation of *Generali* technical experts, he was also engaged on the front of the professional syndicate of Austrian actuaries, who in those years were debating how to compile tables of mortality for Austria and Hungary[18].

More concise was the publication by *Ras*, that in the past had found its reference instead in the English actuarial culture. It presented its tables of

[18] For more details see Assicuarzioni Generali (1931), p. 224. Graf's important role is documented in Graf (1906). The substantial return of *Generali* to the Gompertz-Makeham model was illustrated in Zimmermann and Hafner (2007), especially p. 255 and footnote 46; and Zimmermann and Hafner (2006), especially pages 541–542.

mortality (*Tables of the Riunione*)[19], drawn up in 1908 by Luigi Riedel, then a young official who would become a manager in the life branch twenty years later. Similarly to Graf, he represents a later generation compared to Laudi-Lazarus, which by virtue of its scientific background, could take advantage of solid theoretical bases, formalised through academic teaching. Born in 1877 (not many years separated him then from Vinzenz Bronzin, born in 1872), Riedel had graduated from the Polytechnic in Vienna and in 1897 obtained the title of "authorised insurance surveyor". The same title was also bestowed a few years later upon Guido Voghera, the mathematician (and leading representative of the Trieste intelligentsia, in contact with Umberto Saba and Italo Svevo) whom Bronzin in 1910 – holding his skills in high esteem – would call him to teach at the Academy of Commerce after taking on the direction of the school that trained in Trieste managers and executives for the banking and insurance sector[20]. The great expansion on the industrial plan was accompanied by the need for a technical education that was more and more up to date[21].

It can therefore be concluded that, if the financial world in Trieste (within which speculation and security coexisted in an uncommon balance) enjoyed surrounding itself with an impenetrable veil of silence and confidentiality to safeguard that control of information that was an essential part of its perfect command of market mechanisms, the new bases of scientific-technical knowledge of an actuarial type were not confined simply to the closed environment of the managers, but were part of a larger circulation, an element that is not secondary in that culture that had penetrated and was largely distributed in the civil fabric that made of the Trieste under Habsburg rule a truly European centre.

References

Ara A, Magris C (1987) Un identità di frontiera, 2nd edn. Einaudi, Torino

Asquini A (1926) Il giudizio arbitrale presso la Borsa di Trieste. La Tipolito editrice, Padua/Trieste

[19] See Riunione Adriatica di Sicurtà in Trieste (1908). Over the course of this research, it was not possible to track down the corresponding Italian version, that was certainly published.

[20] His professional resume is contained in Subak (1917), p. 289. Voghera had been suspended from teaching in the Italian gymnasium, an independent school run not by the State but by the City, due to respectability issues with his personal life.
His figure as an intellectual, his studies, his work as a teacher in the memories of his son Giorgio Voghera, see Voghera (1980), pp. 191–212.

[21] The Academies of Commerce in Austria were regarded as schools that could provide a high-level education: see the considerations of a US observer, who had carried out a survey in Europe on behalf of the American Bankers' Association, James (1893). In the early twentieth century the development of knowledge in the field of insurance made it necessary to update school curricula. A spokesman of this trend in Germany was one of the leading theoreticians on insurance, Alfred Manes, see Manes (1903). Bronzin's 1908 work is undoubtedly influenced by this climate.

Assicurazioni Generali (1906a) Onorevole Signore! (letter to the shareholders) 5th November 1906. Archivio Storico di Banca Intesa, patrimonio Banca Commerciale Italiana, Segretaria generale, Cartella 4, Fascicolo 4, Compagnia di Assicurazioni Generali

Assicurazione Generali (1906b) Il funzionamento matematico delle Assicurazioni Generali in Trieste. Editrice la Compagnia, Trieste

Assicurazioni Generali (1909) Archivio Storico di Banca Intesa, patrimonio Banca Commerciale Italiana, Segretaria generale, Cartella 4, Fascicolo 5, Compagnia di Assicurazioni Generali. Banca Commerciale Italiana, Venice branch of Comit, 1st December 1909. Venice

Assicurazioni Generali (1915) Rapporti e bilanci per l'anno 1914. Editrice la Compagnia, Trieste

Assicuarzioni Generali (1931) 1831–1931. Il centenario delle Assicurazioni Generali. Editrice la Compagnia, Trieste

Associazione Caffe' Trieste (1991) Cent'anni di caffè 1891 Trieste 1991. Tipolito Stella, Trieste

Basilio F (1914) Origine e sviluppo del nostro diritto marittimo. Trani Editore, Trieste

Beltrami D (1959) I prezzi nel Portofranco e nella Borsa merci di Trieste dal 1825 al 1890. In: Archivio economico dell'unificazione italiana, Vol. VIII, Fascicolo 2. ILTE, Turin

Berta G (1990) Capitali in gioco. Cultura economica e vita finanziaria nella City di fine Ottocento. Marsilio, Venice

Borsa di Trieste (1906) Statuto. Trieste

Borsa di Trieste (1912) Statuto. Trieste

Borsa Valori di Trieste (1908) Corsi di liquidazione stabiliti dalla Direzione di Borsa. Archivio di Stato di Trieste, Sec. XIX–XX (unfiled, temporary numbering), Envelope 4 (1), January. Trieste

Borsa Valori di Trieste (1913a) Letter to the Stock Exchange Management underwritten by all its components. Archivio di Stato di Trieste, Sec. XIX–XX (unfiled, temporary numbering), Envelope 12 (2), 17th March. Trieste

Borsa Valori di Trieste (1913b) Prezzo corrente compilato dalla Direzione di Borsa con la cooperazione del Gremio dei sensali di Borsa. Archivio di Stato di Trieste, Envelope 12 (2), 24th March. Trieste

Bronzin V (1908) Theorie der Prämiengeschäfte. Franz Deuticke, Leipzig/ Vienna

Camera di Commercio e d'Industria di Trieste (1878) Statuto della Borsa Mercantile di Trieste. Tipografia del Lloyd Austriaco, Trieste

Crump A (1899) Teoria delle speculazioni di Borsa, traduzione di Luigi Einaudi. Unione Tipografico-Editrice Torinese, Turin ("Biblioteca dell'economista") (Original edition: Crump A (1874) The theory of stock exchange speculation. Longmans, Green, Reader & Dyer, London)

Curtin P D (1988) Commercio e cultura dall'antichità al Medioevo. Laterza, Bari/ Rome

de Antonellis Martini L (1968) Portofranco e communità etnico-religiose nella Trieste settecentesca. Giuffrè, Milan

Deputazione di Borsa (1901) Usi di piazza. Tipografia Morterra, Trieste

Direzione di Borsa (1880) Norme e condizioni per la regolazione delle operazioni in effetti divise e valute alla Borsa di Trieste. Editrice la Direzione di Borsa, Trieste

Dorn A (1873) I tribunali arbitrali di Borsa. Tipografia Figli di C. Amati, Trieste

Feis H (1977) Finanza internazionale e stato. Europa banchiere del mondo 1870-1914. Etas Libri, Milan (Originally published in 1972, Yale)

Filini S (1921) Borse e mercati di Trieste. In: Il risorgimento economico della Venezia Giulia nella sua sintesi storico-illustrativa. Published by the author, Trieste/ Milan, pp. 101–114

Fornasin A (2003) La Borsa e la Camera di Commercio di Trieste (1755–1914). In: Finzi R, Panariti L, Paniek G (2003) Storia economica e sociale di Trieste, Vol. 2. Lint, Trieste, pp. 143–189

Graf J (1906) Die Fortschritte auf dem Gebiete des Unterrichts in Versicherungs-Wissenschaft in Österreich. In: Berichte, Denkschriften und Verhandlungen des Fünften Internationalen Kongresses für Versicherungs-Wissenschaft. Herausgegeben von Alfred Manes, Vol. II. Mittler und Sohn, Berlin, pp. 409–422

Hafner W, Zimmermann H (2006) Vinzenz Bronzin's Optionspreismodelle in theoretischer und historischer Perspektive. In: Bessler W (ed) Banken, Börsen und Kapitalmärkte. Festschrift für Hartmut Schmidt zum 65. Geburtstag. Duncker & Humblot, Berlin, pp. 733–758

James E J (1893) Education of business men in Europe. American Bankers' Association, New York, pp. 3–52

Manes A (1903) Versicherungs-Wissenschaft auf deutschen Hochschulen. E.S. Mittler und Sohn, Berlin

Michel B (1976) Banques et banquiers en Autriche au début du XX.e siècle. Fondation nationale des sciences politiques, Paris

Millo A (1989) L'élite del potere a Trieste. Una biografia collettiva 1891–1938. Franco Angeli, Milan

Millo A (1998) Storia di una borghesia. La famiglia Vivante a Trieste dall'emporio alla guerra mondiale. Libreria Editrice Goriziana, Gorizia

Millo A (2001) La formazione delle élites dirigenti. In: Finzi R, Paniek G (2001) Storia economica e sociale di Trieste, Vol. 1. Lint, Trieste, pp. 382–388

Millo A (2003) Il capitalismo triestino e l'impero. In: Finzi R, Panariti L, Paniek G (2003) Storia economica e sociale di Trieste, Vol. 2. Lint, Trieste, pp. 125–142

Millo A (2004) Trieste, le assicurazioni, l'Europa. Arnoldo Frigessi di Rattalma e la Ras. Franco Angeli, Milan

Millo A (2005) Dalle origini [della camera di commercio] all'abolizione del porto franco (1850–1891). In: Il palazzo della borsa vecchia di Trieste tra arte e storia, 1800–1980. Camera di Commercio Industria e Artigianato, Trieste, pp. 274–275

Pfleger F J, Gschwindt L (1899) La riforma delle Borse in Germania, traduzione di Luigi Einaudi. Unione Tipografico-Editrice Torinese, Turin ("Biblioteca dell'economista")

Piccoli G (1882) Elementi di diritto sulle borse e sulle operazioni di borsa secondo la legge austriaca e le norme della Borsa triestina. Stabilimento Artistico-Tipografico G. Caprin, Trieste

Poitras G (2006) Pioneers of financial economics: contributions prior to Irving Fischer. Edward Elgar Publishing, Cheltenham

Riunione Adriatica di Sicurtà in Trieste (1908) Die Sterblichkeitstafeln der k.k. priv. Riunione Adriatica di Sicurtà in Triest und ihre tabellarische Auswertung zu einem Zinsfuße von 3 1/2%. Buchdruckerei des österreichischen Lloyd, Trieste

Riunione Adriatica di Sicurtà in Trieste (1915) Rapporti e bilanci del 76° esercizio 1914. S.n.t., Trieste

Sapelli G (1990a) Trieste italiana. Mito e destino economico. Franco Angeli, Milan

Sapelli G (1990b) Uomini e capitali nella Trieste dell'Ottocento. In: L'impresa come soggetto storico. Il Saggiatore, Milan, pp. 221–270

Slataper S (1989) Il mio Carso. Rizzoli, Milan (1st edition published in 1912, Libreria della Voce, Florence)

Subak G (1917) Cent'anni di insegnamento commerciale. La sezione commerciale della I.R. Accademia di Commercio e Nautica di Trieste. Trieste

Voghera G (1980) Biografia di Guido Voghera. In: (Dello stesso) Gli anni della psicanalisi. Studio Tesi, Pordenone, pp. 191–212

Zappa G (1994) La tecnica della speculazione di Borsa. Utet, Turin (1st edition published in 1952)

Zimmermann H, Hafner W (2006) Vincenz Bronzin's option pricing theory: contents, contribution, and background. In: Poitras (2006), pp. 238–264

Zimmermann H, Hafner W (2007) Amazing discovery: Vincenz Bronzin's option pricing models. Journal of Banking and Finance 31, pp. 531–546

13 The Cultural Landscape of Trieste at the Beginning of the 20th Century – an Essay

Giorgio Gilibert* and Francesco Magris**

In this paper, we explore the cultural and economic landscape of the city of Trieste at the beginning of the 20th century. Our aim is to study whether and to what extent it might have influenced and inspired Vinzenz Bronzin's *Theorie der Prämiengeschäfte* (*Theory of Premium Contracts*) and the other related works by the Austrian economist and mathematician. We establish the deep reciprocal links existing between the – at that time rising – cultural identity of Trieste as it appears in the works of its literary elite and the tumultuous economic development the city was experiencing. It is not indeed a mere coincidence that Trieste has been one of the birthplaces of the literature of the crisis of the bourgeoisie and that its writers took inspiration – although without being always aware of it – from the great intuitions in fields such as the natural sciences, mathematics and economics. At the same time, it seems to us unlikely that Vinzenz Bronzin did not take advantage in his groundbreaking contribution to the Theory of Premium Contracts from the widespread literary engagement, as well as from the effervescent economic environment characterizing the city of Trieste at that time. We therefore argue that besides its contribution to the literature, Trieste has also been a great intellectual laboratory in economics and other sciences, although sometimes neglected, and the case of Bronzin – maybe the most significant – is nevertheless not the only one.[1]

13.1 Introduction: The Problem of Cultural Identity

In an article that appeared in "La Voce[2]" in 1909, Scipio Slataper – the writer who three years later would create, would invent, the literary and poetic landscape of Triestine-ness – wrote that "Trieste has no cultural traditions". This somewhat peremptory declaration – unfair, but nevertheless true at a deeper level

* Università degli Studi di Trieste, Italy. *giorgio.gilibert@econ.units.it*
** Université d'Evry-Val-d'Essonne, France. *francesco.magris@univ-evry.fr*

[1] It is impossible to provide a comprehensive bibliography – given the vast number of historical, cultural, scientific, economic and literary studies concerning Trieste and Venezia Giulia – for an article dedicated in part to Bronzin, in part to scientific culture, and in part to Triestine literature. We provide a selected bibliography in the appendix to this essay.

[2] A literary review lasting a few decades across the 19th and the 20th century to which many intellectual spirits of Trieste contributed. The articles appeared in Italian, although Trieste was then under the Austro-Hungarian Empire. The review consituted an ideal laboratory for the formation of the cultural identity of Trieste.

– not only overlooks Vinzenz Bronzin's *Theorie der Prämiengeschäfte* (Theory of Premium Contracts), published the year before in Vienna: it seems unaware, too, that in 1909 there already existed (and had already been filed away or forgotten, waiting to be rediscovered decades later as masterpieces) Svevo's[3] first two novels, *A life* (1892) and *Senility* (1898). These two works breathe that twilight atmosphere of the individual, the decline of conventional man and bourgeois culture, something which Slataper perhaps cannot understand, despite his inspired grasp of Ibsen, which prompted him to write his great essay on the Norwegian writer, because he aspired to found a culture, and therefore a unity of values, rather than observe the disintegration of every universalistic *Kultur*.

However, apart from his incomprehension of Svevo – something he has in common with a number of famous Italian critics in later years – the young Slataper shrewdly sensed that the distinctiveness of Trieste – the specific quality of that peculiar cultural melting pot which is at the same time an archipelago of cultures both different from and ignorant of one another – had not yet found its cultural expression, its literary expression, and not even its own self-awareness. And it is this culture which he, together with an extraordinary team of a few gifted young friends, wished to establish, and he did so by giving the first literary example of it with *Il mio Carso* (1912), whose first three paragraphs all begin with the words "I would like to tell you" – i.e. exorcising any temptation to lie.

He would like to tell his readers, namely Italians, that he was born in a hut on the Carso, or in an oak forest in Croatia, or on the Moravian[4] plain. He would like to give them to understand that he is not Italian and that he has only "learned" the language in which he is writing and that it does not soothe him but rather awakens in him "the desire to return to my own country because here I feel rotten". But instead his "shrewd and perceptive" readers, he adds, would immediately realise that he is "a poor Italian seeking to barbarize his solitary anxieties", one of their brothers intimidated, at most, by their culture and their astuteness.

In the bitter, testy lyricism of his book, Slataper, his sincerity overcoming any impulse to rhetoric, identifies Triestine-ness with the awareness of and admiration for a real but indefinable difference, genuine when experienced in the interiority of feeling, but immediately suspect when proclaimed and exhibited. The heritage and the echoes of other civilisations, which Slataper feels converging within himself and which make him an Italian – albeit a particular Italian – are roots and sap so fused in his person as not to be clearly definable. The obtuse, sneering readers are wrong not to perceive what really makes him different, though any formulation of it – were that possible – would inevitably be false. Slataper was born neither on the Carso, nor in Croatia, nor in Moravia,

[3] Svevo's most important novel remains "The conscience of Zeno". Svevo was an Italian Jew whose real name was Ettore Schmitz. He decided to change name in order to stress his double belonging to Italian culture and to the Swabian one.

[4] At that time Croatia and Moravia were under the Austro-Hungarian Empire. Today, Croatia is an independent country and Moravia a part of the Czech Republic.

Italian was his only language and his real nationality, even though the latter includes a multinational mix, as his name, moreover, suggests: it is a Slav name. In a letter to Gigetta, he would say "You know that I am Slav, German and Italian", and in 1915 he would die, a volunteer in the Italian army, for the cause of the Italianness of Trieste, even though he had culturally and politically been a critic of Irredentism.

13.2 Culture and Humanities in Trieste

In 1909, a culture existed in Trieste, solid and dignified indeed, but insufficient for that spreading Triestine socio-economic reality, vital and composite, and above all insufficient for its implacable contradictions. It was a culture made up of erudite traditions shot through with national passions, historical studies of the fatherland, local memories, a provincial humanism replete with decorum, honest and old-fashioned even though rich in such meticulous historiographic studies as those of Pietro Kandler. There is also a fervour of cultural activity as, for example, the *Società di Minerva*[5] or, for the Germans, the *Schillerverein*, or later, and with greater difficulty, the cultural activity, especially music and theatre, of the Slovene community of Trieste, such as the reading room (*čitalnice*) or the *Glasbena Matica*, the music school. There was a civic reality rich in cultural circles and societies, in libraries, newspapers, publishing enterprises and schools belonging to the different communities. To give some examples: the Minerva had opened a school in French, English, German, Hungarian and neo-Greek in 1872; between 1863 and 1902, there were 560 daily papers and periodicals (83,7% Italian, 5,9% Slav, 5,6% German, 2,6% Greek, 1,1% French, 1,1% Latin, Spanish, bilingual and multilingual); in 1906, there was even an Albanian newspaper; there were many bookshops, German included, such as the *Schimpff*. Moreover, the most important foreign papers were read in a wide variety of languages thanks to the cafés, the reading rooms and the lecture series. From the end of the 18th centuries, newspapers like the *Triester Weltkorrespondent* and the *Triester Kaufmannsalmanach*, both commercial newspapers, began to include information about Italian literature. Between 1838 and 1840, the Italian newspaper *La Favilla* and the German *Adria* commited themselves to a reciprocal exchange of cultural information, an aim pursued open-mindedly by the *Journal des Őesterreichischen Lloyd*[6], by its Italian version *Giornale del Lloyd*, by the *Osservatore triestino* and the *Illustriertes Familienbuch des Ősterreichischen Lloyd*.

This information testifies to the existence of various communities – apart from the autochthonous Slovene, Greek, Serb, Croatian, Armenian, not to speak

[5] The *Società di Minerva* was a literary circle around which gravitated many influential cultural personalities. It played an important role in the spreading of Italian identity.

[6] Lloyd Adriatico is a ship-owning company that is still active. Today, it is a public company, having faced many economic problems and for that reason nationalised.

of the Jewish, all highly important on the political, economic and cultural plane, a melting pot of Italian-ness of people of different origin. There was a real circulation, a real meeting of different elements within the civic fabric: *Lloyd Austriaco*, which Bruck – the businessman who was to become one of Franz Joseph's ministers – had seen as the instrument to make Trieste the great economic centre of the vast Danubian-Central European area, became the promoter, for instance, of one of the finest editions of the Italian classics. With regard to this vital cultural reality, the literature is totally inadequate, anachronistic and poor: a modest even though ample production of Italian lyric poetry, which echoed the stylistic forms and themes of Italian literature from decades earlier, and settled into its delayed late-classical or late-Romantic positions, enlivened by the generally patriotic, *Risorgimento* Italian spirit, but totally detached from the turbulent and at times also dramatic political and economic reality of Trieste.

The same can be said of the literary production in German, even more modest and more removed from the life of the city, as was, for that matter, the society that recognised itself in the *Schillerverein.* For example, a poet like Robert Hamerling lived for years in Trieste without knowing the city, without being known by it, and without being in the least influenced by it in his late-Romantic production. The *Racconti del Litorale* of Moritz Horst, pseudonym of Anna Schimpff, does not go beyond the conventional description of the Italo-German, Slovene Triestine *koinè*. Similar things may be said of the Italian poets – Revere, Besenghi degli Ughi, Fachinetti, Picciola or Pitteri, imitators of Carducci and Pascoli to name but a few – and even more of still more modest story-tellers, among whom there is not the slightest awareness of that tumultuous, contradictory Triestine reality which for Slataper had to be – and in reality would become – the sap of an extraordinary literature, without roots and thus particularly suitable to express an uprootedness which seemed to be the general existential condition of the world, at least of the Western world; without identity, or an identity uncertain and contradictory, which would become one of the most significant forms of the fragmentary, disturbing and disturbed, contemporary identity *tout court.*

To trivialise matters in a simplifying but essential synthesis, the reality of Trieste was based on a contradiction which at the same time undermined it, that is to say, on the contradiction between its economic vitality, connected with its belonging to the multinational Habsburg Empire whose great port it was, and the culture produced by that reality but not yet aware of itself. This was an Italian culture and historically it started off in the direction of irredentism, towards the spiritual need to detach itself from the Empire so as to become part of Italy, thereby realizing its own cultural vocation while denying its birthplace.

Trieste, as is known, had been transformed from a small and largely insignificant Italian municipality into a cosmopolitan, commercial city, thanks to the measures of the Emperor Charles VI and of Maria Theresa for the port – 1717, free navigation in the Adriatic; 1719, Free Port – and thanks also to the influx of enterprising businessmen arriving from all over Europe, in particular Central Europe. Often without real culture, they were nevertheless gifted with the sanguine vitality of an emerging class. This "Triestine nation", as the historians call it, incorporated into the Italian element all these composite elements of diverse nationalities. Up until the end of the 19th century, more or less, this same Triestine nation conceived of its own Italian-ness in cultural terms. Later, however, it began to feel it as a political objective. So irredentism was born, with all the lacerations that entailed, and which were pointed out, with unparalleled clarity, in Angelo Vivante's great book *Irredentismo adriatico*. Published in the same year as *Il mio Carso* it defines, as far as political and economic analysis is concerned, that rift between economic reality and irredentist ideology which characterises the Triestine bourgeoisie.

Hence the paradox whereby the greatest Italian patriots of Trieste – many of whom died fighting for Italy as volunteers in the First World War and after whom many of the streets in the city are named – bear surnames that are German, Slav, Greek, Armenian and, in particular, Jewish. The Jewish community, consisting of families from various parts of Europe, played an outstanding role in the economic, cultural and political life of Trieste and for the most part identified with the Italian cause. Thus was born what Slataper calls "the double soul" of Trieste, which is simultaneously the greatness and the tragedy of Trieste:

> "The city is Italian. And it is the seaport for German interests".

And he continues by saying that the commercial goods and the different origins of the new people nourish Trieste but also create

> "the torment of two natures colliding to cancel each other out: the commercial and the Italian. And Trieste can block neither of the two: it is its double soul; it would kill itself. Everything commercial is necessary and a violation of Italian-ness; increase in the former is damage to the latter" (Slataper 1954, p. 45).

Slataper writes that "the historical task of Trieste is to be the crucible and the propagator of civilisation, of three civilizations" – Italian, German and Slav – and he realises that, underlying this possibility of being a crucible – a real crucible which he also wants to help become aware of itself, namely through culture and letters – there is no Apollo, poetry and literature, but rather Mercury, god of commerce. This misalliance between Apollo and Mercury nevertheless brings about an uneasy insecurity, a trans-evaluation, and makes of Trieste an ambiguous "place of transition" where "everything is double or triple". The "wheeler-dealer character" of Trieste bears down upon the atmosphere of the city "like grey lead", conferring upon it – again in Slataper's words – "a distinctive anxiety". In a city bereft of cultural traditions, characterised by a new bourgeoisie well-nigh ignorant of culture, the literature that lies outside the humanistic pantheon of patriotic letters knows no institutionalisation, takes on none of the dignity of an activity, but is cultivated like a secret vice, between the pauses and the intervals of social and working existence. The place for literature is not the old-fashioned, classicising literary salon but rather the office, Svevo's desk at the Banca Union[7], the back of Saba's bookshop[8], or the tavern, as in the case of Joyce.

Just like Dublin (which is precisely why Joyce found in Trieste a second homeland, as beloved and as unbearable as Ireland), Trieste became a capital of poetry thanks to its painful rifts and to the poverty of its 19th century cultural traditions. Peripheral as regards the great trends of 19th century civilisation, it became a cultural spearhead of the crisis born of that organic civilisation's own crisis and, in this particular case, of the intellectual crisis of Trieste itself which reflects it. The writer conceals himself behind the merchant, but every merchant is a potential writer. The commercial soul is in conflict with the Italian on the economic plane, and with the poetic on the spiritual plane.

"In every merchant", Slataper said, "there is latent a metaphysical ache". But this "soul in torment" is poetry, the "agony [...] of contrary forces and exhausting longings and cruel struggles and desertions" which is the drama that constitutes Trieste: "This", continued Slataper, "is Trieste: composed of tragedy. Anything which it obtains with the sacrifice of life reduces its distinctive anxiety. Peace must be sacrificed to express it, but to express it [...] well, Trieste is a Triestine: it should require a Triestine art. Trieste cannot throttle its 'double soul', its 'two natures', because then it would perish" (Slataper 1954, p. 46).

Slataper understood that it is not from the outdated culture of the institutions but rather from this lack of culture that a new literature and, in a wider sense, a Triestine culture, could and should be born. The name of Slataper serves, for convenience, to indicate the whole gamut of writers of his time: not only the two great ones, Svevo and Saba, who precisely because they are great transcend and in part lie beyond the 'Slataperian' problems, but the likes of Stuparich, Marin, Spaini, and later Quarantotti Gambini, and later still many others, who would make of Triestine literature an important chapter in 20th century European literature as a whole. It is the "abstract and planned" city – as Dostoevsky said of St Petersburg, a similar product of governmental decisions rather than a process of organic development – which gives birth to the Trieste which is so rich in contrasts and which can find its *raison d'être* only in those contrasts and in their insolubility, an insolubility which in turn can find its own *raison d'être* only in literature.

The writers experienced its heterogeneity thoroughly, its multiplicity of irreducible elements to be resolved in a unity. They understood that Trieste – like the Habsburg Empire of which it formed a part – was a model for the

[7] This is the private merchant bank in which Svevo had been working for several decades and where he took advantage to learn about the commercial life that was gaining ground at that time.
[8] A bookshop that still trades, although it is not run by Saba's heirs any more.

heterogeneity and contradictoriness of modern civilisation as a whole, bereft of any central foundation or unity of values. Svevo and Saba made of Trieste a seismographic station for the spiritual earthquakes preparing to wreak havoc on the world. From a bourgeois civilisation *par excellence*, whose history has essentially been that of its middle-class rise and fall, there issues forth with Svevo an extraordinary poetry of the crisis of the contemporary individual, a poetry that is ironic and tragic, crystal clear and elusive, which hides its own disillusioned acuteness behind an amiable reticence. Like Musil's Austrian who was – said Musil himself – an Austro-Hungarian minus the Hungarian, namely the result of a subtraction, so too the Triestine finds it hard to define himself in positive terms. It is easier to proclaim what he is not, what distinguishes him from every other reality, rather than state his identity. All this could produce, and in fact would produce, a great literature; it would also produce a complacent mannerism – but that would come later.

The meeting of cultures: Trieste – as often happens with a border city, instead of being a bridge to meet the other, builds a wall of the border to keep him out – is also an archipelago of cultures that are ignorant of one another, even though in practical terms, as regards the ethnic component, they are mixed together. With its great literature, Trieste would become a highly sensitive outpost of the crisis of culture and the culture of the crisis assailing Europe, thanks to its position in the Habsburg Empire. "The real Austria was the whole world" says Musil ironically in *Der Mann ohne Eigenschaften*,[9] because in it emerged with vivid particularity the epochal crisis of the West (Musil 1930, § 43). When, in Musil's novel, the Committee for Parallel Action seeks – in order to celebrate the Emperor's birthday – the central idea, the first principle upon which Austria (that is, European civilisation) is founded, it is not to be found. The empire lays bare the emptiness of all reality, which is "founded on air, lives on air".

A Triestine bourgeoisie essentially devoid of culture but happy and vital produced, as has been said, an extremely problematic literature, a literature of crisis and malaise as well as the irony with which to circumvent them. With Slataper, with his generation and with his remarkable gamut of Italian writers who studied in Rome and Florence and at the same time in Vienna and Prague, and who also translated (the first Italian translator of Kafka was one of them: Alberto Spaini), this new literature was born, and with it an exceptionally important Triestine culture. But this cultural dawn, which for Slataper had also to be a dawn of the whole city and not solely of its literature, coincides with the sunset or the beginning of the sunset of that Triestine reality, composite and contradictory, which gave birth to that literature. The red of the dawn is also the red of the sunset; the great Triestine literature is born when it begins to express in real terms that actuality in which its roots are sunk, but when it is born, that actuality begins to perish. That cultural ground was in crisis before it knew it. To

[9] It is worthwhile emphasizing that Musil never went to Trieste. However he was quite familiar with the culture of the city.

give an example: in 1901–1902, only 30 newspapers were printed in Trieste, whereas there were 117 in 1891–1900 and 163 in 1871–1880.

13.3 Economic Values in Trieste

That statement of Slataper's regarding the lack of Triestine traditions of culture is also rebellious in tone, provocative of the young generation in the forefront that in some way had to assert itself and its own culture over the radical negation of the preceding one. The historical significance of Slataper's statement consists precisely in its one-sidedness, proper to any individual or group that wishes to found a new culture and which must therefore deny the preceding culture, with the sting of that iconoclastic impulse necessary to avant-garde movements.

The culture of a city, strictly speaking, is neither identified with nor exhausted by its artistic, literary or philosophical production alone. Culture indicates a style of life, a mentality, a particular way of living, working, welcoming contacts or rejecting them, cultivating or not cultivating interests of various sorts, which naturally embrace spiritual values like art or music in particular, but do not finish there. From this point of view, that middle class devoid of cultural traditions had a culture of its own, which Slataper does not take into particular consideration. Such was, for instance, the purpose of the unforced coalescing and integrating of the Italian language, capable of absorbing the manifold and lively components of the other ethnic groups, even though Trieste had never had that linguistic and cultural pluralism spread throughout the very different social classes which characterised, for example, a city like Fiume[10] (Rijeka), in which it was said that "even the stupidest person was born with four languages". There was not in Trieste that symbiosis between different cultures which was found, for instance, in Dalmatia, where for example even Trumbić, the Croatian politician, declared that he thought in Italian while at the same time wanting to remain Croatian – and was, in fact, a fiercely patriotic nationalist.

The multinational, multilingual component in Trieste for the most part characterised a somewhat restricted élite and was tied to a family dimension in particular. Konstantin von Economo, for instance, Triestine representative of the great medical school of Vienna, "spoke Greek with his father, German with his mother, French with his sister Sophie and his brother Demetrio and Triestine, namely Italian, with his brother Leo" – so Loris Premuda relates, historian of science and of medicine in particular (Premuda 1977, p. 1327). Actually, the Triestine dialect – a Venetian dialect with some terms of German and Slav origin – was a vehicle of integration which had rapidly transformed the new arrivals into "natives". In Giani Stuparich's novel *Un anno di scuola*, Edda Marty, the German girl who attends the Triestine high school before the First World War –

[10] Fiume is the Italian name of the city. After Word War II, it underwent annexation by the new-born Yugoslavia and was named Rijeka. Today it belongs to Croatia and has kept the same name.

the first girl to attend the high school – very soon discovers in the local parlance a more natural way of communicating, even with her German father: "She soon learnt the language. After two years she was speaking like a native" (Stuparich 1961, p. 77).

Cristo Tzaldaris, Alberto Spaini's school-fellow "who read Homer as we read Dante", as Spaini himself testified, made his first declaration of love – he a Greek, to a Greek cousin – in Triestine. This culture derived its most profound substance from its encounter with the great "historical" culture of the Austro-Hungarian monarchy, namely with German culture, and from the contribution of Jewish civilisation. Moreover, it was neither only nor strictly nor even predominantly literary, but rather spread its roots in other directions: in the tradition of medical and scientific studies (omitted by Slataper, in accordance with the traditional humanistic perspective which does not take the sciences into consideration); in an impressive musical education; and in the practice of the *musizieren*, the well-established tradition of chamber music cultivated by the middle class families. Music culture would be one of the richest components of the local culture, not only for the presence of composers (such as, to give but a few examples, Smareglia, Busoni and Dallapiccola – or, in the Slovene camp, Kogoj and Merkù) and for a tradition of remarkable interpreters, perpetuated in recent years by the Trio di Trieste, but also for the tradition of high attendance at concerts and operas.

There are in particular two components of the vigorous Triestine reality that contribute in a special way to forming that ground from which its literature would spring. One was the maritime activity: the great shipping companies – Cosulich, Gerolimich, Martinolich, Tarabocchia, Premuda, for the most part originating from Lussino (now Mali Losinj in Croatia) but rooted in Trieste, with their commercial lines and then passenger ships operating throughout the world, especially with North America (the first departure of a liner of the Austro-American passenger service on the Trieste-New York route took place on May 23rd 1904). The other was financial activity, in particular, banking and insurance. The insurance companies ranged from that "old insurance company" of 1766 and such later giants as *Assicurazioni Generali* or *RAS*,[11] in a city which for example in 1832 possessed a good 22 maritime insurance companies; and there were the banks – such as, for instance, the *Banca Commerciale Triestina* or the branch of *Credit Anstalt*, that "battleship of Trieste banking" which the historian of economics and Italian irredentist Mario Alberti wanted to work, like the insurance Companies, for the benefit of Italy. Meanwhile, on the Austrian side, a scholar like Escher, commissioned by the Chamber of Commerce of Trieste, was expounding the idea of a Trieste that must be the instrument of Austrian control of Suez and Gibraltar, to the exclusion of Italy.

Trieste was a city of marine industries and nautical academies, of

[11] *Assicurazioni Generali* is an insurance company and is today the biggest in Italy and among the most important in Europe. *RAS* is an insurance company that is still active. In 2005, *RAS* was integrated into the German Allianz Group.

legendary figures of financial activity like Giacomo de Gabbiati or Masino Levi, genius of insurance finance, whose unforgettable portrait shows him with a policy in hand and a pen, rather like a Mephistopheles proposing the ancient pact; a city, too, of characters who would move on from Trieste to have a role in the economic and political life of the Empire, like Bruck, or figures such as Baron Revoltella, vice-president of the Suez Canal Company of which he was also a promoter, and director of *Assicurazioni Generali*; later made Baron thanks to his economic merits (Geldadel), he was a philanthropic backer of the homonymous Triestine museum of fine arts and of the *Scuola Superiore di Commercio Revoltella* which was the nucleus of the University of Trieste – not by chance a nucleus which was in fact the Faculty of Economics and Commerce – which Joyce, famous for his delight in playing on names, called the "Revolver University" (in Italian *rivoltella* means *revolver*). Revoltella was also the author of the volume *La compartecipazione dell'Austria al commercio mondiale. Considerazioni e proposte*, 1864, in which he criticised the politics of the Austro-Hungarian Empire intent on expanding into the neighbouring east (the future occupation and annexation of Bosnia-Herzegovina) and suggested instead a commercial expansion into India to rival Britain (Revoltella 1864, pp. 30–45).

It was these economic problems intertwining with political ones – the anti-irredentist position of Angelo Vivante or the nationalist position of Mario Alberti in his book *Trieste e la sua fisiologia economica* (1916) – which create a lively intellectual atmosphere. Trieste was a city which had seen a notable connection between local entrepreneurship and the Habsburg administration, between interested organisations (the Stock Exchange and its Deputation, the real organ of self-government of the commercial class of Trieste and therefore of the city, or the so-called Consiglio Ferdinandiano, or public institutions such as the governorship of Trieste or the Austrian bureaucracy. A substantial economic role was played by the Chamber of Commerce, created in 1850 and redefined in 1868. Enrico Escher, mentioned earlier, was owner of a great forwarding house, another branch that flourished considerably in Trieste. In short, Trieste was a city which had seen in general a culture, or better, an economic attitude directed towards a temperate and pragmatic free trade, which did not exclude state intervention (indeed, required it at certain moments) and whose insurance companies pursued innovative strategies aimed at a modern company structure.

Generali and *RAS* become the biggest companies in the whole Empire on the eve of the First World War, directing their preference towards non-speculative investments such as safe-return loans, like state bonds and public debentures. Representatives of the Triestine *haute bourgeoisie* rose to high economic roles in the Empire; one such was Arminio Brunner, heir of a family that from trade moved into insurance, and who became chairman of a group of companies of imperial proportions. Figures like Marco Besso, president of *Generali*, author of memoirs giving a fresh picture of this Trieste devoted to Mercury rather than Apollo. Slovene banking companies also emerged at this time.

This busy, practical world was very lively, but found no literary expression, except in isolated examples, such as the brilliant observations of the Grand Enlightenment thinker Antonio de Giuliani on the role of Trieste in the development of Europe or, in the middle of the 19th century, the enjoyable and acute observations of Sartorio on the port and economy of Trieste. But the real, true literary description of this world would emerge just a little later, when it was all over, as a recollection rather than description or portrait of a current Trieste. To give but one example, there is Bettiza's[12] novel *Il fantasma di Trieste* (1958), with its portrayal of the family of traders to which the protagonist belongs, and its vivid description of a mercantile Trieste.

There is, certainly, a great writer who has transformed this economic and economic-cultural reality of Trieste into an imposing metaphor for the human condition and contemporary nihilism: Italo Svevo. Rooted in that vigorous and thriving Triestine commercial reality, Svevo sensed the void, the abyss, the vertigo that lay behind and below those prosperous commercial affairs, the noughts (economic and existential) hidden in the figures of the balance sheets of the commercial houses, in the profits and losses such as those Guido makes a mess of in Chapter Seven of *The Conscience of Zeno* – "Story of a commercial association" – which is one of the great pages in which the mathematical game of speculation becomes the disquieting poetry of life and its demonic.

That chapter is the story of the speculation, muddle, cunning, misfortune, fortuitousness that together destroy Guido, the deceiver deceived by his unscrupulous reliance upon his own calculations. The commercial high school *Pasquale Revoltella*, where Guido says he learnt how to set up a commercial enterprise, ironically becomes a school of confusion, subterfuge and ruin. The double-entry book-keeping, almost a *leitmotif* in the story, becomes the register of fraud and in particular of life's chaos (symbolised by the irrational oscillation of prices, source of wealth and misfortune) and of the ploys by which men seek to control and amend it. Money seems, in its volatility, the symbol of the uncertainty of existence and at the same time a strong and capricious power, like Fate.

This story of profits and losses, but especially of calculations and registers, of attempts to rectify on paper (balance sheets, contracts, bills of exchange, banker's drafts, cheques) life's difficulties and defeats, is interwoven with the larger story of the characters, their loves, passions and jealousies. The unreality of those speculative manoeuvres and of those falsified balance sheets becomes the doleful, fraudulent unreality of life itself, which seems to exist on a closed account.

Later on, other great Central European writers such as Musil and Broch will make of economics – especially its mathematical dimension – a metaphor for the nothingness underlying everything, and for the recklessness, both irrational and vital, with which the man without qualities and without values confronts it. In *The Conscience of Zeno*, too, economics appears as vitality,

[12] Enzo Bettiza is an Italian novelist and journalist.

irrational and amoral, but toughened in the savage struggle for existence. The war, the terrible First World War, brings Zeno wealth, because he becomes the man prepared to buy, and living becomes this universal buying. Life, as Zeno observes, is truly original.

13.4 Conclusion: Bronzin and the Austrian Imprint

Who knows whether Svevo and Bronzin ever met by chance in Piazza Hortis[13], through which they frequently passed and where Bronzin used to teach? Bronzin was rooted in that sturdy Triestine reality, especially in the school, and in solid scientific preparation which he, as opposed to Svevo, did not make an object of irony.

And so this cultural ground remains outside the Slataperian consideration, which is more specifically linked to the work of Vinzenz Bronzin or from which it is born. There exists in Trieste, particularly at the scholastic level, a strong Austrian imprint, especially in the *liceo scientifico*, at that time called *Realschule*, namely a school that, as its highly significant title bespeaks, is concerned precisely with reality, with real, concrete things.

The schools of the Empire were profoundly rooted in this study of "realia", of reality in this healthy, vigorous, positive attention dedicated to things, just as also at a higher level Austrian literature, in its extraordinary and innovative description of the devastating crisis that changed the world between the end of the 19th century and the first decades of the 20th century, was culturally fed not, for instance, like the Italian culture and many others, by philosophy or idealistic systems, but rather by science, by mathematics and by the crisis at the foundations of mathematics. It is not by chance that in Musil's novels it is mathematics that offers the metaphors wherewith to describe the world and its devastation. Bronzin had followed the lessons of Boltzmann, that Boltzmann who plays so eminent a role in science, who also wrote poetry and then committed suicide at Duino just outside Trieste in 1906, victim of one of those crises of depression that persecuted him. But the collective European imagination was profoundly caught by Rilke's stay in Duino and was quite ignorant of Boltzmann in Duino – something curious given also the tragic nature of his end.

Bronzin was a classic product of Habsburg culture, in terms also of the symbiosis in his ability and, indeed, scientific genius, especially in mathematics, and knowledge of literature and the classics, of which it is said he remembered entire passages by heart. But it is clear that an author of manuals of political arithmetic, not to speak of that book which contains the formula of financial mathematics so revolutionary for its time – and which has precisely aroused

[13] Piazza Hortis is one of the larger squares in Trieste. Beside it, there is a big public library which has for some years housed the Joyce Laboratory under the direction of Prof. Renzo Crivelli.

interest in him after so many years – cannot even be taken into consideration as representative and brilliant representative of a general culture. He taught political and commercial arithmetic at the *Accademia di Commercio e Nautica di Trieste*, and was head of a commercial technical institute. He had studied at the Vienna Polytechnic. Trieste had a great, albeit ignored scientific culture, which certainly did not stop with Bronzin and his generation; one need not recall only Bruno de Finetti, but in general a whole tradition of economic and, especially, mathematical studies, with specific reference perhaps to financial mathematics.

Perhaps this is the culture most alive today in Trieste, with the establishing of such prestigious scientific institutions as ICTP[14] and, in particular, SISSA[15], institutions of great international, worldwide importance. In this sense Bronzin, who in his extremely long life succeeded in witnessing a time which we can still in some way consider contemporary with our own (he died in the early 1970s), can be seen as a kind of tutelary deity of that Triestine culture, hidden in the shadows.

Certainly Bronzin, from an existential point of view, appears a figure rooted in that Central European culture of which Trieste was a centre and which is also a human style characterised by a singular symbiosis of methodical order, secret and anarchic eccentricity of the heart and predilection for half-light and anonymity. Bronzin carried out basic studies, never thought of entering a context that was socially and culturally more well-known; for example, he remained outside the nascent *Revoltella* university although it was so close to his mathematical interests, preferring to teach at the *Istituto Tecnico Professionale Nautico* or at the *Istituto Tecnico Commerciale*, both working on profound studies and rapping the knuckles of unruly or dim-witted pupils: he resembles so many immortal characters in Austrian literature, from the poor musician of Grillparzer to Kafka's employees, characters who unite a methodical passion for order with the choice of the shadow, of dissimulation, of not appearing, like other almost-forgotten scientists of Trieste, such as Francesco de Grisogono with his invention of a universal system of calculations.

Vinzenz Bronzin calculated the system making it possible to know in what month and day Easter would fall for successive millennia; who knows whether he would have been able to calculate the moment in which his formula would win a Nobel Prize.

[14] A scientific laboratory devoted to bio-genetics and medical studies. In particular, it is engaged in the training of scientists from developing countries.

[15] A scientific laboratory devoted to theoretical physics whose reputation is recognized worldwide. Every year, it takes in hundreds of scientists from all over the world.

References

Apih E (1988) Trieste. Laterza, Bari
Ara A, Magris C (1982) Trieste un'identità di frontiera. Einaudi, Turin
Bosetti G (1984) Trieste. Cahiers du Cercic 3. Université de Grenoble, Grenoble
de Castro D (1981) La questione di Trieste. Edizioni Lint, Trieste
Finzi R, Magris C, Miccoli G (eds) (2002) Il Friuli – Venezia Giulia. Einaudi, Turin
Finzi R, Panjek G (eds) (2003) Storia economica e sociale di Trieste, Vol. 2. Edizioni Lint, Trieste
Musil R (1930) Der Mann ohne Eigenschaften, Vol. 1, Part 2. Rowohlt, Berlin
Premuda L (1977) La formazione intellettuale e scientifica di Constantin von Economo. Rassegna di Studi Psichiatrici 6
Revoltella P (1864) La compartecipazione dell'Austria al commercio mondiale. Considerazioni e proposte. Tipografia del Lloyd Austriaco, Trieste
Sapelli G (1990) Trieste italiana. Mito e destino economico. F. Angeli, Milan
Slataper S (1954) Scritti politici. Mondadori, Milan
Stuparich G (1961) Un anno di scuola. Einaudi, Turin

14 Trieste: A Node of the Actuarial Network in the Early 1900s

Ermanno Pitacco*

The scope of the actuarial research in Trieste, especially among the insurance companies operating in Trieste, is described. Particular attention is placed on the period around the turn of the century, namely from the last 1800s to the early 1900s, during which Professor Bronzin proposed his innovative ideas. However, some early contributions dating back to the previous part of the 19th century, as well as selected contributions from the 1920s and the 1930s are also addressed, the latter in particular with regard to the heritage of the early "actuarial school" in Trieste.

14.1 Introduction

The term "actuarial" (and hence expressions like "actuarial mathematics", "actuarial techniques", "actuarial tools", and so on) refers to the analysis of (some) quantitative aspects of the insurance activity. Typical topics are the assessment of the cost and the calculation of the price (or "premium") of insurance products, the management of premiums throughout the policy duration and thus the relevant investment, the analysis of expected profits, the assessment of the risk profile of a specific portfolio or a whole insurance company, as well as the analysis of reinsurance arrangements.

Actuarial mathematics and actuarial techniques require the definition and the use of models formally describing various features of the insurance activity. It follows that the development of actuarial tools strictly depends on:

- the evolution of the insurance business and consequent needs;
- the development of formal tools (provided by probability theory, statistics, financial mathematics, and so on) required to build up actuarial models;
- the availability of statistical data (e.g. mortality and disability in life insurance, frequency of claim in general insurance, and so on) needed to implement actuarial calculation models providing premiums, profits, etc., as the outputs.

As Haberman (1996) notes, life insurance techniques and non-life insurance (as, for example, marine insurance) techniques had quite different historical

* Università degli Studi di Trieste, Italy. *ermanno.pitacco@econ.units.it*

evolutions. Non-life insurance began with marine insurance, probably in northern Italy about the end of the 12th century. The first policies in marine insurance, involving the payment of premiums to specialized underwriters, probably date from the first half of the 14th century. Despite this long history, actuarial contributions to non-life insurance are more recent, the starting point being reasonably represented by a work on marine insurance by Nicholas Bernoulli, dated 1709 (see Haberman 1996). Most of the following contributions to non-life insurance mathematics can be more appropriately placed in what we now call "risk theory", as general problems (e.g. the impact of portfolio size on the risks of an insurance business) are mainly focussed, rather than problems specifically interesting the management of a non-life business (e.g. claim reserving, experience rating, and so on). The spread of contributions of the latter type date from the beginning of the 1900s. It follows that a special attention should be devoted to some early contributions concerning specific non-life issues (as we will see in Section 2).

As mentioned above, the history of life insurance mathematics and techniques is quite different. After the early seminal contributions in the second half of the 17th century (see, for example, Haberman 1996 and Hald 1987), a continuous progress down to the present day can be discerned, though with important shifts in the focus of actuarial studies, especially in the last decades.

As regards the scope of this chapter in particular, the following points should be stressed (for instance, see Zimmermann and Hafner 2007):

- in the 19th century, Trieste was an important harbour (belonging to the Austro-Hungarian Empire);
- the insurance business (and in particular commercial insurance and marine insurance) could benefit from the flourishing situation of Trieste;
- a number of insurance companies were established in Trieste during the 19th century, and, among these, *Assicurazioni Generali* and *Riunione Adriatica di Sicurtà* (briefly, *RAS*);
- besides insurance business strictly related to commercial activities, life insurance was in a favourable situation also because of the lack of a public pension system providing old-age benefits (namely, life annuities).

In this chapter, since we aim at providing a description of the economic and scientific background of Bronzin's work, special attention is placed on the period around the turn of the century (Section 3), namely from the late 1800s to the early 1900s. However, some early contributions dating back to the previous part of the 19th century (Section 2), as well as selected contributions from the 1920s and the 1930s are also addressed (Section 4), the latter in particular with regard to the heritage of the early "actuarial school" in Trieste.

After some remarks concerning the life insurance market around 1900 (Section 5), the nature and the targets of actuarial contributions in the periods addressed are finally discussed (Sections 6 and 7), specifically to stress the innovative features of Bronzin's work, while trying at the same time to understand the lack of recognition for his original ideas.

14.2 The Antecedents

When we analyse the insurance activity in the 1700s or in the first decades of the 1800s, the distinction between the role of the "manager" and the specific role of the "technician", strictly working in the actuarial field, can be a difficult task. For this reason, we start our review by citing some contributions which may (at least to some extent) be of interest to actuarial science although, in a modern perspective, the actuarial contents may seem rather weak.

Giuseppe Lazzaro Morpurgo, born in Gorizia in 1759, was one of the leading figures in the insurance business in Trieste in the first decades of the 19th century. His collaboration with *Giacomo de' Gabbiati*, a lawyer in Trieste, led to the construction of a tariff for fire insurance. The tariff was based on six rating classes, depending on risk factors such as the location of the building, use of the building, and other aspects. The premium rates were in the range of 0.15 to 0.50 percent of the value assured. Deductibles and maximum amounts were also included in the tariff.

Between 1830 and 1834, Morpurgo also published three volumes dealing with marine insurance, fire insurance and life insurance. Moreover, in a publication dated 1835, Morpurgo described the technical structure of a fund which, thanks to voluntary contributions from wealthy citizens, could pay life annuities and other benefits to needy people.

During his professional career, *Giuseppe Lazzaro Morpurgo* worked mainly in the field of insurance. The *Azienda Assicuratrice*, which introduced fire insurance and hail insurance in Trieste, was established in 1822 as a result of Morpurgo's initiative, and he also organized the technical bases for these insurance products. In 1831, Morpurgo took on the management of *Ausilio Generale di Sicurezza*, the insurance company which was the forebear of *Assicurazioni Generali*. Morpurgo died in Trieste in 1835. For more information about the work of *Giuseppe Lazzaro Morpurgo*, the reader should consult the book published by Assicurazioni Generali (1931).

Vitale Laudi, born in Trieste in 1837, was an actuary in the classical sense. He was awarded a degree in Mathematics at the University of Padua in 1859. In 1861, he started collaborating with *Assicurazioni Generali*, first as a consultant, later as an employee. At the same time, he was also a teacher of mathematics in the *Civica Scuola Reale Superiore* in Trieste, and stopped teaching only in 1878, when appointed manager of the life office of *Assicurazioni Generali.*

Laudi's collaboration with *Wilhelm Lazarus*, a German actuary based in Hamburg, led to the compilation in 1905 of the so-called LL life table. The LL table was based on the mortality registered by seventeen English and Scottish life offices in the period between 1839 and 1843. The data set resulted from 40,616 policies, with 3,928 insured dying in those years. The crude mortality rates were graduated by using the Lazarus law, a generalization of the *Gompertz-Makeham* law, consisting in adding a negative exponential term expressing the (decreasing) mortality at very young ages to the *Gompertz-Makeham* law. In practice, the Lazarus law coincides with the *Gompertz-Makeham* law beyond the age of 20. Indeed, the subsequent table produced in 1907 by *Julius Graf*, the so-called G table, was compiled graduating the company's data with the classical *Gompertz-Makeham* law. In spite of this, in our opinion the Lazarus law maintains its conceptual importance, as it constitutes an early attempt towards the definition of a law representing the age-pattern of mortality over the whole life span. It is interesting to note that, at the same time, the Danish actuary *Thorvald Thiele* proposed a mortality law consisting of three terms, a positive exponential term to represent senescent mortality (like in the original *Gompertz-Makeham* law), a "Gaussian" term to represent the young-adult mortality peak, and a negative exponential term like in the Lazarus proposal.

Laudi also dealt with various scientific and technical topics in the field of life insurance, other than the construction of life tables; for instance, the calculation of actuarial values for time-continuous life annuities, and the calculation of premiums for last-survivor benefits.

Vitale Laudi and *Wilhelm Lazarus* may be considered the "founders" of actuarial techniques for life insurance in *Assicurazioni Generali*. In fact, the need for solid mathematical and statistical bases emerged from the growing importance of the life business, which in turn was a consequence of *Assicurazioni Generali's* strategy and the action of some of its managers, *Marco Besso* in particular.

Laudi died in Trieste in 1901. More information about the scientific and professional work of *Vitale Laudi* (and *Wilhelm Lazarus*) is provided by Graf (1905); see also Sofonea (1968).

Marco Besso was a prominent figure in the insurance scene over the last decades of the 19th century and the beginning of the 20th century. Born in Trieste in 1843, Besso entered *Assicurazioni Generali* as the company's representative in Rome. In 1878, he became secretary general of the company, inaugurating a period of modernisation and diversification. Subsequently, Besso guided *Assicurazioni Generali* as president from 1909 until his death in 1920. Besso was not just a rigorous organizer, but also a visionary involved in establishing a multinational group with offices even in Asia and Oceania.

Even though the work of *Marco Besso* as an insurer cannot properly be included in the actuarial framework, he did leave some interesting publications in the field of insurance and pension techniques. In particular, he published a paper on the occupational pension schemes of northern Italy's railways, and contributed to the reorganization of a friendly society in Milan. It is also worth citing Besso (1887), describing the evolution of life insurance in the second half of the 19th century.

For more information about the role of *Marco Besso* in *Assicurazioni Generali*, and in the insurance field in general, the reader may consult Assicurazioni Generali (1931).

14.3 Around the Turn of the Century

A number of contributions to actuarial mathematics and actuarial techniques were provided around the turn of the century by actuaries of the two big insurance companies in Trieste, namely *Assicurazioni Generali* and *RAS*. It should be noted that many actuaries employed in these insurance companies undertook their actuarial education in Vienna, attending a specific two-year course in the *Wiener Technische Hochschule* (for more information about teaching of insurance sciences in Austria, see Graf 1906).

Leone Spitzer was employed as an actuary in *RAS* in 1892, later becoming the life office manager in the same company. His actuarial work mainly concerned the compilation of life tables, as witnessed, for example, by two papers presented at the International Congress of Actuaries in Berlin in 1906 (see Spitzer 1906a, 1906b), dealing respectively with mortality bases for deferred life annuities and with female mortality.

Julius Altenburger, who was usually based in Budapest, also worked for some years at *RAS* in Trieste. In particular, Altenburger tackled the problem of finding a computationally effective method for the calculation of the (total) mathematical reserve of a life portfolio (see Altenburger 1898). The proposed method was adopted by *RAS* in 1895 (and by other life insurance companies as well), and remained in use until the spread of the Hollerith systems in the 1930s, which enabled the calculation of the portfolio reserve as the sum of the individual policy reserves.

Other contributions by Altenburger concern various topics of life insurance and actuarial techniques, including the role of the supervisory activity from a technical perspective (Altenburger 1909a), life assurance policies for substandard lives (Altenburger 1909c) and the calculation of surrender values (Altenburger 1909d). Finally, in Altenburger (1909b), he discussed the problem of setting up a special reserve in order to face risks due to the uncertainty in the technical bases (what we now call the "uncertainty risk"), namely mortality and interest rate assumptions.

Luigi Riedel, born in Janowitz (Moravia) in 1877, was hired as chief actuary of *RAS* in 1900, later attaining the position of life office manager. An important share of his professional and scientific activity was devoted to the actuarial aspects of disability insurance, and the relevant technical bases. In particular, an interesting contribution (see Riedel 1909) concerns the so-called inception-select mortality of disabled lives, namely the dependence of the probabilities of dying on time spent in the current disability spell. Among the results of his work as an actuary for *RAS*, the construction of the life table

"*Riunione*" (based on the company mortality experience in the years from 1876 to 1900) and the technical bases for pension funds are noteworthy.

The analysis of the mortality risk and the calculation of appropriate safety loadings facing this risk has constituted an important topic since the origins of life insurance mathematics and is also of practical interest. The contribution by *Federico Zalai* (see Zalai 1909), an actuary at *Assicurazioni Generali* in Trieste, falls within this scope.

Mortality risk was also addressed by *Pietro Smolensky*, a prominent figure in the actuarial scene, as we will see in next section. In Smolensky (1909), the impact of the distribution of sums assured on the portfolio riskiness is analysed; he specifically addresses the possibility of a higher mortality among policies with higher amounts assured (and thus the risk of adverse selection).

We conclude the list of contributions dated around the turn of the century by citing the work by Julius Graf (1909), in which the use of mortality laws for describing the age pattern of mortality is explored.

The works by Graf (1905, 1909) suggest some interesting remarks about the nature of the demographical models adopted in life insurance calculations. Early actuarial models for life insurance, proposed between the end of the 17th century and the middle of the 18th century, were based on a time-discrete setting. To some extent, this was a natural consequence of the link between the models themselves and the first life tables, e.g. the Halley table; see for example Pitacco (2004b). An important step towards age-continuous modelling follows from the early mortality "laws", originating from the fitting of mathematical formulae to mortality data. As Haberman (1996) notes, a new era for the actuarial science started in 1825 with the law proposed by *Benjamin Gompertz*, the pioneer of a new approach to survival modelling. Following the probabilistic structure laid down thanks to mathematical formulae fitting the experienced mortality, both actuarial theory and actuarial practice adopted an age-continuous approach to life insurance problems. In 1869, *Wesley Woolhouse* wrote the first complete presentation of life insurance mathematics on an age-continuous basis, considering sums assured payable at the moment of death as well as annuities payable continuously. On the application side, it is worth noting, for instance, that the life office of *Assicurazioni Generali* in Trieste at the beginning of the 20th century was equipped with a tariff system constructed on an age-continuous basis; see Graf (1905). The underlying survival model, as already mentioned, was based on the *Gompertz-Makeham* law.

14.4 Beyond World War I: Selected Contributions (up to 1932)

A number of interesting contributions were provided after World War I by actuaries working in Trieste. To some extent, these contributions reveal the heritage of the early actuarial school in Trieste. At the same time, new problems were explored and innovative ideas emerged, showing the vitality of the actuarial group located in Trieste.

In choosing the cut-off date for this section, we had various aspects in mind. Firstly, in 1932 the second national congress of insurance science was held in Trieste, and such an event in our opinion demonstrates the maturity of the local actuarial community. Secondly, in the 1920s and 1930s, new theoretical interests contributed to the development of actuarial science; our cut-off date allows us to note some early contributions in this field. Finally, because of the racial laws promulgated in Italy in 1938 and 1939, many Jews emigrated, towards the end of the 1930s, and this caused a dramatic reduction in the size of many professional and cultural communities, including the actuarial community.

In this paper, we focus only on a small selection of the numerous contributions to actuarial research which we consider representative of that period.

The coexistence in actuarial literature of strictly practical problems and theoretical issues (although suggested by practical problems or in any case susceptible to practical applications) is evident, in particular in the period we are now addressing. The work of *Mosè Jacob*, an actuary of the *Assicurazioni Generali* team, born in Nadvorna (Ukraine) in 1900, clearly witnesses this trend in the actuarial research.

In a paper published by the *Giornale dell'Istituto Italiano degli Attuari* (see Jacob 1930a), Jacob deals with the splitting of life insurance contracts into the risk and the saving components. Besides the interest in recognizing the two roles of the life insurance policies (and the endowment insurance in particular), namely covering the risk of death and accumulating an amount at maturity, it should be noted that this subject is still an important issue, especially in the framework of the new accounting standards requiring the so-called unbundling of insurance contracts.

Profits and losses originating from an insurance policy depending on the insured's lifetime, are analysed in Jacob (1930b), following a rigorous mathematical approach.

When defining an actuarial model for representing benefits and calculating premiums and reserves, age and time can be taken either as discrete or as continuous variables (see also the remarks at the end of Section 3). There are points in favour and points against both approaches. For example, working in a continuous context allows us to describe the age pattern of mortality through parametric models (namely laws, e.g. the *Gompertz-Makeham* law). Conversely, problems arise when describing time-discrete benefits (as, for example, annuities paid out on a yearly or a monthly basis) in a time-continuous context. The Stieltjes integral, as shown by Jacob (1932a), overcomes these difficulties by capturing both probabilities concentrated in specific points of time and probabilities over intervals. Hence, the use of the Stieltjes integral leads to a unified representation of both time-discrete and time-continuous benefits, and hence a unifying approach to actuarial problems in life insurance.

The actuarial work of *P. Smolensky* ranged over a wide set of problems: theoretical aspects of mathematical reserves (Smolensky 1923), practical issues of reserve calculation (Smolensky 1930a), technical bases for disability benefits (Smolensky 1927) as well as the impact of adverse selection on portfolio risk (Smolensky 1930b). Smolensky also dealt with historical aspects of life insurance (see Smolensky 1931b); this topic will be addressed in Section 5.

In the field of mortality modelling, Smolensky proposed the use of the so-called "compact tables" (see Smolensky 1932). In the calculation of the mathematical reserve of an endowment insurance at a given time t, three variables related to age and duration should be accounted for, namely the insured's age x at policy issue, the time t elapsed since policy issue, the policy term n. By using various numerical examples, Smolensky showed that, for any given value of n, the effect of t on the value of the mathematical reserve is much stronger than the effect of the entry age x. Hence, Smolensky proposed the use of a life table in which mortality only depends on time t, and, conversely, is assumed to be independent of x. Advantages clearly lay in the reduction in complexity of the calculation problem, moving from a three-dimensional space (defined by the coordinates x, t, n) to a two-dimensional space (defined by t, n).

Of course, advantages in computational tractability are nowadays negligible, thanks to the computing capacity commonly available. Notwithstanding this, the idea of a "compact model" still has importance, for example, for expressing the effect of time elapsed since disability inception, which, from statistical evidence, appears to be higher than the effect of age, on both the probability of recovery and the probability of death for disabled people.

A novel interest in the organization of data sets arose in the 1920s and 1930s thanks to the availability of new computing machines. Such interest is witnessed by a paper by de Finetti et al. (1932) dealing with statistical procedures for substandard lives, implemented by storing the relevant information on data cards. A paper by Tolentino and de Finetti (1932), which focuses on statistical features of the reserve calculation through computing machines, constitutes another interesting example.

As mentioned above, the coexistence of practical problems and theoretical issues clearly appears in the actuarial literature of the first decades of the 1900s. Further, we can find papers in which problems arising in the insurance practice are tackled with rigorous formal methods. The contributions by de Finetti and Obry (1932) and Jacob (1932b) both deal with problems related to surrendering, and the calculation of surrender values in particular. We briefly mention the approach proposed in de Finetti and Obry (1932). The paper aims at finding "coherent" rules for surrender values, which do not allow the policyholder to obtain advantage by withdrawing immediately after the payment of a (periodic) premium. Then, the paper extends the concept of coherence to the whole tariff system of a life office, aiming at singling out "arbitrage" possibilities for the insured, which could arise from the combination of several insurance covers. For more information about de Finetti's contributions to the actuarial science, see for example Pitacco (2004a).

The reader interested in contributions provided by the actuarial community in Trieste in the following decades (up to the 1950s) can consult Daboni and Pitacco (1983).

14.5 The Life Insurance Market: Some Remarks

The history of life insurance and the history of actuarial mathematics are, of course, strictly connected, as already mentioned in Section 1. For example, the development of new insurance products requires the intervention of actuarial skills, as regards, in particular, the choice of the technical bases, the construction of formulae for pricing and reserving, and so on.

Dealing with the history of life insurance around 1900 is beyond the scope of this paper but some remarks about the life insurance market at the end of the 19th century and in the first decades of the 20th century may be of interest, especially if referred to the local context. Some very interesting material is provided by two papers by Smolensky (see Smolensky 1931a, 1931b). We will only focus on some issues emerging from these works.

An interesting historical insight into the evolution of life insurance products throughout the 19th century is provided by Smolensky (1931b). Looking at the policies sold in Trieste, the author notes a "standardization" process, and in particular the progressive shift from a large variety of policies, to some extent tailored on the insured's needs, to a very small set of standard products, a large part of which consisting of the classical endowment insurance.

It is worth noting that to some extent, an inverse process is currently developing. Indeed, many modern insurance products are designed as "packages", whose items may be included or not in the product actually purchased by the client. An important example is provided by the so-called "variable annuities", which may include a more or less comprehensive set of guarantees (e.g. the guarantee of a minimum death benefit, the guarantee of a minimum interest rate in the accumulation process, etc.).

Smolensky (1931a) focuses on the dramatic competition in the life insurance markets, especially in some Central European countries. Competition leads to a reduction in premium levels, discounts on commissions, etc., which in turn lead to a lack of confidence on the part of the policyholder. Such was the case in Austria and Hungary, where the situation was faced through specific agreements among insurance companies, which aimed in particular at fixing a minimum premium level and prohibiting insurance products including rider benefits (e.g. premium waiver in the case of disability) that were not properly priced.

14.6 The Main Targets of Actuarial Mathematics Around 1900

Sections 2 to 4 depict the main topics of actuarial research around 1900 with a local focus on Trieste. The main issues discussed at that time may be summarized as follows:

a) *Mortality and disability*. A great effort was devoted to the construction of life tables (see Graf 1905, Smolensky 1932, Spitzer 1906b). The use of parametric models rather than life tables was also discussed (see Graf 1905, 1909). Practical problems concerning mortality assumptions for substandard lives were also dealt with (see Altenburger 1909c). With regard to disability, great attention was placed on the compilation of disablement tables and mortality tables for disabled insured individuals (see Riedel 1909, 1932 and Smolensky 1927).
b) *Calculation problems and tractability*. Finding tractable computational procedures was an extremely important issue one hundred years ago, for obvious reasons. So, great effort was devoted, for example, to suitable procedures for portfolio reserve calculation (see Altenburger 1898, Smolensky 1930a). Moreover, reducing the dimension of calculation problems by neglecting some non-critical variables, was also an important issue (see Smolensky 1932).
c) *Actuarial problems arising from policy conditions*. Among technical problems related to policy conditions, the calculation of surrender values has always constituted a crucial issue (see Altenburger 1909d, de Finetti and Obry 1932, Jacob 1932b). In the current scenario, conditions concerning the annuitization of the sum at maturity also constitute a critical issue, in particular because of the uncertainty in future mortality trends. However, attention was devoted also one century ago to the choice of mortality bases for deferred life annuities (e.g. see Spitzer 1906a).
d) *Risk and saving; financial profits*. Understanding the “role” of a life insurance company is an important research focus in the economics of insurance. Actuarial methods can provide useful tools for analysing these aspects, leading specifically to the splitting of a life business into its saving and risk components (see Jacob 1930a). The saving side of life insurance business generates financial profits, the expected values of which can be quantified by using actuarial methods (see Zalai 1931).
e) *Generalizing actuarial models*. As mentioned at the end of Section 3, early actuarial models for calculating premiums and reserves were based on age patterns of mortality as given by life tables. Hence, it was quite natural that the actuarial model subsequently adopted should be an age-discrete one. An important step towards age-continuous modelling followed from the early mortality laws originated from the fitting of mathematical formulae to mortality data. From a mathematical point of view, features of age-discrete

and age-continuous models are quite different. The definition of a general model capturing both the modelling styles is thus not a trivial matter. Interesting results can be achieved by using appropriate and versatile analytical tools, such as the Stieltjes integral (see Jacob 1932a).

f) *Risks in life insurance*. A more detailed discussion of this issue will be developed in the following part of this section. Here, we shall just stress that actuaries were of course well aware of the presence of risks in the management of a life portfolio. However, focus was concentrated on risks arising from random fluctuations of mortality over time (for example, see Jacob 1930b), and the consequent need for safety loadings (see in particular Zalai 1909). Impact of adverse selection on the randomness of portfolio results was also addressed (see Smolensky 1909, 1930b). Works dealing with risk transfers via reinsurance can also be placed in this framework (see Tolentino 1932). Although the interest of actuaries was concentrated on the risk of random fluctuations in mortality, problems related to a non appropriate choice of the life table were also singled out (see Altenburger 1909b), and this proves awareness about the presence of what we now call the risk of systematic deviations from the expected mortality pattern.
g) *Data processing*. The availability of electro-mechanical processing systems suggested new ways of considering insurance data and related formatting (for example, see de Finetti et al. 1932, Tolentino and de Finetti 1932).

Firstly, we note that the work carried out by the actuarial community in Trieste, in both the theoretical and the practical field, only addressed life insurance topics. This restriction, however, is perfectly in line with the evolution of actuarial science, as pointed out in Section 1. Secondly, research efforts by the local scientific community can be more easily appreciated if we relate their contributions to the development of actuarial science over time, and in particular to the state of art in that period. As a consequence, we place special emphasis on two topics of outstanding importance in the field of life insurance, namely the approaches to the assessment of mortality risks, and the awareness of crucial aspects in the investment of the liquidity generated by a life insurance portfolio.

Mortality risk assessment. The calculation procedures, adopted for determining premiums and reserves by the authors we have considered so far, rely – from a modern perspective – on "deterministic" actuarial models, as only expected values are actually addressed. However, it should be noted that progression towards a "stochastic" approach to life insurance mathematics began at the end of the 18th century. In 1786, *Johannes Tetens* first addressed the analysis of mortality risk inherent in an insurance portfolio. The evidence of the role of $\sqrt{N}$ in determining the riskiness of a portfolio, where N denotes the number of policies in the portfolio itself, can be traced back to Tetens's contribution. In particular, as pointed out by Haberman (1996), Tetens showed that the risk in absolute terms increases as the portfolio size N increases, whereas the risk in respect of each insured decreases in proportion to $\sqrt{N}$. From a modern point of view, Tetens' ideas constitute a pioneering contribution to individual risk theory.

The stochastic approach to life insurance problems made further progress, thanks to seminal contributions through the following centuries. Important work in the second half of the 19th century came from *Carl Bremiker* and *Karl Hattendorff* (see Haberman 1996, Pitacco 2004b). Both Bremiker and Hattendorff focussed specifically on the problem of facing adverse fluctuations in mortality. The need for an appropriate fund and, respectively, for a convenient safety loading of premiums emerged in their contributions.

Despite the direction towards stochastic modelling adopted by a number of significant contributions, a deterministic approach to mortality was still being used around 1900, and is frequently used even in current actuarial practice, in particular for calculating premiums according to the well known equivalence principle. It is worthwhile stressing that adopting a deterministic approach to actuarial calculations is to some extent underpinned by the nature of the insurance process, which consists in "transforming" individual risks through aggregation, so lowering the relevant impact, as proved by Tetens. Thus, advantages provided by "large" portfolio sizes in respect of random fluctuations risk partially justify the traditional deterministic setting for premium and reserve calculations.

However, this justification can be accepted under the assumption that only the risk of random fluctuations in the mortality of insured lives is allowed for. In a more general context, the existence of risk components other than random fluctuations must be recognized, and special attention should be devoted to the risk of systematic deviations arising from the uncertainty in representing future mortality patterns.

A "genuine" stochastic approach to actuarial calculations requires an explicit focus on random variables and related probability distributions. More specifically, an appropriate approach should rely on the random remaining lifetime of an individual aged x, T_x, and the related probability distribution, often assigned in terms of the survival function (referred to the random total lifetime T_0), $S(t) = \Pr\{T_0 > t\}$.

The expression of the random present value (e.g. at policy issue) of the insured benefits as a function of the remaining lifetime T_x (x being the age at policy issue) comes from de Finetti (1950, 1957), and Sverdrup (1952), and constitutes the starting point of a sound stochastic approach based on individual lifetimes (see also Pitacco 2004b).

Investments. Early contributions to stochastic modelling in life insurance did not allow for sources of risk other than mortality. In particular, the idea of a random financial result will be achieved after the seminal contribution of *Louis Bachelier* in 1900, concerning the stochastic modelling of investment problems. It is worth noting, however, that stochastic finance would enter the life insurance actuarial context much later, specifically thanks to the work of *F. M. Redington* (1952), who addressed the principles of life business valuation.

It has been stressed that traditional actuarial mathematics is the "mathematics of insurer's liabilities", rather than the "mathematics of insurer's assets and liabilities". Some comments may enhance the understanding of the rationale underlying this remark. According to the principles of scientific life insurance, as stated by *James Dodson* in 1755, life insurance companies have to build up large reserves when a sequence of level premiums, paid by the policyholder, faces expected costs which increase as the attained age increases, because of the increasing probability of death. The reserves can be seen from two different points of view. Looking at future policy years, the (individual) reserve constitutes the insurer's liability, net of future premiums. Conversely, looking at past policy years, the reserve can be thought as the fund arising from the accumulation of premiums exceeding the expected costs.

Level premiums, of course, must be calculated on the basis of assumptions concerning both the mortality and the rate of interest expected to be earned on such funds over the whole policy duration. Thus, the investment of the funds of a life insurance company became an extremely important issue. Despite this crucial aspect, the focus of actuarial studies was concentrated, over a very long period, on only the liability side, whilst the uncertainty regarding the performance of the assets constituting the funds was accounted for just by summarizing future rates of interest via "prudential" estimates (that is, "low" interest rates). Moreover, the need for a special reserve was stressed (for example, see Altenburger 1909b), in order to face an unanticipated behaviour on the part of interest rates.

The importance of investment issues (or "asset allocation" to use current terminology) was clearly perceived by insurers and actuaries, of course. For example, in the United Kingdom, as Haberman (1996) notes, *Arthur Bailey* in 1862 proposed five principles (known as "canons" in the British actuarial literature) for the selection of investments.

The state of the art we have described so far can help us understand why important contributions in the field of finance were disregarded at the beginning of the 20th century, and for many following decades as well. Clearly, the contribution by Bachelier and, in particular as regards the actuarial community in Trieste, the contribution by Bronzin can be placed among these.

14.7 Final Remarks

Scientific and technical contributions produced by the actuarial community in Trieste, from the second half of the 1800s up to 1932, have been presented and discussed, in the light also of the evolution of actuarial studies over time. It has been stressed how issues related to investment risks were basically disregarded, at least in a formal, probabilistic sense, even though the importance of investment issues was clearly perceived by insurers and actuaries. This scenario can help in understanding why important contributions (namely, those provided by Bachelier and Bronzin) were overlooked.

Further, the historical "closure" of actuarial science compared to other scientific sectors, such as financial economics and corporate finance, should be stressed. On this point, and some related issues, the reader can refer to the interesting paper by Bühlmann (1997). In more recent times, the need for importing concepts and methods from these and other areas arose, because of new standards in assessing life portfolio performance, new solvency requirements, new accounting principles, etc. However, this led to a rather confusing overlap between methods and various terminologies. Only in very recent times has a harmonization process started, which one hopes will lead to a more satisfactory definition within a general framework of (almost) all the quantitative tools needed in the insurance business.

In particular, as regards relationships between financial economics and actuarial studies, the following points should be stressed: Bühlmann (1997) notes that "[...] it is difficult to understand why the approaches and solutions developed for today's financial sector [...] did not originate from the breeding ground of actuarial thinking". Conversely, as Whelan (2002) notes, at the start of the 20th century actuaries were in a perfect position to develop a science of finance, and this for various reasons:

- a very good knowledge of statistics and probability theory;
- high educational standards;
- the need to solve new problems in the insurance field.

Why did actuaries not develop a science of finance at the start of the 20th century? A likely reason might be the following one: a number of problems had to be solved in the field of life insurance and, more generally, in the framework of insurance of the person (as seen in Section 6). The expression "insurance of the person" denotes a wide set of insurance products in which benefits are linked to contingencies concerning the life of the insured (whether one or more person). In other words, also disability annuities, sickness benefits, accident cover, etc., that is, the products currently grouped under the label "health insurance" are included in this framework.

As a result, efforts were concentrated on the creation of probabilistic models and statistical bases needed for pricing and reserving in relation to disability insurance products. In the European context, the works by Karup (1893), Hamza (1900) and Du Pasquier (1912, 1913) constitute important steps in the development of actuarial mathematics for disability insurance.[1] In a local context, the works by Riedel (1909, 1932), for example, witness the interest for disability modelling.

[1] See also Seal (1977), Haberman (1996) and Haberman and Pitacco (1999).

As seen in the previous sections, actuaries were also involved in solving other problems in the field of life insurance; for example, the definition of "reasonable" surrender values and, more in general, the design of policy conditions, the calculation of portfolio reserves via tractable computational procedures, etc. On the other hand, the financial structure of life insurance products was rather simple, at least when compared to some structures recently adopted. While we are currently used to deal with "flexible" products (in which flexibility is achieved, for example, by linking the benefits to inflation indexes, or to the value of investment fund units), increases in benefits were, in past times, mainly realized through profit participation and bonus mechanisms.

In conclusion, problems other than those related to the finance of life insurance products probably attracted the interest of actuaries, specifically at the start of the 20th century.

At all events, actuaries anticipated major ideas in the field of financial economics, as noted by Whelan et al. (2002), but these ideas were not sufficiently developed and were anyway not disseminated. A good example of this is the rule of thumb for option pricing (see Whelan 2002).

As Whelan (2002) notes, "it was as if actuarial science in the 20th century developed in a parallel world, complete with its own symbols and language". Reciprocally, the actuarial world for a long time rejected interesting opportunities offered by new findings in other scientific fields, and the field of finance in particular.

Integration between actuarial science and various other disciplines also interested in insurance has recently reached a satisfactory degree, in particular thanks to the new approaches suggested by Enterprise Risk Management (also involving teaching aspects; see for example Pitacco 2007). Nevertheless, integration is a long-lasting process, and several achievements (in terms of language, formal notation, etc.) are still in the future.

References

The following list of references includes various contributions provided by the "actuarial school" of Trieste, from the end of the 1800s to the first decades of the 1900s. Clearly, this bibliography is largely incomplete, in particular as far as the period 1918–1932 is concerned. Nevertheless, we hope that it may define the main thrusts of actuarial research in Trieste in the period we have focussed on.

Altenburger J (1898) On the grouping of endowment assurances for valuation. Journal of the Institute of Actuaries 34, pp. 150–153

Altenburger J (1909a) Die staatliche Beaufsichtigung der Lebensversicherungsanstalten vom technischen Standpunkte. In: Gutachten, Denkschriften und Verhandlungen des Sechsten Internationalen Kongresses für Versicherungs-Wissenschaft, Vol. 1. Vienna, pp. 189–237

Altenburger J (1909b) Das Problem des mathematischen Risikos; die Sicherheitsreserven bei Versicherungsanstalten. In: Gutachten, Denkschriften und Verhandlungen des Sechsten Internationalen Kongresses für Versicherungs-Wissenschaft, Vol. 1. Vienna, pp. 958–964

Altenburger J (1909c) Kurze Bemerkungen zur Versicherung minderwertiger Leben. In: Gutachten, Denkschriften und Verhandlungen des Sechsten Internationalen Kongresses für Versicherungs-Wissenschaft, Vol. 1. Vienna, pp. 1341–1348

Altenburger J (1909d) Berechnung der Polizzenwerte bei vorzeitiger Vertragslösung. In: Gutachten, Denkschriften und Verhandlungen des Sechsten Internationalen Kongresses für Versicherungs-Wissenschaft, Vol. 2. Vienna, pp. 171–184

Assicurazioni Generali (eds) (1931) Die Jahrhundertfeier der Assicurazioni Generali. Assicurazioni Generali, Trieste (Available in Italian as: Il centenario delle Assicurazioni Generali 1831–1931. Trieste)

Besso M (1887) Progress of life assurance throughout the world, from 1859 to 1883. Journal of the Institute of Actuaries 26, pp. 426–437

Bühlmann H (1997) The actuary: the role and limitations of the profession since the mid-19th century. ASTIN Bulletin 27, pp. 165–171

Daboni L, Pitacco E (1983) Gli studi statistici ed attuariali nel Friuli-Venezia Giulia. In: La ricerca scientifica. Enciclopedia Monogr. del Friuli-Venezia Giulia, Primo Aggiornamento. Istituto per l'Enciclopedia del Friuli-Venezia Giulia, Udine, pp. 531–550

de Finetti B (1950) Matematica attuariale. Quaderni dell'Istituto per gli Studi Assicurativi 5. Trieste, pp. 53–103

de Finetti B (1957) Lezioni di Matematica Attuariale. Edizioni Ricerche, Rome

de Finetti B, Obry S (1932) L'optimum nella misura del riscatto. In: Atti del II Congresso Nazionale di Scienza delle Assicurazioni, Vol. 2. Trieste, pp. 99–123

de Finetti B, Sereni A, Winternitz L (1932) Progetto di scheda meccanografica per le statistiche dei rischi tarati. In: Atti del II Congresso Nazionale di Scienza delle Assicurazioni, Vol. 3. Trieste, pp. 63–73

Du Pasquier L G (1912) Mathematische Theorie der Invaliditätversicherung. Mitteilungen der Vereinigung schweizerischer Versicherungsmathematiker 7, pp. 1–7

Du Pasquier L G (1913) Mathematische Theorie der Invaliditätversicherung. Mitteilungen der Vereinigung schweizerischer Versicherungsmathematiker 8, pp. 1–153

Graf J (1905) Die Rechnungsgrundlagen der k.u.k priv. Assicurazioni Generali in Triest. Assicurazioni Generali, Trieste (Available in Italian as: Il funzionamento matematico delle Assicurazioni Generali in Trieste. Published in 1906, Trieste)

Graf J (1906) Das Unterrichtswesen in Österreich betreffend die Pflege der VersicherungsWissenschaften. In: Berichte, Denkschriften und Verhandlungen des Fünften Internationalen Kongresses für Versicherungs-Wissenschaft, Vol. 2. Berlin, pp. 397–424

Graf J (1909) Welche Vorteile kann die Annahme einer analytischen Funktion für die Absterbeordnung in technischer Beziehung bieten? In: Gutachten, Denkschriften und Verhandlungen des Sechsten Internationalen Kongresses für Versicherungs-Wissenschaft, Vol. 2. Vienna, pp. 429–437

Haberman S (1996) Landmarks in the history of actuarial science. Actuarial Research Paper No. 84, Department of Actuarial Science and Statistics, City University, London

Haberman S, Pitacco E (1999) Actuarial models for disability insurance. Chapman & Hall, London

Hald A (1987) On the early history of life insurance mathematics. Scandinavian Actuarial Journal, pp. 4–18

Hamza E (1900) Note sur la théorie mathématique de l'assurance contre le risque d'invalidité d'origine morbide, sénile ou accidentelle. In: Comptes Rendus du Troisième Congrès International d'Actuaries. Paris, pp. 154–203

Jacob M (1930a) Rischio e risparmio nelle assicurazioni vita. Giornale dell'Istituto Italiano degli Attuari 1, pp. 196–207

Jacob M (1930b) Sulla teoria del rischio matematico. In: Comptes Rendus du Neuvième Congrès International d'Actuaries, Vol. 2. Stockholm, pp. 345–359

Jacob M (1932a) Sugli integrali di Stieltjes e sulla loro applicazione nella matematica attuariale. Giornale dell'Istituto Italiano degli Attuari 3, pp. 160–181

Jacob M (1932b) Il prezzo di riscatto e la teoria dei capitali accumulati. In: Atti del II Congresso Nazionale di Scienza delle Assicurazioni, Vol. 2. Trieste, pp. 162–179

Karup J (1893) Die Finanzlage der Gothaischen Staatsdiener-Wittwen-Societät am 31 December 1890. Heinrich Morchel, Dresden

Pitacco E (2004a) de Finetti, Bruno. In: Teugels J L, Sundt B (eds) Encyclopedia of actuarial science, Vol. 1. J. Wiley & Sons, Chichester, pp. 421–423

Pitacco E (2004b) From Halley to "frailty": a review of survival models for actuarial calculations. Giornale dell'Istituto Italiano degli Attuari 67, pp. 17–47

Pitacco E (2007) Teaching life insurance mathematics in a risk management perspective: stochastic mortality issues. In: Sensei in het actuariaat. Liber Amicorum voor Prof. Dr. Henk Wolthuis AAG, Universiteit van Amsterdam, pp. 123–146

Redington F M (1952) Review of the principles of life office valuations. Journal of the Institute of Actuaries 78, pp. 286–315

Riedel L (1909) Über die Abhängigkeit der Invalidensterblichkeit von der Dauer der Invalidität. In: Gutachten, Denkschriften und Verhandlungen des Sechsten Internationalen Kongresses für Versicherungs-Wissenschaft, Vol. 2. Wien, pp. 753–758

Riedel L (1932) L'impianto tecnico dell'assicurazione addizionale di invalidità totale abbinata all'assicurazione vita. In: Atti del II Congresso Nazionale di Scienza delle Assicurazioni, Vol. 3. Trieste, pp. 95–115

Seal H L (1977) Studies in the history of probability and statistics. XXXV. Multiple decrements or competing risks. Biometrika 64, pp. 429–439

Smolensky P (1909) Das mathematische Risiko aus der Verteilung der Versicherungssummen auf die Sterbefälle. In: Gutachten, Denkschriften und Verhandlungen des Sechsten Internationalen Kongresses für Versicherungs-Wissenschaft, Vol. 1. Vienna, pp. 765–780

Smolensky P (1923) Le teorie della riserva matematica nell'assicurazione vita. Giornale di Matematica Finanziaria 5, pp. 105–133, pp. 145–168

Smolensky P (1927) Disability benefits in life assurance contracts. In: Transactions of the eighth International Congress of Actuaries, Vol. 2. London, pp. 49–59

Smolensky P (1930a) Sul calcolo delle riserve col metodo dei valori ausiliari. Giornale dell'Istituto Italiano degli Attuari 1, pp. 54–66

Smolensky P (1930b) Sulla teoria del rischio. In: Comptes Rendus du Neuvième Congrès International d'Actuaries, Vol. 2. Stockholm, pp. 360–372

Smolensky P (1931a) La lotta contro gli eccessi della concorrenza nella assicurazione sulla vita. Giornale dell'Istituto Italiano degli Attuari 2, pp. 213–224

Smolensky P (1931b) L'evoluzione della polizza vita a Trieste nel secolo XIX. Giornale dell'Istituto Italiano degli Attuari 2, pp. 516–526

Smolensky P (1932) Sulle tavole compatte di mortalità. In: Atti del II Congresso Nazionale di Scienza delle Assicurazioni, Vol. 3. Trieste, pp. 236–245

Sofonea T (1968) Wilhelm Lazarus attuario delle Assicurazioni Generali. Bollettino delle Assicurazioni Generali 3-4, pp. 63–67

Spitzer L (1906a) Rechnungsgrundlagen für die Versicherung aufgeschobener Leibrenten. In: Berichte, Denkschriften und Verhandlungen des Fünften Internationalen Kongresses für Versicherungs-Wissenschaft, Vol. 1. Berlin, pp. 389–392

Spitzer L (1906b) Ein Beitrag zu den Erfahrungen über die Sterblichkeit der Frauen. In: Berichte, Denkschriften und Verhandlungen des Fünften Internationalen Kongresses für Versicherungs-Wissenschaft, Vol. 1. Berlin, pp. 607–616

Sverdrup E (1952) Basic concepts in life assurance mathematics. Skandinavisk Aktuarietidskrift 3–4, pp. 115–131

Tolentino G (1932) Sul pieno di conservazione nell'assicurazione vita. In: Atti del II Congresso Nazionale di Scienza delle Assicurazioni, Vol. 2. Trieste, pp. 162–179

Tolentino G, de Finetti B (1932) Le esigenze statistiche nella meccanizzazione del calcolo delle riserve per le assicurazioni sulla vita. In: Atti del II Congresso Nazionale di Scienza delle Assicurazioni, Vol. 3. Trieste, pp. 210–220

Whelan S (2002) Actuaries' contribution to financial economics. The Actuary, December 2002, pp. 34–35

Whelan S F, Bowie D C, Hibbert A J (2002) A primer in financial economics. British Actuarial Journal 8, pp. 22–74

Zalai F (1909) Zur Theorie des Risikozuschlages. In: Gutachten, Denkschriften und Verhandlungendes des Sechsten Internationalen Kongresses für Versicherungs-Wissenschaft, Vol. 1. Vienna, pp. 843–853

Zalai F (1931) Sulla relazione fra utile d'interesse (soprainteresse) e premio di assicurazione. Giornale dell'Istituto Italiano degli Attuari 2, pp. 67–78

Zimmermann H, Hafner W (2007) Amazing discovery: Vincenz Bronzin's option pricing models. Journal of Banking and Finance 31, pp. 531–546

Part F
Finance, Economics and Actuarial Science

Introduction

Why is it interesting to study the history of financial modelling? Is there anything we can learn from Bronzin's option pricing models except that he provided an independent attempt to price option contracts based on probabilistic assumptions only a few years after Bachelier's seminal study?

The value of these insights depends on one's perception of the production process of scientific knowledge. Obviously one might argue that the current state of research summarizes the entire time path of scientific discovery, because every scientist has the privilege of "standing on the shoulders of giants" – to quote Isaac Newton[1]. However, the scientific process is complex, sometimes slow and reluctant to adopt unorthodox ideas; it is driven by frictions, personal preferences and judgement of the researcher, and a variety of socio-cultural and economic factors. The sociology of science provides a complex picture of the production of scientific knowledge including parallel discoveries, near misses, or unrecognized spadework and blindness. As a consequence, new ideas and concepts often only gradually emerge in the scientific process, and option pricing is a key example for this insight.[2]

The academic field of finance in general provides a rich field of study for the aforementioned issues. Obviously Harry Markowitz invented mean-variance portfolio theory – but what about the contributions of Andrew Roy and Bruno de Finetti? Who suggested the random walk model for speculative prices – Paul Samuelson, Sidney Alexander, Maurice Kendall, Louis Bachelier, or Jules Regnault? Who deserves the merits for the notion of efficient markets – Eugene Fama, Harry Roberts or Holbrook Working? Who should be credited for the first arbitrage based option pricing model? Obvisously, Black and Scholes – but the critical remark (about riskless profits by continuously rebalancing the hedge position) is explicitly credited to Robert Merton in the original Black-Scholes paper! Apparently, the notion of riskless profits if basic price relationships between financial

[1] "If I can see further than anyone else, it is only because I am standing on the shoulders of giants".

[2] It appears like an ironic twist of fate that the "father" of modern sociology of science, Robert K. Merton, is the biological father of Robert C. Merton, the "father" of modern option pricing.

instruments are violated can be found earlier, e.g. in the work of de Finetti and Bronzin, however without calling it that way, and not in a continuous-time stochastic framework.

In this part of the book, Yvan Lengwiler analyses the foundations of the expected utility paradigm which constitutes the basis of modern finance (as well as game theory) and concludes that "it is interesting to note just how many thinkers have contributed to it, and at the same time to realize that the earliest statements of the theory were the most powerful ones, and were followed by weaker conceptions". Flavio Pressacco's essay highlights Bruno de Finetti's impressive contributions to the field of financial economics including mean-variance analysis, risk aversion, and arbitrage pricing. Amazingly, while de Finetti's contribution to probability theory and actuarial science is widely known, he is not regarded as a pioneer for financial economics.

What makes finance a fascinating field of study is the intermediate position it takes between an exact science (like mathematics and physics) and the "dirty" fields of gambling, speculation, and greed – areas which are typically located in the domain of sociologists and psychologists. There is probably no other field where the most sophisticated mathematical models contrast animal (some would call it irrational) spirits, storytelling and gossip, and emotional public debates as in the field of finance. Financial derivatives have always been at the epicenter of these battles, and the current financial crisis is only the most recent, and probably most drastic, case to exemplify that. It also explains the difficult role of economic analysis between a mathematical and behavioral science. Maybe that a major problem of "modern" option theory is that hedging and pricing models are too detached from the economic and institutional setting – in particular: frictions such as market illiquidity or accounting rules – within which the instruments are traded. Espen Haug observes in his paper that in the old days, not only academics, but also practitioners have used hedging and pricing techniques "much more sophisticated than most of us would have thought".

The historical study of option theory provides not only interesting, but highly relevant insight into the discovery process of scientific knowledge, and most notably, into its determinants. In the field of finance, this process is driven by four particularly important factors:

- Technology and data: the application portfolio theory would not have been possible without the implementation of the optimization algorithms on large scale computers which were available in the 50s; also, financial data sources were indispensable for estimating the required inputs.
- Financial innovation and organized markets: the availability of handy, ready-to-apply option pricing formulas was a prerequisite for trading standardized option contracts; again, technology in terms of programmable pocket calculators was essential to support real-time trading activities in the early 70s.

- Regulation and social values: the public attitude towards financial speculation, and in particular towards the use of derivative instruments, exhibits substantial shifts over time, and is reflected in ever changing regulatory constraints.
- Economic setting: a liberal, market-oriented economic environment which establishes binding norms accepted by – at least – the leading classes of the society is a key prerequisite for the development of knowledge, in terms of education and research, about financial issues.

Much has been written about the role of technology and the emergence of organized exchanges in the history of derivative instruments during the 20th century. A much longer – and broader – perspective is taken in the article by Ernst Juerg Weber who traces the use of derivative contracts back to Mesopotamia, Hellenistic Egypt, and the Roman and Byzantine Empires, and shows how the instruments spread across the European countries after the Renaissance. This long fascinating history not only reveals the economic causes of the transformation of individual derivative contracts to modern exchange-traded financial instruments, but also highlights the impact of legal systems, such as the canon law, and specific regulatory actions released after financial crises on this development. The history of derivatives has to tell us much more than how to price options.

15 A Short History of Derivative Security Markets

Ernst Juerg Weber*

In this chapter the pioneering works on option pricing of Louis Bachelier (1900) and Vinzenz Bronzin (1908) are put into the historical context. The history of derivatives is traced back to the origins of commerce in Mesopotamia in the fourth millennium BC. After the collapse of the Roman Empire, contracts for the future delivery of commodities continued to be used in the Byzantine Empire in the Eastern Mediterranean and they survived in canon law in Western Europe. During the Renaissance, financial markets became more sophisticated in Italy and the Low Countries. Contracts for the future delivery of securities were used on a large scale for the first time in Antwerp and then Amsterdam in the sixteenth century. Derivative trading on securities spread from Amsterdam to England and France at the end of the seventeenth century, and from France to Germany in the early nineteenth century. Around 1870, financial practitioners developed graphical tools to represent derivative contracts. Profit charts made derivatives accessible to young scientists, including Louis Bachelier and Vinzenz Bronzin, who had the mathematical knowledge for the rigorous analysis of derivative pricing.

15.1 Introduction

Modern textbooks in financial economics often misrepresent the history of derivative securities. For example, Hull (2006) suggests that derivatives became significant only during the past 25 years, and that it is only now that they are traded on exchanges.

> "In the last 25 years derivatives have become increasingly important in the world of finance. Futures and options are now traded actively on many exchanges throughout the world" (Hull 2006, p. 1).

Mishkin (2006) is even more adamant that derivatives are new financial instruments that were invented in the 1970s. He suggests that an increase in the volatility of financial markets created a demand for hedging instruments that were used by financial institutions to manage risk. Does he really believe that financial markets were insufficiently volatile to warrant derivative trading before the 1970s?

* University of Western Australia, Australia. *eweber@biz.uwa.edu.au*

> "Starting in the 1970s and increasingly in the 1980s and 90s, the world became a riskier place for the financial institutions described in this part of the book. Swings in interest rates widened, and the bond and stock markets went through some episodes of increased volatility. As a result of these developments, managers of financial institutions became more concerned with reducing the risk their institutions faced. Given the greater demand for risk reduction, the process of financial innovation described in Chapter 9 came to the rescue by producing new financial instruments that helped financial institution managers manage risk better. These instruments, called derivatives, have payoffs that are linked to previously issued securities and are extremely useful risk reduction tools" (Mishkin 2006, p. 309).

The widespread ignorance concerning the history of derivatives is explained by a dearth of research on the history of derivative trading. Even economic historians are not well informed about the long history of derivative markets. A review of three leading economic history journals – the *Journal of Economic History*, the *Economic History Review* and the *European Review of Economic History* – has yielded not a single article in the period from 1990 to 2006 with a title that would indicate that it deals with some aspect of the history of derivative securities. In 2007, the *European Review of Economic History* published an article by Pilar Nogués Marco and Vam Malle-Sabouret on derivatives that were written on East India bonds in London in the eighteenth century. Articles in edited volumes and working papers indicate that economic historians are now turning to the history of derivative markets. Goetzmann and Rouwenhorst (2005) includes an article by Gelderblom and Jonker on derivative trading in Amsterdam from 1550 to 1650, and two volumes edited by Poitras (2006, 2007) contain the so far most comprehensive collection of articles and sources on derivative markets during the past four hundred years.

The history of derivatives has remained unexplored until recently because there are few historical records of derivative dealings. Derivatives left no paper trail because they are private agreements that have been traded in over-the-counter markets for most of their history. Even today, the international commodity and financial markets, which have always been a primary focus of derivative dealings, remain beyond the reach of national statistical offices. Another reason why historical records of derivatives are scant is conceptual. A forward contract has no market value when it is set up, although its notional value may be large. Thus, how should a forward contract be recorded when it is set up? There is naturally no point in recording a zero value. This problem is even more acute with futures contracts whose market value does not deviate much from zero during their entire life. At the end of each day, the value of a futures contract is set back to zero by crediting or debiting the daily change in value to a margin account. The "Triennial Central Bank Survey" of the Bank for International Settlements, which was first published in 1989, for the first time addressed the conceptual and practical difficulties of recording derivative dealings in international over-the-counter markets.

Since there are no official statistics on derivatives, economic historians must rely on other sources that provide evidence that derivatives were used, including laws and regulations, court decisions, charters and business conditions of exchanges and trading companies, and surviving derivative contracts. Undoubtedly, the long history of derivatives is little known because the examination of primary sources is a laborious task that requires special skills. Kindleberger (1996), p. 5, remarked that “Historical research of a comparative sort relies on secondary sources, and cannot seek for primary material only available in archives”. There are not many historians and economists who are experts both in ancient languages and scripts and in financial economics. In this chapter, whenever possible secondary sources are used that quote primary sources, for example Ehrenberg (1928) and Swan (2000). A less reliable source that is also used is the testimony of financial practitioners who lived and worked in the period under consideration, including de la Vega (1688), Houghton (1694), Coffinière (1824) and Proudhon (1857).

The focus in this chapter is on financial institutions and the mechanics of derivative dealings; no attention is paid to the emergence of the random walk hypothesis of asset prices, which provided the mathematical foundation for Bachelier and Bronzin’s work. The origin of the random walk hypothesis is discussed in Jovanovic (2006a) and Preda (2006).

15.2 The Origins of Derivatives in Antiquity

It is now hard to believe that the generic term “derivative”, which stands for all kinds of derivative products, has emerged only very recently, in the 1980s. Swan (2000), p. 5, traces it back to the 1982 New York Federal Court case of “American Stock Exchange vs. Commodity Futures Trading Commission”. A reliable definition of derivatives is crucial for regulators who are in charge of derivative markets, but the rapid development of new derivative products has rendered definitions quickly obsolete. A derivative should not be defined as a financial instrument whose value depends (is derived) from the value of some underlying asset because there is no such asset in the case of weather derivatives, electricity derivatives and the derivatives whose value depended on the outcome of papal elections in the sixteenth century (Swan 2000, p. 142). Therefore, financial textbooks – for example Hull (2006), p. 1 – now define derivatives as financial instruments whose value can depend on “almost any variable”.

Yet, also this definition of a derivative is incomplete because it does not recognize the risk that the counterparty of a derivative contract may default. During the financial crisis in 1987, the standard models of derivative pricing failed because they did not take account of the default risk that arose after the near-failure of Long-Term Capital Management (LTCM). For this reason, Swan

(2000), p. 18, defines a derivative contract as a "promise" whose market value depends, first, on the strength of the promissor's ability to perform and, second, on the value of the underlying asset or variable. Similarly, Moser (2000), p. 279, who investigates the history of clearing arrangements at the Chicago Board of Trade (CBOT), uses a definition of futures contracts that recognizes the non-performance option of contract holders because "many futures-contract terms are best understood as efforts to minimize non-performance costs [...]" Defining a derivative as a promise with a default option is crucial in historical research because differences in legal institutions and customs created wide disparities in non-performance costs across places and time.

Derivative contracts emerged as soon as humans were able to make credible promises. In a commercial environment, it is essential for a credible promise that it is somehow recorded. The invention of writing satisfied the administrative and commercial needs of the first urban society in human history in Mesopotamia in the fourth millennium BC. The first derivative contracts were written in cuneiform script on clay tablets, which, luckily for financial historians, are extremely durable. These derivatives were contracts for future delivery of goods that were often combined with a loan. Van de Mieroop (2005) reproduces a tablet in which a supplier of wood, whose name was Akshak-shemi, promised to deliver 30 wooden [planks?] to a client, called Damqanum, at a future date. The contract was written in the nineteenth century BC.

> "Thirty wooden [planks?], ten of 3.5 meters each, twenty of 4 meters each, in the month Magrattum Akshak-shemi will give to Damqanum. Before six witnesses (their names are listed). The year that the golden throne of Sin of Warhum was made" (van de Mieroop 2005, p. 23).

Swan (2000) displays a tablet from about 1700 BC, in which two farming brothers received from the King's daughter three kurru of barley, which had to be returned at harvest time. The brothers probably used the seed, about 0.9 cubic meters[1], for planting a field.

> "Three kurru of barley, in the seah-measure of Shamash, the mesheque measure, in storage, Anum-pisha and Namran-sharur, the sons of Siniddianam, have received from the naditu-priestess Iltani, the King's daughter. At harvest time they will return the three gur of barley in the seah-measure of Shamash, the mesheque measure, to the storage container from which they took it. Before (two witnesses whose names are listed). Month Ulul, 19th day, year in which King Abieshuh completed the statue of Entemena as god" (Swan 2000, p. 28).

[1] In the second millennium BC and earlier, one kurru (kur, gur) was 300 qa, where one qa was about one liter (Segrè 1944).

This contract may either be viewed as a commodity loan or as a short-selling operation, in which the brothers borrowed barley, used it for planting the crop, and then returned it after harvest. This operation was less innocuous than it looks because the brothers carried some risk. If the crop failed they were required to buy barley in order to be able to return it to the royal granary. This operation would not have been possible without the sophisticated Mesopotamian irrigation system, which reduced the risk of crop failure due to drought. It is also possible that the King's daughter, who represented the state, did not enforce the contract if a widespread crop failure due to climatic conditions or a locust plague led to a famine. In that case the state carried the risk of general crop failure.

Derivatives played an important role in the funding of long-distance trade. Zohary and Hopf (2000), pp. 140–141, maintain that the sesame plant was first cultivated in the Indus Valley between 2250 and 1750 BC. The following tablet, which is from 1809 BC, shows that a Mesopotamian merchant borrowed silver, promising to repay it with sesame seeds "according to the going rate" after six months. He may have used the silver to finance a trading mission to the Indus Valley to obtain sesame seeds. This contract combines a silver loan with a forward sale of sesame seeds.

> "Six shekels silver as a šu-lá loan, Abuwaqar, the son of Ibqu-Erra, received from Balnumamhe. In the sixth month he will repay it with sesame according to the going rate. Before seven witnesses (their names are listed). These are the witnesses to the seal. In month eleven of the year when king Rim-Sin defeated the armies of Uruk, Isin, Babylon, Rapiqum and Sutium, and Irdanene, king of Uruk" (van de Mieroop 2005, pp. 21–22).

While six shekels of silver was a fair amount of money, it seems not to be enough to finance a trading mission from Mesopotamia to the Indus Valley.[2] But six shekels may have been the standard value of a contract, and the merchant may have held more than one contract. Indeed, a sexagesimal numeral system that was based on the number sixty had evolved in Mesopotamia by the end of the fourth millennium BC. If the merchant traded in a range of goods, he may also have concluded similar contracts for other goods to attract more funding.

It is a tragic fact that slave trade was prevalent during much of commercial history. A tablet from 1750 BC provided a slave trader with funding and insurance. At the time when the contract was written, he received 204 2/3 qu of oil in the measure of Shamash. In return, he had to deliver healthy slaves from Gutium after one month, with an option of paying 1/3 mina 2/3 shekels of silver instead of delivering slaves.

[2] Around 1800 BC, the price of a slave was about 24 shekels, the wage of a hired worker was one third of a shekel per month, and it cost one to three shekels to rent a house for a year (Farber 1978). The Eshnunna Code, which was written ca. 2000 BC, stipulated a monthly wage of one shekel.

> "204 2/3 qu of oil in the measure of Shamash, to the value of 1/3 mina 2/3 shekels of silver, as the price for healthy slaves from Gutium, Warad-Marduk son of Ibni-Marduk has received from Utul-Ishtar the troop-commander on the authority of Lu-Ishurra son of Ili-usati. Within one month he shall bring healthy slaves from Gutium. If he does not bring them within one month, Lu-Ish(k)urra son of Ili-usati will repay 1/3 mina 2/3 shekels of silver to the bearer of this tablet. Before (four witnesses whose names are listed). Month Ab, sixth day, year in which King Ammisaduqa, etc." (Swan 2000, p. 29).

This contract provided the slave trader with capital to procure slaves from Gutium. The option to pay 1/3 mina 2/3 shekels of silver limited his loss if he was not able to buy slaves at a price that made the transaction profitable. It also provided insurance against all other hazards of the slave trade, including the risk that the slaves fell ill, they ran away, etc. The counterparty agreed to this transaction if the price of 1/3 mina 2/3 shekels of silver for 204 2/3 qu of oil exceeded the spot price of oil by an amount that was sufficient to adequately compensate for supplying the initial loan of oil and for the risks inherent in the slave trade. The cuneiform tablet gave the slave trader the option to pay silver to the bearer of the tablet. This suggests that the holder of the tablet could transfer the contract to a third party. But not enough is known on Mesopotamian trading practices to determine the significance of the transfer of tablets.

About half a million clay tablets have been found so far, with more than 200,000 being held by the British Museum. The cuneiform digital library initiative (cdli), which is a joint effort of the *Vorderasiatisches Museum Berlin*, the Max Planck Institute for the History of Science and the University of California at Los Angeles (UCLA), has digitalized about 225,000 tablets, making them available on the internet and supplying translations and comments.[3] This provides a research opportunity for economists who are interested in the history of economic institutions. An important economic institution that determines economic outcomes is the market itself. The evolution of markets reflects changing transaction and information costs, which depend on technological advances in transport, information processing and administration. The emergence of contracts for future delivery enhanced the efficiency of agricultural markets in Mesopotamia and they were a prerequisite for the expansion of long-distance trade.

The ascendancy of Greek civilization began around 1000 BC. It is more difficult to document the use of derivatives for Greek commerce than Mesopotamia. Greek philosophers and historians, whose writings profoundly influenced Western civilization, were not interested in commerce. The Greeks did not use a medium for commercial contracts that was as durable as clay tablets, and laws that have survived as inscriptions on murals and columns were

[3] The addresses are: http://cdli.mpiwg-berlin.mpg.de and http://cdli.ucla.edu.

generally hostile to contracts for the future delivery of goods. But it is hard to imagine that farmers were able to fully fund the crop cycle, and merchants had enough capital to finance risky commercial expeditions, while rich individuals found no way to invest their wealth in commercial endeavors that promised a return in the future. The fact that Greek law favored spot transactions does not prove that there were no contracts for future delivery because commercial history is littered with laws and ordinances against derivatives that were ignored by the public. In fact, the Greeks were quite practical in commercial affairs. According to Swan (2000), p. 61, Athens allowed contracts for future delivery in seaborne trade because the city depended on the import of grain from Egypt. Alexander, who invaded the Middle East in the fourth century BC, left the local commercial and legal system intact, which had descended from Mesopotamia. Therefore, the use of derivatives continued in the Middle East under Greek dominance. Hellenistic Egypt is the second period in commercial history from which a large number of commercial contracts has survived because papyrus is almost as durable in the desert climate of Egypt as the earlier clay tablets.

The Romans, who copied much of Greek culture, initially adopted the Greek restrictions on contracts for future delivery. But these restrictions clashed with the commercial realities of the vast Roman Empire, which reached from Britannia to Mesopotamia at its peak. Commodities moved along a network of new roads and the ships of Roman merchants criss-crossed the Mediterranean. The city of Rome, whose population grew to one million people, depended on trade with the provinces, particularly the import of wheat from Northern Africa. During the third century BC, Roman law caught up with commercial practice, providing for contracts for future delivery of goods. Swan (2000), Chapter 3.2, considers the treatment of contracts for future delivery in Roman law. Sextus Pomponius, a lawyer who wrote in the second century AD, distinguished between two types of contracts. The first, *vendito re speratae*, which was void if the seller did not have the goods at the delivery date, provided insurance against crop loss and the hazards of long-distance trade, including the loss of ships in maritime trade. The second, *vendito spei*, was a straightforward forward contract that did not provide for any reprieve to the seller in case he was unable to deliver the goods. It is unclear whether *vendito re speratae* involved the same rights as a modern put option because the seller may have been obliged to deliver the goods if he had them.

Early Roman law upheld the principle of privity of contract, which implies that a contract establishes a relationship that is exclusive to the parties in the contract. A contract was not transferable because a third party was unable to enforce it. For example, a credit contract established an exclusive relationship between lender and borrower. The lender could not assign his right to repayment of principal and interest to someone else because the borrower was only obliged to pay to the initial lender. Similarly, the holder of a contract for future delivery could not sell it because only the holder was entitled to receive goods in the future, and no one else. The principle of privity of contract held back the emergence of security markets in the Roman economy. According to Swan (2000), pp. 80–81, the principle eroded only slowly in a legal process that lasted until the end of the Roman Empire. The legal codes of the East Roman Emperor Theodosius II (401–450) and Byzantine Emperor Justinian (482/83–565) suggest that Rome had developed a law of assignment, which made it possible to trade derivatives over-the-counter after they had been written.

There were no corporations in Roman times, with one notable exception that is documented by Malmendier (2005). Societas publicanorum, which were private companies that tendered for government contracts, issued shares that were widely held by Romans. Cicero, who lived from 106 to 43 BC, commented on the trade in these shares, which is said to have taken place near the Temple of Castor on the Forum Romanum. The trade in these shares indicates some erosion of the principle of privity of contract. The fact that the subscriber to a share could sell it implies that there existed no exclusive relationship between the subscriber and the company. Malmendier (2005) avoids taking a position "on how much of a stock market there was in ancient Rome", and there is no evidence for or against the view that derivatives were written on the shares of societas. The available sources only support the conclusion that Roman derivatives included contracts for future delivery of goods that initially were held until the delivery date and that were traded over-the-counter after some unknown date.

The peoples from Central and Northern Europe that established themselves in the West Roman Empire lacked commercial codes. Instead, Church bodies, which had increasingly assumed administrative functions in the late Roman Empire, continued to apply Roman commercial law during the Dark Ages. Thus, the legal framework for contracts for future delivery remained in place during the Dark Ages, but there was no further progress in the design of derivatives because there was not much need for them in the Medieval economy which was both local and feudal.

15.3 Derivative Markets During the Renaissance

The first security markets emerged during the Renaissance, a period of cultural and economic revival that lasted from the fourteenth to the seventeenth century. During the Renaissance, the Italian city states and the Low Countries were the economically most advanced regions in Europe. In the twelfth century, Italian cities began to issue so-called monti shares. By the thirteenth century, monti shares had become negotiable, making them tradeable in secondary markets.[4] Monti shares were followed by bills of exchange, which provided the medium of exchange in long-distance trade from the fifteenth century until the early twentieth century. The buyer of some commodity accepted a bill of exchange and passed it to the payee instead of sending gold or silver coins. The payee

[4] Pezzolo (2005) discusses the finances of Italian cities and their use of monti shares.

either held on to the bill until maturity or he sold it to a third party. In fact, bills of exchange, whose maturity typically ranged from a few days to 90 days, could pass through many hands. The holder of a bill earned interest because bills were traded at a discount that gradually diminished until maturity.

Contracts for Differences

The main trading centers in Northern Europe were Bruges from the twelfth to the fifteenth century, Antwerp in the sixteenth century, and Amsterdam in the seventeenth century. Around 1540, Antwerp legalized the negotiability of bills of exchange and a royal decree made contracts for future delivery transferable to third parties. At about this time, an important innovation occurred in derivative markets. Merchants discovered that there is no need to settle forward contracts by delivering the underlying asset, as it is sufficient if the losing party compensates the winning party for the difference between the delivery price and the spot price at the time of settlement. Contracts for differences were written on bills of exchange, government bonds and commodities. Although it is likely that similar deals had been done in Bruges and with monti shares in Italy, contracts for differences were used on a large scale for the first time in Antwerp.

The following quote by Cristobal de Villalon (1542) refers to a contract for differences on bills of exchange, which was settled by a cash flow that depended on the exchange rate between bills of exchange in Antwerp and Spain. Since bills of exchange provided the medium of exchange in international trade, the domestic currency price of foreign bills was the exchange rate. Note that the author was accustomed to contracts for future delivery in marine insurance, the Roman *vendito re speratae*.

> "Of late in Flanders a horrible thing has arisen, a kind of cruel tyranny which the merchants there have invented among themselves. They wager among themselves on the rate of exchange in Spanish fairs at Antwerp. They call these wagers *parturas* according to the former manner of winning money at a birth (*parto*) when a man wagers whether the child shall be a boy or a girl. In Castile this business is called *apuestas*, wagers. One wagers that the exchange rate shall be at 2 per cent., premium or discount, another at 3 per cent., etc. They promise each other, to pay the difference in accordance with the result. This sort of wager seems to me to be like Marine Insurance business. If they are loyally undertaken and discharged, there is nought to be said against them. But there are many ruinous tricks practiced therein. [...] This is a great sin" (Cristob(v)al de Villalon 1542. Quoted in Ehrenberg 1928, pp. 243–244).

Contracts for differences were precursors of modern futures contracts. Like contracts for differences, futures contracts are usually settled by paying the difference between the delivery price and the spot price of the underlying asset, instead of delivering the asset itself. But futures have some safeguards that contracts for differences did not posses. Both parties in a futures contract maintain a margin account into which some money must be paid upfront. At the end of each business day, the value of a futures contract is reset to zero by crediting and debiting the change in value that had occurred during the day to the margin accounts. In fact, a futures contract is settled incrementally by daily cash flows between the margin accounts of both parties. If the balance of a margin account falls below some minimum value, there is a margin call and the account holder must provide new funds. The use of margin accounts with daily cash flows reduces the counterparty risk because daily price changes are smaller than cumulated price changes over long periods of time. Unlike modern futures, contracts for differences were settled by a single, potentially large cash flow at some distant date.

After the sack of Antwerp by Spanish troops in 1576, Amsterdam became the leading commercial center in Northern Europe. Amsterdam had a cosmopolitan population with Calvinist fugitives from Antwerp and Jews who were harassed by the Catholic Church and the authorities in Spain and Portugal. The Golden Age of Amsterdam lasted for about 80 years, from 1585 until the mid-seventeenth century. Dutch merchants dealt in a wide range of staples that were imported from Italy, the Baltic, the West Indies (Caribbean) and the East Indies (South East Asia). The financial needs of maritime trade created a supply of forward contracts and securities, including bills of exchange and shares of joint-stock companies. The Dutch East India Company and the Dutch West India Company, which were founded in 1602 and 1621, were the first large enterprises that issued shares as a source of funds. Right from the beginning, share trading involved contracts for differences. In an essay on the speculative activities of Isaac Le Maire (1558–1624), van Dillen (1935), pp. 53 and 58, noted that shares were traded "on term" (for future delivery): "[...] shares sold not only for cash but also on term. This wasn't anything new in Amsterdam, since term sales had been the custom for trade in wheat and herring". He also found that forward contracts on shares were usually settled as contracts for differences: "Instead of delivering the shares, people were content most often to pay the surplus, the difference between trading rates, which had to be settled later". Amsterdam was the first city where derivatives that were based on securities were used freely for a long period of time.

Short-Selling

The foundation of the Dutch East India Company was met with public enthusiasm, which turned into disenchantment when the *Company* developed more slowly than expected. The share price doubled within a few years, but about one half to three quarters of this gain was lost by 1610 (Neal 2005). Reacting to the disappointing performance of the Dutch East India Company, Isaac Le Maire, a fugitive from Antwerp, conducted the first recorded bear attack on an underperforming firm by selling its shares short. Thus, he borrowed shares and he then sold the borrowed shares. This was profitable if he could buy the shares back and return them to the owner at a lower price in the future. Conceptually, there is no big step from a contract for differences to a short-selling operation. In a contract for differences the expected profit depends on the difference between the expected future spot price and the delivery price. In a short-selling operation the expected profit is determined by the difference between the expected future spot price and the current spot price.

Short-selling attracts public scorn when asset prices are falling because it is thought that it creates an extra supply of assets that further depresses prices. In Amsterdam short-selling was banned in 1610. Yet, Kellenbenz (1957), p. xiv, is right that restrictions on short-selling were difficult to enforce. The ban on short-selling was ineffective because it was impractical to determine whether a seller indeed owned the asset to be sold or whether the asset was borrowed. It is hard to imagine how the authorities could have ascertained the ownership of every commodity and financial instrument that was sold in Amsterdam, without severely interfering with the operation of markets. Amsterdam would not have become the foremost merchant city in Northern Europe with such stifling controls.

Options

In the mid-seventeenth century, Amsterdam became entangled in wars with France and England and the plague decimated the city's population. Toward the end of the century, a renewed influx of religious fugitives contributed to the city's recovery. Large numbers of Huguenots – French Protestants – moved to Holland and Switzerland after the *Edict of Fontainebleau* in 1685. It is estimated that by the end of the century, Huguenots accounted for 20 to 25 percent of Amsterdam's population. Financial services contributed much to the revival of the city in the late seventeenth century. Commodity trade, however, had moved to London because England now dominated maritime trade.

In 1688, Joseph de la Vega (ca. 1650–1692) wrote a book on stock trading in Amsterdam, which he gave the suggestive title *Confusion de Confusiones*. In the introduction to the English translation, Hermann Kellenbenz, remarks that it "is a book written in Spanish by a Portuguese Jew, published in Amsterdam, cast in dialogue form [used by Greek philosophers], embellished from start to finish with biblical, historical and mythological allusions, and yet concerned primarily with the stock exchange [...]". De la Vega's work has been translated into several languages and a new Spanish edition was published in 1997; Cardoso (2006) includes a complete list of references. De la Vega was fascinated by options, which he considered to be safer than contracts for differences. At the beginning of his treatise, he notes that a long forward contract can be settled in three ways:

> "First there is the sale of the shares, through which profit or loss will arise according to the purchase price; then there is the hypothecation of the shares to four-fifths of their value (which is done even by the

> wealthiest traders without harm to their credit); and, finally, the buyer may have the shares transferred to his name and make the purchase price payable at the Bank - which can be done only by very wealthy people, because a "regiment" [the standard notional value of a forward contract] today costs more than a hundred thousand ducats" (de la Vega 1688, pp. 5–6).

This quote implies that forward contracts were contracts for differences. The holder of a long forward contract usually did not take delivery of the underlying shares because the notional value of a contract was extremely high, a hundred thousand ducats (3290.75 kilograms of silver).[5] If the holder took delivery, he could pay for the shares by borrowing up to four-fifth of their value, using the shares as collateral (hypothecation). This was done if settling for the difference produced a large loss that would have inconvenienced the holder of the contract. Thus, the first method of settling a long forward contract – the sale of the shares – amounted to settling for the difference; and the second method – hypothecation – was a way out if settling for the difference would bankrupt the holder of the contract; whereas the third method – taking delivery of the shares – was only practical for rich investors.

Forward contracts are risky because the delivery price can differ by a large amount from the spot price at settlement. Therefore, de la Vega (1688) favored options, which he considered new instruments for speculation that were safer than contracts for differences.

> "The price of the shares is now 580, [and let us assume that] it seems to me that they will climb to a much higher price because [...] of the good business of the Company [...] of the prospective dividends [...] Nevertheless, I decide not to buy shares through fear that I might encounter a loss and meet with embarrassment if my calculations should prove erroneous. I therefore turn to the persons who are willing to take [write] options and ask them how much premium they demand for the obligation to deliver shares at 600 each at a certain later date. I come to an agreement about the premium, have it transferred [to the writer of the options] immediately at the Bank, and then I am sure that it is impossible to lose more than the price of the premium. And I shall gain the entire amount by which the price [of the stock] shall surpass the figure of 600 [...] In the case of a decline, however, I need not be afraid and disturbed [...]" (de la Vega 1688, p. 8).

[5] In 1702, one Dutch ducat was 21.16 pennyweights (dwt) of silver, where one pennyweight is 1.555174 grams. Thus, one ducat was 32.91 grams of silver. The letter d in dwt stands for penny (*denarius*), as in the traditional notation for pound/shilling/pence, £/s/d (McCusker 1978, Table 1.1).

After this description of a call option, de la Vega (1688) turns to put options:

> "[...] I can do the same business (in reverse), if I reckon upon a decline in the price of the stock. I now pay premiums for the right to deliver stock at a given price [...]" (de la Vega 1688, p. 8).

Finally, he summarizes the option business:

> "The Dutch call the option business "opsies", a term derived from the Latin word optio, which means choice, because the payer of the premium has the choice of delivering the shares to the acceptor of the premium or demanding them from him, [respectively]" (de la Vega 1688, p. 9).

De la Vega may have looked for a less risky method of speculation because Amsterdam had experienced the first recorded financial bubble, the tulipmania, about half a century before he wrote his book.

15.4 The Tulipmania

Carolus Clusius, an Austrian botanist, who became head of the Botanical Garden in Leiden in the 1590s, introduced tulips in Holland. Tulips, which belong to the indigenous flora of Turkey, quickly became fashionable among the affluent. During a speculative frenzy in 1636–37, some bulbs are said to have been traded at a price equal to the value of a house. The traditional view of the tulipmania, which has been put forward by Mackay (1852), Kindleberger (1996) and others, is that it was a speculative bubble during which the public behaved irrationally. Garber (1989, 2000) and Goldgar (2007) cast doubt on this interpretation, arguing that earlier authors exaggerated price rises and that it was not irrational to invest in tulip bulbs. French (2006) argues that monetary factors created the right conditions for an asset price bubble in Amsterdam in the 1630s.

The speculation with tulip bulbs was done with contracts for differences, which had been used in Holland for about a century by the time of the tulipmania. It is unlikely that speculators were wealthy enough to buy tulip bulbs and hold on to them. Indeed, contracts for differences were controversial because they gave people leverage to speculate. In Antwerp contracts for differences were outlawed shortly after forward contracts had been made transferable, around 1541 (Swan 2000, p. 144). But it is unlikely that this restriction was effective because a forward contract does not show how it will be settled. Even if the contract requires the delivery of the underlying asset, the parties to the contract can informally agree on a cash payment at the delivery date. In Amsterdam contracts for differences were not made illegal, instead, in 1621, 1630 and 1636, three edicts were issued with the intention to undermine contracts for differences by making them unenforceable in the courts (Kellenbenz 1957, p. xiv). However, these edicts did not prevent the use of contracts for differences during the tulipmania. Derivative markets continued to work because the failure to honor a contract made a speculator an outcast, practically excluding him from further dealings. The following quote from de la Vega (1688) shows that most people valued their credit and reputation, although his friend did not fit the norm:

> "There are many persons who refer to the decree [which proclaims the unenforceability of short sales] only when compelled to do so, I mean only if unforeseen losses occur to them in their operations. Other people gradually fulfill their obligations after having sold their last valuables and thus meet with punctuality the reverses of misfortune. But I also knew a friend, a strange man, who recovered from the grief of his loss by pacing up and down in his house, not in order to wake up the dead like Elias, but to bury the living. And after half an hour of such soliloquies he uttered five or six sighs in a tone which betrayed more his relief than his despair. When asked the reason for his joy, which pointed to some sort of compromise that he had come to with his creditors, he answered, 'On the contrary, just this moment I have made up my mind not to pay at all, since my peace of mind and my advantage mean more to me than my credit and my honour'" (de la Vega 1688, p. 7).

In Amsterdam derivative trading was based on reputation because personal business relationships were important in a city whose population grew from about 50,000 to 200,000 people during the seventeenth century.

A consequence of the absence of legal enforcement of derivative contracts was that they were traded only over-the-counter. The default risk of derivative contracts was idiosyncratic because it depended on how strongly people valued their "peace of mind" and "advantage". In addition, the edicts of 1621, 1630 and 1636 were ambiguous, leading to some court cases. For this reason, in Amsterdam contracts for differences did not evolve into futures contracts that were traded anonymously at exchanges, and options did not become warrants. The absence of legal enforcement of derivative contracts may also explain why the tulipmania did not lead to a strong economic recession. Since holders of long forward contracts had the right to repudiate them, there were no widespread bankruptcies when the price of tulips collapsed in 1637. The history of the tulipmania suggests that in derivative markets a moratorium is preferable if enforcing contracts would cause widespread ruin and a recession.

15.5 Great Britain and France in the Eighteenth Century

The development of English financial markets lagged behind continental Europe by about two centuries. During the sixteenth century, England was still a rural-agricultural country that lacked the dynamism of the urban Italian and Dutch societies. In the seventeenth century, the country was held back by political strife, which culminated in the Civil War of 1642–1651. Since Parliament withheld funding, the King financed a floating (short-term) debt by imposing compulsory loans and borrowing from a motley crew of money dealers, gold smiths and bankers. English public finances were a shambles, preventing a market for government debt in the seventeenth century. The political turmoil also retarded the evolution of commercial law. Swan (2000), p. 171, found a court case that indicates that the negotiability of bills of exchange was a matter of contention as late as 1736, two hundred years after bills of exchange had become negotiable in the Low Countries. Finally, the shares of joint-stock companies did not play a significant role until the 1690s, although the first joint-stock companies had emerged in England at about the same time as in Amsterdam. The *Royal Exchange*, which had been established by Sir Thomas Gresham in the 1560s, was a commodity exchange.

In the Revolution of 1688, a group of Parliamentarians offered the crown jointly to Mary and her husband William of Orange, both grandchildren of James I of England. The couple lived in Holland where William held the office of *Stadtholder*. The move of William and Mary from Amsterdam to London had a profound impact on English society. Parliamentary rule was strengthened, setting England on course toward a constitutional monarchy.[6] North and Weingast (1989) attribute the evolution of British financial markets to the constitutional changes that established secure property rights in the 1690s. Public finances were reformed, leading to the establishment of the Bank of England in 1694 and the introduction of Exchequer (Treasury) bills in 1696. The Bank of England, which celebrated its Dutch heritage in 2002, discounted bills of exchange and it monetized the floating public debt by buying Exchequer bills. These financial reforms gave rise to a money market in which bills of exchange and Exchequer bills were traded. At the same time, there were improvements in the capital market. In the 1690s, a large number of joint-stock companies was founded whose shares were traded in the stock market, using the same techniques as in Amsterdam. Gerderblom and Jonker (2005) conclude:

> "The financiers following William [of Orange] to Britain possessed a full range of financial techniques, and for which they found a ready market indeed. This transfer of knowledge formed the basis of derivatives trading in London, firmly linking Amsterdam's pioneering

[6] Jardine (2008) portrays how English society benefited from the administrative, commercial and scientific achievements of the Dutch.

work to the emergence of modern markets" (Gerderblom and Jonker 2005).

John Houghton (1645–1705), a pharmacist, trader and publisher, included several articles on options in his weekly periodical *A Collection for Improvement of Agriculture and Trade*. The *Collection*, printed as a single folio sheet, included commercial and financial information, advertisements and a brief article.[7] The purpose of the articles on options, which appeared in June and July 1694, was to explain the new techniques of option trading to the readership. Murphy (2008), who draws attention to Houghton's periodicals, analyzes the financial ledgers of Charles Blunt, a financial broker. She confirms that a well functioning option market had evolved in London by the early 1690s, in which both call options – known as "refusals" – and put options were traded.

After the successful financial reforms in the 1690s, the British government blundered when it took part in the creation of the South Sea Company in 1711. The South Sea Company was given the exclusive right to trade with South America (not the South Pacific), including the slave trade between Africa and South America. This right turned out to be illusory because Spain restricted trade between South America and Great Britain to a single ship per year in the Treaty of Utrecht in 1713, and even the slave trade was not profitable for the *Company* because local agents siphoned off large sums of money. Instead, the South Sea Company became a vehicle for the financing of long-term government debt, which may have been the government's intention all along. The *Company* issued shares and it bought government bonds, which were inadmissible for discounting at the Bank of England. But this was an unattractive business because the public could buy government bonds directly. The idea seems to have been that the Bank of England would control the money market and the South Sea Company would dominate the capital market.

The combination of a colonial trading monopoly with public finances proved to be a disaster, leading to the South Sea bubble in 1719. Exaggerated expectations of future returns from trade with South America drove the share prices far above the value of government bonds held by the *Company*. It seemed that the South Sea Company had achieved the impossible, funding the long-term government debt and, at the same time, enriching shareholders by issuing shares whose value rose above the funded government debt.[8] The apparent success of the South Sea Company led to a wave of new joint-stock companies with

[7] The *Collection* included prices of "actions" (shares) of the *East India*, *Africa* and *Hudson's Bay* companies, exchange rates and the price of bullion. John Houghton published two periodicals with similar names: *A Collection of Letters for the Improvement of Husbandry and Trade* (monthly from September 1681 to 1683) and *A Collection for Improvement of Agriculture and Trade* (weekly from 1692 to 1703). See the entry of Anita McConnell (2004) on John Houghton in the *Oxford Dictionary of National Biography (DNB)*. McCutcheon (1923) focused on Houghton's work as a book-reviewer.

[8] Dale et al. (2005) find evidence for irrational investor behavior, whereas Shea (2007a) rejects irrationality. Dale et al. (2007) provide a rejoinder.

dubious business plans, which tried to cash in on the public's seemingly insatiable appetite for shares. In April 1720, shortly before the South Sea bubble burst, the government restricted the establishment of new joint-stock companies. The limitation on new joint-stock companies, which remained in force until 1825, was a futile attempt to support the price of the shares of the South Sea Company by reducing the overall supply of shares.

During the South Sea bubble, the tools of speculation included call and put options, and there was an innovation, a warrant-like instrument. The South Sea Company issued partially paid shares that subscribers could buy by making several installment payments. Shea (2007b) maintains that these shares were compound call options because the payment of an installment gave the subscriber the right to pay the next installment, thus keeping alive the option to eventually own the share. If the share price fell, the subscriber could refuse to make the next installment payment, forfeiting the option on the shares. The partially paid shares of the South Sea Company were warrants because the privileged position of the South Sea Company made them so fungible that they were traded in a secondary market.

The economic aftermath of the South Sea bubble remains contentious. Schumpeter (1939), pp. 250–251, claims that there was no major economic downturn after the South Sea bubble, but Carswell (1960) argues that the bubble had severe economic repercussions, delaying the onset of the Industrial Revolution by almost half a century. Kindleberger (1984), pp. 282–283, and (1996), p. 191, who avoids taking a position on the economic consequences of the South Sea bubble, notes that "London stopped growing from 1720 to 1750". There is reason to believe that the economic downturn after the South Sea bubble was more severe than after the tulipmania. Unlike in Amsterdam, speculators could not easily abandon a contract. The more rigorous enforcement of financial contracts in Great Britain led to bankruptcies when the bubble burst. To avoid the worst, the Bank of England belatedly and "grudgingly" bailed out the South Sea Company (Kindleberger 1984, p. 282).

In 1734, the British Parliament passed the "Sir John Barnard's Act", which declared contracts for the future delivery of securities to be "null and void". Fines amounted to £500 for "refusals" and "putts" and £100 for short-selling operations. The *Act* applied only to derivatives on securities because, as debated in Parliament, it was feared that commodity markets would move back to Amsterdam if contracts for the future delivery of commodities were outlawed in London. Adam Smith (1766) realized that the Sir John Barnard's Act did not prevent derivative dealings in security markets.

> "This practice of buying stock by time is prohibited by the government, and accordingly, tho' they should not deliver up the stocks they have engaged for, the law gives no redress. There is no natural reason why 1000 £ in stocks should not be delivered or the delivery of it enforced, as well as 1000 £ worth of goods. But after the South Sea

> scheme this was thought upon as an expedient to prevent such practices, tho' it proved ineffectual. In the same manner all laws against gaming never hinder it, and tho' no redress for a sum above 5 £, yet all the great sums that are lost are punctually paid. Persons who game must keep their credit, else no body will deal with them. It is quite the same in stock jobbing. They who do not keep their credit will soon be turned out, and in the language of Change Alley be called a lame duck" (Smith 1766, pp. 537–538).

The Sir John Barnard's Act made derivative contracts on securities unenforceable in the courts. As a consequence, Great Britain moved to a system of derivative trading with securities that was based on reputation, similar to that in Amsterdam a century earlier. The restriction on derivatives that involved securities explains why shares were traded in the Exchange Alley and not at the Royal Exchange. Share trading took place in the Exchange Alley because derivatives on securities were illegal. Thus, share traders were not banished from "the august surroundings of the second Royal Exchange" to "the shady precincts of Exchange Alley and nearby coffee houses", as maintained by Swan (2000), pp. 188–189. Instead, share traders avoided the Royal Exchange because they could not deal with options and conduct short-selling operations in the open. Commodity traders, however, stayed at the Royal Exchange because there were no restrictions on contracts for the future delivery of commodities.

The South Sea bubble was the first financial crisis with an international scope – being called the Mississippi bubble in France. The shares of the Compagnie des Indes, which had absorbed the Mississippi Company and the Banque Royale in 1719, were even more prone to speculation than those of the South Sea Company. Like its British counterpart, the French company possessed a colonial trading monopoly and it funded the Royal treasury by issuing shares. In addition, the French company discounted bills of exchange and it issued bank notes, the business that was assigned to the Bank of England in London. The Compagnie des Indes was the brain child of John Law (1671–1729), who had fled Scotland after being sentenced to death in 1694 for killing an adversary in a duel. Niehans (1990), p. 48, opined that Law "became influential for classical monetary theory in two respects, (1) by being the first to assign paper money an important economic role, and (2) by providing a dramatic example for the disasters that may result from the failure to have a correct understanding of this role". Law put forward the "real-bills doctrine", which, as discussed in Niehans (1990), pp. 48–51, and Weber (2003), does not provide an effective constraint on the issue of paper money. Murphy (2006) provides an introduction to Law's monetary and financial innovations. The price of shares of the Compagnie des Indes rose about 20-fold, whereas the shares of the South Sea Company rose only about six to seven-fold. Speculation was more intense in Paris than in London because unrealistic expectations on the prospects of colonial trade were reinforced by an inflationary overissue of paper money. After the collapse of the bubble in 1720, Law, who had been appointed as French finance minister a few months earlier, fled the country, spending his final years as an impoverished gambler in Venice. The timing of the collapse in share prices – May in Paris and September in London – suggests that the panic spread from Paris to London. Kindleberger (1996), pp. 111–112, indicates that other financial centers were affected, including Amsterdam and Hamburg.

Coffinière (1824), pp. 1–50, reviewed the restrictions on derivative trading that were imposed in the wake of the financial collapse in Paris. On August 30, 1720, the State Council stripped the privilege to deal in financial markets from the sixty security dealers. Over the next five years, a series of laws and ordinances established a stock exchange with at first twenty and then again sixty authorized dealers. The purpose of the French legislation was to confine security and commodity dealings to the premises of the stock exchange in order to control activities. This is just what share traders in London feared the most, to be forced to work at the Royal Exchange. Article 17 of a State Council Decision of September 24, 1724, restricted all dealings in securities and commodities to the privileged dealers "in order to prevent short-sales". Despite the threat of heavy fines, unauthorized people visited the stock exchange, trading took place outside the exchange building in some restaurants, and deals for future delivery were common. In 1736, a police order banned thirty persons from the stock exchange, imposing a fine of 6000 livres on each.

The French Revolution, which upheld the principle of freedom of trade, initially led to the abolishment of the guild-like privileges of the authorized dealers, but the "Commercial Code" of 1807 and supporting legislation returned to a regulatory framework that was virtually indistinguishable to that of the preceding century. Dealings in securities and commodities were again restricted to authorized dealers at the stock exchange. Article 321 and 422 of the "Penal Code" of 1810 imposed fines and prison terms on wagers with government bonds, which were contracts for differences. But trading continued outside the stock exchange in some restaurants. The preamble to a police order of January 24, 1823, bears witness to the futility of more than a century of legislation against derivative trading in Paris. Note that the State Council Decisions of September 24, 1724, and August 7, 1785, remained in force after the French Revolution.

> "Since the Police-Prefect has been informed that the laws and ordinances on the stock exchange are often circumvented, that many people meet at several places, especially at the Tortonic Coffee House, to deal with bills of exchange, money and commodities, interfering without authorization with the business of security and commodity dealers; considering that these infractions can only be explained by a lack of knowledge of the law or a disregard of it; considering Articles 1, 2 and 25 of the Decree of July 1, 1801; – (2) Article 1 of that of March 19, 1801; – (3) Articles 76, 78, 79, 85, 86, 87,

> 88 of the Commercial Code; – (4) the State Decisions of September 24, 1724 (Article 12) and August 7, 1785 (Article 182); – further considering Article 3 of the Government Decision of June 16, 1802; [...]" (Coffinière 1824, p. 47. Translated by E. J. Weber).

After all these weighty considerations and listing a century of futile legislation, the Police-Prefect once more outlawed derivatives, and trading in securities and commodities was restricted to authorized dealers at the stock exchange – again to no avail. As in Great Britain, derivatives continued to be traded informally outside the premises of the exchange, based on reputation with no recourse to the court system. This made people more cautious with whom they dealt, and it avoided the spread of bankruptcies when there were speculative excesses. In the eighteenth and nineteenth centuries, European governments lacked both the will and political power to suppress financial transactions between enterprising individuals.

15.6 Derivative Markets in the Nineteenth Century

In the early nineteenth century, a wave of derivative trading encompassed France that was based on government bonds. After the defeat of Napoleon in 1815, the Allied powers – Great Britain, Prussia, Austria and Russia – asked for financial compensation for a quarter of a century of war in Europe. Although France had lost the war and there had been a hyperinflation during the revolutionary period, the French government gained surprisingly quickly access to domestic and international financial markets. This made it possible to pay for the reparations with a mix of taxes and borrowing that was politically and economically less damaging than relying on exorbitant taxes without borrowing. At the same time, the growth in public debt created a market for government bonds, which provided a pool of fungible assets for derivative trading.

The remarkable recovery of investor confidence in French public debt was caused by several favorable circumstances. After the collapse of the Napoleonic regime, France continued to benefit from Napoleon's monetary and fiscal reforms. Napoleon had stabilized the French currency, reforming public finances and establishing the Bank of France. It is a popular myth that Napoleon was a fiscal conservative because he did not borrow much. Actually, he found it hard to borrow because European banking houses perceived him as a dangerous adventurer with uncertain prospects. In any case, Napoleon's early military campaigns were self-financing because he plundered the treasuries of occupied countries. The loot from the city of Bern financed the campaign in Egypt, a mode of finance that pained the Bernese aristocrats for some time. White (2001) also points to political factors that explain the relatively smooth transition of government after Napoleon. The goal of the four Allied powers, all monarchies, was to restore the Bourbon monarchy and not to destroy France. Even during the peace negotiations, Great Britain became an ally of France against Prussia and Russia, whose territorial claims in Eastern Europe threatened to unsettle the balance of power in Europe. Thus, at the end of the Napoleonic Wars, France had a stable currency, the public debt was small, the government was accepted as legitimate at least by monarchists, and France was supported by Great Britain in the peace negotiations. These circumstances were more favorable than those in Germany after World War I.

White (2001) reckons that the French reparation payments were "in most dimensions somewhat smaller than the post-World War I German reparations" but "larger than any other nineteenth and twentieth century indemnities". As a consequence of the reparation payments, the French public debt that was funded by long-term bonds rose from 1.3 billion francs in 1814 to 4.2 billion francs in 1821 (White 2001, Table 4). This made the French public debt the second highest in the world, behind Great Britain whose total interest bearing public debt was 570 million pounds in 1820, or about 14.4 billion francs (Barro 1997, p. 511). The British public debt had expanded during the eighteenth century and, unlike Napoleon, the British government had been able to raise funds in the capital market to finance the war effort.[9]

In the 1820s, derivative trading with government bonds flourished in Paris.[10] Coffinière (1824) and Proudhon (1857) wrote manuals on the techniques of derivative trading and the regulatory framework. Proudhon (1857), Chapter V, subdivided contracts for future delivery (*négotiations à terme*) into forward contracts (*marchés fermes*) and options (*marchés à primes, marchés libres*). A call option is called an *achat à prime* and a put option is a *vente à prime*. He also considered repurchase agreements, which were called *reports*. Both manuals were widely read but their style is bizarre, albeit for different reasons. Coffinière (1824) expressed moral outrage about the uses of contracts for future delivery that were settled by paying differences. He emphasized time and again that these activities were illegal because they were tantamount to wagers and illegal gambling. The police order against derivative trading, whose preamble was cited above, was issued in January 1823. Coffinière, who was an advocate (solicitor), could not afford to give the appearance that he supported illegal financial transactions.

By the time Proudhon (1857) published his manual, derivative trading involved a wide range of government bonds and shares. The second part of the manual includes a long list of securities that were traded at the Paris Stock Exchange in the 1850s. Yet, the regulatory framework had not kept up with the expansion of derivative markets in the first half of the nineteenth century. Proudhon (1857), p. 47, noted that the government of Louis-Philippe had put up with derivative trading in the *Café Tortoni* and the *Passage de l'Opéra*, but the

[9] Wright (1999) presents estimates on British government borrowing during wars from 1750 to 1815.

[10] See also Flandreau (2003), Lagneau-Ymonet and Riva (2008) and Riva and White (2008) on derivative markets in Paris in the nineteenth century.

police cleared the *Cercle du Boulevard des Italiens* of derivate traders in 1849 and the *Passage de l'Opéra* and the *Casino* in 1853. The purpose of the police action was to protect the monopoly of the authorized security dealers at the stock exchange who earned hefty monopoly rents. Despite the large expansion in trading volumes, their number had been frozen at sixty for 150 years! In the mid-1850s, the authorities yielded and the stock exchange opened its doors to the public, charging a modest entrance fee. Proudhon (1857), p. 81, also reports that contracts for future delivery were now lawful if the delivery date did not exceed two months (one month for railway shares). Hence, unlike Coffinière in 1824, Proudhon (1857) felt no need to hide the purpose of his manual, which he called *Manuel du Spéculateur à la Bourse*.

Proudhon's manual on speculation is unusual because its author hated the stock exchange. In 1853-54, he had accepted the commission to write the manual because he needed money. The first two editions were published anonymously and, only when the success of the book had been established, he put his name on the third edition. It was an odd decision by the booksellers *MM. Garnier Frères* to ask Proudhon to write a manual on derivative trading. Proudhon was a well known social philosopher who had collaborated with Karl Marx until, after falling out with Marx, he developed his own brand of anarchistic socialism. Proudhon's treatment of the contracts for future delivery in Chapter V is more succinct than that of Coffinière, whose book he knew (Proudhon 1857, p. 61). In his book, Proudhon also made valuable contributions to economic theory, anticipating modern information economics. He applied the principal-agent model to the conflict of interest between shareholders and management, and he put forward a model of the stock market in which noise traders interact with well informed professionals. However, all this valuable material is swamped by his polemic against the capitalists and government officials who controlled the stock exchange. Despite his tirades against the stock exchange, the book was popular because Proudhon, who survived on journalism, was a seductive writer who appealed to a base instinct of his readers – envy.

Stock Market Terminology in Central Europe

Between the sixteenth and the eighteenth centuries, in several German cities exchanges sprang up for the trade with bills of exchange. Most exchanges served a local clientele, but Hamburg maintained links with Amsterdam and the Hanseatic cities in the Baltic in the seventeenth century, and Frankfurt gained in importance in the second half of the eighteenth century. In the nineteenth century, the development of German security markets followed the same pattern as in France. Bonds of German states were first introduced at exchanges, and shares of railways, banks, insurance companies and industrial companies followed later. In 1806, the exchange in Berlin started to quote government bonds, two years later 21 government bonds were listed. In 1840, shares of three railways were added, and by 1848 there were 44 of them. In the second half of the nineteenth century, the number of listed securities grew rapidly: 163 in 1867,

358 in 1870, 1273 in 1894, and more than 2000 in 1906. In Frankfurt the number of securities rose from 20 in 1800 to 1104 in 1900 (all figures are from Schanz 1906).

Zurich is typical for the development of financial markets in a small city in central Europe. In 1850, the exchange rates for bills of exchange from 13 cities and the shares of two banks – the *Bank in Zürich* and the *Bank in St. Gallen* – were listed in the *Tagblatt der Stadt Zürich*. Within a few years, corporate bonds were introduced at the exchange and the number of shares rose markedly. In 1856, the *Neue Zürcher Zeitung* listed 13 exchange rates, bonds of six railways, and shares of eight railways and six banks. Figure 15.1 reproduces a leaflet published by the *Schweizerische Kreditanstalt* (*Credit Suisse*) on January 4, 1867, which includes quotes for the three categories of securities that were traded at exchanges: bills of exchange (*Wechsel*) on top, bonds (*Obligationen*) in the middle, and shares (*Actien*) at the bottom. There were 15 exchange rates, 10 bonds, and eight shares of railways and industrial companies. The exchange rates for Basel, Genf (Geneva) and St. Gallen were 100, as one would expect with a single currency. Note that the exchange rate for Triest, the home of Vinzenz Bronzin, is specially mentioned in the table. On September 3, 1869, the first issue of the *Wechsel- und Effekten-Cursblatt von Zürich* includes a bond of the Swiss federal government. In the first half of the nineteenth century, government bonds had been unimportant in Switzerland because of the political fragmentation of the country. In addition there was an American government bond, and two foreign shares from *Crédit Lyonnais* and *Gaze Belge*. In 1869, 59 bonds and shares were traded at the exchange in Zurich. All listings are reproduced in Schmid and Meier (1977), pp. 61–99.

Wechsel-Kurse der Schweizer. Kreditanstalt
in Conto Corrent.
Zürich, 4. Januar 1867.

	Brief.		Geld.	
	Kurze Sicht.		Sicht bis 3 Monat.	
Amsterdam	$213\frac{1}{2}$	timbré.	213	÷ $4\frac{1}{5}$ %
Antwerpen u. Brüssel	100	timbré.	$99\frac{7}{8}$	» 3 %
Augsburg	$212\frac{1}{3}$	—	$211\frac{3}{5}$	» $4\frac{1}{2}$ %
Basel	100	timbré.	100	» $4\frac{1}{2}$ %
Berlin u. Leipzig	$371\frac{1}{2}$	—	370	» $4\frac{1}{2}$ %
Frankfurt a./M.	$212\frac{1}{4}$	—	$211\frac{3}{4}$	» $3\frac{1}{2}$ %
Genua u. Turin	—	timbré.	—	» —
Genf	100	timbré.	100	» $4\frac{1}{2}$ %
Hamburg	$187\frac{3}{4}$	timbré.	$187\frac{1}{3}$	» 4 %
Italienische Bankplätze	—	timbré.	—	» —
London	25. 20	—	$25.17\frac{1}{2}$	» $3\frac{1}{2}$ %
Mailand	—	timbré.	—	» —
Paris, Lyon u. Marseille	100	timbré.	100	» 3 %
St. Gallen	100	—	100	» $4\frac{1}{2}$ %
Wien u. Triest	—	—	—	» —

Disconto: $4\frac{1}{2}$ %. Nebenplätze 5 à $5\frac{1}{2}$ %.

Disconto-Abzug wenigstens { 3 Tage bei Wechseln auf Winterthur, Basel, St. Gallen.
10 » » » » alle andern Plätze.

Effecten-Kursblatt der Schweizer. Kreditanstalt.

Obligationen: Kurs pro %, Marchzinsen extra.	Verzinsung.	Rückzahlung.	Ausgeboten.	Gesucht.	Begeben
5 % Schweiz. Nordost-Bahn	31. März. 30. Sept.	1868/1888	—	$100\frac{1}{2}$	101
$4\frac{1}{2}$ % » »	31. Jan. 31. Juli.	1865/1879	—	—	—
*$4\frac{1}{2}$ % » »	28. Febr. 31. Aug.	1872/1892	95	$94\frac{1}{2}$	95
4 % » »	30. April. 31. Oct.	1870/1890	—	—	—
*4 % » »	28. Febr. 31. Aug.	1872/1892	—	—	—
*5 % Schweiz. Central-Bahn	Ganzjährlich, diverse Termine.	Div. Term.	—	—	$100\frac{1}{2}$
*$4\frac{1}{2}$ % » »	10. Mai. 10. Nov.	1877	—	—	—
5 % Exportgesellschaft	31. Dec.	1873/1878	100	—	100
$5\frac{1}{4}$ % Henggeler Graff. & Cie.	30. Juni. 31. Dec.	1876/1879	100	—	—
$4\frac{1}{2}$ % Schweiz. Nordost-Bahn Emission 1865.	31. Mai. 30. Nov.	1877/1895	95	$94\frac{1}{2}$	95

*Mit Coupons, zahlbar auch auf süddeutschen Plätzen à 28 Kr. resp. 8 Sgr. pr. 1 Fr.

Actien: Kurs pro Stück, inclusive Coupons.	Dividendenzahlung. à compte Dividenden.	Restdividend	Ausgeboten.	Gesucht.	Begeben
Schweiz. Nordost-Bahn*	2 % 30. Juni.	3 Jan.	635	625	$627\frac{1}{2}$
» Central-Bahn	2 % 31. Aug.	15. April.	485	430	—
Banque Commerc. Genevoise	4 % 31. Dec.	1 Trimest.	500	495	500
Basler Handelsbank	2 % 15. Sept.	Im März.	420	410	415
Schweiz. Kreditanstalt	$2\frac{1}{2}$ % 31. Aug.	31. März.	—	570	570
» Export-Gesellschaft	5 % 31. März.	30. Juni.	—	—	—
» Rückversich.-Gesell.	—	1. Mai.	—	—	—
Zürcher Gasgesellschaft	$2\frac{1}{2}$ % im Mai.	Im Nov.	—	—	—

Fig. 15.1 "Kursblatt" for bills of exchange, bonds and shares published by *Credit Suisse* on January 4, 1867

Derivative trading spread from France to Central Europe. Coffinière's book was translated into German and published in Berlin in 1824, and a sanitized German summary of Proudhon's book was published in Zurich in 1857. The anonymous editor highlighted Proudhon's concern with the precarious position of shareholders, using a new title "The Stock Exchange, Stock Exchange Operations and Deceptions, and the Position of Shareholders and the Public". In Germany contracts for future delivery were called *Zeitgeschäfte*, which Emery (1896), p. 46, fn. 2, translated as "time-contracts".[11] Contracts for future delivery were subdivided into forward contracts (*fest abgeschlossene Geschäfte, feste Geschäfte, Fixgeschäfte*) and options (*Prämiengeschäfte, Dontgeschäfte*). A literal translation of *Prämiengeschäfte* is "premium businesses", which points to the premium that is paid for an option. In France, Switzerland and Austria the premium on an option was also called *dont*. The terms for call option (*Geschäft mit Vorprämie*) and put option (*Geschäft mit Rückprämie*) failed to describe these transactions. This was even worse for the four positions that can be taken in option markets: long call (*Kauf mit Vorprämie*), short call (*Verkauf mit Vorprämie*), long put (*Verkauf mit Rückprämie*) and short put (*Kauf mit Rückprämie*). Therefore, Bronzin (1908) introduced a more intuitive terminology: long call (*Wahlkauf*), short call (*Zwangsverkauf*), long put (*Wahlverkauf*) and short put (*Zwangskauf*). In addition, Moser (1875) and Bronzin (1908) mentioned a straddle (*Stellgeschäfte, Stellagen*) and *Nochgeschäfte*. „*Noch*" means "again". In a "*Wahlkauf mit m-mal Noch*", an investor at the same time buys a share and *m* call options on the share. Thus, he has the right to buy another *m* shares in the future. Similarly a "*Wahlverkauf mit m-mal Noch*" combines a sale of a share with *m* long puts on it.

Profit Charts

By the mid-nineteenth century, many publications on derivatives competed for the public's attention. But these publications were ill-suited as manuals for derivative trading because the authors, who often had a background in law, overemphasized regulations that were largely ineffective, and derivatives were explained with the help of tedious numerical examples. In effect, virtually no advance had taken place in the professional discussion of derivatives since de la Vega had published *Confusion de Confusiones* in Amsterdam in 1688. By the mid-nineteenth century, the shortcomings of the financial literature held back the development of derivative markets. A verbatim discussion of contracts for future delivery stretches the possibilities of everyday language, and the use of numerical examples is not suitable for the analysis of combinations of derivative contracts. The straddle was discussed as a separate contract because the authors did not notice that it combined positions in call and put options, and combinations of derivative contracts that produced more complicated payoffs were

[11] Emery (1896) gives some space to Proudhon (1857) at the beginning of his treatise on futures markets in the United States.

beyond the reach of the financial literature. Cohn (1867), pp. 3 and 36, who became Professor of Economics at the Federal Institute of Technology (ETH) in Zurich, still relied on Coffinière (1824) in his doctoral dissertation on the difference business.[12]

The invention of profit charts, which occurred around 1870, contributed much to the understanding of derivative contracts. Profit charts clarified the nature of forward contracts and options and they made it possible to combine derivatives in novel ways, achieving payoffs that had hitherto been impossible. The invention of profit charts was a decisive step in the evolution of derivative markets. They made it possible to explain a derivative contract with a single graph instead of long-winded explanations, numerical example and tables. Both Bachelier (1900) and Bronzin (1908) used profit charts in their works. It is unlikely that Bachelier and Bronzin, who had studied mathematics and physics, would have turned to the analysis of option pricing if profit charts had not provided an easy way for young scientists, who lacked experience in financial markets, to learn about derivatives.

The first profit charts were published by Lefèvre (1873) and Moser (1875). Jovanovic (2006b) reproduces four charts from Lefèvre (1873): a long forward contract (*achat ferme*), a long call option (*achat à prime dont*), a straddle which combines a long put with a long call, and a complex operation. The graph simplified the presentation of a straddle, which Lefèvre cumbersomely called "*achat à prime direct contre vente à prime inverse*". Figures 15.2 to 15.4 reproduce profit charts from Moser's book, which includes many more charts. Figure 15.2 displays a long call option on top and a short call option at the bottom, and Fig. 15.3 shows a straddle on top and a long contract with 2-times *Noch* at the bottom. In the contract with *Noch* it is assumed that a person buys a share and two call options on the share with a strike price of 61, paying 60 for the entire package. As there is no premium involved in a transaction with *Noch*, the price of 60 equals the sum of the share's spot price and two premiums for the call options. Moser (1875) used the profit charts to investigate the relationships between various derivative contracts. The top panel in Fig. 15.4 shows how a long forward contract can be combined with a long put option to create the profit of a long call option (solid line), and in the bottom panel a long put option and a long call option are combined to produce a straddle (solid line).

[12] Gustav Cohn (1840–1919) wrote several books on public finance and transportation economics. He completed the doctoral dissertation at the University of Leipzig in 1867. From 1875 to 1884, he held the chair of economics at the Federal Institute of Technology (ETH) in Zurich, and afterwards he moved to the University of Göttingen.

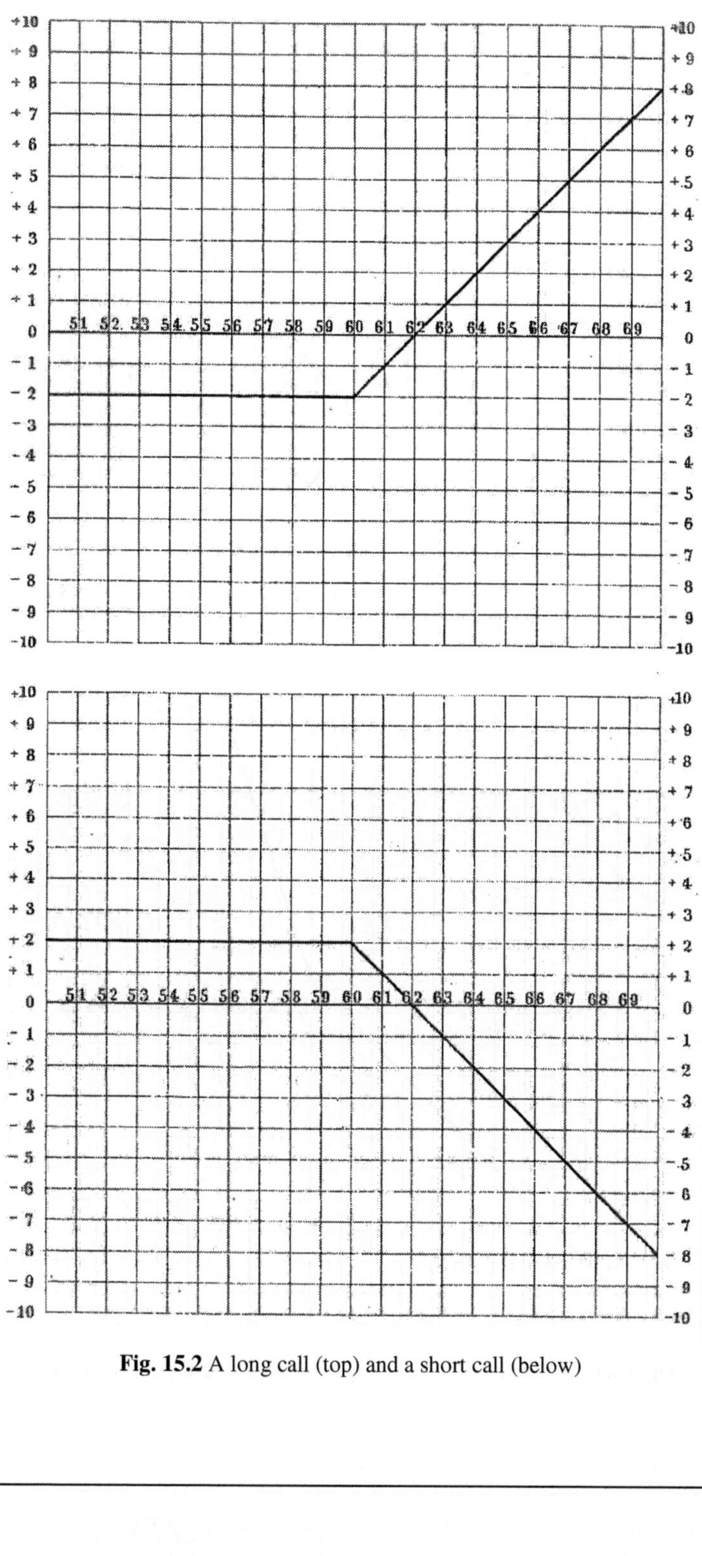

Fig. 15.2 A long call (top) and a short call (below)

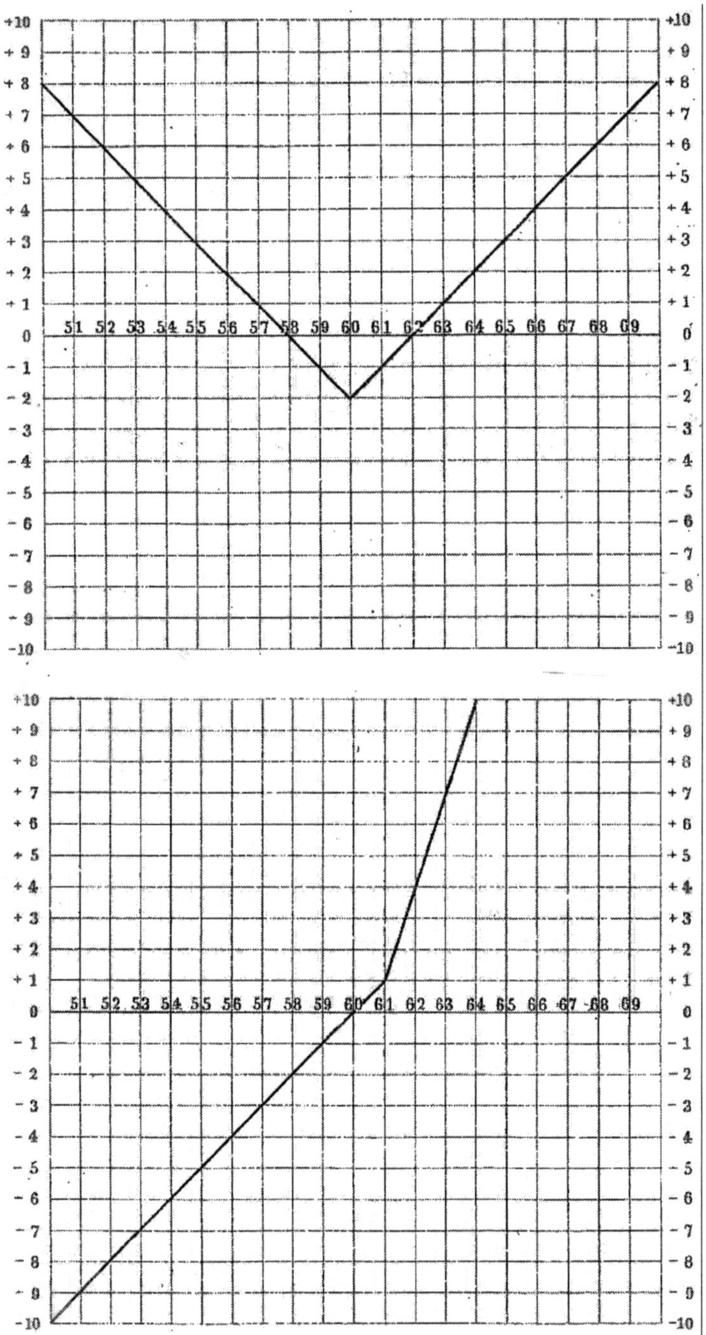

Fig. 15.3 A straddle (top) and a long contract with 2-times *Noch* (below)

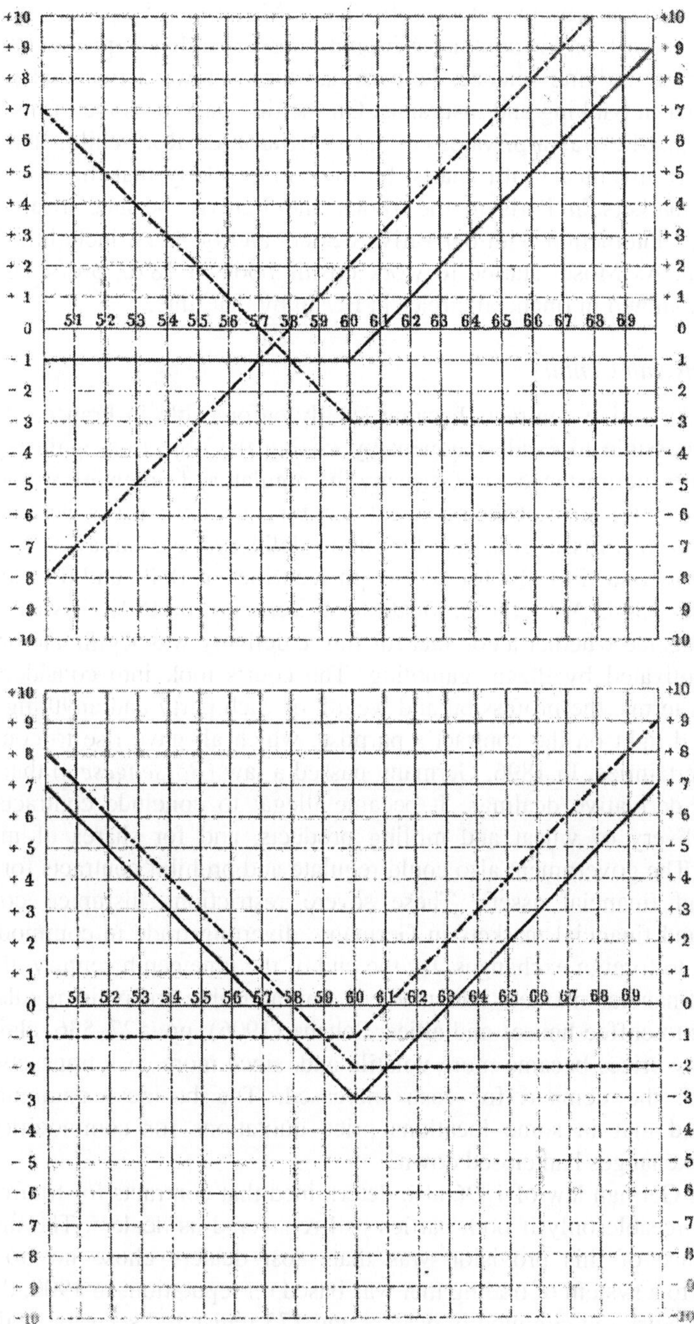

Fig. 15.4 A synthetic long call using a long forward contract and a long put (top) and a synthetic straddle using a long put and a long call (below)

It is unclear who invented profit charts. Moser (1875), p. V, mentions that he started to work on his book in 1870, but Lefèvre published profit charts before Moser. After studying science, Lefèvre had turned toward financial journalism and a career in banking and insurance. On the title page of some of his works he mentions that he was a private secretary of Baron de Rothschild. It is possible that Lefèvre invented profit charts, but it is more likely that they originated in financial markets in Paris in the 1860s and Lefèvre became aware of them through his interaction with derivative dealers and bankers, including Baron de Rothschild. As Moser started to work on his book in 1870, profit charts must have been known in financial circles in Berlin by that time.

Late Nineteenth Century

In 1885, derivative contracts became legally enforceable in France, although it was still possible to evade payment by raising the objection against gambling under some circumstances. In Germany the regulatory framework was similar to that in France for most of the nineteenth century, i.e. derivatives were traded in a legal limbo. In Prussia contracts for future delivery were outlawed for Spanish government bonds in 1836, for all foreign securities in 1840, and for securities of railways in 1844. After the unification of Germany in 1871, it was up to the courts to decide whether a contract for future delivery was legitimate or whether it was motivated by illegal gambling. The courts took into consideration the contract's terms, the profession and wealth of each party and anything else that might shed light on the contract's purpose, which all gave rise to considerable legal uncertainties. In 1896, Germany passed a law (*Börsengesetz*) that severely restricted derivative dealings. It became illegal to conclude contracts for the future delivery of wheat and milling products, and for shares of mines and factories. The government also could regulate and prohibit contracts for all other goods and financial assets. These severe restrictions disrupted commodity markets and financial markets in Germany, diverting trade in commodities and securities to foreign exchanges. By the end of the nineteenth century, the size of German financial markets had made it impracticable to avoid regulations by moving into coffee houses and allies. Schanz (1906), pp. 527–536, claimed that commodity prices became more volatile and, since more cash transactions were conducted, the demand for cash increased. The business community also complained that in some locations price quotations for commodities ceased because exchanges had closed down.

The German law of 1896 also determined that contracts for future delivery were enforceable only if both parties had registered as dealers. The unintended consequence of this provision was that most dealers chose not to register, returning to a system of trading that was based on reputation. In 1900, there were only 212 registered commodity dealers and 175 registered security dealers at all 29 German exchanges. But German commodity and financial markets had long outgrown the small-town conditions of pre-industrial derivative trading, where reputation based trading worked well. The presence of a large number of persons whose contracts were not enforceable caused problems because people had become accustomed to trading anonymously. Schanz (1906), p. 533, maintains that during the downturn in stock prices in the spring of 1900, many unregistered persons, including merchants and bankers, simultaneously bought shares forward and sold them forward. Allegedly, they then abandoned the position that produced a loss, thus taking advantage of the fact that their contracts were legally nonbinding. The German restrictions on derivative trading were a self-inflicted wound on the German economy at the turn of the nineteenth to the twentieth century. Although the German government again relaxed some regulations, Germany lacked an effective regulatory framework for derivative markets and the allocation of risk in the economy at the beginning of the twentieth century.

15.7 Conclusion

The history of derivatives is as old as the history of commerce. Farmers, manufacturers and merchants face risks because the production and distribution of goods takes time. Prices may change between the time the production decision is made and the sale of goods, and unforeseen circumstances may arise during the production process and distribution of goods. Forward contracts remove the price risk of future transactions, and options limit the risk of future transactions to the option premium. An efficient allocation of the risk of future transactions increases output because it enhances specialization among producers both locally and between distant markets.

In this chapter, the history of derivatives from antiquity to the time of Louis Bachelier and Vinzenz Bronzin is traced. Contracts for future delivery of goods spread from Mesopotamia to Hellenistic Egypt and the Roman world. After the collapse of the Roman Empire, contracts for future delivery continued to be used in the Byzantine Empire in the Eastern Mediterranean and they survived in canon law in Western Europe. During the Renaissance, financial markets became more sophisticated in Italy and the Low Countries. An important financial innovation were securities, which were issued as a source of funds by merchants (bills of exchange), governments (bonds) and joint-stock companies (shares). The first derivatives on securities were written in the Low Countries in the sixteenth century. Derivative trading on securities spread from Amsterdam to England and France at the turn of the seventeenth to the eighteenth century, and from France to Germany in the early nineteenth century.

During the process of writing this chapter, two issues arose that should be investigated further by someone who has access to the sources and the skills to use these sources. The first issue is the role of Sephardic Jews in the spread of derivatives from Antiquity, across the divide of the Middle Ages, to the Low Countries. Swan (2000), pp. 105–107, argues that during the Middle Ages derivatives continued to be used in monasteries and at fairs under the auspices of the Church because derivatives survived in canon law, which was influenced by

Roman law. This argument fails to explain why derivatives on securities emerged in the Low Countries in the sixteenth century, and not in Italian city states where securities (monti shares) had become negotiable much earlier, in the thirteenth century. Certainly, canon law must have been more influential in Catholic Italy between the thirteenth and fifteenth centuries than in the Protestant Low Countries in the sixteenth century.

An alternative hypothesis is that derivatives were introduced in the Low Countries by Sephardic Jews, who lived in Spain and Portugal and whose ancestry lay in Mesopotamia. Jews had prospered in Spain under Moslem rule from the eighth to the twelfth century. During the Christian reconquest of Spain, they were in and out of favor with rulers, depending on political and economic expediency. In 1492, Jews were either expelled from Spain or forcibly converted to Christianity. Sephardic Jews were transported to Northern Africa and the Eastern Mediterranean, and a significant group moved to Portugal, where they had the misfortune to be expelled again in 1497. From Portugal they fled to Northern Europe, including the Low Countries. Both Isaac Le Maire (1558–1624), who conducted the short-selling operation against the Dutch East India Company, and Joseph de la Vega (ca. 1650–1692), who wrote *Confusion de Confusiones*, belonged to the community of exiled Sephardic Jews in Amsterdam. The comment of Cristobal de Villalon (1542), which was reproduced in Section 3, shows that contracts for differences were used both in Spain and the Low Countries.[13] It is a promising hypothesis that Sephardic Jews carried derivative trading from Mesopotamia to Spain during Roman times and the first millennium AD, and to the Low Countries in the sixteenth century. The hypothesis that derivative trading spread from Mesopotamia via Spain to the Low Countries should be investigated by an economic historian with a background in finance who has access to Spanish archives and knowledge of Arabic, Hebrew, Latin and Spanish. Given these demanding requirements, it is not surprising that nobody has so far considered the role of Sephardic Jews in the spread of derivatives.

The second issue that needs further investigation is the role of banks in derivative markets. Not much is known on the use of derivatives by banks, but there is reason to believe that bankers and banks were at the forefront of derivative trading during the eighteenth and nineteenth centuries. Banks underwrote government bonds and shares of joint-stock companies and they invested in these securities. The business with securities (*Effektengeschäft*) was highly profitable and it is likely that it involved deals that were settled at a future date. Since personal relationships remained important, derivatives continued to be traded over-the-counter until the nineteenth century. This provided an

[13] Cristobal de Villalon was a Spanish humanist. His writings include a book on Spanish grammar (*Gramática Castellana*), which was published in Antwerp in 1558. The moral outrage that he expressed about contracts for differences may have been a ruse to elude the Inquisition. Similarly, Coffinière (1824) feigned moral outrage to protect his reputation as an advocate (Section 6). Nothing is known on de Villalon's ancestry.

opportunity for well connected banking houses, for example *Bank Rothschild*, which operated informal derivative markets either in-house or between banks. Mayer Amschel Rothschild (1744–1812), who founded the *Bank Rothschild* in Frankfurt, sent his sons Nathan, James, Salomon and Carl to London (1798), Paris (1812), Vienna (1820) and Naples (1821) to open banks; first-born Amschel stayed in Frankfurt. Reputation based derivative trading survived until the nineteenth century because it was supported by a strong constituency of security dealers and bankers.

The information on derivative dealings of banks is scarce because they kept operations secret as far as possible and their customers valued privacy. Many banks operated as sole proprietors and partnerships, with no need to divulge information to shareholders and the public. The following circumstantial evidence suggests that banks were active in derivative markets during the nineteenth century. (1) Henri Lefèvre, who – as mentioned in Section 6 – published the first profit charts for options, was a private secretary of Baron de Rothschild in Paris. (2) Bankers jealously guarded the profitable business with securities. The *Bank in Zürich*, which issued bank notes, was founded with the help of private banking houses in 1836. Bleuler (1913), p. 30, fn. 1, argues that the *Bank in Zürich* did not deal with securities as a concession to private bankers whose support it needed. Indeed, *Bank Rothschild* of Frankfurt subscribed to five percent of the bank's capital at its foundation (Bleuler 1913, p. 26, fn. 1). (3) The Swiss Federal Law on the Issue of Bank Notes of 1881 made it illegal for banks of issue to participate in contracts for future delivery of securities and goods, both on their own account and on account of third parties.[14] To avoid the restriction on derivatives and other regulations, large Swiss banks, the so-called *Grossbanken* which included the *Schweizerische Kreditanstalt* (Credit Suisse), *Bank in Winterthur, Basler Handelsbank* and *Schweizerische Volksbank*, chose not to issue bank notes in the nineteenth century.[15] Derivative dealings of banks and bankers almost certainly surpassed dealings in coffee houses and allies, which attracted the ire of the authorities in Paris and elsewhere. The fact that it is difficult and even impossible to find solid quantitative information on a historical issue does not prove that the issue was not important. This is particularly true in the history of derivative markets and in financial history in general.

[14] Article 16 of the Law applied the restriction on derivative dealings only to banks of issue that specialized in the discount of commercial bills (*Diskontbanken*), and not to banks that kept securities as reserves and state-run cantonal banks. The charters of some small Swiss banks included provisions against time dealings.

[15] The *Bank in Winterthur* and the *Basler Handelsbank* became *UBS*, and *Credit Suisse* absorbed the *Schweizerische Volksbank.* The *Eidgenössische Bank* and the short-lived *Banque Général Suisse* were the only large Swiss banks that issued bank notes for some time. Weber (1988, 1992) deals with the issue of bank notes by Swiss banks in the nineteenth century.

References

Bachelier L (1900, 1964) Théorie de la spéculation. Annales de l'École Normale Supérieure 17, pp. 21–86. English translation in: Cootner P (ed) (1964) The random character of the stock Market Prices. MIT Press, Cambridge (Massachusetts), pp. 17–79. And in: Bachelier L (2006) Louis Bachelier's theory of speculation. Princeton University Press, Princeton
Barro R J (1997) Macroeconomics, 5th edn. MIT Press, Cambridge (Massachusetts)
Bleuler W (1913) Bank in Zürich. Schweizerische Kreditanstalt, Orell Füssli, Zurich
Bronzin V (1908) Theorie der Prämiengeschäfte. Franz Deuticke, Leipzig/Vienna
Cardoso J L (2006) Joseph de la Vega and the confusion de confusiones. In: Poitras (2006, 2007)
Carswell J (1960) The South Sea bubble. Cresset Press, London
Coffinière (1824) Die Stockbörse und der Handel mit Staatspapieren. Aus dem Französischen des Herrn Coffinière mit einem Nachtrage vom Geheimen Rath Schmalz. Schlesingersche Buch- und Musikhandlung, Berlin
Cohn G (1867) Zeitgeschäfte und Differenzgeschäfte. Doctoral dissertation, Philosophische Facultät, Universität Leipzig. Druck von Friedrich Maucke, Jena
Dale R S, Johnson J E, Tang L (2005) Financial markets can go mad: evidence of irrational behaviour during the South Sea bubble. Economic History Review 58, pp. 233–271
Dale R S, Johnson J E, Tang L (2007) Pitfalls in the quest for South Sea rationality. Economic History Review 60, pp. 766–772
de la Vega J (1688) Confusion de confusiones. Amsterdam (English edition with an introduction by the translator, Hermann Kellenbenz, published in 1957 by Baker Library, Harvard Graduate School of Business, Boston (Massachusetts). Spanish edition with an introduction by Gonzales Anes, published in 1997 by Bolsa de Madrid, Madrid)
Ehrenberg R (1928) Capital and finance in the age of the Renaissance (First published as: Das Zeitalter der Fugger. Translated by Lucas H M and published in 1963 by Kelly A M, Bookseller, New York)
Emery H C (1896) Speculation on the stock and produce exchanges of the United States. Doctoral dissertation, Faculty of Political Science, Columbia University, New York (Reprinted in 1968 by AMS Press, New York and in 1969 by Greenwood Press, New York)
Farber H (1978) A price and wage study for Northern Babylonia during the Old Babylonian period. Journal of the Economic and Social History of the Orient XXI, pp. 1–51
Flandreau M, Sicsic P (2003) Crédits à la spéculation et marché monétaire: le marché des reports en France de 1875 à 1914. In: Feiertag O, Margairaz M (eds) (2003) Politiques et pratiques des banques d'émission en Europe (XVII–XXe siècles): Le bicentenaire de la Banque de France dans le perspective de l'identité monétaire européenne. Albin Michel, Paris
French D (2006) The Dutch monetary environment during tulipmania. Quarterly Journal of Austrian Economics 9, pp. 3–14
Garber P M (1989) Tulipmania. Journal of Political Economy 97, pp. 545–560
Garber P M (2000) Famous first bubbles: the fundamentals of early manias. MIT Press, Cambridge (Massachusetts)
Gelderblom O, Jonker J (2005) Amsterdam as the cradle of modern futures trading and options trading, 1550–1650. In: Goetzmann and Rouwenhorst (2005), pp. 189–205
Goetzmann W M, Rouwenhorst K G (eds) (2005) The origins of value: the financial innovations that created modern capital markets. Oxford University Press, Oxford (UK)
Goldgar A (2007) Tulipmania: money, honor, and knowledge in the Dutch golden age. University of Chicago Press, Chicago
Houghton J (1694) Collection for the improvement of agriculture and trade. June and July
Hull J C (2006) Options, futures, and other derivatives, 6th edn. Pearson Education, Upper Saddle River (New Jersey)
Jardine L (2008) Going Dutch: how England plundered Holland's glory. Harper Press, New York

Jovanovic F (2006a) A nineteenth-century random walk: Jules Regnault and the origins of scientific financial economics. In: Poitras (2006, 2007)
Jovanovic F (2006b) Economic instruments and theory in the construction of Henri Lefèvre's science of the stock market. In: Poitras (2006, 2007)
Kellenbenz H (1957) Introduction to the English translation of Joseph de la Vega (1688) Confusion de confusiones. Baker Library, Harvard Graduate School of Business, Boston (Massachusetts)
Kindleberger C P (1984) A financial history of Western Europe. George Allen & Unwin, London
Kindleberger C P (1996, 1978) Manias, panics, and crashes: a history of financial crises, 3rd edn. Basic Books, New York
Lagneau-Ymonet P, Riva A (2008) Les opérations à terme à la bourse de Paris au XIX siècle. In: Stanziani A (forthcoming) Droit et crédit: la France au XIX siècle
Lefèvre H (1873) Physiologie et mécanique sociales. Journal des Actuaires Français 2
Mackay C (1852, 1841) Memoirs of extraordinary popular delusions. Richard Bentley, London, 1841. Office of the National Illustrated Library, 227 Strand, London, 1852 (2nd expanded edn). This book has been reprinted by several publishers.
Malmendier U (2005) Roman shares. In: Goetzmann and Rouwenhorst (2005)
McConnell A (2004) John Houghton. In: Oxford dictionary of national biography (DNB), Vol. 28. Oxford University Press, Oxford
McCusker J J (1978) Money and exchange in Europe and America, 1600–1775. Institute of Early American History and Culture, University of North Carolina Press, Chapel Hill
McCutcheon R P (1923) John Houghton, a seventeenth-century editor and book-reviewer. Modern Philology 20, pp. 255–260
Mishkin F S (2006) The economics of money, banking, and financial markets, 7th edn. (update). Pearson/Addison Wesley, Boston
Moser J (1875) Die Lehre von den Zeitgeschäften. Verlag von Julius Springer, Berlin
Moser J T (2000) Origins of the modern exchange clearing house: a history of early clearing and settlement methods at futures exchanges. In: Telser L G (ed) Classic futures: lessons from the past for the electronic age. Risk Publications, London
Murphy A E (2006) John Law: financial innovator. In: Poitras (2006, 2007)
Murphy A L (2008) Trading options before Black-Scholes: a study of the market in late-seventeenth-century London (accepted for publication in the Economic History Review in 2007, expected to appear in 'Online Early' on the Blackwell-Synergy website in 2008)
Neal L (2005) Venture shares of the Dutch East India Company. In: Goetzmann and Rouwenhorst (2005)
Niehans J (1990) A history of economic theory. Johns Hopkins University Press, Baltimore
North D C, Weingast B R (1989) Constitutions and commitment: the evolution of institutions governing public choice in seventeenth-century England. Journal of Economic History XLIX, pp. 803–832
Pezzolo L (2005) Bonds and government debt in Italian city-states, 1250–1650. In: Goetzmann and Rouwenhorst (2005)
Pilar Nogués Marco, Vam Malle-Sabouret C (2007) East India bonds, 1718–1763: early exotic derivatives and London market efficiency. European Review of Economic History 11, pp. 367–394
Poitras G (ed) (2006, 2007) Pioneers of financial economics: contributions prior to Irving Fisher, Vol. 1 and 2. Edward Elgar Publishing, Cheltenham (UK)
Preda A (2006) Rational investors, informative prices: the emergence of the 'science of financial investments' and the random walk hypothesis. In: Poitras (2006, 2007) (This is a revised version of an article published in History of Political Economy 36, pp. 351–386)
Proudhon P-J (1857) Manuel du spéculateur à la bourse, 5th edn. Librairie de Barnier Frères, Paris (A German summary was published in 1857 as: Die Börse, die Börseoprationen und Täuschungen, die Stellung der Aktionäre und des Gesammt-Publikums. Verlag von Meyer und Zeller, Zürich)

Riva A, White E N (2008) Counterparty risk on the Paris exchange in the nineteenth century. Sixth World Congress of Cliometrics, Edinburgh
Schanz G (1906) Börsenwesen. In: Elster L (ed) Wörterbuch der Volkswirtschaft, Vol. 1. Gustav Fischer, Jena, pp. 497–540
Schmid H R, Meier R T (1977) Die Geschichte der Zürcher Börse. Effektenbörsenverein Zürich, Buchverlag der Neuen Zürcher Zeitung, Zürich
Schumpeter J A (1939) Business cycles: a theoretical, historical and statistical analysis of the capitalist process, Vol. 1. McGraw-Hill, New York
Segrè A (1944) Babylonian, Assyrian and Persian measures. Journal of the American Oriental Society 64, pp. 73–81
Shea G S (2007a) Financial market analysis can go mad (in the search for irrational behaviour during the South Sea bubble). Economic History Review 60, pp. 742–765
Shea G S (2007b) Understanding financial derivatives during the South Sea bubble: the case of the South Sea subscription shares. Oxford Economic Papers 59, Supplement 1, i72–i104
Smith A (1766) Report dated 1766. In: Meek R L et al. (eds) (1978) Lectures on jurisprudence. Clarendon Press, Oxford
Swan E J (2000) Building the global market. A 4000 year history of derivatives. Kluwer Law International, The Hague
van de Mieroop M (2005) The innovation of interest. Sumerian loans. In: Goetzmann and Rouwenhorst (2005)
van Dillen J G (1935) Isaac Le Maire et le commerce des actions de la Compagnie des Indes Orientales. Revue d'Histoire Moderne 5, pp. 121–137. Translated in: Van Dillen J G, Poitras G, Majithia A (2006) Isaac Le Maire and the early trading in Dutch East India Company shares. Published in: Poitras (2006, 2007)
Weber E J (1988) Currency competition in Switzerland, 1826–1850. Kyklos 41, pp. 459–478
Weber E J (1992) Free banking in Switzerland after the liberal revolutions in the nineteenth century. In: Dowd K (ed) The experience of free banking. Routledge, London, pp. 187–205
Weber, E J (2003) The misuse of central bank gold holdings. In: Tcha M (ed) Gold and the modern world economy. Routledge, London, pp. 64–80. (Some balance sheets in this article are wrong. A corrected version of the article is available on SSRN.)
White E N (2001) Making the French pay: the cost and consequences of the Napoleonic reparations. European Review of Economic History 5, pp. 337–365
Wright J F (1999) British government borrowing in wartime, 1750–1815. Economic History Review LII, pp. 355–361
Zohary D, Hopf M (2000) Domestication of plants in the old world: the origin and spread of cultivated plants in West Asia, Europe, and the Nile Valley, 3rd edn. Oxford University Press, Oxford

16 Retrospective Book Review on James Moser: "Die Lehre von den Zeitgeschäften und deren Combinationen" (1875)

Hartmut Schmidt*

James Moser: Die Lehre von den Zeitgeschäften und deren Combinationen. Berlin: Verlag von Julius Springer, 1875. Pp. VIII, 87.

Most readers who study Bronzin's *Theorie der Prämiengeschäfte* today are impressed by its clarity, precision, rigor, and by its closeness to the vast body of related current literature. It is hard to believe that Bronzin's monograph was written hundred years ago. Given this fact, many readers may arrive at the conviction that this unusual piece of German financial literature is absolutely exceptional, unique and solitary in the period before World War I. The scarcity of academic financial writers during this period suggests not to expect any high quality companion publications which are in line with textbooks in use nowadays.

To test this expectation, try the slender monograph on combining positions in single stock futures and options[1] by James Moser. The author reports that he worked from 1870 to 1873 to design these combinations. His starting points are the then traded six standard contracts on single stocks: future, call, put, straddle, *Noch* of the buyer[2] and *Noch* of the seller (right to buy or to sell an additional quantity). Moser discusses the results of combining only two of these, ending up with 51 equations. Each of the combinations results in a standard contract. Obviously, this is a book on duplication. The first equation combines a future

* Universität Hamburg, Germany. *phs@econ.uni-hamburg.de*

[1] It has been argued that "*Prämiengeschäfte*" or "*primes*" are not really options because the buyer of an option must pay the option price in any event. In contrast, the buyer of a prime pays a forfeit or premium if the prime is not exercised. Indeed, Moser does not use the term "option". But he proves on p. 5 that this contrast disappears at closer view. An amount equal to the forfeit is implied in the price of the underlying. So the buyer of the prime must pay this amount, the option price, in any event. Since the primes were paid for at termination, and not at purchase, the bundling of option price and striking price in case of excercise, for payment on settlement day, was convenient and may be interpreted as an arrangement to reduce transaction costs. For a numerical example and a more detailed discussion the reader is referred to Cootner's editorial comments on Bachelier's "Theory of Speculation" in Cootner (1964), pp. 76–77. The term used for puts and calls or options in the U.S. after the Civil War was "privileges" (Kairys and Valerio 1997, p. 1707).

[2] Call of more.

and a call to duplicate a put. Of course, other equations are less familiar, equation 13, for example, combines a future and a call to duplicate a *Noch* of the buyer. Moser claims to be the first person to use equations to present derivatives (p. VI).

To help the reader grasp what the equations for the synthetic positions imply, Moser employs three other methods to present the stock-price dependent profit or loss of standard contracts and their combinations: numerical examples, arbitrage tables,[3] and graphs. The graphs are the now familiar profit diagrams[4] or profit and loss profiles. Moser claims to be the first author to apply "the graphic method" to derivatives (p. V). His graphs make the book look exactly like a part of a modern finance text.

Frequently, claims to premier authorship turned out to be based on a gap in the knowledge of literature. However, concerning profit and loss diagrams, there is support for Moser. Welcker and Kloy wrote in their 1988 book on *Professionelles Optionsgeschäft* that to their knowledge Moser is the originator of the graphic presentation (p. 29). On the same page they point to four later users: Bronzin (1908), Arnold (1964), Schmidt (1981), and Welcker[5] (1986). Influential early users were certainly Fritz Schmidt (1921), pp. 37–60, and Heinrich Sommerfeld (1922), both authors of well known textbooks. Sommerfeld, like Welcker and Kloy, explicitly recognised Moser as the originator of the graphic method (Baghhorn 1978).[6] Today, quite a number of influential users can be added to the Moser list, for example, Copeland and Weston (1979), pp. 377–382, Brealey and Myers (1981), pp. 425–438, Stoll and Whaley (1993), pp. 256–283, and Zimmermann (2006), pp. 391–409. Bachelier (1900)[7] appears second only to Moser. Kruizenga, influenced by Samuelson[8], suggests that "working through the various combinations [...] can be done much easier by using vectors rather than the graphs" (Kruizenga 1964, p. 387). So Malkiel and Quandt (1969) use vectors, not graphs.[9] Still, Moser's graphs have been spreading[10] more widely than Kruizenga's vector notation.

[3] For more recent and improved arbitrage tables see Cox and Rubinstein (1985), pp. 39–41, 135.

[4] Today, two kinds of option graphs are common, profit diagrams, showing profit and loss, and position diagrams (payoff profiles); see Brealey et al. (2006), pp. 545–546. For the standard contracts at Moser's time, there would have been no difference between profit and payoff diagrams. All payments, including option price, were made on the future settlement day. Payoff reflected profit or loss.

[5] In the 1960ies, Arnold, Welcker and Schmidt were advised by Wolfgang Stützel and influenced by his vivid interest in future settlement transactions.

[6] Sommerfeld (1922), p. 6, quoted by Baghhorn (1978), p. 22.

[7] Translation in Cootner (1964), pp. 42–60.

[8] Malkiel and Quandt (1969), p. 46, state that Kruizenga used the method first and that he credited "Paul Samuelson with originating the idea" of vector notation.

[9] Malkiel and Quandt (1969), p. 46, point out the convenience of the vector notation in ascertaining an investor's interest in combinations.

[10] The widespread use of profit diagrams in academic textbooks started after 1970. This reflects the 1970 relaunch of option trading on German exchanges, the opening of the Chicago Board Options Exchange in 1973 and the use of profit diagrams in related trade literature.

Moser presents and comments his combinations. He strictly sticks to his systematic and rigorous analysis. It is up to the reader to ponder about implications and to draw conclusions. For the reader, it is hard to overlook all the arbitrage opportunities. In addition, the book encourages to go beyond the combinations of two standard contracts and to create, by applying the graphic method, synthetic positions by combining three, four or five contracts. Readers may also have wondered how many standard contracts should be traded if they are readily duplicated. Who needs standard contracts in straddles and *Nochs*?

Moser's 1875 monograph impresses by its precision, clarity and timelessness. Is it the solitary contributed by the generation before Bronzin? This question is difficult to answer. More than hundred years have passed, and for a long time during this period future settlement transactions were generally thought to be an unsound and evil practice. For decades they were prohibited on German exchanges. Not surprisingly, there has been no continuous development of this field, neither in theory nor in business.[11] Much of the related materials were considered useless at some point and disposed. Only a few copies of Moser's book can be located. Any companion writings of other authors may be even rarer and still awaiting rediscovery and recognition.

References

Arnold H (1964) Finanzierungsinstrumente und Finanzierungsinstitue als Institutionen zur Transformation von Unsicherheitsstrukturen. Doctoral dissertation, Saarbrücken

Bachelier L (1900) Theory of speculation. Gauthier-Villars, Paris. English translation in: Cootner (1964), pp. 17–78

Baghhorn K (1978) Methoden der Darstellung von Terminpositionen. Degree dissertation, Universität Hamburg, Hamburg

Brealey R, Myers S (1981) Principles of corporate finance, 1st edn. McGraw-Hill, New York

Brealey R, Myers S, Allen F (2006) Corporate finance, 8th edn. McGraw-Hill Irwin, Boston

Bronzin V (1908) Theorie der Prämiengeschäfte. Franz Deuticke, Leipzig/Vienna

Cootner P (ed) (1964) The random character of stock market prices. MIT Press, Cambridge (Massachusetts)

Copeland T E, Weston J F (1979) Financial theory and corporate policy, 1st edn. Addison-Wesley, Reading

Cox J C, Rubinstein M (1985) Option markets. Prentice-Hall, Englewood Cliffs

Kairys J P, Valerio N (1997) The market for equity options in the 1870s. Journal of Finance 52, pp. 1707–1723

Kruizenga R (1964) Introduction to the option contract. In: Cootner (1964), pp. 377–391

Malkiel B G, Quandt R E (1969) Strategies and rational decisions in the securities options market. MIT Press, Cambridge (Massachusetts)

Moser J (1875) Die Lehre von den Zeitgeschäften und deren Combinationen. Verlag von Julius Springer, Berlin

[11] The discontinuity in the U.S. has been explained by the absence of exchange traded options. Kairys and Valerio (1997), p. 1720. The discontinuity in European countries occurred, in contrast, even though options were traded on exchanges for extended periods before and after World War I.

Schmidt F (1921) Die Effektenbörse und ihre Geschäfte. Gloeckner, Leipzig
Schmidt H (1981) Wertpapierbörsen. In: Bitz M (ed) (1981) Bank- und Börsenwesen, Bd 1, Struktur und Leistungsangebot. Vahlen, Munich
Sommerfeld H (1922) Die Technik des börsenmäßigen Termingeschäfts. Spaeth und Linde, Berlin
Stoll H R, Whaley R E (1993) Futures and options, theory and applications. South-Western, Cincinnati
Welcker J (1986) Technische Aktienanalyse, 3rd edn. Verlag Moderne Industrie, Zurich
Welcker J, Kloy J W (1988) Professionelles Optionsgeschäft. Verlag Moderne Industrie, Zurich
Zimmermann H (ed) (2006) Finance compact, 2nd edn. Verlag Neue Zürcher Zeitung, Zurich

17 The History of Option Pricing and Hedging

Espen Gaarder Haug*

This book is mainly about the mathematics of Professor Vinzenz Bronzin and his remarkable book on option pricing, published in 1908. This chapter concerns the wider history of option pricing and hedging where Bronzin's work shines out as a beautiful diamond. The study of the history of option pricing and hedging is much more than simply a study of the ancient past. It reveals more than this: It tells us where we came from, where we are, and possibly even gives us some hints about where we are going or, at least, what direction we should following. The put-call-parity, hedging options with options and some types of market-neutral delta hedging were understood and used at least a hundred years ago and is, in my view, still the foundation of what knowledgeable option traders use today. A careful study of the history, including several somewhat forgotten and ignored ancient sources, several of which have been recently rediscovered, tells us that many of the option traders as well as academics from history were much more sophisticated than most of us would have thought. Here, I will try to give a short (but still incomplete) and, hopefully, useful summary of the history of option pricing and hedging from my viewpoint today. The history of option pricing and hedging is far too complex and profound to be fully described within a few pages or even a book or two, but, hopefully, this contribution will encourage readers to search out more old books and papers and question the premises of modern text books that are often not revised with regard to the history option pricing.

17.1 Option Markets in the "Good Old Days"

The oldest surviving written records on forward contracts are probably Mesopotamian clay tablets dating all the way back to 1750 B.C. More modern derivative markets seems to appear from the 16th century onwards, running from Antwerp via Amsterdam to London, Chicago, and New York (see Gelderblom and Jonker 2003). Kairys and Valerio (1997) describe quite an active market in equity options in New York in the 1870s. Their description is very interesting and informative, but probably takes a wrong turn when they try to look at how the market priced options at that time. They basically conclude, partly based on their use of Black, Scholes and Merton-style methods, that put options were overpriced at that time – a judgement ensuing from their decision to exclude an important tail-event in this period:

* Independent arbitrage trader and author. *espenhaug@mac.com*

> "However, the put contracts benefited from the financial panic that hit the market in September, 1873. Viewing this as a "one-time" event, we repeat the analysis for puts, excluding any unexpired contracts written before the stock market panic" (Kairys and Valerio 1997).

It seems somewhat surprising that anyone would exclude a tail-event from an empirical analysis supporting a final analysis when the importance of accounting for tail events in option pricing and hedging should be "well understood". How tail-events ought to be approached or modelled naturally extends beyond the confines of our discourse and will only be touched on in this chapter.

When Cyrus Field finally succeeded in connecting Europe and America by cable in 1866, the international arbitrage of securities was made possible. Although American securities had already been purchased in considerable volume abroad after 1800, the absence of quick communication placed a definite limit on the amount of active trading in securities that could take place between the London and the New York markets (see Weinstein 1931). Nelson (1904), an option arbitrageur in New York, describes a relatively active international option and securities arbitrage market, where up to 500 messages per hour and typically 2,000 to 3,000 messages per day were sent between the London and the New York market via cable companies. Each message flashed over the wire system in less than a minute. Nelson describes many details about this arbitrage business: the cost of shipping shares, the cost of insuring shares, interest expenses, the possibilities for switching shares directly between someone long securities in New York and short in London and thereby saving shipping and insurance charges, and so forth. Holz (1905) describes several active option markets in Europe in the late 19th century. Deutsch (1910) depicts the different option exchanges in Europe: the London Stock Exchange, the Continental Bourse, the Berlin Bourse, and the Paris Bourse, and how potential arbitrage options were traded between these exchanges.

In a recent paper Mixon (2008) looks at option pricing in the past and compares it with the present. He concludes that:

> "Traders in the nineteenth century appear to have priced options the same way that twenty-first century traders price options. Empirical regularities relating implied volatility to realized volatility, stock prices, and other implied volatilities (including the volatility skew), are qualitatively the same in both eras" (Mixon 2008).

Several partly forgotten and overlooked works on options, will reveal to us that option traders and academics in the past were much more sophisticated than most of us would have thought. Bronzin (1908), who is the focal point of this book, is a clear example of this. We will also look at how many of the hedging and pricing principles used by traders today seem to have developed in a series of steps, many dating back as early as the 20th century.

17.2 The Put-Call-Parity in a Historical Perspective

One of the few surviving texts describing the financial markets in Amsterdam in the 17th century is *Confusión de Confusiones*[1] by Joseph de la Vega (1688). He describes a relatively active derivatives market in his day. Joseph de la Vega diffusely discusses the put-call-parity, even though his book was not intended to be teaching manual on the technicalities of the options market. The put-call-parity is very important as it is in many respects one of the most robust principles used in option pricing and hedging to have withstood the test of time. That is, option traders both then and today have actively use the put-call-parity in their trading.

From reading modern publications, journals, papers and books on options, we might easily get the impression that the put-call-parity was first understood and described by Professor Stoll (1969) in the Journal of Finance. However, looking into several overlooked and recently rediscovered texts, it becomes clear that Stoll only rediscovered what had probably been described in greater detail at least 60 years before his time. Knoll (2004) describes that the use of the put-call-parity for the purpose of avoiding potential usury can be traced back two thousand years. The surviving text from that period is at best obscure in its references to anything similar to the put-call-parity as we know it today from trading and financial economics.

Nelson's (1904) text on option trading, pricing, and hedging has been neglected and somewhat forgotten. He was an option arbitrageur in New York who published a book with the title "The A B C of Options and Arbitrage". He often cites the book written by Higgins (1902) and must clearly have been influenced by the former's writings[2]. Both Nelson, and Higgins can be considered to have written the first paper[3] to describe the put-call-parity in detail – in many ways, in much greater detail than the newly rediscovered authors such as Stoll (1969).

The put-call-parity of ancient literature seems to have served two main purposes:

1. As a pure arbitrage constraint,

[1] Interestingly, de la Vega's text from 1688 is also referred to by Professor Lesser in 1875 in a small booklet in German describing options.

[2] Another book that he refers to is by Castelli (1877).

[3] At least to my knowledge at the time of writing, but further research on the relations between Nelson and Higgins (1902) has to be done.

2. but also as a tool to create calls out of puts, puts out of calls and straddles out of calls or puts for the purpose of hedging options with options. In other words more than simply providing an arbitrage constraint, they provided a very important tool for transferring risk in an optimal and robust way between options, even in cases where no theoretical arbitrage opportunities between put and call options existed.

In order to understand the use of put and call parity in the early 20th century, one should read the whole of Nelson's book together with other texts from that period. Here, I will only offer a few quotations from Nelson (1904):

> "It may be worthy of remark that 'calls' are more often dealt than 'puts' the reason probably being that the majority of 'punters' in stocks and shares are more inclined to look on the bright side of things, and therefore more often 'see' a rise than a fall in prices.
> This special inclination to buy 'calls' and to leave the 'puts' severely alone dose not, however, tend to make 'calls' dear and 'puts' cheap, for it can be shown that the adroit dealer in options can convert a 'put' into a 'call,' a 'call' into a 'put', a 'call o' more' into a 'put-and-call,' in fact any option into another, by dealing against it in the stock. We may therefore assume, with tolerable accuracy, that the 'call' of a stock at any moment costs the same as the 'put' of that stock, and half as much as the put-and-call" (Nelson 1904).

Nelson also describes a series of ways for using the put-call-parity to convert various options into each other, again referring to Higgins (1902):

1. That a call of a certain amount of stock can be converted into a put-and-call of half as much by selling one-half of the original amount.
2. That a put of a certain amount of stock can be converted into a put-and-call of half as much by buying one-half of the original amount.
3. That a call can be turned into a put by selling all the stock.
4. That a put can be turned into a call by buying all the stock.
5. and 6. That a put-and-call of a certain amount of a stock can be turned into either a put or twice as much by selling the whole amount, or into a call of twice as much by buying the whole amount.

A closer study of Nelson's book clearly indicates the use of the put-call-parity both as an arbitrage constraint as well as a tool for hedging options with options.

In modern options literature on the topic of the continuous dynamic delta hedging of Black and Scholes (1973) and Merton (1973), all risk can be removed all the time subject to a series of theoretical assumptions. In their theoretical world, any option can be perfectly replicated by continuous dynamic delta hedging. Here, the put-call-parity is only applied as an arbitrage constraint.

To illustrate the use of the put-call-parity as something more than a simple arbitrage constrain let us take a look at an example. If you, as a market maker, have numerous customers coming who want to buy put options from you, then in the theoretical Black, Scholes and Merton world you can simply manufacture them risk-free based on the continuous dynamic delta hedging replication argument. In the Black, Scholes and Merton world you would not care whether there was someone you could acquire numerous call options from, except in pure arbitrage situations. In the real world, where dynamic delta replication fails to remove most risk, it would be important to obtain calls, if available, and convert them into puts for the purpose of reducing risk. If they were not obtainable, you would need to raise the price on the options, and/ or widen the bid-offer spread to recover from the risk you are unable to hedge away if only using dynamic delta hedging. The original description and use of the put-call-parity is fully consistent with and even "predicts" the theory that supply and demand for options will effect option prices.

Then again, in 1908, Bronzin derived the put-call-parity and seems to have used it as part of his hedging argument in his mathematical option pricing formulas/ models. In 1910 Henry Deutsch[4] described the put-call-parity, but in less detail than Higgins and Nelson. In his Ph.D. thesis at MIT, Kruizenga (1956) (and also Kruizenga 1964) rediscovered the put-call-parity, but this was in many ways less detailed than that of Nelson (1904).

Another neglected arbitrage trader who published a book is Reinach (1961). He describes how option traders hedged short positions in standard options by getting hold of embedded options on the same stock found in convertible bonds. Reinach also points out the importance of the put-call-parity for the options business, and I cite an interesting quotation from his book:

> "Although I have no figures to substantiate my claim, I estimate that over 60 per cent of all calls are made possible by the existence of Converters".

Converters were basically market makers converting puts into calls and calls into puts, and so on, using the put-call-parity. So as we can see, hedging options with options was a very important part of the options business.

We should also remember that the put-call-parity is basically fully consistent with any volatility smile. This is not the case with the Black, Scholes and Merton model, where the continuous delta hedging basically relies on the assumption of normally distributed returns. Bronzin (1908) seems in many ways

[4] The first version of this book was actually published in 1904, I refer to the second edition, published in 1910.

to offer a more flexible model in this respect as he suggested a whole series of distributions, whilst still taking the put-call-parity into account.

17.3 Delta Hedging in a Historical Perspective

Initial market-neutral delta hedging is when you put on a delta hedge just after buying or selling an option that makes the portfolio (option plus the stock) close to risk-neutral for small movements in the asset price. This is also often described as a static market-neutral delta hedge. When it comes to the option traders of previous eras, I actually prefer the description 'initial market-neutral delta hedge' rather than 'static hedge', because we know they often put on an initial delta hedge subsequent to option issue;, but we know little about whether they actually adjusted this hedge later on or not. Initial market-neutral delta option hedging of this kind was already described by Nelson (1904):

> "Sellers of options in London as a result of long experience, if they sell a call, straightway buy half the stock against which the call is sold; or if a put is sold; they sell half the stock immediately" (Nelson 1904).

In London at that time the market standard was the European-style option issued at-the-money. As rediscovered today, the delta for at-the-money options with a short term to maturity is approximately 50 percent, and, naturally, –50 percent for put options. Out-of-the-money options were not often traded in London and were known as "special options". Of course, an option issued at-the-money will typically not stay at-the-money for long. It is unclear whether options were actively traded after issue in London in those days, or whether it was normal to keep the options until expiration.

The standard options in London were actually issued closer to an at-the-money forward; that is, the strike price was set just after the option was dealt and adjusted for cost-of-carrying the underlying stock:

> "The regular London option is always either a put or a call, or both, at the market price of the stock at the time the bargain is made, to which is immediately added the cost of carrying or borrowing the stock until the maturity of the option" (Nelson 1904).

Today we know that the delta for an option with a strike price equal to the forward price (also known as an at-the-money forward) has a theoretical delta very close to 50 percent (naturally -50 percent for put options). Well, we have basically rediscovered what they already knew in the early 20th century. We also know that the delta for approximately at-the-money or at-the-money-forward options is the most stable delta (see Haug 2003 and Haug 2007). The delta for at-the-money options is very robust even if you do not know the future volatility of the underlying asset. This is not the case for out-of-the money options, where the delta is very sensitive to the volatility value used in the model for calculating the delta. Today we also know that the volatility is stochastic and hard to predict.

Nelson (1904) identified more dynamic delta hedging where the option buyer buys and sells stocks against the option over the option's duration. In 1937 Gann also indicated some forms of auxiliary dynamic hedging. However, it is far from clear that they knew what the theoretical or "practical" market-neutral delta for options should be, other than for at-the-money options. Even today, with the latest in option models, we do not really know the correct delta or optimal practical delta. All we know is some theoretical model delta where the delta is very sensitive to the volatility used for any options that not are close to at-the-money; in practice, we do not know the future volatility. Again, especially for out-of-the money options, the delta is very sensitive to the volatility used as input in the model. This is true even with stochastic volatility models. Here, the delta for out-of-the money options is very sensitive both to the volatility level and the volatility of volatility, and both parameters are highly stochastic in practice. In other words, even stochastic volatility models that mainly rely on delta hedging to remove most risk are not robust in practice. And this is even without taking into account the possibility of jumps in the asset price.

In 1960[5] Sidney Fried described empirical relationships between warrants and the common stock price. The author gives several examples of how to try to construct a roughly market-neutral static delta hedge both by shorting warrants and going long on stocks or by buying warrants and shorting stocks. The hedge ratio that Fried described simply seems to be based on a combination of experience, the historical relationship between warrants and the stock price as well as some basic knowledge of the factors effecting the value of the warrant.

Fried's work is in many ways less sophisticated than that of Higgins (1902) and Nelson (1904), but at the same time contributes some new insights when it comes to the empirical relationships existing between the movements of the underlying stock and the price of the warrant.

In their book "Beat the Market" Thorp and Kassouf describe market-neutral delta hedging for any strike price or time to maturity. In 1969 Thorp suggested extending initial market-neutral delta hedging to dynamic discrete delta hedging:

> "We have assumed so far that a hedge position is held unchanged until expiration, then closed out. This static or 'desert island' strategy is not optimal. In practice intermediate decisions in the spirit of dynamic programming lead to considerably superior dynamic strategies. The methods, technical details, and probabilistic summary are

[5] The first version of this booklet was already published in 1949. My comments are based on the 1960 version.

> more complex so we defer the details for possibly subsequent publication" (Thorp 1969).

Another ignored text on delta hedging is a booklet published in 1970 by Arnold Bernhard & Co. It is somewhat unclear exactly who the author is, but it says "Written and Edited by the Publisher and Editors of The Value Line Convertible Survey". The authors describe market-neutral delta hedging for any strike price. The booklet gives several examples of buying convertible bonds or warrants and shorting stocks against them in a market-neutral delta hedge, which the authors call a balanced hedge. The booklet also reprints examples of tables with delta values (hedge ratios) for a series of warrants and convertible bonds that were distributed to traders on Wall Street. The booklet does not describe continuous-time delta hedging.

None of the people who described initial market-neutral delta hedging or discrete dynamic delta hedging before 1973 claimed they could remove all of the risk all the time. In this way, they were closer to the limitations presented in practice.

So far we can conclude that market-neutral delta hedging was well known and used by traders long before 1973. We know that initial market-neutral delta hedging was already actively used in the early nineteen hundreds in London for at-the-money options. Delta hedging was later extended and discussed by several authors.

It is well known today that delta hedging works extremely poorly when there are jumps in the underlying asset (see Haug 2007, Chapter 2, for a detailed discussion on this topic as well as further references). When the underlying asset jumps, it should be noted that the risk from holding options and simultaneously undertaking market-neutral delta hedging is not symmetrical. Hua and Wilmott (1995) give an excellent example of the asymmetry in the delta hedging replication error for long and short option positions. If you are delta hedging a long option position, the worst case scenario for you is that there is no crash. This is actually because delta hedging is inefficient in the presence of jumps; but, if you are long options, you will benefit from the hedging error when the market crashes.

It is interesting to learn from an experienced option arbitrage trader like Nelson, who possessed a basic understanding of market-neutral delta hedging in the early 19th century, that the most experienced option traders of his time had a tendency to be long options rather than short. Though this in no way guarantees the trader a profit or even positive expected returns, it does protect him from blow-ups when delta hedging fails.

Even after 1973, there were several academics who gave Thorp and Kaussouf and their predecessors the credit for having been the first to promote delta hedging, and not Black and Scholes (1973) and Merton (1973). Even a book written in 1975 by a finance academic appears to credit Thorp and Kassouf

(1967) rather than Black and Scholes (1973), although the latter were listed in its bibliography:

> "Sidney Fried wrote on warrant hedges before 1950, but it was not until 1967 that the book 'Beat the Market' by Edward O. Thorp and Sheen T. Kassouf rigorously, but simply, explained the short warrant/long common hedge to a wide audience" (Auster 1975).

17.4 Option Pricing Formulas Before Black, Scholes and Merton

On March 19, 1900, Bachelier defended his doctoral thesis on option pricing/modelling. It was only in 1954 that Leonard Savage[6] and Paul Samuelson rediscovered Bachelier's thesis in a library (see Poundstone 2005). Bachelier's thesis was translated into English and reprinted in a book by Cootner (1964) that was reprinted again in 2000 (see also Davis and Etheridge 2006). His work is widely known today. He derived an option formula not unlike those we see today, but based on the assumption of the asset price being normally distributed. This gives a positive probability for a negative stock price and is not often used for stocks and other assets with limited liability features. The Bachelier formula is given by:

$$c = (S - X)N(d_1) + \sigma\sqrt{T}n(d_1), \tag{17.1}$$

where

$$d_1 = \frac{S - X}{\sigma\sqrt{T}},$$

S = stock price
X = strike price of option
T = time to expiration in years
σ = volatility of the underlying asset price
$N(x)$ = the cumulative normal distribution function
$n(x)$ = the standard normal density function.

Bachelier says little about the hedging of options, but he describes the purchase of a future contract against a short call and draws a profit and loss (P&L) diagram at maturity, clearly demonstrating that this has the same payoff profile as a put, and can thus be seen as a loose description of the put-call-parity. In

[6] See Poundstone (2005) for more details on the rediscovery of Bachelier's work.

addition to this, Bachelier gives several examples of profit and loss profile for options against options, like bull spreads and call-back spreads (buying one call and selling two calls with a higher strike price against it). So already back then, Bachelier clearly had at least some intuition about how using combinations of futures and options could alter the risk-reward profile. Bachelier also describes in quite some detail Brownian motion mathematically.

Bronzin (1908) was also a master of early mathematical option pricing, as recently rediscovered by Hafner and Zimmermann (2007). Bronzin was a professor of mathematics, and his book on option pricing, originally published in German, will certainly be considered a classical treasure of option literature. Bronzin (1908) derived the put-call-parity and also developed several option-pricing formulas based on several alternative distributions of the asset price; these were rectangular, triangular, parabolic and exponential distributions as well as the normal distribution. I will not go into detail on Bronzin here as the rest of the book gives much more detailed information about his work.

Sprenkle (1961)[7] assumed that asset prices were log-normally distributed and that the stock price followed geometric Brownian motion.

$$dS = \mu S dt + \sigma S dz,$$

where μ is the expected rate of return on the underlying asset, σ is the volatility of the rate of return, and dz is a Wiener process, just as in the Black and Scholes (1973) and Merton (1973) analysis. In this way he ruled out the possibility of negative stock prices, consistent with limited liability. Furthermore, he allowed for positive drift in the underlying asset and derived the following option pricing formula based on this:

$$c = Se^{\mu T} N(d_1) - (1-k) X N(d_2), \tag{17.2}$$

where

$$d_1 = \frac{\ln(S/X) + (\mu + \sigma^2/2)T}{\sigma\sqrt{T}},$$

$$d_2 = d_1 - \sigma\sqrt{T},$$

and k is the adjustment for the degree of market-risk aversion.

James Boness (1964) also assumed a log-normal asset price and derived the following formula for the price of a call option:

[7] This is also reprinted in Cootner (1964).

$$c = SN(d_1) - Xe^{-\mu T}N(d_2) \tag{17.3}$$

$$d_1 = \frac{\ln(S/X) + (\mu + \sigma^2/2)T}{\sigma\sqrt{T}}$$

$$d_2 = d_1 - \sigma\sqrt{T}\,.$$

Paul Samuelson (1965) also assumed the asset price follows geometric Brownian motion with positive drift, μ:

$$c = Se^{(\mu-w)T}N(d_1) - Xe^{-wT}N(d_2) \tag{17.4}$$

$$d_1 = \frac{\ln(S/X) + (\mu + \sigma^2/2)T}{\sigma\sqrt{T}}$$

$$d_2 = d_1 - \sigma\sqrt{T}$$

where w is the average rate of growth in the value of the call. This is different from the Boness model in that the Samuelson model can account for the expected return from the option being larger than that of the underlying asset $w > \mu$.

McKean (1965) derived a formula for a perpetual American put option, but without assuming continuous delta hedging and risk neutrality as was later postulated by Merton (1973).

In 1969, Thorp derived an option formula similar to that of Sprenkle (1961) and Boness (1964). In the same paper he mentioned initial market-neutral delta hedging and suggested that discrete dynamic hedging must be superior. References to this paper are surprisingly absent in contemporary options literature. Could it be that it was published in the wrong journal?

An appraisal of early option-pricing literature shows that people were much more sophisticated than we might have thought. With the recent rediscovery of Bronzin, it is remarkable to discover how much was already known in the early 20th century.

17.5 Black, Scholes and Merton 1973

Modern options literature attributes the great breakthrough in option pricing and hedging to Black and Scholes (1973) and Merton (1973). In several modern textbooks, we are led to understand that option markets were hardly developed before 1973 and that option traders only had a few rules of thumbs for option pricing and hedging prior to this date.

It is quite clear that it was not the option-pricing formula itself that Black, Scholes and Merton came up with, but rather a new way of deriving it. The Boness formula is actually identical to the Black, Scholes and Merton 1973 formula, but the way in which Black, Scholes and Merton derived their formula, based on continuous dynamic delta hedging or alternatively based on CAPM allowed them to liberate themselves from the expected rate of return. In other words, it was not the formula itself that is considered to be their great achievement, but rather the method they devised for deriving it. This was also pointed out by Professor Rubinstein (2006):

> "The real significance of the formula to the financial theory of investment lies not in itself, but rather in how it was derived. Ten years earlier the same formula had been derived by Case M. Sprenkle (1962) and A. James Boness (1964)" (Rubinstein 2006).

In other words, the contribution made by Black, Scholes and Merton was essentially to extend the discrete delta hedging argument to continuous hedging and then to use this as an argument for risk-neutral valuation. In their 1973 paper, Black and Scholes refer to Thorp and Kassouf (1967)[8]:

> "One of the concepts that we use in developing our model is expressed by Thorp and Kassouf (1967). They obtain an empirical valuation formula for warrants by fitting a curve to actual warrant prices. Then they use this formula to calculate the ratio of shares of stock options needed to create a hedge position by going long in one security and short in the other. What they fail to pursue is the fact that in equilibrium, the expected return on such a hedge position must be equal to the return on a riskless asset. What we show below is that this equilibrium condition can be used to derive a theoretical valuation formula" (Black and Scholes 1973).

There is no doubt that extending discrete dynamic delta hedging to continuous dynamic delta hedging and using this to argue for risk-neutral valuation was a brilliant mathematical idea. However, option trading must also be based on what we can actually do in practice. Continuous dynamic delta hedging is based on a series of unrealistic assumptions like normally distributed returns, no jumps in the underlying asset price and constant volatility (or at best time-dependent deterministic volatility). Every model is only a model and that there are inconsistencies in some of its assumptions does not preclude its viability. The central question is whether the model is sensitive to breaks in its assumptions. If

[8] But they give no reference to Thorp (1969).

it is not sensitive, then the model can be considered robust; if not, it is typically non-robust. This question is an important issue that Merton (1998) himself pointed out:

> "A broader, and still open, research issue is the robustness of the pricing formula in the absence of a dynamic portfolio strategy that exactly replicates the payoffs to the option security. Obviously, the conclusion on that issue depends on why perfect replication is not feasible as well as on the magnitude of the imperfection. Continuous trading, is, of course, only an idealized prospect, not literally obtainable; therefore, with discrete trading intervals, replication is at best only approximate. Subsequent simulation work has shown that within the actual trading intervals available and the volatility levels of speculative prices, the error in replication is manageable, provided, however, that the other assumptions about the underlying process obtain [...]. Without a continuous sample path, replication is not possible and that rules out a strict no-arbitrage derivation. Instead, the derivation is completed by using equilibrium asset pricing models such as the Intertemporal CAPM Merton 1973 and the Arbitrage Pricing Theory Ross 1976" (Merton 1998).

Today we know that the Black, Scholes and Merton argument in favour of using dynamic delta hedging as an argument for risk-neutral valuation is not robust in practice. Delta hedging works very poorly when there are jumps in the underlying asset price, and jumps occur from time to time (see Haug and Taleb 2008 and Haug 2007, Chapter 2, for a more detailed discussion and supporting references). On the other hand, hedging options with options is very robust both for jumps and stochastic volatility in discrete time as well as in continuous time. Option traders also use delta hedging to remove some risk, but more in the way described and applied before 1973.

The Black, Scholes and Merton model is inconsistent with the volatility smile that we observe in basically any option market. On the other hand, hedging options with options and relying on the put-call-parity predicts that supply and demand for options will affect actual option prices and, therefore, lead to a volatility smile.

In the strict theoretical Black, Scholes and Merton world the implied volatility is the market's best estimate of the future expected volatility (standard deviation) of the underlying asset only. With a volatility smile, different strikes on the same underlying asset and the same time to maturity will typically yield different implied volatilities. Would a trader change his estimate of future volatility in the underlying asset simply because he changed the strike of the option? Clearly not. Many option traders and academics like to think of the volatility smile simply as a way to adjust or fix the Black, Scholes and Merton model to work better in practice. I used to think of it this way as well. That was before I carefully studied the history of option pricing and hedging. It now looks to me as though most of the robust hedging and pricing principles that knowledgeable option traders rely on were described and discovered in a series of steps before Black, Scholes and Merton. Whereby the last adaptation to further develop discrete dynamic delta hedging and see it culminate in continuous delta hedging seems to be the only method that an option trader is unable to usefully apply in practice, sophistocated though its mathematical basis may be. Nevertheless, I am sure this will provoke an ongoing discussion (see also Derman and Taleb 2005, Haug 2007, Haug and Taleb 2008, Hyungsok and Wilmott 2008).

We should also ask ourselves how so much knowledge from the past could be overlooked and partly forgotten? Modern option literature clearly makes no reference to many of the early discoveries in options pricing and hedging. Several reasons, I think, may be offered in answer to this question. Herbert Filer, in his book, first published in 1959, describes what must be considered reasonably active options markets in New York and Europe in the 1920s and early 1930s. Filer also mentions that during World War II no trading took place on the European Exchanges because they were closed. London options trading did not return until 1958. This may, in fact, be one of the reasons why much of the early options literature was partly forgotten and overlooked. In addition, it may also be that many academics tend to only look for references in a specific selection of academic journals which they collectively consider as being relevant and reliable: This, though, is a moot point.

17.6 Conclusion

We can conclude that option traders and academics in the past were much more sophisticated than most of us would have thought. Option pricing and hedging seems to have developed in a series of steps rather than with one or two big discoveries in the 1970s. We know from historical sources that market-neutral delta hedging, the put-call-parity, hedging options with options, and several mathematical option pricing formulas were known by the early 1900s, and were discussed and extended later. More than one hundred years ago, Bachelier (1900) and Bronzin (1908) published option pricing formulas which were very similar to those we use today. Almost every hedging and pricing technique used for options today was already known and used prior to 1973.

The history of option pricing is far more interesting than I would have initially supposed. Visiting libraries and antiquarian bookstores is an exiting hobby; there are possibly a few more historical diamonds to be found there. Personally, I prefer to divide research work on the history of options and derivatives into two parts:

1. What I would like to call derivatives archaeology: This is the more physical and very practical part of actually digging out forgotten and overlooked texts from libraries, antiquarian bookstores – even looking for clay tablets at potential archaeological sites. This is extremely fascinating and a great break from just sitting at your desk, reading and writing.
2. The second and equally important part consists in interpreting the historical records. This can be a long journey, as well, hunting for evidence in texts written in foreign or even ancient languages, which are hard to translate and where pages are possibly missing. After translating the texts, we then have to try to interpret them in the context of their time.

The recovery of Bronzin papers is a tour-de-force of financial archaeology. His work has now been translated and made accessible to a large number of interested people through the publication of this book. I will encourage more people to take up an interest in the history of option pricing and hedging, with financial archaeological investigations and the interpretation of the sources that are currently available.

References

Auster R (1975) Option writing and hedging strategies. Exposition Press, New York

Bachelier L (1900) Théorie de la speculation. Annales Scientifiques de l' Ecole Normale Supérieure, Ser. 3, 17, Paris, pp. 21-88. English translation in: Cootner P (ed) (1964) The random character of stock market prices. MIT Press, Cambridge (Massachusetts), pp. 17–79

Bernhard A (1970) More profit and less risk: convertible securities and warrants. Written and edited by the publisher and editors of 'The Value Line Convertible Survey'. Arnold Bernhard & Co., New York

Black F, Scholes M (1973) The pricing of options and corporate liabilities. Journal of Political Economy 81, pp. 637–654

Boness A (1964) Elements of a theory of stock-option value. Journal of Political Economy 72, pp. 163–175

Bronzin V (1908) Theorie der Prämiengeschäfte. Franz Deuticke, Leipzig/Vienna

Castelli C (1877) The theory of options in stocks and shares. F.C. Mathieson, London

Cootner P (ed) (1964) The random character of stock market prices. MIT Press, Cambridge (Massachusetts)

Davis M, Etheridge A (2006) Louis Bachelier's theory of speculation: the origins of modern finance. Princeton University Press, Princeton

de la Vega J (1688) Confusión de confusiones. Reprinted in: Fridson M S (ed) (1996) Extraordinary popular delusions and the madness of crowds & Confusión de confusiones. J. Wiley & Sons, New York

Derman E, Taleb N (2005) The illusion of dynamic delta replication. Quantitative Finance 5, pp. 323–326

Deutsch H (1910) Arbitrage in bullion, coins, bills, stocks, shares and options, 2nd edn. Effingham Wilson, London

Filer H (1959) Understanding put and call options. Popular Library, New York

Fried S (1960) The speculative merits of common stock warrants. RHM Associates, New York

Gann W D (1937) How to make profits in puts and calls. Lambert Gann Publishing Co., Washington
Gelderblom O, Jonker J (2003) Amsterdam as the cradle of modern futures and options trading, 1550–1650. Working Paper, Utrecht University, Utrecht
Hafner W, Zimmermann H (2007) Amazing discovery: Vincenz Bronzin's option pricing models. Journal of Banking and Finance 31, pp. 531–546
Haug E G (2003) Know your weapon, Part 1 and 2. Wimott Magazine, May and August
Haug E G (2007) Derivatives: models on models. J. Wiley & Sons, New York
Haug E G, Taleb N N (2008) Why we never used the Black-Scholes and Merton formula. Wilmott Magazine, January
Higgins L R (1902) The put-and-call. E. Wilson, London
Holz L (1905) Die Prämiengeschäfte. Doctoral dissertation, Universität Rostock. Rostock
Hua P, Wilmott P (1995) Modelling market crashes: the worst-case scenario. Working Paper, Oxford Financial Research Centre
Hyungsok A, Wilmott P (2008) Dynamic hedging is dead! Long live static hedging. Wilmott Magazine, January
Kairys J P, Valerio N (1997) The market for equity options in the 1870s. Journal of Finance 52, pp. 1707–1723
Knoll M (2004) Ancient roots of modern financial innovation: the early history of regulatory arbitrage. Working Paper 49, University of Pennsylvania Law School, Philadelphia
Kruizenga R J (1956) Put and call options: a theoretical and market analysis. Unpublished doctoral dissertation, Massachusetts Institute of Technology. Cambridge (Massachusetts)
Kruizenga R J (1964) Introduction to the option contract. In: Cootner P (ed) (1964) The random character of stock market prices. MIT Press, Cambridge (Massachusetts), pp.377–391
Lesser E (1875) Zur Geschichte der Prämiengeschäfte. Universität Heidelberg
McKean H P (1965) A free boundary problem for the heat equation arising from a problem in mathematical economics. Industrial Management Review 6, pp. 32–39
Merton R C (1973) Theory of rational option pricing. Bell Journal of Economics and Management Science 4, pp. 141–183
Merton R C (1998) Application of option-pricing theory: twenty-five years later. American Economic Review 3, pp. 323–349
Mixon S (2008) Option markets and implied volatility: past versus present. Journal of Financial Economics, Forthcoming
Nelson S A (1904) The A B C of options and arbitrage. The Wall Street Library, New York
Poundstone W (2005) Fortune's formula. Hill and Wang, New York
Reinach A M (1961) The nature of puts & calls. The Book-Mailer, New York
Rubinstein M (2006) A history of the theory of investments. J. Wiley & Sons, New York
Samuelson P (1965) Rational theory of warrant pricing. Industrial Management Review 6, pp. 13–31
Sprenkle C (1961) Warrant prices as indicators of expectations and preferences. Yale Economics Essays 1, pp. 178–231
Stoll H (1969) The relationship between put and call prices. Journal of Finance 24, pp. 801–824
Thorp E O (1969) Optimal gambling systems for favorable games. Review of the International Statistics Institute 37, pp. 273–293
Thorp E O, Kassouf S T (1967) Beat the market. Random House, New York
Weinstein M H (1931) Arbitrage to securities. Harper Brothers, New York

18 The Early History of Option Contracts

Geoffrey Poitras*

This chapter discusses the history of option contracts from ancient times until the appearance of *Theorie der Prämiengeschäfte* by Vinzenz Bronzin in 1908. The history examines the use of contracts with option features prior to the introduction of trade in free standing option contracts on the Antwerp bourse during the 16th century. Descriptions of the Amsterdam share option market by de la Vega in the 17th century and de Pinto in the 18th century are reviewed. The specific language of a late 17th century English option contract is provided in detail. The development and practice of option trading in the 18th and 19th centuries, as reflected in merchant manuals of that period, is examined. The article concludes with an overview of late 19th century option trading in securities and commodities.

18.1 What Are Option Contracts?

By standard definition, an option contract grants the right, but not the obligation, to buy or sell a real asset, commodity or security at a later date, under stated conditions. This contingent claim can be 'free standing', as with put and call options traded on the Chicago Board Option Exchange, or bundled with other features, as in a convertible bond indenture.[1] In ancient times, goods transactions contracts with embedded option features were important to commerce. The development of exchange trading for free standing option contracts took place from the 16th to 18th centuries. It is likely that trading in both forward and option contracts was a common event on the Antwerp bourse during the 16th century. By the mid-17th century, the active trade in such contracts on the Amsterdam bourse featured a sophisticated clearing process. In England, trading in both options and forward contracts was an essential activity in London's

* Simon Fraser University, Canada. *poitras@sfu.ca.* Thanks to Franck Jovanovic for helpful information on 19th century French option trading.

[1] The rudimentary, single event insurance contracts used up to the 17th century also qualify as options within this definition. The connection between put option and insurance contracts is not examined here. The 'free standing' terminology is consistent with Statement of Financial Accounting Standard #133 issued by the Financial Accounting Standards Board in the US. Alternative terminology is also used, e.g., Poitras (2000) refers to 'pure derivative securities'. For decades, the accounting profession has grappled with the difficulties of distinguishing between possibly equivalent cash flows from portfolios including combinations of 'free standing derivatives' and the underlying real asset, security or commodity.

Exchange Alley by the late 17th century.[2] Despite this, prior to the mid-19th century, options trading was a relatively esoteric activity confined to a specialized group of traders.

The use of contracts with option features is not a modern development. The basis for such features arises from the fundamental process of exchange in markets. This process involves two steps. First, buyers and sellers agree on a market clearing price for the goods involved in the transaction. Second, the exchange is completed, typically with a cash payment being made in exchange for adequate physical delivery of the goods involved. In many transactions, time can separate the pricing agreement, the cash settlement or the delivery of goods. For example, a forward credit sale involves immediate pricing, delivery at maturity of the forward contract and settlement at an even later date. Commercial agreements in early markets often included option-like features that were bundled into a loosely structured agreement that was governed largely by merchant convention. For example, because trading on samples was common in medieval goods markets, an agreement for a future sale would typically have a provision that would permit the purchaser to refuse delivery if the delivered goods were found to be of inadequate quality when compared to the original sample. As reflected in notarial protests stretching back to antiquity, disagreement over what constituted satisfactory delivery was a common occurrence.[3]

The contract for the German *Prämiengeschäfte* differs from the options traded in modern markets which have inherited characteristics associated with historical features of US option trading. Following Emery (1896), p. 53, the *Prämiengeschäfte* "may be considered as an ordinary contract for future delivery with special stipulation that, in consideration of a cash payment, one of the parties has the right to withdraw from the contract within a specified time".[4] As such, this option is a feature of a forward contract with a fee to be paid at delivery if the option is exercised. Circa 1908 on the Paris and Berlin bourses, the premium payment at maturity was fixed by convention and the 'price' would

[2] There are numerous instances of explicit and implicit call or conversion provisions in 14th to 18th century security issues. For example, the Venetian *prestiti* had a call provision that allowed for principal value to be repaid at par, as finances permitted. Various 18th century government debt restructuring plans involved the introduction of conversion provisions. For example, there was the conversion of English government life annuities, issued under William III and Queen Anne, into long annuities, or John Law's Mississippi scheme which introduced conversion provisions for exchanging French government debt obligations into Compagnie des Indes stock. Options features have even been attached to bank notes, as in the option clause included on the notes issues by Scottish banks from 1730–1765 which reserved the right to suspend specie payment for a period up to six months, with interest to be paid in the interval (Gherity 1995).

[3] Some of the earliest examples of written language, the Sumerian cuneiform tablets, contain such notarial protests. See, for example, http://www.sfu.ca/~poitras/Brit_Mus.ZIP which provides a picture of a Sumerian tablet circa 1750 BC from the British Museum collection: "A letter complaining about the delivery of the wrong grade of copper after a Gulf voyage".

[4] Emery (1896), p. 51–53, provides a number of references to late 19th century German and French sources on options trading that would have been accessible to V. Bronzin. The connection between German and English terminology is also discussed (p. 91).

be determined by the setting the exercise price relative to the initial stock or commodity price. In Castelli (1877), p. 7, the premium to be paid at maturity "fluctuates according to the variations of the Stock to be contracted". In contrast, the modern call option is a tradeable 'privilege' of 'refusal' with fixed terms where an agreed upon fee would be paid in advance.[5] In the modern approach, both puts and refusals are buyer's options. The seller writes the options. If the option is a feature of a forward contract, a call option arises because the buyer for future delivery can refuse to take delivery, a put option arises because a seller for future delivery can withdraw.[6]

18.2 Ancient Roots of Option Contracts

Evidence that the use of option contracts was acceptable in ancient times appears during the Greek civilization. Aristotle in his *Politics* provides a reference to the use of options involving a successful speculation by the philosopher Thales. Aristotle's specific reference to Thales in *Politics*:

> "There is, for example, the story which is told of Thales of Miletus. It is a story about a scheme for making money, which is fathered on Thales owing to his reputation for wisdom; but it involves a principle of general application. He was reproached for his poverty which was supposed to show the usefulness of philosophy; but observing from his knowledge of meteorology (so the story goes) that there was likely to be a heavy crop of olives [next summer], and having a small sum at his command, he paid down earnest-money, early in the year, for the hire of all the olive-presses in Miletus and Chios; and he managed, in the absence of any higher offer, to secure them at a low rate. When the season came, and there was a sudden and simultaneous demand for a number of presses, he let out the stock he had collected at any rate he chose to fix; and making a considerable fortune he succeeded in proving that it is easy for philosophers to become rich if they so desire, though it is not the business which they are

[5] Various alternative terms such as 'privileges' or 'premiums' are used to describe option contracts. While trade publications such as Castelli (1877) and Deutsch (1904) refer to "options", this usage is in conflict with the use of 'option' in the various late 19th century US 'anti-option' legislation proposals that refer to contracts where delivery is not obligatory; this would include both futures and options contracts. As a consequence, sources such as Emery (1896) refer to privileges and futures. Similarly, 'premiums' also identify the element that distinguishes futures from options.

[6] Following Deutsch (1904), p. 170, "Options to deliver stocks and shares ["puts"] are not quoted in Paris". Deutsch goes on to observe that this is "not of much importance" because a call combined with a sale of the stock produces a put. As such, the 'privilege' to 'put' a commodity back to the seller on the delivery date, at the initial purchase price, could also be obtained by the payment of a 'premium' on the settlement date.

really about" (Aristotle 1984, Book I, Chapter 11, Section 5–10).[7]

Unfortunately, this often referenced Aristotelan anecdote is somewhat lacking. For example, it is not clear how Thales, who seems to have been a pure speculator rather than an olive grower, was able to accurately forecast the bumper olive crop in Miletus six months in advance. The precise nature of the contract is also not clear. Presumably, the payment of "earnest-money" was to take options on the use of all available olive presses in the surrounding area for the harvest season, rather than as a down payment associated with a forward contract. What if the bumper crop had not materialized? Would Thales still be required to take up the presses even though he was not able to lease the presses at a substantial premium? Aristotle rationalizes the limited examination of the details of the transaction: "the various forms of acquisition [...] minutely and in detail might be useful for practical purposes; but to dwell long upon them would be in poor taste" (Aristotle 1984, Book I, Chapter 11, Section 5).

Another often quoted ancient reference to a transaction with an option feature can be found in Genesis 29 of the Bible where Laban offers Jacob an option to marry his youngest daughter Rachel in exchange for seven years labour. The story illustrates an important difficulty associated with options trading in early markets: the possibility of delivery failure. After completing the requisite seven years labour required to complete payment of the option premium, Jacob was to discover that Laban would renege on the agreement and only offer Jacob his elder daughter Leah for marriage. Fortunately for Jacob, the then socially acceptable practice of polygamy permitted the eventual completion of the transaction and Jacob's subsequent marriage to Rachel. There is some debate over the validity of this example as an options contract. In particular, it was Hebrew custom for a suitor to make payment when desiring marriage and this payment could be made in labour, instead of goods (Malkiel and Quandt 1969, p. 7–8). This would make the transaction a forward, rather than an option, contract.

While Aristotlean and Biblical anecdotes provide interesting evidence of options contracting in ancient times, tracing the evolution of options through time is complicated by the similarity of options contracts to other types of agreements such as gambles, and the embedding of option features in contracts

[7] Aristotle goes on to say: "The story is told as showing that Thales proved his own wisdom; but [...] the plan he adopted – which was, in effect, the creation of a monopoly – involves a principle which can be generally applied in the art of acquisition" (Aristotle 1984, Book I, Chapter 11, Section 5). A further connection is made to a Sicilian who cornered the cash market for iron by buying up all available supplies. Aristotle questioned the use of derivative securities transactions to manipulate the cash market without recognizing that Thales may have benefited in the absence of any monopoly. This reflects the relative lack of understanding that ancient writers had concerning speculative transactions.

for the future purchase or sale of a commodity or security.[8] Some method of contracting for forward delivery has been an essential feature of commerce since antiquity (e.g., Poitras 2000, Chapter 9, Bell et al. 2007). With the expansion of trade and the rise in the importance of urban centres, forward contracting became essential to urban merchants contracting with agricultural producers for crops prior to harvest or with fisherman for catches prior to arrival in port.[9] Such contracts would have a range of implicit and, possibly, explicit buyer and seller option provisions that related to delivery dates, acceptable quality at delivery, and so on. As noted, the two most important buyer options concerned 'refusal' to take delivery and the privileges of 'putting' the deliverable back to the seller at a predetermined price. A key point in the development of option contracts is where market liquidity was sufficient to permit the securitization of contingent claims associated with the privleges of 'put' and 'refusal'. As early as Ehrenberg (1928), it has been recognized that this required the emergence of sufficient speculative trading to sustain market liquidity.

18.3 The Antwerp Exchange

The evolution of trading in free standing option contracts revolved around two important elements: enhanced securitization of the transactions; and the emergence of speculative trading. Both these developments are closely connected with the concentration of commercial activity, initially at the large medieval market fairs and, later, on the bourses. Though it is difficult to attach specific dates to the process, considerable progress was made by the Champagne fairs with the formalization of the *lettre de foire* and the bill of exchange, e.g., Munro (2000). The sophisticated settlement process used to settle accounts at the Champagne fairs was a precursor of the clearing methods later adopted for exchange trading of securities and commodities. Over time, the medieval market fairs came to be surpassed by trade in urban centres such as Bruges (De Roover 1948, Van Houtte 1966) and, later, in Antwerp and Lyons. Of these two centres, Antwerp was initially most important for trade in commodities while Lyons for trade in bills. Fully developed bourse trading in commodities emerged in Antwerp during the second half of the 16th century (Tawney 1925, p. 62-65, Gelderblom and Jonker 2005). The development of the Antwerp commodity

[8] Further to the discussion in note 2, the government debt issues in the 18th century provide, arguably, the most productive period for inclusion of the widest variety of option provisions in debt issues, e.g., Marco and Malle-Sabouret (2007), Shea (2007b), Cohen (1953).

[9] The medieval era was not without restrictions on forward contracting. Emery (1896), p. 34, reports that sales of grain prior to threshing or of herring before being caught were forbidden in the German *Hanse* cities in 1417. Similar ordinances were also reported in England in 1357. Such known instances are consistent with the ethics of medieval scholasticism that condemn unearned profits including, but not limited to, interest on money loans (usury), e.g., Poitras (2000), Chapter 3. Gelderblom and Jonker (2005) provides details of 16th Dutch restrictions on forward contracting.

market provided sufficient liquidity to support the development of trading in 'to arrive' contracts. Due to the rapid expansion of seaborne trade during the period, speculative transactions in 'to arrive' grain that was still at sea were particularly active. Trade in whale oil, herring and salt was also important (Gelderblom and Jonker 2005, Barbour 1950, Emery 1895). Over time, these contracts came to be actively traded by speculators either directly or indirectly involved in trading that commodity but not in need of either taking or making delivery of the specific shipment.

Van der Wee (1977) examines the emergence of forward and option contract trading on the new Antwerp Exchange that opened in 1531. This exchange was initially intended for both commercial and financial transactions, but commercial contracts were increasingly transacted on the "English Exchange", which opened one hour before the monetary exchange. The gradual separation of goods and commodity transactions from finance provided a trading environment that facilitated the development of both commercial and financial contracting. The Antwerp Exchange was the model that Thomas Gresham used to establish a similar Exchange in London in 1571 (De Roover 1949). The concentration of liquidity on the Antwerp Exchange furthered speculative trading centered around the important merchants and large merchant houses that controlled either financial activities or the goods trade. The milieu for such trading was closely tied to medieval traditions of gambling:

> "Wagers, often connected with the conclusion of commercial and financial transactions, were entered into on the safe return of ships, on the possibility of Philip II visiting the Netherlands, on the sex of children as yet unborn etc. Lotteries, both private and public, were also extremely popular, and were submitted as early as 1524 to imperial approval to prevent abuse" (Van der Wee 1977).

With the Antwerp Exchange providing a systematic and organized environment for speculation, trading in 'to arrive' contracts evolved into trade in 'futures' contracts where the forward contracts involved standardized transactions in fictitious goods for a future delivery and payment that was settled by the payment of 'differences'.[10] Purchasers of such contracts would speculate on the rise in prices before the due date. If such a rise occurred, the goods would then be sold and the speculator pocketed the difference in price. This 'difference dealing' was also conducted by goods vendors, selling for future delivery betting that prices would fall. In commodities where prices were volatile, especially

[10] The identification of this early trade as 'futures' contracting is found in Gelderblom and Jonker (2005). This approach is at variance with the conventional view that futures trading began in Chicago in the 19th century or the less conventional view that such trading began in the 18th century Japanese rice market (Schaede 1989). In what follows, the distinction between futures contracts and forward contracts will not be explored. Futures and forwards will both be referred to as 'time bargains'.

grain, whale oil, salt and herring, such speculation became common.[11] The development of an active market in time bargains facilitated the emergence of "premium transactions" where: "The buyer made a contract for future delivery at a fixed price, but with the condition that he could reconsider after two or three months: he could then withdraw from the contract provided that he paid a premium to the vendor (*stellegelt*)" (van der Wee 1977). While financial speculators on the Antwerp exchange also used option contracts to gamble on the rise or fall of exchange rates at the Castilian or Lyons fairs, speculation in the bill of exchange market did not typically involve option contracting, e.g., De Roover (1944), Munro (2000) and Poitras (2009).[12]

18.4 Option Trading in 17th Century Amsterdam

The collapse of Antwerp in 1585 and the resulting diaspora of important merchants contributed substantially to the rise of the important financial and commodity exchanges in Amsterdam and in London, where the Royal Exchange was established in 1571. While Amsterdam had developed as an important commercial center prior to 1585 (van Dillen 1927, Gelderblom and Jonker 2005), the establishment of a permanent building for the Amsterdam bourse in 1611 marks a symbolic beginning of Dutch commercial supremacy. During the 17th and 18th centuries, trading of forward and option contracts on the Amsterdam exchange exhibited many essential features of exchange trading in modern derivative markets. By the middle of the 17th century trading on the Amsterdam bourse of options on the Dutch East Indies Company (VOC) and, to a lesser extent, the Dutch West Indies Company, had progressed to where puts and calls with regular expiration dates were traded (Wilson 1941, Gelderblom and Jonker 2005).[13] By the 18th century, the trade involved both Dutch joint stock shares and "British funds". This trading on the Amsterdam bourse is the first historical instance of exchange trading in financial derivative securities.

[11] Unger (1980) provides detailed information on the herring industry during this period. The Dutch herring trade to the Baltic was intimately connected to the grain trade to southern Europe. Due to a number of technological developments introduced over the fourteenth to sixteenth centuries, the Dutch herring fleets dominated this trade until the second half of the 17th century. The evolution of the herring fishery depended on increased capital requirements; as a consequence the role of brokers also evolved: "By the mid-fifteenth century the brokers were becoming owners and operators of ships as well. They were merchants with an interest in more assured supplies of preserved fish [...] even individuals with no direct connection with fishing can and did invest in the boats and their supplies" (Unger 1980, p. 258).

[12] Financial transactions revolved around the bill of exchange which involved an initial exchange followed by a re-exchange at a later date in a different location. While various maneuvers were used to reduce or eliminate the uncertain rate on the re-exchange, e.g., De Roover (1944), the sequence of transactions in a bill of exchange transaction is not well suited to the securitization of the associated options.

[13] The acronym VOC is a reference to the English to Dutch translation of the Dutch East India Company, as the Verenigde Oostindische Compagnie.

"With the appearance of marketable British securities, and the application to them of a speculative technique that was already well understood, the Amsterdam bourse became the scene of international finance at its most abstract and most exciting – gambling in foreign securities" (Wilson 1941, p. 79).

While information about option trading in Antwerp is scattered and sparse, detailed accounts of option trading in Amsterdam are available in Josef de la Vega (1688) and Isaac De Pinto (1771b). Both sources discuss options on joint stocks; option trading in commodities is not directly examined suggesting such trade was not a common source of speculative trading. *Confusion de Confusiones* (de la Vega 1688, Fridson 1996) is a remarkable book (Cardoso 2006). Though the central concerns are much broader, de la Vega does make a number of detailed references to options trading on the Amsterdam exchange. There is a general description of the potential gains to options trading: "Give 'opsies' or premiums, and there will be only limited risk to you, while the gain may surpass all your imaginings and hopes". This statement is followed by a somewhat exaggerated claim about the potential gains: "Even if you do not gain through 'opsies' the first time [...] continue to give the premiums for a later date, and it will rarely happen that you lose all your money before a propitious incident occurs that maintains the price for several years" (Fridson 1996, p. 155). Presumably, de la Vega has call options trading in mind, the possibility of trading put options appears later (p. 156).

De la Vega proceeds to describe a crude call option trading strategy: "As the contracts are signed because of the premiums and as the payer of the premiums gains in reputation for his generosity as well as his foresight, keep postponing the terminal dates of your contracts, and keep entering into new ones, so that one contract in time becomes ten, and the business reaches a fine and simple conclusion" (de la Vega 1688, p. 155). The trading strategy described is uninteresting, as it depends on the naive assumption of a relatively constant upward movement in stock prices. However, the references to extension of the option expiration dates, with regular marking-to-market, is interesting. De la Vega takes up the uncertain legal interpretation of option contracts at a later point (p. 183) and explicitly recognizes that the Dutch restriction on short sales could impact put and call options differently.[14] The reference to extending

[14] De la Vega's well reasoned discussion (p. 183) of the legal implications of option contracts stands in stark contrast to his naive views on profitable option trading strategies: "As to whether the regulation [banning short sales] is applicable to option contracts, the opinions of experts diverge widely. I have not found any decision that might serve as a precedent, though there are many cases at law from which one [should be able to] draw a correct picture. All legal experts hold that the regulation is applicable to both the seller and buyer [of the contract]. In practice, however, the judges have often decided differently, always freeing the buyer from the liability while holding the seller [to the contract] [...] If [...] the opinion is correct that it applies only to the seller, the regulation will be of no use to me [as a person wanting to seek shelter] when I receive call premiums, for in this case I am in fact a seller; but it will help me if I have received a put premium, as I am then the buyer of stocks. With regard to the put premium [...] law and legal opinion, the regulation and the reasons for the decisions are contradictory. The theory remains uncertain, and one cannot tell which way the adjudication tends" (de la Vega 1688).

contracts is further elaborated in de la Vega's discussion of the *rescontre* system (p. 181), a major technical innovation in securities trading that emerged between 1650-1688, when the Dutch introduced quarterly settlements of share transactions on the Amsterdam bourse.[15] Prior to this time settlement procedures had been less formal. A key feature of the *rescontre* was the concentration of liquidity that, for example, permitted prolongations to be done more readily (Dickson 1967, p. 491, Van Dillen 1927).

De la Vega goes on to describe an even more naive trading strategy: "If you are [consistently] unfortunate in all your operations and people begin to think that you are shaky, try to compensate for this defect by [outright] gambling in the premium business, [i.e., by borrowing the amount of the premiums]. Since this procedure has become general practice, you will be able to find someone who will give you credit [and support you in difficult situations, so you may win without dishonor]" (de la Vega 1688, p. 155). The possibility that the losses may continue is left unrecognized. However, recognition of a "general" practice of borrowing funds to make option premium payments reflects the speculative mentality that motivated some option purchases. The extension of funds to settle positions appears to be tied into the *rescontre* settlement process. The bulk of option market participants appear to have been speculators, attracted primarily by the urge to gamble, usually "men of moderate wealth indulging in a little speculation" (Wilson 1941, p. 105). In contrast, drawing from De Pinto (1762), Wilson observes that for trading conducted on the Amsterdam bourse during the 18th century had evolved to where: "Options were the province of the out-and-out gamblers" (Wilson 1941, p. 84).[16]

---

[15] The term '*rescontre*' was derived from the practice of Dutch merchants to "indicate that a bill had been paid by charging it to a current account – '*solvit per rescontre*' as distinct from '*per banco*', '*per wissel*' and so on" (Dickson 1967, p. 491, Mortimer 1762, p. 28n). Wilson (1941, p. 83 provides the following description of the rescontre settlement process: "The technique of speculation in the British Funds at Amsterdam ... was a kind of gamble carried on every three months: no payments were made except on *rescontre* (settlement or carry-over), i.e., the period for which funds were bought or sold and for which options were given or taken. *Rescontredag* (contango day) occurred four times a year, and on these occasions representatives of the speculators gathered round a table to regulate or liquidate their transactions, and to make reciprocal payments for fluctuations or surpluses. Normally these fluctuations were settled without the actual value of the funds in question being paid – only real investors paid cash for their purchases. Speculative buyers paid to sellers the percentage by which the funds had fallen since the last contango day, or alternatively received from them the percentage by which funds had risen in the same interval. After surpluses had been paid, new continuations were undertaken for the following settlement. In such a prolongatie (continuation) the buyer granted the seller a certain percentage (a contango rate) to prolong his purchase to the next *rescontre*: in this way he stood the chance of benefiting by a rise in quotations in the interval, without tying up his capital: he was only bound to pay any possible marginal fall".

[16] Wilson (1941), p. 84–85, describes the options trade: "A *prime à délivrer* [a call] was the option which A gave to B, obliging him to deliver on the following *rescontre* certain English securities – say £1000 East India shares – at an agreed price. If the speculation of the giver of the option was unsuccessful, he merely lost his option: if, on the other hand, the funds rose, he had the benefit of the rise. The *prime à recevoir* [a put] was the option given by A to B by which B

18.5 Tulipmania: Option Trading in Commodity Markets?

In contrast to the availability of primary sources concerning the trade in options contracts for financial securities on the Amsterdam bourse – joint stock, government debt issues and the like – there is a scarcity of sources on such trade in commodities. There are a number of possible reasons for the lack of sources, e.g., Gelderblom and Jonker (2005), p. 200. The lack of significant price variability, the practice of using forward contracts with terms either in years or a few days, and the inability of speculators not connected to the trade to handle physical delivery acted to restrict speculative participation in the commodities market. The trade in securities did not have these features.[17] While the tulipmania of 1634–1637 has attracted considerable modern attention and debate associated with whether the event qualifies as a 'speculative bubble', the primary sources associated with the tulipmania also provide insight into the use of forward and option contracts in the 17th century Dutch commodities trade. In the process of considering these sources, some modern misperceptions regarding the role that option contracts played in the tulipmania can be clarified.

The tulipmania was precipitated by the entrance, around the end of 1634, of purely speculative buyers into the tulip market which, prior to this time, had been conducted among merchants directly involved in the tulip trade. Following Posthumus:

> "People who had no connection with bulb growing began to buy [...] Among these were weavers, spinners, cobblers, bakers, and other small tradespeople, who had no knowledge whatsoever of the subject. About the end of 1634 [...] the trade in tulips began to be general, and in the following months the non-professional element increased rapidly" (Posthumus 1929, pp. 438–439).

The speculators were attracted by the specific characteristics of the tulip market: the significant separation in time of the purchase agreement from the delivery and payment provided a commodity where speculative buyers of bulbs, not intending to take delivery, could trade with sellers that did not possess the bulb on the purchase agreement date. Payment and delivery considerations did not enter until it was certain that the actual tulip bulb was available for possession.

> "At the height of business most transactions took place without any basis in goods. Each succeeding buyer tried to sell his ware for

was pledged to take from A on *rescontre* £1000 East India shares, say, at an agreed price. B became, in fact, a kind of insurance for A, obliged to make good to him the margin by which the funds might diminish in the interval".

[17] Emery (1896), p. 80–81, explores the reasons that speculative privilege trading is concentrated in stocks. Among the reasons, Emery stresses the importance of greater price variability in stocks relative to produce. Also, options on produce tend to have shorter terms to maturity.

> higher prices; and, in the general excitement, one could make a profit – at least on paper – of several thousand florins in a few days. The craze spread rapidly with these high profits. All classes of population ended by taking part in it – intellectuals, the middle classes, and the labourers" (Posthumus 1929, p. 440).

Due to the vagaries of tulip growing (e.g., Garber 1989), option contracts are well suited to trading of tulips for forward delivery. However, based on the fairly detailed record of the types of contracts used (Posthumus 1929, Poitras 2000, Chapter 10), merchant practice in the tulip trade of the time was to use forward contracts tailored to the needs of trade rather than option contracts. A number of different contracting methods were used, from the "promises and vouchers" of the most speculative and uninformed traders, to the formal notarized written contracts of tulip dealers. Some are quite basic, such as: "Sold to N.N. a quarter of Witte Kroonen for the sum of 525 gld. when the delivery takes place; and four cows at once, which may be now taken from the stable and led to the seller's house" (Posthumus 1929, p. 458). A more detailed example for the sale of a piece good is:

> "I, the undersigned, acknowledge to have bought from N.N., on conditions hereunder mentioned, one Gouda of 48 aces standing planted in N.N.'s garden, for the sum of 520 gld. in sterling. But in case 8 days after the notifying, the buyer were not to come to take the bulb, the seller may take it out of the ground, in the presence of two praiseworthy persons, and seal it in a box. And if a fortnight after this, the bulb has not been fetched by the buyer, the seller may sell it anew. If he gets more for it, the first buyer will not profit by it, and, when less, has to pay the difference. In case of any obscurity or misunderstanding or dispute arising out of this transaction, it will remain with two praiseworthy people, who know these things and who live in the place or town, where this transaction has taken place. And by default of payment of the aforesaid sum, I hereby engage all my goods, movable and immovable, submitting same in the power of all rights and magistrates; all this without arch or cunning. Have signed this. Act in Haarlem on December 12th, 1636" (Posthumus 1929, p. 456).

Perhaps some speculative fringe players in the tulipmania engaged in pure gambles that were configured as free standing options transactions. However, such deals, if any were ever done, were only obscure incidents in the tulipmania.[18]

[18] The basic mechanics of tulip production argue against widespread option trading for those directly involved in the tulip trade. Tulip growers wanted to sell bulbs for future delivery, not to take option premiums. Due to potential and actual limitations in the supply of bulbs, other

The relevance of option contracts to the tulipmania arises from the legal outcomes associated with the collapse of prices from a peak which is usually traced to February 3, 1637. By the end of February 1637, there was widespread default on forward contracts. After a short period of political and legal wrangling, the bulk of contracts outstanding at the time of the collapse were voided on the basis of "appeals to Frederick" (De Marchi and Harrison 1994). Such appeals referenced the anti-speculative 1630 and 1636 edicts of Stadholder Frederick Henry that permitted a contract to be repudiated if the 'short' did not have possession of the commodity at the time the contract for sale was entered. These edicts reinforced and clarified similar edicts going back to 1610 which were initially aimed at the speculative trade in shares (Kellenbenz 1957, p. 136). Significantly, where the courts determined that payments of differences were to be made, the forward contracts were to be interpreted as implied option contracts with payments by the longs to be made in the 1–5% range of the actual losses, consistent with the conventional size of refusal premiums. Hence, even though the contracts were written as forward contracts, the legal environment of the time interpreted such contracts to reflect the historical practice of merchants in the commodities trade permitting the buyer's option to refuse delivery.

18.6 London Option Trading

Following the Glorious Revolution of 1688, many of the speculative practices used in Amsterdam were adopted in England where stock trading had a highly developed spot market by the mid-1690s. Dutch investors and speculators also conducted a considerable amount of their British securities trading outside the Amsterdam bourse at various locations in London, such as on the Royal Exchange and in Exchange Alley where curb and coffeehouse trading was conducted. After a collapse of share prices in 1696, dealing in shares of joint stock companies, especially so-called "stockjobbing" activities, left the Royal Exchange and business was conducted in other locations, most notably in coffeehouses such as Jonathan's located in Exchange Alley near the Royal Exchange. While it is not possible to precisely date the beginning of the regular three month *rescontre* for time bargains and options on stock in London, there is considerable evidence that it was firmly established by the middle of the 18th century, prior to the formal establishment of the London Stock Exchange (1773). Trading in stock options was also widespread though the full impact of option trading in market events such as the collapse of 1696 or the infamous South Sea Bubble is unclear.[19]

potential market participants were not in a position to quote call option prices.

[19] The intricate dealings that were involved in the South Sea Bubble are discussed in various sources, including: Morgan and Thomas (1962), Chapter 2; Mackay (1852), Chapter 2; Wilson (1941), Chapter IV; Hoppit (2002); Shea (2007a).

Unlike modern day markets, the process for purchase and settlement in the 18th century gave rise to 'stockjobbing' associated with the forward trading of securities. Following Mortimer:[20]

> "The mischief of it is, that under this sanction of selling and buying the funds for time for foreigners – Brokers and others, buy and sell for themselves, without having any interest in the funds they sell, or any cash to pay for what they buy, nay even without any design to transfer, or accept, the funds they sell or buy for time. The business thus transacted, has been declared illegal by several acts of parliament, and this is the principal branch of STOCK-JOBBING" (Mortimer 1761, p. 32).

The history of stockjobbing in England reflected considerable and generally disapproving interest in Parliament. A number of attempts were made to regulate stockjobbing, starting in 1697 with an Act "To Restrain the number and ill Practice of Brokers and Stockjobbers".[21] In addition to restricting the number of practices of commodity brokers, this Act was designed to deal with three main difficulties associated with the trade in shares: unscrupulous promotion activities; manipulation of prices for shares; and, misuse of options. The pressures to further regulate stockjobbers intensified leading to the Bubble Act of 1720 and, following the South Sea Bubble, to the passage of "An Act to prevent the infamous Practice of Stock-jobbing" in 1733, also known as Barnard's Act. While this Act contained substantial penalties for speculative trading in options and time bargains, the Act was quite ineffective in restricting this trade. However, Barnard's Act was successful in removing legal protection for these transactions, making the broker a principal in speculative transactions, responsible for completion of transaction in the event of default by a client. The ensuing increased need for honesty and integrity in these speculative dealings was a significant factor leading a loose knit group of brokers to form the London Stock Exchange.

The first documented instance of a stock option contract traded in London is for 1687. Though Houghton (1694) reproduces examples of printed options

[20] Mortimer makes no reference to the use of options in stockjobbing activities, giving some support to the position that Barnard's Act of 1734 was effective in deterring this activity. In contrast to Mortimer, another early source – Defoe (1719) – makes no reference to forward trading, using examples which usually relate to cash transactions, for example, using false rumours to influence the stock price, the idea being to buy low on negative rumours and selling high on positive rumours (pp. 139–140). However, it is not clear that Defoe had the best grasp of the financial transactions which were being done.

[21] A broker in this period was an intermediary or mutual agent who served as a witness, for a commission, to contracts between two parties. In London, brokers had to be licensed and sworn. While much of the commodity and joint stock business was conducted through brokers, dealing was not confined to sworn brokers and, at various times, many unlicensed dealers operated in the market.

contracts for both a put and a refusal, it was also common practice to use covenants and indentures drawn up by scriveners, and the surviving contract is of this type. Following Dickson (1967), p. 491, the earliest surviving English option contract is dated July 29, 1687, a covenant by Sir Bazill Firebrass of Mark Lane to deliver £1,000 East India stock at 200 to Sir Thomas Davill on or before March 1, 1688, in return for a premium of 150 guineas. Similar contracts from the summer of 1691 were used by Sir Stephen Evance, a leading banker, King's Jeweller, and Chairman of the Royal Africa Company. The contracts were mostly in shares of the Company of White Paper Makers, with smaller amounts in African and East India stock. In each contract Evance was undertaking to deliver stock in six months' time at a given price with a stated option premium of roughly 20%.

18.7 Houghton on London Option Contracts

Houghton's 1694 contributions to his circular *A Collection for the Improvement of Husbandry and Trade* can be fairly recognized as containing possibly the first coherent and balanced description of early stock trading in London, e.g., Neal (1990), p. 17, though the description provided by Houghton is so brief that Cope (1978), p. 4, credits Mortimer (1761) with being the "first detailed description of the market". Though Houghton (1694) does provide some description of stock trading, the most significant contribution is on the specific subject of options trading. For seven weeks in June and July 1694, Houghton dedicated the first page of his circular to discussing stock trading. About 2½ of the seven weeks are dedicated to trading in "puts and refusals". On June 22, 1694, Houghton provides the following insightful discussion of the profit to be obtained from call option trading:

> "The manner of managing the Trade is this: The Monied Man goes among the *Brokers*, [which are chiefly upon the *Exchange*, and at *Jonathan's* Coffee House, sometimes at *Garaway's* and at some other Coffee Houses] and asks how *Stocks* go? [...] Another time he asks what they will have for Refuse of so many Shares: That is, How many Guinea's a Share he shall give for liberty to Accept or Refuse such Shares, at such a price, at any time within Six Months, or other time they shall agree for.
> For Instance; When *India* Shares are at Seventy Five, some will give Three Guinea's a Share, Action, or Hundred Pound, down for Refuse at Seventy Five, any time within Three Months, by which means the Accepter of the Guinea's, if they be not called for in that time, has his Share in his own Hand for his Security; and the Three Guinea's, which is after the rate of Twelve Guinea's profit in a year for Seventy Five Pound, which he could have sold at the Bargain making if

> he had pleased; and in consideration of this profit, he cannot without Hazard part with them the mean time, tho' they shall fall lower, unless he will run the hazard of buying again at any rate if they should be demanded; by which many have been caught, and paid dear for, as you shall see afterwards: So that if Three months they stand at stay, he gets the Three Guinea's, if they fall so much, he is as he was losing his Interest, and whatever they fall lower is loss to him.
> But if they happen to rise in that time Three Guinea's, and the charge of Brokerage, Contract and Expence, then he that paid the Three Guinea's demands the Share, pays the Seventy Five Pounds, and saves himself. If it rises but one or two Guinea's, he secures so much, but whatever it rises to beyond what it cost him is Gain. So that in short, for a small hazard, he can have his chance for a very great Gain, and he will certainly know the utmost his loss can be; and if by their rise he is encouraged to demand, he does not matter the farther advantage the Acceptor has, by having his Money sooner than Three Months to go to Market with again; so in plain *English*, one gives Three Guinea's for all the profits if they should rise, the other for Three Guinea's runs the hazard of all the losses if they should fall" (Houghton 1694, June 22).

This insightful description is quite remarkable in that, unlike de la Vega or De Pinto, Houghton was not an active participant in the market; Houghton was "not much concern'd in Stocks, and therefore (had) little occasion to Apologize for Trading therein" (Houghton 1694, June 8).

An important, but overlooked, feature of Houghton's 1694 discussion appears in the contributions of June 29 and July 6 where samples of put and call option contracts are given in detail. That standard contracts were available indicates that the market was well developed and that brokers, in conjunction with notaries, were the likely vehicles for executing trades. Examination of the specific clauses in these contracts provides useful information about option trading practices.[22] In the June 29, 1694 circular, Houghton provides a sample contract for a 'refusal' or call option, how "for Security to the giver out of Guinea's, the Acceptor gives him a contract in these or like words":

> "In consideration of Three Guinea's to me A.B. of London, Merchant, in hand paid by C.D. of London, Factor, at and before the Sealing and Delivery hereof, the Receipt whereof I do hereby ac-

[22] From de la Vega's sketchy description of Amsterdam options contracts, it is likely that Houghton's English contract was similar to those traded in Amsterdam: "For the options business there exists another sort of contract form, from which it is evident when and where the premium was paid and of what kind are the signatories' obligations. The forms of hypothecating are different also. Stamped paper is used for them, upon which the regulations concerning dividends and other details are set down, so that there can be no doubt and disagreement regarding the arrangements" (de la Vega 1688, p. 182).

> knowledge, I the said A.B. do hereby for my self, my Heirs, Executors and Administrators, covenant, promise, and agree to and with the said C.D. his Executors, Administrators and Assigns, that I the said A.B. my Executors, Administrators or Assigns shall and will transfer, or cause to be transferred to the said C.D. his Executors, Administrators or Assigns, one Share in the Joint stock of the Governor and Company of Merchants of London, trading to the East-Indies, within Three Days next after the same shall be demanded, as herein after is mentioned, together with all Dividends, Profits, and Advantages whatsoever, that shall after the Date hereof be voted, ordered, made, arise or happen thereon, or in respect thereof [if any shall be] Provided the said C.D. his Executors, Administrators or Assigns shall make demand of the said One Share personally by Word of Mouth of me, my Executors or Administrators, or by a Note in Writing under his or their Hand, and leave such Note unto or for me, my Executors or Administrators, at my now dwelling House situated in Cornhill, London, at any time on or before the Nineteenth day of September now next coming. And also pay, or cause to be paid, or to the Use of me the said A.B. my Executors, Administrators or Assigns, for the said One Share, and Dividends as aforesaid, within the said Three Days next after demand, the full Summ of Seventy five pounds of lawful Money of England, at the place where the Transfer Book belonging to the said Company shall for the time being be kept, together with all Advance-Money [if any shall be]. But if the said C.D. his Executors, Administrators or Assigns shall not demand the said One Share, as aforesaid, within the time aforesaid; and also pay, or cause to be paid to, or to the Use of me, my Executors, Administrators or Assigns, the said Summ of Seventy five Pounds, and all Advance Money, as aforesaid, at the place of refund, within the said Three Days next after such Demand, then this present Writing to be utterly void and of none Effect. And the said Three Guinea's to remain to me the said A.B. my Executors and Administrators for ever. Witness my Hand and Seal the Nineteenth Day of June, Anno Dom 1694 and in the Sixth Year of the Reign of King William and Queen Mary of England, &c.
> Sealed and Delivered in the Presence of E.F. G.H. A.B" (Houghton 1694, June 29).

Upon signing of the contract and payment of the three guineas, the Acceptor then provides the purchaser with a receipt for payment.

The first useful piece of information in Houghton's sample contract is the price, three guineas for a three month call option, with exercise price of seventy-five. Though Houghton does give weekly quotes for East India stock, a price is not available for June 19. Houghton quotes prices for June 15 and 22 at £73, so

£75 could represent an option that is at-the-money. This is consistent with the option practices observed by Cope (1978), p. 8, where the "price at which the option was exercisable was the same as, or very close to, the price of the stock for ready money when the option was arranged". Houghton does not provide details of how the option price is determined. Kairys and Valiero (1997) report that US stock option pricing in the 1870's kept the premium constant and adjusted the exercise price, quoting call prices as the difference between the the exercise price and the cash stock price. This may have been the case here, as a cash stock price of £74 would make the option slightly out-of-the-money. For the late 19th century, Emery (1896), p. 81, indicates that the option writers had a preference for near-the-money transactions in order to "get larger privilege money". The premium would be increased if the stock price volatility increased.

The next point of interest concerns the description of the parties. The writer of the option is described as "A.B., my Heirs, Executors and Administrators" while the purchaser is "C.D. his Executors, Administrators or Assigns". This wording binds the writer to the contract, whether in death or bankruptcy, while permitting C.D. to 'assign' the contract to another party. The well-developed case law on negotiable instruments, e.g., Munro (2000), is found to apply to the option contract with the result that the option purchaser could resell the contract to another party, prior to the expiration date. While this feature substantially enhances potential market liquidity, the mechanism for assigning a contract, particularly where there has been a significant change in the price and dividends and other advantages have been paid in the interim, is unclear. In contrast, the regular *rescontre* settlement used in Amsterdam trading significantly reduced the element of default risk. In addition, regular settlement dates facilitate the use of European options with premium payment at maturity.

Modern exchange traded options contracts, such as those traded on the Chicago Board Options Exchange, are American style, that is, the option can be exercised at any time up to and including the expiration date, and are not dividend-payout protected. Houghton's sample contract provides information about related features at his time. The sample contract contains the agreement to transfer the share together with "all Dividends, Profits, and Advantages whatsoever, that shall after the Date hereof be voted, ordered, made, arise or happen thereon". Taking the "Date hereof" to be the date the option contract is signed, this feature provides what in modern terms is known as 'dividend payout protection'. This feature is combined with the feature that, upon proper notification, the writer agrees to sell one share of stock "at any time on or before the Nineteenth day of September". The Houghton option contract is American-style with dividend-payout protection.

Perhaps the most important theoretical result in the modern study of option pricing is the Black-Scholes formula (Black and Scholes 1973). As originally presented, this formula provides a closed form solution for the price of a European call option on a non-dividend paying stock. Hence, even though most traded options are American, the European feature plays an important theoretical role. As conventionally presented, a European option can only be exercised on the expiration date. In general, the price of an American option is equal to the price of a European option, plus an additional non-negative early exercise premium. An American *call* option on a non-dividend paying security is a special case where the early exercise premium is zero because, in the absence of transactions costs, the option will never be exercised early. Significantly, inclusion of a dividend payout protection provision in the option contract converts the option valuation problem for a dividend paying security to the non-dividend paying case.

What has all this to do with Houghton? The origins of the European and American features in options contracts are obscure, though early sources such as Bachelier (1900) indicate that the European feature predates the American. What Houghton provides is evidence that late 17th century option contracts were transferable, dividend payout protected, American options with premium payments up front and settlement that required physical delivery of the security. If settlement was to be made by payment of differences, this was not stated in the contract. Yet, in the absence of transactions costs, an American call option with dividend payout protection will not rationally be exercised early; it will always be more profitable to sell the option.[23] This effectively equates the American option to a European option. Instead of restricting exercise to the expiration date, the late 17th century London option contract was structured with transferability and dividend payout protection provisions that made early exercise unprofitable resulting in irrelevance of the American feature.

A number of other less significant features of Houghton's option contract that are of some modern interest can also be identified. In particular, modern exchange traded option contracts permit cash settlement, in lieu of the exchange of stock for money. The Houghton contract only allows for the actual purchase of stock. The possibility of a *rescontre* method of settlement is not admitted, though De la Vega's option contracts would seem to be designed for *rescontre* trading. There is also a provision in Houghton's contract for advance money, which may have been akin to a margin account, to ensure that the option purchaser actually has sufficient funds to complete the transaction. However, why this would be required in an options transaction is unclear. Finally, as evidenced by the issue of a receipt, the option contract did require that the three guinea premium be paid up front. The possibility of delaying the premium payment until the expiration date is not admitted.

[23] Early exercise for a dividend payout protected put option can occur if the security price is sufficiently close to zero that there is insufficient potential for further increase in the put value due to further reduction in the stock price. In this case, the put can be exercised and the profit invested at interest. In Houghton's time, the securities on which options were traded had prices that were sufficiently above zero that the early exercise event had such a low probability that the early exercise premium for the put can also be set to zero.

18.8 Restrictions on Options Trading

The modern perception of option contracts as a sophisticated risk management tool is not consistent with the long history of attempts to impose legal restrictions on options trading. The basis for such restrictions is the close correspondence between option contracts and gambles. In Roman times, games of chance played for money were forbidden under penalty of a fine fixed at four times the value of the stakes. Such a law was unusual in relatively permissive Roman society but was considered necessary as gambling was a social obsession. However, the laws on gambling were not unambiguous. Gambling on certain activities, such as horse races and gladiatorial combat, was permitted and the general gambling restriction was suspended during the week-long Saturnalia festival. Enforcement of gambling laws was lax and gaming conducted at private clubs was generally overlooked. This historical perception of gambling is reflected in the history of restrictions on options trading. Because such contracts were often employed for gambling purposes, parties to the contract could not expect the protection of the courts if the transaction did not go as planned. Brokers and other agents with public recognition or registration were not permitted to facilitate such contracts. As a consequence, options trading was usually restricted to a private transactions between individuals where professional or social reputation was used to control the risk of contract default.

During the emergence of trade in free standing option contracts, the conventional legal view was that, while technically a gambling transaction, such contracts could be entered into by private parties willing to conduct such business without the guarantee that the courts could be used to enforce such contracts. However, in periods of speculative excess, the abuse of option contracts produced a subsequent demand for regulation. By the 1690s, an organized options market had emerged in London in support of the increasing number of joint stock issues.[24] Houghton provides the following account of a market manipulation involving options:

> "But the great *Mystery* of all is, That some Rich Men will join together, and give money for REFUSE, or by Friendship, or some other way, strive to secure all the Shares in a Stock, and also give Guinea's for Refuse of as many Shares more as Folk will sell, that have no Stock: and a great many such they are, that believe the Stock will not rise so high as the then Price, and Guinea's receiv'd or they shall buy before it does rise, which they are mistaken in; and then such takers of Guinea's for Refuse as have no Stock, must buy of the other that have so many Shares as they have taken Guinea's for the

[24] The early history of options trading in England can be found in Morgan and Thomas (1962). An early discussion can be found in Duguid (1901). Barnard's Act was repealed in 1860.

> Refuse of, at such Rates as they or their Friends will sell for; tho' Ten or Twenty times the former Price" (Houghton 1694, July 13).

In modern parlance, this is a classic example of a short squeeze being executed against uncovered call option writers. The Act of 1697 limited some of the potential abuses that were perpetrated with options, but did not eliminate such trading. This left forward trading as the favoured vehicle for manipulating security prices, an undesirable outcome of the "villanous" practice of stockjobbing.

There was considerable disagreement in the broker community about whether options transactions were reputable. While potentially useful in some trading contexts, reputable brokers felt that options contributed to the speculative excesses common in the early financial markets. While trading in options and time bargains did contribute to the most important English financial collapse of the 18th century, the South Sea Bubble of 1720, this event was due more to the cash market manipulations of "John Blunt and his friends" (Morgan and Thomas, Chapter 2). In any event, dealing in time bargains and, especially, options were singled out as practices that were central to "the infamous practice of stock-jobbing". In 1721, legislation aimed at preventing stockjobbing passed the Commons but was not able to pass the Lords. It was not until 1733 that Sir John Barnard was able to successfully introduce a bill under the title: "An Act to prevent the infamous Practice of Stock-jobbing". This Act is generally referred to as Barnard's Act.

The abuses associated with stockjobbing were due, at least partly, to the standard market practice of a significant settlement lag for purchases of joint stock. While there was a cash market conducted, often at or near the company transfer office, dealing for time had a legitimate basis in the practical difficulties associated with executing a stock transfer. This meant that when stock was sold for time, the short position had a considerable lead time to deliver the security. Trading involved establishing a price for future delivery of stock and paying a small deposit against the future delivery. In cases where the selling broker did have possession of the underlying stock when the transaction was initiated, there was little or no speculative element in the time bargain. However, this was not the case when the seller did not possess the stock. In addition, the purchaser for time did not usually have to take possession of the stock at delivery but, rather, could settle the difference between the agreed selling price and the stock price on the delivery date.

Barnard's Act (1733) was designed to regulate those features of stock dealings associated with excessive speculation, e.g., Morgan and Thomas (1962), p. 62. The main provision of the Act states: "All contracts or agreements whatsoever by or between any person or persons whatsoever, upon which any premium or consideration in the nature of a premium shall be given or paid for liberty to put upon or deliver, receive, accept or refuse any public or joint stock, or other public securities whatsoever, or any part, share or interest therein, and also all wagers and contracts in the nature of wagers, and all contracts in the nature of puts or refusals, relating to the then present or future price or value of any stock or securities, as aforesaid, shall be null and void". A penalty of £500 was levied on any person, including brokers, who undertook any such bargain. All bargains were to be "specifically performed and executed", stock being actually delivered and cash "actually and really given and paid", and with a £100 penalty for anyone settling a contract by paying or receiving differences. It was further provided: "whereas it is a frequent and mischievous practice for persons to sell and dispose of stocks and securities of which they are not possessed"; anyone doing so would incur a penalty of £500. There is disagreement among modern writers, such as Cope (1978) and Dickson (1967), concerning the extent to which Barnard's Act actually limited options trading. That it had some impact is evident. However, the extent of the impact is less clear.

Despite Barnard's Act making options trading illegal, options trading continued to the point where, in 1820, a controversy over the trading of stock options nearly precipitated a split in the London Stock Exchange.[25] A few members of the Exchange circulated a petition discouraging options trading. The petition passed, and members formally agreed to discourage options trading. However, when an 1823 committee of the Exchange followed up on this with a proposal to implement a rule forbidding Exchange members from dealing in options (which was already illegal under Barnard's Act), a substantial number of members voted against. A dissident group even began raising funds for a new Exchange building. In the end, the trading ban rule was rejected because options trading was a significant source of profits for numerous Exchange members who did not want to see that business lost to outsiders.

18.9 Put-Call Parity and the Pricing of Options Contracts

What methods were used for pricing option contracts? The limited information that is available for trading on the Amsterdam bourse, for example, De la Vega's *Confusion* (1688) and De Pinto's *Jeu d'Actions en Hollande* (1771), indicates that options were used primarily for speculating and not for risk management by cash market participants. By the middle of the 17th century, speculative trading on both time bargains and options in Amsterdam had progressed to the point where gains or losses on positions were settled on *rescontre* (settling day) without delivery of the cash securities, and positions could be carried forward to the next *rescontre*. By the late 17th century a regular monthly (changing to quarterly) *rescontre* process was in place. In the absence of a primary source directly concerned with the methods of pricing of derivative securities, it is still possible to infer that while prices were, at times, determined by forces of supply and demand, there was also some understanding and application of the concept

[25] Cope (1978) takes a somewhat different view of these events.

of cash-and-carry arbitrage, especially for time bargains (Wilson 1941, pp. 83–84).[26]

Unlike time bargains, arbitrage requirements seem to have had less impact on option prices. Wilson (1941), p. 122, for example, provides quotes for options on East India Company and South Sea Company shares in 1719 that reflect some pricing inefficiencies. Consistent with information from Kairys and Valerio (1997) for US option markets in the 1870's, option prices reflect a general pricing advantage for writers, supporting the view that most buyers were "out-and-out gamblers".[27] Option writers quoted prices at premiums consistent with exploiting market sentiments. The tendency of options trading, at least in England, to be concentrated among less reputable brokers (Morgan and Thomas 1962, pp. 61–62) and to be associated with market manipulation also argues against sophisticated understanding of option pricing. However, there is evidence that option writers did understand put-call parity and, as a consequence, could have created fully hedged written option arbitrage profits. Put-call parity is an arbitrage-based relationship between the price of put and call options. For practical purposes, put-call parity is, arguably, the most important distribution-free property of option prices. Both de la Vega (1688) and De Pinto (1771a) contain statements indicating that put-call parity was understood, as it applied in specific circumstances of late 17th century and 18th century Amsterdam option markets. The exact specification of put-call parity depends on the underlying commodity being traded and the restrictions imposed on the arbitrage transactions, for example, transactions costs, timing of transactions, and the difference between lending and borrowing rates.

Assuming perfect markets, at any time $t = 0$ put-call parity for European options written on a spot position in a non-dividend paying security can be stated:

$$P_0[X,T] = C_0[X,T] + \frac{X}{1+rT} - S_0$$

where $C_0[X,T]$ and $P_0[X,T]$ are the $t = 0$ prices of call and put options with exercise price X and time to expiration T (measured in fractions of a year), r is

[26] Wilson (1941), Chapter III (iii) and Chapter IV (v), provides a useful summary of De la Vega, De Pinto and some correspondence between David Leeuw and Peter Crellius.

[27] By definition, a 'gambler' is willing to undertake trades that have a negative expected value. While this definition raises a number of difficulties, e.g., the Friedman-Savage paradox, it is sufficient for present purposes.

the annualized interest rate and S_0 is the security price at $t=0$.[28] In the absence of market imperfections, put-call parity has to hold because, if not, then it is possible to execute an arbitrage. For example, if $P < C + (X/(1+rT)) - S$ then the following trades can be executed: write the call, borrow $X/(1+rT)$, buy the put and buy the stock. By assumption, this transaction would generate positive cash flow at $t=0$, yet the value of the position will always be zero at $t=T$.

Modern textbook presentations of put-call parity use European options on a spot security to motivate the explanation of put-call parity because the underlying arbitrage trades are more intuitive. Recognizing that stock could be traded on both a cash and a forward basis, similar arbitrage conditions apply to options written on forward contracts. The precise statement of put-call parity in this case depends on whether the forward contract underlying the transaction will mature on the expiration date of the option, permitting delivery of the spot commodity, or whether a forward contract is to be delivered on the option expiration date. For de la Vega and De Pinto the exchange traded options typically corresponded to forward contracts with the same expiration date. In this case, put-call parity requires:

$$P_0[X,T] = C_0[X,T] - \left\{ \frac{F[0,T]-X}{1+rT} \right\}$$

The arbitrage condition is slightly different from the spot case because taking a position in the security no longer involves a $t=0$ cash flow associated with purchasing the security.

For example, if $P[X,T] < C[X,T] - (F[0,T]-X)/(1+rT)$ then the arbitrageur will buy the put, write the call, take a long forward position in the security at $F[0,T]$ and borrow $\{F[0,T]-X\}$ if $F[0,T] < X$ that will convert to an investment in the fixed income security if $F[0,T] > X$. The intuition behind the net investment if $F[0,T] > X$ is that, if the call is in the money, then the put will be out of the money, and there will be money left over after the proceeds from the written call position have been used to purchase the put. This surplus is invested in a riskless, zero coupon, fixed income security maturing at

[28] An European option can only be exercised on the expiration date. An American option has the additional feature that it can be exercised at any time up to and including the expiration date. Being intimately connected to the *rescontre* settlement process, the options being examined by de la Vega and De Pinto were European options. As stated the options are written for one unit of stock though for modern options contracts, such as those traded on the Chicago Board Options Exchange, 100 units of stock is the typical contract size. More generally, C and P would be the option premium paid for the contract of Q units of stock, the bond would have par value QX and Q units of stock would be traded.

T. Similarly, if the put is in the money, the call will be out of the money and the proceeds from writing the call will be insufficient to purchase the put so funds have to be borrowed to fully fund the arbitrage at $t = 0$. This follows by definition because an arbitrage is a riskless trading strategy requiring no net investment of funds.

Neither de la Vega or De Pinto directly discuss the put-call parity condition or the underlying arbitrages. What is presented is a 'conversion' strategy that converts a call option position to a put option. De la Vega describes the strategy as follows:

> "I come to an agreement about the [call] premium, have it transferred [to the taker of the options] immediately at the Bank, and then I am sure that it is impossible to lose more than the price of the premium. And I shall gain the entire amount by which the price [of the stock] shall surpass the figure of 600 [...] In case of a decline, however, I need not be afraid and disturbed about my honor nor suffer fright which could upset my equanimity. If the price of shares hangs around 600, I [may well] change my mind and realize that the prospects are not as favorable as I had presumed. [Now I can do one of two things.] Without danger I [can] sell shares [against time], and then every amount by which they fall means a profit [...] and with a rise in price I could lose only the bonus [premium]" (de la Vega 1688, p. 156).

In effect, this says that a long position in a call at $C[X,T]$ combined with a short forward contract at $F[0,T](=X)$ produces a position with a payoff equal to that of a long position in a put at $P[X,T]$. Because the options involved are both at the money, this strategy reduces to the replication strategy underlying put-call parity for at-the-money options written on forward contracts with the same expiration date as the option contracts.

As an aside, the second strategy suggested by de la Vega for a trader confronted with a change in expectations about the future movement in prices is also of interest. De la Vega (1688), p. 156, suggests that "if I reckon upon a decline in the price of stock", then the trader with a long call position ought to "now pay premiums for the right to deliver stock at a given price". In modern terms, De la Vega is suggesting that the trader undertake a straddle, in this case a combination of a long call with a long put, both options being at-the-money. De la Vega provides no further discussion of the strategy. There is no recognition that the straddle is not a bet on the direction of stock prices but, rather, is a play on volatility. In effect, an at-the-money straddle is a bet that the actual future volatility of prices will be greater than the volatility implicit in the quoted option premiums. Merchant manuals from the 19th century also recognize straddle trading. Making reference to Castelli (1877), Emery observes: "A 'straddle' is much more common in securities than in produce. A straddle reading at the market price in a fluctuating security would rarely be sold, and then only at a very high price, but in more stable stocks they are not infrequent" (Emery 1896, p. 81).

Writing over eighty years after de la Vega, it is not surprising that De Pinto has a much more developed understanding of options trading. De Pinto also has an example with a trader, Paul, holding a long position in a call option, in this case with an exercise price of 150. De Pinto considers what happens if "the speculation stops":

> "Another transaction, more curious, is to convert this premium to deliver, which was betting for an increase, into a premium to receive. First we thought the stock was going to increase a lot, we paid 2½% to deliver at 150. The stock took indeed some value, but we heard that the cause for this increase has disappeared. Therefore, we sell on the Closed Market for the same *rescontre* £1000 at 150 and we convert by this process the premium to deliver into a premium to receive" (De Pinto 1771b, p. 300).

In this case, the recognition of the put-call parity relationship is explicit. De la Vega goes on to describe a more sophisticated variation of this strategy. After the initial call option has been successful and the stock price has risen to 155, the trader can lock in the 5% profit and create a put option by shorting the forward contract at 155.

18.10 The Extent of Option Trading

Prior to the financial collapse associated with the Mississippi scheme, Paris was on a path to be included with London and Amsterdam as a key European financial center. Despite the political and economic importance of France, various French characteristics retarded the development of financial markets during the 17th century. France tended to be a nation of small farmers; the explorers and traders that brought glory to her neighbors were relatively absent. It was the state that dominated economic development rather than the individual entrepreneurs that thrived in Holland and, after the Glorious Revolution, in England. Major state sponsored commercial ventures – such as Richelieu's Company of One Hundred Associates (1627) and Colbert's Company of the West Indies (1664) – were relatively unsuccessful compared to similar efforts by the Dutch and English. At the time of the Mississippi scheme, Paris lacked the central bourse that characterized trade in London and Amsterdam. Despite these drawbacks, the economic importance of France meant that Paris was an integral part of the international commercial network and that trading practices similar to those used in London and Amsterdam were the norm in financial markets, e.g., Neal and Quinn (2001).

In the absence of a central bourse, stock trading and other financial activities such as trading bills of exchange took place at different locales around Paris. At the time of the Mississippi scheme, between 1716 and 1720, stock trading was centered in the Rue Quincampoix. It was here that John Law established the offices of the *Compagnie des Indes* (Mississippi Company) for the issue of shares in the company and, as a consequence, the legendary throngs gathered at the peak of share prices to purchase "*les primes*", effectively at-the-money six month warrants to purchase a share of company stock (Murphy 1997, p. 213–217). It is one of the ironies of the Mississippi scheme that Law issued *primes* to undermine the stockjobbing by private traders – in this case trading of three to six month time bargains in company stock at prices (12000–14000 *livres* per share) considerably above the price (10000 *livres*) that the stock had achieved at that point in the speculative bubble. Law reasoned that by issuing large amounts of *primes* with an exercise price of 10000 *livres*, this trade would be ended. What Law did not anticipate was that the speculation had progressed to where shareholders would rush to sell a share at 10000 to raise cash to purchase *primes* at a premium of 1000 that granted the right to buy 10 shares in the future at 10000 each. The resulting downward pressure on cash share prices led, ultimately, to the collapse of the scheme.

The issuing of *primes* by the *Compagnie des Indes* at the height of the Mississippi scheme speculation is, perhaps, the most remarkable event in the history of option contracts. The extent of the Mississippi scheme went far beyond the considerable losses of investors. For two generations and longer, the French were wary of financial securities such as bank notes, letters of credit and company shares. While there were government efforts to organize the share market, such as a 1724 order authorizing the creation of a stock exchange in Paris, scepticism of joint stock financing was widespread. At the 1785 peak of an *agioteur* driven speculative frenzy on the Paris bourse (Taylor 1962), the bear speculator Étienne Clavière was able to commission the great French revolutionary, orator and politician M. le comte de Mirabeau (1749-1791) to produce anti-agiotage polemics and tracts designed to support an uncovered bear squeeze of longs with forward contracts (*vente à terme*). The squeeze involved spreading negative sentiment, depressing the cash price in order to permit the bear syndicate to purchase shares for values well below the delivery price. Because it is difficult to sustain the negative sentiment, the squeeze would have been difficult if the forward contracts had option features.

The closing of the Paris Bourse and the abolition of French joint stock companies were two consequences of the turmoil of 1793. These events mark a symbolic end to the rudimentary financial transactions of the 18th century, just as the official recognition of the new-style Paris Bourse in 1801 marks the beginning of the more sophisticated and accepted option trading practices that concerned Bronzin (1908). While important merchant manuals of the 18th century, such as Jacques Savary, *Dictionnaire Universel de Commerce* (1730) and Malachy Postlethwayt *The Universal Dictionary of Trade and Commerce* (1751), have detailed discussion of the trade in *actions*, there are no entries for privileges, *prime à délivrer* or *prime à recevoir*; premiums; *jeu d'actions*; or puts and refusals. With the exception of Houghton (1694), the important sources on the 17th and 18th century stock options trade are either sufficiently obscure or were part of the numerous legislative attempts to regulate or abolish the trade. It is not until the second half of the 19th century that knowledge and understanding of options trading moved outside the narrow confines of a small group of specialized traders and gradually acquired increased reputation in Europe.

Though primary sources are scarce, it is likely that privilege trading in the US was present from the late 18th century beginnings of trade in securities, perhaps earlier in the produce markets. Over time, this trade developed differently from Europe due to differing settlement practices. In the US, "each day is a settling day and a clearing day for transactions of the day before [...] This is a marked difference from European practice" where "trading for the account" (*Prolongationsgeschäfte*) involves monthly or fortnightly settlement periods with allowance for continuation of the position until the next settlement date (Emery 1896, p. 82). The continuation process for a buyer seeking to delay delivery involves the immediate sale of the stock being delivered and the simultaneous repurchase for the next settlement date. As this transaction would involve the lending of money, an additional 'contango' payment would typically be required. As a consequence of these settlement differences, in the US (American) options developed with fixed exercise prices, possible exercise prior to delivery and premiums paid in advance. In Europe, premiums for (European) options would be due on the scheduled future delivery date which coincided with a regular settlement date, exercise could only take place on the delivery date and the exercise price would be adjusted to determine a market clearing 'price' for the option at the time of purchase.

18.11 Option Trading at the End of the 19th Century

The history of economic thought on option contracts is sparse. Relatively little of substance on the theory of option pricing was written until the appearance of Bachelier (1900; Dimand and Ben-El-Mechaiekh 2006) and Bronzin (1908; Zimmermann and Hafner 2006), though Lefèvre (1874; Jovanovic 2006) does introduce valuation using expiration date profit diagrams. Significantly, each of these sources is continental European. Prior to this time, there is some evidence that market participants had a subtle understanding of option pricing, though market convention rather than competitive pricing was more important for determining actual premiums paid, e.g., Cope (1978), p. 8. For a variety of reasons, including a history of speculative abuses, option trading was held in low esteem by the bulk of stock and commodity market participants, especially in the

US. As a consequence, the trade was generally conducted by a specialized group traders catering to a relatively small clientele. Circa the end of the 19th century, trading in privileges was only conducted in the after market and on 'the curb' as such trading was prohibited on all US stock and commodity exchanges.

The increased popularity of options trading during the 19th century can be traced to the dramatic expansion of stock issues associated with railway, canal and industrial expansion. For example, on the Paris bourse the number of share issues increased from 7 in 1800 to 63 in 1830 and 152 by 1853. As indicated in Viaene (2006), this led to a considerable expansion in the trading of puts and calls which was a natural outcome of the 'trading for account' process. At some point, this trade expanded to include retail investors. While important merchant manuals from the first half of the century such as Tate (1820) contain no discussion of options, similar manuals at the time of Bronzin (1908), such as Deutsch (1904), do contain a detailed discussion indicating active trading of options on stocks and shares in Paris and, to a lesser extent, in London and Berlin. Evidence of the pace at which option trading evolved is found in the passing mention that options initially receive in the trade publication by Cohn (1874). Castelli (1877), p. 2, identifies "the great want of a popular treatise" on options as the reason for undertaking a detailed treatment of mostly speculative option trading stategies. In a brief treatment, Castelli uses put-call parity in an arbitrage trade combining a short position in "Turks 5%" in Constantinople with a written put and purchased call in London. The trade is executed to take advantage of "*enormous contangoes* collected at Constantinople" (pp. 74–77), effectively interest payments on the balance raised by the short position.

In the US, the views of option trading were more circumspect. By the end of the 19th century, all US stock and produce exchanges had banned option trading, though some trade did take place in other venues. Evidence for such trade in stock options is provided by Kairys and Valerio (1997), where an 1873–1875 sample of over-the-counter US option contacts is examined. This sample was obtained from advertisements in the *Commercial and Financial Chronicle*. The prices were only ask quotes, exclusive of bids, and were aimed at generating business from buyers of options. The option prices were found to favor the option writer. Following the European practice, these contracts determined prices by keeping the premium constant and adjusting the exercise price:

> "Whereas current option prices are quoted after fixing the strike price, the cost of a privilege was fixed at $1.00 per share for all contracts and the strike price was adjusted to reflect current market conditions. Furthermore, the strike price was expressed as a spread from the current spot price of the underlying stock with the understanding that the spread was then the "price" that was quoted for the privilege contract. Based on Emery (1896), this method of pricing options was also customary in the Chicago grain markets where contract maturities varied from one day to a week. This indicates the prevalence of

European practices in the US option market at this time" (Kairys and Valerio 1997, p. 1709).

Kairys and Valerio (1997), p. 1719, pose the question: why did the option markets fail to develop further given the apparent level of refinement? Unfortunately, the explanations provided are lacking. In contrast, Emery provides a more insightful explanation for the disappearance of stock options trading:

> "In the last few years [...] privileges have been less common than they formerly were. The trade in privileges depends chiefly upon a few men of large means. The public buy, but seldom sell, privileges, and if the men who are accustomed to dealing in that way stop selling, the field for such practices becomes very circumscribed" (Emery 1896, p. 80).

The disappearance of the 'men of large means' in 1875 is possibly due to the substantial deterioration in the public perception of options induced by the stock projector Jacob Little's use of options to manipulate the price of Erie stock in that year. According to Clews: "Mr. Little had been selling large blocks of Erie stock on seller's option, to run from six to twelve months" (Clews 1915, p. 10). The resulting attempt to corner the stock and squeeze Little is one of the fascinating stories of the 19th century robber barons. The upshot was, yet again, a public black eye for stock option trading in the US and the imposition of a restriction on the maximum term of stock option contracts to sixty days.

References

Aristotle (1984) The politics. Translated and with an introduction, notes and glossary by Carnes Lord. University of Chicago Press, Chicago

Bachelier L (1900) Théorie de la speculation. Annales Scientifiques de l' Ecole Normale Supérieure, Ser. 3, 17, Paris, pp. 21–88. English translation in: Cootner P (ed) (1964) The random character of stock market prices. MIT Press, Cambridge (Massachusetts), pp. 17–79

Barbour V (1950) Capitalism in Amsterdam in the 17th century. University of Michigan Press, Ann Arbor (Michigan)

Bell A, Brooks C, Dryburgh P (2007) Interest rates and efficiency in medieval wool forward contracts. Journal of Banking and Finance 31, pp. 361–380

Black F, Scholes M (1973) The pricing of options and corporate liabilities. Journal of Political Economy 81, pp. 637–659

Bronzin V (1908) Theorie der Prämiengeschäfte. Franz Deuticke, Leipzig/Vienna

Cardoso J (2006) Joseph de la Vega and the 'Confusion de confusiones'. In: Poitras G (ed) (2006) Pioneers of financial economics: contributions prior to Irving Fisher, Vol. 1. Edward Elgar Publishing, Cheltenham (UK), pp. 64–75

Castelli C (1877) The theory of "options" in stocks and shares. F. Mathieson, London

Clews H (1915) Fifty years in Wall Street. Irving Publishing, New York (Reprinted in 1973 by Arno Press)
Cohen J (1953) The element of lottery in British government bonds, 1694–1919. Economica, pp. 237–246
Cohn M (1874) The London Stock Exchange in relation with the foreign bourses. The stock exchange arbitrageur. Effingham Wilson, London
Cope S (1978) The stock exchange revisited: a new look at the market in securities in London in the eighteenth century. Economica 45, pp. 1–21
Courtadon G (1982) A note on the premium market for the Paris Stock Exchange. Journal of Banking and Finance 6, pp. 561–505
Defoe D (1719) The anatomy of exchange alley or a system of stockjobbing. Reprinted in: Francis J (1850) Chronicles and characters of the stock exchange, 1st American edn. Crosby and Nichols, Boston
de la Vega J (1688) Confusion de confusiones. Reprinted in: Fridson M (ed) (1996) Extraordinary popular delusions and the madness of crowds; and, Confusion de confusiones. J. Wiley & Sons, New York, pp. 147–214
de Marchi N, Harrison P (1994) Trading 'in the wind' and with guile: the troublesome matter of the short selling of share in seventeenth-century Holland. In: De Marchi N, Morgan M (eds) Higgling: transactors and their markets in the history of economics. Annual Supplement to History of Political Economy 26, pp. 47–65
de Pinto I (1771a) An essay on circulation of currency and credit in four parts and a letter on the jealousy of commerce. Translated with annotations by Baggs S (1774), London (Reprinted in 1969 by Gregg International Publishers)
de Pinto I (1771b) Jeu d'actions en Hollande, Amsterdam (Reprinted in 1969 by Gregg International Publishers)
de Roover R (1944) What is dry exchange? A contribution to the study of English mercantilism. Journal of Political Economy 52, pp. 250–266
de Roover R (1948) Banking and credit in medieval Bruges. Harvard University Press, Cambridge (Massachusetts)
de Roover R (1949) Gresham on foreign exchange. Harvard University Press, London
Deutsch H (1904) Arbitrage in bullion, coins, bills, stocks, shares and options, 3rd edn (1933). Effingham Wilson, London
Dickson P (1967) The financial revolution in England. St. Martin's Press, New York
Dimand R, Ben-El-Mechaiekh H (2006) Louis Bachelier. In: Poitras G (ed) (2006) Pioneers of financial economics: contributions prior to Irving Fisher, Vol. 1. Edward Elgar Publishing, Cheltenham (UK), pp. 225–237
Ehrenberg R (1928) Capital and finance in the age of the renaissance. Jonathan Cape, London (Translated from the German by Lucas H M)
Emery H (1896) Speculation on the stock and produce exchanges of the United States. Columbia University Press, New York (Reprinted in 1968 by AMS Press, New York)
Fridson M (ed) (1996) Extraordinary popular delusions and the madness of crowds; and, Confusion de confusiones. J. Wiley & Sons, New York
Garber P (1989) Tulipmania. Journal of Political Economy 97, pp. 535–560
Gelderblom O, Jonker J (2005) Amsterdam as the cradle of modern futures and options trading, 1550–1630. In: Goetzmann W M, Rouwenhorst K G (eds) (2005) The origins of value: the financial innovations that created modern capital markets. Oxford University Press, Oxford (UK), pp. 189–205
Gherity J (1995) The option clause in Scottish banking, 1730–65: a reappraisal. Journal of Money, Credit and Banking 27, pp. 713–727
Hoppit J (2002) The myths of the South Sea Bubble. Transactions of the Royal Historical Society 12, pp. 141–165

Houghton J (1692–1703) A collection for improvement of husbandry and trade. Taylor, Hindmarsh, Clavell, Rogers and Brown, London (Reprinted in 1969 by Gregg International Publishers)

Jovanovic F (2006) Economic instruments and theory in the construction of Henri Lefevre's 'science of the stock market'. In: Poitras G (ed) (2006) Pioneers of financial economics: contributions prior to Irving Fisher, Vol. 1. Edward Elgar Publishing, Cheltenham (UK), pp. 169–190

Kairys J, Valerio N (1997) The market for equity options in the 1870s. Journal of Finance 52, pp. 1707–1723

Kellenbenz H (1957) 'Introduction' to de la Vega Confusion de confusiones. Reprinted in: Fridson M (ed) (1996) Extraordinary popular delusions and the madness of crowds; and, confusion de confusiones. J. Wiley & Sons, New York, pp. 125–146

Lefèvre H (1874) Principes de la science de la bourse. Publication de l'Institut Polytechnique. Paris

Mackay C (1852) Extraordinary popular delusions and the madness of crowds, 2nd edn. Reprinted in 1980 by Bonanza Books, New York

Malkiel B, Quandt R (1969) Strategies and rational decisions in the securities options market. MIT Press, Cambridge (Massachusetts)

Marco P, Malle-Sabouret C (2007) East India bonds, 1718-1763: early exotic derivatives and London market efficiency. European Review of Economic History 11, pp. 367–394

Morgan V, Thomas W (1962) The stock exchange. St. Martins Press, New York

Mortimer T (1762) Everyman his own broker; or a guide to exchange alley, 5th edn. S. Hooper, London

Munro J (2000) English 'backwardness' and financial innovations in commerce with the low countries, 14th to 16th centuries. In: Stabel P, Blondé B, Greve A (eds) (2000) International trade in the low countries (14th–16th centuries). Garant, Leuven/Apeldoorn, pp. 105–167

Murphy A (1997) John Law, economic theorist and policy-maker. Clarendon Press, Oxford

Neal L (1990) The rise of financial capitalism, international capital markets in the age of reason. Cambridge University Press, Cambridge

Neal L, Quinn S (2001) Networks of information, markets, and institutions in the rise of London as a financial centre, 1660–1720. Financial History Review 8, pp. 7–26

Poitras G (2000) The early history of financial economics, 1478–1776. Edward Elgar Publishing, Cheltenham (UK)

Poitras G (ed) (2006) Pioneers of financial economics: contributions prior to Irving Fisher, Vol. 1. Edward Elgar Publishing, Cheltenham (UK)

Poitras G (2009) Arbitrage: historical perspectives. In: Cont R (ed) The encyclopedia of quantitative finance. J. Wiley & Sons, New York (forthcoming)

Posthumus N (1929) The tulipmania in Holland in the years 1636 and 1637. Journal of Economics and Business History 1, pp. 434–466

Postlethwayt M (1751) The universal dictionary of trade and commerce, 4th edn (1774). John and Paul Napton, London

Rich E, Wilson C (1977) The Cambridge economic history of Europe, Vol. 5. Cambridge University Press, London

Savary des Bruslons J (1730) Dictionnaire universel de commerce, Vol. 3. Chez Jacques Etienne, Paris

Schaede U (1989) Forwards and futures in Tokugawa-period Japan. Journal of Banking and Finance 13, pp. 487–513

Shea G (2007a) Financial market analysis can go mad (in the search for irrational behaviour during the South Sea bubble). Economic History Review 60, pp. 742–765

Shea G (2007b) Understanding financial derivatives during the South Sea bubble: the case of the South Sea subscription shares. Oxford Economic Papers 59, pp. 73–104

Tate W (1820) The modern cambist: forming a manual of foreign exchanges, in the different operations of bills of exchange and bullion, 6th edn (1848). Effingham Wilson, London

Tawney R (1925) 'Introduction' to a discourse upon usury by T. Wilson (1572). Reprinted in 1962 by Frank Cass, London

Taylor G (1962) The Paris Bourse on the eve of the French Revolution. American Historical Review 67, pp. 951–977

Unger R (1980) Dutch herring, technology and international trade in the seventeenth century. Journal of Economic History 40, pp. 253–280

Van der Wee H (1977) Monetary, credit and banking systems. In: Rich E, Wilson C (1977) The Cambridge economic history of Europe, Vol. 5. Cambridge University Press, London, pp. 240–392

Van Dillen J (1927) Termijnhandel te Amsterdam in de 16de en 17de eeuw. De Economist 76, pp. 503–523

Van Houtte J (1966) The rise and decline of the market of Bruges. Economic History Review XIX, pp. 29–47

Viaene A (2006) Les marchés à terme et conditionnels à la Bourse. In: Gallais-Hamonno G (ed) Le marché financier français au XIXè siècle: aspects quantitatifs des acteurs et des instruments à la Bourse de Paris, Vol. 2. Les Publications de la Sorbonne, Paris, pp. 571–602

Wilson C (1941) Anglo-Dutch commerce and finance in the eighteenth century. Reprinted in 1966 by Cambridge University Press, London

Zimmermann H, Hafner W (2006) Vincenz Bronzin's option pricing theory: contents, contribution, and background. In: Poitras G (ed) (2006) Pioneers of financial economics: contributions prior to Irving Fisher, Vol. 1. Edward Elgar Publishing, Cheltenham (UK), pp. 238–264

19 Bruno de Finetti, Actuarial Sciences and the Theory of Finance in the 20th Century

Flavio Pressacco*

In this paper, we discuss the idea of the high relevance of an economic-oriented approach to an important but little-known aspect of B. de Finetti's scientific production. We claim that through this approach, de Finetti was able to provide groundbreaking contributions in some fundamental paradigms of the economic theory of the 20th century such as mean variance, expected utility and risk aversion, arbitrage free pricing.

19.1 Introduction

Bruno de Finetti was born in 1906 in Innsbruck,[1] where his father, a leading civil engineer was engaged in the construction of railway lines. His parents were Italian, but at that time citizens of the Austrian empire, living in the regions of the north-eastern part of Italy which became part of the Italian nation only after the end of the First World War. De Finetti spent his childhood in Trieste and youth in Trento, revealing a precocious talent for mathematics. His mother's dream, especially after the untimely death of her husband, was that the young Bruno could in some way follow in his father's footsteps, so he enrolled at the Faculty of Sciences at the Politecnico of Milan in 1923. But he loved mathematics and after two years decided, despite stiff opposition from his mother (de Finetti F 2000), to move to the Faculty of Applied Mathematics at the new State University in Milan. There, he graduated in 1927. But even before this, he showed himself to be ingenious: the previous year saw the publication of his first paper in the scientific journal, Metron: "Considerazioni matematiche sull'eredità mendeliana" (de Finetti 1926) which attracted the attention of leading European mathematicians.[2] And a few years after that first paper, de Finetti acquired a reputation as a top-level mathematician. Today, about 80 years later, de Finetti is universally known as one of the great mathematicians and the founder of the theory of subjective probability, as well as a refined scholar of actuarial sciences. Yet until recently only a few people in Italy and even fewer abroad (except for

* Università degli Studi di Udine, Italy. *flavio.pressacco@uniud.it*

[1] Main bibliographical notes about de Finetti may be found in de Finetti (1981), by himself and in the volume jointly edited by U.M.I. and A.M.A.S.E.S. on occasion of the centenary of his birth (de Finetti 2006, pp. XI–XIV). See also the obituary prepared by Daboni (1987) on occasion of the commemoration (Bollettino U.M.I. 1987).

[2] Among others Darmois, Hadamard and Lotka. See de Finetti (2006), pp. 15–16.

some friends of the Italian actuarial academic circles as e.g. P. Boyle, H. Bühlmann and H. Gerber) have been fully aware of the outstanding relevance of the contribution he gave to the foundations of economics under uncertainty and to the foundations of the modern theory of finance. The goal of this paper is to offer a historical critical discussion of such contributions along with a tentative explanation of the reasons they remained so long neglected and unknown.[3] And, since de Finetti spent a long period of his academic and professional life in Trieste after 1931, it will be clear that the atmosphere of Trieste as well as some of its institutions played a fundamental role in the fascinating story of the evolution of de Finetti's ideas about theoretical and applied economics.

The framework of the paper is as follows. Section 2 gives a sketch of the pervasive role of economic thinking in the subjective probability approach. Section 3 describes the dominant influence of Pareto's ideas on de Finetti's point of view concerning pure economics. Section 4 introduces the relevance both from a practical and theoretical side of the actuarial world on de Finetti's professional and scientific life, with particular concern to the topic of the gambler's ruin problem. Section 5 debates de Finetti's priority in introducing the mean variance approach to face financial decisions under uncertainty in the context of proportional reinsurance (de Finetti 1940). Section 6 discusses de Finetti's early intuitions on the expected utility approach which may be found in the second part of de Finetti (1940). Section 7 reviews de Finetti's original introduction of the theory of risk aversion in connection with the expected utility paradigm. In Section 8, something is said of de Finetti's self-perception as a forerunner economist, with proper account of his self-criticism about some conclusions originally found in de Finetti (1940). Finally conclusions come in Section 9.

19.2 The Influence of Ulisse Gobbi

Let us begin by saying that in his first paper we already find the main characteristics of de Finetti's vision of mathematics. According to his own biographical note[4] on the occasion of his 75th birthday, mathematics is to be seen "both as a tool for applications (in physics, engineering, biology, economics and statistics) and to investigate conceptual and critical issues, rather than as a formalism or abstract matter or axiomatic dedicated to itself". I would like to add that he regarded mathematics as the key to understanding the universe, but having spent his youth in a Central European setting, this meant not only the inanimate, material world, but also the behaviour of human beings and human institutions. And in turn, this explains why he was so prone to the influence of economic thought.

This immanent attitude was early revealed by his decision to attend, as a young student of the Politecnico of Milan, a free course in Insurance Economics

[3] On this topic, see also Pressacco (2006a, 2006b).
[4] de Finetti (1981), p. XVIII.

(actually a course in the economics of uncertainty) given by Ulisse Gobbi; surely at that time an unusual decision for a student of sciences. Luckily for the history of science, Gobbi turned out to be a very good teacher: many years later, de Finetti himself wrote that that course left an enduring mark in his mind[5].

The influence of the economic way of thinking was immediate and very strong. It played a decisive role in the definition of the probability of an event as the price of an investment (in de Finetti's terminology, a 'bet') with random (gross) return; precisely 1 if the event verifies and 0 otherwise.

This definition is indeed the pillar of de Finetti's innovative subjective approach to probability (see de Finetti 1931). Note that the price is subjective but not arbitrary as at that price the evaluator should be ready to accept both the long position (buyer-better) and the short one (seller-bank) in the investment (in the bet).[6]

More generally, the whole building of the subjective approach was based on economic grounds. Indeed de Finetti showed that all fundamental theorems of probability may be derived as consequences of a proper coherency condition on probability assessments (that is, prices) regarding logically connected events (investments). And coherency in turn relies entirely upon an economic reasoning. Indeed de Finetti claims that a person is coherent in evaluating the probabilities of some events if for any group of bets a competitor makes on whichever set of events among those considered, it is not possible that the gain of the competitor be in any case positive. To my knowledge, the first clear assertion of this idea appears in de Finetti (1931), p. 313.

It is worth making two points here. First of all, the above idea of coherency means nothing but arbitrage-free pricing, so that de Finetti's approach may be regarded as an early (individual) version of the (market) arbitrage-free pricing approach which more than forty years later would become, through the work of Black and Scholes (1973) and their closed-form formulas for option pricing, a pillar of the theory of modern finance and a booster of the exchange market for derivatives. Secondly, we have here an example of methodological inversion. It is customary for mathematicians to apply their skills to economic problems; the reverse, that is use of economic ideas to obtain groundbreaking results in the field of applied mathematics, is rather unusual. Not for de Finetti who made wide use of this approach (tool) to tackle otherwise involved mathematical problems in a simple way.

[5] According to his own words in de Finetti (1969), p. 26, footnote 3: "I appreciated it very much, and it left me with an enduring memory of lessons opening new horizons for me".

[6] We point out that this approach resembles an old pricing idea of the scholastics. Looking for a just price (*justum pretium*) of an asset, they suggested that an economic agent should not charge more for an asset (as a seller) than he himself would be willing to pay for it (as a buyer).

19.3 The Influence of Vilfredo Pareto

Besides Gobbi, another social scientist had an outstanding influence on de Finetti's thinking about economics: V. Pareto. Let us recall that de Finetti considered mathematics a fundamental tool to understand and explain the behaviour of human beings and human institutions. Then it is not surprising that in the 1930s, he too took part in the general effort to understand and analyze the foundations of economic theory which characterized the tumultuous decade. In doing so, he largely resorted to the work and thinking of V. Pareto. The latter was a many-sided scientist, well known as one of the leading members of the so called Lausanne school of Economics[7], also labeled the Mathematical school, due to its stress on mathematical tools. Despite the fact that de Finetti did not feel himself to be an economist, he too should be considered as an upholder of the mathematical school. In support of this assertion let us consider the following sentence:

> "the laws of economics are mathematic laws, and economists must give to their research and results the accuracy of a system of equations" (de Finetti 1935b, p. 228).

At the end of his meditations on the foundations of economic theory, de Finetti was convinced that any approach to pure and applied economics should be based only on the powerful pillars of two Paretian concepts: ophelimity (reflecting an ordinal system of preferences of economic agents) and optimum (set of the allocations which, under a plurality of evaluation criteria, may be changed only worsening the situation at least with respect to one criterion)[8].

On the other side, in line with his applicative guidelines, he worked on an analytic characterization of the optimum set and in 1937 wrote two milestone papers concerning the issue (de Finetti 1937a, 1937b). By the end of the decade he could safely be considered one of the leading experts of the theory of optimum, both on the technical mathematical side as well as on applications to economic theory.

19.4 The *Generali* Insurance and the Gambler's Ruin Problem

Going back now to the beginning of the decade, another important occurrence took place: in 1931 he was taken on by *Generali* Insurance, one of the world's leading insurance companies (then as now). As head of the research department,

[7] Other leading members of the Lausanne school were A. Cournot (the founder) and L. Walras.

[8] de Finetti's point of view concerning the foundations of economics and in particular the related ideas of Pareto may be found in his three papers: de Finetti (1935a, 1935b, 1936). For a detailed discussion of this topic see sections 3 and 4 of Pressacco (2006b).

he found the opportunity there to tackle concrete insurance problems, while at the same time keeping in touch with the world of actuarial sciences, whose national and international meetings he regularly attended from the beginning of the decade. Of course, in treating actuarial problems he had a big advantage in bringing his enormous culture in probability theory, coupled with his great ability to apply mathematical tools.

An important example of this synergy between mathematics, probability theory and actuarial sciences is given by de Finetti's treatment of the gambler's ruin problem applied to insurance companies.

Let us briefly recall that in the classical approach going back to the origin of probability calculus (de Moivre), gambler's ruin models consider an infinite sequence of fair games (with zero expectation conditionally to any past sequence of the game) played by two agents. The main result of the theory was that the probability of asymptotic ruin of each player was the ratio between the opponent's initial wealth and the global initial wealth of both players. Hence in the asymmetric case (with only one strong player endowed with unlimited wealth), came the sure ruin of the other weak player (as the ratio tends to one).

Tailoring this theory to the ruin probability of an insurance company, de Finetti treated the last as a weak gambler with finite wealth facing an asymmetric game versus a community of insured people seen as a unique player with infinite wealth. But in difference to the classical problem, the company's ruin is not certain because the sequence of games is not fair any more. Indeed, the safety loadings induce positive expectation, so the game becomes advantageous for the weak player.

In this modified scenario, de Finetti (1939) obtains the following result: let us denote by G_h the company's random gain from its h year portfolio and by β a coefficient satisfying for any integer h the condition $E(\exp(-\beta G_h)) = 1$; then a company with initial wealth W_0 which follows a strategy to insure a sequence of single periods independent portfolios whose random gains are characterized by the common coefficient β, has an asymptotic ruin probability $p = \exp(-W_0 \beta)$. The reciprocal of β is named by de Finetti the risk level of each year portfolio. This was a groundbreaking result in the branch of actuarial sciences known as collective risk theory. Indeed it launched a bridge between the classical, Scandinavian school (see Lundberg 1909, Cramer 1930) and a modern preference-based approach. [9]

[9] Other members of the Italian actuarial school gave relevant contributions to the theory of risk. See Cantelli (1917) and Ottaviani (1940).

19.5 The Mean Variance Approach in Finance

These human events, cultural propensities and technical results concerning Pareto optimum and the gambler's ruin were the background of an extraordinary paper "Il problema dei pieni", written by de Finetti at the end of the 1930s, surely one of the most relevant writings in the theory of modern finance.

Indeed, as recently recognized by leading scholars of modern finance (see Markowitz 2006 and Rubinstein 2006a), this paper contains the core of the mean variance approach to financial decisions under uncertainty and the seed of the theory of expected utility in economic decisions; that is, two fundamental paradigms of the economic science of the 20th century.

In 1938, the Italian National Research Council announced a competition for the best work on the subject: "On the maximum amount which an insurance company may accept as its own retained risk. Theoretical contributions with reference to the real insurance world, taking into account reinsurance opportunities". De Finetti participated and, not surprisingly, was awarded the first prize. In his statement, the problem was seen as a proportional reinsurance one, with decision variables the retention quotas of each risk of the company's portfolio.

The core of de Finetti's approach was that, under proportional reinsurance, each additional reinsurance has a twofold effect. It lowers the risk of the retained portfolio, but at the same time lowers its profitability. Risk and profitability may as a good proxy be captured respectively by the variance (a quadratic function of the retention quotas) and by the expectation (a linear function) of the retained portfolio's profit. And in line with his economic ideas, this looked like a typical two-criteria (mean-variance) optimum problem, contrary to the approach prevailing at that time in actuarial circles, exclusively concerned with the control of risk.

This was the original proposal to apply the mean-variance approach to face portfolio problems under uncertainty. And as we shall see it was not only a matter of methodological innovation. Looking for a system to solve concrete reinsurance problems, de Finetti offered a procedure to obtain the optimum set which may be considered as a precursor of the celebrated critical line algorithm (CLA) by Markowitz. It is interesting to present de Finetti's reasoning in some detail in order to offer an idea of his ability to capture in a very simple way the essence of an intriguing problem combining intuition and rigour in order to obtain meaningful solutions.

An insurance company is faced with n risks (policies). The net profit of these risks is represented by a vector of random variables with expected value $m := m_i > 0,\ i = 1,...,n$ and a non singular covariance matrix $V := \sigma_{ij},\ i, j = 1,...,n$. The company has to choose a proportional reinsurance or retention strategy specified by a retention vector x. The retention strategy is feasible if $0 \leq x_i \leq 1$ for all i. A retention x induces a random profit with expected value $E = x^T m$ and variance $V = x^T V x$. A retention x is by definition mean variance efficient or Pareto optimum if for no feasible retention y we have both $x^T m \leq y^T m$ and $x^T Vx \geq y^T Vy$, with at least one inequality strict. Let X^* be the set of optimal retentions.

De Finetti looked at the set of feasible retentions as represented by the points of the n dimensional unit cube. The set X^* is a path in this cube. It connects the natural starting point, the vertex 1 of full retention (with largest expectation), to the opposite vertex 0 of full reinsurance (zero retention and hence minimum null variance).

De Finetti argued that the optimum path must be the one which at any point x^* of X^* moves in such a way to get locally the largest benefit measured by the ratio decrease of variance over decrease of expectation.

To translate this idea in an operational setting de Finetti introduced the so called key functions:

$$F_i(x) = \frac{1}{2} \cdot \frac{\partial V / \partial x_i}{\partial E / \partial x_i} = \sum_j x_j \cdot \frac{\sigma_{ij}}{m_i}, \qquad i = 1, \ldots, n$$

which intuitively capture the benefit coming at x from a small (additional or initial) reinsurance of the i-th risk. The connection between the efficient path and the key functions is then straightforward: move in such a way to provide additional or initial reinsurance only to the set of those risks giving the largest benefit (that is with the largest value of the key function). If this set is a singleton, the direction of the optimum path is obvious, otherwise the direction should be the one preserving the equality of the key functions among all the best performers.

Given the form of the key functions it was easily seen that this implied a movement on a segment of the cube characterized by the set of equations $F_i(x) = \lambda$ for all the current best performers. Here λ plays the role of the benefit parameter. And we should go on this segment until the key function of another non efficient risk matches the current value of the benefit parameter, thus becoming a member of the efficient set. Accordingly at this point the direction of the efficient path is changed; indeed it is defined by a new set of equations, with the addition of the equation of the newcomer risk. Through a repeated sequential application of this matching logic, de Finetti was able to define the whole efficient set, offering closed form formulas for the no-correlation case and giving a largely informal sketch of the sequential procedure in case of correlated risks.

From a historical point of view, it is interesting to note that this groundbreaking contribution appeared at the beginning of the 2nd World War in Italian in an actuarial journal so that it went unobserved to researchers in financial economics. In the following decade, Markowitz published his milestone papers (Markowitz 1952, 1956, 1959) on mean variance portfolio selection, which brought him the Nobel prize in Economics in 1990 and the reputation of being the founder of modern finance. Meanwhile, de Finetti's paper fell into oblivion.

Only recently, thanks to the work of de Finetti scholars[10], have leading economists begun to recognize the importance of de Finetti's paper. Note the words of M. Rubinstein in (2006a), for instance:

> "It has recently came to the attention of economists in the English-speaking world that among de Finetti's papers is a treasure trove of results in economics and finance written well before the works of the scholars that are traditionally credited with these ideas [...] de Finetti's 1940 paper anticipating much of mean variance portfolio's theory later developed by H. Markowitz",

and of Markowitz himself in (2006):

> "It has come to my attention that in the context of choosing optimum reinsurance levels, de Finetti essentially proposed mean variance portfolio analysis using correlated risks".

Additionally, Markowitz underlined that de Finetti had worked out a special case of the so-called global optimality conditions in quadratic programming, which Kuhn and Tucker (1951) developed at the beginning of the thirties thus paving the way for the critical line algorithm[11].

To complete this historical review we should recall also that Markowitz pointed out that de Finetti overlooked the (let us say irregular) case in which at some step it is not possible to find a matching point along an optimum segment before one of the currently partially reinsured variables reaches one of its boundary values (0 or less likely 1). Hence he concluded that "de Finetti did not solve the problem of correlated risks" and that "to get a solution for the proportional reinsurance problem in the general case advanced programming techniques must be applied" (Markowitz 2006).

Even if literally correct, this sentence seems to me rather ungenerous. It has been shown (see Pressacco and Serafini 2007) that a procedure coherently based on the key functions approach suggested by de Finetti is able to generate the critical line algorithm and hence the mean variance optimum set of any proportional reinsurance problem.

Even more exciting it could be seen that, despite the fact that de Finetti did not explore the asset portfolio selection problem at all, his ideas are in direct close relation with the mean variance optimum portfolio. Indeed, Pressacco and Serafini (2008) show that, through a proper reformulation of the key functions, it is possible to build a procedure, mimicking the one suggested by de Finetti for the reinsurance case, to obtain something analogous to the critical line algorithm

[10] Rubinstein (2006b) quotes verbal notification from C. Albanese, L. Barone and F. Corielli and the paper by Pressacco (1986).

[11] Only recently, it has been found that Karush (1939) discovered the "optimality conditions" more than ten years before Kuhn and Tucker.

and a simple and meaningful characterization of the optimum mean variance portfolio (not only in the classical problem but also in case of additional upper and lower bound collective constraints) in a natural and straightforward way.

19.6 De Finetti and the Expected Utility Approach: Early Intuitions

What we said in the previous chapter would be enough to qualify de Finetti's work of 1940 as an outstanding paper in the theory of finance. Yet the second part of the paper also contains very interesting ideas which we will present and discuss in this chapter.

After having defined the optimum set for each single period problem de Finetti faced the problem to select a single best. And to achieve this, he moved to a multiperiod horizon, aiming to choose a retention strategy consistent with a given acceptable asymptotic ruin probability.

On the basis of the gambler's ruin background, his proposal was simply to fix the retentions at a level corresponding to the risk coefficient granting the desired level of ruin probability. Without entering in technical details, we signal here that for example in the toy model with normal no correlated risks in each year it is $\lambda\beta = 2$ and $x_i = \min\left(2m_i / \beta V_i ; 1\right)$.

According to this approach the issue is mathematically clear, but rather obscure as to its true economic meaning. Only after a careful reflection could it be realized that organizing a sequence of portfolios characterized by a common coefficient β is for the company equivalent to accepting a sequence of indifferent games under exponential utility with risk aversion coefficient β, that is formally with $u(x) = 1 - \exp(-\beta x)$.

Thus it could be said that the second part of the de Finetti paper of 1940 is to be considered an unconscious anticipation of the application of the expected utility paradigm and in particular the founder of the vast actuarial literature concerning the so called zero utility principle[12].

19.7 The Theory of Risk Aversion

At that time de Finetti was not aware of the importance of his suggestions. He clearly perceived it only some years later, after reading the fundamental work (von Neumann and Morgenstern 1944), where a neo-Bernoullian theory of

[12] For a comprehensive survey on this topic see Heilpern (2003).

measurable (up to linear transforms) utility, concerning preferences among random variables, was coherently exposed[13].

Hence recognizing the connections between his early intuitions and the new paradigm, he was able to define some key concepts of the expected utility theory in another groundbreaking paper (de Finetti 1952). In detail and with the aim of defining proper measures of risk aversion associated with a given cardinal utility function $u(x)$, he introduced three new tools linking expected utility and risk aversion.

Precisely: the absolute risk aversion function $\alpha(x)=-u''(x)/u'(x)$, invariant to linear transforms of u; the probability premium defined as the difference between winning and losing probability which renders a bet of amount h indifferent; the risk premium defined as the sure loss indifferent to a fair bet of amount h.

He then proved (or, rather, gave a sketch of the proof) that both the above premiums are (at least for "small" values of h) directly proportional to the value of the starting wealth of the risk aversion function (de Finetti 1952, p. 700). He showed precisely that the probability premium is $(1/2)h\alpha$ while the risk premium is $(1/2)h^2\alpha$.

In addition he recognized the exponential utility $u(x)=1-\exp(-\alpha x)$ as the one associated with an attitude of constant (for any initial wealth x) risk aversion at the level α, and linked such attitude to the asymptotic theory of risk, with the explicit assertion that "the classical criterion of the risk level (applied in the second part of de Finetti 1940) is coincident with the utility criterion under constant risk aversion". Note that the criterion is to be intended here in the zero utility sense rather than in the optimizing one[14].

Finally he asserted that it would be $u(x)=\ln(x)$ for $\alpha(x)=1/x$ and $u(x)=-x^{1-c}$ for $\alpha(x)=c/x$, in this way also highlighting utility functions characterized by hyperbolic absolute risk aversion, nowadays linked to the concept of constant relative risk aversion.

All these tools and concepts are of major relevance in the foundations of economics, and universally credited to papers by Arrow (1971) and Pratt (1964), written well after de Finetti's paper.

[13] As well known, the von Neumann-Morgenstern theory may be considered a rigorous version of an old approach suggested more than two centuries early by Bernoulli and more recently by Ramsey (1926, 1931).

[14] It would be easy to check that in the toy model the retentions of a utility maximizer would be exactly one half the ones of the company following the zero utility principle. It immediately follows that the ruin probability of the utility maximizer with risk aversion β is $\exp(-W2\beta)$.

The claim for this primacy also came from de Finetti's Italian scholars[15] in the 1980s (see Daboni and Pressacco 1987, de Ferra and Pressacco 1986, and Montesano 1991), and only recently found international imprimatur, once again through Rubinstein (2006a):

> "In 1952, anticipating K. Arrow and J. Pratt by over a decade, he formulated the notion of absolute risk aversion, used it in connection with risk premia for small bets and discussed the special case of constant risk aversion".

19.8 De Finetti's Attitude Towards His Fundamental Papers

A couple of comments are now in order concerning the attention that de Finetti himself devoted to two groundbreaking papers, namely de Finetti (1940) and de Finetti (1952). His attitude was completely different. On the one hand, he expressed the regret of not having being able to apply the expected utility approach sooner. Indeed, some time later he wrote:

> "this way to introduce and define expected utility was very close to the one proposed by myself [in 1930]. The difference was that I intended to base only the concept of probability on this idea, without considering utility. The source of my reluctance came from motivations that I now recognize as groundless [...] I looked upon the idea of Pareto to give up measurable utility as a valuable progress to the scientific thinking, and I did not like to take a backward step at this point [...] Hence a self-critical attitude not for a personal concern, but rather as a warning about the difficulties in avoiding unconscious mental obstructions, coming even from those fighting against them" (de Finetti 1969, p. 67, 69).

Note that the regret is not referred to the lack of timely awareness of the role of expected utility and risk aversion in actuarial applications, but to the very same inability to anticipate (in the 1930s) the approach of von Neumann-Morgenstern!

On the other hand, he never claimed his primacy in the mean variance approach. Apparently, he treated it as a mere note in actuarial sciences and negligible from an economic point of view. Enlightening proof of this is that "Il prob-

[15] We note that, following on from their teacher, the first-generation scholars Daboni, de Ferra (de Ferra 1964) and Fürst (Fürst 1963) were forerunners of the application of utility theory to financial and actuarial problems. For a systematic treatment of the actuarial applications see Daboni (1988). Daboni (1984) developed also an alternative axiomatic treatment of the utility theory based on the theorem of representation of the monotone associative means of de Finetti, Nagumo and Kolmogorof, see de Finetti (1931b).

lema dei pieni" is not included in the long list of papers connected to economics given by de Finetti himself at the end of de Finetti (1969), p. 335. A possible explanation of the puzzle of de Finetti's non-appreciation of de Finetti (1940) may be found in a critical stance he later assumed towards the core results of the paper. Indeed, in some subsequent papers he expressed a couple of strong criticisms regarding the practical conclusions about the control of risk through reinsurance strategies given in the original paper. Quite probably, having concentrated his attention on these shortcomings, he was then induced to a wrong under-evaluation of the great methodological worth of his paper.

The first critique came from his sudden subsequent preference for a cooperative approach to reinsurance over a single company point of view. This implied reciprocal reinsurance treaties between a network of companies rather than unilateral reinsurance decisions. Following this line, in another paper (de Finetti 1942) de Finetti was able to define conditions granting the optimality of pool quota treaties; that is, joint agreements under which each company should retain a constant (company specific) quota of all portfolios of initial risks. In turn, this result was the forerunner of an important branch of actuarial literature; see e.g. Borch (1962, 1974), Bühlmann (1970), Bühlmann and Gerber (1978), as well as of relevant literature concerning risk exchanges in state contingent markets where trading of Arrow-Debreu securities takes place (see Arrow 1953).

Some time later, de Finetti raised a strong critique regarding the practical suggestions emerging from the collective risk theory, specifically concerning the idea that the expected level of free capital of an insurance company should increase beyond any limit because of the contribution of the (retained gains coming from) safety loadings.

Then he suggested decisions criteria based on the control of the asymptotic ruin probability be abandoned and an alternative strategy chosen, inspired by the maximization of the expectation of the company's value for the shareholders.

In a paper presented by him on the occasion of an international congress of actuaries (1957), that value came from the present value of dividends' stream distributed according to a barrier strategy (that is, distributing the excess of the free capital over the desired level of the barrier at the end of each exercise). Once more, this marked an innovative approach to a key financial paradigm: the so called managerial approach to risk theory, later extended and refined by many authors, most notably by Borch (1968, 1974, 1984), undoubtedly the strongest supporter of this approach; see also Pressacco (1989).

19.9 Conclusions

In this paper, we introduced and discussed the idea of the high relevance of an economic-oriented approach on a large part of de Finetti's scientific production. This approach allowed de Finetti to provide some groundbreaking contributions in fundamental scientific paradigms of the 20th century such as mean-variance, expected utility and risk aversion, arbitrage free pricing and optimal decisions under uncertainty. These paradigms were central both in theory as well as in the real world (investment funds, options and other derivatives) of modern finance. A positive role in this picture was surely played by his experience in the insurance sector and the connected close contact with the theory and practice of actuarial sciences. Despite the fact that most of these contributions were until recently neglected or unknown to a large part of the scientific community, we think it enough to conclude with de Finetti's doubts as to his own work:

> "am I an economist, or did I at least make some mathematical discovery useful to bring about innovations in economic theory?" (de Finetti 1969, p. 25)

is far from the truth: he really was a leading and innovative researcher in both fields.

References

Arrow K J (1953) Le role des valeurs borsieres pour la repartition la meilleure des risques. Colloques International CNRS 40, pp. 41–88

Arrow K J (1971) The theory of risk aversion. Essays in the theory of risk bearing. Markham, Chicago, pp. 90–120

Black F, Scholes M (1973) The pricing of options and corporate liabilities. Journal of Political Economy 81, pp. 637–659

Borch K (1962) Equilibrium in a reinsurance market. Econometrica 30, pp. 424–444

Borch K (1968) The rescue of an insurance company after ruin. The Astin Bulletin 5, pp. 280–292

Borch K (1974) The mathematical theory of insurance. Lexington Books, London

Borch K (1984) An alternative dividend policy for an insurance company. Mitteilungen der Vereinigung Schweizerischer Versicherungsmathematiker 2, pp. 201–206

Bühlmann H (1970) Mathematical methods in risk theory. Springer, New York

Bühlmann H, Gerber H U (1978) Risk bearing and the reinsurance market. The Astin Bulletin 10, pp. 12–24

Cantelli F P (1917) Su due applicazioni di un teorema di G. Boole alla statistica matematica. In: Atti della Reale Accademia Nazionale Lincei, Ser. V, 26. Rome, pp. 295–302

Cournot A (1838) Recherches sur le principes mathematiques de la théorie des richesses. L. Hachette, Paris

Cramer H (1930) On the mathematical theory of risk. Skandia, Stockholm

Daboni L (1984) On the axiomatic treatment of the utility theory. Metroeconomica XXXVI, pp. 281–287

Daboni L (1987) De Finetti's obituary. Bollettino della Unione Matematica Italiana, Ser. VII, 1-a, pp. 283–308

Daboni L (1988) Lezioni di tecnica attuariali delle assicurazioni contro i danni. Lint, Trieste

Daboni L, Pressacco F (1987) Mean variance, expected utility and ruin probability in reinsurance decisions. Probability and Bayesian Statistics, Viertl. Plenum Press, pp. 121–128

de Ferra C (1964) Una applicazione del criterio dell'utilità nella scelta degli investimenti. Giornale Istituto Italiano Attuari 27, pp. 51–70

de Ferra C, Pressacco F (1986) Contributi alla teoria delle decisioni. In: Atti del convegno Ricordo di Bruno de Finetti. Dipartimento di Matematica Bruno de Finetti, Trieste, pp. 171–179
de Finetti B (1926) Considerazioni numeriche sull'ereditarietà mendeliana. Metron 1, pp. 3–41
de Finetti B (1931a) Sul significato soggettivo della probabilità. Fundamenta Mathematicae 17, pp. 298–329
de Finetti B (1931b) Sul concetto di media. Giornale Istituto Italiano Attuari 2, pp. 19–46
de Finetti B (1935a) Il tragico sofisma. Rivista Italiana di Scienze Economiche 7, pp. 362–382
de Finetti B (1935b) Vilfredo Pareto di fronte ai suoi critici odierni. Nuovi Studi di Diritto. Economia e Politica 4, pp. 225–244
de Finetti B (1936) Compiti e problemi dell'economia pura. Giornale Istituto Italiano Attuari 7, pp. 316–326
de Finetti B (1937a) Problemi di optimum. Giornale Istituto Italiano Attuari 8, pp. 48–67
de Finetti B (1937b) Problemi di optimum vincolato. Giornale Istituto Italiano Attuari 8, pp. 112–126
de Finetti B (1939) La teoria del rischio e il problema della rovina dei giocatori. Giornale Istituto Italiano Attuari 10, pp. 41–51
de Finetti B (1940) Il problema dei pieni. Giornale Istituto Italiano Attuari 11, pp. 1-88 (English translation in: Barone L (2006) The problem of full risk insurances, Ch. 1: 'The problem in a single accounting period'. Journal of Investment Management 4, pp. 19–43)
de Finetti B (1942) Impostazione individuale e impostazione collettiva del problema della riassicurazione. Giornale Istituto Italiano Attuari 13, pp. 28–33
de Finetti B (1952) Sulla preferibilità. Giornale degli economisti e Annali di Economia 6, pp. 685–709
de Finetti B (1957) Su una impostazione alternativa della teoria collettiva del rischio. Transaction XVth International Congress of actuaries 2. Mallon, New York, pp. 433–443
de Finetti B (1969) Un matematico e l'economia. F. Angeli, Milan (Reprinted in 2005 by Giuffrè, Biblioteca IRSA)
de Finetti B (1981) Scritti (1926–1930). CEDAM Editore, pp. XV–XXIV
de Finetti B (2006) Opere scelte. A cura Unione Matematica Italiana e Associazione Matematica Applicata alle Scienze Economiche e Sociali, Vol. 1. Edizioni Cremonese, Rome
de Finetti F (2000) Alcune lettere giovanili di B. de Finetti alla madre. Nuncius 15, pp. 721–740
Fürst D (1963) Considerazioni su utilità e teoria dei giochi sulla base di un particolare esempio. In: Bruno de Finetti. Un matematico e l'economia. F. Angeli, Milan, pp. 144-173 (Reprinted by Giuffrè, Biblioteca IRSA)
Heilpern S (2003) A rank dependent generalization of zero utility principles. Insurance: Mathematics & Economics 33, pp. 67–73
Karush W (1939) Minima of functions of several variables with inequalities as sideconstrainst. Doctoral dissertation, Department of Mathematics, University of Chicago, Chicago
Kuhn H W, Tucker A W (1951) Non linear programming. In: Neyman J (ed) Proceedings of the Second Berkeley Symposium on Mathematics, Statistics and Probability. University of California Press, Berkeley
Lange O (1942) The foundations of welfare economics. Econometrica 10, pp. 215–228
Lintner J (1965) The valuation of risky assets and the selection of risky investments in stock portfolios and capital budgets. The Review of Economics and Statistics 47, pp. 13–37
Lundberg F (1909) Zur Theorie der Rückversicherung. Transactions of the International Congress of Actuaries
Markowitz H (1952) Portfolio selection. Journal of Finance 6, pp. 77–91
Markowitz H (1956) The optimization of quadratic functions subject to linear constraints. Naval Research Logistic Quarterly 3, pp. 111–133
Markowitz H (1959) Portfolio selection: efficient diversification of investments. J. Wiley & Sons/ Yale University Press

Markowitz H (2006) De Finetti scoops Markowitz. Journal of Investment Management 4, pp. 5–18

Montesano A (1991) Measures of risk aversion with expected and non expected utility. Journal of Risk and Uncertainty 4, pp. 271–283

Ottaviani G (1940) La teoria del rischio del Lundberg e il suo legame con la teoria classica del rischio. Giornale Istituto Italiano Attuari 11, pp. 163–189

Pratt J (1964) Risk aversion in the small and in the large. Econometrica 32, pp. 132–136

Pressacco F (1986) Separation theorems in proportional reinsurance. In: Goovaerts M et al (eds) Insurance and Risk Theory. D. Reidel Publishing, Dordrecht, pp. 209–215

Pressacco F (1989) A managerial approach to risk theory: some suggestions from the theory of financial decisions. Insurance: Mathematics & Economics 8, pp. 47–56

Pressacco F (2006a) Bruno de Finetti, le scienze attuariali e la teoria della finanza nel XX secolo. Assicurazioni LXXIII, No. 1, pp. 3–12

Pressacco F (2006b) The interaction between economics and mathematics in de Finetti thought and its relevance in finance, decision theory and actuarial sciences. Giornale Istituto Italiano Attuari LXIX, pp. 7–32

Pressacco F, Serafini P (2007) The origins of the mean variance approach in finance. Decision in Economics and Finance 30, pp. 1–17

Pressacco F, Serafini P (2008) New insights on portfolio selection from de Finetti suggestions. Preprint

Ramsey F P (1926) Truth and probability. In: Ramsey F P (1931) The Foundations of Mathematics and other Logical Essays, Ch. VII. R. B. Braithwaite, London, pp. 156–198

Rubinstein M (2006a) B. de Finetti and mean variance portfolio selection. Journal of Investment Management 4, pp. 3–4

Rubinstein M (2006b) A history of the theory of investments. J. Wiley & Sons, New York

von Neumann J, Morgenstern O (1944) Theory of Games and Economic Behavior. Princeton University Press, Princeton

20 The Origins of Expected Utility Theory

Yvan Lengwiler*

This short contribution is not about Vinzenz Bronzin or about option pricing. Rather, the topic I would like to address is another important piece of economic theory, namely the theory of expected utility maximization. It is interesting to note just how many thinkers have contributed to it, and at the same time to realize that the earliest statements of the theory were the most powerful ones, and were followed by weaker conceptions. It just took the field of economics a surprisingly long time to grasp its full potential. I believe that the history of this great piece of theory is instructive, because it is an example of a powerful idea that was assimilated only very slowly and in a roundabout fashion.

20.1 Introduction

Expected utility theory consists of two components. The first component is that people use or should use the expected value of the utility of different possible outcomes of their choices as a guide for making decisions. I say "use or should use" because the theory can be interpreted in a positive or a normative fashion. With "expected value" we mean the weighted sum, where the weights are the probabilities of the different possible outcomes. This component, which I discuss in section 2, goes back to the Blaise Pascal's writings of mid-17th century.

The second component is the idea or insight that more of the same creates additional utility only with a decreasing rate. This assumption of decreasing marginal utility plays a very central role in economics in general, but as we will see, is actually older than the marginalist school with which we would typically associate this idea. I discuss some of the contributions of the marginalist school in section 3.

In section 4, I talk about the additional insight that is possible by combining both components. It is this combination that gives rise to the concept of risk aversion and implies the demand for diversification and insurance. When we use the term "expected utility theory", we typically mean the combination of these two components.

Section 5 is a digression into the problems connected with unbounded utility functions. These problems relate to Pascal's original writings, but may also be relevant for the way we use expected utility theory today.

---

* Universität Basel, Switzerland. *yvan.lengwiler@unibas.ch*
I thank Heinz Zimmermann and Ralph Hertwig for useful remarks.

20.2 Pascal and God

The first component is old, very old. In fact, it is as old as probability theory itself. In the mid-17th century, Blaise Pascal (1670) presented a peculiar argument explaining why believing in god is rational, and not believing is not rational. This argument, known as "Pascal's wager", is an arbitrage or hedging argument. I do not know the psychological or social circumstances that Pascal was subject to when proposing this argument, but to me it seems quite far-fetched and artificial, especially since it can easily be invalidated, even within the framework of expected utility maximization that Pascal proposes. The wager works as follows. Consider a binomial world: either god exists or god does not exist. You have to decide on which of these two cases you bet by choosing whether to be religious or not. Pascal proposes the following payoffs:

	god exists	god does not exist
living as if god exists	$-C+\infty$	$-C$
living as if god does not exist	$U-\infty$	U

U is the utility provided by an earthly life unconstrained by religion. C is the disutility from living a god-abiding life.[1] Pascal argues that both, C and U, are finite, whereas the stakes are infinite in the case that god exists, simply because afterlife is infinitely longer than earthly life. If god exists, believers will spend an eternal afterlife in heaven, collecting an infinite amount of utility; non-believers will receive infinite disutility by spending eternity in hell. Obviously, if the prior probability of god existing is strictly positive (even if arbitrarily small), choosing to be religious is the best reply. So, people should choose to be religious simply in order to hedge the risk of eternal damnation and bet on the possibility of eternal bliss.

Pascal's wager has generated a lively debate in philosophy, maybe in part because there are so many obvious arguments against it. One obvious, and in my view devastating objection, is the many gods objection.[2] It runs as follows: maybe there is a god, but it is unclear what type of god it is. Several types are advertised on earth right now: there is the christian faction, the muslim faction, the hindu faction, all of them with various sub-types, and also several smaller enterprizes. How would a god, type-X, treat an atheist compared with a believer of a god, type-Y? Of course, one could try to worship all the proposed gods, but

[1] Actually, the sign of C is not important. Whether living a religious life provides positive or negative utility is immaterial because the absolute level of utility has no meaning. The assumption is simply that $-C<U$. Pascal argues that despite this assumption it is still rational to be religious.

[2] Diderot (1875–1877) is generally acclaimed to be the first to make this objection by noting that "An Imam could reason just as well this way".

would portfolio diversification work in this case? Maybe god demands exclusive devotion?

More generally, if nothing is known about god, it is essentially random what the right thing to do is. Maybe god dislikes obedient believers in general but prefers critical minds, and thus treats atheists the best? Or maybe he just likes people with blue hair. So we should all color our hair or wear a wig?

Another argument, which I have not read before, but which comes naturally to an economist, is discounting. Let a stay in heaven yield a flow of g utils, and a stay in hell yields a flow of $-h$ utils. Similarly, a stay on earth without religious constraints yields a flow of u utils, and with constraints it yields a flow of $-c$ utils. The person discounts future utils with a rate of r. Let T be the remaining length of the person's earthly life (assumed, for simplicity, not to be stochastic). Then Pascal's payoff matrix presents itself as follows,

	god exists	god does not exist
living as if god exists	$-C+G$	$-C$
living as if god does not exist	$U-H$	U

where

$$C := \int_0^T c\exp(-rt)dt = \frac{c}{r}(1-\exp(-rT)), \qquad G := \int_T^\infty g\exp(-rt)dt = \frac{g}{r}\exp(-rT),$$

$$U := \int_0^T u\exp(-rt)dt = \frac{u}{r}(1-\exp(-rT)), \qquad H := \int_T^\infty h\exp(-rt)dt = \frac{h}{r}\exp(-rT),$$

are the present values of the different kinds of lives and afterlives. Let p be the probability that god exists. After a few manipulations we conclude that being religious is the best reply if and only if

$$p > p^* := \frac{u+c}{g+h}(\exp(rT)-1).$$

Without discounting $(r=0)$ we are back at Pascal's wager: any strictly positive probability of god's existence $(p>0)$ rationalizes to be religious, because, in that case, $p^*=0$. But with discounting $(r>0)$, this is no longer true, because now $p^*>0$. This means that god has to be *sufficiently probable* in order for an individual to rationally choose to be religious. The reason why this happens is that, despite the fact that afterlife is by assumption eternal, *the slightest amount* *of discounting makes the present value of afterlife finite.*[3]

Actually, it is somewhat interesting to study how the threshold probability, p^*, changes with the remaining length of life. According to the above formula, young people (large T) would need better evidence for the existence of god in order to be religious than old people (small T), because p^* is decreasing in T. As death approaches ($T \to 0$), the required probability vanishes ($p^* \to 0$), and so eventually it becomes rational for everyone to be a theist. The reason for this effect is that the relative weight of life before death compared to potential afterlife eventually vanishes as life comes to an end.

Now, all of this is, I think, quite ridiculous. The wager is interesting for us not as an argument for religion, but because, to my knowledge, Pascal, who is one of the founding fathers of probability theory, is the first scholar to explicitly propose the expected utility of possible outcomes of a given choice as a decision rule. Thus, we conclude that this first component of expected utility theory is as old as probability theory itself.

20.3 Decreasing Marginal Utility

The second component – the assumption that marginal utility is a decreasing function – is the hallmark of the marginalist revolution that took place in 19th century economics, but which also bears fruit in other areas.

Fechner (1860), following the work of Weber (1851), developed a research program, which he called psycho-physics, that tried to relate stimulus to sensation in a quantitative fashion. By how much does the sensation of light or loudness of touch change as a result of brighter light, louder sound, or more pressure? He concluded from his experiments that Bernoulli's logarithmic specification, to which he refers (and which we discuss in the next section) was a generally valid principle: let x be stimulus and let u be sensation, then the Weber-Fechner law says that the *just noticeable difference* ("*eben merkliche Unterschied*"), that is, the smallest increase in stimulus, dx, that leads to a noticeable difference of sensation, du, is proportional to the level of the stimulus. Formally, $kdx = xdu$, or $u(x) = k \ln(x)$. A hundred years later, Stevens (1961) challenged the Weber-Fechner law and proposed, instead, a power specification, $u(x) = k(x - x_0)^b$.[4] To an economist, it is difficult to understand how one could make a big fuss about these specifications, since both specifications feature constant relative risk aversion, and economists are not interested in absolute utility scales. This is, of course, very different for psycho-

[3] Pascal argues as follows: one bets one certain life against one uncertain afterlife. But because afterlife (if it exists) is eternal, the payoff in afterlife swamps all other payoffs (Pascal 1670, § 233). Discounting invalidates this conclusion.

[4] This, in turn, has not passed unchallenged either, see Florentine and Epstein (2006).

physicists, who are looking for a *quantitative* relation.

In the economic field, Dupuit (1844, 1853) was the first to derive from the general concept of decreasing marginal utility the idea of a decreasing demand function. By clearly distinguishing the utility generated by the last used unit from the total utility he also developed the concept of the consumer's rent. Without reference to Dupuit, Gossen (1854) deduced from the idea of decreasing marginal utility the conclusion that an individual would optimally allocate his income in such a way that the marginal contribution of money to utility would be equal for all possible uses of money. In other words, if p_i is the price of good i, and du_i is the marginal utility of good i for a given person, then du_i/p_i should be the same for all commodities i for a given person. This is Gossen's most significant "second law" and is the same as the first order condition of utility maximization subject to a budget constraint, assuming price-taking behavior. Yet, Gossen's work was without any consequence because no one read his book. This work may have passed by unnoticed due to poor marketing. His position as a retired public servant was probably not helpful either in promoting his notability amongst academics. Jevons reports that none of the academics of the time who thought they were proficient in German economics had heard of Gossen (see § 28 of the preface to the second edition of Jevons 1871). It was finally Jevons who discovered Gossens' book in 1878. He acknowledged that Gossen had preceded him, but it was Jevons' theory of exchange that influenced the discussion at the time.

Significant progress was achieved by Walras (1874) and by Edgeworth (1881). Walras analyzed a complete system of multiple markets, assuming price-taking behavior by each individual person. From the aggregation of individuals' budget constraints he derived the famous Walras' Law, stating that if $n-1$ markets are in equilibrium, then the n-th market is necessarily also in equilibrium. This was, of course, the foundation of general equilibrium theory. Edgeworth, on the other hand, analyzed multiple bilateral exchange. He realized that many allocations would be possible in equilibrium (the contract curve), but conjectured that as competition intensifies, the set of equilibria should shrink. The existence of a Walras equilibrium was later proved formally by Arrow and Debreu (1954), and the validity of Edgeworth's core convergence conjecture was established by Debreu and Scarf (1963).

All these authors shared a common device: they used abstract, unspecified utility functions.[5] Consequently, the resulting equilibria possessed only rudimentary structure. This lack of structure finally led the field into a dead end. All that economists were able to show was that an abstract economy had an abstract equilibrium, and that the equilibrium allocation would satisfy certain properties (such as efficiency). But, except for simple toy models, it was

[5] Jevons, however, fully acknowledged the need to be concrete: "We cannot really tell the effect of any change in trade or manufacture until we can with some approach to truth express the laws of the variation of utility numerically" (Jevons 1871, Chapter IV, § 105).

impossible in general to construct an equilibrium and see what it looked like. The Sonnenschein-Mantel-Debreu theorem (Sonnenschein 1973, Mantel 1974, Debreu 1974) can be seen as the tombstone of abstract general equilibrium theory. It says that general equilibrium theory is compatible with everything and therefore is not falsifiable. Consequently, it is not a scientific theory in the sense of Popper (1966). Scientific orthodoxy requires more structure and more concrete assumptions, which are, ideally, empirically supported.

20.4 Cramer and Bernoulli Knew it All

The combination of the two components discussed above produces the very powerful theory of expected utility as we know and use it today. It is surprising to realize that all of this was already known in the 18th century, long before the marginalist revolution in economics. In discussing the St. Petersburg paradox, Gabriel Cramer, in a letter written in 1728, proposed to evaluate gambles by considering the expected utility of the money gained, where the utility would be measured as the square root of the payout. Ten years later, Daniel Bernoulli proposed to use the logarithm. It is quite striking to read the few lines in which Bernoulli lays out the ideas of expected utility theory (I quote from the English translation):

> "If the utility of each possible profit expectation is multiplied by the numbers of ways it can occur, and we then divide the sum of these products by the total number of cases, a mean utility (moral expectation) will be obtained, and the profit which corresponds to this utility will equal the value of the risk in question" (Bernoulli 1954, § 4).
> "However, it hardly seems plausible to make any precise generalizations since the utility of an item may change with circumstances. Thus, though *a poor man generally obtains more utility than does a rich man from an equal gain*, it is nevertheless conceivable, for example, that a rich prisoner who possesses two thousand ducats but needs two thousand ducats more to purchase his freedom, will place higher value on a gain of two thousand ducats than does another man who has less money than he. Though innumerable examples of this kind may be constructed, they represent exceedingly rare exceptions. We shall, therefore, do better to consider what usually happens, and in order to perceive the problem more correctly we shall assume that there is an imperceptibly small growth in the individual's wealth which proceeds continuously by infinitesimal increments. Now it is highly probable that *any increase in wealth, no matter how insignificant, will always result in an increase in utility which is inversely proportionate to the quantity of goods already possessed*" (Bernoulli 1954, § 5, first emphasis added).

In the first quote, Bernoulli proposes Pascal's principle.[6] In the second quote, he first proposes the general principle of decreasing marginal utility, and then also proposes a specific functional form, namely $du = x^{-1}dx$, or in other words, $u(x) = \ln(x)$.

Bernoulli then goes on to explain that what matters is not the gain in the particular gamble, but the total wealth of the individual, where zero wealth is defined as the subsistence level:

> "[...] nobody can be said to possess nothing at all in this sense unless he starves to death. For the great majority the most valuable portion of their possessions so defined will consist in their productive capacity, this term being taken to include even the beggar's talent: a man who is able to acquire ten ducats yearly by begging will scarcely be willing to accept a sum of fifty ducats on condition that he henceforth refrain from begging or otherwise trying to earn money. For he would have to live on this amount, and after he had spent it his existence must also come to an end. I doubt whether even those who do not possess a farthing and are burdened with financial obligations would be willing to free themselves of their debts or even to accept a still greater gift on such a condition. But if the beggar were to refuse such a contract unless immediately paid no less than one hundred ducats and the man pressed by creditors similarly demanded one thousand ducats, we might say that the former is possessed of wealth worth one hundred, and the latter of one thousand ducats, though in common parlance the former owns nothing and the latter less than nothing" (Bernoulli 1954, § 5).

Bernoulli lays out a very modern concept of wealth here: wealth is not the stock of assets a person owns, but rather the ability to generate an income stream. More precisely, it is the amount that the individual would be willing to trade in exchange for his ability to generate future income. This is not exactly the net present value of lifetime income, because the individual's preferences are used to value risky cash flows at different points in time instead of market prices, but it does come close to it.

It is surprising that 110 years before Gossen wrote his little-read book, 120 years before Fechner formulated his law, and 130 years before Jevons formulated his theory of exchange, two great mathematicians had already formulated a superior decision-theory. I say 'superior' because Cramer's and Bernoulli's formulation contained both components – expected utility and decreasing marginal utility –, not the second component alone. This construction is capable

[6] Interestingly, Bernoulli does not refer to Pascal's wager, even though the idea is the same. I do not know whether Bernoulli was not aware of Pascal's *Pensées* (which seems hard to imagine), or whether it was just not as usual as it is today to explicitly acknowledge previous thinkers.

of dealing with situations involving risk. In fact, their theory was designed for this case. Gossen's, Fechner's and Jevons' theories are not capable of addressing the exchange of risky bets.

Bernoulli's work was known to Fechner and Jevons – they both refer to him –, but these scholars did not realize that Bernoulli's formulation was superior. Jevons writes:

> "The variation of utility has not been overlooked by mathematicians, who had observed, as long ago as the early part of last century - before, in fact, there was any science of Political Economy at all - that the theory of probabilities could not be applied to commerce or gaming without taking notice of the very different utility of the same sum of money to different persons. [...] Daniel Bernoulli, accordingly, distinguished in any question of probabilities between the *moral expectation* and the *mathematical expectation*, the latter being the simple chance of obtaining some possession, the former the chance as measured by its utility to the person. Having no means of ascertaining numerically the variation of utility, Bernoulli had to make assumptions of an arbitrary kind, and was then able to obtain reasonable answers to many important questions. It is almost self-evident that the utility of money decreases as a person's total wealth increases; if this be granted, it follows at once that gaming is, in the longrun, a sure way to lose utility; that every person should, when possible, divide risks, that is, prefer two equal chances of £50 to one similar chance of £100; and the advantage of insurance of all kinds is proved from the same theory" (Jevons 1871, chapter 4, § 125).

It is evident from this quote that Jevons perfectly appreciated some fundamental implications of expected utility theory, such as the soundness of diversification and the demand for insurance. He failed, however, to fully spell out these implications in any further detail. Had he combined expected utility theory with his own theory of exchange, he would have reached a theory of the exchange of risky gambles, and he might have become the founder of what we call finance today.

20.5 Unbounded Utility

Menger (1934) pointed out that the utility function must be bounded, for otherwise it may fail to yield finite expected utility with some distributions, and thus there may be no maximizer. Menger also pointed out that, for the same reason, the logarithmic or the square root functions do not really resolve the St. Petersburg paradox. Because these utility functions are unbounded, one can always find a distribution of the payoff that yields infinite expected utility. In order to prevent this, given arbitrary distributions of the payoff, the utility function itself has to be bounded. Pascal's wager suffers, of course, precisely from the fact that the construction yields infinite expected utility, and thus can lead to unconvincing conclusions.

Arrow (1965) concluded that relative risk aversion must approach a value smaller than one as wealth approaches zero, and must approach a value greater than one as wealth grows indefinitely, if the utility function is bounded. Thus, relative risk aversion must be globally increasing, although it can be locally decreasing: "Thus, broadly speaking, the relative risk aversion must hover around 1, being, if anything, somewhat less for low wealths and somewhat higher for high wealths" (Arrow 1965, p. 37). Essentially, any bounded utility function must hover around the logarithmic function, although the logarithmic function itself is not a valid utility function because it is unbounded. Arrow is again very clear:

> "[...] if, for simplicity, we wish to assume a constant relative risk aversion, then the appropriate value is one. As can easily be seen, this implies that the utility of wealth equals its logarithm, a relation already suggested by Bernoulli" (Arrow 1965, p. 37).

Ten years before Menger noted the need for a bounded utility function, Charles Jordan also argued for a bounded utility function on different grounds. He explicitly refers to the psycho-physics literature and then argues:

> "[...] while accounting for the threshold of sensations, it (Bernoulli's specification) asserts that there is no upper limit for them. The sensations increase, it states, indefinitely with the stimuli. But we know that this is not true [...]" (Jordan 1924, § 12).

He then proposes an alternative specification,

$$u(x) = \lambda\left[1 - \frac{x_0 + a}{x + a}\right].$$

$u(x_0) = 0$, and Jordan interprets x_0 as the "threshold of [...] cautiousness". x_0 and λ can be understood just as normalizations, with λ being a scaling factor and x_0 determining the absolute level of utility. Unlike psycho-physicists, economists have no interest in absolute utility levels or scales. Moreover, absolute and relative risk aversion are unaffected by these two coefficients, so for economic applications we may just as well set $\lambda = 1$ and $x_0 = 0$.

Jordan's specification is interesting because the range of this utility function is bounded (it is the unit interval). Relative risk aversion is also bounded and is monotonically increasing from 0 to 2.[7] Relative risk aversion at the point $x = a$ is 1. Thus, Jordan's utility function "hovers around the logarithmic function" in the sense of Arrow, because it features bounded relative risk aversion around unity. To my knowledge, this utility function has not been used by economists, despite its interesting properties.

The axiomatization of the theory that was provided by von Neumann and Morgenstern (1944) as an appendix to their work on game theory does not allow for outcomes that are associated with infinite levels of utility. Thus, the theory is not strictly compatible with Cramer or Bernoulli, or with Pascal. But that is exactly why it is immune to the absurdity of Pascal's wager. Some generalizations are possible, if we restrict the distributions of the random variables. Ryan (1974) and Arrow (1974) work out cases where utility functions that are unbounded above may still be admissible. However, they show that one still needs either a lower bound on the utility or on the first derivative of utility, so either $u(0)$ or $u'(0)$ must be finite. Both conditions are not met by the popular constant relative risk aversion specification that we routinely use in economics and finance. Strictly speaking, these specifications are not covered by the theory.

20.6 Back to the Roots

Today, we very often use the constant relative risk aversion specification, i.e. the power or the log function. It is not without irony that the field has found that the original specification that was proposed by Cramer (power function) and by Bernoulli (log) are actually quite useful. These are also the specifications that have shaped psycho-physics, with the Weber-Fechner law being Bernoulli's specification, and Steven's formula being a generalization of Cramer's proposal. Jevons had called Bernoulli's specification an "assumption of an arbitrary kind" (see quotation above), but even if this choice was arbitrary in the sense of not being founded upon experiments, it still demonstrates great intuition or insight.

The Sonnenschein-Mantel-Debreu result was a wake-up call. Economics is now more interested in concrete models. In that sense, economics has moved closer to psycho-physics. This is also demonstrated by the fact that experiments have become a widely used method in economics in the more recent past. In this sense, the program to use experiments in economics could be labelled "econophysics", though the term seems to be taken already (Mantegna and Stanley 1999).

The move away from abstract theories that have too little structure to yield interesting (falsifiable) results, and towards more concrete models is also a move back to the roots, so to speak, because when economists use expected utility

[7] In fact, relative risk aversion is proportional to the utility level, $-xu''(x)/u'(x)=2u(x)$.

theory today, they are, it seems to me, closer to Cramer and Bernoulli than to Gossen and Jevons.

References

Arrow K J (1965) Aspects of the theory of risk-bearing. Yrjö Jahnsson Foundation, Helsinki

Arrow K J (1974) The use of unbounded utility functions in expected-utility maximization: response. Quarterly Journal of Economics 88, pp. 136–138

Arrow K J, Debreu G (1954) Existence of an equilibrium for a competitive economy. Econometrica 22, pp. 265–290

Bernoulli D (1954) Exposition of a new theory on the measurement of risk. Econometrica 22, pp. 23–36 (Originally published in 1738 as 'Specimen theoriae novae de mensura sortis', St. Petersburg)

Debreu G (1974) Excess demand functions. Journal of Mathematical Economics 1, pp. 15–21

Debreu G, Scarf H (1963) A limit theorem on the core of an economy. International Economic Review 4, pp. 235–246

Diderot D (1875-1877) Pensées philosophiques, Vol. 1 (LIX)

Dupuit J (1844) De la mesure de l'utilité des travaux publics. Annales des Ponts et Chaussées 8

Dupuit J (1853) De l'utilité et de la mesure. Journal des Économistes 12, pp. 1–27

Edgeworth F Y (1881) Mathematical psychics. Kegan Paul & Co., London

Fechner G T (1860) Elemente der Psychophysik. Breitenkopf und Härtel, Leipzig

Florentine M, Epstein M (2006) To honor Stevens and repeal his law (for the auditory system). Invited talk, International Society for Psychophysics

Gossen H H (1854) Entwickelung der Gesetze des menschlichen Verkehrs, und der daraus fließenden Regeln für menschliches Handeln. F. Vieweg, Braunschweig

Jevons W S (1871) The theory of political economy, 1st edn. Macmillan and Co. (2nd edn published 1879)

Jordan C (1924) On Daniel Bernoulli's 'moral expectation' and on a new conception of expectation. The American Mathematical Monthly 31, pp. 183–190

Mantegna R N, Stanley H E (1999) An introduction to econophysics. Cambridge University Press, Cambridge (UK)

Mantel R R (1974) On the characterization of aggregate excess demand. Journal of Economic Theory 7, pp. 348–353

Menger K (1934) Das Unsicherheitsmoment in der Wertlehre – Betrachtungen im Anschluß an das sogenannte Petersburger Spiel. Zeitschrift für Nationalökonomie 5, pp. 459–485

Pascal B (1670) Pensées. Republished several times, for instance 1972 in French by Le Livre de Poche, Paris and 1995 in English by Penguin Classics, London

Popper K R (1966) Logik der Forschung. Mohr Siebeck, Tübingen

Ryan T M (1974) The use of unbounded utility functions in expected-utility maximization: comment. Quarterly Journal of Economics 88, pp. 133–135

Sonnenschein H (1973) Do Walras' identity and continuity characterize the class of community excess demand functions? Journal of Economic Theory 6, pp. 345–354

Stevens S S (1961) To honor fechner and repeal his law. Science 133, pp. 80–86

von Neumann J, Morgenstern O (1944) Theory of games and economic behavior. Princeton University Press, Princeton

Walras L (1874) Éléments d'économie politique pure, ou théorie de la richesse sociale. Corbaz, Lausanne

Weber E H (1851) Die Lehre vom Tastsinne und Gemeingefühle auf Versuche gegründet. F. Vieweg, Braunschweig

21 An Early Structured Product: Illustrative Pricing of Repeat Contracts

Heinz Zimmermann*

An innovative contribution of Bronzin's (as well as Bachelier's) treatise is the pricing of "repeat contracts" (in German: *Noch-Geschäfte*).[1] These contracts had some popularity in the 19th century and were used until the early decades of the past century. However, although they were covered by all major finance textbooks[2] and encyclopedias in these days, their practical significance as well as their economic role remain somehow obscure. In this chapter, the pricing of the option component of repeat contract is addressed from the perspective of modern option pricing (the binomial and Black-Scholes models), and the numerical results are compared to those from Bronzin's and Bachelier's anlysis. The relative size of the repeat premiums is extremely close between the models.

21.1 Characterization

Repeat contracts represent simple combinations a forward transaction with a bundle (multiples) of ordinary call and put options. However, given some of their complexities (i.e. the determination of the exercise price and the premium) and the way how the premium of the option component was charged against the forward price as well as the exercise price in some "user friendly way", they can be regarded as forerunners of the structured products issued in today's financial markets.

The option-part of the contract, subsequently called "repeat option", gives the holder of a forward contract the right, by paying a premium N_m (the *Noch*-premium), to *repeat* the forward transaction m times at maturity at the exercise price $B+N_m$ (in case of a forward purchase), or $B-N_m$ (in case of a forward sale). In Bronzin's notation, B is the forward price. The case $m=1$ is also called "option to double", the case $m=2$ is an "option to triple", and so on.

Apparently, the repeat premium N_m serves two functions: It is the price the buyer has to pay to purchase the option as in the case of simple options, but it is

* Universität Basel, Switzerland. *heinz.zimmermann@unibas.ch*

[1] See Bronzin (1908), pp. 30–37 for a description and basic analytical characterization of the contracts, and Bachelier (1900), pp. 55–57.

[2] Moser (1875), Siegfried (1892), Holz (1905), Fürst (1908), Stillich (1909), Granichstaedten-Czerva (1915), Leitner (1920), Meithner (1924), Sommerfeld (1929) and others provide descriptions of the operation of repeat contracts. See also die literature referenced in the chapter of Schmidt (2009) in this *Volume*.

also the markup added to (or subtracted from) the forward price in fixing the exercise price of the option. Unfortunately, the practice was to *combine* the two functions in that the repeat premium was unconditionally added to (subtracted from) the forward price when the forward transaction was executed; in other words, the forward price of the fixed (unconditional) part of the *Noch*-contract was actually $B \pm N_m$.[3] So, the typical description of the contract reads, in the referenced old textbooks, as follows:

- a fixed commitment to buy/sell a given quantity (the contract size) at $B \pm N_m$
- the option to repeat the transaction m times at the "same price" (i.e. the exercise price $B \pm N_m$)

While fully correct, the two separate functions of the repeat premium (as option price, as well as part of the exercise price, and how they are contractually related) are far from obvious at first glance in these characterizations, and only a few textbook authors made this distinction transparent; notable examples are Leitner (1920), p. 622, Sommerfeld (1929), pp. 126 f., and apparently, Bronzin and Bachelier.

In the following section, the pricing problem is shortly analytically described. The advantage of the binomial model in determining the repeat premium is illustrated in Section 3, and Section 4 uses the Black-Scholes model to numerically solve the pricing problem. Some final remarks in Section 5 conclude the chapter.

21.2 The Pricing Problem

The twin function of the repeat premium N_m complicates the determination of the size of fair premium. A fundamental restriction in computing the premium is

$$N_m = mP_1, \tag{21.1}$$

where P_1 is the price of a simple "skewed" (non-ATM) call option. Bronzin shows that this condition must hold by arbitrage (pp. 48-50, equation 15), but this follows immediately from the value additivity principle. Since the repeat premium increases with the number of repeats, so does the exercise price (in the case of a repeat call[4]). But call options prices are a decreasing function of the exercise price. Therefore, there are two opposite effects of the number of repeats

[3] This is consistent with the general practice in these days to pay the option premium *at expiration* of the contract.

[4] The subsequent analysis is about repeat *call* options; the analysis of put options is straightforward.

upon the premium, so that intuition suggested that the premium is a concave function of the number of repeats.

More specifically, the valuation problem for a repeat call option can be stated, in Bronzin's notation, as[5]

$$N_m = mP_1 = m \int_{N_m}^{\infty} (\tilde{x} - N_m) f(x) dx, \tag{21.2a}$$

where $f(x)$ is the probability (or pricing) density of $\tilde{x}$, which stands for the deviation of the market price at maturity from the forward price. In the following, we adapt the more familiar notation of modern option pricing and define the following variables:

- S_T Underlying market price at maturity T;
- F Forward price, $F = S\exp(rT)$, where S is the current underlying market price and r is the continuously compounded riskfree rate (less dividends, if any);
- X Exercise price of the option;
- C Current price of a simple call option with exercise price X;

For the repeat call-option, the exercise price is defined by $X = F + N_m$. Therefore, the valuation equation (21.2a) can be restated as

$$N_m = mC = m \int_{X}^{\infty} (\tilde{S}_T - X) f(S_T) dS_T = m \int_{F+N_m}^{\infty} (\tilde{S}_T - F - N_m) f(S_T) dS_T \tag{21.2b}$$

where, obviously, no closed-form solution of N_m is available in general. In the simplified case of binomial market price movements, however, an explicit solution is possible and illustrative pricing results can be derived, as is shown next.

21.3 Binomial Pricing

The binomial model provides a natural starting point to study the pricing of the repeat premium. The advantage of the model is that it provides a closed form

[5] In the following, we adapt the notation of Bronzin, except that we add the subscript m to the repeat option premium N.

solution for the premium, and thereby a simple analysis of the factors affecting it. The following notation is used:

S	Current stock price (e.g. 1.00);
u	Up-factor of the stock price, i.e. one plus the simple upstate return (e.g. 1.2);
d	Down-Factor, i.e. one plus the simple downstate return (e.g. 0.8);
R	One plus the simple riskfree interest rate (e.g. 1.05);
F	Forward price, $F = SR$ (based on the previous values = 1.05);
m	Multiplier of an m-repeat contract (e.g. 2 for an option to triple);
N_m	the repeat ("*Noch*") premium;
q	Risk-neutral upstate probability.

The payoff in the upstate is

$$m[uS - F - N] = m[uS - SR - N] = m[S(u-R) - N],$$

while the payoff in downstate is zero by construction. We assume a single binomial price movement and a maturity one time unit (e.g. year).

Under the risk-neutral probability q, the value of the repeat premium is given by

$$N_m = \frac{q \times m[S(u-R) - N_m]}{R}$$

which can be easily solved

$$N_m = \frac{mS(u-R)q}{R + mq}, \tag{21.3}$$

and replacing the risk-neutral probability by the arbitrage condition $q = \dfrac{R-d}{u-d}$ implies

$$N_m = \frac{mS(u-R)\dfrac{R-d}{u-d}}{R + m\dfrac{R-d}{u-d}} = \frac{m\,S(u-R)(R-d)}{R(u-d) + m(R-d)} \tag{21.4}$$

The relationship between the repeat premium and the number of repeats is given by

$$\frac{\partial N_m}{\partial m}=\frac{SR(u-R)(R-d)(u-d)}{\left[R(u-d)+m(R-d)\right]^2}>0$$

which is strictly positive, but decreasing in m. Thus, the repeat premium is a positive, concave function of the number of repeats.

Typically, repeat premiums are expressed as multiples of at-the-money call prices, where at-the-money is defined by $X=F$ (exercise price = forward price). The at-the money call price is given by

$$C_{ATM}=\frac{q[Su-F]}{R}=\frac{q[Su-SR]}{R}=\frac{q\left[S(u-R)\right]}{R} \tag{21.5}$$

so that the Repeat/ATM-ratio is

$$\frac{N_m}{C_{ATM}}=\frac{mS(u-R)q}{R+mq}\times\frac{R}{q\left[S(u-R)\right]}=\frac{1}{\frac{1}{m}+\frac{q}{R}} \tag{21.6}$$

The following example highlights the formula: Assuming a stock price of 1, a simple interest rate of 5% (R=1.05) and volatility factors of 1.3 and 0.8, respectively, the risk neutral probability is 0.5, and an option-to double (m=1) costs

$$N_1=\frac{1\times1\times(1.3-1.05)\times0.5}{1.05+2\times0.5}=0.081$$

while an option to triple the contract size (m=2) costs

$$N_2=\frac{2\times1\times(1.3-1.05)\times0.5}{1.05+2\times0.5}=0.122$$

Notice that the exercise price of the repeat option is 1.05+0.081=1.131 in the first example, and 1.05+0.122=1.172 in the second. The Repeat/ATM ratio for the option to triple is then

$$\frac{N_2}{C_{ATM}}=\frac{1}{\frac{1}{2}+\frac{0.5}{1.05}}=1.024,$$

implying almost equality of the two prices. For an option to quadruple, we have 1.235, and so on; see Table 21.1 for the other numerical values.

Table 21.1 Binomial pricing of repeat options I (based on u and d)

m		1	2	3	4	5	10
N_m		0.081	0.122	0.147	0.164	0.176	0.207
C_{ATM}		0.119	0.119	0.119	0.119	0.119	0.119
Ratios	N_m / C_{ATM}	0.677	1.024	1.235	1.377	1.479	1.736
	N_m / N_1	–	1.512	1.824	2.033	2.183	2.562

Assumptions: S =1, u =1.3, d =0.8, R =1.05, T =1.

21.3.1 Modified Binomial Pricing

In order to analyze the impact of the volatility of the price process on the repeat premium in the binomial framework, we can specify the up- and downstate volatility factors with the well-known Cox-Ross-Rubinstein approximation

$$u = e^{\sigma\sqrt{T}} = \frac{1}{d}$$

where σ is the standard deviation of the log price changes of the limiting normal distribution. Thereby we use the following approximations

$$RT = e^{rT} \approx 1 + rT \text{, with } r = \ln R$$

$$u = e^{\sigma\sqrt{T}} \approx 1 + \sigma\sqrt{T} + \frac{1}{2}\sigma^2 T \text{, and}$$

$$d = e^{-\sigma\sqrt{T}} \approx 1 - \sigma\sqrt{T} + \frac{1}{2}\sigma^2 T$$

where we drop terms of higher asymptotic order than T. Making these substitutions in equation (21.3) and multiplying out terms, we get

$$N_m = \frac{mS\sigma^2 T}{2\sigma\sqrt{T} + m\left(\sigma\sqrt{T} - \frac{1}{2}\sigma^2 T + rT\right)}$$

and after rearranging terms

$$N_m = S \times \frac{1}{\frac{1}{\sigma\sqrt{T}}\left(1+\frac{2}{m}+\frac{r}{\sigma}\sqrt{T}\right)-\frac{1}{2}}$$

and finally, setting $T=1$ (as in Section 21.3), we have

$$N_m = S \times \frac{1}{\frac{1}{\sigma}\left(1+\frac{2}{m}+\frac{r}{\sigma}\right)-\frac{1}{2}} \tag{21.7}$$

Using the same numerical values as those before (in the text), but using a standard deviation of σ=0.3 instead of the up- and down volatility factors, we get for the option to triple

$$N_2 = 1 \times \frac{1}{\frac{1}{0.2}\left(1+\frac{2}{2}+\frac{\ln 1.05}{0.2}\right)-\frac{1}{2}} = 0.149,$$

which is larger than in the previous example (0.122). Recognizing the well-known approximation of the risk-neutral probability $q \approx \frac{1}{2}+\frac{1}{2}\frac{r-0.5\sigma^2 T}{\sigma\sqrt{T}}$, we approximate the at-the-money option price (21.5) by substituting q and $R \approx 1+r$

$$C_{ATM} = \frac{q\left[S(u-R)\right]}{R} = \left(\frac{1}{2}+\frac{1}{2}\frac{r-0.5\sigma^2}{\sigma}\right)S\frac{\sigma-\left(r-0.5\sigma^2\right)}{1+r} \tag{21.8}$$

and the Repeat/ATM ratio follows immediately. The impact of the volatility σ can now be easily analysed; see Table 21.2 for numerical examples. It is apparent that for typical numbers of repeats (up to 3 or 4), the Repeat/ ATM is very robust against alternative specifications of volatility.

Table 21.2 Binomial pricing of repeat options II (Approximation based on σ)

Panel A σ =20%

m		1	2	3	4	5	10
N_m		0.064	0.093	0.110	0.122	0.130	0.149
C_{ATM}		0.093	0.093	0.093	0.093	0.093	0.093
Ratios	N_m / C_{ATM}	0.681	0.999	1.183	1.303	1.387	1.594
	N_m / N_1	-	1.466	1.736	1.912	2.036	2.339

Panel B σ =30%

m		1	2	3	4	5	10
N_m		0.100	0.149	0.179	0.198	0.212	0.247
C_{ATM}		0.143	0.143	0.143	0.143	0.143	0.143
Ratios	N_m / C_{ATM}	0.696	1.042	1.249	1.387	1.485	1.730
	N_m / N_1	-	1.497	1.794	1.992	2.133	2.484

Additional assumptions: S =1, R =1.05, T =1.

21.4 Black-Scholes Pricing

The Black-Scholes model provides a natural framework to price repeat options in a lognormal setting. The model assumes that the underlying market price is governed by a geometric Wiener process, which implies that the market price at maturity is lognormally distributed. The risk-neutral distribution of $\ln\frac{S_T}{S}$ has mean $\left(r-\frac{1}{2}\sigma^2\right)T$ and variance $\sigma^2 T$. Recognizing that an m -repeat call option corresponds to m regular call options with exercise price $F+N_m$, where N_m is the repeat premium, the solution of

$$N_m = m\times\left[S\,N(z_1)-(F+N_m)\,e^{-rT}\,N(z_2)\right], \tag{21.9}$$

$$\text{with } z_1=\frac{\ln\frac{S}{F+N_m}+\frac{1}{2}\sigma^2T}{\sigma\sqrt{T}},\quad z_2=z_1-\sigma\sqrt{T}$$

must be solved numerically; $N(.)$ is the cumulative standard normal density. A set of illustrative prices is found in Table 21.3. Again, the ratios are not much sensitive with respect to the assumed volatility, but the numerical values are quite different from those in the Binomial approximation in Section 21.2.1. Obviously, the Black-Scholes values are more reliable in a continuous hedging framework.

Table 21.3 Black-Scholes pricing of repeat options

	σ =20% C_{ATM} =0.0797			σ =30% C_{ATM} =0.1192		
m	N_m	$\frac{N_m}{C_{ATM}}$	$\frac{N_m}{N_1}$	N_m	$\frac{N_m}{C_{ATM}}$	$\frac{N_m}{N_1}$
1	0.057	0.720	-	0.0870	0.7300	-
2	0.092	1.163	1.61	0.1417	1.1886	1.62
3	0.118	1.485	2.06	0.1820	1.5267	2.09
4	0.138	1.740	2.41	0.2141	1.7958	2.46
5	0.155	1.949	2.70	0.2408	2.0198	2.76
10	0.211	2.660	3.69	0.3326	2.7895	3.82

Additional assumptions: $S=1$, $R=1.05$, $T=1$.

21.4.1 Comparison with the Bachelier and Bronzin Models

Although the models of Bachelier and Bronzin[6] are based a normal, instead of a lognormal, distribution of the underlying market price, it is amazing to see how close their numerical values are to those derived before. In Table 21.4, we display the Repeat/ ATM-ratios for the first two multiples taken from Bronzin (1908) and Bachelier (1900) and compare them with those derived from the Black-Scholes model assuming an interest rate of zero. It is evident that the ratios differ very little (less than 5%). The same is true for the ratio between the repeat premiums. This is an interesting observation and demonstrates the practical suitability of Bronzin's simple model, and distributional assumption, for modeling actual prices for a "complex" derivative product.

[6] In the following, we just stick to Bronzin's normal "law of error" formula. A comparison of the repeat premiums across the different distributional assumptions is provided in Chapter 5, Section 7, Table 5.6.

Table 21.4 Repeat option prices: A comparison between Bachelier, Bronzin and Black-Scholes

		Repeat/ ATM-Ratio $\frac{N_m}{C_{ATM}}$		Ratio $\frac{N_2}{N_1}$
m		*1*	2	
Bachelier (1900)		0.6921	1.0955	1.58
Bronzin (1908)*		0.6919	1.0938	1.58
Black-Scholes	σ =20%	0.7113	1.1428	1.60
Black-Scholes	σ =30%	0.7212	1.1682	1.62

*Vales derived from the normal law of error (i.e. the normal distribution)
Additional assumptions: $T=1,\ R=1$

The question about the volatility assumption of Bronzin and Bachelier naturally arises. Interestingly, no assumption is necessary in their setting! The reason is that both authors assume *i)* a zero interest rate[7] and *ii)* a normal distribution, as stated before. This makes it possible to use a simplified expression for the at-the-money option price, namely (in Bronzin's setting, equation 44)[8]

$$P=\frac{1}{2h\sqrt{\pi}}=\frac{\sigma}{\sqrt{2\pi}} \tag{21.10}$$

where we adapt Bronzin's notation for easier comparison (P refers to the at-the-money option price, and $h=\frac{1}{\sigma\sqrt{2}}$ is called the precision modulus). Apparently, the at-the-money option price is entirely determined by the assumed volatility. Therefore, Bronzin uses this formula to substitute the volatility

$$\sigma=P\sqrt{2\pi}$$

completely out in the repeat option-formula. Specifically, the author shows that the Repeat/ATM-ratio, $R=\frac{N_m}{P}$, satisfies the condition

$$R=\frac{e^{-\frac{R^2}{4\pi}}}{\frac{1}{m}+\psi\left(\frac{R}{2\sqrt{\pi}}\right)} \tag{21.11}$$

[7] Given the institutional setting in these days, where the option premium was mostly paid at maturity, this assumption was justified.
[8] This is discussed in Chapter 5, Section 5.5.4.

under the normal "law of error" (normal distribution), where $\psi(\varepsilon)=\frac{1}{\sqrt{\pi}}\int_{\varepsilon}^{\infty}e^{-t^2}dt$ is the cumulative density tabulated in the Appendix of Bronzin's book. The author derives numerical ("trial and error") solutions of this equation, with the numerical values shown in Table 21.4.

We could, of course, try to apply the same "trick" in our Black-Scholes derivation, but this does not work out correctly. As shown in Chapter 5, Section 5.5.4, under a lognormal assumption and a non-zero interest rate, we would at-best get an approximation. But apparently, as the comparison between Tables 21.3 and 21.4 demonstrates, the relative price structure between the derived option prices is surprisingly stable.

21.5 Why Repeat Contracts?

Interestingly, the motivation for using repeat contracts was not widely discussed in the financial literature in the 19th century, and the contracts have disappeared in the first half of the 20th century without commentaries in the standard textbooks. Critical remarks can be found about the potential intransparency which repeat contracts cause on the underlying markets[9], although one would expect rather the contrary due to the commitment of the selling parties to buy or sell additional quantities of the underlying security or commodity. For example, a possible information effect could emerge from the fact that disclosure about open interest, number of traded contracts etc. was limited or inexistent at many exchanges, in comparison to contemporary markets. Repeat contracts could have served as a substitute for this missing information, because they provide information about the liquidity on the underlying market in the future. This could be of some value in spot markets which are exposed to substantial quantity risks (crop failures, natural disasters, and the like).

However, in general, one would expect a rather limited economic effect of repeat options due to the fact that the options included in the repeat contract can be easily traded (and thus priced) separately from the forward contract. It seems somehow implausible to assume that investors did not recognize that additive feature of the contracts. Schmidt (2008) in this *Volume* concludes similarly: "Readers may also have wondered how many standard contracts should be traded if they are readily duplicated. Who needs standard contracts in straddles and "*Nochs*"?"

[9] See for example Stillich (1909), p. 172. Original text: „*Das Nochgeschäft hat den Nachteil, dass es den Markt verschleiert. Niemand weiss, in welchem Umfange die Börse in dem einen oder andern Papier in Anspruch genommen werden wird, ob eine, zwei oder drei Millionen verlangt oder geliefert werden müssen. Dadurch wird das Urteil über Angebot und Nachfrage und die daraus resultierende Preisbestimmung erschwert*".

However, given that only a few sources in the relevant literature (quoted at the beginning of this Chapter) were explicit about the decomposition of the contracts, it might well be the case that issuers could capitalize from structuring attractively sounding "packages" of forward and option components, similarly to the structured products of our days. A key common characteristic of the repeat contracts and today's structured products is the attempt to "hide" the price of the option component; in the case of repeat options this is accomplished by augmenting or decreasing the forward price, i.e. to offset the premium of the repeat option by "slightly adjusting" the fixed price of the transaction. In our days, issuers of structured products play the same game by including the price of downside protection in the limited upside potential (i.e. indirectly also by finding the appropriate exercise price of the put option), or by inflating the promised return of the product (the "coupon") beyond the riskfree rate by incurring invisible downside risks.

Did the package appear attractive for hedgers or speculators, due to inexistent alternatives to buy the options separately, or due to intransparency about the structure (the pricing) of the contracts? Of course, financial markets were neither extremely "complete" nor transparent or "efficient" compared to our days[10], and it could well be the case that the contracts analyzed here were used to exploit some of the frictions in the trading mechanism or inefficiencies in the pricing structure. A few (however vague) remarks about this possibility can be found some of the quoted works.[11]

In order to analyze whether repeat contracts were used to improve hedging opportunities or to exploit pricing inefficiencies, it would be necessary to know more about the underlying risks, assets, or commodities on which the contracts were issued, and about the empirical pricing characteristics of the traded

[10] There is no reason to believe that markets were not efficient with respect to the informational structure, technology, and frictions (including currencies, quotation standards, product characteristics) in these days. The statement in the text refers to inefficiencies which appear unfamiliar from today's perspective. Indeed, there were several handbooks available providing valuable practical information on the practices of security trading, fees and transaction costs, trading hours, quotation principles etc. prevalent at the major stock exchanges, and suggesting arbitrage strategies. A major reference was Otto Swoboda's manual, which was first published in 1894 and included more than 700 pages, and pretended (according to the title of the book) to cover the practices at "all stock exchanges worldwide" (*Usancen sämtlicher Börsenplätze der Welt*). It was regularly updated and expanded by various authors; e.g. a (completely revised) 17th edition was published in 1928 and included three volumes. See Swoboda (1894) and (1928). Therefore, arbitrage transactions across exchanges and countries seem having played an important role in these days.

[11] For example, *Saling's Börsenpapiere* (see Siegfried 1892) contains a detailed description of how repeat contracts can be used to hedge a premium contract (i.e. a forward contract plus an option to step back); however, the transaction only makes sense if one of the contracts is mispriced. This is underpinned by a vague statement about the inconsistency of the premiums (call and put prices) with the prevailing forward price, i.e. a violation of the put-call-parity. Fürst (1908) gives numerous numerical examples and rules-of-thumb how to replicate and hedge repeat contracts with *Stella* contracts (a combination of call and put option) and forwards. No deeper economic understanding is however provided.

contracts. It would also be interesting to explore who, or what institutions, were actually issuing the contracts, and whether they were traded on exchanges or over-the-counter. These and many more questions could be part of a fascinating research agenda on the history of financial engineering.

References

Bachelier L (1900, 1964) Théorie de la spéculation. Annales Scientifiques de l' Ecole Normale Supérieure, Ser. 3, 17, Paris, pp. 21–88. English translation in: Cootner P (ed) (1964) The random character of stock market prices. MIT Press, Cambridge (Massachusetts), pp. 17–79

Bronzin V (1908) Theorie der Prämiengeschäfte. Franz Deuticke, Leipzig/Vienna

Fürst M (1908) Prämien-, Stellage- und Nochgeschäfte. Verlag der Haude- & Spenerschen Buchhandlung, Berlin

Granichstaedten-Czerva R (1915) Die Prämiengeschäfte. Vienna

Holz L (1905) Die Prämiengeschäfte. Doctoral dissertation. Decker, Berlin

Leitner F (1920) Das Bankgeschäft und seine Technik, 4th edn. Sauerländer, Frankfurt

Meithner K (1924) Abschluss und Abwicklung der Effektengeschäfte im Wiener Börsenverkehr. Veröffentlichungen des Banktechnischen Institutes für Wissenschaft und Praxis an der Hochschule für Welthandel in Wien. Vienna

Moser J (1875) Die Lehre von den Zeitgeschäften und deren Combinationen. Verlag von Julius Springer, Berlin

Schmidt H (2009) Retrospective book review on James Moser: Die Lehre von den Zeitgeschäften und deren Combinationen (1875). This Volume

Siegfried R (ed) (1892) Die Börse und die Börsengeschäfte. Sahling's Börsen-Papiere, 6th edn, 1st Part. Verlag der Haude- & Spenerschen Buchhandlung, Berlin

Sommerfeld H (1929) Die Technik des börsenmässigen Termingeschäfts, 2nd edn. Industrieverlag Spaeth & Linde, Berlin/ Vienna

Stillich O (1909) Die Börse und ihre Geschäfte. Karl Curtius, Berlin

Swoboda O (1928) Die Arbitrage in Wertpapieren, Wechseln, Münzen und Edelmetallen. Handbuch des Börsen-, Münz- und Geldwesens sämtlicher Handelsplätze der Welt, 17th edn. Verlag der Haude- & Spenerschen Buchhandlung, Berlin

Swoboda O (1984) Die kaufmännsiche Arbitrage. Eine Sammlung von Notitzen und Usancen sämtlicher Börsenplätze der Welt. Verlag der Haude- & Spenerschen Buchhandlung, Berlin

Biographical Notes on the Contributors

Elena Esposito is a professor of sociology at the University Reggio Emilia, Italy, Facoltà di Scienze della Comunicazione e dell'Economia. She studied sociology and philosophy at the Universities Bologna, Italy, and Bielefeld, Germany. Her research fields include sociological systems theory, sociology of financial markets, and the role of time in economics.

Giorgio Gilibert is a professor of political economy at the University of Trieste, Italy. His fields to interest include theory of capital, economic history, and history of economic thought.

Wolfgang Hafner is a finance historian, free-lance researcher, and author. He studied economic and social history at the University of Zurich. His field of interest include – among other issues – the history of financial markets and derivatives.

Espen Gaarder Haug has worked in derivatives trading and research for more than 18 years. He has a PhD degree from the Norwegian University of Science and Technology. He is the author of two books on option models and is interested in the history of option pricing.

Yvan Lengwiler is a professor of economic theory at the University of Basel, Switzerland. He studied economics at the Universtity of St.Gallen, Switzerland, and Princeton University, NJ, USA. His fields to interest include asset pricing, monetary policy, and auction theory.

Francesco Magris is an associate professor at the University of Evry, France. His fields of interest include the theory of economic fluctuations, economics of migrations, public economy, and history of economic thought.

Anna Millo is an assistant professor for contemporary history at the Department of Politics at the University of Bari. Her field of interest include the history of the leading classes in Europe from the 19th to the 20th century.

Ermanno Pitacco is a professor of actuarial mathematics in the Faculty of Economics, University of Trieste, and Academic Director of the Master in Insurance and Risk Management at the MIB School of Management in Trieste. He studied business economics at the University of Trieste, and actuarial science and statistics at the University of Rome “La Sapienza”. Main fields of scientific interest are life and health insurance mathematics, pension mathematics, longevity risk, and portfolio valuation.

Geoffrey Poitras is a professor of finance at Simon Fraser University, Vancouver, Canada. He studied economics at Dalhousie University and McMaster University in Canada before completing a PhD in economics from Columbia University. His fields of interest include risk management, business ethics, and securities analysis.

Flavio Pressacco is a professor of mathematics for finance at the University of Udine, Italy, and current Chairman of AMASES, the Italian Association of Mathematics applied to Social and Economic Sciences. He studied economics at the University of Trieste, Italy. His field of interest include decision theory applied to economics and finance, portfolio theory and derivatives pricing.

Josef Schiffer is a free-lance writer who studied history and German literature at the University of Graz/Austria. He was an editor of the “Vienna Edition” of Ludwig Wittgenstein’s writings in Cambridge/UK, and a research fellow in the *Sonderforschungsbereich* “Modernity” at Graz University.

Hartmut Schmidt was a professor of finance and banking at University of Hamburg and Syracuse University. He studied in Freiburg, Köln and Saarbrücken. Most of his publications focus on securities markets.

Eremigius Von Prosecco is a professor of philosophical speculation at the Bacchus College in Amarone. He studied at Bronzin University and specializes in financial inventions and mental constructions in financial markets.

Ernst Juerg Weber is an associate professor of economics at the University of Western Australia. After studying economics at the University of Zurich and the University of Rochester N.Y., USA, he taught at the University of Zurich, the California State University, and the Victoria University of Wellington, New Zealand. His research deals with monetary economics, macroeconomics, and financial history.

Heinz Zimmermann is a professor of finance at the University of Basel, Wirtschaftswissenschaftliches Zentrum, Switzerland. He studied economics at the University of Bern, Switzerland, and Rochester N.Y., USA. His fields of interest include asset pricing, derivative markets, and corporate finance.